# Introduction to Programming

Learn to program in Java with data structures, algorithms,
and logic

D1571447

**Nick Samoylov**

BIRMINGHAM - MUMBAI

# Introduction to Programming

**Commissioning Editor:** Aaron Lazar
**Acquisition Editor:** Denim Pinto
**Content Development Editor:** Nikhil Borkar
**Technical Editor:** Subhalaxmi Nadar
**Copy Editor:** Safis Editing
**Project Coordinator:** Ulhas Kambali
**Proofreader:** Safis Editing
**Indexer**: Aishwarya Gangawane
**Graphics:** Tania Dutta
**Production Coordinator:** Arvindkumar Gupta

First published: June 2018

Production reference: 1140618

Published by Packt Publishing Ltd.
Livery Place
35 Livery Street
Birmingham
B3 2PB, UK.

ISBN 978-1-78883-912-9

www.packtpub.com

*To my wife Luda, without whom I would not do anything useful to others and to my colleagues, especially Doug Galligan and Kaushlendra Singh, who taught me a lot.*

# Contributors

## About the author

**Nick Samoylov** graduated from the Moscow Institute of Physics and Technology, has worked as a theoretical physicist, and learned to program a tool for testing his mathematical models. After the demise of the USSR, Nick created and successfully ran a software company, but was forced to close it following pressure from the government and criminal elements. In 1999, with his wife Luda and two daughters, he emigrated to the USA and has been living in Colorado ever since, working as a Java programmer. In his free time, Nick likes to write and hike in the Rocky Mountains.

*Our CenturyLink "Photons" team, their friendship, technical advice, and support made this book possible. The team leader Kurt DeSchazer always seeks to improve and build something useful. Our managers Jim Gatley, Katie Feiman, Mike Gibson and architect Rich Cerami created a productive environment that benefited our customers and the company. My wife Luda helped me to make the text more readable and precise.*

# About the reviewers

**Dr. Srinivas Padmanabhuni**, the past president of ACM India, prior to cofounding Tarah Technologies, was Associate Vice President heading research at Infosys until October 2015. He has over 15 years' experience in IT and has given over 100 expert invited talks in the US, China, Australia, Canada, Singapore, UK, and India, including ivy league universities such as CMU, Purdue, and RUC.

**Aristides Villarreal Bravo** is a Java developer, a member of the NetBeans Dream Team, and a Java User Groups leader. He lives in Panama. He has organized and participated in various conferences and seminars related to Java, JavaEE, NetBeans, the NetBeans platform, free software, and mobile devices. He is the author of jmoordb and tutorials and blogs about Java, NetBeans, and web development.

Aristides has participated in several interviews on sites about topics such as NetBeans, NetBeans DZone, and JavaHispano. He is a developer of plugins for NetBeans.

*My mother, father, and all my family and friends.*

# Packt is searching for authors like you

If you're interested in becoming an author for Packt, please visit `authors.packtpub.com` and apply today. We have worked with thousands of developers and tech professionals, just like you, to help them share their insights with the global tech community. You can make a general application, apply for a specific hot topic that we are recruiting an author for, or submit your own idea.

`mapt.io`

Mapt is an online digital library that gives you full access to over 5,000 books and videos, as well as industry leading tools to help you plan your personal development and advance your career. For more information, please visit our website.

# Why subscribe?

- Spend less time learning and more time coding with practical eBooks and Videos from over 4,000 industry professionals

- Improve your learning with Skill Plans built especially for you

- Get a free eBook or video every month

- Mapt is fully searchable

- Copy and paste, print, and bookmark content

# PacktPub.com

Did you know that Packt offers eBook versions of every book published, with PDF and ePub files available? You can upgrade to the eBook version at `www.PacktPub.com` and as a print book customer, you are entitled to a discount on the eBook copy. Get in touch with us at `service@packtpub.com` for more details.

At `www.PacktPub.com`, you can also read a collection of free technical articles, sign up for a range of free newsletters, and receive exclusive discounts and offers on Packt books and eBooks.

# Table of Contents

# Preface

The purpose of this book is to give the readers a solid understanding of Java fundamentals, leading them through a series of practical steps from the basics to real programming. The discussion and the examples aim to stimulate professional intuition, using well-proven programming principles and practices.

After finishing this book, you will be able to do the following:

- Install Java Virtual Machine and run it
- Install and configure your integrated development environment (editor)
- Write, compile, and execute Java programs and tests
- Understand and use Java language fundamentals
- Understand and apply object-oriented design principles
- Master the most frequently used Java constructs

## Who this book is for

The targeted audience is those who would like to pursue a career in modern Java programming and the novice to intermediate Java programmer who would like to refresh their knowledge of the latest Java version.

## What this book covers

Chapter 1, *Java Virtual Machine (JVM) on Your Computer*, introduces Java as a language and as a tool. It describes the motivation for Java creation, its history, its editions, architectural principles, and components. It also outlines the Java marketing position and the main areas of application. Then, a sequence of practical steps walk you through the process of Java machine installation and configuration on your computers and through its usage and main commands.

Chapter 2, *Java Language Basics*, introduces the basic concepts of Java as an Object Oriented Programming (OOP) language. You will learn about classes, interfaces, objects, and their relations, along with OOP concepts and features.

Chapter 3, *Your Development Environment Setup*, explains what development environment is and guides you through its configuration and tuning. It also has an overview of popular editors and build frameworks. The step-by-step instructions help the reader to create their own development environment, and configure it, including the setting of a classpath and using it in practice.

Chapter 4, *Your First Java Project*, uses everything that was learned so far and guides the reader through the process of writing a program and developer's test and running them.

Chapter 5, *Java Language Elements and Types*, familiarizes the reader with Java language elements: identifiers, variables, literals, keywords, separators, comments, and similar ones. It also describes types—both primitive and reference. Special attention is applied to class String, enum types, and arrays.

Chapter 6, *Interfaces, Classes and Objects Construction*, explains the most important aspects of Java programming—Application Programming Interface (API), object factories, method overriding, hiding, and overloading. The usage of keywords this and super is also introduced here. The chapter concludes with the discussion of final classes and methods.

Chapter 7, *Packages and Accessibility (Visibility)*, introduces the notion of a package and teaches the reader how to create and use it for better code clarity. It also describes different levels of accessibility (visibility) of classes and class members—methods and properties. It concludes with the discussion of the key OOP design concept of an encapsulation.

Chapter 8, *Object-Oriented Design (OOD) Principles*, presents a higher-level view on Java programming. It discusses the criteria of a good design and provides a guide to the well-proven OOD principles. It also demonstrates code examples that illustrate the discussed principles.

Chapter 9, *Operators, Expressions, and Statements*, helps you dive deeper into three core elements of Java programming: operators, expressions, and statements. You will see the list of all Java operators, learn details about the most popular ones, and be able to execute specific examples that illustrate the key aspects of each of them.

Chapter 10, *Control Flow Statements*, describes Java statements that allow building a program flow according to the logic of the implemented algorithm, including conditional statements, iterative statements, branching statements, and exceptions.

Chapter 11, *JVM Processes and Garbage Collection*, allows the reader to look under the hood of JVM and see that it is more complex than just program runner. It executes several service threads in addition to the application threads. One of the service threads executes an important mission of releasing the memory from unused objects.

Chapter 12, *Java Standard and External Libraries*, provides an overview of the most popular libraries included with JDK and the external ones. Brief examples demonstrate the library capabilities. The chapter also guides users how to find a library on the internet.

Chapter 13, *Java Collections*, introduces you to Java collections with code examples that demonstrate their usage.

Chapter 14, *Managing Collections and Arrays*, introduces you to classes that allow you to create, initialize, and modify collections and arrays. They also allow the creation of unmodifiable and immutable collections. Some of these classes belong to Java standard libraries, others to popular Apache Commons libraries.

Chapter 15, *Managing Objects, Strings, Time, and Random Numbers*, demonstrates classes and utilities from Java Standard Library and Apache Commons that every programmer has to master in order to become an effective coder.

Chapter 16, *Database Programming*, explains how to write Java code that can manipulate—insert, read, update, and delete—data in a database. It also provides a short introduction to SQL language and basic database operations.

Chapter 17, *Lambda Expressions and Functional Programming*, explains the concept of a functional programming. It provides an overview of functional interfaces that come with JDK and explains how to use them in lambda expressions.

Chapter 18, *Streams and Pipelines*, introduces the reader to the powerful concept of data stream processing. It explains what streams are, how to process them using lambda expressions, and how to build processing pipelines. It also shows how easily you can organize stream processing in parallel.

Chapter 19, *Reactive Systems*, provides an overview and the prospects for your future professional work. As more data gets processed and services become more sophisticated, the need for more adaptive, highly scalable, and distributed processes grows exponentially, and this is what we will address in this chapter—how such a software system looks in practice.

# To get the most out of this book

No prior knowledge of Java programming is expected from a reader, although some understanding of what programming is would help them to get the most from this book.

# Download the example code files

You can download the example code files for this book from your account at `www.packtpub.com`. If you purchased this book elsewhere, you can visit `www.packtpub.com/support` and register to have the files emailed directly to you.

You can download the code files by following these steps:

1. Log in or register at `www.packtpub.com`.
2. Select the **SUPPORT** tab.
3. Click on **Code Downloads & Errata**.
4. Enter the name of the book in the **Search** box and follow the onscreen instructions.

Once the file is downloaded, please make sure that you unzip or extract the folder using the latest version of:

- WinRAR/7-Zip for Windows
- Zipeg/iZip/UnRarX for Mac
- 7-Zip/PeaZip for Linux

The code bundle for the book is also hosted on GitHub at `https://github.com/PacktPublishing/Introduction-to-Programming`. We also have other code bundles from our rich catalog of books and videos available at `https://github.com/PacktPublishing/`. Check them out!

# Download the color images

We also provide a PDF file that has color images of the screenshots/diagrams used in this book. You can download it here: `https://www.packtpub.com/sites/default/files/downloads/IntroductiontoProgramming_ColorImages.pdf`.

# Conventions used

There are a number of text conventions used throughout this book.

`CodeInText`: Indicates code words in text, database table names, folder names, filenames, file extensions, pathnames, dummy URLs, user input, and Twitter handles. Here is an example: "Mount the downloaded `WebStorm-10*.dmg` disk image file as another disk in your system."

A block of code is set as follows:

```
html, body, #map {
 height: 100%;
 margin: 0;
 padding: 0
}
```

When we wish to draw your attention to a particular part of a code block, the relevant lines or items are set in bold:

```
[default]
exten => s,1,Dial(Zap/1|30)
exten => s,2,Voicemail(u100)
exten => s,102,Voicemail(b100)
exten => i,1,Voicemail(s0)
```

Any command-line input or output is written as follows:

```
$ mkdir css
$ cd css
```

**Bold**: Indicates a new term, an important word, or words that you see on screen. For example, words in menus or dialog boxes appear in the text like this. Here is an example: "Select **System info** from the **Administration** panel."

Warnings or important notes appear like this.

Tips and tricks appear like this.

# Get in touch

Feedback from our readers is always welcome.

**General feedback**: Email feedback@packtpub.com and mention the book title in the subject of your message. If you have questions about any aspect of this book, please email us at questions@packtpub.com.

**Errata**: Although we have taken every care to ensure the accuracy of our content, mistakes do happen. If you have found a mistake in this book, we would be grateful if you would report this to us. Please visit www.packtpub.com/submit-errata, selecting your book, clicking on the Errata Submission Form link, and entering the details.

**Piracy**: If you come across any illegal copies of our works in any form on the internet, we would be grateful if you would provide us with the location address or website name. Please contact us at copyright@packtpub.com with a link to the material.

**If you are interested in becoming an author**: If there is a topic that you have expertise in and you are interested in either writing or contributing to a book, please visit authors.packtpub.com.

# Reviews

Please leave a review. Once you have read and used this book, why not leave a review on the site that you purchased it from? Potential readers can then see and use your unbiased opinion to make purchase decisions, we at Packt can understand what you think about our products, and our authors can see your feedback on their book. Thank you!

For more information about Packt, please visit packtpub.com.

# Java Virtual Machine (JVM) on Your Computer

# 1

This book will be your guide to achieving an intermediate level of Java programming skills. Programming is not just about knowing the language syntax. It is also about the tools and sources of information necessary to write, compile, and execute a program or run a whole software system. The first step on this road is to learn the important components of Java, including **Java Development Kit (JDK)** and **Java Virtual Machine (JVM)**.

This chapter will introduce Java as a language and a tool, and establish the most important terminology. It will also describe the motivation behind Java's creation, cover its history, editions, versions, and technologies, and outline Java's marketing position and main areas of application. Then, a sequence of practical steps will walk readers through the process of Java installation and configuration on their computers, and introduce the main Java commands.

In this chapter, we will cover the following topics:

- What is Java?
- Java platforms, editions, versions, and technologies
- Java SE Development Kit (JDK) installation and configuration
- Main Java commands
- Exercise – JDK tools and utilities

# What is Java?

Since this book is written for beginners, we will assume that you know almost nothing about Java. But even if you do know something, or even a lot, it is always helpful to review the basics, even if it's just so you can feel good about yourself by appreciating how much you have mastered already. So, we will start by defining the terms Java, JVM, compilation, bytecode, and more.

# Basic terms

When talking about Java, people use Java, JVM, JDK, SDK, and Java platform as synonyms. The legal definition treats Java as *Sun's trademark for a set of technologies*, but we typically do not think about Java as a trademark. Most often, when somebody says Java, they mean a programming language that is used by humans to express sets of instructions (programs) that can be executed by a computer (not directly, but after the program is compiled/transformed into code that a computer understands). The human-readable Java program is called **source code**, and the computer-readable program (after all transformations) is called **binary code**, because it is expressed only using 1 and 0.

You can find the complete **Java Language Specification** (description) at `https://docs.oracle.com/javase/specs/`. It is much more accessible than one might expect, and it can be helpful even for a novice, especially if one uses it as a reference document. Do not feel discouraged by the formal language of the first few sections. Read what you can and come back later, as your understanding of Java grows and the motivation for deeper and more precise definitions increases.

 JVM is a program that translates byte code of Java `.class` files into binary machine code and sends it to a microprocessor for execution.

Have you noticed that there are two similar terms, *bytecode* and *byte code*? In conversation, the difference is hardly noticeable, so people use them interchangeably. But there is a difference. *Byte code* (or *Byte Code*, to be precise) is a language that can be executed by a special program called JVM. By contrast, *bytecode* is the format (each instruction occupies one byte, thus the name) of the instructions generated by the Java compiler (another program) that reads the human-readable source code and transforms it into Byte Code.

Bytecode is a binary code expressed in the format JVM understands. JVM then reads (loads, using a program called **class loader**) bytecodes, transforms the instructions into binary code (instructions in a format a particular computer microprocessor, where JVM is running, understands), and passes the result to the CPU, a microprocessor that executes it.

A class is a file (with the extension .class) produced by the Java compiler (from the source code in a file with the same name and the extension .java). There are more than a dozen JVM implementations, created by different companies, but we will be focusing on Oracle JVM's implementation, which is called **HotSpot**. In Chapter 11, *JVM Processes and Garbage Collection*, we will look more closely at JVM's functionality, architecture, and processes.

On the same page as the Java Language Specification (https://docs.oracle.com/javase/specs), you can find the Java Virtual Machine Specification. We recommend that you use it as a source of references for the terminology and for the understanding of JVM functionality.

> JDK is a collection of software tools and supporting libraries that allow for the creation and execution of Java language programs.

Since Java 9, applets (components that can be executed in a browser) are not supported anymore, so we will not talk much about them. An application is a Java program that can be (after compilation) executed on a computer where JVM is installed. So, JDK includes at minimum a compiler, JVM, and **Java Class Library** (JCL)—a collection of ready-to-use procedures that can be called by an application. But in reality, it has many other tools and utilities that can help you to compile, execute, and monitor a Java application. The subset of JDK that includes JVM, JCL, class loader, and supporting files allows the execution (running) of bytecode. Such a combination is called the **Java Runtime Environment** (JRE). Each Java application is executed in a separate JVM instance (copy) that has its own allocated computer memory, so two Java applications cannot talk to each other directly, but only via the network (web-services and similar means).

> **Software Development Kit** (**SDK**) is a collection of software tools and supporting libraries that allow the creation of an application using a certain programming language. SDK for Java is called JDK.

So, when people use SDK in reference to JDK, they are correct, but not precise.

The Java platform is composed of a compiler, JVM, supporting libraries, and other tools from JDK.

The supporting libraries in the preceding definitions are Java standard libraries, also called **JCL**, and are necessary for executing bytecode. If a program requires some other libraries (not included in JCL), they have to be added at compilation time (see `Chapter 3`, *Your Development Environment Setup*, which describes how to do it) and included in the generated bytecode. Java platform can be one of the four: **Java Platform Standard Edition (Java SE), Java Platform Enterprise Edition (Java EE), Java Platform Micro Edition (Java ME)**, or **Java Card**. There used to be the JavaFX Platform, too, but it has been merged into Java SE since Java 8. We will talk about the differences in the next section.

Open JDK is a free and open source implementation of Java SE.

These are the most basic terms. Other terms will be introduced as needed throughout the book, in the corresponding contexts.

# History and popularity

Java was first released in 1995 by Sun Microsystems. It was derived from C and C++, but did not allow users to manipulate computer memory on a very low level, which is the source of many difficulties, including memory leak related issues, that C and C++ programmers experience if they are not very careful about it. Java stood out due to its simplicity, portability, interoperability, and safety net, which allowed it to become one of the most popular programming languages. It is estimated that as of 2017, there are close to 20 million programmers in the world (close to 4 million of them are in the US), and approximately half of them use Java. And there are good reasons to believe that the need for software developers, including Java developers, will only grow in the future. So, studying Java looks like a step towards a stable career. And learning Java is not actually very difficult. We will show you how to do it; just continue reading, thinking, and trying all the suggestions in practice on your computer.

Java was conceived as a facility that allows users to *write once, run anywhere* – that is another term to explain and understand. It means that compiled Java code can run on all computers with operating systems that support Java, without the need for recompilation. As you understand already, *support Java* means that for each operating system, an interpreter exists that can transform bytecode into binary code. That's how *run anywhere* is implemented: anywhere where a Java interpreter is available.

After the concept proved to be popular and Java was firmly established as one of the major players among other object-oriented languages, Sun Microsystems made much of its JVM free and open source software, governed by the GNU **General Public License** (**GPL**). In 2007, Sun Microsystems made all of its JVM's core code available under free and open source distribution terms, except for a small portion of code to which Sun did not have the copyright. In 2010, Oracle acquired Sun Microsystems and declared itself *a steward of Java technology with a relentless commitment to fostering a community of participation and transparency.*

Today, Java is used in many areas, most prominently in Android programming and other mobile applications, in various embedded systems (various chips and specialized computers), desktop **Graphical User Interface** (**GUI**) development, and a huge variety of web applications, including network applications and web services. Java is also widely used for scientific applications, including the rapidly expanding areas of machine learning and artificial intelligence.

# Principles

There were five primary goals in the creation of the Java language, according to *Design Goals of the Java* $^{TM}$ *Programming Language* (`http://www.oracle.com/technetwork/java/intro-141325.html`). The Java language had to be:

- **Object-oriented and familiar**: This meant that it had to look like C++, but without unnecessary complexities (we will discuss the term object-oriented in `Chapter 2`, *Java Language Basics*)
- **Architecture-neutral and portable**: This meant the ability to use JVM as the environment that isolates the language (source code) from the knowledge of each particular operating system (often called the platform)
- **High performance**: It should work on par with the leading programming languages of the time

- **Interpreted**: It can be moved to an executing phase without linking (creating a single executable file from multiple `.class` files), thus allowing a quicker write-compile-execute cycle (modern JVMs, though, are optimized to keep the binary version of the often used `.class` files, to avoid repeating interpretation)
- **Multithreaded**: It should allow several concurrent execution jobs (threads), such as downloading an image and processing other user commands and data at the same time
- **Dynamic**: Linking should happen during execution
- **Secure**: It had to be well protected from an unauthorized modification at runtime

The result proved these goals to be well-defined and fruitful, because Java became one of the main languages of the internet era.

# Java platforms, editions, versions, and technologies

In everyday discussions, some programmers use these terms interchangeably, but there is a difference between Java platforms, editions, versions, and technologies. This section is focuses on explaining it.

## Platforms and editions

We hear the term *platform* almost every day. Its meaning changes depending on the context, but in the most general sense, it means a device or environment that allows someone to do something. It serves as a foundation, an environment, a platform. In the information technology realm, a platform provides an operating environment where a software program can be developed and executed. An operating system is a typical example of a platform. Java has its own operating environment, which comes, as we have mentioned in the previous sections, in four platforms (and six editions):

- **Java Platform Standard Edition (Java SE)**: This is the edition most people mean when they say Java. It includes JVM, JCL, and other tools and utilities that allow for the development and deployment of Java applications on desktops and servers. In this book, we are going to stay within the boundaries of this edition, and will mention the other editions only in this section.

- **Java Platform Enterprise Edition** (**Java EE**): This is composed of Java SE, servers (computer programs that provide services to the applications), enhanced libraries, code samples, tutorials, and other documentation for developing and deploying large-scale, multitiered, and secure network applications.
- **Java Platform Micro Edition** (**Java ME**): This is a small-footprint (using little resources) subset of Java SE, with some specialized class libraries for developing and deploying Java applications for embedded and mobile devices – phones, personal digital assistants, TV set-top boxes, printers, sensors, and so on. There is also a variation of Java ME for Android programming (with its own JVM implementation), developed by Google. It is called **Android SDK**.
- **Java Card**: This is the smallest of the Java platforms, for developing and deploying Java applications onto small embedded devices, such as smart cards. It comes in two editions (quotes are taken from the official Oracle documentation found at `http://www.oracle.com/technetwork/java/embedded/javacard/documentation/javacard-faq-1970428.html#3`):
    - **Java Card Classic Edition**, which *targets smart cards as deployed today on all vertical markets, based on ISO7816 and ISO14443 communication.*
    - **Java Card Connected Edition**, which is developed *to support a web application model, with servlets running on the card, and TCP/IP as basic protocol* and *runs on high-end secure microcontrollers, typically based on a 32-bit processor and supporting a high-speed communication interface like USB.*

# Versions

Since its first release in 1996, Java has evolved through nine major versions:

- JDK 1.0 (January 23, 1996)
- JDK 1.1 (February 19, 1997)
- J2SE 1.2 (December 8, 1998)
- J2SE 1.3 (May 8, 2000)
- J2SE 1.4 (February 6, 2002)
- J2SE 5.0 (September 30, 2004)
- Java SE 6 (December 11, 2006)
- Java SE 7 (July 28, 2011)

- Java SE 8 (March 18, 2014)
- Java SE 9 (September 21, 2017)
- Java SE 10 (March 20, 2018)

There are several suggestions regarding changing the Java versioning scheme. Since Java 10, a new time-based versioning $YEAR.$MONTH of JDK has been introduced. Also, a new Java version is planned to be released every six months, in March and in September of each year. So, Java 11 will be released in September 2018, with JVM version 18.9. We will show you how to display which JDK version you are using shortly.

# Technologies

The word technology is overloaded. Programmers use it for almost anything. If you look at Oracle's list of Java technologies (`https://www.oracle.com/java/technologies/index.html`), you will find the following list:

- **Embedded**, which includes all of the previously listed Java platforms except for Java EE, with some modifications, usually with a smaller footprint and other optimizations
- **Java SE**, which covers Java SE and Java SE Advanced, which includes Java SE and some monitoring and management tools for an enterprise level (larger than just a development computer) installation
- **Java EE**, as described previously
- **Cloud**, which includes cloud-based reliable, scalable, and elastic services

But in the Oracle glossary (`http://www.oracle.com/technetwork/java/glossary-135216.html`), the following technologies are added to the list:

- **JavaSpaces**: A technology that provides distributed persistence
- **Jini Technology**: An **Application Programming Interface** (**API**) that enables the networking of devices and services automatically

Elsewhere, on the front page of the Oracle Java 10 documentation (`https://docs.oracle.com/javase/10`), client technologies are listed as follows:

Client Technologies

JavaFX and Swing (JDK 8)
Java Accessibility Guide

Meanwhile, in the Oracle Java tutorial (`https://docs.oracle.com/javase/tutorial/getStarted/intro/cando.html`), **Java Web Start** and **Java Plug-In** are mentioned as deployment technologies *for deploying your applications to end users.*

However, the biggest list of Java technologies that Oracle provides is on the page dedicated to the Technology Network (`http://www.oracle.com/technetwork/java/index.html`). In addition to Java SE, Java SE Advanced and Suite, Java Embedded, Java EE, Java FX, and Java Card, there are also listed **Java TV**, **Java DB**, and **Developer Tools**. If you go to the Java SE or Java EE pages, under the **Technologies** tab, you will find more than two dozens APIs, and various software components listed as technologies, too. So, one should not be surprised to find anywhere any kind of list of Java technologies.

It seems that anything related to Java has been called a technology at least once, somewhere. To avoid further confusion, from now on, in this book, we will try to avoid using word technology.

# Java SE Development Kit (JDK) installation and configuration

From now on, every time we talk about Java, we mean Java SE version 10. We will refer to it as Java 10, or Java, or JDK, used as synonyms, unless otherwise specified.

## Where to start

Before you can do any Java development on your computer, you will need JDK installed and configured. In order to do this, search the internet for the JDK download and select any link that starts with `https://www.oracle.com/`. The best, as of this writing, should be `http://www.oracle.com/technetwork/java/javase/downloads/index.html`.

If you follow the preceding link, you will see this section:

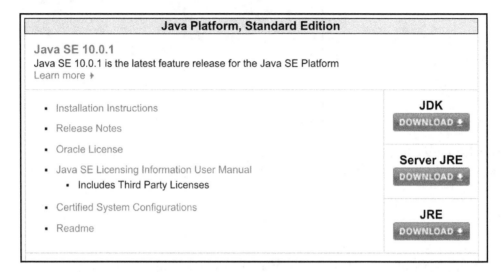

Let us call this page *Page1*, for further references. Now, you can click the **Download** link under **JDK**. The other two download links offer JRE, which, as you know already, only allows you to run already compiled Java programs; we need to write a program, compile it into bytecode, and then run it.

# The page with Java installers

After you click, you will see a page (*Page2*) with this section:

## Java SE Development Kit 10.0.1

You must accept the Oracle Binary Code License Agreement for Java SE to download this software.

○ Accept License Agreement   ◉ Decline License Agreement

| Product / File Description | File Size | Download |
|---|---|---|
| Linux | 305.97 MB | ⬇jdk-10.0.1_linux-x64_bin.rpm |
| Linux | 338.41 MB | ⬇jdk-10.0.1_linux-x64_bin.tar.gz |
| macOS | 395.46 MB | ⬇jdk-10.0.1_osx-x64_bin.dmg |
| Solaris SPARC | 206.63 MB | ⬇jdk-10.0.1_solaris-sparcv9_bin.tar.gz |
| Windows | 390.19 MB | ⬇jdk-10.0.1_windows-x64_bin.exe |

These are the Java installers for different **operating systems** (**OS**). You need to choose the one that fits your OS and click the corresponding link (do not forget to click **Accept License Agreement** using the radio button; if in doubt, read the license agreement via the link **Oracle Binary Code License Agreement for Java SE**). For Linux, there are two installers – one in Red Hat Package Manager Format (.rpm), and one that is just an archived (.tar) and compressed (.gz) version. Also, noticed that in this list, there are only installers for 64-bit operating systems. As of this writing, it is not clear yet if the 32-bit version is to be dropped officially, although it was available as an early access build.

Select the installer that you need, and download it.

# How to install

Now is the time to install Java, which basically consists of the following four steps:

1. Expand the installer
2. Create directories
3. Copy files into these directories
4. Make the Java executables accessible without typing the full path

To find the detailed installation instructions, go back to *Page1* and click on the **Installation Instructions** link. Find the link for your operating system and follow the provided steps, but choose only those that are related to JDK.

Eventually, you will come to the point when you are able to run the command java -version, which will display the following:

```
demo> java -version
java version "10.0.1" 2018-04-17
Java(TM) SE Runtime Environment 18.3 (build 10.0.1+10)
Java HotSpot(TM) 64-Bit Server VM 18.3 (build 10.0.1+10, mixed mode)
demo>
```

As you can see, it shows the version for Java as **10.0.1**, and for JRE and JVM as **18.3 (build 10.0.1)**. It is not clear yet if future versions of Java, JRE, and JVM are going to follow the same format.

Anyway, if the `java -version` command displays the version you tried to install, it means that you have installed Java correctly and can now enjoy working with it. From now on, every time a new version comes out, you are going to be prompted to upgrade, and you can do it by just clicking the provided link. Alternatively, you can go to the page with the installers (*Page2*), download the corresponding installer, launch it, and repeat the process already familiar to you.

In practice, though, programmers do not upgrade their Java installation every time. They keep their development version the same as the Java in their production environment (in order to avoid potential incompatibility). If they would like to play with a new version before upgrading the production, they might have two versions of Java installed on their computer, in parallel. In Chapter 3, *Your Development Environment Setup*, you will learn how to do this, and how to switch between them.

# Main Java commands

In the previous section, you saw one example of a Java command, the one that displays the JVM version. By the way, the command `java` starts the JVM, and is used to run bytecodes of the compiled Java programs (we will demonstrate how to do this in detail in Chapter 4, *Your First Java Project*).

## The JVM execution command

Now, if you only run `java`, the output will display the short version of help. Since it is quite long, we will show it in several parts. Here is the first section:

```
demo> java
Usage: java [options] <mainclass> [args...]
           (to execute a class)
    or java [options] -jar <jarfile> [args...]
           (to execute a jar file)
    or java [options] -m <module>[/<mainclass>] [args...]
       java [options] --module <module>[/<mainclass>] [args...]
           (to execute the main class in a module)

Arguments following the main class, -jar <jarfile>, -m or --module
<module>/<mainclass> are passed as the arguments to main class.
```

It shows three ways to run JVM:

- To execute a class, a `.class` file that contains bytecode
- To execute a jar file, a file with the extension `.jar` that contains `.class` files (may be even the whole application) in a ZIP format, which also includes a Java-specific manifest file
- To execute the main class in a module (a group of `.class` files and other resources that is better structured than a `.jar` file), typically an application, or a part of it

As you can see, in each of the preceding commands, a main class has to be supplied explicitly. It is the `.class` file that has to be executed first. It acts as the main entrance into the application, and starts the chain of loading other classes (as they are needed) to run the application. An example of such a command would be:

```
java MyGreatApplication
```

In fact, this means that there is a file, `MyGreatApplication.class`, in the current directory, but we should not specify the file extension. Otherwise, JVM will look for the file `MyGreatApplication.class.class`, which it will not find, of course, and fail to run anything.

In this book, we are not going to use any of these commands explicitly, and will leave it up to the editor to run it behind the scenes, because a modern editor does not just help write and modify the source code; it can also compile and execute the written code. That's why it is called not just the editor, but the **Integrated Development Environment** (**IDE**).

Nevertheless, we will continue to overview all of the `java` command options, so you will have an idea what is going behind the scenes in your IDE. To enjoy car driving, one does not need to know the details of the engine's inner workings, but it is helpful to have some idea about the principles of its operation. Besides, as your professional level grows and the applications you work on grow too and have to handle many requests, you will need to adjust the JVM configuration, so here is the first sneak peek under the hood.

Here is the next section of the output of the `java` command:

```
where options include:

    -d32          Deprecated, will be removed in a future release
    -d64          Deprecated, will be removed in a future release
    -cp <class search path of directories and zip/jar files>
    -classpath <class search path of directories and zip/jar files>
    --class-path <class search path of directories and zip/jar files>
                  A : separated list of directories, JAR archives,
                  and ZIP archives to search for class files.
    -p <module path>
    --module-path <module path>...
                  A : separated list of directories, each directory
                  is a directory of modules.
    --upgrade-module-path <module path>...
                  A : separated list of directories, each directory
                  is a directory of modules that replace upgradeable
                  modules in the runtime image
    --add-modules <module name>[,<module name>...]
                  root modules to resolve in addition to the initial module.
                  <module name> can also be ALL-DEFAULT, ALL-SYSTEM,
                  ALL-MODULE-PATH.
    --list-modules
                  list observable modules and exit
```

In the preceding screenshot, you can see two deprecated options followed by options related to classpath and module path. The last two are very important options. They allow the specifying of the location of the classes your application consists of, and the location of the libraries your application uses. The latter can be classes written by you or third-party libraries.

The concept of modules is out of the scope of this book, but module path is used very similarly to the classpath. The classpath option tells JVM where to look for the classes, while the module path tells JVM about the location of the modules. It is possible to use both in the same command line.

For example, let us assume that you have the file MyGreatApplication.class (which contains the bytecode of your program, MyGreatApplication.java) stored in the directory dir2, which is a subdirectory of the directory dir1, and your terminal window currently shows the content of the directory dir1:

```
demo> ls -l
total 0
drwxr-xr-x  2 ab54696  staff  68 Dec  9 10:33 dir2
drwxr-xr-x  2 ab54696  staff  68 Dec  9 10:33 dir3
drwxr-xr-x  2 ab54696  staff  68 Dec  9 10:51 dir4
demo>
```

As you can see, there is another directory, `dir3`, which we created to store another file, `SomeOtherProgram.class`, that is used by your application. We also put in `dir4` a library of other supporting `.class` files, collected in `SomeLibrary.jar`. The command line to run your application then looks like this:

```
java –cp dir2:dir3:dir4/SomeLibrary.jar  MyGreatApplication //on Unix
java –cp dir2;dir3;dir4\SomeLibrary.jar  MyGreatApplication //on Windows
```

Alternatively, we can put `SomeOtherProgram.class` and `MyGreatApplication.class` in `some.jar` or a `some.zip` file, and place it in `dir5`. Then, the command will take one of the following forms:

```
java –cp dir4/SomeLibrary.jar:dir5/some.zip MyGreatApplication //Unix
java –cp dir4/SomeLibrary.jar:dir5/some.jar MyGreatApplication //Unix
java –cp dir4\SomeLibrary.jar;dir5\some.zip MyGreatApplication //Windows
java –cp dir4\SomeLibrary.jar;dir5\some.jar MyGreatApplication //Windows
```

Instead of `–cp`, we could use the options `–classpath` or `––class-path`. They are just three different conventions, so that people used to one of them can write a command line intuitively. None of the styles are better or worse than the others, although each of us has preferences and opinions. If neither of the classpath options is used, JVM looks for classes only in the current directory. Some of the classes (standard libraries) are always located in certain directories of Java installation, so there is no need to list them with a classpath option. We will talk about setting the classpath in more detail in `Chapter 3`, *Your Development Environment Setup*.

The next section of the `java` command output lists options that allow for validating that everything is set correctly before actually executing the application:

```
-d <module name>
--describe-module <module name>
                describe a module and exit
--dry-run       create VM and load main class but do not execute main method.
                The --dry-run option may be useful for validating the
                command-line options such as the module system configuration.
--validate-modules
                validate all modules and exit
                The --validate-modules option may be useful for finding
                conflicts and other errors with modules on the module path.
```

Since modules are outside of the scope of this book, we are skipping these and moving on to the next section of the output:

```
-D<name>=<value>
               set a system property
-verbose:[class|module|gc|jni]
               enable verbose output
-version       print product version to the error stream and exit
--version      print product version to the output stream and exit
-showversion   print product version to the error stream and continue
--show-version
               print product version to the output stream and continue
--show-module-resolution
               show module resolution output during startup
-? -h -help
               print this help message to the error stream
--help         print this help message to the output stream
-X             print help on extra options to the error stream
--help-extra   print help on extra options to the output stream
```

The -D option allows for setting a parameter with a value that is accessible to the application. It is often used to pass some values or flags to the application, which the application can use to change its behavior. If more information needs to be passed, then the .properties file is used (with many flags and various values), while the location of the property file is passed with the option -D. It is completely up to the programmer what has to be in the .properties file or in the value passed with the option -D. But there are best practices related to the application configuration, which also depend on the particular framework or libraries you are using. You will learn them over time, and these practices are beyond the beginner programmer course.

The -verbose option provides more information (than we have seen on these screenshots) and some specific data, depending on the flags class, module, gc, or jni, where **gc** stands for **garbage collector**, which will be discussed in Chapter 11, *JVM Processes and Garbage Collection*. For the other flags, you can read the official Oracle documentation, but chances are, you will not use them anytime soon.

The -version option displays the version of Java that is installed. This is very useful from day one, because it allows for checking, at any time, what version of Java is currently in use. In the previous section, we demonstrated how to do it, and the output it produces. When a new version of Java is released, many programmers install it in parallel with the one they are currently using, and switch between them, either to learn new features or to start writing code for a new version, while maintaining the old code written for the old version. You will learn how to have two versions of Java installed on the same computer, and how to switch between them, in Chapter 3, *Your Development Environment Setup*.

We will skip the module-related options.

The rest of the options in the preceding screenshot are related to the help. The options -?, -h, -help, and --help display what we are showing in these screenshots, and the options -X and --help-extra provide additional information. You can try all of them on your own.

The last section of the help output looks as follows:

```
    -ea[:<packagename>...|:<classname>]
    -enableassertions[:<packagename>...|:<classname>]
                    enable assertions with specified granularity
    -da[:<packagename>...|:<classname>]
    -disableassertions[:<packagename>...|:<classname>]
                    disable assertions with specified granularity
    -esa | -enablesystemassertions
                    enable system assertions
    -dsa | -disablesystemassertions
                    disable system assertions
    -agentlib:<libname>[=<options>]
                    load native agent library <libname>, e.g. -agentlib:jdwp
                    see also -agentlib:jdwp=help
    -agentpath:<pathname>[=<options>]
                    load native agent library by full pathname
    -javaagent:<jarpath>[=<options>]
                    load Java programming language agent, see java.lang.instrument
    -splash:<imagepath>
                    show splash screen with specified image
                    HiDPI scaled images are automatically supported and used
                    if available. The unscaled image filename, e.g. image.ext,
                    should always be passed as the argument to the -splash option.
                    The most appropriate scaled image provided will be picked up
                    automatically.
                    See the SplashScreen API documentation for more information
    @argument files
                    one or more argument files containing options
    -disable-@files
                    prevent further argument file expansion
To specify an argument for a long option, you can use --<name>=<value> or
--<name> <value>.
```

We will not discuss these options. Just note how to use the long option (with two hyphens) explained in the last preceding line.

# The compilation command

As mentioned earlier, a program written in Java is called a source code, and is stored in a `.java` file. The compilation command `javac` reads it and creates a corresponding `.class` file with Java Byte Code.

Let us run the command `javac` without specifying a `.java` file. It will show help. Let us review it in sections:

```
demo> javac
Usage: javac <options> <source files>
where possible options include:
  @<filename>                    Read options and filenames from file
  -Akey[=value]                  Options to pass to annotation processors
  --add-modules <module>(,<module>)*
            Root modules to resolve in addition to the initial modules, or all modul
es
            on the module path if <module> is ALL-MODULE-PATH.
  --boot-class-path <path>, -bootclasspath <path>
            Override location of bootstrap class files
  --class-path <path>, -classpath <path>, -cp <path>
            Specify where to find user class files and annotation processors
  -d <directory>                 Specify where to place generated class files
  -deprecation
            Output source locations where deprecated APIs are used
```

The help tells us that this command has the following format:

```
javac <options> <source files>
```

To compile just a few files, one can list them in the command line after options (if the file is not in the current directory, one has to prepend the filename with an absolute or relative path). Listed files are separated by colons (`:`) for Oracle Solaris, or semicolons (`;`) for Windows, and can be directories, `.jar` files, or `.zip` files. It is also possible to list all source files in a file and provide this filename using the `@filename` option (see the preceding screenshot). But do not try to remember all of this. You will rarely (if ever) run the commands `java` or `javac` explicitly. You will probably use an IDE that will do it for you (see Chapter 3, *Your Development Environment Setup*). That is also the reason we are going to skip most of the options listed in the preceding screenshot and will mention only two of them: `--class-path` (or `-classpath`, or `-cp`), which specifies where to find the `.class` files required by the currently compiled code, and `-d`, which indicates where to put the created `.class` files.

Here is the next section of `javac` help:

```
-encoding <encoding>         Specify character encoding used by source files
-endorseddirs <dirs>         Override location of endorsed standards path
-extdirs <dirs>              Override location of installed extensions
-g                           Generate all debugging info
-g:{lines,vars,source}       Generate only some debugging info
-g:none                      Generate no debugging info
-h <directory>
        Specify where to place generated native header files
--help, -help                Print this help message
--help-extra, -X             Print help on extra options
-implicit:{none,class}
        Specify whether or not to generate class files for implicitly referenced
files
-J<flag>                     Pass <flag> directly to the runtime system
--limit-modules <module>(,<module>)*
        Limit the universe of observable modules
--module <module-name>, -m <module-name>
        Compile only the specified module, check timestamps
--module-path <path>, -p <path>
        Specify where to find application modules
--module-source-path <module-source-path>
        Specify where to find input source files for multiple modules
--module-version <version>
        Specify version of modules that are being compiled
```

The only option from the preceding screenshot that we will mention here is `--help` (or `-help`), which provides the same help message that we are going through now.

Finally, the last section of `javac` help is as follows:

```
-nowarn                      Generate no warnings
-parameters
        Generate metadata for reflection on method parameters
-proc:{none,only}
        Control whether annotation processing and/or compilation is done.
-processor <class1>[,<class2>,<class3>...]
        Names of the annotation processors to run; bypasses default discovery pr
ocess
--processor-module-path <path>
        Specify a module path where to find annotation processors
--processor-path <path>, -processorpath <path>
        Specify where to find annotation processors
-profile <profile>
        Check that API used is available in the specified profile
--release <release>
        Compile for a specific VM version. Supported targets: 6, 7, 8, 9
-s <directory>               Specify where to place generated source files
-source <release>
        Provide source compatibility with specified release
--source-path <path>, -sourcepath <path>
        Specify where to find input source files
--system <jdk>|none          Override location of system modules
-target <release>            Generate class files for specific VM version
--upgrade-module-path <path>
        Override location of upgradeable modules
-verbose                     Output messages about what the compiler is doing
--version, -version          Version information
-Werror                      Terminate compilation if warnings occur
```

We have already described the option `--source-path` (or `-sourcepath`). The option `-verbose` asks the compiler to provide a more detailed report about what it is doing, while the option `--version` (or `-version`) displays the JDK version:

```
demo> javac -version
javac 10.0.1
demo>
```

# Command jcmd and other commands

There are more than a dozen other Java commands (tools and utilities) that you will only start using probably after several years of professional programming, if at all. They are all described in the Oracle Java documentation online. Just search the Java utilities and tools.

Among them, we find only one command that is very useful from day one of Java programming. It is the command `jcmd`. If you run it, it displays all of the Java processes (JVM instances) that are running on your computer. In this example, you can see three Java processes, with the process IDs **3408**, **3458**, and **3454**:

```
demo> jcmd
3408 org.jetbrains.idea.maven.server.RemoteMavenServer
3458 jdk.jcmd/sun.tools.jcmd.JCmd
3454 org.jetbrains.jps.cmdline.Launcher /Applications/IntelliJ IDEA CE.app/Conte
nts/lib/util.jar:/Applications/IntelliJ IDEA CE.app/Contents/lib/httpclient-4.5.
2.jar:/Applications/IntelliJ IDEA CE.app/Contents/lib/jna-platform.jar:/Applicat
ions/IntelliJ IDEA CE.app/Contents/lib/log4j.jar:/Applications/IntelliJ IDEA CE.
app/Contents/lib/maven-aether-provider-3.3.9-all.jar:/Applications/IntelliJ IDEA
 CE.app/Contents/lib/idea_rt.jar:/Applications/IntelliJ IDEA CE.app/Contents/lib
/resources_en.jar:/Applications/IntelliJ IDEA CE.app/Contents/lib/netty-all-4.1.
13.Final.jar:/Applications/IntelliJ IDEA CE.app/Contents/lib/openapi.jar:/Applic
ations/IntelliJ IDEA CE.app/Contents/lib/commons-codec-1.9.jar:/Applications/Int
elliJ IDEA CE.app/Contents/lib/guava-21.0.jar:/Applications/IntelliJ IDEA CE.app
/Contents/lib/jps-model.jar:/Applications/IntelliJ IDEA CE.app/Contents/lib/nano
xml-2.2.3.jar:/Applications/IntelliJ IDEA CE.app/Contents/lib/jgoodies-forms.jar
:/Applications/IntelliJ IDEA CE.app/Contents/lib/aether-1.1.0-all.jar
3455 com.packt.javapath.App
```

Process **3408** runs the Maven server (your IDE will typically start it). Process **3458** is our running of `jcmd`. And process **3454** is an editor (IDE) IntelliJ IDEA that is running the small demo application `com.packt.javapath.App`.

This way, you can always check to see if there is a runaway Java process on your computer. If you would like to stop it, you can use a **Task Manager**, or the command `kill`, which requires PID.

Knowledge of PID is also needed when you would like to monitor your Java application. We will talk about that in `Chapter 11`, *JVM Processes and Garbage Collection*.

With this, we complete our overview of Java commands. As we already mentioned, your IDE will use all of these commands behind the scenes, so you will probably never use them unless you do production support (which is several years out, after you start learning Java). But we feel that you need to know them, so that you can connect the dots of the Java development process.

# Exercise – JDK tools and utilities

On your computer, find the Java installation directory, and list all of the commands (tools and utilities)—the executables—present there.

 You are in the right spot if you see `java` and `javac` among other executables.

# Answer

Here is the list of all of the executables installed with Java 10.0.1:

```
demo> cd /Library/Java/JavaVirtualMachines/jdk-10.jdk/Contents/Home/bin
demo> ls
appletviewer   javac          jconsole       jimage         jps            jweblauncher   rmiregistry    wsgen
idlj           javadoc        jcontrol       jinfo          jrunscript     keytool        schemagen      wsimport
jaotc          javap          jdb            jjs            jshell         orbd           serialver      xjc
jar            javapackager   jdeprscan      jlink          jstack         pack200        servertool
jarsigner      javaws         jdeps          jmap           jstat          rmic           tnameserv
java           jcmd           jhsdb          jmod           jstatd         rmid           unpack200
demo>
```

One of the ways to find this directory is to look at the value of the environment variable `PATH`. For example, on a Mac computer, Java is installed in the directory `/Library/Java/JavaVirtualMachines/jdk-10.jdk/Contents/Home/bin`.

The Oracle documentation that describes the JVM installation location can be found at `https://www.java.com/en/download/help/version_manual.xml`.

# Summary

In this chapter, you have learned the most important Java related terms—JVM, JDK, SDK, Java platform, and others, covering the main phases of a Java program's life cycle, from source code to bytecode to execution. You also learned about Java's history, the motivation behind its creation, its editions, and its versions. The practical steps and advice provided have helped you to install Java on your computer and exercise its main commands, `java`, `javac`, and `jcmd`. For more details, you were referred to the official Oracle documentation. The ability to find and understand this documentation is a prerequisite for a successful career as a Java programmer, so we recommend that you follow all of the provided links and do some related searching on the internet, so that you feel comfortable finding good sources of information.

In the next chapter, we will dive into Java as a programming language, and will cover the basics. This will become a foundation (or a jumping board, if you will) for the following chapters. If you are new to Java, we recommend that you continue reading without skipping, because each chapter is built on knowledge from the previous one. Even if you have some Java exposure, it is always helpful to review the basics again. *Repetitio est mater studiorum (Repetition is the mother of study/learning)*, says a Latin proverb.

# Java Language Basics

2

Now that you have a general idea about Java and its related terms and tools, we will start discussing Java as a programming language.

This chapter will introduce the basic concepts of Java as an **object-oriented programming (OOP)** language. You will learn about classes, interfaces, and objects, and their relations. You will also learn the concepts and features of OOP.

In this chapter, we will cover the following topics:

- The basic terms in Java programming
- Classes and objects (instances)
- Class (static) and object (instance) members
- Interface, implementation, and inheritance
- OOP concepts and features
- Exercise – Interface versus abstract class

We call them basics because they are the founding principles of Java as a language, and there is more to learn before you can start programming professionally. For those who are learning Java for the first time, learning the basics of Java is a steep slope to climb, but the path becomes easier thereafter.

## The basic terms of Java programming

The notion of Java programming basics has many interpretations. Some tutorials assume the basics to be the same for any object-oriented language. Others discuss syntax and basic language elements and grammar rules. Yet others reduce the basics to the value types, operators, statements, and expressions that allow computations.

Our view of Java basics consists of some elements from each of the earlier approaches. The only criteria for the selection we used were practicality and a gradual increase of complexity. We will start with simple definitions in this section, and then dive deeper into them in the subsequent sections.

# Byte code

In the broadest terms, a Java program (or any computer program for that matter) means a sequential set of instructions for a computer, that tell it what to do. Before executing on a computer, a program must be compiled from a human-readable, high-level programming language into a machine-readable binary code.

In the case of Java, the human-readable text, called a source code, is stored in a `.java` file and can be compiled into byte code by the Java compiler `javac`. Java byte code is the instruction set for JVM. The byte code is stored in a `.class` file and can be interpreted and compiled into binary code by, JVM or, more specifically, by the **Just-In-Time** (**JIT**) compiler used by JVM. The binary code is then executed by a microprocessor.

An important feature of byte code is that it can be copied from one machine and executed on another machine's JVM. That is what Java portability means.

# Defects (bugs) and their severity and priority

The word *bug*, with the meaning of *little faults and difficulties*, existed as early as the 19th century. The origin of this word is unknown, but it looks as if the verb *to bug* in a sense *to annoy* comes from that feeling of a pesky bothering coming from an insect—a bug—that buzzes around and threatens to bite you or something. The word was applied to programming defects as soon as a computer was first built.

The defects vary by their severity – the degree of the effect they have on the program execution, or its results. Some defects are quite insignificant, like a format, in which the data are presented for a human. It would be another matter if the same data have to be consumed by some other system that could not process data presented in such a format. Then such a defect may be qualified as critical, because it would not allow the system to complete the data processing.

 The severity of a defect depends on how it affects the program, not on how difficult it is to fix it.

Some defects may force the program to exit before it has achieved the desired result. For example, a defect may lead to the exhaustion of memory or another resource, and cause JVM to shut down.

The defect priority, how high the defect is on the to-do list, generally corresponds to the severity. But some low severity defects may be prioritized higher because of a customer perception. For example, the grammar error on a website, or a typo that may be perceived as offensive.

> A defect's priority typically corresponds to its severity but sometimes, the priority may be increased based on customer perception.

# Java program dependencies

We also mentioned that a program may require the use of other programs and procedures that are already compiled into bytecodes. For JVM to find them, you must list the corresponding `.class` files in the `java` command using the `-classpath` option. Several programs and procedures make up a Java application.

The other programs and procedures used by the application for its tasks are called application dependencies.

Notice that JVM does not read a `.class` file until some other class code requests it. So, it well may be that some of the `.class` files listed on a classpath are never used if the conditions under which they are needed never happen during the application's execution.

# Statements

A statement is a language construct that can be compiled into a set of instructions to a computer. The closest analogy from everyday life to a Java statement is a sentence in the English language, a basic unit of language that expresses a complete thought. Every statement in Java must end with a `;` (semi-colon).

Here is an example of a declaration statement:

```
int i;
```

The preceding statement declares a variable `i` of type `int` which stands for *integer* (see `Chapter 5`, *Java Language Elements and Types*).

Here is an expression statement:

```
i + 2;
```

The preceding statement adds 2 to the value of the existing variable i. When declared, an int variable is assigned a value of 0 by default, so the result of this expression is 2, but it is not stored. That is why it is often combined with declaration and assignment statements:

```
int j = i + 2;
```

This tells the processor to create the variable j of type int and assign to it a value that is equal to the current value assigned to the variable i increased by 2. In Chapter 9, *Operators, Expressions, and Statements*, we will discuss statements and expressions in more detail.

# Methods

A Java method is a group of statements that are always executed together with the purpose of producing a certain result in response to a certain input. A method has a name, either a set of input parameters or no parameters at all, a body inside { } brackets, and a return type or void keyword that indicates that message does not return any value. Here is an example of a method:

```
int multiplyByTwo(int i){
   int j = i * 2;
   return j;
}
```

In the preceding code snippet, the method name is multiplyByTwo. It has one input parameter of type int. The method name and the list of parameter types are together called **method signature**. The number of input parameters is called **arity**. Two methods have the same signature if they have the same name, the same arity, and the same sequence of types in the list of input parameters.

That was a rewording of the definition of a method signature taken from Java Specification, section *8.4.2 Method Signature*. On the other hand, in the same specification, one can encounter the phrases such as: *several methods with the same name and signature, method* getNumberOfScales *in class* Tuna *has a name, signature, and return type*, and similar. So, beware; even the specification's authors sometimes do not include method name into the notion of the method signature, and don't be confused if other programmers follow suit.

The same preceding method can be re-written in many styles and with the same result:

```
int multiplyByTwo(int i){
    return i * 2;
}
```

Another style is as follows:

```
int multiplyByTwo(int i){ return i * 2; }
```

Some programmers prefer the most compact style, to be able to see as much code as possible on the screen. But that could decrease another programmer's ability to understand the code, which could lead to programming defects.

Another example is a method without input parameters:

```
int giveMeFour(){ return 4; }
```

It is quite useless. In reality, a method without parameters would read data from a database, for example, or from another source. We showed this example just to demonstrate the syntax.

Here is an example of code that does nothing:

```
void multiplyByTwo(){ }
```

The preceding method does nothing and returns nothing. The syntax requires indicating the absence of a return value using the keyword `void`. In reality, methods without return values are often used to record data to a database or to send something to a printer, to an email server, to another application (using web-services, for example), and so on.

And just for a complete overview, here is an example of a method with many parameters:

```
String doSomething(int i, String s, double a){
    double result = Math.round(Math.sqrt(a)) * i;
    return s + Double.toString(result);
}
```

The above method extracts a square root from the third parameter, multiplies it to the first parameter, converts the result into a string, and attaches (concatenates) the result to the second parameter. The types and methods from the class `Math` used will be covered in `Chapter 5`, *Java Language Elements and Types*. These calculations do not make much sense and are provided just for illustration purposes.

# Classes

All methods in Java are declared inside of structures called **classes**. A class has a name and a body in brackets { }, where methods are declared:

```
class MyClass {
    int multiplyByTwo(int i){ return i * 2; }
    int giveMeFour(){ return 4; }
}
```

Classes also have fields, often called properties; we will talk about them in the next section.

# The Main class and the main method

One class serves as an entry to a Java application. It has to be specified in the `java` command while launching the application:

**java -cp <location of all .class files> MyGreatApplication**

In the preceding command, `MyGreatApplication` is the name of the class that serves as the starting point of the application. When JVM finds the file `MyGreatApplication.class`, it reads it into the memory and looks in it for a method called `main()`. This method has a fixed signature:

```
public static void main(String[] args) {
    // statements go here
}
```

Let's break the preceding code snippet into pieces:

- `public` means that this method is accessible to any external program (see Chapter 7, *Packages and Accessibility (Visibility)*)
- `static` means that there is only one copy of the method exists in all the memory (see the following section)
- `void` means it returns nothing
- `main` is the method name
- `String[] args` means it accepts an array of String values as an input parameter (see Chapter 5, *Java Language Elements and Types*)

- // means it is a comment, ignored by JVM and placed here only for humans (see Chapter 5, *Java Language Elements and Types*)

The preceding main() method does nothing. If run, it will execute successfully but produce no result.

You may also see the input parameters written as follows:

```
public static void main(String... args) {
  //body that does something
}
```

It looks like a different signature, but in fact, it is the same. Since JDK 5, Java has allowed the *last parameter* of the method signature to be declared as a sequence of parameters of the same type of the variable arity. This is called **varargs**. Inside the method, one can treat the last input parameter as an array String[], whether it was declared as an array explicitly or as a varargs. You will be fine if you never use varargs in your life. We are telling you about it just so you can avoid confusion while reading other peoples' code.

One last, important feature of the main() method is the source of its input parameter. There is no other code that calls it. It is called by JVM itself. So, where do the parameters come from? One could guess that the command line is the source of the parameter values. In the java command, so far, we assumed that no parameters were passed to the main class. But if the main method expects some parameters, we can construct the command line as follows:

```
java -cp <location of all .class files> MyGreatApplication 1 2
```

This means that inside the main() method, the value of the first element of the input array args[0] will be 1, while the value of the second element of the input array args[1] will be 2. Yes, you noticed it right, the count of the elements in an array starts with 0. We will discuss this further in Chapter 5, *Java Language Elements and Types*. The result will be the same whether the main() method signature is described using an array String[] args explicitly or by using varargs String... args.

The code in the main() method then calls methods in the same main .class file or in the other .class files listed with the -classpath option. In the following section, we will see how such calls can be done.

# Classes and objects (instances)

A class is used as the template for creating objects. When an object is created, all fields and methods declared in the class are copied into an object. The combination of field values in an object is called **object state**. The methods provide object behavior. An object is also called an instance of a class.

Each object is created by using the operator `new` and a constructor that looks like a special kind of method. The primary duty of a constructor is to set an initial object state.

Let's us now have a closer look at Java classes and objects.

# Java classes

Java classes are stored in `.java` files. Each `.java` file may contain several classes. They are compiled by the Java compiler `javac` and stored in `.class` files. Each `.class` file contains one compiled class only.

Each `.java` file contains only one `public` class. The keyword `public` in front of the class name makes it accessible from the classes in other files. The filename must match the public class name. The file can contain other classes too, they are compiled into their own `.class` file, but they can be accessed only by the public class that gave its name to the `.java` file.

This is what the content of the file `MyClass.java` might look like:

```java
public class MyClass {
  private int field1;
  private String field2;
  public String method1(int i){
    //statements, including return statement
  }
  private void method2(String s){
    //statements without return statement
  }
}
```

It has two fields. The keyword `private` makes them accessible only from inside the class, from its method. The preceding class has two methods – one public and one private. The public method is accessible by any other class, while the private method is accessible only from other methods of the same class.

This class seems to not have a constructor. So, how are the states of the objects based on this class going to be initialized? The answer is that, in fact, each class that does not define its constructor explicitly but gets a default one—without parameters. And here are two examples of constructors added explicitly—one without parameters, another with a parameter:

```
public class SomeClass {
  private int field1;
  public MyClass(){
    this.field1 = 42;
  }
  //... other content of the class - methods
  //    that define object behavior
}

public class MyClass {
  private int field1;
  private String field2;
  public MyClass(int val1, String val2){
    this.field1 = val1;
    this.field2 = val2;
  }
  //... methods here
}
```

In the preceding code snippet, the keyword `this` indicates the current object. Its usage is optional. We could write `field1 = val1;` and achieve the same result. But it is a good practice to use the keyword `this` to avoid confusion, especially when (and programmers often do this) the name of the parameter is the same as the name of the field, such as in the following constructor:

```
public MyClass(int field1, String field1){
  field1 = field1;
  field2 = field2;
}
```

Adding the keyword `this` makes the code more friendly to human eyes. And sometimes, this is needed. We will discuss such cases in `Chapter 6`, *Interfaces, Classes, and Objects Construction.*

A constructor can also call the methods of this or any other accessible class:

```
public class MyClass {
  private int field1;
  private String field2;
  public MyClass(int val1, String val2){
    this.field1 = val1;
    this.field2 = val2;
    method1(33);
    method2(val2);
  }
  public String method1(int i){
    //statements, including return statement
  }
  private void method2(String s){
    //statements without return statement
  }
}
```

If a class does not define a constructor explicitly, it gets a default constructor from the default base class `java.lang.Object`. We will explain what it means in the upcoming *Inheritance* section.

A class can have several constructors with different signatures that can be used to create objects with different states if an application logic requires it. Once an explicit constructor with parameters is added to a class, the default constructor is not accessible unless it is added explicitly too. To clarify, this class has only one—default—constructor:

```
public class MyClass {
  private int field1;
  private String field2;
  //... other methods here
}
```

And this class has only one constructor too, but does not have a default one:

```
public class MyClass {
  private int field1;
  private String field2;
  public MyClass(int val1, String val2){
    this.field1 = val1;
    this.field2 = val2;
  }
  //... other methods here
}
```

This class has two constructors—with and without parameters:

```
public class MyClass {
  private int field1;
  private String field2;
  public MyClass(){ }
  public MyClass(int val1, String val2){
    this.field1 = val1;
    this.field2 = val2;
  }
  //... other methods here
}
```

The preceding constructor without parameters does nothing. It is provided only for the convenience of the client code that needs to create an object of this class but does not care about the particular initial state of the object. In such cases, JVM creates the default initial object state. We will explain what the default state is in `Chapter 6`, *Interfaces, Classes, and Objects Construction*.

Each object of the same class, created by any constructor, has the same methods (same behavior) even if its state (values assigned to the fields) is different.

This information about Java classes is enough for a beginner. Nevertheless, we would like to also describe some other classes that can be included in the same `.java` file, so that you will recognize them in other people's code. These other classes are called **nested classes**. They can be accessed only from the classes in the same file.

The class we have previously described – the only one public class in the `.java` file – is also called a top-level class. It can include a nested class called an inner class:

```
public class MyClass { // top-level class
  class MyOtherClass { // inner class
    //inner class content here
  }
}
```

A top-level class can also include a static (more about static members in the next section) nested class. A `static` class is not called an inner class, just a nested class:

```
public class MyClass { // top-level class
  static class MyYetAnotherClass { // nested class
    // nested class content here
  }
}
```

Any method can include a class that can be accessed only within the method. It is called a local class:

```
public class MyClass { // top-level class
  void someMethod() {
    class MyInaccessibleAnywhereElseClass { // local class
      // local class content here
    }
  }
}
```

A local class is not very often used, but not because it is useless. Programmers just do not remember how to create a class that is needed inside one method only and create an external or inner class instead.

The last but not the least kind of a class that can be included in the same file as a public class is called an anonymous class. It is a class without a name that allows the creation of an object in-place that can override the existing method or implement an interface. Let's us assume that we have the following interface, `InterfaceA`, and the class `MyClass`:

```
public interface InterfaceA{
  void doSomething();
}
public class MyClass {
  void someMethod1() {
    System.out.println("1. Regular is called");
  }
  void someMethod2(InterfaceA interfaceA) {
    interfaceA.doSomething();
  }
}
```

We can execute the following code:

```
MyClass myClass = new MyClass();
myClass.someMethod1();
myClass = new MyClass() {      //Anonymous class extends class MyClass
  public void someMethod1(){              // and overrides someMethod1()
    System.out.println("2. Anonymous is called");
  }
};
myClass.someMethod1();
myClass.someMethod2(new InterfaceA() { //Anonymous class implements
  public void doSomething(){     //  InterfaceA
```

```
    System.out.println("3. Anonymous is called");
    }
});
```

The result is going to be:

1. **Regular is called**
2. **Anonymous is called**
3. **Anonymous is called**

We do not expect the reader to understand the preceding code in full detail yet. We hope that the reader will be able to do it after reading this book.

This was a long section, with a lot of information. Most of it is just for reference, so do not feel bad if you do not remember everything. Just revisit this section after you have finished the book and acquired some practical experience with Java programming.

A few more introductory sections follow. Then Chapter 3, *Your Development Environment Setup*, will lead you through the configuration of the development tools on your computer, and in Chapter 4, *Your First Java Project*, you will start writing code and execute it - the moment every software developer remembers.

A few more steps, and you can call yourself a Java programmer.

# Java object (class instance)

One often reads—and Oracle documentation is not an exception—that an object is *used to model the real-world objects*. Such a view originates from before the days of object-oriented programming. At that time programs had a common or global area to store intermediate results. If not carefully managed, different subroutines and procedures—that's what methods were called then—modified those values, stepping on each other's toes and making it very difficult to trace defects. Naturally, programmers tried to regulate the access to the data and to make the intermediate results accessible only to certain methods. A bundle of methods and the data only they can access started to be known as an object.

Such constructs were also seen as models of the real-world objects. All the objects around us probably have some kind of an inner state, but we do not have access to it and know only how the objects behave. That is, we can predict how they will react to this or that input. Creating private fields in a class (object) that can be accessed only from the methods of the same class (object) seemed to be the solution to the hidden object state. With that, the original idea of modeling the real-world objects was carried along.

But after the years of object-oriented programming, many programmers realized that such a view can be misleading and actually quite harmful when one tries to apply it consistently to all kinds of software objects. For example, an object can carry values used as the parameters of an algorithm that has nothing to do with any real-world object but has everything to do with a computational efficiency. Or, as another example, an object that brings back the results of a computation. Programmers often call it a **data transfer object** (**DTO**). It has nothing to do with a real-world object unless stretches the definition of a real-world object, but that would be, well, a stretch.

A software object is simply a data structure in computer memory where the actual values are stored. Is memory a real-world object? The physical memory cells are, but the information they carry does not represent the cells. It represents the values and methods of a software object. And this information about an object is not even stored in a continuous memory area: object state is stored in an area called heap, while methods are stored in the method area, which, depending on the JVM implementation, may or may not be part of the heap.

An object, in our experience, is an integral part of the process of computation, which more often than not does not operate on models of real-world objects. An object is used to pass around values and methods, which are sometimes related and sometimes not. The set of methods and values might be grouped in one class for just a convenience or any other consideration.

To be fair, sometimes the software objects do represent models of real-world objects. But the point is that it is not always the case. With that, let us not consider software objects as models of real-world objects, unless they really are. Instead, let us look at how the objects are created and used and how they can help us to build a useful functionality – an application.

As we described in the previous section, an object is created based on a class, using the keyword `new` and a constructor – either the default or one that is declared explicitly. Consider, for example, the following class:

```
public class MyClass {
  private int field1;
  private String field2;
  public MyClass(int val1, String val2){
    this.field1 = val1;
    this.field2 = val2;
  }
```

```
public String method1(int i){
  //statements, including return statement
}
//... other methods are here
}
```

If we have this class, we can write the following in the method of some other class:

```
public AnotherClass {
  ...
  public void someMethod(){
    MyClass myClass = new MyClass(3, "some string");
    String result = myClass.method1(2);
  }
  ...
}
```

In the preceding code, the statement MyClass myClass = new MyClass(3, "some string"); creates an object of class MyClass, using its constructor and the keyword new, and assigns the reference of the newly created object to the variable myClass. We have chosen an identificator of the object reference that matches the name of the class with the first letter in a lower case. It is just a convention and we could have chosen another identificator (like boo, for example) with the same result. In Chapter 5, *Java Language Elements and Types*, we discuss identificators and variables in more detail. As you can see in the next line in the preceding example, once a reference is created we can use it to access public members of the newly created object.

Any Java object is created only one way: by using the keyword (operator) new and a constructor. This process is also called **class instantiation**. The reference to the object can be passed around as any other value (as a variable, parameter, or returned value), and every code that has access to the reference can use it to access the public members of the object. We will explain what public members are in the following section.

# Class (static) and object (instance) members

We have mentioned the term public members in relation to an object. We have also used the keyword static while talking about the main() method. We also stated that a member that is declared static can have only one copy in JVM memory. Now, we are going to define all that, and more.

# Private and public

The keywords `private` and `public` are called **access modifiers**. There are also default and `protected` access modifiers, but we will talk about them in Chapter 7, *Packages and Accessibility (Visibility)*. They are called access modifiers because they regulate accessibility to (sometimes also called visibility of) classes, methods, and fields, from outside the class, and also because they modify the declaration of the corresponding class, method, or field.

A class can be private when it is a nested class only. In the preceding *Java class* section, we did not use an explicit access modifier for nested classes (thus, we used the default one), but we could have made them private if we would like to allow access to these classes only from the top-level class and siblings.

A private method or private field can be accessed only from within the class (object) where it is declared.

By contrast, a public class, method, or field can be accessed from any other class. Notice that a method or field cannot be public if the enclosing class is private. Which makes sense, doesn't it? If the class itself is inaccessible publicly, how can its members be public?

# Static members

A class can be declared static only when it is a nested class. Class members—methods and fields—can be static too, as long as the class is not anonymous or local. Any code can access a static member of a class without creating a class instance (object). We saw such an example in previous sections when we used the class `Math` in one of the code snippets. A static class member is also called a class variable in case of the field or a class method in case of a method. Notice that these names contain the word `class` as an adjective. That is because a static member is associated with a class, not a class instance. It means that there is only one copy of a static member that can exist in JVM memory, although many instances (objects) of the class can be created and reside there at any moment in time.

Here is another example. Let's assume we have the following class:

```
public class MyClass {
  private int field1;
  public static String field2;
  public MyClass(int val1, String val2){
    this.field1 = val1;
    this.field2 = val2;
  }
```

```
   public String method1(int i){
     //statements, including return statement
   }
   public static void method2(){
     //statements
   }
   //... other methods are here
 }
```

From any method of any other class, the public static members of the preceding `MyClass` class can be accessed as follows:

```
MyClass.field2 = "any string";
String s = MyClass.field2 + " and another string";
```

The result of the preceding operations will be the assigning to the variable s of the value `any string and another string`. The `String` class will be discussed further in `Chapter 5`, *Java Language Elements and Types*.

Similarly, one can access a public static method `method2()` of the class `MyClass` as follows:

```
MyClass.method2();
```

The other methods of the class `MyClass` can still be accessed via an instance (object):

```
MyClass mc = new MyClass(3, "any string");
String someResult = mc.method1(42);
```

Obviously, there is no need to create an object of class `MyClass` if all its members are static.

Nevertheless, sometimes it is possible to access a static member using the object reference. The following code may work – it depends on the implementation of the `javac` compiler. If it works, it produces the same result as the preceding code:

```
MyClass mc = new MyClass(3, "any string");
mc.field2 = "Some other string";
mc.method2();
```

Some compilers provide a warning saying something like *static member being accessed by instance reference,* but they still let you do it. Others produce the error *cannot make a static reference to the non-static method/field* and force you to correct your code. The Java specification does not regulate such a case. But it is not a good practice to access a static class member via a reference to an object because it makes the code ambiguous for a human reader. So, you are better off avoiding doing that even if your compiler is more forgiving.

# Object (instance) members

A non-static class member is also called an instance variable in case of the field or an instance method in case of a method. It can be accessed only via reference to the object followed by a dot "." We have seen several such examples already.

In line with the long-established tradition, the fields of an object are usually declared private. If necessary, the methods set() and/or get() are provided to access such private values. They are often called setters and getters as they set and get values of private fields. Here is an example:

```java
public class MyClass {
  private int field1;
  private String field2;
  public void setField1(String val){
    this.field1 = val;
  }
  public String getField1(){
    return this.field1;
  }
  public void setField2(String val){
    this.field2 = val;
  }
  public String getField2(){
    return this.field2;
  }
  //... other methods are here
}
```

Sometimes, it is necessary to make sure that the object state cannot be changed. To support such a case, programmers use a constructor to set the state and remove setters:

```java
public class MyClass {
  private int field1;
  private String field2;
  public MyClass(int val1, String val2){
    this.field1 = val1;
    this.field2 = val2;
  }
  public String getField1(){
    return this.field1;
  }
}
```

```
public String getField2(){
  return this.field2;
}
//... other non-setting methods are here
}
```

Such an object is called immutable.

# Method overloading

Two methods with the same name but different signatures represent method overloading. Here is an example:

```
public class MyClass {
  public String method(int i){
    //statements
  }
  public int method(int i, String v){
    //statements
  }
}
```

The following is not allowed and will cause a compilation error, because return values are not a part of the method signature and cannot be used to distinguish one method from another if they have the same signature:

```
public class MyClass {
  public String method(int i){
    //statements
  }
  public int method(int i){ //error
    //statements
  }
}
```

Yet, this is allowed, because the methods have different signatures:

```
public String method(String v, int i){
  //statements
}
public String method(int i, String v){
  //statements
}
```

# Interface, implementation, and inheritance

Now, we are stepping into the most significant area of Java programming – the heavily used Java programming terms of interface, implementation, and inheritance.

## Interface

In everyday life, the word interface is quite popular. Its meaning is very close to the role Java interface plays in programming. It defines the public face of an object. It describes how it is possible to interact with the object and what can be expected of it. It hides inner class workings and exposes only method signatures with return values and access modifiers. An interface cannot be instantiated. An object of an interface type can be created only by creating an object of a class that implements this interface (interface implementation will be covered more thoroughly in the next section).

For example, look at the following class:

```java
public class MyClass {
  private int field1;
  private String field2;
  public MyClass(int val1, String val2){
    this.field1 = val1;
    this.field2 = val2;
  }
  public String method(int i){
    //statements
  }
  public int method(int i, String v){
    //statements
  }
}
```

Its interface is as follows:

```java
public interface MyClassInterface {
  String method(int i);
  int method(int i, String v);
}
```

So, we could write `public class MyClass implements MyClassInterface {...}`. We will talk about it in the next section.

Since an interface is a *public* face, the method access modifier `public` is assumed by default and can be omitted.

An interface does not describe how the object of the class can be created. To discover that, one must look at the class and see what the signatures of the constructors it has are. One can also check and see if public static class members are present that can be accessed without creating an object. So, an interface is only the public face of a class *instance*.

Let's cover the rest of interface capabilities. According to the Java Specification, *The body of an interface may declare members of the interface, that is, fields, methods, classes, and interfaces.* If you are confused and asking what the difference between an interface and a class is, you have a legitimate concern which we are going to address now.

Fields in the interface are implicitly public, static, and final. The modifier `final` means their values cannot be changed. By contrast, in a class, the implicit (default) access modifier of a class itself, its fields, methods, and constructors is package-private, which means it is visible only within its own package. Packages are named groups of related classes. You will learn about them in `Chapter 7`, *Packages and Accessibility (Visibility)*.

A method in the body of an interface may be declared default, static, or private. The purpose of the default method will be explained in the next section. A static method can be accessed from anywhere via the interface name and the dot " . ". Private methods can be accessed only by other methods inside the same interface. By contrast, the default access modifier for the methods in classes is package-private.

As for the classes declared inside an interface, they are implicitly static. They are also public and can be accessed without an instance of an interface, which is impossible to create anyway. We are not going to talk more about such classes because they are used in very particular areas that are beyond the scope of this book.

Similarly to a class, an interface allows the declaration of an inner or nested interface inside its body. It can be accessed from outside like any static member, using the top-level interface with the dot " . ". We would like to remind you that an interface is public by default and cannot be instantiated, and thus is static by default.

There is one last very important term related to interfaces. A method signature listed in the interface without an implementation is called an **abstract method** and the interface itself is called **abstraction** because it abstracts, summarizes, and removes the signatures from the implementation. An abstraction cannot be instantiated. As an example, if you put the keyword `abstract` in front of any class and try to create its object, the compiler will throw an error even if all the methods in the class are not abstract. In such a case, the class behaves as an interface with the default methods only. Yet, there is a significant difference in their usage, which you will see after reading the upcoming *Inheritance* section of this chapter.

We will talk more about interfaces in Chapter 6, *Interfaces, Classes, and Objects Construction*, and cover their access modifiers in Chapter 7, *Packages and Accessibility (Visibility)*.

# Implementation

An interface can be implemented by a class, which means that the class has a body for each of the abstract methods listed in the interface. Here is an example:

```java
interface Car {
  double getWeightInPounds();
  double getMaxSpeedInMilesPerHour();
}

public class CarImpl implements Car{
  public double getWeightInPounds(){
    return 2000d;
  }
  public double getMaxSpeedInMilesPerHour(){
    return 100d;
  }
}
```

We named the class CarImpl to indicate that it is an implementation of the interface Car. But we could name it any other way we like.

Both interface and its class implementation can have other methods too without causing a compiler error. The only requirement for the extra method in the interface is that it has to be default and have a body. Adding any other method to a class does not interfere with the interface implementation.  For example:

```java
interface Car {
  double getWeightInPounds();
  double getMaxSpeedInMilesPerHour();
  default int getPassengersCount(){
    return 4;
  }
}

public class CarImpl implements Car{
  private int doors;
  private double weight, speed;
  public CarImpl(double weight, double speed, int doors){
    this.weight = weight;
    this.speed = speed;
```

```
      this.dooes = doors;
  }
  public double getWeightInPounds(){
    return this.weight;
  }
  public double getMaxSpeedInMilesPerHour(){
    return this.speed;
  }
  public int getNumberOfDoors(){
    return this.doors;
  }
}
```

If we now create an instance of a class `CarImpl`, we can call all the methods we have declared in the class:

```
CarImpl car = new CarImpl(500d, 50d, 3);
car.getWeightInPounds();            //Will return 500.0
car.getMaxSpeedInMilesPerHour(); //Will return 50.0
car.getNumberOfDoors();            //Will return 3
```

That was not surprising.

But, here is something you might not have expected:

```
car.getPassengersCount();            //Will return 4
```

This means that by implementing an interface class acquires all the default methods the interface has. That is the purpose of the default methods: to add functionality to all classes that implement the interface. Without it, if we add an abstract method to an old interface, all current interface implementations will trigger a compiler error. But, if we add a new method with the modifier default, the existing implementations will continue working as usual.

Now, another nice trick. If a class implements a method with the same signature as the default method, it will `override` (a technical term) the behavior of the interface. Here is an example:

```
interface Car {
  double getWeightInPounds();
  double getMaxSpeedInMilesPerHour();
  default int getPassengersCount(){
    return 4;
  }
}

public class CarImpl implements Car{
```

```
   private int doors;
   private double weight, speed;
   public CarImpl(double weight, double speed, int doors){
     this.weight = weight;
     this.speed = speed;
     this.dooes = doors;
   }
   public double getWeightInPounds(){
     return this.weight;
   }
   public double getMaxSpeedInMilesPerHour(){
     return this.speed;
   }
   public int getNumberOfDoors(){
     return this.doors;
   }
   public int getPassengersCount(){
     return 3;
   }
 }
```

If we use the interface and class described in this example, we can write the following code:

```
CarImpl car = new CarImpl(500d, 50d, 3);
car.getPassengersCount();          //Will return 3 now !!!!
```

If not all of the abstract methods of the interface have been implemented the class must be declared abstract, and cannot be instantiated.

The purpose of an interface is to represent its implementations – all objects of all the classes that have implemented it. For example, we could create another class that implements the Car interface:

```
public class AnotherCarImpl implements Car{
   public double getWeightInPounds(){
     return 2d;
   }
   public double getMaxSpeedInMilesPerHour(){
     return 3d;
   }
   public int getNumberOfDoors(){
     return 4;
   }
   public int getPassengersCount(){
       return 5;
```

```
    }
}
```

Then we can let the `Car` interface represent each of them:

```
Car car = new CarImpl(500d, 50d, 3);
car.getWeightInPounds();             //Will return 500.0
car.getMaxSpeedInMilesPerHour();     //Will return 50.0
car.getNumberOfDoors();              //Will produce compiler error
car.getPassengersCount();            //Still returns 3 !!!!

car = new AnotherCarImpl();
car.getWeightInPounds();             //Will return 2.0
car.getMaxSpeedInMilesPerHour();     //Will return 3.0
car.getNumberOfDoors();              //Will produce compiler error
car.getPassengersCount();            //Will return 5
```

Several interesting observations can be made from looking at the preceding code snippet. First, when the variable `car` is declared as an interface type (not a class type as in the previous example), one cannot call a method not declared in the interface.

Second, the `car.getPassengersCount()` method returns 3 the first time. One could have expected it to return 4, because `car` was declared as an interface type and one could have expected the default method to work. But, in fact, the variable `car` refers the object of class `CarImpl`, and that is why the class implementation of the `car.getPassengersCount()` method is executed.

Working with an interface, you should remember that the signatures come from the interface, but the implementation comes from a class, or from a default interface method if the class does not implement it. Here shines another feature of default methods. They serve both as a signature that can be implemented and as an implementation if the class does not implement it.

If there are several default methods in an interface, it is possible to create private methods accessible only by the default methods of the interface. They can be used to contain common functionality instead of repeating it in every default method. The private methods cannot be accessed from outside the interface.

With that, we can now reach the summit of Java basics complexity. After this, and all the way to the end of the book, we will only be adding some details and building up your programming skills. It will be a walk on a high altitude plateau - the longer you walk, the more comfortable you feel. But, to get to that height, we need to climb the last uphill pitch; inheritance.

# Inheritance

A class can acquire (inherit) all the non-private non-static members, so that when we use the object of this class, we cannot have any idea where these members actually reside – in this class or in the class from which they were inherited. To indicate inheritance, the keyword `extends` is used. For example, consider the following classes:

```
class A {
  private void m1(){...}
  public void m2(){...}
}

class B extends class A {
  public void m3(){...}
}

class C extends class B {
}
```

In this example, the objects of classes B and C behave as if each of them has methods m2() and m3(). The only limitation is that a class can extend one class only. Class A is a base (or parent) class for both class B and class C. Class B is a base class for class C only. And, as we have mentioned already, each of them has the default base class `java.lang.Object`. Classes B and C are subclasses of class A. Class C is also a subclass of class B.

By contrast, an interface can extend to many other interfaces at the same time. If AI, BI, CI, DI, EI, and FI are interfaces, then the following is allowed:

```
interface AI extends BI, CI, DI {
  //the interface body
}
interface DI extends EI, FI {
  //the interface body
}
```

In the preceding example, the interface AI inherits all the non-private non-static signatures of the interfaces BI, CI, DI, EI, and FI, and any other interfaces that are base interfaces of the interfaces BI, CI, DI, EI, and FI.

Coming back to the topic of the previous section, *Implementation*, a class can implement many interfaces:

```
class A extends B implements AI, BI, CI, DI {
  //the class body
}
```

This means that class A inherits all non-private non-static members of class B and implements the interfaces AI, BI, CI, and DI, as well as their base interfaces. The ability to implement multiple interfaces comes from the fact that the preceding example would have exactly the same result if re-written like this:

```
interface AI extends BI, CI, DI {
  //the interface body
}

class A extends B implements AI {
  //the class body
}
```

The extended interface (class) is also called superinterface (superclass) or parent interface (parent class). The extending interface (class) is called a child interface (child class) or subinterface (subclass).

Let's illustrate this with examples. We start with an interface inheritance:

```
interface Vehicle {
  double getWeightInPounds();
}

interface Car extends Vehicle {
  int getPassengersCount();
}

public class CarImpl implements Car {
  public double getWeightInPounds(){
    return 2000d;
  }
  public int getPassengersCount(){
    return 4;
  }
}
```

The class CarImpl in the preceding code must implement both signatures (listed in the interface Vehicle and in the interface Car), because from its perspective they both belong to the interface Car. Otherwise, a compiler will complain, or class CarImpl has to be declared abstract (and cannot be instantiated).

Now, let us look at another example:

```java
interface Vehicle {
  double getWeightInPounds();
}

public class VehicleImpl implements Vehicle {
  public double getWeightInPounds(){
    return 2000d;
  }
}

interface Car extends Vehicle {
  int getPassengersCount();
}

public class CarImpl extends VehicleImpl implements Car {
  public int getPassengersCount(){
    return 4;
  }
}
```

In this example, the class `CarImpl` does not need to implement the abstract method `getWeightInPounds()` because it has inherited the implementation from the base class `VehicleImpl`.

One consequence of the described class inheritance is usually not intuitive for a beginner. To demonstrate it, let us add the method `getWeightInPounds()` to the class `CarImpl`:

```java
public class VehicleImpl {
  public double getWeightInPounds(){
    return 2000d;
  }
}

public class CarImpl extends VehicleImpl {
  public double getWeightInPounds(){
    return 3000d;
  }
  public int getPassengersCount(){
    return 4;
  }
}
```

In this example, we do not use interfaces, for simplicity. Because the class `CarImpl` is a child of the class `VehicleImpl`, it can behave as an object of class `VehicleImpl` and this code will compile just fine:

```
VehicleImpl vehicle = new CarImpl();
vehicle.getWeightInPounds();
```

The question is, what value do you expect to be returned in the second line of the preceding snippet? If you guessed 3,000, you are correct. If not, do not feel embarrassed. It takes time to get used to it. The rule is that the reference of a base class type can refer to an object of any of its children. It is widely used for overriding base class behaviors.

The summit is close. Only one step is left, although it brings something that you probably won't have expected if you did not know anything about Java before reading this book.

# The java.lang.Object class

So, here is a surprise. Each Java class, by default (without an explicit declaration), extends the class `Object`. To be precise, it is `java.lang.Object`, but we have not introduced packages yet and will only be talking about them in `Chapter 7`, *Packages and Accessibility (Visibility)*.

All Java objects inherit all the methods from it. There are ten of them:

- `public boolean equals (Object obj)`
- `public int hashCode()`
- `public Class getClass()`
- `public String toString()`
- `protected Object clone()`
- `public void wait()`
- `public void wait(long timeout)`
- `public void wait(long timeout, int nanos)`
- `public void notify()`
- `public void notifyAll()`

Let's briefly visit each of these methods.

Before we do that, we would like to mention that you can override their default behavior in your classes, and re-implement them any way you need, which programmers often do. We will explain how to do this in Chapter 6, *Interfaces, Classes, and Objects Construction.*

# The equals() method

The method equals() of the java.lang.Object class looks like this:

```
public boolean equals(Object obj) {
  //compares references of the current object
  //and the reference obj
}
```

Here is an example of its usage:

```
Car car1 = new CarImpl();
Car car2 = car1;
Car car3 = new CarImpl();
car1.equals(car2);    //returns true
car1.equals(car3);    //returns false
```

As you can see from the preceding example, the implementation of the default method equals() compares only memory references that point to the addresses where the objects are stored. That is why the references car1 and car2 are equal – because they point to the same object (same area of the memory, same address), while the car3 reference points to another object.

A typical re-implementation of the equals() method uses an object's state for comparison instead. We will explain how to do this in Chapter 6, *Interfaces, Classes, and Objects Construction.*

# The hashCode() method

The hashCode() method of the java.lang.Object class looks like this:

```
public int hashCode(){
  //returns a hash code value for the object      _
  //based on the integer representation of the memory address
}
```

The Oracle documentation states that, if two methods are the same according to the default behavior of the `equals()` method described previously, then they have the same `hashCode()` return value. Which is great! But unfortunately, the same document states that it is possible that two different (according to the `equals()` method) objects can have the same `hasCode()` return value. That is why programmers prefer to re-implement the `hashCode()` method and use it while re-implementing the `equals()` method instead of using the object state. The need to do it does not arise very often though, and we are not going into the details of such an implementation. If interested, you can find good articles about it on the internet.

# The getClass() method

The `getClass()` method of the `java.lang.Object` class looks like this:

```
public Class getClass(){
   //returns object of class Class that has
   //many methods that provide useful information
}
```

The most commonly used piece of information from this method is the name of the class that was the template for the current object. We will get into why one may need it in `Chapter 6`, *Interfaces, Classes, and Objects Construction*. The name of the class can be accessed via the object of the class `Class`, returned by this method.

# The toString() method

The `toString()` method of the `java.lang.Object` class looks like this:

```
public String toString(){
   //return string representation of the object
}
```

This method is typically used to print the content of the object. Its default implementation looks like this:

```
public String toString() {
   return getClass().getName()+"@"+Integer.toHexString(hashCode());
}
```

As you can see, it is not very informative, so programmers re-implement it in their classes. This is the most commonly re-implemented method of the class `Object`. Programmers practically do it for each of their classes. We will explain more about the `String` class and its methods in `Chapter 9`, *Operators, Expressions, and Statements.*

# The clone() method

The `clone()` method of the `java.lang.Object` class looks like this:

```
protected Object clone(){
  //creates copy of the object
}
```

The default result of this method returns a copy of the object fields as-is, which is fine if the values are not an object reference. Such values are called **primitive type**, which we will define precisely in `Chapter 5`, *Java Language Elements and Types.* But if an object field holds a reference to another object, only the reference itself will be copied, not the referred object itself. That is why such a copy is called a shallow one. To get a deep copy, one has to re-implement the `clone()` method and follow all the references of the tree of objects that can be quite a widespread. Fortunately, the `clone()` method is not used very often. In fact, you may never encounter a need to use it.

While reading this, you may wonder, what happens to an object when it is used as a method parameter. Is it passed inside the method as a copy using the `clone()` method? If so, is it passed as a shallow or a deep copy? The answer is, neither. Only a reference to the object is passed in as the parameter value, so all the methods that receive the same object reference can access the same area of the memory where the object state is stored.

This presents a potential risk for unexpected data modification and subsequent data corruption – bringing them to an inconsistent state. That is why, while passing around an object, programmers have to always be aware that they are accessing values that may be shared across other methods and classes. We will talk more about this in `Chapter 5`, *Java Language Elements and Types* and expand on it in `Chapter 11`, *JVM Processes and Garbage Collection* while talking about threads and concurrent processing in general.

# The wait() and notify() methods

The `wait()`, and `notify()` methods and their overloaded versions are used for communication between threads—the lightweight processes for concurrent processing. Programmers do not re-implement these methods. They just use them to increase the throughput and performance of their applications. We will go into more details about the `wait()` and `notify()` methods in `Chapter 11`, *JVM Processes and Garbage Collection*.

Now, congratulations are in order. You have stepped on the summit of Java basics complexity and will now continue walking horizontally, adding details and practicing the acquired knowledge. You have constructed in your head a framework of Java knowledge while reading the first two chapters. Don't feel frustrated if not everything is clear of if you forget something. Keep reading, and you will have many opportunities to refresh your knowledge, extend it, and retain it for a longer run. It is going to be an interesting journey with a nice reward at the final destination.

# OOP concepts

Now, we can talk about concepts that will make more sense to you, compared to presenting them before you learned the main terminology and saw the code examples. These concepts are:

- Object/class: This keeps the state and behavior together
- Encapsulation: It hides the state and details of the implementation
- Inheritance: It propagates behavior/signatures down the chain of class/interface extensions
- Interface: It isolates signatures from their implementations
- Polymorphism: This allows an object to be represented by multiple implemented interfaces and any of the base classes, including `java.lang.Object`.

By now, you are familiar with all of the above, so this is going to be mostly a summary, adding only a few details. That's how we learn – from observing specific facts, building a bigger picture, and improving that picture as new observations come in. We do it all the time, don't we?

# Object/class

A Java program and an entire application can be written without creating a single object. Just use the `static` keyword in front of every method and every field of a class you are creating and call them from the static `main()` method. You will be limited in your programming capabilities. You will not be able to create an army of objects that can work in parallel doing a similar job on their own copy of data, for example. But your application will still work.

Besides, in Java 8, functional programming features were added that allow us to pass around functions the same way an object can be passed. So, your object-less application could be quite capable. And several languages without object creating capabilities were used very effectively. Yet, after object-oriented languages proved to be useful and became popular, the first being Smalltalk, several traditionally procedural languages—PHP, Perl, Visual Basic, COBOL 2002, Fortran 2003, and Pascal, to name a few—added object-oriented capabilities.

As we just mentioned, Java also extended its features into covering functional programming, thus blurring the borders between procedural, object-oriented, and functional languages. Yet, the presence of classes and the ability to use them to create objects is the first of the concepts that a programming language must support in order to be classified as object-oriented.

# Encapsulation

Encapsulation—the ability to make data and functions (methods) inaccessible from outside or have controlled access—was one of the primary drivers for creating object-oriented languages. Smalltalk was created on the idea of messages passing between objects, which is done in both Smalltalk and Java when one object calls a method on another object.

Encapsulation allows invocation of services of an object without knowing how those services are implemented. It reduces the software's system complexity and increases its maintainability. Each object does its job without the need to coordinate the changes in the implementation with its clients, so long as it does not violate the contract that is captured in the interface.

We will discuss encapsulation in further detail in `Chapter 7`, *Packages and Accessibility (Visibility)*.

# Inheritance

Inheritance is another OOP concept supported by every object-oriented language. It is usually described as the ability to reuse the code, which is a true but often misunderstood statement. Some programmers assume that inheritance claims to be able to reuse code *between applications*. In our experience, code reusability between applications can be accomplished without inheritance and is more dependent on the functional similarity between applications than the particular programming language feature. It is more related to the skill of the extracting common code into a shared reusable library than anything else.

In Java, or any other object-oriented language, inheritance allows the reuse of common functionality, implemented in a base class, *across its children*. It can be used for bringing modularity and improving code reusability across applications by assembling base classes into a common shared library. But in practice, such an approach is rarely used because each application usually has such particular requirements that a common base class is either too simplistic and effectively useless or carries many methods specific to each of the applications. Besides, in `Chapter 6`, *Interfaces, Classes, and Objects Construction*, we will show that reusability is much easier achieved using an aggregation, which is based on using independent objects instead of inheritance.

Together with an interface, inheritance makes polymorphism possible.

# Interface (abstraction)

Sometimes OOP concept of an interface is also called abstraction because an interface summarizes (abstracts) the public description of an object behavior from the details of its implementation and hides (abstracts) it. An interface is an integral part of an encapsulation and polymorphism, but important enough to be stated as a separate concept. Its significance will become especially apparent in `Chapter 8`, *Object-Oriented Design (OOD) Principles*, when we discuss the transition from a project idea and vision to the specific programming solution.

Interface and inheritance provide the foundation for polymorphism.

# Polymorphism

From the code examples we have provided, you have probably already realized that an object has all the methods that are listed in the implemented interfaces and all the non-private non-static methods of its base classes, including `java.lang.Object`. Like a person with many citizenships, it can pass as an object of any of its base classes or implemented interfaces. This language capability is called a polymorphism (from *poly* – many and *morphos* – form).

Please note that in broad terms, method overloading—when a method with the same name can have different behavior depending on its signature—exhibits polymorphic behavior too.

# Exercise – Interface versus abstract class

What is the difference between an interface and an abstract class? We did not talk about it, so you will need to do some research.

 After the default methods of interfaces were introduced in Java 8, the difference shrunk significantly, and is negligible in many cases.

# Answer

An abstract class can have a constructor, while an interface cannot.

An abstract class can have a state, while an interface cannot. The fields of an abstract class can be private and protected, while in an interface, fields are public, static, and final.

An abstract class can have method implementation with any access modifiers, while implemented default methods in an interface are public only.

If the class you would like to amend extends to another class already, you cannot use an abstract class, but you can implement an interface, because a class can extend to only one other class but can implement multiple interfaces.

# Summary

In this chapter, you have learned the foundational concepts of Java and of any object-oriented programming language. You now have an understanding of classes and objects as the basic building blocks of Java, know what static and instance members are, and know about interface, implementation, and inheritance. That was the most complex and challenging exercise of this beginner chapter, and brought the reader to the core of Java language, introducing the language framework we are going to use throughout the rest of the book. The exercise allowed the reader to get exposure to the discussion about the differences between an interface and an abstract class, which has become much narrower after Java 8's release.

In the next chapter, we will turn to practical matters of programming. The reader will be guided through the concrete steps of installing the necessary tools and configuring the development environment on their computer. After that, all the new ideas and software solutions will be demonstrated, with specific code examples.

# Your Development Environment Setup

# 3

By now, you probably have a pretty good idea of how to compile and execute a Java program on your computer. Now, it is time to learn how to write a program. This chapter is the last step before you can do it. Because you need to set up your development environment first, this chapter is going to explain what a development environment is, and why you need it. Then, it will guide you through configuration and tuning, including the setting of a classpath. On the way, an overview of popular editors and specific advice on IntelliJ IDEA will be provided.

In this chapter, we will cover the following topics:

- What is a development environment?
- Setting the classpath
- IDEs overview
- How to install and configure IntelliJ IDEA
- Exercise – Installing NetBeans

## What is the development environment?

The development environment is a set of tools installed on your computer that allows you to write Java programs (applications) and tests for them, to share the source code with your colleagues, and to compile the source and run it. We will discuss each of the development tools and stages of the development process in this chapter.

# Java editor is your main tool

A Java-supporting editor is the center of a development environment. In principle, you can use any text editor to write a program and store it in a `.java` file. Unfortunately, a regular text editor does not warn you about Java language syntax errors. That is why a specialized editor that supports Java is a better choice for writing Java programs.

A modern Java language editor is not just a writing tool. It also has the ability to integrate with the JVM installed on the same computer, and use it to compile the application, execute it, and much more. That is why it is called not just an editor, but an IDE. It can integrate with other development tools, too, so you do not need to exit the IDE in order to store the source code on the remote server of a source control system, for example.

Another huge advantage of Java IDEs is that they can remind you about language possibilities and help you to find a better way to implement the required functionality.

IDE also supports code refactoring. This term means a code change for better readability, reusability, or maintainability, without affecting its functionality. For example, if there is a block of code used in several methods, one can extract it in a separate method and use it everywhere, instead of duplicating code. Another example is when the name of a class, method, or variable is changed to a more descriptive one. Using a regular editor would require you to find all of the places where the old name is used manually. An IDE does it for you.

Another helpful feature of an IDE is the ability to generate the boilerplate code of a class, and standard methods, such as a constructor, getters, setters, or the `toString()` method. It increases programmer productivity by keeping their focus on what is important.

So, make sure that you are comfortable with the IDE of your choice. As a programmer, you're going to work with your IDE editor for most of your working hours.

# Source code compilation

An IDE uses the `javac` compiler installed on your computer to find all Java-language syntax errors. Caught early, such errors are much easier to correct than if they are found after the application is already running in the production environment.

Not all programming languages can be supported this way. It is possible for Java, because Java is a strictly-typed language, which means that it needs to declare a type for every variable before one can use it. You saw `int` and `String` types in the examples in `Chapter 2, Java Language Basics`. After that, if you try to do something that is not allowed with the variable for its declared type, or try to assign another type to it, the IDE will warn you, and you can revisit it or insist on the way you have written the code (when you know what you are doing).

Despite the similar name, JavaScript, by contrast, is a dynamically-typed language, which allows for declaring a variable without defining its type. That's why a Java novice can develop a much more complex and fully functional application from the very beginning, while a complex JavaScript code remains a challenge, even for an experienced programmer, and still does not reach the level of complexity that Java code can.

By the way, one of the reasons for Java's popularity, although it was introduced later than C++, was—paradoxically—the limitation it imposed on object type manipulation. In Java, the risk of making difficult-to-trace runtime errors is much smaller than in C++.
The runtime errors are those code issues that cannot be found by the IDE at compile-time, based on the language syntax only.

# Code sharing

IDE integrates with code sharing systems, too. Collaboration on the same code requires placing the code in a common shared location, called a **source code repository** or version control repository, where it can be accessed by all the team members. One of the most well-known shared repositories is a web-based version-control repository—GitHub (`https://github.com/`). It is based on the Git version-control system (`https://en.wikipedia.org/wiki/Git`). Other popular source control systems include CVS, ClearCase, Subversion, and Mercurial, to name a few.

An overview and guidance on such systems are outside of the scope of this book. We mention because they are being an important part of the development environment.

# Code and test execution

Using an IDE, you can even execute an application, or its tests. To accomplish that, IDE first compiles the code using the `javac` tool, then executes it using JVM (the `java` tool).

An IDE also allows us to run an application in a debug mode, when the execution can be paused at any statement. It allows the programmer to examine the current values of the variables, which is often the most efficient way to find dreaded runtime errors. Such errors usually are caused by unexpected intermediate values assigned to a variable during execution. The debug mode allows us to walk along the offensive execution path slowly, and see the conditions that cause the problem.

One of the most helpful aspects of IDE functionality is its ability to maintain the classpath or manage dependencies, which we are going to discuss in the next section.

# Setting the classpath

In order for `javac` to compile the code and for `java` to execute it, they need to know the location of the files that compose the application. In Chapter 2, *Java Language Basics*, while explaining the format of the `javac` and `java` commands, we described how the `-classpath` option allows you to list all of the classes and third-party libraries your application is using (or, in other words, depends on). Now, we will talk about setting this list.

# Manual setting

There are two ways to set it:

- Via the `-classpath` command-line option
- Via the `CLASSPATH` environment variable

We will describe how to use the `-classpath` option first. It has the same format in the `javac` and `java` commands:

```
-classpath dir1;dir2\*;dir3\alibrary.jar   (for Windows)

javac -classpath dir1:dir2/*:dir3/alibrary.jar    (for Lunix)
```

In the preceding example, dir1, dir2, and dir3 are folders that contain the files of the application and the third-party .jar files the application depends on. Each can include a path to the directory, too. The path can be absolute or relative to the current location where you run this command.

If a folder does not contain .jar files (it has only .class files, for example), it is enough to have only the folder name listed. Both tools—javac and java—will look inside the folder when searching for a particular file. A dir1 folder provides such an example.

If a folder contains .jar files (with .class files inside), then you can do one of two things:

- Specify a wildcard, *, so that all the .jar files in that folder will be searched for a requested .class file (the preceding dir2 folder is such an example)
- List each .jar file separately (the alibrary.jar file stored in the dir3 folder is such an example)

The CLASSPATH environment variable serves the same purpose as the -classpath command option. The format of the list of file locations, specified as a value of the CLASSPATH variable, is the same as the list set with the -classpath option described earlier. If you use CLASSPATH, you can run the javac and java commands without the -classpath option. If you use both, then the value of CLASSPATH is ignored.

To see the current value of the CLASSPATH variable, open a Command Prompt or Terminal and type echo %CLASSPATH% for Windows OS or echo $CLASSPATH for Linux. Chances are you will get back nothing, which means that the CLASSPATH variable is not used on your computer. You can assign a value to it using the set command.

It is possible to include the CLASSPATH value with the -classpath option:

```
-classpath %CLASSPATH%;dir1;dir2\*;dir3\alibrary.jar (for Windows)

-classpath $CLASSPATH:dir1:dir2/*:dir3/alibrary.jar (for Lunix)
```

Notice that the javac and java tools are part of JDK, so they know where to find the Java standard libraries coming with JDK, and there is no need to specify the standard libraries' .jar files on the classpath.

An Oracle tutorial for how to set a classpath is provided at https://docs.oracle.com/javase/tutorial/essential/environment/paths.html.

# Searching on the classpath

Whether -classpath or CLASSPATH is used, the classpath value presents the list of .class and .jar files. The javac and java tools always search the list from left to right. If the same .class file is listed several times (inside several folders or .jar files, for example), then only its first copy will be found. If several versions of the same library are included in the classpath, it may cause a problem. For example, a newer version of a library might never be found if it is listed in the classpath after the older version.

Also, the libraries themselves can depend on other .jar files and their particular versions. Two different libraries may require the same .jar file, but of different versions.

As you can see, with many files listed on the classpath, their management can quickly become a full-time job. The good news is that you probably don't need to worry about it, because IDE will set the classpath for you.

# IDE sets the classpath automatically

As we already mentioned, the javac and java tools know where to find the standard libraries that come with the JDK installation. If your code uses other libraries, you need to tell IDE which libraries you need, so IDE can find them and set the classpath.

To accomplish that, IDE uses a dependency-managing tool. The most popular dependency-managing tools today are Maven and Gradle. Since Maven has been around longer than Gradle, all major IDEs have this tool, either built-in or integrated via a plug-in. A plug-in is a piece of software that can be added to an application (IDE, in this case) to extend its functionality.

Maven has an extensive online repository that stores practically all existing libraries and frameworks. To tell an IDE with a built-in Maven capability which third-party libraries your application needs, you have to identify them in the file called pom.xml. IDE reads what you need from the pom.xml file and downloads the required libraries from the Maven repository to your computer. Then, IDE can list them on the classpath while executing the javac or java command. We will show you how to write pom.xml content in Chapter 4, *Your First Java Project*.

Now is the time to choose your IDE, install it, and configure it. In the next section, we will describe the most popular IDEs.

# There are many IDEs out there

There are many IDEs available that you can use free of charge: NetBeans, Eclipse, IntelliJ IDEA, BlueJ, DrJava, JDeveloper, JCreator, jEdit, JSource, jCRASP, and jEdit, to name a few. Each of them has followers who are convinced that their choice is the best, so we are not going to argue. It is a matter of preference, after all. We will concentrate on the three most popular ones—NetBeans, Eclipse, and IntelliJ IDEA. We will use the IntelliJ IDEA free Community Edition for our demonstrations.

We recommend reading the documentation about these and other IDEs, and even trying them out, before making your final choice. For your initial research, you can use the Wikipedia article at `https://en.wikipedia.org/wiki/Comparison_of_integrated_development_environments#Java`, which has a table comparing many modern IDEs.

# NetBeans

NetBeans was first created in 1996 as a Java IDE student project at Charles University in Prague. In 1997, a company was created around the project, and produced commercial versions of the NetBeans IDE. In 1999, it was acquired by Sun Microsystems. In 2010, after the acquisition of Sun Microsystems by Oracle, NetBeans became part of the open source Java products produced by Oracle, with a contribution from a large community of developers.

NetBeans IDE became the official IDE for Java 8 and could be downloaded together with JDK 8 in the same bundle; see `http://www.oracle.com/technetwork/java/javase/downloads/jdk-netbeans-jsp-142931.html`.

In 2016, Oracle decided to donate the NetBeans project to the Apache Software Foundation, stating that it was *opening up the NetBeans governance model to give NetBeans constituents a greater voice in the project's direction and future success through the upcoming release of Java 9 and NetBeans 9 and beyond.*

There are NetBeans IDE versions for Windows, Linux, Mac, and Oracle Solaris. It enables coding, compiling, analysis, running, testing, profiling, debugging, and deployment of all Java application types – Java SE, JavaFX, Java ME, web, EJB, and mobile applications. Besides Java, it supports multiple programming languages in particular, C/C++, XML, HTML5, PHP, Groovy, Javadoc, JavaScript, and JSP. Because the editor is extensible, it is possible to plug in support for many other languages.

It also includes an Ant-based project system, support for Maven, refactoring, version control (supports CVS, Subversion, Git, Mercurial, and ClearCase), and can be used for working with cloud applications.

# Eclipse

Eclipse is the most widely used Java IDE. It has an extensive plug-in system that grows all the time, so it is not possible to list all its features. Its primary use is for developing Java applications, but plugins also allow us to write code in Ada, ABAP, C, C++, C#, COBOL, D, Fortran, Haskell, JavaScript, Julia, Lasso, Lua, NATURAL, Perl, PHP, Prolog, Python, R, Ruby, Rust, Scala, Clojure, Groovy, Scheme, and Erlang. Development environments include the Eclipse **Java development tools** (**JDT**) for Java and Scala, Eclipse CDT for C/C++, and Eclipse PDT for PHP, among others.

The name *Eclipse* was invented in reference to the competition with Microsoft Visual Studio, which Eclipse was to eclipse. The subsequent versions were named after the moons of Jupiter—Callisto, Europa, and Ganymede. A version named after Galileo—the discoverer of those moons—followed. Then, two sun-themed names—Helios of Greek mythology, and Indigo, one of the seven colors of the rainbow (which is produced by the sun)—were used. The version after that, Juno, has a triple meaning: a Roman mythological figure, an asteroid, and a spacecraft to Jupiter. Kepler, Luna, and Mars continued the astronomy theme, and then Neon and Oxygen came from the names of chemical elements. Photon represents a return to sun-themed names.

Eclipse also enables coding, compiling, analysis, running, testing, profiling, debugging, and deployment of all Java application types and all major platforms. It also supports Maven, refactoring, major version control systems, and cloud applications.

The huge variety of available plugins may be a challenge for a novice, and, occasionally, even to a more experienced user, for two reasons:

- There is usually more than one way to add the same functionality to the IDE, by combining similar plug-ins of different authors

- Some plug-ins are incompatible, which may create a difficult-to-solve problem and force us to rebuild the IDE installation again, especially when a new release comes out

# IntelliJ IDEA

The IntelliJ IDEA paid version is definitely the best Java IDE on the market today. But even the free Community Edition has a strong position among the three leading IDEs. In the following Wikipedia article, you can see a table that nicely summarizes the difference between paid Ultimate and free Community Editions: `https://en.wikipedia.org/wiki/IntelliJ_IDEA`

It was developed by the JetBrains (formerly known as IntelliJ) software company, which has around 700 employees (as of 2017) in six offices in Prague, Saint Petersburg, Moscow, Munich, Boston, and Novosibirsk. The first version, released in January 2001, was one of the first available Java IDEs with integrated advanced code-navigation and code-refactoring capabilities. Since then, this IDE has been known for its *Deep insight into your code*, as the authors state when describing the product features on their website at `https://www.jetbrains.com/idea/features`.

Like the other two IDEs described earlier, it enables coding, compiling, analysis, running, testing, profiling, debugging, and the deployment of all Java application types and all major platforms. Like the two previous IDEs, it also supports Ant, Maven, and Gradle, as well as refactoring, major version-control systems, and cloud applications.

In the next section, we will walk you through the installation and configuration of IntelliJ IDEA Community Edition.

# Installing and configuring IntelliJ IDEA

The following steps and screenshots will demonstrate the IntelliJ IDEA Community Edition installation on Windows, though the installation is not much different for Linux or macOS.

# Downloading and installing

You can download the IntelliJ IDEA Community Edition installer from `https://www.jetbrains.com/idea/download`. After the installer has downloaded, launch it by double-clicking on it or right-clicking and selecting the **Open** option from the menu. Then, walk through the following screens, accepting all of the default settings by clicking the **Next>** button, unless you need to do something different. Here is the first screen:

You can use the **Browse...** button and select any location for a **Destination Folder**, or just click **Next>** and accept the default location on the following screen:

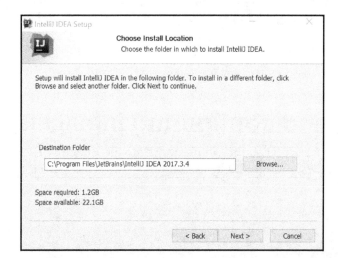

Check **64-bit launcher** (unless your computer supports 32-bits only) and `.java` on the following screen:

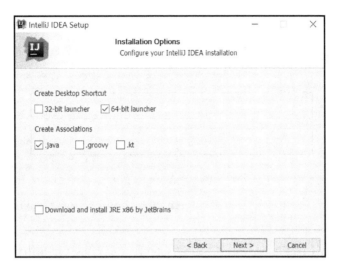

We will assume that you have JDK installed already, so there is no need to check **Download and install JRE** on the previous screenshot. If you have not installed JDK yet, you can check **Download and install JRE**, or install JDK by following the steps described in `Chapter 1`, *Java Virtual Machine (JVM) on Your Computer*.

The following screen allows you to customize the entry in your start menu, or you can just accept the default options by clicking on the **Install** button:

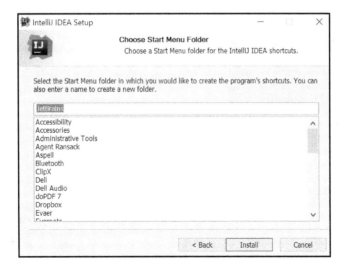

It will take the installer some time to finish the installation. The progress bar on the following screen will give you an idea of how much time is left for the process to complete:

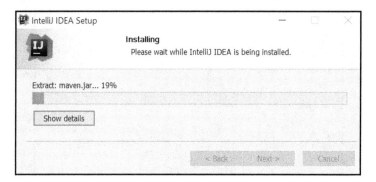

After the installation has complete, and the **Next>** button becomes clickable, use it to get to the next screen.

Check the **Run IntelliJ IDEA** box on the next screen, and click the **Finish** button:

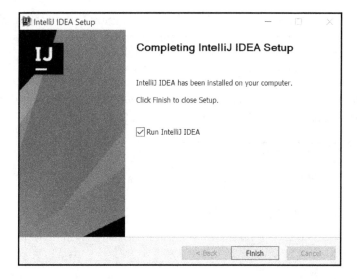

The installation is completed and we can now start configuring the IDE.

# Configuring IntelliJ IDEA

When IntelliJ IDEA starts for the very first time, it asks you about the settings you might have from the previous IDE version:

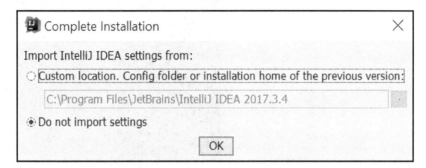

Since it is your first IntelliJ IDEA installation, click **Do not import settings**.

The next screen or two also show only once – at the first launch of the newly installed IDE. They will ask whether you accept the JetBrains privacy policy, and whether you would like to pay for the license or prefer to continue using the free Community Edition or free trial (this depends on the particular download you get). Answer the questions whichever way you prefer, and, if you accept the privacy policy, the following screen will ask you to chose a theme—white (*IntelliJ*) or dark (*Darcula*).

We have chosen the dark theme, as you will see on our demo screens. But you can select whatever you prefer and then, change it later, if you so desire:

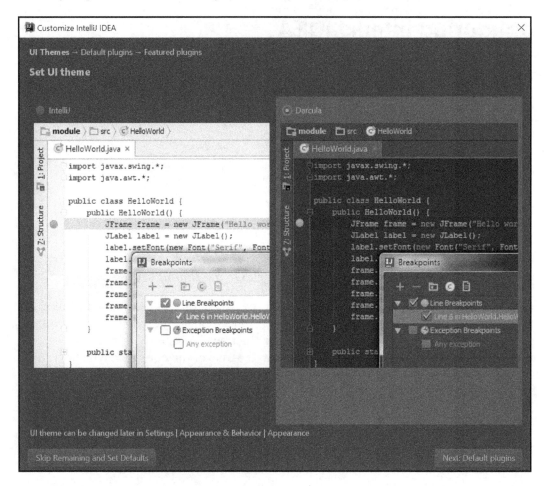

On the above screen, at the bottom, you can see two buttons: **Skip Remaining and Set Deafults** and **Next: Default plugins**. If you click **Skip Remaining and Set Defaults**, you will skip the chance to configure some settings now, but you can do it later. For this demo, we will click the **Next: Default plugins** button and then show you how to revisit the settings later.

Here is the screen with the default settings options:

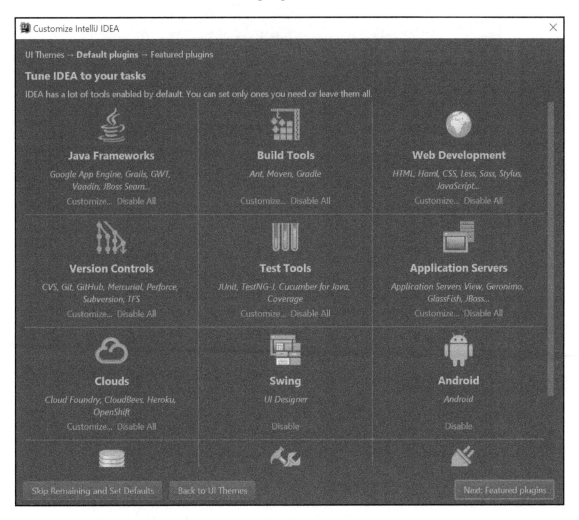

You can click any **Customize...** link on the preceding screen and see the possible options, then return back. We will use only three of them—**Build Tools**, **Version Control**, and **Test Tools**. We will start with **Build Tools** by clicking **Customize...**:

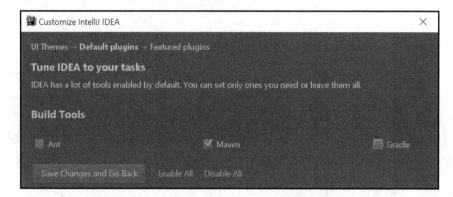

We are going to leave the **Maven** option checked, but the presence of other checks does not hurt , and can even help, if you would like to explore the related functionality later.

Click **Save Changes and Go Back**, then click the **Customize...** link under the **Version Controls** symbol:

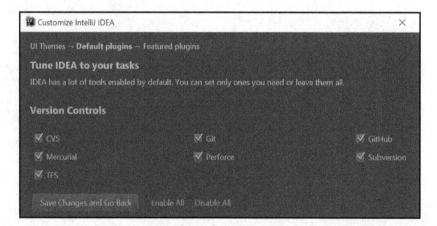

We will talk a bit about source control tools (or version control tool, as they are also called) later, but full treatment of this subject is outside the scope of this book. On the preceding screen, you can check the box with the version-control system you know you are going to use. Otherwise, leave all of the boxes checked, so the version-control system will be integrated automatically, as soon as you open a code-source tree checked out from one of the listed tools.

Click **Save Changes and Go Back**, then click the **Customize...** link under the **Test Tools** symbol:

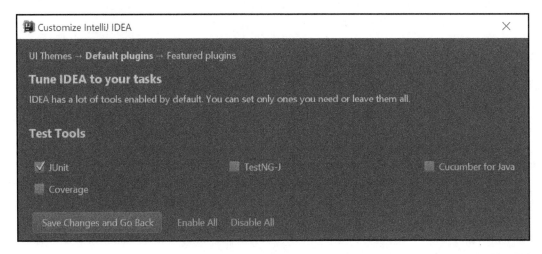

On the preceding screen, we are going to leave only the **JUnit** checkbox checked, because we would like to have our demo configuration clear of unnecessary distractions. But you can leave everything checked. It does not hurt to have other options available. Besides, you may decide to use other options in the future.

As you have seen, in principle, we did not need to change any of the default settings. We have only done it to show you the available capabilities.

Click **Save Changes and Go Back**, then click the **Next: Featured plugins** button, and then the **Start using IntelliJ IDEA** button.

 If you have not configured IDE at the installation time or did something different and would like to change the configuration, you can do so later.

We will explain how to access the configuration settings in IntelliJ IDEA after installation and provide the corresponding screenshots in Chapter 4, *Your First Java Project*.

# Exercise – Installing NetBeans IDE

Download and install NetBeans IDE.

# Answer

As of the time of writing, the page for downloading the latest version of NetBeans is `https://netbeans.org/features/index.html`.

After the download is complete, launch the installer. You might get a message that advises you to use the `--javahome` option when launching the installer. Find the corresponding installation instructions, and do that. The NetBeans version expected a certain version of Java, and a mismatch may cause installation or running problems.

If the installer launches without warning, you can just follow the wizard until the screen states **Installation completed successfully** and has the **Finish** button. Click the **Finish** button, then run NetBeans. You are ready to start writing Java code using the NetBeans IDE. After reading `Chapter 4`, *Your First Java Project*, try to create a similar project in NetBeans, and see how you like it compared to IntelliJ IDEA.

# Summary

Now you know what the development environment is and what tools you need on your computer to start coding. You have learned how to configure an IDE and what it does for you behind the scenes. You now have an idea of what to look for when selecting your IDE.

In the next chapter, you will start using it to write and compile code and test for it. You will learn what a Java project is, how to create and configure one, and how to execute your code and test it without leaving your IDE, which means that you will become a Java programmer.

# Your First Java Project

**4**

In the previous chapters, you learned quite a few things about Java, including its basic aspects, and main tools. Now, we are going to apply the knowledge acquired to complete and take the first step toward a real-life program—creating a Java project. We will show you how to write application code, how to test it, and how to execute the main code and its tests.

In this chapter, we will cover the following topics:

- What is a project?
- Creating a project
- Writing and building application code
- Executing and unit testing an application
- Exercise: JUnit `@Before` and `@After` annotations

# What is a project?

Let's start with the definition and origin of the term project.

# Definition and origin of project

The term *project*, according to an English by Oxford Dictionaries, is *an individual or collaborative enterprise that is carefully planned to achieve a particular aim*. The term was adopted by the designers of IDEs to mean the collection of files that compose an application. That is why the term project is often used as a synonym for an application, too.

# Project-related terms

The files that constitute the project are stored in the directories of a filesystem. The top-most directory is called the *project root directory*, and the rest of the project directories form a tree underneath it. That's why a project can also be seen as a tree of directories that contain all of the .java files and other files that comprise the source code of an application and its tests. Non-Java files are usually called `resources`, and are stored in a directory with the same name.

Programmers also use the terms *source code tree*, *source code*, or just *source*, as synonyms for aproject.

When a project uses the classes of another project, they are packaged in a .jar file and usually constitute a *library* (a collection of, more or less, independent classes) or *framework* (a system of classes designed to work together in support of certain functionalities). The difference between a library and a framework does not affect how your project accesses its classes, so from now on, we will call all of the third-party .jar files used by the project libraries for brevity. In the *Maven project configuration* section, we will show you how to access such libraries, if your code needs them.

# A project's life cycle

The Java project life cycle consists of the following phases (steps, stages):

- Feasibility: when a determination is made on whether to proceed with the project or not
- Requirements-gathering and high-level design
- Class-level design: *the first phase of the development phases*
- Project creation
- Writing application code and its unit tests
- Project building: code compilation
- Storing the source code in a remote repository and sharing it with other programmers
- Project packaging: gathering .class files and all the supporting non-Java files into a .jar file that is commonly called a *project artifact* or just an *artifact*
- Project installation: saving the artifact in a binary repository (also called *an artifactory*), from where it can be retrieved and shared among other programmers. This phase is the last one of the development phases

- Project deployment and execution in a test environment; placing the artifact into an environment where it can be executed and tested under the condition similar to production, *this is the testing phase*
- Project deployment and execution in the production environment: *this is the first phase of the production (also called maintenance) phases*
- Project enhancement and maintenance:fixing the defects and adding new features to the application
- Shutting down the project after it is not needed anymore

In this book, we cover only four project phases:

- Project design (see Chapter 8, *Object-Oriented Design (OOD) Principles*)
- Project creation
- Writing application code and its unit tests
- Project building, which is a code compilation using the javac tool

We will show you how to perform all these phases using the IntelliJ IDEA Community edition, but similar procedures are available with other IDEs, too.

To build the project, IDE uses Java Compiler (the javac tool) and a dependency managing tool. The latter sets the values of the -classpath option in the javac and java commands. The three most popular dependency managing tools are Maven, Gradle, and Ant. IntelliJ IDEA has a built-in Maven capability and does not require installing an external dependency managing tool.

# Creating a project

There are several ways to create a project in IntelliJ IDEA (or any other IDE, for that matter):

- Using a project wizard (see the *Creating a project using a project wizard* section)
- Reading the existing source code from the filesystem
- Reading the existing source code from the source-control system

In this book, we will walk you through the first option only—using a project wizard. The other two options are just point-and-read, in one step, and do not require much of an explanation. After you learn how to create a project manually, you will understand what happens behind the scenes, during the automatic creation from the existing source.

# Creating a project using a project wizard

When you start IntelliJ IDEA except for the first time, it will show you a list of already created projects. Otherwise, you will see the following screen only:

The three options – **Import Project**, **Open**, and **Check out from Version Control** – allow you to work on an existing project. We are not going to use them in this book.

Click the **Create New Project** link, which brings you to the first screen of the project-creation wizard. Choose **Java** in the upper-left corner, then click the **New** button in the upper-right corner, and select the location of the JDK installed on your computer. After that, click the **OK** button in the bottom-right corner.

On the next window, do not select anything, and just click the **Next** button:

You don't see the **Next** button in the preceding screenshot because it is at the bottom of the actual screen, and the rest is empty space, which we decided not to show here.

On the next screen, enter the project name (typically, your application name) in the upper field, as shown here:

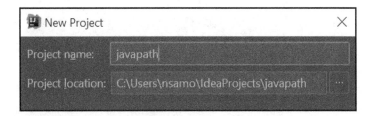

For our demo code, we have chosen the project (application) name to be `javapath`, in the sense of the path to the Java programming. Click the **Finish** button at the bottom of the preceding screen, and you should see something like this:

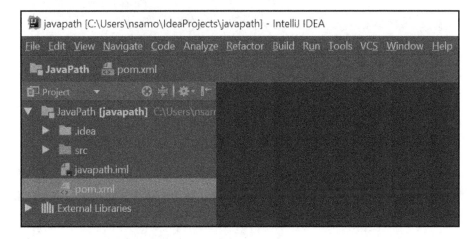

If you don't see the project structure in the left pane, click **View** (in the top-most menu), then **Tool Windows**, then **Project**, as shown in the following screenshot:

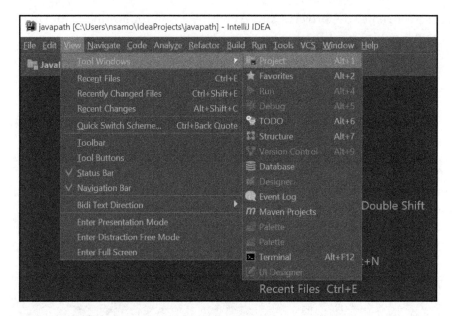

Now you should be able to see the project structure:

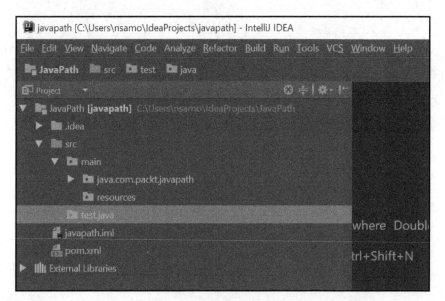

The preceding project includes:

- The `.idea` directory that holds the IntelliJ IDEA settings for your project
- The `src` directory, with subdirectories:
  - `main`, which will hold your application files in its `java` subdirectory (for `.java` files) and `resources` subdirectory (for other types of files),
  - `test`, which will hold the tests for your application in its `java` (for `.java` files) and the `resources` subdirectory (for other types of files).
- The `javapath.iml` file, which is another IntelliJ IDEA file with project configurations
- The `External Libraries` directory, which holds all of the libraries your project is using

In the preceding screenshot, you can also see the `pom.xml` file. This file is used to describe other libraries your code requires. We will explain how to use it in the *Maven project configuration* section. IDE generated it automatically, because in the previous chapter, while configuring the IDE, we indicated our desire to integrate with Maven in the IDE default settings. If you have not done that, you can now right-click on the project name (`JavaPath`, in our case) and select **Add Framework Support**:

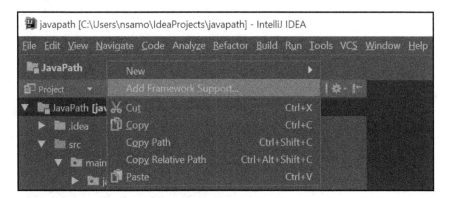

Then, you will be presented with the screen where you can select **Maven**:

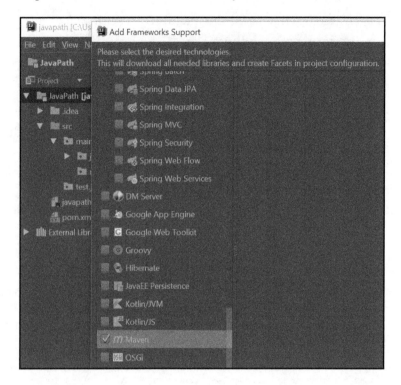

Click the **OK** button, and the pom.xml file will be created. The same steps should be followed if the pom.xml file does not have the Maven symbol, as in the preceding screenshots. Here is how it looks after Maven support is added:

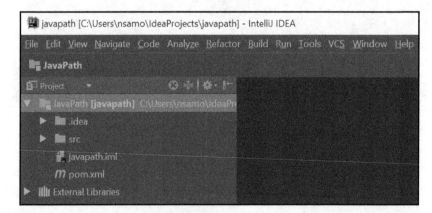

Another way to trigger `pom.xml` creation is to respond to a small window in the lower-right corner that pops up with various suggestions, including **Add as Maven Project** (it means that the code dependencies are going to be managed by Maven):

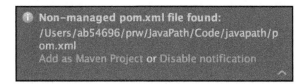

If you have missed clicking the preceding link, you can still recover the suggestion by clicking the link at the bottom line:

It will bring the suggestion back into the bottom-left corner of the screen:

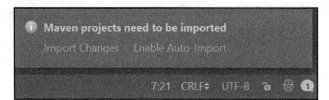

Click on the **Add as Maven Project** link, and the `pom.xml` file will be created.

Another helpful suggestion looks like the following:

We recommend that you click the **Enable Auto-Import** link. It will allow IDE to support your project even better, by relieving you from having to do certain things manually.

If none of the preceding methods work for you, it is always possible to create the pom.xml file manually. Just right-click on the project name (JavaPath) in the left pane, select **New**, select **File**, then type the filename, pom.xml, and click the **OK** button.

# Maven project configuration

As we have already mentioned, Maven helps to compose the javac and java commands when you compile and run your application. It sets the value of the –classpath option. To accomplish it, Maven reads the list of libraries your project needs from pom.xml. It is your responsibility to correctly specify these libraries. Otherwise, Maven will not be able to find them.

By default, the pom.xml file is located in the project root directory. That is also the directory where IDE runs the javac command and sets the src/main/java directory on the classpath so that javac can find the source files of your project. It puts the compiled .class files in the target/classes directory into the root directory too, and sets this directory on the classpath while executing the java command.

Another function of pom.xml is to describe your project so that it can be uniquely identified among all other projects on your computer, and even among all other projects on the internet. That is what we are going to do now. Let's look inside the pom.xml file:

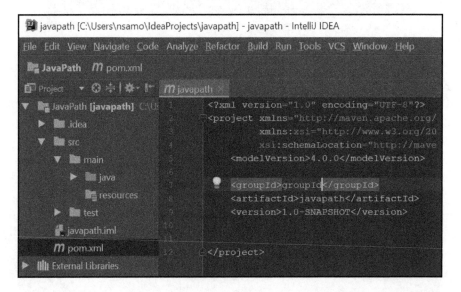

You can see the three XML tags that identify your project:

- `groupId` identifies a group of projects within an organization or an open source community
- `artifactId` identifies a particular project within the group
- `version` identifies the version of the project

The value set in the `groupId` tag has to follow the package-naming convention, so now, we need to explain what a package is. A package is the biggest structural unit of the Java application. Each package groups related Java classes. Two different classes in different packages can have the same name. That's why a package is also called a namespace.

The package name has to be unique. It enables us to identify a class correctly, even when a class with the same name exists in other packages listed on the classpath. The package can have several subpackages. They are organized in a hierarchy similar to the directory structure of a filesystem. The package that contains all the other packages is called a top-level package. Its name is used as the `groupId` tag value of the `pom.xml` file.

The package-naming convention requires that the top-level package name is based on the internet domain name (in reverse order) of the organization that created the package. For example, if the domain name is `oracle.com`, then the top-level package name has to be `com.oracle` followed by (after a dot, .) the project name. Alternatively, a subdomain, a department name, or any other project group can be inserted between the reversed domain name and project name. Then, other subpackages follow.

Many packages of JDK standard libraries, start with `jdk`, `java`, or `javax`, for example. But the best practice is to follow the described naming convention defined in section $6.1 of the Java Specification (`https://docs.oracle.com/javase/specs`).

Selecting a unique package name may be problematic when an open source project starts without any organization in mind. In such cases, programmers often use `org.github.<author's name>` or something similar.

In our project, we have a top-level `com.packt.javapath` package. By doing so, we took a bit of a risk, because another Packt author may decide to start the packages with the same name. It would be better to start our packages with `com.packt.nicksamoylov.javapath`. This way, the author's name would resolve the possible conflict, unless, of course, another author with the same name starts writing Java books for Packt. But, we decided to take the risk for brevity. Besides, we do not think that the code we are creating in this book will be used by another project.

So, the `groupId` tag value for our project will be `com.packt.javapath`.

The `artifactId` tag value is typically set to the project name.

The `version` tag value contains the project version.

The `artifactId` and `version` are used to form a `.jar` filename during the project packaging. For example, if the project name is `javapath` and the version is `1.0.0`, the `.jar` filename will be `javapath-1.0.0.jar`.

So, our `pom.xml` will now look like this:

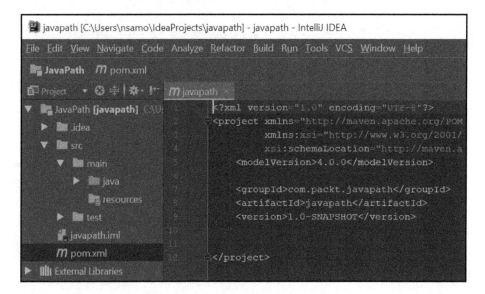

Notice the `-SNAPSHOT` suffix in the version. Its usefulness becomes apparent only when you are going to share the same project with other programmers. But we will explain it now, so that you understand the purpose of this value. When an artifact of a project (a `.jar` file) is created, its name will be `javapath-1.0-SNAPSHOT.jar`. The presence of `-SNAPSHOT` in the filename indicates that it is a work in progress and the code is changing from build to build. This way, other Maven-managed projects that use your artifact will download it every time a timestamp on the `.jar` file changes.

When the code stabilizes and the changes become rare, you can set the version value to `1.0.0` and change it only when the code changes and a new project version is released—`javapath-1.0.0.jar`, `javapath-1.0.1.jar`, or `javapath-1.2.0.jar`, for example. Then, a other projects that use the javapath `.jar` file do not download a new file version automatically. Instead, the programmers of another projects can read the release notes of each new version and decide whether to use it or not; a new version may introduce changes that are not desirable, or are incompatible with their application code. If they decide they need a new version, they set it in the `pom.xml` file in the `dependencies` tag of their project, and Maven downloads it for them.

In our `pom.xml` file, there is no `dependencies` tag yet. But it can be placed anywhere inside of the `<project>...</project>` tags. Let's look at a few examples of dependencies in a `pom.xml` file. We can add them to the project now, because we are going to use them later, anyway:

```
<dependencies>
  <dependency>
    <groupId>org.junit.jupiter</groupId>
    <artifactId>junit-jupiter-api</artifactId>
    <version>5.1.0-M1</version>
  </dependency>
  <dependency>
    <groupId>org.postgresql</groupId>
    <artifactId>postgresql</artifactId>
    <version>42.2.2</version>
  </dependency>
  <dependency>
    <groupId>org.apache.commons</groupId>
    <artifactId>commons-lang3</artifactId>
    <version>3.4</version>
  </dependency>
</dependencies>
```

The first `org.junit.jupiter` dependency refers to a `junit-jupiter-api-5.1.0-M1.jar` file that contains the `.class` files necessary for writing tests. We will use it in the next section, *Writing an application code and tests*.

The second `org.postgresql` dependency refers to a `postgresql-42.2.2.jar` file that allows us to connect and work with the PostgreSQL database. We will use this dependency in `Chapter 16`, *Database Programming*.

The third dependency refers to the `org.apache.commons` file, `commons-lang3-3.4.jar`, that contains many small, very useful methods called utilities, some of which we are going to use generously, for various purposes.

Each of these `.jar` files is stored in a repository on the internet. By default, Maven will search its own central repository, located at `http://repo1.maven.org/maven2`. The vast majority of the libraries you need are stored there. But in the rare case that you need to specify other repositories—in addition to the Maven central one—you can do it as follows:

```
<repositories>
  <repository>
    <id>my-repo1</id>
    <name>your custom repo</name>
    <url>http://jarsm2.dyndns.dk</url>
  </repository>
  <repository>
    <id>my-repo2</id>
    <name>your custom repo</name>
    <url>http://jarsm2.dyndns.dk</url>
  </repository>
</repositories>
```

Read the Maven guides for more details on Maven at `http://maven.apache.org/guides`.

With the `pom.xml` file configured, we can start writing code for our first application. But before that, we would like to mention how you can customize the configuration of IntelliJ IDEA to match your preferences for the look and feel and other features of the IDE.

# Changing IDE settings at any time

You can change IntelliJ IDEA settings and project configuration any time, to adjust the appearance and behavior of the IDE to the style most comfortable for you. Take your time and see what you can set on each of the following configuration pages.

To change the configuration of IntelliJ IDEA itself:

- On Windows: click **File** on the top-most menu, then select **Settings**
- On Linux and macOS: click **IntelliJ IDEA** on the top-most menu, then select **Preferences**

The configuration screen that you access will look similar to the following:

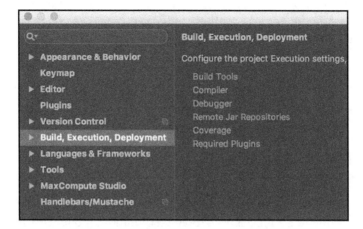

Click around and see what you can do here, so that you know the possibilities of your IDE.

To change project specific settings, click **File**, then select **Project Structure**, and see the available settings and options. Notice that the same screen can be accessed by right-clicking on the project name (in the left pane) and then selecting **Open Module Settings**.

After you have established your own style and know your preferences, you can set them as the default settings for the IDE configuration via **File | Other Settings | Default Settings**.

The default project structure can be also set via **File | Other Settings | Default Project Structure**. These default settings will be applied automatically, every time you create a new project.

With that out of our way, we can start writing our application code.

# Writing an application code

This is the most interesting activity of a programmer's profession. And that is the purpose of this book – to help you write Java code well.

Let's start with the requirements for your first application. It should take an integer number as an input, multiply it by 2, and print the result in the following format: `<the input number> * 2 = <result>`.

Now, let's come up with the design. We will create the `SimpleMath` class with the `multiplyByTwo(int i)` method that will accept an integer and return the result. This method will be called by the `main()` method of the `MyApplication` class. The `main()` method should:

- Receive an input number from a user
- Pass the input value into the `multiplyByTwo(int i)` method
- Get back the result
- Print it on a screen in the required format

We will also create tests for the `multiplyByTwo(int i)` method, to make sure that the code we have written works correctly.

We will start by creating directories that will hold our `.java` files. The directory path must match the package name of each class. We have talked about a package already, and set the top-level package name as a `groupId` value. Now, we will describe how to declare it in the `.java` files.

# Java package declaration

Package declaration is the first line of any Java class. It starts with the `package` keyword, followed by the package name. The `javac` and `java` tools search for a class on a classpath using a fully qualified class name, which is a class name with the package name appended in front of it. For example, if we put the `MyApplication` class in the `com.packt.javapath.ch04demo` package, the fully qualified name of this class will be `com.packt.javapath.ch04demo.MyApplication`. As you could guess, `ch04demo` stands for the *demo code* of Chapter 4. This way, we can use the same class name in different chapters, and they will not clash. That is how the package name serves the purpose of unique identification of a class on a classpath.

Another function of the package is to define the location of the `.java` files, relative to the `src\main\java` directory (for Windows) or the `src/main/java` directory (for Linux). The package name must match the path to the files that belong to this package:

**src\main\java\com\packt\javapath\ch04demo\MyApplication.java** (for Windows)

**src/main/java/com/packt/javapath/ch04demo/MyApplication.java** (for Linux)

Any mismatch between the package name and the file location triggers a compilation error. When you create a new class using an IDE wizard (after right-clicking on the package name), IDE adds the correct package declaration as the first line of the `.java` file automatically. But if you create a new source file without using IDE, then it is your responsibility to match the package name and the `.java` file location.

It is possible to not have a package name declared if the `.java` file resides in the `src\main\java` directory (for Windows) or the `src/main/java` directory (for Linux). Java specification calls such a package a default package. Using the default package is practical for only a small or temporary application, because as the number of classes grows, a flat list of a hundred, or even a thousand, files becomes unmanageable. Besides, if you write code to be used by other projects, these other projects will not be able to refer to your classes without a package name. In `Chapter 7`, *Packages and Accessibility (Visibility)*, we will talk more about this.

The directory tree of the `.class` files is created by the `javac` tool during compilation, and it mirrors the directory structure of the `.java` files. Maven creates a `target` directory in the project root directory with a `classes` subdirectory in it. Maven then specifies this subdirectory as the output location of the generated files, with a `-d` option in the `javac` command:

```
//For Windows:
javac -classpath src\main\java -d target\classes
                        com.packt.javapath.ch04demo.MyApplication.java

//For Linux:
javac -classpath src/main/java -d target/classes
                        com.packt.javapath.ch04demo.MyApplication.java
```

During the execution, the `.class` files' location is set on the classpath:

```
//For Windows:
java -classpath target\classes com.packt.javapath.ch04demo.MyApplication

//For Linux:
java -classpath target/classes com.packt.javapath.ch04demo.MyApplication
```

With the knowledge of the package declaration, its function, and its relation with the directory structure, let's create our first package.

# Creating a package

We assume that you have created the project by following the steps in the *Creating a project using a project wizard* section. If you have closed your IDE, please start it again, and open the created project by selecting `JavaPath` in the list of **Recent projects**.

When the project is open, click on the `src` folder in the left pane, then click on the `main` folder. You should see the `java` folder now:

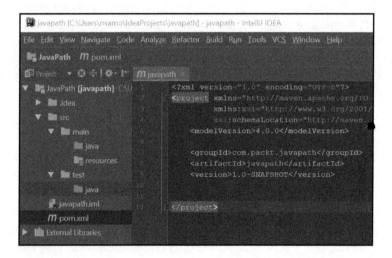

Right-click on the `java` folder, select the **New** menu item, and then select the **Package** menu item:

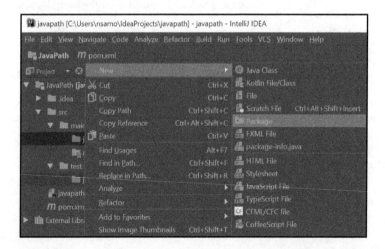

Type `com` in the pop-up window:

Click the **OK** button. The `com` folder will be created.

Right-click on it in the left pane, select the **New** menu item, then select the **Package** menu item, and type `packt` in the pop-up window:

Repeat the process and create the `javapath` folder under the `packt` folder, and then the `ch04demo` folder under the `javapath` folder. After
the `com.packt.javapath.ch04demo` package is in place, we can create its member—the `MyApplication` class.

# Creating the MyApplication class

To create a class, right-click on the `com.packt.javapath.che04demo` package in the left pane, select the **New** menu item, then select the **Java Class** menu item, and type `MyApplication` in the pop-up window:

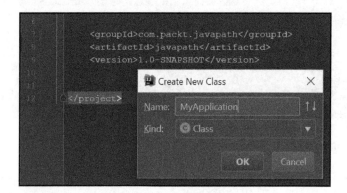

Click the **OK** button, and the class will be created:

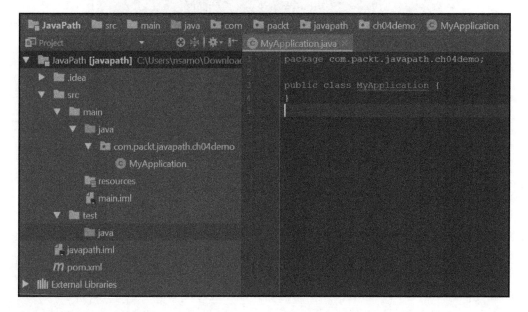

The name of the `MyApplication` class in the right pane is faded. That is how IntelliJ IDEA indicates that it is not used anywhere yet.

# Building the application

Behind the scenes, the IDE compiles the code you are writing every time you change it. For example, try to remove the first letter, M, in the name of the class in the right pane. IDE will immediately warn you about the syntax error:

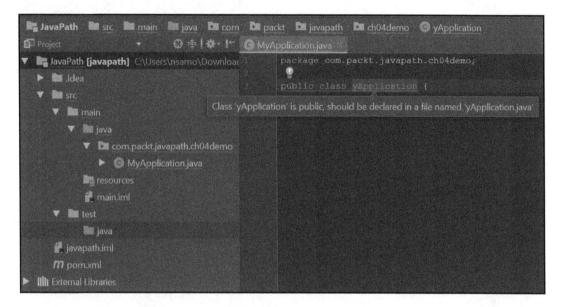

If you navigate your mouse to the red bubble, or any red line that underscores the class declaration in the preceding screenshot, you will see the **Class 'yApplication' is public, should be declared in a file named 'yApplication.java'** message. You may recall that we talked about it in Chapter 2, *Java Language Basics*.

 Each .java file contains only one public class. The file name must match the public class name.

Because IDE compiles the code after every change, in the case of a small number of .java files, building a project explicitly is not necessary. But when the size of the application increases, you might not notice that something went wrong.

That's why it is a good practice to request IDE to recompile (or build, in other words) all of the .java files of your application from time to time, by clicking **Build** in the top-most menu and selecting the **Rebuild Project** menu item:

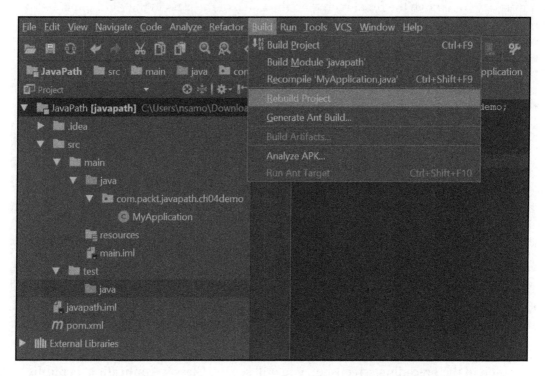

You may have noticed other related menu items: **Build Project** and **Build Module 'javapath'**. A module is a way to bundle classes across packages. But using modules is outside the scope of this book. **Build Project** recompiles only the classes that have been changed, and those that use the changed classes. It makes sense to only use it for a very big application, when the build time is significant. **Rebuild Projects**, on the other hand, recompiles all of the .java files, whether they were changed or not, and we recommend that you always use it. That way, you can be sure that every class is rebuilt, and no dependency was missed.

After you click on **Rebuild Projects**, you will see a new `target` folder appear in the left pane:

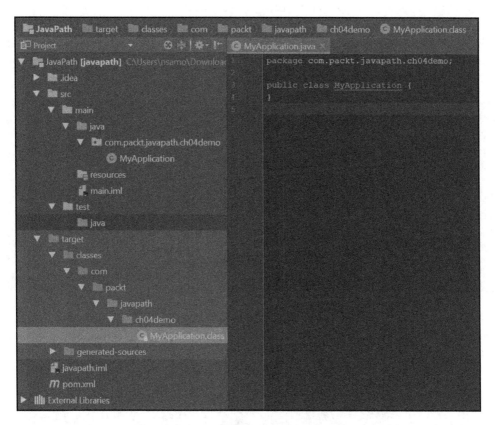

That is where Maven (and the built-in Maven used by IntelliJ IDEA) stores the `.class` files. You may have noticed that the `javac` tool creates a folder for each part of the package name. That way, the tree of compiled classes reflects exactly the tree of the source classes.

Now, before continuing code writing, we are going to perform a trick that will make your source tree look simpler.

# Hiding some files and directories

If you prefer not to see the IDE-specific files (`.iml` files, for example) or temporary files and directories (the `target` folder, for example), you can configure IntelliJ IDEA to not show them. Just click on **File | Settings** (on Windows) or **IntelliJ IDEA | Preferences** (on Linux and macOS), then click the **Editor** menu item in the left column, and then **File Types**. The resulting screen will have the following section:

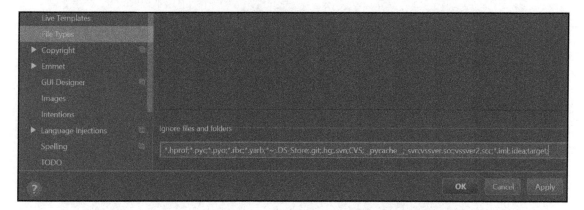

At the bottom of the screen, you can see the **Ignore files and folders** label and the input field with the file name patterns. Add the following to the end of the list: `*.iml;.idea;target;`. Then, click the **OK** button. Now, your project structure should look like this:

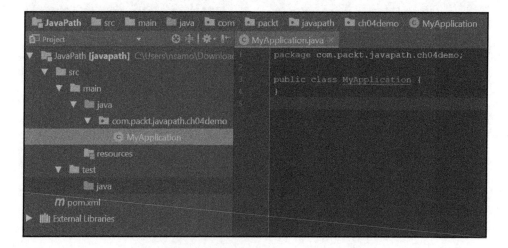

It shows only the application source files and third-party libraries (under **External Libraries**).

# Creating the SimpleMath class

Let's now create another package, `com.packt.javapath.math`, and the `SimpleMath` class in it. The reason for this is that in the future, we plan to have several, similar math-related classes in this package, and other, non-math-related classes in other packages.

In the left pane, right-click on the `com.packt.javapath.ch04demo` package, select **New**, then click **Package**. Type `math` in the provided input field, and click the **OK** button.

Right-click on the `math` package name, select **New**, then click **Java Class**, type `SimpleMath` in the provided input field, and click the **OK** button.

You should have created a new `SimpleMath` class that looks like this:

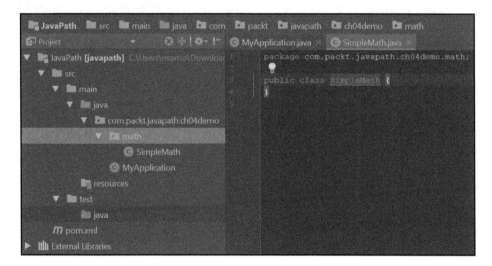

# Creating methods

First, we add the following method to the `SimpleMath` class:

```
public int multiplyByTwo(int i){
   return i * 2;
}
```

Now, we can add the code that uses the preceding method to the `MyApplication` class:

```
public static void main(String[] args) {
   int i = Integer.parseInt(args[0]);
   SimpleMath simpleMath = new SimpleMath();
   int result = simpleMath.multiplyByTwo(i);
   System.out.println(i + " * 2 = " + result);
}
```

The preceding code is pretty straightforward. The application receives an integer as an input parameter from the first element of the `String[] args` input array. Notice that the first element in the Java array has the index 0, not 1. The argument comes as a string, and has to be converted (parsed) to an `int` type by using the `parseInt()` static method of the `java.lang.Integer` class from a standard Java library. We will talk about Java types in Chapter 5, *Java Language Elements and Types*.

Then, an object of the `SimpleMath` class is created, and the `multiplyByTwo()` method is called. The returned result is stored in the `result` variable of the `int` type, and then printed out in the required format using the `java.lang.System` class of a standard Java library. This class has an `out` static property that holds a reference to an object of the `java.io.PrintStream` class. The `PrintStream` class, in turn, has the `println()` method, which prints the result to a screen.

# Executing and unit testing an application

There are several ways to execute our new application. In the *Building the application* section, we saw that all of the compiled classes are stored by IntelliJ IDEA (using the built-in Maven) in the `target` folder. This means that we can execute the application by using the `java` tool and listing the folder target with the `-classpath` option.

To do that, open a Command Prompt or Terminal window and go to the root directory of our new project. If you are not sure where it is, look at the top line of the IntelliJ IDEA window that shows the full path to it. Once you are in the project root directory (it is the folder where the `pom.xml` file is located), run the following command:

```
demo> java -cp target/classes com.packt.javapath.ch04demo.MyApplication 2
2 * 2 = 4
demo>
```

In the preceding screenshot, you can see that the `-classpath` option (we used the short version, `-cp`, instead) has listed the directory where all of the classes are compiled. After that, we have typed the name of the `com.packt.javapath.ch04demo.MyApplication` main class, because we have to tell the `java` tool which class is an entry point to the application and contains the `main()` method. Then, we have typed 2 as an input parameter to the main class. As you may recall, the `main()` method expects it to be an integer.

When we run that command, the result shows the output in the expected format: 2 * 2 = 4.

Alternatively, we could collect all of the compiled classes in a `myapp.jar` file and run a similar `java` command with the `myapp.jar` file listed on the classpath:

```
demo> cd target/classes
demo> jar cf myapp.jar .
demo> java -cp myapp.jar com.packt.javapath.ch04demo.MyApplication 2
2 * 2 = 4
demo>
```

In the preceding screenshot, you can see that we entered the `target` folder and its `classes` subfolder first, then collected its content (all of the compiled classes) into the `myapp.jar` file with the `jar` command. Then, we typed the `java` command and listed the `myapp.jar` file with the `-classpath` option. Since the `myapp.jar` file is in the current directory, we do not include any directory path. The result of the `java` command was the same as before: 2 * 2 = 4.

Another way to get to the project root directory is to just open a terminal window from IDE. In IntelliJ IDEA, you can do it by clicking on the **Terminal** link in the bottom-left corner:

Then, we can type all of the preceding commands in the Terminal window inside the IDE.

But there is an even easier way to execute the application from the IDE without typing all of the preceding commands, which is the recommended way during the project development phase. It is your IDE, remember? We will demonstrate how to do it in the next section.

# Executing the application using the IDE

In order to be able to execute an application from the IDE, some configuration has to be set the first time. In IntelliJ IDEA, if you click on the top-most menu item, click **Run**, and select **Edit Configurations...**, you will see the following screen:

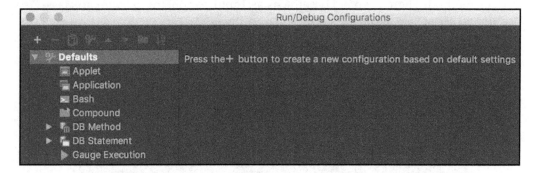

Click the plus (+) symbol in the upper-left corner, and type the values in the new window:

Type `MyApplication` (or any other name you like) in the **Name** field.

Type `com.packt.javapath.ch02demo.MyApplication` in the **Main class** field.

Type 2 (or any other number you like) in the **Program arguments** field.

Check the **Single instance only** checkbox in the upper-right corner. It will ensure that you will have only one instance of your application running at all times.

After filling in all the described values, click the **OK** button in the bottom-right corner.

Now, if you open the `MyApplication` class, you will see two green arrows – one at the class level, and another at the `main()` method:

```
MyApplication.java
1        package com.packt.javapath.ch04demo;
2
3        import com.packt.javapath.ch04demo.math.SimpleMath;
4
5   ▶    public class MyApplication {
6
7 ▶ @ ┐      public static void main(String[] args) {
8               int i = Integer.parseInt(args[0]);
9               SimpleMath simpleMath = new SimpleMath();
10              int result = simpleMath.multiplyByTwo(i);
11              System.out.println(i + " * 2 = " + result);
12          }
13
14      }
15
```

Click on any of these green arrows, and your application will be executed.

The result will be shown in the bottom-left corner of IntelliJ IDEA. A window with the title **Run** will open, and you will see the result of the application execution. If you have typed `2` in the **Program arguments** field, the result should be the same: `2 * 2 = 4`.

# Creating a unit test

Now, let's write a test for the `multiplyByTwo()` method of the `SimpleMath` class, because we would like to make sure that the `multiplyByTwo()` method works as expected. Such tests are useful as long as the project exists, because you can run them every time the code is changed, and verify that the existing functionality has not been changed accidentally.

A method is the smallest testable part of an application. That's why such a test is called a unit test. It is a good idea to have a unit test for each method that you create (except the trivial ones, such as getters and setters, for example).

We will use a popular test framework called JUnit. There are several versions of it. At the time of this writing, version 5 is the latest one, but versions 3 and 4 are still actively used. We will use version 5. It requires Java 8 or later, and we assume that on your computer, you have installed Java 9, at least.

As we have already mentioned, in order to use a third-party library or a framework, you need to specify it as a dependency in the pom.xml file. As soon as you do it, the Maven tool (or the built-in Maven feature of the IDE) will look for the corresponding .jar file in the Maven repository online. It will download that .jar to your local Maven repository in the .m2 folder, which was automatically created in the home directory on your computer. After that, your project can access it and use it at any time.

We have already set values in pom.xml for the dependency on JUnit 5 in the *Maven project configuration* section. But, let's assume that we have not done it yet, in order to show you how programmers usually do it.

First, you need to do some research and decide which framework or library you need. For example, after searching the internet, you may have read JUnit 5 documentation (http://junit.org/junit5) and figured that you need to set the Maven dependency on junit-jupiter-api. With that, you can search the internet again, and this time, look for maven dependency junit-jupiter-api, or just maven dependency junit 5. Chances are, the first link in your search results will bring you to the following page:

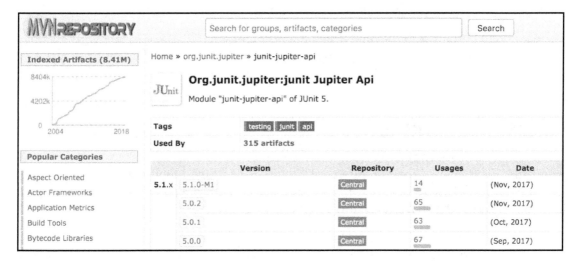

Select any version you like (we have chosen the latest, **5.1.0-M1**) and click on it.

A new page will be opened, which tells you how to set the dependency in `pom.xml`:

Alternatively, you can go to the Maven repository site (`https://mvnrepository.com`) and type `junit-jupiter-api` in its search window. Then, click on one of the provided links, and you will see the same page.

If you did not add the `junit-jupiter-api` dependency while reading the Chapter 3, *Your Development* Environment *Setup*, you can do it now by copying the provided dependency into your `pom.xml` file inside the `<dependencies></dependencies>` tag:

```xml
MyApplication.java    m javapath
1     <project xmlns="http://maven.apache.org/POM/4.0.0" xmlns:xsi="http://www.w3.org/2001/XM
2       xsi:schemaLocation="http://maven.apache.org/POM/4.0.0 http://maven.apache.org/maven-v
3       <modelVersion>4.0.0</modelVersion>
4
5       <groupId>com.packt.javapath</groupId>
6       <artifactId>javapath</artifactId>
7       <version>1.0-SNAPSHOT</version>
8
9       <dependencies>
10
11          <!-- https://mvnrepository.com/artifact/org.junit.jupiter/junit-jupiter-api -->
12          <dependency>
13              <groupId>org.junit.jupiter</groupId>
14              <artifactId>junit-jupiter-api</artifactId>
15              <version>5.1.0-M1</version>
16              <scope>test</scope>
17          </dependency>
18
19      </dependencies>
20
21    </project>
22
```

Now, you can use the JUnit framework to create a unit test.

In IntelliJ IDEA, the `junit-jupiter-api-5.1.0-M1.jar` file is also listed in the `External Libraries` folder, in the left pane. If you open the list, you will see that there are two other libraries that were not specified in the `pom.xml` file: `junit-latform-commons-1.0.0-M1.jar` and `opentest4j-1.0.0.jar`. They are there because `junit-jupiter-api-5.1.0-M1.jar` depends on them. That is what Maven does—it discovers all of the dependencies and downloads all necessary libraries.

Now, we can create a test for the `SimpleMath` class. We will use IntelliJ IDEA to do it. Open the `SimpleMath` class and right-click on the class name, then select **Go To**, and click on **Test**:

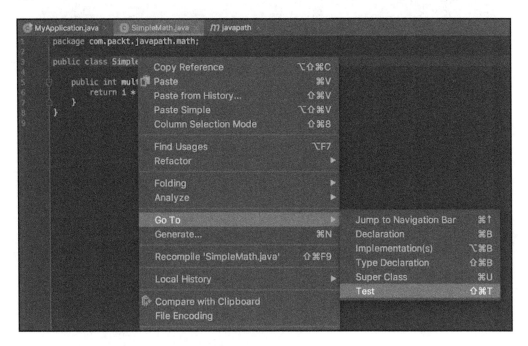

You will get a small pop-up window:

Click on **Create New Test...** and the following window will allow you to configure the test:

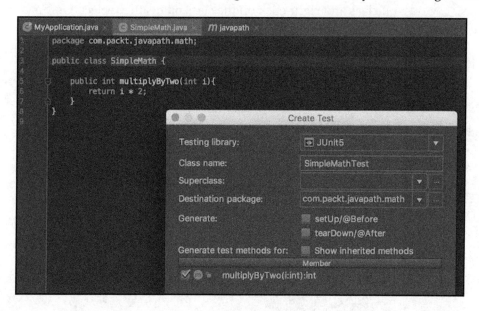

There is built-in support for JUnit 5 in IntelliJ IDEA. In the preceding screen, select **JUnit5** for **Testing library**, and check the checkbox for the `multiplyByTwo()` method. Then, click the **OK** button in the bottom-right corner. The test will be created:

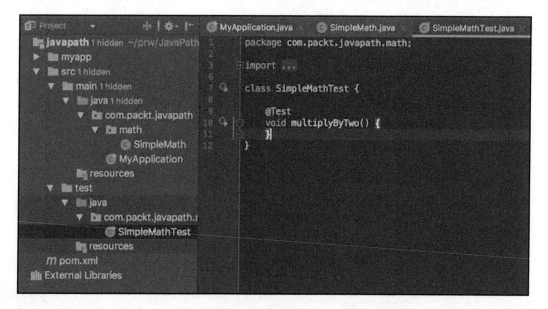

Notice that in the left pane, under the `test/java` folder, a package structure is created that matches the package of the `SimpleMath` class exactly. In the right pane, you can see the `SimpleMathTest` test class with one test (empty, so far) for the `multiplyByTwo()` method. The test method can have any name, but it has to have `@Test` in front of it, which is called an annotation. It tells the test framework that this is one of the tests.

Let's implement the test. For example, we can do it like this:

```
package com.packt.javapath.math;

import ...

@DisplayName("My first test case")
class SimpleMathTest {

    @Test
    @DisplayName("Happy path")
    void multiplyByTwo(){
        SimpleMath simpleMath = new SimpleMath();
        int i = 2;
        int result = simpleMath.multiplyByTwo(i);
        assertEquals( expected: 4, result);
    }
}
```

As you can see, we have created an object of the `SimpleMath` class and called the `multiplyByTwo()` method with a parameter of 2. We know that the correct result has to be 4, and we check the result using the `assertEquals()` method that comes from the JUnit framework. We also added the `@DisplayName` annotation to the class and to the test method. You will see what this annotation does shortly.

Let's now modify the `mutliplyByTwo()` method in the the `SimpleMath` class:

```
package com.packt.javapath.math;

public class SimpleMath {

    public int multiplyByTwo(int i){
        return i * 2 + 1;
    }
}
```

Instead of just multiplying by 2, we also add 1 to the result, so our test will break. It is a good practice to run a test on the incorrect code, first, so we can make sure that our test catches such errors.

# Executing the unit test

Now, let's go back to the `SimpleMathTest` class, and run it by clicking on one of the green arrows. The green arrow on the class level runs all of the test methods, while the green arrow on the method level runs only that test method. Since we have only one test method, so far, it does not matter which arrow we click. The result should look like this:

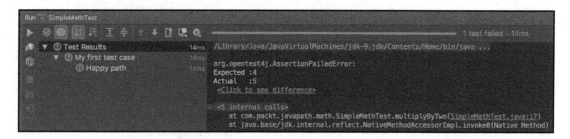

That is exactly what we hoped to see: the test expected to a result equal to 4, but got 5, instead. It provides us with a level of confidence that our test works correctly.

Notice in the left pane, we can see the display names that came from the `@DisplayName` annotations—that was the purpose of those annotations.

Also, click on each of the blue links in the right pane to see what they do. The first one provides more detailed information about expected and actual results. The second link brings you to the line of the test, where the assertion is located that has failed the testis located, so you can see the exact context and correct what went wrong.

Now, you can go to the `SimpleMath` class again and remove the 1 that we added. Then ,click on the green triangle in the upper-left corner (see the preceding screenshot). It means *rerun the test*. The result should look like this:

By the way, you may have noticed that our screenshots and the path to the project have slightly changed. It happened because we are now taking the screenshots from IntelliJ IDEA running on macOS, so we can cover Windows and macOS. As you can see, the appearance of IntelliJ IDEA screens look principally the same on Windows as on the macOS system.

# How many unit tests are enough?

This is always the question any programmer thinks about every time a new method is written or an old method is modified—How many unit tests are enough to make sure that the application is thoroughly tested, and what kind of tests should they be? Typically, it is not enough to have one test for each method of the application. There are usually many aspects of functionality that have to be tested. But each test method should test only one aspect, so it is easier to write it and to understand.

For example, for our simple `multiplyByTwo()` method, we could add another test (we would call it `multiplyByTwoRandom()`) that picks a random integer number as an input into the method and does it a hundred times. Or, we could think about some extreme numbers, such as 0 and negative numbers, and see how our method works with them (we could call them `multiplyByZero()` and `multiplyByNegative()`, for example). Another test would be to use a very big number – bigger than half the biggest integer Java allows (we will talk about such limits in Chapter 5, *Java Language Elements and Types*). We might also think about adding the check of the passed-in parameter value inside the `multiplyByTwo()` method, and throwing an exception if the passed-in parameter is bigger than half the maximum integer. We will talk about exceptions in Chapter 10, *Control Flow Statements*.

You can see how quickly the number of unit tests, for the simplest method can grow. Imagine how many unit tests can be written for a method that does much more than our simple code.

We don't want to write too many unit tests, either, because we need to maintain all this code for the rest of the project's life. In the past, on more than only one occasion, a big project became too expensive to maintain, only because too many complex unit tests were written that added little or no value. That's why often, after the project code stabilizes and works in production for some time, and if there is a reason to think that it has too many unit tests, the team revisits them and makes sure that there are no useless tests, duplicates, or anything else quite obvious.

Writing good unit tests that work quickly and test the code thoroughly is a skill that comes with experience. In this book, we will use every opportunity to share the best practices of unit testing with you, so that by the end of this book, you will have some experience in this very important area of professional Java programming.

# Exercise – JUnit @Before and @After annotations

Read the JUnit user guide (`https://junit.org/junit5/docs/current/user-guide`) and the class `SampleMathTest` two new methods:

- One that is executed only once before any test method is run
- One that is executed only once after all the test methods were run

We did not talk about it, so you would need to do some research.

# Answer

For JUnit 5, the annotations that can be used for this purpose are `@BeforeAll` and `@AfterAll`. Here is the demonstration code:

```java
public class DemoTest {
  @BeforeAll
  static void beforeAll(){
    System.out.println("beforeAll is executed");
  }
  @AfterAll
  static void afterAll(){
    System.out.println("afterAll is executed");
  }
  @Test
  void test1(){
    System.out.println("test1 is executed");
  }
  @Test
  void test2(){
    System.out.println("test2 is executed");
  }
}
```

If you run it, the output will be:

```
beforeAll is executed
test1 is executed
test2 is executed
afterAll is executed
```

# Summary

In this chapter, you learned about Java projects, and how to set them up and use them for writing your application code and unit tests. You also learned how to build and how to execute application code and unit tests. Basically, that is what a Java programmer does most of the time. In the rest of the book, you will gain more detailed knowledge of the Java language, the standard libraries, and third-party libraries and frameworks.

In the next chapter, we will dive deeper into Java language elements and types, including `int`, `String`, and `arrays`. You will also learn what an identifier is and how to use it as a variable's name, as well as information about Java-reserved keywords and comments.

# 5
# Java Language Elements and Types

This chapter starts a systematic introduction to Java with a definition of language elements—identifiers, variables, literals, keywords, separators, and comments. It also describes Java types—primitive types and reference types. Special attention is applied to the `String` class, `enum` types, and arrays.

In this chapter, we will cover the following topics:

- What are the Java language elements?
- Comments
- Identifiers and variables
- Reserved and restricted keywords
- Separators
- Primitive types and literals
- Reference types and String
- Arrays
- Enum types
- Exercise – Variable declarations and initializations

# What are the Java language elements?

As with any programming language, Java has a grammar that is applied to the language elements. The elements are building blocks used to compose language structures that allow the programmer to express intent. Elements themselves have different levels of complexity. Lower-level (simpler) elements enable building higher-level (more complex) ones. For a more detailed and systematic treatment of Java grammar and language elements, please see the Java Specification (`https://docs.oracle.com/javase/specs`).

In this book, we start with input elements that belong to one of the lowest levels. They are called **input elements** because they serve as input to the Java compiler.

# Input elements

Java input elements, according to the Java Specification, can be one of the following three:

- **Whitespace**: This can be one of these ASCII characters--SP (space), HT (horizontal tab), or FF (form feed, also called page break)
- **Comment**: A free-formed text that is not processed by the compiler but transferred into the bytecode as-is, so programmers use a comment to add a human-readable explanation to the code as they write it. A comment can include a whitespace, but it is not recognized as an input element; it is processed as a part of the comment only. We will describe the grammar rules for a comment and show some examples in the *Comments* section.
- **Token**: This can be one of the following:
  - **Identifier**: Will be described in the *Identifiers and variables* section.
  - **Keyword**: Will be described in the *Reserved and restricted keywords* section.
  - **Separator**: Will be described in the *Separators* section.
  - **Literal**: Will be described in the *Primitive types and literals* section. Some literals can include a whitespace, but it is not recognized as an input element; the whitespace is processed as a part of the literal only.
  - **Operator**: Will be described in `Chapter 9`, *Operators, Expressions, and Statements*.

Input elements are used to compose more complex elements, including types. Some of the keywords are used to denote types, and we will also discuss them in this chapter.

# Types

Java is a strongly typed language, which means that any variable declaration must include its type. Type limits the value a variable can hold and how this value can be passed around.

All types in Java are divided into two categories:

- **Primitive types**: Described in the *Primitive types and literals* section
- **Reference types**: Described in the *Reference types and String* section

Some of the reference types require more attention, either because of their complexity or other particulars that have to be explained to avoid future confusion:

- **Arrays**: Described in the *Arrays* section
- **String** (the uppercase first character indicates it is the name of a class): Described in the *Reference types and String* section
- **Enum types**: Described in the *Enum types* section

# Comments

The Java Specification provides the following information about comments:

> *"There are two kinds of comments:*
> */* text */*
> *A traditional comment: all the text from the ASCII characters /* to the ASCII characters */*
> *is ignored (as in C and C++).*
> *// text*
> *An end-of-line comment: all the text from the ASCII characters // to the end of the line is*
> *ignored (as in C++)."*

Here is an example of comments in the `SimpleMath` class that we have written already:

```
public class SimpleMath {
  /*
    This method just multiplies any integer by 2
    and returns the result
  */
  public int multiplyByTwo(int i){
    //Should we check if i is bigger than 1/2 of Integer.MAX_VALUE ?
    return i * 2; // The magic happens here
  }
}
```

The comments do not affect the code in any way. They are just programmer's notes. Also, don't confuse them with JavaDoc or another documentation generating system.

# Identifiers and variables

Identifiers and variables are among the most often used elements of Java. They are closely coupled because every variable has a name and the name of a variable is an identifier.

## Identifier

An identifier is the first in the list of Java tokens. It is a sequence of symbols, each may be a letter, a dollar sign $, an underscore, _, or any digit 0-9. The restrictions are as follows:

- The first symbol of an identifier cannot be a digit
- A single-symbol identifier cannot be an underscore _
- An identifier cannot have the same spelling as a keyword (see the *Reserved and restricted keywords* section)
- An identifier cannot be a Boolean literal `true` or `false`
- An identifier cannot be spelled as a special type `null`

If any of the above restrictions is violated, a compiler generates an error.

In practice, the letters used for an identifier are usually taken from the English alphabet – lowercase or uppercase. But it is possible to use other alphabets, too. You can find the formal definition of the letters that can be included in the identifier in section 3.8 of the Java Specification (`https://docs.oracle.com/javase/specs`). Here is the list of the examples from that section:

- `i3`
- αρετη
- `String`
- `MAX_VALUE`
- `isLetterOrDigit`

To show the variety of possibilities, we can add two more examples of legal identifiers:

- `$`
- `_1`

# Variable

A variable is a storage location, as the Java Specification puts it in the *Variables* section. It has a name (an identifier) and an assigned type. A variable refers to the memory where a value is stored.

The Java Specification has provision for eight kinds of variables:

- **Class variable**: A static class member that can be used without creating an object
- **Instance variable**: A non-static class member that can be used only via an object
- **Array component**: An array element (see the *Arrays* section)
- **Method parameter**: An argument passed to a method
- **Constructor parameter**: An argument passed to a constructor when an object is created
- **Lambda parameter**: An argument passed to a lambda expression. We will talk about it in Chapter 17, *Lambda Expressions and Functional Programming*
- **Exception parameter**: It is created when an exception is caught, we will talk about it in Chapter 10, *Control Flow Statements*
- **Local variable**: A variable declared inside a method

From a practical point of view, all eight kinds of variables can be summarized as follows:

- A class member, static or not
- An array member (also called a component or an element)
- A parameter of a method, constructor, or lambda expression
- An exception parameter of a catch-block
- A regular local code variable, the most common kind

Most of the time, when programmers talk about a variable, they mean the last kind. It can refer to a class member, class instance, parameter, exception object, or any other value necessary for the code you are writing.

# Variable declaration, definition, and initialization

Let's look at the examples first. Let's assume we have these three lines of code consecutively:

```
int x;   //declartion of variable x
x = 1;   //initialization of variable x
x = 2;   //assignment of variable x
```

As you can guess from the preceding example, variable initialization is assigning the first (initial) value to a variable. All subsequent assignments cannot be called an initialization.

A local variable cannot be used until initialized:

```
int x;
int result = x * 2;   //generates compilation error
```

The second line of the preceding code will generate a compilation error. If a variable is a member of a class (static or not) or a component of an array and not initialized explicitly, it is assigned a default value that depends on the variable's type (see the *Primitive types and literals* and *Reference types and String* sections).

A declaration creates a new variable. It includes the variable type and name (identifier). The word **declaration** is a technical term used in the Java Specification, section 6.1 (https://docs.oracle.com/javase/specs). But some programmers use word definition as the synonym for declaration because the word definition is used in some other programming languages (C and C++, for example) for a type of statement that does not exist in Java. So, be aware of it and assume they mean declaration when you here *definition* applied to Java.

Most of the time, when writing Java code, programmers combine declaration and initialization statements in one. For example, a variable of the int type can be declared and initialized to hold integer 1, as follows:

```
int $ = 1;
int _1 = 1;
int i3 = 1;
int αρετη = 1;
int String = 1;
int MAX_VALUE = 1;
int isLetterOrDigit = 1;
```

The same identifiers can be used to declare and initialize a variable of the String type to hold abs:

```
String $ = "abc";
String _1 = "abc";
String i3 = "abc";
String αρετη = "abc";
String String = "abc";
String MAX_VALUE = "abc";
String isLetterOrDigit = "abc";
```

As you may have noticed, in the preceding examples, we used the identifiers from the examples of the *Identifier* section.

# Final variable (constant)

A final variable is a variable that, once initialized, cannot be assigned to another value. It is denoted by the `final` keyword:

```
void someMethod(){
   final int x = 1;
   x = 2; //generates compilation error
   //some other code
}
```

Nevertheless, the following code will work just fine:

```
void someMethod(){
   final int x;
   //Any code that does not use variable x can be added here
   x = 2;
   //some other code
}
```

The preceding code does not generate a compilation error because the local variable is not initialized to a default value automatically in a declaration statement. Only the class, instance variable, or array component is initialized to a default value if the variable is not initialized explicitly (see the *Primitive types and literals* and *Reference types and String* sections).

When a final variable refers to an object, it cannot be assigned to another object, but the state of the object assigned can be changed at any time (see the *Reference types and String* section). The same applies to a variable that refers an array, because an array is an object (see the *Arrays* section).

Since a final variable cannot be changed, it is a constant. It is called a constant variable if it has a primitive type or a type of `String`. But Java programmers apply the term constant usually to the class-level final static variables, and call the local final variable just final variable. The identifier of class-level constants by convention is written in capital letters. Here are a few examples:

```
static final String FEBRUARY = "February";
static final int DAYS_IN_DECEMBER = 31;
```

Such constants look very similar to the following constants:

```
Month.FEBRUARY;
TimeUnit.DAYS;
DayOfWeek.FRIDAY;
```

But the preceding constants are defined in a special kind of class, called `enum`, although for all practical purposes, all constants behave similarly in the sense that they cannot be changed. One just has to check the type of a constant in order to know what methods its class (type) provides.

# Reserved and restricted keywords

A keyword is the second of Java tokens listed in the *Input types* section. We have seen several Java keywords already—`abstract`, `class`, `final`, `implements`, `int`, `interface`, `new`, `package`, `private`, `public`, `return`, `static`, and `void`. Now we will present the full list of the reserved keywords. These keywords cannot be used as identifiers.

## Reserved keywords

Here is the list of all 49 keywords of Java 9:

| abstract | class | final | implements | int |
|----------|-------|-------|------------|-----|
| interface | new | package | private | public |
| return | static | void | if | this |
| break | double | default | protected | throw |
| byte | else | import | synchronized | throws |
| case | enum | instanceof | boolean | transient |
| catch | extends | switch | short | try |
| char | for | assert | do | finally |
| continue | float | long | strictfp | volatile |
| native | super | while | _ (underscore) | |

The keywords are used for different Java elements and statements, and cannot be used as identifiers. The `goto`, `const`, and _ (underscore) keywords are not used as keywords yet, but they might in the future Java releases. For now, they are just included in the list of the reserved keywords to prevent their use as an identifier. But they can be a part of an identifier among other characters, for example:

```
int _ = 3; //Error, underscore is a reserved keyword
int __ = 3; //More than 1 underscore as an identifier is OK
int _1 = 3;
int y_ = 3;
int goto_x = 3;
int const1 = 3;
```

The `true` and `false` words look like keywords and cannot be used as identifiers, but in fact they are not Java keywords. They are Boolean literals (values). We will define what a literal is in the *Primitive types and literals* section.

And there is another word that looks like a keyword but is in fact a special type—`null` (see the *Reference types and String* section). It also cannot be used as an identifier.

# Restricted keywords

There are ten words that are called restricted keywords: `open`, `module`, `requires`, `transitive`, `exports`, `opens`, `to`, `uses`, `provides`, and `with`. They are called restricted because they cannot be identifiers in the context of a module declaration, which we will not discuss in this book. In all other places, it is possible to use them as identifiers. Here is one example of such usage:

```
int to = 1;
int open = 1;
int uses = 1;
int with = 1;
int opens =1;
int module = 1;
int exports =1;
int provides = 1;
int requires = 1;
int transitive = 1;
```

However, it is a good practice not to use them as identifiers anywhere. There are plenty of other ways to name a variable.

# Separators

A separator is the third of the Java tokens listed in the *Input types* section. Here are all twelve of them, in no particular order:

```
;   { }   ( )   [ ]   ,   .   ...   ::   @
```

# Semicolon ";"

By now, you are quite familiar with the usage of the separator ; (semicolon). Its only job in Java is to terminate a statement:

```
int i;  //declaration statement
i = 2;  //assignment statement
if(i == 3){    //flow control statement called if-statement
  //do something
}
for(int i = 0; i < 10; i++){
  //do something with each value of i
}
```

# Braces "{}"

You have seen the separators { } (braces) around the class:

```
class SomeClass {
  //class body with code
}
```

You have also seen braces around method bodies:

```
void someMethod(int i){
  //...
  if(i == 2){
    //block of code
  } else {
    //another block of code
  }
  ...
}
```

The braces are also used to denote a block of code in control-flow statements (see Chapter 10, *Control Flow Statements*):

```
void someMethod(int i){
  //...
  if(i == 2){
    //block of code
  } else {
    //another block of code
  }
  ...
}
```

And they are used to initialize arrays (see the *Arrays* section):

```
int[] myArray = {2,3,5};
```

There are also a few other rarely used constructs where braces are used.

# Parentheses "()"

You have also seen the usage of separators () (parentheses) to keep the list of method parameters in the method definition and method invocation:

```
void someMethod(int i) {
  //...
  String s = anotherMethod();
  //...
}
```

They are also used in control-flow statements (see Chapter 10, *Control Flow Statements*):

```
if(i == 2){
  //...
}
```

During typecasting (see the *Primitive types and literals* section), they are put around the type:

```
long v = 23;
int i = (int)v;
```

As for setting the precedence of an execution (see Chapter 9, *Operators, Expressions, and Statements*), you should be familiar with it from basic algebra:

```
x = (y + z) * (a + b).
```

# Brackets "[]"

The separators [] (brackets) are used for arrays declaration (see the *Arrays* section):

```
int[] a = new int[23];
```

# Comma ","

The comma , is used for the separation of method parameters, listed in parentheses:

```
void someMethod(int i, String s, int j) {
  //...
  String s = anotherMethod(5, 6.1, "another param");
  //...
}
```

A comma can also be used to separate variables of the same type in the declaration statement:

```
int i, j = 2; k;
```

In the preceding example, all three variables, i, j, and k, are declared to be of the int type, but only variable j is initialized to 2.

The use of a comma in a looping statement serves the same purpose of the declaration of multiple variables (see Chapter 10, *Control Flow Statements*):

```
for (int i = 0; i < 10; i++){
   //...
}
```

# Period "."

The separator . (period) is used to separate parts of the package name, as you have seen in the com.packt.javapath example.

You also have seen how the period was used to separate an object reference and the method of that object:

```
int result = simpleMath.multiplyByTwo(i);
```

Similarly, if a simpleMath object had a public property of a, it could be referred to as simpleMath.a.

# Ellipsis "..."

The separator . . . (ellipsis) is used only for varargs:

```
int someMethod(int i, String s, int... k){
  //k is an array with elements k[0], k[1], ...
}
```

The preceding method can be called in any of the following ways:

```
someMethod(42, "abc");          //array k = null
someMethod(42, "abc", 42, 43);  //k[0] = 42, k[1] = 43
int[] k = new int[2];
k[0] = 42;
k[1] = 43;
someMethod(42, "abc", k);       //k[0] = 42, k[1] = 43
```

In Chapter 2, *Java Language Basics*, while talking about the main() method, we explained the concept of varargs (variable arguments) in Java.

# Colons "::"

The separator : : (colons) is used for method reference in lambda expressions (see Chapter 17, *Lambda Expressions and Functional Programming*):

```
List<String> list = List.of("1", "32", "765");
list.stream().mapToInt(Integer::valueOf).sum();
```

# At sign "@"

The separator @ (at sign) is used to denote an annotation:

```
@Override
int someMethod(String s){
  //...
}
```

You have seen several examples of an annotation when we created a unit test in Chapter 4, *Your First Java Project*. There are several predefined annotations in the Java standard libraries (@Deprecated, @Override, and @FunctionalInterface, to name a few). We are going to use one of them (@FunctionalInterface) in Chapter 17, *Lambda Expressions and Functional Programming*.

The annotations are metadata. They describe classes, fields, and methods, but they themselves are not executed. The Java compiler and JVM read them and treat the described class, field, or method in a certain way depending on the annotation. For example, in `Chapter 4`, *Your First Java Project*, you saw how we used the `@Test` annotation. Adding it in front of a public non-static method tells JVM that it is a test method that has to be run. So, if you execute this class, the JVM will run only this method.

Or, if you use the `@Override` annotation in front of a method, the compiler will check to see whether this method actually overrides a method in a parent class or not. If the matching signature of a non-private non-static class is not found in any of the class parents, the compiler will raise an error.

It is also possible to create new custom annotations (JUnit framework does exactly that), but this topic is outside the scope of this book.

# Primitive types and literals

Java has only two kinds of variable types: primitive types and reference types. A primitive type defines what kind of value the variable can hold and how big or small this value can be. We will discuss primitive types in this section.

A reference type allows us to assign only one kind of value to the variable – the reference to the memory area where an object is stored. We will discuss the reference types in the next section, *Reference types and String*.

Primitive types can be divided into two groups: the Boolean type and the numeric types. The numeric-types group can be split further into integral types (`byte`, `short`, `int`, `long`, and `char`) and floating-point types (float and double).

Each primitive type is defined by a corresponding reserved keyword, listed in the *Reserved and restricted keywords* section.

# The Boolean type

The Boolean type allows a variable to have one of two values: `true` or `false`. As we mentioned in the *Reserved keywords* section, these values are Boolean literals, which means they are values that represent themselves directly – without a variable. We will talk more about literals in the *Primitive type literals* section.

Here is an example of a b variable declaration and initialization to the value true:

```
boolean b = true;
```

And here is another example of assigning a true value to the b Boolean variable using an expression:

```
int x = 1, y = 1;
boolean b = 2 == ( x + y );
```

In the preceding example, in the first line, two variables, x and y, of the int primitive type are declared and each assigned a value of 1. In the second line, a Boolean variable is declared and assigned the result of the 2 == ( x + y ) expression. Parentheses set the precedence of execution as follows:

- Calculate the sum of values assigned to the x and y variables
- Compare the result with 2, using the == Boolean operator

We will study operators and expressions in Chapter 9, *Operators, Expressions, and Statements*.

Variables of the Boolean are used in control-flow statements and we will see many examples of their usage in Chapter 10, *Control Flow Statements*.

# Integral types

Values of Java integral types occupy different amounts of memory:

- byte: 8 bit
- char: 16 bit
- short: 16 bit
- int: 32 bit
- long: 64 bit

All of them, except `char`, are signed integer. The sign value (`0` for minus "–" and `1` for plus "+") occupies the first bit of the binary representation of the value. That is why a signed integer can hold, as a positive number, only half of the value an unsigned integer can. But it allows a signed integer to hold a negative number, which an unsigned integer cannot do. For example, in case of the `byte` type (8 bit), if it were an unsigned integer, the range of the values it could hold would be from 0 to 255 (including 0 and 255) because 2 to the power of 8 is 256. But, as we have said, the `byte` type is a signed integer, which means the range of values it can hold is from -128 to 127 (including -128, 127, and 0).

In the case of the `char` type, it can hold values from 0 to 65,535 inclusive because it is an unsigned integer. This integer (called a code point) identifies a record in the Unicode table (`https://en.wikipedia.org/wiki/List_of_Unicode_characters`). Each Unicode table record has the following columns:

- **Code point**: A decimal value – a numeric representation of the Unicode record
- **Unicode escape**: A four-digit number with the `\u` prefix
- **Printable symbol**: A graphic representation of the Unicode record (not available for control codes)
- **Description:** A human-readable description of the symbol

Here are five records from the Unicode table:

| Code point | Unicode escape | Printable symbol | Description |
|---|---|---|---|
| 8 | \u0008 | | Backspace |
| 10 | \u000A | | Line feed |
| 36 | \u0024 | $ | Dollar sign |
| 51 | \u0033 | 3 | Digit three |
| 97 | \u0061 | a | Latin small letter A |

The first two are examples of a Unicode that represents control codes that are not printable. A control code is used to send a command to a device (a display or a printer, for example). There are only 66 such codes in the Unicode set. They have code points from 0 to 32 inclusive and from 127 to 159 inclusive. The rest of 65,535 Unicode records have a printable symbol – a character that the record represents.

The interesting (and often confusing) aspect of the char type is that a Unicode escape and a code point can be used interchangeably, except when the variable of the char type is involved in an arithmetic operation. In such a case, the value of code point is used. To demonstrate it, let's look at the following code snippet (in the comments, we have captured the output):

```
char a = '3';
System.out.println(a);         //  3
char b = '$';
System.out.println(b);         //  $
System.out.println(a + b);     //  87
System.out.println(a + 2);     //  53
a = 36;
System.out.println(a);         //  $
```

As you can see, variables a and b of the char type represent the 3 and $ symbols and are displayed as these symbols as long as they are not involved in an arithmetic operation. Otherwise, only the code point values are used.

As you can see from the five Unicode records, the 3 character has a code point value of 51, while the $ character has a code point value of 36. That is why adding a and b produces 87, and adding 2 to a results in 53.

In the last line of the example code, we have assigned a decimal value of 36 to the a variable of the char type. It means we have instructed JVM to assign the character with a code point of 36, which is the $ character, to the a variable.

And that is why the char type is included in the group of integral types of Java – because it acts as a numeric type in arithmetic operations.

The range of values each of the primitive types can hold is as follows:

- byte: From -128 to 127, inclusive
- short: From -32,768 to 32,767, inclusive
- int: From -2.147.483.648 to 2.147.483.647, inclusive
- long: From -9,223,372,036,854,775,808 to 9,223,372,036,854,775,807, inclusive
- char: From '\u0000' to '\uffff' inclusive, that is, from 0 to 65,535, inclusive

You can access the maximum and minimum values of each type any time, using a corresponding wrapper class of each primitive type (we will talk about wrapper classes in more detail in `Chapter 9`, *Operators, Expressions, and Statements*). Here is one way to do it (in the comments, we have shown the output):

```
byte b = Byte.MIN_VALUE;
System.out.println(b);      //  -127
b = Byte.MAX_VALUE;
System.out.println(b);      //   128

short s = Short.MIN_VALUE;
System.out.println(s);      // -32768
s = Short.MAX_VALUE;
System.out.println(s);      //  32767

int i = Integer.MIN_VALUE;
System.out.println(i);      // -2147483648
i = Integer.MAX_VALUE;
System.out.println(i);      //  2147483647

long l = Long.MIN_VALUE;
System.out.println(l);      // -9223372036854775808
l = Long.MAX_VALUE;
System.out.println(l);      //  9223372036854775807

char c = Character.MIN_VALUE;
System.out.println((int)c); // 0
c = Character.MAX_VALUE;
System.out.println((int)c); // 65535
```

You may have noticed the `(int)c` construct. It is called **casting**, similar to what happens during a movie production when an actor is tried for a particular role. The value of any primitive numeric types can be converted into the value of another primitive numeric type, provided it is not bigger than the maximum value of the target type. Otherwise, an error will be generated during program execution (such an error is called a runtime error). We will talk more about conversion between primitive numeric types in Chapter 9, *Operators, Expressions, and Statements*.

A casting between numeric types and the `boolean` type is not possible. A compile-time error will be generated if you try to do that.

# Floating-point types

In the Java Specification, the floating-point types (`float` and `double`) are defined as:

> *"The single-precision 32-bit and double-precision 64-bit format IEEE 754 values."*

It means that the `float` type occupies 32 bits and the `double` type takes 64 bits. They represent positive and negative numerical values with a fractional part after the dot ".": `1.2`, `345.56`, `10.`, `-1.34`. By default, in Java, a numeric value with a dot in it is assumed to be of the `double` type. So, the following assignment causes a compilation error:

```
float r = 23.4;
```

To avoid the error, one has to indicate that the value has to be treated as a `float` type by appending the `f` or `F` character at the value, as follows:

```
float r = 23.4f;
or
float r = 23.4F;
```

The values themselves (`23.4f` and `23.4F`) are called literals. We will talk more about them in the *Primitive type literals* section.

The minimum and maximum value can be found the same way as we did for integral numbers. Just run the following snippet of code (in the comments, we have captured the output we got on our computer):

```
System.out.println(Float.MIN_VALUE);   //1.4E-45
System.out.println(Float.MAX_VALUE);   //3.4028235E38
System.out.println(Double.MIN_VALUE);  //4.9E-324
System.out.println(Double.MAX_VALUE);  //1.7976931348623157E308
```

The range of negative values is the same as the range of the positive numbers, only with the minus sign – in front of each number. Zero can be either `0.0` or `-0.0`.

# Default values of primitive types

After a variable is declared and before it can be used, a value has to be assigned to it. As we have mentioned in the *Variable declaration, definition, and initialization* section, a local variable must be initialized or assigned a value explicitly. For example:

```
int x;
int y = 0;
x = 1;
```

But if the variable is declared as a class field (static), an instance (non-static) property, or an array component and is not initialized explicitly, it is initialized automatically with a default value. The value itself depends on the type of the variable:

- For the `byte`, `short`, `int`, and `long` types, the default value is zero, 0
- For the `float` and `double` types, the default value is positive zero, 0.0
- For the `char` type, the default value is \u0000 with point code zero
- For the `boolean` type, the default value is `false`

# Primitive type literals

A literal is the fourth of the Java tokens listed in the *Input types* section. It is the representation of a value. We will discuss literals of reference types in the *Reference types and String* section. And now we will talk about primitive type literals, only.

To demonstrate literals of primitive types, we will use a `LiteralsDemo` program in the `com.packt.javapath.ch05demo` package. You can create it by right-clicking on the `com.packt.javapath.ch05demo` package, then selecting **New | Class**, and typing the `LiteralsDemo` class name, as we have described in `Chapter 4`, *Your First Java Project*.

Among primitive types, literals of the `boolean` type are the simplest. They are just two: `true` and `false`. We can demonstrate it by running the following code:

```
public class LiteralsDemo {
  public static void main(String[] args){
    System.out.println("boolean literal true: " + true);
    System.out.println("boolean literal false: " + false);
  }
}
```

The result will look as follows:

```
boolean literal true: true
boolean literal false: false
```

These are all possible Boolean literals (values).

Now, let's turn to a more complex topic of the literals of the `char` type. They can be as follows:

- A single character, enclosed in single quotes
- An escape sequence, enclosed in single quotes

The single-quote, or apostrophe, is a character with Unicode escape `\u0027` (decimal code point 39). We have seen several examples of `char` type literals in the *Integral types* section when we demonstrated the `char` type behavior as a numeric type in arithmetic operations.

Here are some other examples of the `char` type literals as single characters:

```
System.out.println("char literal 'a': " + 'a');
System.out.println("char literal '%': " + '%');
System.out.println("char literal '\u03a9': " + '\u03a9'); //Omega
System.out.println("char literal '™': " + '™'); //Trade mark sign
```

If you run the preceding code, the output will be as follows:

```
char literal 'a': a
char literal '%': %
char literal 'Ω': Ω
char literal '™': ™
```

Now, let's talk about the second kind of `char` type literal – an escape sequence. It is a combination of characters that acts similarly to control codes. In fact, some of the escape sequences include control codes. Here is the full list:

- \ b (Backspace BS, Unicode escape `\u0008`)
- \ t (Horizontal tab HT, Unicode escape `\u0009`)
- \ n (Line feed LF, Unicode escape `\u000a`)
- \ f (Form feed FF, Unicode escape `\u000c`)
- \ r (Carriage return CR, Unicode escape `\u000d`)
- \ " (Double quote ", Unicode escape `\u0022`)
- \ ' (Single quote ', Unicode escape `\u0027`)
- \ \ (Backslash \, Unicode escape `\u005c`)

As you can see, an escape sequence always starts with a backslash (\). Let's demonstrate some of the escape sequences usages:

```
System.out.println("The line breaks \nhere");
System.out.println("The tab is\there");
System.out.println("\"");
System.out.println('\'');
System.out.println('\\');
```

If you run the preceding code, the output will be as follows:

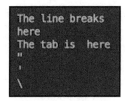

As you can see, the \n and \t escape sequences act only as control codes. They are not printable themselves but affect the display of the text. Other escape sequences allow the printing of a symbol in the context that would not allow it to be printed otherwise. Three double or single quotes in a row would be qualified as a compiler error, as well as a single backslash character if being used without a backslash.

By comparison with the char type literals, the float-points literals are much more straightforward. As we have mentioned before, by default, a 23.45 literal has the double type and there is no need to append the letter d or D to the literal if you would like it to be of the double type. But you can, if you prefer to be more explicit. A float type literal, on the other hand, requires appending the letter f or F at the end. Let's run the following example (notice how we use \n escape sequence to add a line break before the output):

```
System.out.println("\nfloat literal 123.456f: " + 123.456f);
System.out.println("double literal 123.456d: " + 123.456d);
```

The result looks as follows:

```
float literal 123.456f: 123.456
double literal 123.456d: 123.456
```

The floating-point type literals can also be expressed using e or E for scientific notation (see https://en.wikipedia.org/wiki/Scientific_notation):

```
System.out.println("\nfloat literal 1.234560e+02f: " + 1.234560e+02f);
System.out.println("double literal 1.234560e+02d: " + 1.234560e+02d);
```

The result of the preceding code looks as follows:

```
float literal 1.234560e+02f: 123.456
double literal 1.234560e+02d: 123.456
```

As you can see, the value remain the same, whether presented in a decimal format or a scientific one.

The literals of the byte, short, int, and long integral types have the int type by default. The following assignments do not cause any compilation errors:

```
byte b = 10;
short s = 10;
int i = 10;
long l = 10;
```

But each of the following lines generates an error:

```
byte b = 128;
short s = 32768;
int i = 2147483648;
long l = 2147483648;
```

That is because the maximum value the byte type can hold is 127, the maximum value the short type can hold is 32,767, and the maximum value the int type can hold is 2,147,483,647. Notice that, although the long type can a value as big as 9,223,372,036,854,775,807, the last assignment still fails because the 2,147,483,648 literal has the int type by default but exceeds the maximum int type value. To create a literal of the long type, one has to append the letter l or L at the end, so the following assignment works just fine:

```
long l = 2147483648L;
```

It is a good practice to use capital L for this purpose because lowercase letter l can be easily confused with the number 1.

The preceding examples of integral literals are expressed in a decimal number system. But the literals of the `byte`, `short`, `int`, and `long` types can also be expressed in the binary (base 2, digits 0-1), octal (base 8, digits 0-7), and hexadecimal (base 16, digits 0-9 and a-f) number systems. Here is the demonstration code:

```
System.out.println("\nPrint literal 12:");
System.out.println("- bin 0b1100: "+ 0b1100);
System.out.println("- oct    014: "+ 014);
System.out.println("- dec     12: "+ 12);
System.out.println("- hex    0xc: "+ 0xc);
```

If we run the preceding code, the output will be:

```
Print literal 12:
- bin 0b1100: 12
- oct    014: 12
- dec     12: 12
- hex    0xc: 12
```

As you can see, a binary literal starts with `0b` (or `0B`), followed by the value 12 expressed in a binary system: 1100 (=$2^0*0 + 2^1*0 + 2^2*1 + 2^3*1$). An octal literal starts with 0, followed by the value 12 expressed in an octal system: 14 (=$8^0*4 + 8^1*1$). The decimal literal is just `12`. The hexadecimal literal starts with `0x` (or with `0X`), followed by value 12 expressed in a hexadecimal system—c (because in the hexadecimal system the symbols a to f (or A to F) map to decimal values 10 to 15).

Adding a minus sign (–) in front of a literal makes the value negative, no matter which numeric system is used. Here is a demonstration code:

```
System.out.println("\nPrint literal -12:");
System.out.println("- bin 0b1100: "+ -0b1100);
System.out.println("- oct    014: "+ -014);
System.out.println("- dec     12: "+ -12);
System.out.println("- hex    0xc: "+ -0xc);
```

If you run the preceding code, the output will be as follows:

```
Print literal -12:
- bin 0b1100: -12
- oct    014: -12
- dec     12: -12
- hex    0xc: -12
```

And, to complete our discussion of primitive type literals, we would like to mention the possible usage of the underscore (_) inside a primitive type literal. In the case of a long number, breaking it into groups helps to quickly estimate its magnitude. Here are a few examples:

```
int speedOfLightMilesSec = 299_792_458;
float meanRadiusOfEarthMiles = 3_958.8f;
long creditCardNumber = 1234_5678_9012_3456L;
```

Let's see what happens when we run the following code:

```
long anotherCreditCardNumber = 9876____5678_____9012____1234L;
System.out.println("\n" + anotherCreditCardNumber);
```

The output of the previous code would be as follows:

```
9876567890121234
```

As you can see, one or many underscores are ignored if placed between digits inside a numeric literal. An underscore in any other location would cause a compilation error.

# Reference types and String

When an object is assigned to a variable, this variable holds the reference to the memory where the object resides. From a practical standpoint, such a variable is handled in the code as if it is the object it represents. The type of such a variable can be a class, an interface, an array, or a special `null` type. If `null` is assigned, the reference to the object is lost and the variable does not represent any object. If an object is not used anymore, JVM removes it from the memory in the process called **garbage collection**. We will describe this process in Chapter 11, *JVM Processes and Garbage Collection*.

There is also a reference type called type variable used for the declaration of a type parameter of a generic class, interface, method, or constructor. It belongs to the area of Java generic programming that is outside of the scope of this book.

All objects, including arrays, inherit all the methods from the `java.lang.Object` class described in Chapter 2, *Java Language Basics*.

A variable that refers to an object of the `java.lang.String` class (or just `String`) is a reference type, too. But, in certain respects, the `String` object behaves as a primitive type, which might be confusing at times. That is why we will dedicate a section in this chapter to the `String` class.

Also, the enum type (a reference type as well) requires special attention and we describe it at the end of this section in the *Enum types* subsection.

# Class types

A variable of the class type is declared using the corresponding class name:

```
<Class name> variableName;
```

It can be initialized by assigning to it `null` or an object (an instance) of the class whose name is used for the declaration. If the class has a superclass (also called a parent class) from which it inherits (extends), the name of the superclass can be used for the variable declaration. It is possible because of Java polymorphism, described in Chapter 2, *Java Language Basics*. For example, if a `SomeClass` class extends `SomeBaseClass`, both of the following declarations and initializations are possible:

```
SomeBaseClass someBaseClass = new SomeBaseClass();
someBaseClass = new SomeClass();
```

And, since every class extends the `java.lang.Object` class by default, the following declarations and initializations are possible too:

```
Object someBaseClass = new SomeBaseClass();
someBaseClass = new SomeClass();
```

We will talk more about assigning child class object to a base class reference in Chapter 9, *Operators, Expressions, and Statements*.

# Interface types

A variable of an interface type is declared using the corresponding interface name:

```
<Interface name> variableName;
```

It can be initialized by assigning to it `null` or an object (an instance) of the class that implemented the interface. Here is an example:

```
interface SomeInterface{
    void someMethod();
}
interface SomeOtherInterface{
    void someOtherMethod();
}
class SomeClass implements SomeInterface {
    void someMethod(){
        . . .
    }
}
class SomeOtherClass implements SomeOtherInterface{
    void someOtherMethod(){
        . . .
    }
}
SomeInterface someInterface = new SomeClass();
someInterface = new SomeOtherClass(); //not possible, error
someInterface.someMethod();           //works just fine
someInterface.someOtherMethod();   //not possible, error
```

We will talk more about assigning child type to a base type reference in `Chapter` 9, *Operators, Expressions, and Statements.*

# Arrays

An array in Java is a reference type and extends (inherits from) the `Object` class, too. An array contains components that have the same type as the declared array type or the type whose values can be assigned to the array type. The number of components may be zero, in which case the array is an empty array.

An array component has no name and is referenced by an index, which is a positive integer or zero. An array with n components is said to have *length of n*. Once an array object is created, its length never changes.

An array declaration starts with a type name and empty brackets `[]`:

```
byte[] bs;
long[][] ls;
Object[][] os;
SomeClass[][][] scs;
```

The number of bracket pairs indicates the number of dimensions (or the nesting depth) of the array.

There are two ways to create and initialize an array:

- By creation expression, using the `new` keyword, type name, and brackets with the length of each dimension in each pair of brackets; for example:

```
byte[] bs = new byte[100];
long[][] ls = new long [2][3];
Object[][] os = new Object[3][2];
SomeClass[][][] scs = new SomeClass[3][2][1];
```

- By array initializer, using a comma-separated list of values of each dimension, surrounded by braces, for example:

```
int[][] is = { { 1, 2, 3 }, { 10, 20 }, { 3, 4, 5, 6 } };
float[][] fs = { { 1.1f, 2.2f, 3 }, { 10, 20.f, 30.f } };
Object[] oss = { new Object(), new SomeClass(), null, "abc" };
SomeInterface[] sis = { new SomeClass(), null, new SomeClass() };
```

As you can see from these examples, a multidimensional array can contain arrays of different lengths (the `int[][] is` array). Also, a component type value can be different from the array type as long as the value can be assigned to the variable of the array type (the `float[][] fs`, `Object[] is`, and `SomeInterface[] sis` arrays).

Because an array is an object, its components are initialized every time an array is created. Let's consider this example:

```
int[][] is = new int[2][3];
System.out.println("\nis.length=" + is.length);
System.out.println("is[0].length=" + is[0].length);
System.out.println("is[0][0].length=" + is[0][0]);
System.out.println("is[0][1].length=" + is[0][1]);
System.out.println("is[0][2].length=" + is[0][2]);
System.out.println("is[1].length=" + is[0].length);
System.out.println("is[1][0].length=" + is[1][0]);
System.out.println("is[1][1].length=" + is[1][1]);
System.out.println("is[1][2].length=" + is[1][2]);
```

If we run the preceding code snippet, the output will be as follows:

```
is.length=2
is[0].length=3
is[0][0].length=0
is[0][1].length=0
is[0][2].length=0
is[1].length=3
is[1][0].length=0
is[1][1].length=0
is[1][2].length=0
```

It is possible to create a multidimensional array without initializing some of the dimensions:

```
int[][] is = new int[2][];
System.out.println("\nis.length=" + is.length);
System.out.println("is[0]=" + is[0]);
System.out.println("is[1]=" + is[1]);
```

The result of this code running is as follows:

```
is.length=2
is[0]=null
is[1]=null
```

The missing dimension can be added later:

```
int[][] is = new int[2][];
is[0] = new int[3];
is[1] = new int[3];
```

The important point is that a dimension has to be initialized before it can be used.

# Default value of a reference type

The default value of a reference type is `null`. It means that if a reference type is a static class member or an instance field and not assigned an initial value explicitly, it will be initialized automatically and assigned the value of `null`. Please note that, in the case of an array, this applies to the array itself and to its reference type components.

# Reference type literals

The `null` literal indicates the absence of any assignment to a reference type variable. Let's look at the following code snippet:

```
SomeClass someClass = new SomeClass();
someClass.someMethod();
someClass = null;
someClass.someMethod(); // throws NullPointerException
```

The first statement declares the `someClass` variable and assigns to it a reference to the object of the `SomeClass` class. Then a method of this class is called using its reference. The next line assigns the `null` literal to the `someClass` variable. It removes the reference value from the variable. So, when in the next line, we try to call the same method again, we get back `NullPointerException`, which happens only when a reference used is assigned the `null` value.

The `String` type is a reference type, too. This means that the default value of a `String` variable is `null`. The `String` class inherits all the methods from the `java.lang.Object` class as any other reference type does, too.

But in some respects, objects of the `String` class behave as if they are of a primitive type. We will discuss one such case—when the `String` object is used as a method parameter—in the *Passing reference type values as method parameters* section. We will discuss other cases of `String` behaving like a primitive type now.

Another feature of the `String` type that makes it look like a primitive type is that it is the only reference type that has more literals than just `null`. The type `String` can also have a literal of zero or more characters enclosed in double quotes—`""`, `"$"`, `"abc"`, and `"12-34"`. The characters of the `String` literal may include escape sequences, too. Here are a few examples:

```
System.out.println("\nFirst line.\nSecond line.");
System.out.println("Tab space\tin the line");
System.out.println("It is called a \"String literal\".");
System.out.println("Latin Capital Letter Y with diaeresis: \u0178");
```

If you execute the preceding code snippet, the output will be as follows:

```
First line.
Second line.
Tab space    in the line
It is called a "String literal".
Latin Capital Letter Y with diaeresis: Ÿ
```

But, in contrast with the `char` type literals, `String` literals do not behave like numbers in an arithmetic operation. The only arithmetic operation applicable to the `String` type is an addition, and it behaves like a concatenation:

```
System.out.println("s1" + "s2");
String s1 = "s1";
System.out.println(s1 + "s2");
String s2 = "s1";
System.out.println(s1 + s2);
```

Run the preceding code and you will see the following:

```
s1s2
s1s2
s1s1
```

Another particular characteristic of `String` is that an object of the `String` type is immutable.

# String immutability

One cannot change the `String` type value assigned to a variable without changing the reference. There are several reasons why JVM authors decided to do that:

- All `String` literals are stored in the same common memory area, called string pool. Before a new `String` literal is stored, the JVM checks whether such a literal is already stored there. If such an object exists already, a new object is not created and the reference to the existing object is returned as the reference to a new object. The following code demonstrates this situation:

```
System.out.println("s1" == "s1");
System.out.println("s1" == "s2");
String s1 = "s1";
System.out.println(s1 == "s1");
```

```
System.out.println(s1 == "s2");
String s2 = "s1";
System.out.println(s1 == s2);
```

In the preceding code, we use the == relational operator, which is used to compare values of primitive types and references of reference types. If we run this code, the result will be as follows:

You can see that the various comparisons of literals (directly or via a variable) consistently yield true if two literals have the same spelling, and produce false if the spelling is different. This way, long String literals are not duplicated and the memory is used better.

To avoid concurrent modification of the same literal by different methods, every time we attempt to change the String literal, a copy of the literal with the change is created, while the original String literal remains untouched. Here is the code that demonstrates it:

```
String s1 = "\nthe original string";
String s2 = s1.concat(" has been changed");
System.out.println(s2);
System.out.println(s1);
```

The concat() method of the String class adds another String literal to the original value of s1 and assigns the result to the s1 variable. The output of this code is as follows:

```
the original string has been changed

the original string
```

As you can see, the original literal assigned to `s1` did not change.

- Another reason for such a design decision is security – one of the highest-priority goals JVM's authors had in mind. `String` literals are widely used as username and passwords to access an application, database, and server. Immutability of the `String` value makes it less susceptible to an unauthorized modification.
- Yet another reason is that there are certain calculation-intensive procedures (the `hashCode()` method in the `Object` parent class, for example) that could be quite taxing in the case of long `String` values. By making the `String` object immutable, such a calculation could be avoided if it was already performed on the value with the same spelling.

That is why all methods that modify a `String` value return the `String` type, which is the reference to a new `String` object that carries the result. The `concat()` method in the preceding code is a typical example of such a method.

The matter becomes a bit more complicated in the case where a `String` object is created not from the literal, but using the `String` constructor, `new String("some literal")`. In such a case, the `String` object is stored in the same area where all objects of all classes are stored, and every time a `new` keyword is used, another chunk of memory (with another reference) is allocated. Here is the code that demonstrates it:

```
String s3 = new String("s");
String s4 = new String("s");
System.out.println(s3 == s4);
```

If you run it, the output will be as follows:

```
false
```

As you can see, despite the same spelling, the objects have different memory references. To avoid confusion and to compare the `String` objects by their spelling only, always use the `equals()` method of the `String` class. Here is the code that demonstrates its usage:

```
System.out.println("s5".equals("s5"));    //true
System.out.println("s5".equals("s6"));    //false
String s5 = "s5";
System.out.println(s5.equals("s5"));      //true
System.out.println(s5.equals("s6"));      //false
String s6 = "s6";
System.out.println(s5.equals(s5));        //true
System.out.println(s5.equals(s6));        //false
```

```
String s7 = "s6";
System.out.println(s7.equals(s6));      //true
String s8 = new String("s6");
System.out.println(s8.equals(s7));      //true
String s9 = new String("s9");
System.out.println(s8.equals(s9));      //false
```

If you run it, the result will be:

```
true
false
true
false
true
false
true
true
false
```

We added the results as the comments to the preceding code for your convenience. As you can see, the equals() method of the String class returns true or false based only on the spelling of the value, so use it all the time when spelling comparison is your goal.

By the way, you may remember that the equals() method is defined in the Object class—the parent class of the String class. The String class has its own equals() method that overrides the method with the same signature in the parent class as we have demonstrated in Chapter 2, *Java Language Basics*. The source code of the equals() method of the String class looks as follows:

```
public boolean equals(Object anObject) {
  if (this == anObject) {
    return true;
  }
  if (anObject instanceof String) {
    String aString = (String)anObject;
    if (coder() == aString.coder()) {
      return isLatin1() ?
              StringLatin1.equals(value, aString.value)
            : StringUTF16.equals(value, aString.value);
    }
  }
  return false;
}
```

As you can see, it compares references first and, if they point to the same object, returns `true`. But, if the references are different, it compares the spelling of the values, which actually happens in the `equals()` method of the `StringLatin1` and `StringUTF16` classes.

The point we would like you to take away is that the `equals()` method of the `String` class is optimized by performing the comparison of references first and, only if not successful, it comparing the values themselves. Which means there is no need to compare references in the code. Instead, for `String` type object comparison, always use the `equals()` method only.

With that, we are moving to the last of the reference types we will discuss in this chapter—the `enum` type.

# Enum types

Before describing the `enum` type, let's look at one of the use cases as the motivation for having such a type. Let's assume we would like to create a class that describes `TheBlows` family:

```
public class TheBlows {
  private String name, relation, hobby = "biking";
  private int age;
  public TheBlows(String name, String relation, int age) {
    this.name = name;
    this.relation = relation;
    this.age = age;
  }
  public String getName() { return name; }
  public String getRelation() { return relation; }
  public int getAge() { return age; }
  public String getHobby() { return hobby; }
  public void setHobby(String hobby) { this.hobby = hobby; }
}
```

We have set the default hobby as `biking` and will allow to change it later, but other properties have to be set during object construction. That would fine, except we do not want to have more than four members of this family in the system, as we know all the members of `TheBlows` family very well.

To impose these restrictions, we decided to create all possible objects of the `TheBlows` class up-front and make the constructor private:

```java
public class TheBlows {
  public static TheBlows BILL = new TheBlows("Bill", "father", 42);
  public static TheBlows BECKY = new TheBlows("BECKY", "mother", 37);
  public static TheBlows BEE = new TheBlows("Bee", "daughter", 5);
  public static TheBlows BOB = new TheBlows("Bob", "son", 3);
  private String name, relation, hobby = "biking";
  private int age;
  private TheBlows(String name, String relation, int age) {
    this.name = name;
    this.relation = relation;
    this.age = age;
  }
  public String getName() { return name; }
  public String getRelation() { return relation; }
  public int getAge() { return age; }
  public String getHobby() { return hobby; }
  public void setHobby(String hobby) { this.hobby = hobby; }
}
```

Now only the four instances of the `TheBlows` class exist and no other object of this class can be created. Let's see what happens if we run the following code:

```java
System.out.println(TheBlows.BILL.getName());
System.out.println(TheBlows.BILL.getHobby());
TheBlows.BILL.setHobby("fishing");
System.out.println(TheBlows.BILL.getHobby());
```

We will get the following output:

Similarly, we can create the `TheJohns` family with three family members:

```java
public class TheJohns {
  public static TheJohns JOE = new TheJohns("Joe", "father", 42);
  public static TheJohns JOAN = new TheJohns("Joan", "mother", 37);
  public static TheJohns JILL = new TheJohns("Jill", "daughter", 5);
  private String name, relation, hobby = "joggling";
  private int age;
  private TheJohns(String name, String relation, int age) {
    this.name = name;
```

```
      this.relation = relation;
      this.age = age;
    }
    public String getName() { return name; }
    public String getRelation() { return relation; }
    public int getAge() { return age; }
    public String getHobby() { return hobby; }
    public void setHobby(String hobby) { this.hobby = hobby; }
  }
```

While doing that, we noticed a lot of commonalities in these two classes and decided to create a `Family` base class:

```
public class Family {
  private String name, relation, hobby;
  private int age;
  protected Family(String name, String relation, int age, String hobby) {
    this.name = name;
    this.relation = relation;
    this.age = age;
    this.hobby = hobby;
  }
  public String getName() { return name; }
  public String getRelation() { return relation; }
  public int getAge() { return age; }
  public String getHobby() { return hobby; }
  public void setHobby(String hobby) { this.hobby = hobby; }
}
```

Now the `TheBlows` and `TheJohns` classes can be substantially simplified after extending the `Family` class. Here's how the `TheBlows` class can now look:

```
public class TheBlows extends Family {
  public static TheBlows BILL = new TheBlows("Bill", "father", 42);
  public static TheBlows BECKY = new TheBlows("Becky", "mother", 37);
  public static TheBlows BEE = new TheBlows("Bee", "daughter", 5);
  public static TheBlows BOB = new TheBlows("Bob", "son", 3);
  private TheBlows(String name, String relation, int age) {
    super(name, relation, age, "biking");
  }
}
```

And that is the idea behind the `enum` type—to allow the creating of classes with a fixed number of named instances.

The enum reference type class extends the `java.lang.Enum` class. It defines the set of constants, each of them an instance of the enum type it belongs to. The declaration of such a set starts with the enum keyword. Here is an example:

```
enum Season { SPRING, SUMMER, AUTUMN, WINTER }
```

Each of the listed items—SPRING, SUMMER, AUTUMN, and WINTER—is an instance of Season. They are the only four instances of the Season class that can exist in an application. No other instance of the Season class can be created. And that is the reason for the creation of the enum type: it can be used for cases when the list of instances of a class has to be limited to the fixed set, such as the list of possible seasons.

The enum declaration can also be written in a camel-case style:

```
enum Season { Spring, Summer, Autumn, Winter }
```

But the all-uppercase style is used more often because, as we mentioned earlier, the static final constant's identifiers in Java programming are written this way by convention, in order to distinguish them from the non-constant variable. And enum constants are static and final implicitly.

Let's review an example of the Season class usage. Here is a method that prints different messages, depending on the season:

```
void enumDemo(Season season){
  if(season == Season.WINTER){
    System.out.println("Dress up warmer");
  } else {
    System.out.println("You can drees up lighter now");
  }
}
```

Let's see what happens if we run the following two lines:

```
enumDemo(Season.WINTER);
enumDemo(Season.SUMMER);
```

The result will be as follows:

```
Dress up warmer
You can drees up lighter now
```

You probably have noticed that we used an == operator that compares references. That is because the enum instances (as all static variables) exist uniquely in memory. And the equals() method (implemented in the java.lang.Enum parent class) brings the same result. Let's run the following code:

```
Season season = Season.WINTER;
System.out.println(Season.WINTER == season);
System.out.println(Season.WINTER.equals(season));
```

The result will be:

The reason for this is that the equals() method of the java.lang.Enum class is implemented as follows:

```
public final boolean equals(Object other) {
   return this == other;
}
```

As you can see, it does exactly the same comparison of two objects references – this (the reserved keyword that refers the current object) and the reference to another object. If you wonder why the parameter has the Object type, we would like to remind you that all reference types, including enum and String, extend java.lang.Object. They do it implicitly.

Other useful methods of java.lang.Enum are as follows:

- name(): Returns the enum constant's identifier as it is spelled when declared.
- ordinal(): Returns the integer that corresponds to the position of the enum constant when declared (the first in the list has an ordinal value of zero).
- valueOf(): Returns the enum constant object by its name.
- toString(): Returns the same value as the name() method by default, but can be overridden to return any other String value.
- values(): A static method you will not find in the documentation of the java.lang.Enum class. In the Java Specification, section 8.9.3 (https://docs.oracle.com/javase/specs), it is described as implicitly declared and the Java Tutorial (https://docs.oracle.com/javase/tutorial/java/javaOO/enum.html) states that the compiler *automatically adds some special methods when it creates an enum.*

Among them, a static `values()` method that returns an array containing all of the values of the `enum` in the order they are declared.

Let's look at an example of their usage. Here is the `enum` class we will use for the demo:

```
enum Season {
   SPRING, SUMMER, AUTUMN, WINTER;
}
```

And the following is the code that uses it:

```
System.out.println(Season.SPRING.name());
System.out.println(Season.SUMMER.ordinal());
System.out.println(Enum.valueOf(Season.class, "AUTUMN"));
System.out.println(Season.WINTER.name());
```

The output of the preceding snippet is as follows:

The first line is the output of the `name()` method. The second—is the return value of the `ordinal()` method: the SUMMER constant is the second in the list, so its ordinal value is 1. The third line is the result of the `toString()` method applied to the `enum` constant of AUTUMN returned by the `valueOf()` method. And the last—is the result of the `toString()` method applied to the WINTER constant.

The `equals()`, `name()`, and `ordinal()` methods are declared `final` in `java.lang.Enum`, so they cannot be overridden and are used as-is. The `valueOf()` method is static and not associated with any class instance, so it cannot be overridden. The only method we can override is the `toString()` method:

```
enum Season {
   SPRING, SUMMER, AUTUMN, WINTER;
   public String toString() {
     return "The best season";
   }
}
```

If we run the preceding code again, the result is as follows:

Now, you can see that the `toString()` method returns the same result for each constant. If necessary, the `toString()` method can be overridden for each constant. Let's look at this version of the `Season` class:

```
enum Season2 {
   SPRING,
   SUMMER,
   AUTUMN,
   WINTER { public String toString() { return "Winter"; } };
   public String toString() {
      return "The best season";
   }
}
```

We have overridden the `toString()` method for the `WINTER` constant only. If we run the same code snippet again, the result will be as follows:

As you can see, the old version of `toString()` is used for all constants, except `WINTER`.

It is also possible to add any property (and getters and setters) to `enum` constants and associate each of them with corresponding values. Here is one example:

```
enum Season {
   SPRING("Spring", "warmer than winter", 60),
   SUMMER("Summer", "the hottest season", 100),
   AUTUMN("Autumn", "colder than summer", 70),
   WINTER("Winter", "the coldest season", 40);

   private String feel, toString;
   private int averageTemperature;
   Season(String toString, String feel, int t) {
      this.feel = feel;
      this.toString = toString;
```

```
       this.averageTemperature = t;
    }
    public String getFeel(){ return this.feel; }
    public int getAverageTemperature(){
        return this.averageTemperature;
    }
    public String toString() { return this.toString; }
}
```

In the preceding example, we have added three properties to the `Season` class: `feel`, `toString`, and `averageTemperature`. We have also created a constructor (a special method used to assign the initial values of an object state) that takes these three properties and adds getters and `toString()` methods that return values of these properties. Then, in parentheses after each constant, we have set the values that are going to be passed to the constructor when this constant is created.

Here is a demo method that we are going to use:

```
void enumDemo(Season season){
    System.out.println(season + " is " + season.getFeel());
    System.out.println(season + " has average temperature around "
                            + season.getAverageTemperature());
}
```

The `enumDemo()` method takes the `enum Season` constant and constructs and displays two sentences. Let's run the preceding code for each season, like this:

```
enumDemo2(Season3.SPRING);
enumDemo2(Season3.SUMMER);
enumDemo2(Season3.AUTUMN);
enumDemo2(Season3.WINTER);
```

The result will be as follows:

```
Spring is warmer than winter
Spring has average temperature around 60
Summer is the hottest season
Summer has average temperature around 100
Autumn is colder than summer
Autumn has average temperature around 70
Winter is the coldest season
Winter has average temperature around 40
```

The enum class is a very powerful tool that allows us to simplify the code and make it better protected from runtime errors because all possible values are predictable and can be tested in advance. For example, we can test the SPRING constant getters using the following unit test:

```
@DisplayName("Enum Season tests")
public class EnumSeasonTest {
  @Test
  @DisplayName("Test Spring getters")
  void multiplyByTwo(){
    assertEquals("Spring", Season.SPRING.toString());
    assertEquals("warmer than winter", Season.SPRING.getFeel());
    assertEquals(60, Season.SPRING.getAverageTemperature());
  }
}
```

Granted, the getters don't have much code to make a mistake. But if the enum class has more complex methods or the list of the fixed values comes from some application requirements document, such a test will make sure we have written the code as required.

In the standard Java libraries, there are several enum classes. Here are a few examples of constants from those classes that can give you a hint about what is out there:

```
Month.FEBRUARY;
TimeUnit.DAYS;
TimeUnit.MINUTES;
DayOfWeek.FRIDAY;
Color.GREEN;
Color.green;
```

So, before creating your own enum, try to check and see whether the standard libraries already provide a class with the values you need.

# Passing reference type values as method parameters

One important difference between the reference types and primitive types that merits special discussion is the way their values can be used in a method. Let's see the difference by example. First, we create the SomeClass class:

```
class SomeClass{
  private int count;
  public int getCount() {
```

```
        return count;
    }
    public void setCount(int count) {
        this.count = count;
    }
}
```

Then we create a class that uses it:

```
public class ReferenceTypeDemo {
    public static void main(String[] args) {
        float f = 1.0f;
        SomeClass someClass = new SomeClass();
        System.out.println("\nBefore demoMethod(): f = " + f +
                            ", count = " + someClass.getCount());
        demoMethod(f, someClass);
        System.out.println("After demoMethod(): f = " + f
                            + ", count = " + someClass.getCount());
    }
    private static void demoMethod(float f, SomeClass someClass){
        //... some code can be here
        f = 42.0f;
        someClass.setCount(42);
        someClass = new SomeClass();
        someClass.setCount(1001);
    }
}
```

Let's look inside demoMethod() first. We have made it very simple for demo purposes, but assume it does more, and then assigns a new value to the f variable (parameter) and sets a new count value on the object of the SomeClass class. Then this method attempts to replace the passed-in reference with a new value that points to a new SomeClass object with another count value.

In the main() method, we declare and initialize the f and someClass variables with some values and print them out, then pass them as the parameters to the demoMethod() method and print the values of the same variables again. Let's run the main() method and see the results that should look like the following:

```
Before demoMethod(): f = 1.0, count = 0
After demoMethod(): f = 1.0, count = 42
```

To understand the difference, we need to take into account these two facts:

- Values to a method are passed by copy
- Value of a reference type is a reference to a memory where the referred object resides

That is why when the primitive value (or `String`, which is immutable as we have explained already) is passed in, the copy of the actual value is created, so the original value cannot be affected.

Similarly, if the reference to an object is passed in, only its copy is accessible to the code in the method, so the original reference cannot be changed. That is why our attempt to change the original reference value and make it refer another object did not succeed, either.

But the code inside the method is able to access the original object and change its count value using the copy of the reference value because the value still points to the same memory area where the original object resides. That is why code inside the method is able to execute any method of the original object, including those methods that change the object's state (values of the instance fields).

This change of an object state, when it was passed in as a parameter, is called a side-effect and is sometimes used, when the following occurs:

- A method has to return several values but it is not possible to do it via returned construct
- The programmer is not skilled enough
- A third-party library or a framework utilizes the side-effect as the primary mechanism of getting back the result

But the best practices and design principles (the Single Responsibility Principle in this case, which we will discuss in `Chapter 8`, *Object-Oriented Design (OOD) Principles*) guide programmers to avoiding side-effects, if possible, because side effects often lead to a not-very-readable (for a human) code and subtle runtime effects that are difficult to identify and fix.

One has to distinguish a side effect and a code design pattern called Delegation Pattern (`https://en.wikipedia.org/wiki/Delegation_pattern`), when the methods invoked on the passed-in objects are stateless. We will talk about design patterns in `Chapter 8`, *Object-Oriented Design (OOD) Principles*.

Similarly, a side effect is possible when an array is passed in as a parameter. Here is the code that demonstrates it:

```
public class ReferenceTypeDemo {
  public static void main(String[] args) {
    int[] someArray = {1, 2, 3};
    System.out.println("\nBefore demoMethod(): someArray[0] = "
                                          + someArray[0]);
    demoMethod(someArray);
    System.out.println("After demoMethod(): someArray[0] = "
                                          + someArray[0]);
  }
  private static void demoMethod(int[] someArray){
    someArray[0] = 42;
    someArray = new int[3];
    someArray[0] = 43;
  }
}
```

The result of the preceding code execution is as follows:

```
Before demoMethod(): someArray[0] = 1
After demoMethod(): someArray[0] = 42
```

You can see that despite the fact that, inside the method, we were able to assign a new array to the passed-in variable, the assignment of value 43 affected only the newly created array, but had no effect on the original array. Yet, the change of an array component using the passed-in copy of the reference value is possible because the copy still points to the same original array.

And, to close the discussion about reference types as method parameters and possible side effects of that, we would like to demonstrate that the String type parameter—because of the String value immutability—behaves like a primitive type when passed in as a parameter. Here is the demo code:

```
public class ReferenceTypeDemo {
  public static void main(String[] args) {
    String someString = "Some string";
    System.out.println("\nBefore demoMethod(): string = "
                                          + someString);
    demoMethod(someString);
    System.out.println("After demoMethod(): string = "
                                          + someString);
  }
  private static void demoMethod(String someString){
```

```
        someString = "Some other string";
    }
}
```

The preceding code yields the following results:

```
Before demoMethod(): string = Some string
After demoMethod(): string = Some string
```

The code inside the method was not able to change the original parameter value. The reason for that is not – as in the case of a primitive type – that the parameter value was copied before being passed into the method. The copy, in this case, still pointed to the same original String object. The actual reason is that changing a String value does not change the value, but creates another String object with the result of the change. That is the String value immutability mechanism as we have described it in the *String type and literals* section. The reference to this new (changed) String object assigned to the copy of the reference value passed in and has no effect on the original reference value that still points to the original String object.

With that, we conclude the discussion about Java reference types and String.

# Exercise – Variable declarations and initializations

Which of the following statements are correct:

1. int x = 'x';
2. int x1 = "x";
3. char x2 = "x";
4. char x4 = 1;
5. String x3 = 1;
6. Month.MAY = 5;
7. Month month = Month.APRIL;

# Answer

1, 4, 7

# Summary

The chapter provided the foundation for the discussion of more complex Java language constructs. Knowledge of Java elements, such as identifiers, variables, literals, keywords, separators, comments and types—primitive and reference—is indispensable for Java programming. You also had a chance to learn about several areas that can be sources of confusion if not understood properly, such as the String type immutability and possible side effects when a reference type is used as a method parameter. Arrays and enum types were also explained in detail, enabling the reader to use these powerful constructs and increase the quality of their code.

In the next chapter, the reader will be introduced the most common terms and coding solutions of Java programming—**Application Programming Interface** (**API**), object factories, method overriding, hiding, and overloading. Then the discussion about the design of a software system and the advantage of aggregation (vs inheritance) will bring the reader into the realm of best design practices. The overview of Java data structures will conclude the chapter, providing the reader with practical programming advice and recommendations.

# Interfaces, Classes, and Object Construction

**6**

This chapter explains to readers the most important aspects of Java programming: **Application Programming Interfaces** (**APIs**), object factories, method overriding, hiding, and overloading. An explanation of the design advantage of aggregation (versus inheritance) follows, starting the discussion around software system design. The chapter concludes with an overview of Java data structures.

In this chapter, we will cover the following topics:

- What is an API?
- Interface and object factory as APIs
- Overriding, hiding, and overloading
- The `this` and `super` keywords
- Constructors and constructor overloading
- Final variable, final method, and final class
- Object association (aggregation)
- Exercise – Restricting a class instantiation to a single shared instance

## What is an API?

The term **Application Programming Interface** (**API**) is a specification of protocols, procedures, and services that can be used as building blocks by a programmer to implement a required functionality. An API may represent a web-based system, operating system, database system, computer hardware, or software library.

In addition to that, in everyday life, the term API is often applied to the system that implements the specification. For example, you might be familiar with Twitter APIs (`https://developer.twitter.com/en/docs`) or Amazon APIs (`https://developer.amazon.com/services-and-apis`), or you might have worked with devices (sensors) that are able to respond to a request by providing the data (measurement results). So, when programmers say *we can use an Amazon API*, they mean not only the description of the provided procedures, but the services themselves.

In Java, we have also a few variations of the term *API usage* that we would like to identify and describe in the following subsections.

# Java APIs

Java APIs include two big groups of APIs and libraries that implement them:

- Java core packages (`http://www.oracle.com/technetwork/java/api-141528.html`) that come with the Java installation and are included in the JDK
- Other frameworks and libraries that can be downloaded separately, such as Apache Commons APIs (`https://commons.apache.org`), for example, or the three libraries we have already included as dependencies in the Maven `pom.xml` file of our demo project. The vast majority of them can be found in the Maven repository (`https://mvnrepository.com`), but a variety of new and experimental libraries and frameworks can be found eslewhere.

# Command line APIs

A command line API describes the command format and its possible options that can be used to execute the application (tool). We have seen such examples when we talked about using the tools (applications) `java` and `javac` in Chapter 1, *Java Virtual Machine (JVM) on Your Computer*. We even built our own application in Chapter 4, *Your First Java Project*, defined its API, and described its command line API as accepting an integer as a parameter.

# HTTP-based APIs

A web-based application often provides an HTTP-based API using a variety of protocols (`https://en.wikipedia.org/wiki/List_of_web_service_protocols`) that allow access to the application functionality via the internet. HTTP stands for Hypertext Transfer Protocol, which is an application protocol for distributed information systems that serves as the foundation of data communication for the **World Wide Web** (**WWW**).

The two most popular web service protocols are:

- XML-based **SOAP** (Simple Object Access Protocol) protocol
- JSON-based REST or RESTful (**REpresentational State Transfer**) style over HTTP protocol

Both describe how functionality (services) can be accessed and incorporated into the application. We do not describe web services in this book.

# Software component API

A software component may be a library, an application subsystem, an application layer, or even a single class--something that can be used directly from Java code by invoking its methods. An API of a software component looks like an interface that describes method signatures which can be invoked on the objects of classes that implement the interface. If the component has public static methods (which do not require objects and can be invoked using classes only), these methods have to be included in the API description as well. But for a complete description of the component API, as we have mentioned already in `Chapter 2`, *Java Language Basics*, the information about how the objects of the component can be created should be part of the API description, too.

In this book, we are not going beyond application boundaries and will use the term API only in the sense of a software component API, as described previously. And, we will call the entities that implement an API (the services that the API describes) by their names: application subsystem, application layer, library, class, interface, and methods.

That is why we started an API-related discussion about interfaces and object factories that complement each other and, together with static methods, compose a complete description of a software component API.

# Interface and object factory as API

The noun abstract means a content summary of a book, article, or formal speech. The adjective abstract means existing in thought or as an idea, but not having a physical or concrete existence. The verb to abstract means to consider (something) theoretically or separately from something else.

That is why an interface is called an abstraction—because it captures only method signatures and does not describe how the result is achieved. Various implementations of the same interface—different classes—may behave quite differently, even if they receive the same parameters and return the same results. The last statement is a loaded one because we have not defined the term behavior. Let's do it now.

 The behavior of a class or its objects is defined by the actions its methods perform and the results they return. If a method returns nothing (void), it is said that such a method is used only for its side effects.

Such a view implies that a method that returns a value has a direct (not a side) effect. However, it can have a side effect, too, by sending a message to another application, for example, or storing data in a database. Ideally, one has to try and capture the side-effect in the method name. If that is not easy because the method does many things, it may indicate the need to break such a method into several better-focused ones.

The statement that two implementations of the same method signature can have different behavior makes sense only when the method name does not capture all the side effects, or the author of the implementations did not honor the meaning of the method name. But even when the behavior of different implementations is the same, the code itself, the libraries it uses, and how effectively it works may be different.

Why it is important to hide the implementation details we will explain in Chapter 8, *Object-Oriented Design (OOD) Principles*. For now, we will just mention that the clients' isolation from the implementation allows the system to be more flexible in adopting new versions of the same implementation or in switching to a completely different one.

# Interface

We talked about interfaces in `Chapter 2`, *Java Language Basics*, so now we will just look at some examples. Let's create a new package, `com.packt.javapath.ch06demo.api`. Then, we can right-click `com.packt.javapath.ch06demo.api`, open **New** | **Java Class**, select **Interface**, type `Calculator`, and click the **OK** button. We have created an interface and can add to it a method signature, `int multiplyByTwo(int i)`, so the result looks like this:

```
Calculator.java
package com.packt.javapath.ch06demo.api;

public interface Calculator {

    int multiplyByTwo(int i);

}
```

This will be the public face of every class that implements this interface. In real life, we would not use the package name `api` and use `calculator` instead, as it is more specific and descriptive. But we are discussing the term "API" and that is the reason we decided to name the package this way.

Let's create another package, `com.packt.javapath.ch06demo.api.impl`, which will hold all implementations of `Calculator` and other interfaces that we will add to the `com.packt.javapath.ch06demo.api` package. The first implementation is the `CalulatorImpl` class. By now, you should know already how to create the `com.packt.javapath.ch06demo.api.impl` package and the `CalulatorImpl` class in it. The result should look like this:

```
Calculator.java    CalculatorImpl.java
package com.packt.javapath.ch06demo.api.impl;

import com.packt.javapath.ch06demo.api.Calculator;

class CalculatorImpl implements Calculator {

    public int multiplyByTwo(int i){
        System.out.println(CalculatorImpl.class.getName());
        return i * 2;
    }
}
```

We have put implementations in the package one level deeper than `api`, thus indicating that those are details that should not be exposed to the users of the API we create.

In addition, we need to write a test and use it to make sure our functionality is correct and convenient for users. Again, we assume that by now you know how to do it. The result should look like this:

```
Calculator.java        CalculatorImpl.java        CalculatorTest.java
1    package com.packt.javapath.ch06demo.api;
2
3    import org.junit.jupiter.api.Test;
4
5    public class CalculatorTest {
6
7        @Test
8        void multiplyByTwo() {
9        }
10   }
11
```

Then, we add the missing test body and annotations as follows:

```
@DisplayName("API Calculator tests")
public class CalculatorTest {
  @Test
  @DisplayName("Happy multiplyByTwo()")
  void multiplyByTwo(){
    CalculatorImpl calculator = new CalculatorImpl();
    int i = 2;
    int result = calculator.multiplyByTwo(i);
    assertEquals(4, result);
  }
}
```

This code serves us not only as the functionality test; it can also be viewed as an example of a client code the API users would write. So, the test helps us to see our API from a client perspective. Looking at this code, we realize that we were not able to completely hide the implementation. The CalculatorImpl class is still accessed by the client directly, even if we change the line that creates the object to the following:

```
Calculator calculator = new CalculatorImpl();
```

This means that if case we change the signature of the CalculatorImpl constructor or switch to another implementation of the same interface (let it be called AnotherCalculatorImpl), the client code has to be changed, too. To avoid it, programmers use classes called object factories.

# Object factory

The purpose of an object factory is to hide the details of object creation so that the client does not need to change the code if the implementation changes. Let's create a factory that produces `Calculator` objects. We will put it in the same package, `com.packt.javapath.ch06demo.api.impl`, as the implementations of the `Calculator` interface reside in:

And we can change the test (client code) to use this factory:

```
@DisplayName("API Calculator tests")
public class CalculatorTest {
  @Test
  @DisplayName("Happy multiplyByTwo()")
  void multiplyByTwo(){
    Calculator calculator = CalculatorFactory.createInstance();
    int i = 2;
    int result = calculator.multiplyByTwo(i);
    assertEquals(4, result);
  }
}
```

With that, we have achieved our goal: the client code does not have any notion of the classes that implement `Calculator` interface. We can, for example, change the factory so that it creates objects of another class:

```
public static Calculator create(){
  return AnotherCalculatorImpl();
}
```

The `AnotherCalculatorImpl` class may look like this:

```
class AnotherCalculatorImpl  implements Calculator {
  public int multiplyByTwo(int i){
    System.out.println(AnotherCalculatorImpl.class.getName());
    return i + i;
  }
}
```

This `multiplyByTwo()` method adds two values instead of multiplying the input parameter by 2.

We also can make the factory read the configuration file and instantiate the implementation based on the configuration file values:

```
public class CalculatorFactory {
  public static Calculator create(){
    String whichImpl =
      Utils.getStringValueFromConfig("calculator.conf", "which.impl");
    if(whichImpl.equals("multiplies")){
      return new CalculatorImpl();
    } else if (whichImpl.equals("adds")){
      return new AnotherCalculatorImpl();
    } else {
      throw new RuntimeException("Houston, we have a problem. " +
        "Unknown key which.impl value " + whichImpl + " is in config.");
    }
  }
}
```

We did not talk about the `if...else` constructions or about the `RuntimeException` class yet (see `Chapter 10`, *Control Flow Statements*). And, we will discuss the `Utils.getStringValueFromConfig()` method shortly. But, we hope you understand what this code does:

- Reads the configuration file
- Instantiates the class depending on the value of the `which.impl` key
- Exits the method by throwing an exception (thus informing the client that there is a problem that has to be resolved) if there is no class that corresponds to the value of the `which.impl` key

And here is how the configuration file `calculator.conf` may look:

```
{
    "which.impl": "multiplies"
}
```

 This is called **JavaScript Object Notation (JSON)** format, which is based on key-value pairs separated by a colon (`:`). You can read more about JSON at `http://www.json.org/`.

The `calculator.conf` file resides in the `resources` directory (a subdirectory of the `main` directory). Maven, by default, places the content of this directory on the classpath, so it can be found by the application.

To tell the factory to use another `Calculator` implementation, we need to do only the following:

- Change the value of the key `which.impl` in the file `calculator.conf`
- Change the factory `create()` method to instantiate the new implementation based on this new value

It is important to notice that the client code (`CalculatorTest` class) is not affected when we switch `Calculator` implementation. That is the advantage of hiding the implementation details from the client code using the interface and object factory class.

Now, let's look inside the `Utils` class and its `getStringValueFromConfig()` method.

# Reading configuration file

By looking at the real-life implementation of the `getStringValueFromConfig()` method, we are jumping ahead of your knowledge of Java and Java libraries. So we do not expect you to understand all the details, but we hope this exposure will give you an idea about how things are done and what are we aiming at in our course.

# Using the json-simple library

The `getStringValueFromConfig()` method is located in the `Utils` class, which we have created to read the values from the `.conf` file. This class has the following code:

```java
import org.json.simple.JSONObject;
import org.json.simple.parser.JSONParser;
import org.json.simple.parser.ParseException;

public class Utils {
    private static JSONObject config = null;
    public static String getStringValueFromConfig(String configFileName,
                                                   String key){
      if(config == null){
        ClassLoader classLoader = Utils.class.getClassLoader();
        File file =
            new File(classLoader.getResource(configFileName).getFile());
        try(FileReader fr = new FileReader(file)){
          JSONParser parser = new JSONParser();
          config = (JSONObject) parser.parse(fr);
        } catch (ParseException | IOException ex){
          ex.printStackTrace();
          return "Problem reading config file.";
        }
      }
      return config.get(key) == null ? "unknown" : (String)config.get(key);
    }
}
```

First of all, please notice the technique called caching. We check the value of the `config` static class field first. If it is not `null`, we use it. Otherwise, we find the `config` file on the classpath using the same class loader that was used to load the known class we passed in as a parameter. We parse the config file, which means breaking it into key-value pairs. The result is the reference to the generated object of the `JSONObject` class we assign to the `config` field (cache it so the next time it will be available to use).

 That is the caching technique, used to avoid wasting time and other resources. The drawback of this solution is that any change to the configuration file requires restarting the application so the file can be read again. In our case, we assumed it is acceptable. But in other cases, we could add a timer and refresh the cached data after the defined period of time has passed, or do something similar.

To read the config file, we use the `FileReader` class from the Apache Commons library (`https://commons.apache.org/proper/commons-io`). To let Maven know that we need this library, we have added the following dependency to the `pom.xml` file:

```
<dependency>
  <groupId>commons-io</groupId>
  <artifactId>commons-io</artifactId>
  <version>2.5</version>
</dependency>
```

To process data in JSON format, we use JSON.simple library (released under Apache License, too) and have added the following dependency to `pom.xml`:

```
<dependency>
  <groupId>com.googlecode.json-simple</groupId>
  <artifactId>json-simple</artifactId>
  <version>1.1</version>
</dependency>
```

The `JSONObject` class stores key-value pairs presented in JSON format. If the passed-in key is not present in the file, the object of the `JSONObject` class returns the value `null`. In such a case, our `getStringValueFromConfig()` method returns a `String` literal unknown. Otherwise, it casts the return value to `String`. We can do it because we know that the value can be assigned to a variable of `String` type.

 The `<condition>? <option1> : <option2>` construct is called a ternary operator. It returns `option1` when the condition is true, and otherwise returns `option2`. We will talk about it more in `Chapter 9`, *Operators, Expressions, and Statements*.

# Using the json-api library

Alternatively, we could use another JSON processing API and its implementation:

```
<dependency>
  <groupId>javax.json</groupId>
  <artifactId>javax.json-api</artifactId>
  <version>1.1.2</version>
</dependency>
<dependency>
  <groupId>org.glassfish</groupId>
  <artifactId>javax.json</artifactId>
  <version>1.1.2</version>
</dependency>
```

Then the code of the `getStringValueFromConfig()` method would look slightly different:

```
import javax.json.Json;
import javax.json.JsonObject;
import javax.json.JsonReader;
public class Utils {
    private static JsonObject config = null;
    public static String getStringValueFromConfig(String FileName,
                                                            String key){
      if(config == null){
        ClassLoader classLoader = Utils.class.getClassLoader();
        File file = new File(classLoader.getResource(fileName).getFile());
        try(FileInputStream fis = new FileInputStream(file)){
          JsonReader reader = Json.createReader(fis);
          config = reader.readObject();
        } catch (IOException ex){
          ex.printStackTrace();
          return "Problem reading config file.";
        }
      }
      return config.get(key) == null ? "unknown" : config.getString(key);
    }
}
```

This second implementation requires a bit less code and uses a more consistent camel case style (`JsonObject` versus `JSONObject`). But, since their performance is not very different, which library to use is largely a matter of a personal preference.

# Unit test

Let's create a unit test that proves the method works as expected. By now, you should be able to create a `UtilsTest` class in the `test/java/com/packt/javapath/ch06demo` directory (or in the `test\java\com\packt\javapath\ch06demo` directory in the case of the Windows). The test should look like this:

```
@DisplayName("Utils tests")
public class UtilsTest {
  @Test
  @DisplayName("Test reading value from config file by key")
  void getStringValueFromConfig(){
    //test body we will write here
  }
}
```

Next, we add
the `test/resources/utilstest.conf` file (`test\resources\utilstest.conf` for
Windows):

```
{
  "unknown": "some value"
}
```

It will play the role of a `config` file. With that, the test code looks as follows:

```
@Test
@DisplayName("Test reading value from config file by key")
void getStringValueFromConfig(){
   String fileName = "utilstest.conf";
   String value = Utils.getStringValueFromConfig(fileName, "some value");
   assertEquals("some value", value);

   value = Utils.getStringValueFromConfig(fileName, "some value");
   assertEquals("unknown", value);
}
```

We test two cases:

- The returned value should be equal `some value` in the first case
- The value should come back as `unknown` if the key does not exist in the config file

We run this test and observe the success. To make sure, we can also change
the `utilstest.conf` file settings to the following:

```
{
  "unknown": "another value"
}
```

This should cause the test to fail the first case.

Let's revisit the Calculator API.

# Calculator API

Based on the previous discussion, we can describe the Calculator API in the
`Calculator` interface as follows:

```
public interface Calculator {
   int multiplyByTwo(int i);
}
```

```
static Calculator createInstance(){
  return CalculatorFactory.create();
}
```

If the constructor of the `Calculator` implementation requires parameters, we would add them to the `create()` factory method and to the `createInstance()` static method of the interface.

When only one implementation of the `Calculator` interface exists, the previous API declaration would be enough. But when you give the client a choice of two or more implementations, as we have described previously, then the API should also include the description of `calculator.conf` configuration file.

The configuration description would have to list all possible values of the `which.impl` key (`multiplies` and `adds`, in our case). We would also need to explain how the implementations are different so that the programmer who uses our calculator could make an informed choice.

If that sounds like too much, then you might step back and look at your API design again because it is probably not well focused and tries to cover too many things. Consider breaking such an API into several simpler APIs. Describing each of these smaller APIs is easier both to write and to understand.

For example, here is how the configuration description can be added to an interface in our case:

```
public interface Calculator {
  int multiplyByTwo(int i);
  static Calculator createInstance(){
    return  CalculatorFactory.create();
  }
  String CONF_NAME = "calculator.conf";
  String CONF_WHICH_IMPL = "which.impl";
  enum WhichImpl{
    multiplies, //use multiplication operation
    adds        //use addition operation
  }
}
```

As you can see, we have captured the configuration filename in a constant, as well as the configuration key name. And we have created an `enum` for all possible values of the key. We have also added an explanation of the difference between the implementations as a comment. If the explanation is too long, the comment can provide a reference to documentation, a website name, or a URL, for example.

Since there are two implementations and two possible values in the configuration file, we need to run our unit test `CalculatorTest` twice—for each possible value of the configuration—to make sure that both implementations work as expected. But we do not want to change the configuration inside the deliverable software component itself.

That is when the `test/resources` directory (`test\resources` for Windows) comes into play again. Let's create a `calculator.conf` file in it and add the following lines to the `CalculatorTest` test, which will print the current settings in that file:

```
String whichImpl =
    Utils.getStringValueFromConfig(Calculator.CONF_NAME,
                                   Calculator.CONF_WHICH_IMPL);
System.out.println(Calculator.CONF_WHICH_IMPL + "=" + whichImpl);
```

The `CalculatorTest` code should look as follows:

```
void multiplyByTwo() {
  WhichImpl whichImpl =
      Utils.getWhichImplValueFromConfig(Calculator.CONF_NAME,
                                        Calculator.CONF_WHICH_IMPL);
  System.out.println("\n" + Calculator.CONF_WHICH_IMPL +
                                        "=" + whichImpl);
  Calculator calculator = Calculator.createInstance();
  int i = 2;
  int result = calculator.multiplyByTwo(i);
  assertEquals(4, result);
}
```

Let's also add a line that prints out the class name of each implementation:

```
public class CalculatorImpl implements Calculator {
  public int multiplyByTwo(int i){
    System.out.println(CalculatorImpl.class.getClass().getName());
    return i * 2;
  }
}
public class AnotherCalculatorImpl implements Calculator {
  public int multiplyByTwo(int i){
    System.out.println(AnotherCalculatorImpl.class.getClass().getName());
    return i + i;
  }
}
```

If we set the value of `which.impl` (in the `calculator.conf` file in the `test` directory) to `adds`, it will look like this:

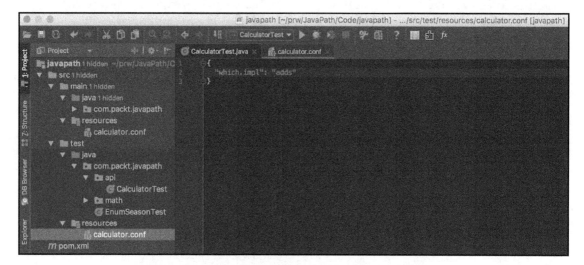

And the result of the `CalculatorTest` test will be:

```
which.impl=adds
com.packt.javapath.api.impl.AnotherCalculatorImpl

Process finished with exit code 0
```

The output tells us three things:

- The value of `which.impl` in `calculator.conf` was set to `adds`
- The corresponding implementation of `AnotherCalculatorImpl` was used
- The invoked implementation worked as expected

Similarly, we can run our unit test for the `calculator.conf` file set to `multiplies`.

The result looks very good, but we still can improve the code and make it less susceptible to error, if sometime in the future somebody decides to enhance the functionality by adding a new implementation or something similar. We can take advantage of the constants added to the `Calculator` interface and make the `create()` factory method more protected from a human mistake:

```
public static Calculator create(){
    String whichImpl = Utils.getStringValueFromConfig(Calculator.CONF_NAME,
```

```
                                       Calculator.CONF_WHICH_IMPL);
    if(whichImpl.equals(Calculator.WhichImpl.multiplies.name())){
      return new CalculatorImpl();
    } else if (whichImpl.equals(Calculator.WhichImpl.adds.name())){
      return new AnotherCalculatorImpl();
    } else {
      throw new RuntimeException("Houston, we have a problem. " +
                    "Unknown key " + Calculator.CONF_WHICH_IMPL +
                    " value " + whichImpl + " is in config.");

    }
  }
```

Just to make sure that the test doing its job, we change the value in
the calculator.conf file in the test directory to add (instead of adds) and run the test
again. The output will be as follows:

```
which.impl=add

java.lang.RuntimeException: Houston, we have a problem. Unknown key which.impl value add is in config.
```

The test failed, as was expected. It gives us a level of confidence that the code works and
doesn't just always show success.

Yet, the code can be improved to become more readable, more testable, and less susceptible
to human errors when it is modified or expanded. Using the knowledge of the enum
functionality, we can write a method that converts the value of the key which.impl in
the calculator.conf file to one of the constants (instances) of the class enum WhichImpl.
To do it, we add this new method to the class Utils:

```
WhichImpl getWhichImplValueFromConfig(String configFileName, String key){
  String whichImpl = getStringValueFromConfig(configFileName, key);
  try{
    return Enum.valueOf(WhichImpl.class, whichImpl);
  } catch (IllegalArgumentException ex){
    throw new RuntimeException("Houston, we have a problem. " +
                  "Unknown key " + Calculator.CONF_WHICH_IMPL +
                  " value " + whichImpl + " is in config.");
  }
}
```

This code is based on the usage of the method `getStringValueFromConfig()`, which we have tested already and know it works as expected. The construct `try...catch` allows us to capture and process situations when some code (the method `Enum.valueOf()` in this case) encounters a condition it cannot resolve and throws an exception (we will learn more about this in `Chapter 10`, *Control Flow Statements*). One has to read the Java API documentation in order to know that the method `Enum.valueOf()` can throw an exception. For example, here is a quote from the documentation about the method `Enum.valueOf()`:

> *"Throws: IllegalArgumentException - if the specified enum type has no constant with the specified name or the specified class object does not represent an enum type"*

It is a good idea to read the API documentation of any third-party class you are going to use. In our code, we catch it and throw a new exception with our own wording for consistency.

As you would expect, we have also written a unit test for the method `getWhichImplValueFromConfig()` and added it to `UtilsTest`:

```
@Test
@DisplayName("Test matching config value to enum WhichImpl")
void getWhichImpValueFromConfig(){
  String confifFileName = "utilstest.conf";
  for(int i = 1; i <= WhichImpl.values().length; i++){
    String key = String.valueOf(i);
    WhichImpl whichImpl =
        Utils.getWhichImplValueFromConfig(confifFileName, key);
    System.out.println(key + "=" + whichImpl);
  }
  try {
    WhichImpl whichImpl =
        Utils.getWhichImplValueFromConfig(confifFileName, "unknown");
    fail("Should not get here! whichImpl = " + whichImpl);
  } catch (RuntimeException ex){
    assertEquals("Houston, we have a problem. " +
                "Unknown key which.impl value unknown is in config.",
                ex.getMessage());
  }
  try {
    WhichImpl whichImpl =
        Utils.getWhichImplValueFromConfig(confifFileName, "some value");
    fail("Should not get here! whichImpl = " + whichImpl);
  } catch (RuntimeException ex){
    assertEquals("Houston, we have a problem. " +
                "Unknown key which.impl value unknown is in config.",
```

```
                    ex.getMessage());
    }
  }
```

To support this test, we have also added two more entries to the `utilstest.conf` file:

```
{
  "1": "multiplies",
  "2": "adds",
  "unknown": "unknown"
}
```

This test covers three cases:

- If all the constants from the `enum WhichImpl` are present in the config file, the method `getWhichImplValueFromConfig()` works just fine—it finds each of them and does not throw an exception
- If the key passed into the method `getWhichImplValueFromConfig()` is not from `enum WhichImpl`, the method throws an exception with the message `Houston, we have a problem. Unknown key which.impl value unknown is in config`
- If the key passed into the method `getWhichImplValueFromConfig()` is not present in the config file, the method throws an exception with the message `Houston, we have a problem. Unknown key which.impl value unknown is in config`

When we have confidence that this method works as expected, we can rewrite the factory method `create()` as follows:

```
public static Calculator create(){
  WhichImpl whichImpl =
    Utils.getWhichImplValueFromConfig(Calculator.CONF_NAME,
                                Calculator.CONF_WHICH_IMPL);
  switch (whichImpl){
    case multiplies:
      return new CalculatorImpl();
    case adds:
      return new AnotherCalculatorImpl();
    default:
      throw new RuntimeException("Houston, we have another " +
                "problem. We do not have implementation for the key " +
                Calculator.CONF_WHICH_IMPL + " value " + whichImpl);
  }
}
```

The `switch()` construct is quite straightforward: it directs the execution thread to the code block under the case that matches the corresponding value (more about it in `Chapter 10`, *Control Flow Statements*).

The benefit of creating and using the method `getWhichImplValueFromConfig()` is that the `create()` method became much cleaner and focused on one task only: creating the right object. We will talk about the *Single Responsibility Principle* in section *So many OOD principles and so little time* of `Chapter 8`, *Object-Oriented Design (OOD) Principles*.

We have captured the Calculator API in one place—the interface `Calculator` —and we have tested it and proved that it works as designed. But there is another possible API aspect—the last one—we have not covered, yet.

# Adding static methods to API

Each of the classes that implement the `Calculator` interface may have static methods in addition to the instance methods defined in the interface. If such static methods could be helpful to the API's users, we should be able to document them in the `Calculator` interface, too, and that is what we are going to do now.

Let's assume that each of the implementations of the `Calculator` interface has a static method, `addOneAndConvertToString()`:

```
public class CalculatorImpl implements Calculator {
  public static String addOneAndConvertToString(double d){
    System.out.println(CalculatorImpl.class.getName());
    return Double.toString(d + 1);
  }
  //...
}
public class AnotherCalculatorImpl implements Calculator {
  public static String addOneAndConvertToString(double d){
    System.out.println(AnotherCalculatorImpl.class.getName());
    return String.format("%.2f", d + 1);
  }
  //...
}
```

Notice that the methods have the same signature but slightly different implementations. The method in `CalculatorImpl` returns the result as is, while the method in `AnotherCalculatorImpl` returns the formatted value with two decimal places (we will show the result shortly).

Usually, static methods are called via a dot-operator applied to a class:

```
String s1 = CalculatorImpl.addOneAndConvertToString(42d);
String s2 = AnotherCalculatorImpl.addOneAndConvertToString(42d);
```

But, we would like to hide (encapsulate) from an API client the implementation details so that the client code continues to use only the interface `Calculator`. To accomplish that goal, we will use the class `CalculatorFactory` again and add to it the following method:

```
public static String addOneAndConvertToString(double d){
  WhichImpl whichImpl =
      Utils.getWhichImplValueFromConfig(Calculator.CONF_NAME,
                                  Calculator.CONF_WHICH_IMPL);
  switch (whichImpl){
    case multiplies:
      return CalculatorImpl.addOneAndConvertToString(d);
    case adds:
      return AnotherCalculatorImpl.addOneAndConvertToString(d);
    default:
      throw new RuntimeException("Houston, we have another " +
              "problem. We do not have implementation for the key " +
              Calculator.CONF_WHICH_IMPL + " value " + whichImpl);
  }
}
```

As you may have noticed, it looks very similar to the factory method `create()`. We also used the same values of the `which.impl` property—multiplies and adds—as identification of the class. With that, we can add the following static method to the `Calculator` interface:

```
static String addOneAndConvertToString(double d){
  return CalculatorFactory.addOneAndConvertToString(d);
}
```

As you can see, this way we were able to hide the names of the classes that implemented the interface `Calculator` and the static method `addOneAndConvertToString ()`, too.

To test this new addition, we have expanded code in `CalculatorTest` by adding these lines:

```
double d = 2.12345678;
String mString = "3.12345678";
String aString = "3.12";
String s = Calculator.addOneAndConvertToString(d);
if(whichImpl.equals(Calculator.WhichImpl.multiplies)){
  assertEquals(mString, s);
```

```
  } else {
    assertNotEquals(mString, s);
  }
  if(whichImpl.equals(Calculator.WhichImpl.adds)){
    assertEquals(aString, s);
  } else {
    assertNotEquals(aString, s);
  }
```

In the test, we expect one value of `String` type, in case of `WhichImpl.multiplies` and the same value in a different format (only two decimal places) in the case of `WhichImpl.adds`. Let's run `CalculatorTest` with the following setting in `calculator.conf`:

```
{
  "which.impl": "adds"
}
```

The result is:

```
which.impl=adds
com.packt.javapath.api.impl.AnotherCalculatorImpl
com.packt.javapath.api.impl.AnotherCalculatorImpl

Process finished with exit code 0
```

And when we set `calculator.conf` to the value `multiplies`, the result is as follows:

```
which.impl=multiplies
com.packt.javapath.api.impl.CalculatorImpl
com.packt.javapath.api.impl.CalculatorImpl

Process finished with exit code 0
```

With that, we complete the discussion on the Calculator API.

# The API is complete

The final version of our API looks as follows:

```
public interface Calculator {
  int multiplyByTwo(int i);
  static Calculator createInstance(){
    return  CalculatorFactory.create();
  }
```

```
    static String addOneAndConvertToString(double d){
      return  CalculatorFactory.addOneAndConvertToString(d);
    }
    String CONF_NAME = "calculator.conf";  //file name
    String CONF_WHICH_IMPL = "which.impl"; //key in the .conf file
    enum WhichImpl{
      multiplies, //uses multiplication operation
                  // and returns addOneAndConvertToString()
                  // result without formating
      adds    //uses addition operation
              // and returns addOneAndConvertToString()
              // result with two decimals only
    }
  }
```

This way, we maintain the single source of record—the interface that captures all the API details. If more details are needed, the comments may refer to some external URL with full documentation that describes each of the `Calculator` implementations. And, to repeat what we have said already at the beginning of this section, the method name should describe all the side effects the method produces.

In practice, programmers try to write small, well-focused methods and capture everything the method does in its name, but they rarely add more than abstract signatures to an interface. And when they talk about APIs they usually mean only abstract signatures, which is the most important aspect of an API. But we think it is a good idea to also document all other API aspects in one place.

# Overloading, overriding, and hiding

We have already mentioned method overriding and explained it in Chapter 2, *Java Language Basics*. Method overriding is replacing the methods implemented in a parent class (or default methods implemented in an interface) with the methods of the same signatures in the child class (or in the class that implements the interface, or in the child interface correspondingly). Method overloading is creating several methods with the same name and different parameters (thus, different signatures) in the same class or interface. In this section, we will discuss overriding and overloading the members of an interface, a class, and a class instance in more detail and will explain what hiding is as well. We start with an interface.

# Interface method overloading

We already said in Chapter 2, *Java Language Basics*, that in addition to abstract methods, an interface can have default methods and static members—constants, methods, and classes.

If an abstract, default, or static method `m()` already exists in an interface, one cannot add another method `m()` with the same signature (method name and list of parameter types). So, the following examples generate compilation errors because each pair of methods has the same signature, while the access modifier (`private`, `public`), `static` or `default` keywords, returned value type, and implementation are not part of the signature:

```
interface A {
  int m(String s);
  double m(String s);
}
interface B {
  int m(int s);
  static int m(int i) { return 42; }
}
interface C {
  int m(double i);
  private double m(double s) { return 42d; }
}
interface D {
  int m(String s);
  default int m(String s) { return 42; }
}
interface E {
  private int m(int s) { return 1; };
  default double m(int i) { return 42d; }
}
interface F {
  default int m(String s) { return 1; };
  static int m(String s) { return 42; }
}
interface G {
  private int m(double d) { return 1; };
  static int m(double s) { return 42; }
}
interface H {
  default int m(int i) { return 1; };
  default double m(int s) { return 42d; }
}
```

To create a different signature, one has either to change the method name or change the list of parameter types. Having two or more methods with the same method name and different parameter types constitutes method overloading. Here are a few examples of legitimate method overloading in an interface:

```
interface A {
   int m(String s);
   int m(String s, double d);
   int m(double d, String s);
   String m(int i);
   private double m(double d) { return 42d; }
   private int m(int i, String s) { return 1; }
   default int m(String s, int i) { return 1; }
}
interface B {
   static int m(String s, int i) { return 42; }
   static int m(String s) { return 42; }
}
```

Overloading is applied to inherited methods, too, which means that the following overloading of non-static methods is not different from the previous example:

```
interface D {
   default int m(int i, String s) { return 1; }
   default int m(String s, int i) { return 1; }
}
interface C {
   default double m(double d) { return 42d; }
}
interface B extends C, D {
   int m(double d, String s);
   String m(int i);
}
interface A extends B {
   int m(String s);
   int m(String s, double d);
}
```

You have probably noticed that we have changed the private methods to default in the previous code. We did it because otherwise the private access modifier makes the method inaccessible to a child interface and thus cannot be overloaded in a child.

As for the static methods, the following combinations of static and non-static methods, although allowed, do not constitute overloading:

```
interface A {
  int m(String s);
  static int m(String s, double d) { return 1 }
}
interface B {
  int m(String s, int i);
  static int m(String s) { return 42; }
}
interface D {
  default int m(String s, int s) { return 1; }
  static int m(String s, double s) { return 42; }
}
interface E {
  private int m() { return 1; }
  static int m(String s) { return 42; }
}
```

Static methods belong to a class (and thus exist uniquely in the application), while non-static methods are associated with an instance (and a method copy is created for each object).

For the same reason, static methods of different interfaces do not overload each other, even if the interfaces have a parent-child relationship:

```
interface G {
  static int m(String s) { return 42; }
}

interface F extends G {
  static int m(String s, int i) { return 42; }
}
```

Only the static methods that belong to the same interface can overload each other, while non-static interface methods can be overloaded even if they belong to different interfaces, provided they have parent-child relations.

# Interface method overriding

By contrast with overloading, which happens with the static and non-static methods of signatures that are different but have the same name, method overriding happens only with non-static methods and only when they have exactly the same signature.

Another difference is that the overriding method resides in the child interface, while the overridden method belongs to the parent interface. The following are examples of method overriding:

```
interface D {
  default int m(String s) { // does not override anything
    return 1;
  }
}

interface C extends D {
  default int m(String d) { // overrides method of D
    return 42;
  }
}
```

The class that implements interface C directly and does not implement the method m() will get the implementation of this method from interface C and will not get the implementation of this method from interface D. Only the class that implements interface D directly and does not implement the method m() will get the implementation from interface D.

Notice that we use the word directly. By saying that class X implements interface C directly, we mean that class X is defined as follows: class X implements C. If interface C extends D, then class X implements interface D as well, but not directly. That is an important distinction because the methods of interface C in such a case can override the methods of interface D that have the same signature, thus making them inaccessible for class X.

While writing code that depends on overriding, a good practice would be to use the annotation @Override which expresses the programmer's intent. The Java compiler and an IDE that uses it then check whether overriding took place and generates an error if the method with this annotation does not override anything. Here are some examples:

```
interface B {
  int m(String s);
}
interface A extends B {
  @Override              //no error
  int m(String s);
}
interface D {
  default int m1(String s) { return 1; }
}
interface C extends D {
  @Override              //error
```

```
   default int m(String d) { return 42; }
}
```

The error will help you notice that the method in the parent interface is spelled differently (m1() versus m()). And here is another example:

```
interface D {
   static int m(String s) { return 1; }
}
interface C extends D {
   @Override                    //error
   default int m(String d) { return 42; }
}
```

This example generates an error because an instance method cannot override a static method and vice versa. Also, a static method cannot override a static method of the parent interface because each static method of an interface is associated with the interface itself, not with a class instance:

```
interface D {
   static int m(String s) { return 1; }
}
interface C extends D{
   @Override                    //error
   static int m(String d) { return 42; }
}
```

But a static method in a child interface can hide the static method with the same signature in a parent interface. In fact, any static member—a field, a method, or a class—can hide the corresponding static member of the parent interface, direct parent or not. We will discuss hiding in the next section.

# Interface static member hiding

Let's look at the following two interfaces:

```
interface B {
   String NAME = "B";
   static int m(String d) { return 1; }
   class Clazz{
      String m(){ return "B";}
   }
}

interface A extends B {
```

```
    String NAME = "A";
    static int m(String d) { return 42; }
    class Clazz{
      String m(){ return "A";}
    }
  }
```

Interface B is a parent (also called superinterface or base interface) of interface A (called a derived interface, child interface, subinterface, or subtype). All the members of an interface are `public` by default. Interface fields and classes are also `static` by default. So, all members of interfaces A and B are `public` and `static`. Let's, run the following code:

```
  public static void main(String[] args) {
    System.out.println(B.NAME);
    System.out.println(B.m(""));
    System.out.println(new B.Clazz().m());
  }
```

The result will be as follows:

As you can see, the effect looks like overriding, but the mechanism that produces it is hiding. The difference is more prominent in the case of the hiding of class members, which we will discuss in the next section.

# Class member hiding

Let's look at these two classes:

```
  class ClassC {
    public static String field = "static field C";
    public static String m(String s){
      return "static method C";
    }
  }

  class ClassD extends ClassC {
    public static String field = "static field D";
    public static String m(String s){
      return "static method D";
    }
  }
```

They have two static members each—a field and a method. With that, look at the following code:

```
System.out.println(ClassD.field);
System.out.println(ClassD.m(""));
System.out.println(new ClassD().field);
System.out.println(new ClassD().m(""));
ClassC object = new ClassD();
System.out.println(object.field);
System.out.println(object.m(""));
```

Stop reading and try to guess what will the output be.

Here is the same code with numbers of lines and the output (captured in the comments):

```
1 System.out.println(ClassD.field);          //static field D
2 System.out.println(ClassD.m(""));           //static method D
3 System.out.println(new ClassD().field);     //static field D
4 System.out.println(new ClassD().m(""));      //static method D
5 ClassC object = new ClassD();
6 System.out.println(object.field);           //static field C
7 System.out.println(object.m(""));            //static method C
```

The output of the first two lines was probably expected. Lines 3 and 4 are not as intuitive, but probably also make sense. Any object of a class should be able to access class members. Nevertheless, it is not recommended to access static members via an object because such code hides the fact that the accessed members are static, which makes the code less readable and may lead to unnecessary object creation. Same applies to lines 6 and 7. And, just to reiterate what we have discussed in Chapter 2, *Java Language Basics*, lines 5, 6, and 7 demonstrate that we are able to assign the object of ClassD to the reference of type ClassC because ClassC is the parent class, and all the children (of all generations) of a class have the same type as the parent class. This means that a child can have many types inherited from all its parents—direct and indirect. It looks like genetic inheritance, doesn't it?

So, you can see static members of a child class (also called a derived class, extended class, subclass, or subtype) can hide the static members of its parent (also called a base class or superclass).

There are two differences between hiding fields and hiding methods. A static field:

- Hide an instance variable
- Even hide a field with the same name but different type

Here are the allowable cases for hiding, described previously:

```
class ClassC {
  public static String field1 = "instance field C";
  public String m1(String s){
    return "instance method C";
  }
}
class ClassD extends ClassC {
  public String field1 = "instance field D";
  public String m1(String s){
    return "instance method D";
  }
}
```

To demonstrate it, we can run the following code:

```
System.out.println(new ClassD().field1);
System.out.println(new ClassD().m1(""));
ClassC object1 = new ClassD();
System.out.println(object1.m1(""));
System.out.println(object1.field1);
System.out.println(((ClassD)object1).field1);
```

Again, you can stop reading now and guess what the output will be.

Here are the results:

```
1 System.out.println(new ClassD().field1);          //instance field D
2 System.out.println(new ClassD().m1(""));           //instance method D
3 ClassC object1 = new ClassD();
4 System.out.println(object1.m1(""));                //instance method D
5 System.out.println(object1.field1);                //instance field C
6 System.out.println(((ClassD)object1).field1);//instance field D
```

As you can see, line 5 outputs the value of the static variable `ClassC.field1` although the field with the same name, `field1`, exists in `ClassD`, too. Even if we change `field1` in `ClassC` to non-static, the same result will be displayed: line 5 prints out the value of the field using the declared type of the reference `object1`, not the actual type of the object assigned to it. To make matters even more complicated, as we have stated before, the type of the field `field1` in `ClassC` may be different from the type of field with the same name in `ClassD`, and the effect of public field hiding will still be the same.

To avoid confusion, always follow these two best practices:

- Write the identifier of a static variable in uppercase characters, while the identifier of an instance variable should be in lowercase
- Try to never allow public access to the instance fields; make them private and access to their values via getters and setters, instead:

```
class ClassC {
  private String field1 = "instance field C";
  public String getField(){ return field1; }
  public void setField(String s){ field1 = s; }
  public String m1(String s){
    return "instance class C";
  }
}
class ClassD extends ClassC {
  private String field1 = "instance field D";
  public String getField(){ return field1; }
  public void setField(String s){ field1 = s; }
  public String m1(String s){
    return "instance class D";
  }
}
```

This way, in the case of overriding or hiding, you will have only one set of rules related to methods. It is much simpler and more straightforward. Besides, you can have better control over the values of the private fields. For example, you can add code to the setter that makes sure that the field is never assigned `null` or another undesirable value.

# Instance method overriding

Since, as we have seen in the previous section, class (or static) members cannot override each other but only hide, we can talk about overriding instance members, only. We have also already established that instance fields hide each other and the rules of field hiding are quite different from the much simpler rules of method overriding, so the best practice would be to not expose instance fields and access their values via getters and setters only. This way, instance member overriding is reduced to instance method overriding, and that is what we are going to describe in this section.

The rules for instance method overriding are not different than the rules for interface default method overriding: a method in a child class overrides the method in a parent class with the same signature. If the signatures are different, but the method name is the same, the method is overloaded, not overridden. So, if you would like to override a method, it is always advisable to add the `@Override` annotation to the method to make sure it is not just overloaded silently.

As we have established earlier, too, a static method in a child class cannot override an instance method from the parent class. It makes class instance overriding rules much simpler than interface overriding rules.

One important feature to note is that constructors, although they look like methods, are not methods or even members of the class. A constructor doesn't have a return type and has the same name as the class. Therefore, a constructor cannot be overridden, but it can be overloaded. Its only purpose is to be called when a new instance of the class (object) is created.

With that, we move to the last subsection of the *Overloading, overriding, and hiding* section: instance method overloading.

# Instance method overloading

For instance method overloading, there are just two statements to describe it:

- For a non-static method to be overloaded, it has to have the same name and a different set of parameter types as another non-static method of the same class or the class that has a parent-child relationship with the class that contains the overloaded method
- A private non-static method can be overloaded only by a non-static method of the same class.

So, here is an example of method overloading:

```
void m() {
  // some code
}
int m(String s){
  // some code
  return 1;
}
void m(int i){
  // some code
}
```

```
int m(String s, double d){
    // some code
    return 1;
}
int m(double d, String s){
    // some code
    return 1;
}
```

As you can see, the name of the overloaded method stays the same, but the number of parameters, their type, or the sequence of parameter types, must be different. Otherwise, it is not overloading and the compiler will generate an error. The returned type does not play any role in the overloading. It can be the same or different.

To look at it from another perspective, all the overloaded methods are considered different. In the previous example, we could just give a different name to each method and have exactly the same code behavior. So, overloading is useful when you have several methods with the same functionality (that's why you don't want to change the method name), but different parameters or different parameter types.

Here is one possible case of overloading use. You might remember one of the first classes we created was called `SimpleMath`:

```
public class SimpleMath {
    public int multiplyByTwo(int i){
        return i * 2;
    }
}
```

Then, we might want to add to it another method that, for user convenience, will accept a number as a `String` type: `multiplyByTwo(String s)`. We could do it the following way:

```
public class SimpleMath {
    public int multiplyByTwo(int i){
        return 2 * i;
    }
    public int multiplyByTwo(String s){
        int i = Integer.parseInt(s);
        return 2 * i;
    }
}
```

Or, if we would like to keep the complicated code of multiplying by two in one place (so we can change it in one place only if there is a need to modify it), we could write the following:

```
public class SimpleMath {
    public int multiplyByTwo(int i){
        return 2 * i;
    }
    public int multiplyByTwo(String s){
        int i = Integer.parseInt(s);
        return multiplyByTwo(i);
    }
}
```

A constructor cannot be overloaded in the same manner:

```
public class SimpleMath {
    private int i;
    private String s;
    public SimpleMath() {
    }
    public SimpleMath(int i) {
        this.i = i;
    }
    public SimpleMath(String s) {
        this.s = s;
    }
    // Other methods that use values of the fields i and s
    // go here
}
```

With that, we conclude the topic of overloading, overriding, and hiding. It is time to explain in more detail the use of the keywords this (used earlier) and super (not used yet), and talk more about constructors.

# This, super, and constructors

The keyword this provides a reference to the current object. The keyword super refers to the parent class object. A constructor is used to initialize the object state (values of the instance fields). It can be accessed using the keywords new, this, or super.

# Keyword this and its usage

We saw several examples of its usage in a constructor similar to the following:

```
public SimpleMath(int i) {
  this.i = i;
}
```

It allows us to clearly distinguish between the object property and local variable, especially when they have the same name.

Another use of the keyword `this` can be demonstrated in the implementation of the method `equals()` in the following `Person` class:

```
public class Person {
  private String firstName;
  private String lastName;
  private LocalDate dob;
  public Person(String firstName, String lastName, LocalDate dob) {
    this.firstName = firstName;
    this.lastName = lastName;
    this.dob = dob;
  }
  public String getFirstName() { return firstName; }
  public String getLastName() { return lastName; }
  public LocalDate getDob() { return dob; }

  @Override
  public boolean equals(Object other){
    if (other == null) return false;
    if (this == other) return true;
    if (!(other instanceof Person)) return false;
    final Person that = (Person) other;
    return this.getFirstName().equals(that.getFirstName()) &&
           this.getLastName().equals(that.getLastName()) &&
           this.getDob().equals(that.getDob());
  }
}
```

The reason we need to override the `equals()` method in the parent class `java.lang.Object` (which is the default parent class for all Java classes) is that we would like two objects of the class `Person` to be equal not only when they are actually the same object, but also when the value of each property of one object is the same as the value of the corresponding property of another object. As you can see, we have added an annotation `@Override` to make sure that this method does override the method `equals()` in the parent class `java.lang.Object`. Otherwise, if we make a mistake in the method signature, it may just overload the method `equals()` in the class `java.lang.Object` or, if we make mistake in the method name, be added as just another unrelated to the `equals()` method and we never know about it or would struggle to understand why two different objects of class `Person` are not equal, although all their property values are the same.

The first line checks if the passed in reference value is `null`. If yes, the returned value is `false` because, obviously, the current (`this`) object is not `null`.

The second line of our method `equals()` checks the equality of the references and returns `true` if they refer the same object. This is the same way the default `equals()` method in the parent class `Object` works.

The third line of our method `equals()` checks if the object `other` is an instance of the class `Person`. We need this line because in the next line we are casting the object `other` to the type `Person` in order to be able to access the getters of `Person`. If the object `other` cannot be cast to the type `Person` (which means the reference `other` does not refer an object that has class `Person` as a direct or indirect parent) the fourth line will throw an exception and break the flow of the execution (JVM will exit with an error). So, we check and make sure that the object `other` has the class `Person` in its ancestry and will not break the execution flow during casting.

The last line of our new method, `equals()`, is a Boolean expression (we will talk about such expressions in `Chapter 9`, *Operators, Expressions, and Statements*) that compares the values of three properties of the current object with the corresponding values of another object and returns `true` only if each of the three fields have the same value in both objects.

Let's create a unit test for our new method, `equals()`:

```
public class PersonTest {
  @Test
  void equals() {
    LocalDate dob = LocalDate.of(2001, 01, 20);
    LocalDate dob1 = LocalDate.of(2001, 01, 21);

    Person p = new Person("Joe", "Blow", dob);
```

```
        assertTrue(p.equals(p));
        assertTrue(p.equals(new Person("Joe", "Blow", dob)));

        assertFalse(p.equals(new Person("Joe1", "Blow", dob)));
        assertFalse(p.equals(new Person("Joe", "Blow1", dob)));
        assertFalse(p.equals(new Person("Joe", "Blow", dob1)));
        assertFalse(p.equals( new Person("Joe1", "Blow1", dob1)));
    }
}
```

As you can see, we have created two objects for different dates of birth. Then, we create a `Person` object and compare it:

- To itself—should be equal
- To another object with the same state (property values)—should be equal
- To another object with the first name different only—should not be equal
- To another object with the last name different only —should not be equal
- To another object with the date of birth different only —should not be equal
- To another object with all property values different—should not be equal

We run this test and get the green color of success.

But then, we decide to test what happens if one or all the values are `null` and add the following lines to the test:

```
assertFalse(p.equals(null));
assertFalse(p.equals(new Person(null, "Blow", dob)));
assertFalse(p.equals(new Person("Joe", null, dob)));
assertFalse(p.equals(new Person(null, null, dob)));
assertFalse(p.equals(new Person(null, null, null)));

assertTrue(new Person(null, "Blow", dob)
    .equals(new Person(null, "Blow", dob)));
assertTrue(new Person("Joe", null, dob)
    .equals(new Person("Joe", null, dob)));
assertTrue(new Person("Joe", "Blow", null)
    .equals(new Person("Joe", "Blow", null)));
assertTrue(new Person(null, null, null)
    .equals(new Person(null, null, null)));
```

First, we compare the existing object with all properties not `null` and a new object that has either one property or all properties set to `null`. We expect the first four comparisons to tell us the objects are not equal. Then, we compare two objects with the same state that have one or all values set to `null`. We expect all the pairs to be reported as equal.

If we run the test, here is what we get:

```
java.lang.NullPointerException
    at com.packt.javapath.ch06demo.Person.equals(Person.java:57) <4 internal calls>
    at com.packt.javapath.ch06demo.PersonTest.equals(PersonTest.java:35)
    at java.base/jdk.internal.reflect.NativeMethodAccessorImpl.invoke0(Native Method)
```

The error (a `NullPointerExceptions`) indicates that we are trying to call a method on a reference that is not assigned yet (has a `null` value) in line 57 of the class `Person`. Here is that line:

```
return this.getFirstName().equals(that.getFirstName()) &&
       this.getLastName().equals(that.getLastName()) &&
       this.getDob().equals(that.getDob());
```

We realize that all the getters return a `null` value when we call them on the method `equals()`, which is the source of `NullPointerException`. We need to change either our implementation of the method `equals()` (taking into account the possibility of a `null` value) or change the implementation of the constructor (and not allow the values passed in to be `null`). Very often, the decision can be made based on the business requirements. For example, is it possible, that in the data we are going to process there could be a person without a first name, last name, date of birth, or even any of these values? The last one—a person without any properties—is probably not realistic. Yet, the real data often comes with errors and the question we might ask our business folks (also called domain experts) is how the code should process such cases. Then, we change the code to reflect the new requirements.

Let's assume they have told us that one or even two properties can be `null` and we should handle such cases as if they are not `null`. But, they said, we should not process a case when all the properties are `null`.

After reviewing the new requirements, we go to the domain experts again and suggest, for example, that we convert `null` values of `String` type into the empty literal `""` and the `LocalDate` type into the date as of January 1, zero years, but only when not all values are `null`. We skip the person data when all the values are `null` after adding a corresponding record to a log file. They suggest we allow the first and last name to be `null` and convert them to the empty `String` type literal `""`, but do not process a person without a date of birth and make a record of such a case in a log file. So, we change the constructor as follows:

```
public Person(String firstName, String lastName, LocalDate dob) {
    this.firstName = firstName == null ? "" : firstName;
    this.lastName = lastName == null ? "" : lastName;
```

```
    this.dob = dob;
    if(dob == null){
        throw new RuntimeException("Date of birth is null");
    }
}
```

And our test section that handles the null values changes to the following:

```
assertFalse(p.equals(null));
assertFalse(p.equals(new Person(null, "Blow", dob)));
assertFalse(p.equals(new Person("Joe", null, dob)));
assertFalse(p.equals(new Person(null, null, dob)));
try {
    new Person("Joe", "Blow", null);
} catch (RuntimeException ex){
    assertNotNull(ex.getMessage());
    //add the record ex.getMessage() to the log here
}

assertTrue(new Person(null, "Blow", dob)
    .equals(new Person(null, "Blow", dob)));
assertTrue(new Person("Joe", null, dob)
    .equals(new Person("Joe", null, dob)));
assertTrue(new Person(null, null, dob)
    .equals(new Person(null, null, dob)));
```

We run it and get the green color of success.

That was an example of the use of the keyword `this`. We will show another example in the *Constructors* section. And there is a very important case of the use of the keyword `this` at the end of the *Final variable* section, too. You do not want to miss it! Otherwise, it can be a source of bugs that are very difficult to find.

And now, we will explain how the keyword `super` is used.

# Keyword super and its usage

The keyword `super` represents the parent class object. To demonstrate its usage, let's create a programming model of a vehicle, a truck, and a car. Let's start with a vehicle. The class that models it calculates the speed of the vehicle it can reach in a specified period of time, in seconds. It looks as follows:

```
public class Vehicle {
    private int weightPounds, horsePower;
    public Vehicle(int weightPounds, int horsePower) {
```

```
        this.weightPounds = weightPounds;
        this.horsePower = horsePower;
    }
    protected int getWeightPounds(){ return this.weightPounds; }
    protected double getSpeedMph(double timeSec, int weightPounds){
        double v =
            2.0 * this.horsePower * 746 * timeSec * 32.174 / weightPounds;
        return Math.round(Math.sqrt(v) * 0.68);
    }
}
```

The class has two properties set by the constructor and two protected methods. Protected is an access modifier that means the method can be accessed only by the children of this class. We will talk more about access modifiers in Chapter 7, *Packages and Accessibility (Visibility)*.

The Car and Truck classes(which model a car and a truck) can extend this class and inherit the two protected methods, so they can be used for calculating the car and truck speed. There are other possible ways to organize code. Generally, using aggregation (setting the Vehicle object as a field value of the Car and Truck classes ) is preferred, unless one has a reason to have a common parent (we will talk about this in Chapter 8, *Object-Oriented Design (OOD) Principles*). But for now, let's assume that we have a good reason to use inheritance, so we can demonstrate the use of the keyword super. And it sort of makes sense, in general: a car and a truck are both vehicles, aren't they?

So, here is how the class Truck looks:

```
public class Truck extends Vehicle {
    private int payloadPounds;
    public Truck(int payloadPounds, int weightPounds, int horsePower) {
        super(weightPounds, horsePower);
        this.payloadPounds = payloadPounds;
    }
    public void setPayloadPounds(int payloadPounds) {
        this.payloadPounds = payloadPounds;
    }
    protected int getWeightPounds(){
        return this.payloadPounds + getWeightPounds();
    }
    public double getSpeedMph(double timeSec){
        return getSpeedMph(timeSec, getWeightPounds());
    }
}
```

The class has one property: the current payload weight the truck has. It factors in the speed calculations. The heavier the payload, the longer it takes the truck to reach the same speed. Since the payload weight may change any time after the object is created, the setter for the payload weight is provided, and the protected method getWeightPounds() returns the total weight of the vehicle with its payload. The main method and the purpose of all the modeling is the method getSpeedMph(), which returns the truck's speed (in miles per hour) it can reach in timeSec seconds after it starts.

But, we now discuss the use of the keyword super. You probably noticed that it was already included in the constructor. As you can guess, it represents the constructor of the parent class. In such cases, the keyword super has to be the first line of the child constructor. We will talk about it in the next section, *Constructors*.

And here is the class that models car speed:

```
public class Car extends Vehicle {
  private int passengersCount;
  public Car(int passengersCount, int weightPounds, int horsePower) {
    super(weightPounds , horsePower);
    this.passengersCount = passengersCount;
  }
  public void setPassengersCount(int passengersCount) {
    this.passengersCount = passengersCount;
  }

  protected int getWeightPounds(){
    return this.passengersCount * 200 + getWeightPounds(); }
  public double getSpeedMph(double timeSec){
    return getSpeedMph(timeSec, getWeightPounds());
  }
}
```

It looks very similar to the class Truck. The only difference is the way the payload is calculated. It is assumed that each passenger ways 200 pounds. Thus, when the passenger count is set, the payload is calculated as the number of passengers multiplied by 200.

Both classes—Car and Truck—have a defect (also called a bug, or an error). To discover it, let's try to calculate a truck's speed 10 seconds from the start time by running the following code:

```
Truck truck = new Truck(500, 2000, 300);
System.out.println(truck.getSpeedMph(10));
```

If we do that, the result will be a `StackOverflowError` error:

```
Exception in thread "main" java.lang.StackOverflowError
    at com.packt.javapath.ch06demo.transport.Truck.getWeightPounds(Truck.java:14)
    at com.packt.javapath.ch06demo.transport.Truck.getWeightPounds(Truck.java:14)
    at com.packt.javapath.ch06demo.transport.Truck.getWeightPounds(Truck.java:14)
```

A stack is the JVM memory area where the chain of method calls is stored. The last method name called is stored on the top. When the last method called is completed, its name is removed from the top and the next method is executed, and so on until the stack is empty—that is, when the `main()` method is completed—and the application completes its execution (JVM exits).

In our case, the stack grew uncontrollably and eventually overflowed. The JVM could not add another method name on the top of the stack and exited with an error. The reason for such a condition is a recursive call our code requested in this line:

```
protected int getWeightPounds(){
   return this.payloadPounds + getWeightPounds();
}
```

We wanted to add the truck payload to the weight of the vehicle itself, stored as the property in the parent class, but instead told the JVM to call the same method, which calls itself recursively, because this method is overridden and has the same name in the child class. That is where the keyword `super` comes to the rescue. By adding it in front of the method `getWeightPounds()`, we tell the JVM to call not the child's method, but the parent's one:

```
protected int getWeightPounds(){
   return this.payloadPounds + super.getWeightPounds();
}
```

If we run the same code again, we will get the expected result:

```
163.0

Process finished with exit code 0
```

Well, our speed calculating formula seems over-optimistic. But who knows? Maybe by the time the book is printed, electric trucks will be closing in on this speed or hyperloop traffic will get there.

Also, please notice that we have not added `super` in front of the same method in the code that calculates speed:

```
public double getSpeedMph(double timeSec){
    return getSpeedMph(timeSec, getWeightPounds());
}
```

That is because we do not want to call the method of the parent class. Instead, we would like to get the weight from its overridden version in the child class. To make sure, and to avoid confusion by making code more easily readable, we could add the keyword `this` in front of it:

```
public double getSpeedMph(double timeSec){
    return getSpeedMph(timeSec, this.getWeightPounds());
}
```

In fact, that is one of the best practices that we recommend to follow at all times.

That concludes the discussion of the use of the keyword `super`. We will see it again, and the keyword `this`, in the *Constructors* section too, where we are going to explain how the constructors do their job and what a default constructor is.

# Constructors

An object is an instance of a class used as the template for object creation. Each object is defined by its state and behavior. The object's state is defined by the values of its fields (also called properties), the object behavior by its methods. Since all Java objects are descendants of `java.lang.Object`, it is not possible to have an object without state and behavior because every object inherits its methods and some basic state from `java.lang.Object`. But when we talk about application code, classes, and objects this code creates, we mean the methods and state we define in order to build the functionality we want. In this sense, it is possible to have an object without methods. Such objects are usually called data objects, data structures, or data transfer objects. And it is possible to have objects without a state, with methods only. Such objects are often called utilities.

If an object can have a state, the state has to be initialized during object creation. It means that some values have to be assigned to the variables that represent the object fields. This initial assignment can be done either using an assignment operator, =, explicitly or by letting the JVM assign the default values to the object's fields. What these default values are depends on the field type. We have discussed the default value of each type in Chapter 5, *Java Language Elements and Types*. Primitive numeric types have the default type of zero, the Boolean type `false`, and the reference type `null`.

An object is created using the operator new. This operator requires specifying the constructor that has to be used for object creation. The primary duty of a constructor is to initialize the object state. But, there are three cases when an explicit definition of a constructor in the class is not required:

- When neither the object nor any of its parents can have a state (no fields are defined)
- When an initial value is assigned to each field along with the type declaration (int x = 42;)
- When default values are good enough (for example, the field int x; is initialized to the value of zero by default)

How then can an object be created? The operator new expects the constructor. The answer is that in such a case—when there is no constructor explicitly defined in a class—a default constructor is generated for the class by the compiler. This default constructor looks like the following:

```
public ClassName(){
    super();
}
```

As you can see, it does only one thing: calls the constructor (the one without parameters) of the parent class using the keyword super. This parent constructor without parameters may be a default one too, or may be explicitly created. And here resides a possible source of confusion: if a class has an explicitly defined constructor, the default one (without parameters) is not generated automatically. The reason for this limitation is that it puts the programmer in command and lets the class author decide whether to add a constructor without parameters to the class or not. Otherwise, imagine you have created a class, Person, and do not want to allow an instance of this class without certain fields populated. And you do not want these values to be the default ones, but would like to force the client code to populate them explicitly every time a new Person object is created. That's why no constructor is going to be generated automatically behind the scenes as soon as at least one constructor—with or without parameters—is defined in a class. Let's test this behavior. Here are two classes without explicitly defined constructors (or any code at all for that matter):

```
public class Parent {
}
public class Child extends Parent{
}
```

We can run the following code just fine:

```
new Child();
```

It does not do anything, but that is not the point. Let's add a constructor with a parameter to the parent class:

```
public class Parent {
  public Parent(int i) {
  }
}
```

If we try to create an object of the class `Child` again, we will get an error:

Click on the red line to see this error message in IntelliJ, because the compiler error message is not as helpful:

It identifies the explicitly defined constructor (with a parameter of type `int`) as required and its list of parameters as a formal argument list. Meanwhile, a default constructor of the class `Child` attempts (as we described before) to call a no-arguments constructor of the class `Parent` and cannot find one. The error wording is not very clear on that.

So, let's add a constructor without parameters to the class `Parent`:

```
public class Parent {
  public Parent() {
  }
  public Parent(int i) {
  }
}
```

An object of the class `Child` can now be created without any problems. That is how the class author can control the process of object creation.

And if you decide that the `Parent` object has to be created using a constructor with parameters only, you can remove the no-arguments constructor from it again and add to the class `Child` a constructor that calls the `Parent` constructor with parameters:

```
public class Child extends Parent{
  public Child() {
    super(10);
  }
}
```

Or, you can add to the child a constructor with parameters:

```
public class Child extends Parent{
  public Child(int i) {
    super(i);
  }
}
```

Any of these work just fine.

From this demonstration, you have probably realized that in order to create an object of a child, all its parent objects have to be created (and their state initialized) first. And it has to be done starting from the most ancient ancestor. Let's look at the following example:

```
public class GrandDad{
  private String name = "GrandDad";
  public GrandDad() {
    System.out.println(name);
  }
}
public class Parent extends GrandDad{
  private String name = "Parent";
  public Parent() {
    System.out.println(name);
  }
}
public class Child extends Parent{
  private String name = "Child";
  public Child() {
    System.out.println(name);
  }
}
```

Can you guess what the output is going to be if we try to create the child new Child()? If you guessed the GrandDad constructor finishes first, then Parent, then Child, you are correct. Here is the result:

```
GrandDad
Parent
Child
```

The Child constructor calls the Parent constructor, which in turn calls the GrandDad constructor, which calls the java.lang.Object constructor. Only after a parent object has been created (and its constructor has finished doing what it had to do) does the child constructor finish executing, and so on through the chain of parent-child relations.

After thinking a moment, we decide to derive the value of the field name from the class name. Every Java object has a base class, java.lang.Object, which provides access to the class information via the method getClass(). This method returns an object of the class java.lang.Class with all the information about the class used as a template for the object, including its name. Naturally, we first consider using this.getClass().getName() to get the class name inside Child, Parent, and GrandDad. But, if we start the chain of calls by calling new Child() (as we do in our example), the construct this.getClass().getName() always returns the name of the class Child, even when we use the construct in GrandDad.

The reason is that, although the keyword this represents the current object (the GrandDad object, for example, if this is used in GrandDad), the method getClass() returns information *not about the current object*, but about the *runtime* object (the one that was created by the operator new) which is an instance of Child in this case. That is why, in our example, the construct this.getClass().getName() always returns the name of the class Child, whether this construct is used inside Child, Parent, or GrandDad.

But there is another way to access the class information that better suits our needs. We can use the class name explicitly, add the extension .class to it, and only then get the class name. Here is an example:

```
GrandDad.class.getSimpleName(); //always returns "GrandDad"
```

It seems like it's not much different from using the String literal we used before, does it? Nevertheless, it is an improvement because, if the name of the class changes, the value assigned to the variable NAME will change, too, while in the case of a String literal, its value is not tied to the name of the class automatically.

So, we have added a static field NAME with initialization to each of our three classes:

```
public class GrandDad{
  private static String NAME = GrandDad.class.getSimpleName();
  public GrandDad() {
    System.out.println(NAME);
  }
}
public class Parent extends GrandDad{
  private static String NAME = Parent.class.getSimpleName();
  public Parent() {
    System.out.println(NAME);
  }
}
public class Child extends Parent{
  private static String NAME = Child.class.getSimpleName();
  public Child() {
    System.out.println(NAME);
  }
}
```

Notice that we have followed the convention of writing static variable identifiers in uppercase only.

If we call new Child(), the result will be as follows:

If we add a constructor with a parameter, the code will look as follows:

```
public class GrandDad{
  private static String NAME = GrandDad.class.getSimpleName()
  public GrandDad() {
    System.out.println(NAME);
  }
  public GrandDad(String familyName) {
    System.out.println(familyName + ": " + NAME);
  }
}
public class Parent extends GrandDad{
  private static String NAME = Parent.class.getSimpleName()
  public Parent() {
    System.out.println(NAME);
  }
}
```

```
    public Parent(String familyName) {
      System.out.println(familyName + ": " + NAME);
    }
}
public class Child extends Parent{
    private static String NAME = Child.class.getSimpleName()
    public Child() {
      System.out.println(NAME);
    }
    public Child(String familyName) {
      System.out.println(familyName + ": " + NAME);
    }
}
```

The execution of the line `new Child("The Blows")` will now change the output only for the child:

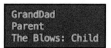

That is because the new child's constructor continues to call the parent's constructor without parameters by default. To engage the new parent's constructor, we need to do it explicitly, using the keyword `super` (we show only the constructors here):

```
public GrandDad(String familyName) {
  System.out.println(familyName + ": " + NAME);
}
public Parent(String familyName) {
  super(familyName);
  System.out.println(familyName + ": " + NAME);
}
public Child(String familyName) {
  super(familyName);
  System.out.println(familyName + ": " + NAME);
}
```

By executing the same line, `new Child("The Blows")`, we get the desired result:

Please notice that the keyword `super` has to be the first line of a constructor. If you try to put it anywhere else, an error will be generated. That is because all the constructors have to be completely executed before any other code can be invoked. All the objects in the parent-child chain have to be created and their state initialized first, starting from the topmost base class.

The last constructor-related feature that we would like to mention here is this: one constructor can call another constructor of the same class by using the keyword `this`. For example, let's say we do not want a family to exist without a family name, but the client code might never be able to supply one. So, we decide to add a default family name to the constructor without parameters:

```
public class Child extends Parent{
   private static String NAME = Child.class.getSimpleName()
   public Child() {
     this("The Defaults");
   }
   public Child(String familyName) {
     super(familyName);
     System.out.println(familyName + ": " + NAME);
   }
}
```

If we execute the line `new Child()` again, we will get the following:

```
The Defaults: GrandDad
The Defaults: Parent
The Defaults: Child
```

As you can see, the constructors of the same class can be overloaded and call each other the same way the methods do. But constructors are not inherited and thus cannot be hidden or overridden. That is just impossible.

As for any other method, it can be overridden if not private or final. What is private; you probably already have an idea. We will talk about it in more detail in Chapter 7, *Packages and Accessibility (Visibility)*. And we will talk about *Final variable* in the next section.

# Final variable, final method, or final class

The use of the keyword `final` and its effects depend on the context. It can make a variable value unchangeable, a method not overridable, or a class not extendable. We will briefly discuss each of this situations.

# Final variable

If a keyword `final` is placed in front of a variable declaration, the value of this variable once assigned (the variable is initialized) cannot be changed. The way a variable can be initialized depends on how the variable is used. There are three kinds of variable usage, and each has different initialization rules:

- A local variable is a variable declared in the block of code; it can be initialized using an assignment in the same statement with the declaration, or sometime later, but only once; here are some examples:

```
class SomeClass{
  private String someValue = "Initial value";
  public void setSomeValue(String someValue) {
    this.someValue = someValue;
  }
  public String getSomeValue() {
    return someValue;
  }
}
public class FinalDemo {
  public static void main(String... args) {
    final SomeClass o = new SomeClass();
    System.out.println(o.getSomeValue());    //Initial value
    o.setSomeValue("Another value");
    System.out.println(o.getSomeValue());    //Another value
    o.setSomeValue("Yet another value");
    System.out.println(o.getSomeValue());    //Yet another value

    final String s1, s2;
    final int x, y;
    y = 2;
    int v = y + 2;
    x = v - 4;
    System.out.println("x = " + x);          //x = 0
    s1 = "1";
    s2 = s1 + " and 2";
    System.out.println(s2);                  // 1 and 2
    //o = new SomeClass();                    //error
    //s2 = "3";                               //error
    //x = 5;                                  //error
    //y = 6;                                  //error
  }
}
```

The primitive types' final variables—after they are initialized the first time—become just constants and cannot be changed (see the last two lines that are commented as error). Similarly, the reference type String type final variable cannot be changed too, because of the String type immutability discussed in Chapter 5, *Java Language Elements and Types*. But other reference type objects, including arrays, are just referred to by the final variables. So, the reference itself cannot be changed (or reassigned) and remains a constant, too. But the state of the referred object can be changed, as demonstrated previously, using an object of SomeClass.

- An instance variable can be initialized using an assignment in the same statement as the declaration (the same way as a local variable), using an instance initialization block, or in a constructor:

```
public class FinalDemo {
  final SomeClass o = new SomeClass();
  final String s1 = "Initial value";
  final String s2;
  final String s3;
  final int i = 1;
  final int j;
  final int k;
  {
    j = 2;
    s2 = "new value";
  }
  public FinalDemo() {
    k = 3;
    s3 = "new value";
  }
  public void method(){
    //this.i = 4;          //error
    //this.j = 4;          //error
    //this.k = 4;          //error
    //this.s3 = "";        //error
    this.o.setSomeValue("New value");
  }
}
```

But, after the initialization, the primitive types and String values of the final instance variable cannot be changed, while the properties of an object (or components of an array) can, similar to the final local variable.

- The (`static`) class final variable can be initialized using an assignment in the same statement as the declaration (the same way as a local or instance variable), or using a static initialization block:

```
public class FinalDemo {
    final static SomeClass OBJ = new SomeClass();
    final static String S1 = "Initial value";
    final static String S2;
    final static int INT1 = 1;
    final static int INT2;
    static {
        INT2 = 2;
        S2 = "new value";
    }
    void method2(){
        OBJ.setSomeValue("new value");
        //OBJ = new SomeClass();
        //S1 = "";
        //S2 = "";
        //INT1 = 0;
        //INT2 = 0;
    }
}
```

As in the cases of local and instance final variables, the static final variables of primitive types and `String` become constants after the first assignment, while the property of an object (or components of an array) can be changed many times later.

If you think you never saw a final variable before this section, please notice that an interface field is final implicitly. Once assigned, it cannot be changed. There are two other kinds of variable that are implicitly final: a variable declared as a resource of a `try...with...resources` statement (we will see examples in Chapter 16, *Database Programming*) and an exception parameter of a multi-catch clause (we will talk about them in Chapter 10, *Control Flow Statements*).

Final variables are important for security, but we are not going to talk about security in this book. Instead, we will see many uses of final variables during the discussion of Java functional programming in Chapter 17, *Lambda Expressions and Functional Programming*.

While reading other people's code, you might notice that the method parameters are declared final:

```
void someMethod(final int i, final String s, final SomeClass o){
    //...
}
```

It is often done with an intent to prevent the side effects of changing values outside the method. But we have demonstrated already in Chapter 5, *Java Language Elements and Types*, of primitive types are passed as copies and their re-assignment changes only the copy, not the original. In the case of the reference type String, we also demonstrated in the same chapter that its value is immutable because, for every String variable reassignment, a new copy of the value is created and the original value is not affected. As for the other reference types, making the reference itself final helps only to prevent an assignment of a new object. But if that is not the case, the reference being final does not prevent a change of properties of the original object outside the method.

So, unless it is really necessary (for anonymous classes, for example, or a few other cases—the compiler and IDE will tell you about them), making these variables final prevents reassigning them a new value only inside the method, and does not help to avoid side effects outside the method.

Some programmers also argue that declaring variables final wherever possible makes the code author's intent easier to understand. That is true, but only if the convention is followed consistently and all variables that can be declared final are declared final. Otherwise, if some variables are declared final and some not (although they could be), the code may be misleading. One could think that the variables without the final keyword in front of them are declared so intentionally because they are reassigned to a different value somewhere. If you are not the code author (or even if you are the code author, but you are looking at the code after a period of time), you can reasonably assume that there might be a branch of logic that takes advantage of a certain variable not being final. You are reluctant to add final to the existing variables because you are not sure if that was just missed or omitted intentionally, which means that the code is not clearer and the idea of more readable code falls apart.

To be fair, there is a class of difficult to discover errors that can be easily avoided if one applies the keyword final wherever one can. Please look at this example:

```
class FinalVariable{
    private int i;
    public FinalVariable() { this.i = 1; }
    public void setInt(int i){
        this.i = 100;
```

```
            i = i;
      }
      public int getInt(){
            return this.i;
      }
}
```

This class has a field `i` that is initialized in the constructor to the value 1. The class also has a getter and setter for this field. In the setter, the programmer made a mistake. Can you spot it? Let's run the following code:

```
FinalVariable finalVar = new FinalVariable();
System.out.println("Initial setting: finalVar.getInt()=" +
                                        finalVar.getInt());
finalVar.setInt(5);
System.out.println("After setting to 5: finalVar.getInt()=" +
                                        finalVar.getInt());
```

In the code, we create an object of class `FinalVariable`. The constructor assigns it the value of 1 and we confirm it using the getter. Then, we try to assign it the value of 5 and expect the getter to return this value. Instead, we get the following output:

```
Initial setting: finalVar.getInt()=1
After setting to 5: finalVar.getInt()=100
```

Let's see what happens if we declare the parameter `final`, as follows:

```
public void setInt(final int i){
   this.i = 100;
   i = i;
}
```

The compiler and IDE would warn us that we are trying to assign the variable `i` to another value. We would see the problem and fix it like this:

```
public void setInt(final int i){
      this.i = 100;
      this.i = i;
}
```

And the code would start behaving as we expected:

```
Initial setting: finalVar.getInt()=1
After setting to 5: finalVar.getInt()=5
```

But there are not many such cases, and soon you are going to learn how to avoid such pitfalls and start adding `this` in front of the instance variable automatically. So, in our opinion, extensive use of the keyword `final` as the way to improve code quality is not justified, but some programmers still prefer doing that, so we leave it as a matter of programming style.

By the way, adding the keyword `final` as a way to improve application performance is reportedly useful in some special cases, but we have not encountered these cases ourselves and thus leave it to those who can demonstrate such a case.

# Final method

The keyword `final` in front of a method makes it impossible to override it in a child class instance or hide if, the method is static. It provides an assurance that the method functionality cannot be changed through overriding. The class `java.lang.Object`, for example, has many of its methods as final.

But if a final method uses non-final ones, this may allow for the backdoor introduction of undesirable changes. Naturally, such considerations are very important for security.

Sometimes, one can read that making methods final can improve code performance. It may be the case, but in some very specific situations and does not seem to help significantly in mainstream programming. For performance improvements, there are usually much better opportunities available, including the proven object-oriented design principles (see `Chapter 8`, *Object-Oriented Design (OOD) Principles*).

All private methods and methods of a final class (which are not inherited) are effectively final because one cannot override them.

# Final class

A class declared final cannot be extended. That is, it cannot have children, which makes all the methods of the class effectively final.

This feature is widely used for security or when a programmer would like to make sure the class functionality cannot be overridden, overloaded, or hidden.

# Exercise – Restricting a class instantiation to a single shared instance

Write a class in such a way that it guarantees that only one object can be created.

## Answer

Here is one possible solution:

```
public class SingletonClassExample {
  private static SingletonClassExample OBJECT = null;

  private SingletonClassExample(){}

  public final SingletonClassExample getInstance() {
    if(OBJECT == null){
      OBJECT = new SingletonClassExample();
    }
    return OBJECT;
  }

  //... other class functionality
}
```

Another solution could be to make the class private inside the factory class and store it in the factory field, similarly to the previous code.

Be aware, though, that if such a single object has a state that is changing, one has to make sure it is acceptable to modify the state and rely on it concurrently, because this object may be used by different methods at the same time.

# Summary

One of the most often used terms, API, was thoroughly discussed in this chapter, as well as the related topics of object factories, overriding, hiding, and overloading. Also, the use of the keywords `this` and `super` was explored in detail and demonstrated during the explanation of constructors. The chapter concluded with an overview of the keyword `final` and its use for local variables, fields, methods, and classes.

In the next chapter, we will describe package and class member accessibility (also called visibility), which will help us to expand on one of the key object-oriented programming concepts, encapsulation. It will lay the foundation for our discussion of object-oriented design principles.

# 7
# Packages and Accessibility (Visibility)

By now, you are already quite familiar with packages. In this chapter, we will complete its description and then discuss different levels of accessibility (also called visibility) of classes and class members – methods and fields. It all will come down to the key concept of object-oriented programming – the encapsulation – and lay the foundation for our discussion of object-oriented design principles.

In this chapter, we will cover the following topics:

- What is importing?
- Static importing
- Interface access modifiers
- Class access modifiers
- Method access modifiers
- Property access modifiers
- Encapsulation
- Exercise – Shadowing

## What is importing?

Importing allows us to specify a fully qualified class or interface name only once at the beginning of the `.java` file, before the class or interface declaration. The format of an import statement is as follows:

```
import <package>.<class or interface name>;
```

For example, look at the following:

```
import com.packt.javapath.ch04demo.MyApplication;
```

From now on, this class can be referred to in the code by its name, `MyApplication`, only. It is also possible to import all the classes or interfaces of a package using the wildcard character (*):

```
import com.packt.javapath.ch04demo.*;
```

Notice that the preceding import statement imports classes and interfaces of the subpackages of the `com.packt.javapath.ch04demo` package. If needed, each subpackage has to be imported separately.

But, before we continue, let's talk about the `.java` file structure and packages.

# Structure of the .java file and packages

As you already know, the package name reflects the directory structure, starting with the project directory that contains the `.java` files. The name of each `.java` file has to be the same as the name of the public class defined in it. The first line of the `.java` file is the package statement that starts with the `package` keyword, followed by the actual package name—the directory path to this file, in which slashes are replaced with dots. Let's look at some examples. We will look primarily at the `.java` file that contains a class definition, but we will also look at files with interfaces and the `enum` class definition because there is a particular type of importing (called static importing) that is primarily used with interfaces and `enum`.

We assume that the `src/main/java` (for Linux) or `src\main\java` (for Windows) project directory contains all the `.java` files, and the definition of the `MyClass` and `MyEnum` classes and the `MyInterface` interface from the package `com.packt.javapath` are stored in the files:

```
src/main/java/com/packt/javapath/MyClass.java (for Linux)
src/main/java/com/packt/javapath/MyEnum.java
src/main/java/com/packt/javapath/MyInterface.java
```

or (for Windows)

```
src\main\java\com\packt\javapath\MyClass.java (for Windows)
src\main\java\com\packt\javapath\MyEnum.java
src\main\java\com\packt\javapath\MyInterface.java
```

The first line of each of these files is as follows:

```
package com.packt.javapath;
```

If we do not import anything, then the next line in each file is a class or interface declaration.

The declaration of the `MyClass` class looks like this:

```
public class MyClass extends SomeClass
        implements Interface1, Interface2, ... {...}
```

It consists of the following:

- An access modifier; one of the classes in the file has to be `public`
- The `class` keyword
- The class name (identifier) that starts with a capital letter by convention
- If the class is a child of another class, the `extends` keyword and the name of the parent class
- If the class implements one or more
  interfaces, the `implements` keyword followed by the comma-separated list of interfaces it implements
- The body of the class (where the fields and methods are defined) surrounded by braces, { }

The declaration of the `MyEnum` class looks like this:

```
public enum MyEnum implements Interface1, Interface2, ... {...}
```

It consists of the following:

- An access modifier; it has to be `public` if it is the only class defined in the file
- The `enum` keyword
- The class name (identifier) that starts with a capital letter by convention
- No `extends` keyword because the enum type extends
  the `java.lang.Enum` class implicitly and, in Java, a class can have only one parent
- If the class implements one or more
  interfaces, the `implements` keyword followed by the comma-separated list of interfaces it implements
- The body of the class (where the constants and methods are defined) surrounded by braces, { }

The declaration of the `MyInterface` interface looks like this:

```
public interface MyInterface extends Interface1, Interface2, ... {...}
```

It consists of the following:

- An access modifier; one of the interfaces in the file has to be `public`
- The `interface` keyword
- The interface name (identifier) that starts with a capital letter by convention
- If the interface is a child of one or more interfaces, the `extends` keyword followed by the comma-separated list of the parent interfaces
- The body of the interface (where the fields and methods are defined) surrounded by braces, `{ }`

Without importing, we would need to refer to each class or interface we are using by its fully qualified name, which includes the package name and class, or interface name. For example, the `MyClass` class declaration would look like this:

```
public class MyClass
            extends com.packt.javapath.something.AnotherMyClass
            implements com.packt.javapath.something2.Interface1,
                    com.packt.javapath.something3.Interface2
```

Or, let's say we would like to instantiate the `SomeClass` class from the `com.packt.javapath.something` package. The fully qualified name of that class would be `com.packt.javapath.something.SomeClass` and its object creation statement would look as follows:

```
com.packt.javapath.something.SomeClass someClass =
                new com.packt.javapath.something.SomeClass();
```

It is too verbose, isn't it? This is where package importing comes to the rescue.

# Single class import

To avoid using the fully qualified class or interface name in the code, we can add an import statement in the space between the package declaration and class or interface declaration:

```
package com.packt.javapath;
import com.packt.javapath.something.SomeClass;
public class MyClass {
  //...
  SomeClass someClass = new SomeClass();
  //...
}
```

As you can see, the import statement allows avoiding usage of the fully qualified class name, which makes the code easier to read.

# Multiple classes import

If several classes or interfaces from the same package are imported, it is possible to import all the package members using the asterisk (*) wildcard character.

If SomeClass and SomeOtherClass belong to the same package, then the import statement may look like this:

```
package com.packt.javapath;
import com.packt.javapath.something.*;
public class MyClass {
  //...
  SomeClass someClass = new SomeClass();
  SomeOtherClass someClass1 = new SomeOtherClass();
  //...
}
```

The advantage of using the asterisk is a shorter list of import statements, but such a style hides the names of the imported classes and interfaces. So, the programmer may not know exactly where they come from. Besides, when two or more packages contain members with the same name, you just have to import them explicitly as a single class import. Otherwise, the compiler will generate an error.

On the other hand, the programmers who prefer wildcard importing, argue that it helps to prevent accidentally creating a class with a name that exists already in one of the imported packages. So, you have to make your own choice when it comes to style and configuring your IDE to use or not use the wildcard importing.

In IntelliJ IDEA, the default style of import is using a wildcard. If you would like to switch to a single class import, click on **File** | **Other Settings** | **Default Settings**, as in the following screenshot:

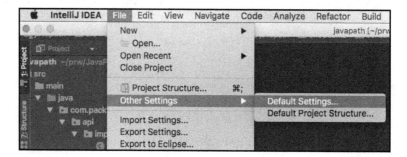

On the screen that opens, select **Editor** | **Java** and check the **Use single class import** checkbox:

There are other settings on this page that you might find useful, so try to remember how to access it.

# Static import

Static import allows importing not just a class or an interface but its public members—fields and methods—individually. If you look in one of our test classes, you will see the following static import statement:

```
import static org.junit.jupiter.api.Assertions.*;
```

This statement allowed us to write the following:

```
Person p = new Person("Joe", "Blow", dob);
assertTrue(p.equals(p));
```

That is instead of writing this:

```
Person p = new Person("Joe", "Blow", dob);
Assertions.assertTrue(p.equals(p));
```

That is one widespread case of static import usage. Another popular case is static importing of constants of an interface or enum. For example, if we have an interface as follows:

```
package com.packt.javapath.api;
public interface Constants {
  String NAME = "name";
}
```

Then, to use its constants, one can import them statically:

```
package com.packt.javapath;
import static com.packt.javapath.api.Constants.*;
public class MyClass {
  //...
  String s = "My " + NAME + " is Joe";
  System.out.println(s);        //Prints: My name is Joe
  //...
}
```

By the way, the same effect could be achieved by importing that Constants interface non-statically and having the class implement it:

```
package com.packt.javapath;
import com.packt.javapath.api.Constants;
public class MyClass implements Constants {
  //...
  String s = "My " + NAME + " is Joe";
  System.out.println(s);        //Prints: My name is Joe
  //...
}
```

This style of implementing an interface in order to use their constants is quite popular among Java programmers.

An example of using static import in order to use the `enum` constants looks similar:

```
import static java.time.DayOfWeek.*;
```

It allows the code to use `DayOfWeek` constants as `MONDAY`, instead of `DayOfWeek.MONDAY`.

# Access modifiers

There are three explicit access modifiers—public, private, and protected—and one implicit (default) access modifier that is implied when no access modifier is set. They can be applied to the top-level class or interface, their members, and constructors. A *top-level* class or interface can include a *member* class or interface. Other *members* of a class or interface are fields and methods. Classes also have *constructors*.

To demonstrate the accessibility, let's create a `com.packt.javapath.Ch07demo.pack01` package that contains two classes and two interfaces:

```
public class PublicClass01 {
  public static void main(String[] args){
    //We will write code here
  }
}

class DefaultAccessClass01 {
}

public interface PublicInterface01 {
  String name = "PublicInterface01";
}

interface DefaultAccessInterface01 {
  String name = "DefaultAccessInterface01";
}
```

We will also create another `com.packt.javapath.Ch07demo.pack02` package with one class in it:

```
public class PublicClass02 {
  public static void main(String[] args){
    //We will write code here
  }
}
```

Each of the preceding classes and interfaces is in its own file:

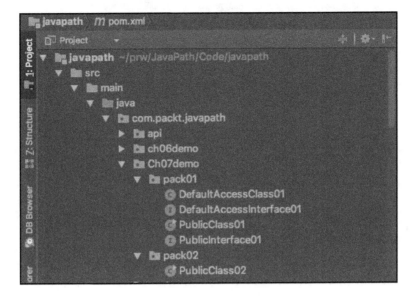

Now we are ready to explore the accessibility of classes, interfaces, their members, and constructors.

# The accessibility of a top-level class or interface

The public class or interface is accessible from anywhere. We can import them and access them from another package:

```
import com.packt.javapath.Ch07demo.pack01.PublicClass01;
import com.packt.javapath.Ch07demo.pack01.PublicInterface01;
//import com.packt.javapath.Ch07demo.pack01.DefaultAccessClass01;
//import com.packt.javapath.Ch07demo.pack01.DefaultAccessInterface01;

public class PublicClass02 {
  public static void main(String[] args){
    System.out.println(PublicInterface01.name);
    PublicClass01 o = new PublicClass01();

  }
}
```

In the preceding code, the two import statements are commented out because they generate an error. That is because in the `DefaultAccessClass01` class and the `DefaultAccessClass01` interface, we did not use the access modifier, which made them accessible only to the members of the same package.

 Without an access modifier, a top-level class or interface can be accessed only by the members of the same package.

Making an access modifier `private` in the declaration of a top-level class or interface make them inaccessible, so using a `private` access modifier for a top-level class or interface does not make sense.

The `protected` keyword cannot be applied to a top level. This limitation is not as obvious. We will see in the next section that `protected` means it is accessible to the package members and the children. So, one could argue that `protected` access can be applicable to a top-level class or interface too. Yet, the Java authors decided not to do it, and the compiler will generate an exception if you try to make a top-level class or interface `protected`.

However, `private` and `protected` access modifiers can be applied to inner classes or interfaces—the members of the top-level class or interface.

## Access to class or interface members

Even when class or interface members are declared public, they cannot be accessed if the enclosing class or interface is inaccessible. So, all of the following discussion will be done under the assumption that the class or interface is accessible.

Members of a class or interface can access other members of the same class or interface no matter what access modifiers they have. Which makes sense, doesn't it? It all happens inside the same enclosing class or interface.

By default, the interface members are public. So, if an interface itself can be accessed, its members without access modifier can be accessed too. And, just to remind you, the interface fields are static and final (constants) by default.

The class members, on the other hand, without an access modifier, are accessible only to the package members. So, the class or interface may be public, but their members are less accessible, if not made public explicitly.

Private class or interface members are accessible only to the other members of the same class or interface. That is the most restricted access possible. Even children of the class cannot access their parents' private members.

Protected package members are accessible to other members of the same package and to the children of the class or interface, which means that protected members can be overridden. And that is often used by programmers as an expression of the intent: they make those members protected that they expect to be overridden. Otherwise, they make them either private or public. Default—no access modifiers—access is rarely used.

**Private**: Allows access from the same class (or interface) only
**No modifier (default)**: Allows access from the same class (or interface) and the same package
**Protected**: Allows access from the same class (or interface), the same package, and any child
**Public**: Allows access from anywhere

The same accessibility rules apply to inner classes and interfaces too. Here is an example of a class that contains inner classes and interfaces:

```
public class PublicClass01 {
    public static void main(String[] args){
        System.out.println(DefaultAccessInterface01.name);
        DefaultAccessClass01 o = new DefaultAccessClass01();
    }
    class DefaultAccessClass{
    }
    protected class ProtectedClass{
    }
    private class PrivateClass{
    }
    interface DefaultAccessInterface {
    }
    protected class ProtectedInterface{
    }
    private class PrivateInterface{
    }
}
```

And here is an interface with an inner class and interface:

```
public interface PublicInterface01 {
   String name = "PublicInterface01";

   class DefaultAccessClass{
   }
   interface DefaultAccessInterface {
   }
}
```

As you can see, only default (public) access is allowed for the inner classes and interfaces of an interface.

And, just to repeat what we have already discussed, we will briefly mention some other related aspects of members accessibility:

- A static nested class (it is an inner class, but is called nested in the case of the static class by convention) cannot access non-static members of the same class, while they can access it
- Being a member of some top-level class, a static nested class can be public, protected, package-accessible (default), or private
- Public, protected, and package-accessible members of a class are inherited by the child

# The constructor's accessibility is the same as any class member

As the title of this section has stated, that is all we can say about the accessibility of a constructor. Naturally, when we talk about constructors, we talk only about classes.

The interesting thing about constructors is their ability to have private access only. It means that a class can provide its own factory method (see Chapter 6, *Interfaces, Classes, and Object Construction*), control how each object is constructed, and even control how many of them can be put into the circulation. The last feature is especially valuable in the case where each object requires access to a certain resource (a file or another database) that has limited support for concurrent access. Here is how the simplest version of such a factory method with a limited number of objects created may look:

```
private String field;
private static int count;
private PublicClass02(String s){
```

```
      this.field = s;
  }
  public static PublicClass02 getInstance(String s){
    if(count > 5){
      return null;
    } else {
      count++;
      return new PublicClass02(s);
    }
  }
}
```

The usefulness of this code is not great and we show it only to demonstrate how a privately accessible constructor can be used. It is possible because each class members can access all other class members no matter their access modifiers.

All the accessibility-related features would be not needed unless they brought some advantages. And that is what we are going to talk about in the next section – about the central concept of object-oriented programming, called encapsulation, which would be impossible without accessibility control.

# Encapsulation

The concept of OOP was born in an effort to manage the increasing complexity of software systems. The concept of data and procedures bundled in an object with controlled access to them (called encapsulation) allows better-organized data and procedures in layers, some of them hidden, others exposed to an access from outside. The accessibility control described in the previous sections was a significant part of it. Together with inheritance, interface (also called abstraction), and polymorphism, encapsulation became one of the central concepts of OOP.

There is often no clear-cut separation of one OOP concept from another. Interfaces help to hide (encapsulate) the implementation details too. Inheritance, with its ability to override and hide methods of the parent classes, adds a dynamic aspect to the accessibility. All these three concepts make it possible to add the concept of polymorphism—the ability of the same object to present itself as a different type, depending on the context (based on inheritance or an implemented interface), or change its behavior based on the data availability (using composition—we will talk about it in Chapter 8, *Object-Oriented Design (OOD) Principles*—or method overloading, hiding, and overriding).

But none of the concepts would be possible without encapsulation. That is why it is the most fundamental among the four concepts of OOP. Chances are, you will hear it mentioned a lot, so we have decided to dedicate this section to the terms often used in the context of an encapsulation based on the advantages it provides:

- Data hiding and decoupling
- Flexibility, maintainability, refactoring
- Reusability
- Testability

# Data hiding and decoupling

When we make object states (values of its fields) and some methods private or impose some other measure of restricted access to the internal object data, we participate in *data hiding*. The user of the object's functionality can call only certain methods based on their accessibility and cannot manipulate the object's internal state directly. The object's users may have no idea how exactly the functionality is implemented and the data is stored. They pass the required input data to the accessible methods and get back the results. This way we *decouple* the internal state from its usage and the implementation details from the API.

Grouping related methods and data in the same class also increases *decoupling*, this time between different areas of functionality.

You may hear the term *tightly coupled* as something that should be allowed only when there is no way to avoid it because it usually means that any change of one part would require a corresponding change of another part. Even in everyday life, we prefer to deal with modularized systems that allow replacing one module only without changing any other component of the rest of the system.

That is why *loose coupling* is usually something programmers prefer although it often comes at the price of not being sure that there will be no unexpected surprises until the system is tested in all possible execution paths. A well-thought-out system of tests that cover the essential use cases usually helps to reduce the chance of a defect propagation in production.

# Flexibility, maintainability, and refactoring

When we talked about decoupling in the previous section, the idea of flexibility and maintainability probably came to mind by association. Loosely coupled systems are more flexible and easier to maintain.

For example, in `Chapter 6`, *Interfaces, Classes, and Object Construction*, we demonstrated a flexible solution when implementing an object factory:

```
public static Calculator createInstance(){
  WhichImpl whichImpl =
      Utils.getWhichImplValueFromConfig(Utils.class,
          Calculator.CONF_NAME, Calculator.CONF_WHICH_IMPL);
  switch (whichImpl){
    case multiplies:
      return new CalculatorImpl();
    case adds:
      return new AnotherCalculatorImpl();
    default:
      throw new RuntimeException("Houston, we have another problem."+
              " We do not have implementation for the key " +
              Calculator.CONF_WHICH_IMPL + " value " + whichImpl);
    }
  }
}
```

It is tightly coupled with its `Calculator` interface (its API) only, but that is inevitable because it is the contract the implementation must honor. As for the implementation inside the factory, it is much freer from any restrictions as long as it adheres to the contract.

We could create an instance of each of the implementations only once and return only that one instance (making each class a singleton). Here is an example of `CalculatorImpl` as a singleton:

```
private static Calculator calculator = null;
public static Calculator createInstance(){
  WhichImpl whichImpl =
      Utils.getWhichImplValueFromConfig(Utils.class,
          Calculator.CONF_NAME, Calculator.CONF_WHICH_IMPL);
  switch (whichImpl){
    case multiplies:
      if(calculator == null){
        calculator = new CalculatorImpl();
      }
      return calculator;
    case adds:
      return new AnotherCalculatorImpl();
    default:
      throw new RuntimeException("Houston, we have another problem."+
              " We do not have implementation for the key " +
              Calculator.CONF_WHICH_IMPL + " value " + whichImpl);
    }
  }
}
```

Or we could add another `Calculator` implementation to the factory as a nested class and use it instead of `CalculatorImpl`:

```
public static Calculator createInstance(){
  String whichImpl =
Utils.getStringValueFromConfig(CalculatorFactory.class,
          "calculator.conf", "which.impl");
  if(whichImpl.equals("multiplies")){
    return new Whatever();
  } else if (whichImpl.equals("adds")){
    return new AnotherCalculatorImpl();
  } else {
    throw new RuntimeException("Houston, we have a problem. " +
            "Unknown key which.impl value " + whichImpl +
            " is in config.");
  }

}

static class Whatever implements Calculator {
  public static String addOneAndConvertToString(double d){
    System.out.println(Whatever.class.getName());
    return Double.toString(d + 1);
  }
  public int multiplyByTwo(int i){
    System.out.println(Whatever.class.getName());
    return i * 2;
  }
}
```

And the client code of this factory would never know the difference unless it prints out information about the class using the `getClass()` method on the object returned from the factory. But that is another story. Functionally, our new implementation of `Whatever` would work as an old one.

And that is actually a common practice—to change internal implementation from one release to another. There are bug fixes, of course, and new functionality added. And as the code of the implementation is evolving, its programmers are constantly watching for the possibility of refactoring. In computer science, factoring is a synonym of decomposition, which is breaking a complex code into simpler parts with the purpose of making the code more readable and maintainable. For example, let's assume we were asked to write a method that accepts two parameters of the String type (each represents an integer) and returns their sum as an integer too. After thinking for a moment, we decided to do it this way:

```
public long sum(String s1, String s2){
    int i1 = Integer.parseInt(s1);
    int i2 = Integer.parseInt(s1);
    return i1 + i2;
}
```

But then we have asked for a sample of possible input values, so we can test our code in the condition close to production. It turned out that some of the values can be up to 10,000,000,000, which exceeds 2,147,483,647 (the maximum Integer.MAX_VALUE int value Java allows). So we have changed our code to the following:

```
public long sum(String s1, String s2){
    long l1 = Long.parseLong(s1);
    long l2 = Long.parseLong(s2);
    return l1 + l2;
}
```

Now our code can handle values up to 9,223,372,036,854,775,807 (which is Long.MAX_VALUE). We deployed the code to production and it worked just fine for several months, used by a big software system that processes statistics. Then the system switched to a new source of data and the code started breaking. We investigated and found out that a new source of data yields values that can include letters and some other characters. We have tested our code for such cases and discovered that the following line throws NumberFormatException:

```
long l1 = Long.parseLong(s1);
```

We discussed the situation with the domain experts and they suggested we record the values that are not integer, skip them, and continue the sum calculations. So, we have fixed our code, as follows:

```
public long sum(String s1, String s2){
   long l1 = 0;
   try{
      l1 = Long.parseLong(s1);
   } catch (NumberFormatException ex){
      //make a record to a log
   }
   long l2 = 0;
   try{
      l2 = Long.parseLong(s2);
   } catch (NumberFormatException ex){
      //make a record to a log
   }
   return l1 + l2;
}
```

We have quickly released the code to production, but for the next release got new requirements: the input String values can contain decimal numbers. So, we have changed the way we process the input String values by assuming they carry decimal values (which cover integer values too) and refactored the code, as follows:

```
private long getLong(String s){
   double d = 0;
   try{
      d = Double.parseDouble(s);
   } catch (NumberFormatException ex){
      //make a record to a log
   }
   return Math.round(d);
}
public long sum(String s1, String s2){
   return getLong(s1) + getLong(s2);
}
```

That is what refactoring does. It restructures the code without changing its API. As new requirements keep coming in, we can change the getLong() method without even touching the sum() method. We also can reuse the getLong() method in other places, and that is going to be the topic of the next section.

# Reusability

Encapsulation definitely makes it easier to achieve reusability because it hides the implementation details. For example, the `getLong()` method we wrote in the previous section can be reused by another method of the same class:

```
public long sum(int i, String s2){
   return i + getLong(s2);
}
```

It can even be made public and used by other classes, like in the following line:

```
int i = new Ch07DemoApp().getLong("23", "45.6");
```

That would be an example of a composition when some functionality is built (composed) using methods of different classes not related by inheritance. And, since it does not depend on the object state (such a method is called stateless), it can be made static:

```
int i = Ch07DemoApp.getLong("23", "45.6");
```

Well, if the method is used concurrently by several other methods at runtime, even such a simple code may need to be protected (synchronized) against parallel usage. But such considerations are outside of the scope of this book. For now, if in doubt, do not make the method static.

If you read about the history of object-oriented programming, you will find that inheritance was originally tasked, among other things, to be the primary mechanism of code reuse. And it does the job. A child inherits (reuses) all the methods of its parent and overrides only those that need to be overridden for the child's specialization.

But in practice, it seems that other reusability techniques, similar to those demonstrated earlier, are more popular, especially for cases when the reused method is stateless. We will talk more about the reasons for that in Chapter 8, *Object-Oriented Design (OOD) Principles*.

# Testability

Code testability is another area where encapsulation helps. If the implementation details were not hidden, we would need to test every single line of code and change the test every time we change any line of the implementation. But hiding the details behind the facade of the API allows us to focus only on the test cases that are required and limited by the set of possible input data (parameter values).

Also, there are frameworks that allow us to create an object that returns a certain result based on the certain value of the input parameters. Mockito is a popular framework that does it (`http://site.mockito.org`). Such objects are called mock objects. They are especially helpful when you need to get certain results from methods of one object to test other methods, but you cannot run the actual implementation of the methods you use as the source of data because you do not have the necessary data in the database, for example, or it requires some complicated setup. To get around the problem, you can replace the actual implementation of certain methods—mock them—with one that returns the data you need unconditionally or in response to certain input data. Without the encapsulation, such simulation of a method behavior may be impossible because the client code would be tied to the specific implementation and you would not be able to change it without changing the client code.

# Exercise – Shadowing

Write the code that demonstrates variable shadowing. We have not talked about it, so you will need to do some research.

## Answer

Here is one possible solution:

```
public class ShadowingDemo {
    private String x = "x";
    public void printX(){
        System.out.println(x);
        String x = "y";
        System.out.println(x);
    }
}
```

If you run `new ShadowingDemo().printX();`, it will print x first, then y because the local variable x in the following line shadows the x instance variable:

```
String x = "y";
```

Please note that shadowing can be a source of a defect or can be used for the benefit of the program. Without it, you would be not able to use a local variable identifier that is already used by an instance variable. And here is another example of a case where variable shadowing helps:

```
private String x = "x";
public void setX(String x) {
   this.x = x;
}
```

The x local variable (parameter) shadows the x instance variable. It allows using the same identificator for a local variable name that has been already used for an instance variable name. To avoid possible confusion, it is recommended to refer to an instance variable using the keyword `this` as we did in the example above.

# Summary

In this chapter, you learned about one of the fundamental features of an object-oriented language – the rules of accessibility of classes, interfaces, their members, and constructors. You now can import classes and interfaces from other packages and avoid using their fully qualified names. All that discussion allowed us to introduce the central concept of OOP—encapsulation. With that, we can start an informed discussion of **object-oriented design (OOD)** principles.

The next chapter presents a higher-level view of Java programming. It discusses the criteria of a good design and provides a guide to the well-proven OOD principles. Each of the design principles is described in detail and illustrated using a corresponding code example.

# Object-Oriented Design (OOD) Principles

# 8

In this chapter, we are going to get back to a high-level view of programming and Java programming in particular. We will show the role of design in the process of a software system, starting with the earliest feasibility phase, going through high-level design, detailed design, and ending with the coding and testing. We will discuss the criteria for a good design and provide a guide to the well-proven OOD principles. The discussion will be illustrated by code examples that demonstrate the application of the main OOD principles.

In this chapter, we will cover the following topics:

- What is the purpose of design?
- Encapsulating and programming to an interface
- Taking advantage of polymorphism
- Decoupling as much as you can
- Preferring aggregation over inheritance
- So many OOD principles and so little time
- Single Responsibility Principle
- Open Closed Principle
- Liskov Substitution Principle
- Interface Segregation Principle
- Dependency Inversion Principle
- Exercise – Design patterns

# What is the purpose of design?

Any project requires planning and a vision of what is going to be built. It is especially important when several members of the same team have to coordinate their activity. But even if you work alone, you have to make some kind of plan, whether it is a design document or just the code you are writing without capturing your ideas in any other form. And that is the purpose of design—to envision the future system clearly enough to be able to start building it.

In the process, the design evolves, changes, and becomes more detailed. Each step of a project life cycle requires something different. And that is what we are going to discuss now—how the purpose of design evolves as the project progresses from the first idea to the complete implementation.

The project steps described here look sequential, but in fact, they are executed with significant overlap. Even more, the agile methodology of software development encourages moving each feature through all the project steps without waiting until all the features of the future product are discovered.

The deliverable, in agile methodology, is not the requirements, design, or any other document, but a functional code deployed to production and producing value (also called a **minimum viable product** (**MVP**)). It has to be accomplished every iteration—in a span of one or two weeks. Then, the feedback loop based on real customer experience allows continuous adjusting of the original vision and drives all the effort to the most valuable solution in the shortest period of time and with a minimal waste of resources.

Many, if not the majority, of modern successful products have been brought to the market this way. Their authors often confess that only a handful of original ideas have been implemented, if any. Life is a great joker, isn't it? It favors those who adapt to a change quicker.

Now, let's walk through the project life cycle and see how the system design evolves along with it.

# The project's feasibility

Decision that a certain project is worth financing has to be made very early. Otherwise, it might not start at all. This means that the decision maker has to be supplied with enough information to provide a level of confidence that the risk is reasonable and worth taking. This information includes high-level requirements, a high-level design, and even prototyping or some other proof that the available technologies can be used for the successful implementation. Based on this data and market research, the project advocates estimate the level of effort, expenses, potential income, and future profit—the mother of all goals.

Even before the project gets a green light, the most critical for the success of the product features are identified, presented in a form that can be communicated to the future customers, and discussed or even tested with them. If the team includes people who did something similar in the past, it definitely helps to shortcut the decision making.

The purpose of this phase is to present the future system in a form that could be understood by all participants and potential customers.

# Requirement gathering and prototyping

As soon as the project is approved and budgeted, the requirement gathering goes ahead full-speed along with the prototype implementation. In fact, the prototype is often used as a tool for requirements-gathering. It helps to discuss specific critical details and avoid misunderstandings.

In this project stage, the high-level design progresses, along with the discovery of more details about the sources of the input information, the processes necessary to consume it (and produce the necessary results), the technologies that can be used to do it, and how the customers may interact with the system.

With more data about the future system, how it might work and be implemented, it is possible to identify obstacles that can impede the progress or make the whole project impossible. So, the decision makers continue to closely watch the results and critically evaluate them.

The purpose of design at this stage is bringing all the incoming data together into a cohesive dynamic picture of the future functioning system. Of the four pillars of OOP, encapsulation and interface are at the forefront of high-level design. The implementation details should be spot-checked in the critical areas and proved to be possible with the selected technologies. But they stay hidden—encapsulated—behind the interface, the latter being focused on the system's interaction with the customers and on the discovery of new functional and non-functional requirements for the implementation.

# High-level design

The most apparent feature of the high-level design is its focus on the system structure on the level of the subsystems and the interfaces between them. If the product has to interact with external systems, the interface and protocol of such interactions are part of the high-level design, too. The architecture is identified and validated as being able to support the design, too.

In the case of a typical mid-size software system, the high-level design can be expressed in the list of packages and their public interfaces. If the system has a graphic user interface, its prototype and wireframes are usually enough.

# Detailed design

Detailed design comes into play as soon as the use cases to be implemented are first identified. The business representatives set priorities for the new product features. The programmers identify and adjust the interfaces to support the first features and start creating classes to implement the first use cases that are going to be delivered in the first iterations.

At first, the implementation may have hardcode (dummy) data in some places. So, the use cases might have a limited range of applications. Still, such an implementation is valuable as it allows executing all the required processes, so the customers in production can test the feature and get a feeling of what to expect. The programmers also create unit tests for each of the implemented methods, even for the dummy ones. At the same time, the use cases are captured in the integration tests that execute scenarios across classes and subsystems.

By the end of the first iteration, the high-priority use cases are implemented and fully tested using the automated tests. The first iteration usually is very busy. But programmers are motivated not to repeat their mistakes this time and typically work with a lot of enthusiasm and higher-than-usual productivity.

The purpose of detailed design is to provide a template for coding. Once the template is established, all the future classes will be mostly cut-and-paste from the existing ones. That is why the first classes are usually implemented by the senior programmers or under their close supervision. While doing that, they try to keep the encapsulation as closed as possible, for having minimal and intuitive interfaces, and for taking advantage of inheritance and polymorphism where possible.

The naming convention is a big part of the first iterations too. It has to reflect the domain terminology and be well understood by all the team members. Thus, the purpose of the design on this stage is to create a pattern for the coding and vocabulary for the project.

# Coding

As you can see, coding has been going since high-level design and possibly even earlier. As the detailed design produces the first results, coding gets more steam. New members can be added to the team, and some of them can be juniors. Adding people to the team is the favorite managerial activity, but it has to be done in a controlled manner so that every new member can be instructed and learn project vocabulary well enough to understand all the business discussions around new product features.

The design activity on this stage is focused on the details of the implementation and its tests. The pattern created during detailed design has to be applied and adjusted as needed. The purpose of the design during coding is to verify all the design decisions made so far and to produce specific solutions expressed as the lines of code. Refactoring is one of the main activities during this phase and several first iterations.

# Testing

By the time the coding is finished, the tests are also written and are run many times. They are usually executed every time a new chunk of changes are committed to a source code repository. Some companies are practicing a continuous integration model when the change, once committed to the source repository, triggers the automated regression and integration testing with subsequent deployment to production environment.

Yet, there are many development teams that still have dedicated test specialists who—after the code is deployed into a test environment—are testing it manually and using some specialized tools.

The design effort in this phase is focused on test coverage, test automation, and integration with other systems, automated or not. Deployment and limited testing (called **smoke testing**) in a production environment is also part of the design effort of this phase.

The purpose of design during testing is to make sure that all the delivered use cases are covered with tests, including negative and non-functional testing. Monitoring and reporting on the system performance are important activities of this phase, too.

# A roadmap to a good design

As we discussed the design evolution in previous section, we have already hinted at the criteria that ensure design quality:

- It has to be flexible enough to adapt to the incoming changes (they are as inevitable as taxes, so you'd better be ready)
- It has to clearly communicate the project structure and specialization of each part
- It has to use well-defined domain terminology
- It has to allow testing parts in isolation and integrated together
- It has to be presented in a form that allows us to discuss it with the future customers and, ideally, is tested by them
- It has to take full advantage of the four OOP concepts—encapsulation, interface, inheritance, and polymorphism

Those are general criteria for any project and any OOP language. But in this book, we introduce Java best practices, so we need to mainly discuss the detailed design, coding, and testing in Java – all related to the last of these criteria. That is what we are going to do now.

# Encapsulating and coding to an interface

We have mentioned encapsulation and interface many times and in different contexts. It was neither accidental nor intentional. It was unavoidable. Encapsulation and interface were born out of necessity to keep the implementation hidden as much as possible. It addresses two problems that plagued early programming:

- Unregulated shared access to the data
- Difficulties in changing the code when the relations between parts are not well structured

OOP is a successful solution. It ensures controlled access to the data (object state) and flexibility (freedom to change) the implementation as needed as long as the interface is not changed. In addition, it helps to organize the design and development of software. After the interfaces are defined, everybody can work on the implementation independently. There is no need to spend time on meetings and discussions if the interfaces do not change.

As we have demonstrated in Chapter 6, *Interfaces, Classes, and Object Construction*, making an object's state private also addressed the difference in accessibility between instance fields and instance methods when inheritance is involved. A child cannot override non-private fields of the parent but only hide them. Only methods can be overridden. To demonstrate the difference, let's create the following three classes:

```
public class Grandad {
  public String name = "Grandad";
  public String getName() { return this.name; }
}

public class Parent extends Grandad {
  public String name = "Parent";
  public String getName() { return this.name; }
}

public class Child extends Parent {
  public String name = "Child";
  public String getName() { return this.name; }
}
```

Each has a public field with the same name and method with the same signature. Now, without looking down the page, try to guess what will be the output of the following code:

```
Grandad grandad = new Child();
System.out.println(grandad.name);
System.out.println(grandad.getName());
```

Here is the screenshot of the output:

```
Grandad
Child
```

This difference often creates confusion and can cause difficult-to-debug errors. To avoid them, we recommend never allowing access to the object state (fields) directly, only via methods (getters and setters at the very least). That is another reason to always keep the state encapsulated.

We will now create a small software modeling system that illustrates the application of the design steps we are discussing. Let's assume that we were tasked with creating a model of traffic that allows calculating the speed of every vehicle based on a typical mix of cars and trucks in a certain city where the model is going to be tested first. The value returned by the model should be the speed (miles per hour) the vehicle reaches after a certain number of seconds. The results will be used for assessing the traffic density on a multi-lane road a few seconds after the traffic light turns green. It will be part of the decision-making during the introduction of new traffic regulations related to the minimum number of passengers (for cars) and the maximum weight of the payload (for trucks).

We definitely simplify possible real-life requirements in order to make the code easier to read. In a real system, such calculations would require more input data and a much more complicated algorithm based on the machine learning modeling. But even the simple system we develop will have all the design aspects that the real-life system has.

After discussing the requirements, the high-level design has identified the API. It has to accept three parameters:

- The number of vehicles
- The number of seconds after all the vehicles began moving
- The vehicle load: number of passengers for cars and the payload for trucks

The last parameter should be optional. It can be one of these:

- Modeled based on the current traffic statistics in the targeted city
- Set to a specific value for the purpose of the evaluation of the effect of the new traffic regulations

The following is the detailed design of the modeling system API located in the com.packt.javapath.ch08demo.traffic package:

```
public interface Vehicle {
    double getSpeedMph(double timeSec);
    static List<Vehicle> getTraffic(int vehiclesCount){
        return TrafficFactory.get(vehiclesCount);
    }
}
public interface Car extends Vehicle {
    void setPassengersCount(int passengersCount);
}
public interface Truck extends Vehicle {
    void setPayloadPounds(int payloadPounds);
}
```

As you can see, we only expose the interface to the client and hide the implementation (more about this in the next section). It allows us the freedom of implementing the interfaces whichever way we think is best as long as it fulfills the contract. And if we change the implementation later, the clients are not required to change their code. That is an example of encapsulation and decoupling the interface from the implementation. As we discussed in the previous chapter, it also facilitates code maintainability, testability, and reusability. More about the latter in the *Preferring aggregation over inheritance* section, although we should point out that inheritance facilitates code reuse too and we will see proof of it in the next section.

By extending the Car and Truck interfaces from the Vehicle interface, we have hinted already that we are going to use polymorphism, and that is what we are going to discuss in the following section.

# Taking advantage of polymorphism

The Car and Truck interfaces are extending (children of) the Vehicle interface. It means that the class that implements the Car interface (let's give such a class the name CarImpl), for example, when instantiated, creates an object that has three types – Vehicle, Car, and CarImpl. These types are similar to passports of a person who is a citizen of three countries. Each citizenship carries specific rights and restrictions, and a person chooses how to present themselves in different situations of international travel, the same way an object of the CarImpl class can be *cast* to any of these types, provided the type is accessible in the code that does the casting. And here is what we mean by type accessibility:

- We have already declared the Car, Truck, and Vehicle interfaces as public, which means that any code of any package can access these types
- We don't want client code able to access the implementations of these interfaces, so we create the com.packt.javapath.ch08demo.traffic.impl package and put all the implementations there without specifying an access modifier (thus using the default access that makes them visible only to other members of the same package)

Here are the implementations of the traffic interfaces:

```
class VehicleImpl implements Vehicle {
  public double getSpeedMph(double timeSec) {
    return 42;
  }
}
class TruckImpl implements Truck {
```

```
    public void setPayloadPounds(int payloadPounds){
    }
}
class CarImpl implements Car {
  public void setPassengersCount(int passengersCount){
  }
}
```

We have created these classes in the `com.packt.javapath.ch08demo.traffic.impl` package with some dummy data—just to make them compile. But the `CarImpl` and `TruckImpl` classes still generate a compilation error because there is the `getSpeedMph()` method listed in the `Vehicle` interface which is not implemented in these two classes. The `Car` and `Truck` interfaces extend the `Vehicle` interface and, thus, inherit its abstract `getSpeedMph()` method.

So, now we need to either implement the `getSpeedMph()` method in each of these two classes or make each of them a child of the `VehicleImpl` class, where this method is implemented already. We have decided that the speed will probably be calculated the same way for a car and for a truck, so extending the `VehicleImpl` class is the way to go. If later we discover that the `CarImpl` or `TruckImpl` class needs a different implementation, we can override the one in the parent class. Here is the new version of the same two classes:

```
abstract class VehicleImpl implements Vehicle {
  public double getSpeedMph(double timeSec){
    return 42;
  }
}
class TruckImpl extends VehicleImpl implements Truck {
  public void setPayloadPounds(int payloadPounds){
  }
}
class CarImpl extends VehicleImpl implements Car {
  public void setPassengersCount(int passengersCount){
  }
}
```

Notice, please, that we have also made the `VehicleImpl` class abstract, which makes it impossible to create an object of the `VehicleImpl` class. Only objects of its children can be created. We did this because we use it as a base class that contains some common functionality, but we are never going to need the generic `Vehicle` object, only a specific one—either `Car` or `Truck`.

We have followed the recommendation of keeping everything as encapsulated as possible. The restricted access can be changed to be more accessible later. And it is easier to do than to restrict access after some client code is written already that relies on the existing level of less-restricted access.

So, back to the `CarImpl` and `TruckImpl` traffic interfaces implementation. They are inaccessible from outside the package, but that is not a problem because the API we have defined does not require it. If the `TrafficFactory` class can access them, that it would be enough. That is why we create the `TrafficFactor` class in the `com.packt.javapath.ch08demo.traffic.impl` package, where it can access both implementations as a member of the same package:

```
package com.packt.javapath.ch08demo.traffic.impl;

import com.packt.javapath.ch08demo.traffic.Vehicle;
import java.util.ArrayList;
import java.util.List;

public class TrafficFactory {
  public static List<Vehicle> get(int vehiclesCount) {
    List<Vehicle> list = new ArrayList();
    return list;
  }
}
```

It does not do much, but it is good enough for the design phase, to make sure that all the classes are in place and have appropriate access before we start coding. We will talk more about the `List<Vehicle>` construct in `Chapter 13`, *Java Collections*. For now, it would be enough to assume it represents a list of objects that implement the `Vehicle` interface.

Now, we can write the following client code:

```
double timeSec = 5;
int vehiclesCount = 4;
List<Vehicle> traffic = Vehicle.getTraffic(vehiclesCount);
for(Vehicle vehicle: traffic){
  System.out.println("Loaded: " + vehicle.getSpeedMph(timeSec));
  if(vehicle instanceof Car){
    ((Car) vehicle).setPassengersCount(0);
    System.out.println("Car(no load): " + vehicle.getSpeedMph(timeSec));
  } else {
    ((Truck) vehicle).setPayloadPounds(0);
    System.out.println("Truck(no load): " + vehicle.getSpeedMph(timeSec));
  }
}
```

The preceding code retrieves any number of vehicles (four, in this case) from `TrafficFactory`. The factory hides (encapsulates) the details of the implementation of traffic modeling. Then, the code iterates over the list in a for-loop (see `Chapter 10`, *Control Flow Statements*) and prints out the speed of each vehicle calculated at the point five seconds after the vehicle has started to move.

The code then demonstrates that the client can change the load the vehicle carries, as was required. For cars, we set the number of passengers to zero, and for trucks, we set their payloads to zero.

We execute this code and get no results because the traffic factory returns an empty list. But the code compiles and runs, and we can start implementing the interfaces. We can give the assignments to different team members and we do not have to worry about coordinating the effort between them as long as they do not change the interface.

After making sure the interface, inheritance, and polymorphism are used to their full (as far as we could do it) capacity, we can turn our attention to the coding details.

# Decoupling as much as you can

We have chosen inheritance for code sharing across different implementations. The result looks as follows. Here is the `VehicleImpl` class:

```
abstract class VehicleImpl implements Vehicle {
  private int weightPounds, horsePower;
  public VehicleImpl(int weightPounds, int horsePower) {
    this.weightPounds = weightPounds;
    this.horsePower = horsePower;
  }
  protected int getWeightPounds(){ return this.weightPounds; }
  protected double getSpeedMph(double timeSec, int weightPounds){
    double v = 2.0 * this.horsePower * 746 * timeSec *
                                    32.174 / weightPounds;
    return Math.round(Math.sqrt(v) * 0.68);
  }
}
```

Notice that some methods have `protected` access, meaning only members of the same package and class children can access them. That is done for better encapsulation, too. Our code clients do not need access to these methods, only children do. And here is one of them:

```
class CarImpl extends VehicleImpl implements Car {
  private int passengersCount;
  public CarImpl(int passengersCount, int weightPounds, int horsePower){
    super(weightPounds , horsePower);
    this.passengersCount = passengersCount;
  }
  public void setPassengersCount(int passengersCount) {
    this.passengersCount = passengersCount;
  }
  protected int getWeightPounds(){
    return this.passengersCount * 200 + super.getWeightPounds();
  }
  public double getSpeedMph(double timeSec){
    return getSpeedMph(timeSec, this.getWeightPounds());
  }
}
```

The `this` and `super` keywords in the preceding code allow us to distinguish which method has to be called – the one in the current child object or the one in the parent object.

The other two aspects of the preceding implementation are worth noticing:

- The access modifier of the `getWeightPounds()` method is set to `protected`. That is because the method with the same signature and `protected` access modifier is declared in the parent, class too. But the overriding method cannot have more restrictive access than the overridden one. Alternatively, to tighten the encapsulation, we could change the method name in `CarImpl` to `getCarWeightPounds()`, for example, and make it private. Then, there would be no need to use the `this` and `super` keywords. But classes of another package cannot access the `protected` method anyway, so we have decided to keep the `getWeightPounds()` name and use the `this` and `super` keywords, admitting that it is just a matter of style.
- The access to the constructor can be made default (package-level), too.

The `TruckImpl` class looks similar to the following code snippet:

```
class TruckImpl extends VehicleImpl implements Truck {
  private int payloadPounds;
  TruckImpl(int payloadPounds, int weightPounds, int horsePower) {
    super(weightPounds, horsePower);
    this.payloadPounds = payloadPounds;
  }
  public void setPayloadPounds(int payloadPounds) {
    this.payloadPounds = payloadPounds;
  }
  protected int getWeightPounds(){
    return this.payloadPounds + super.getWeightPounds();
  }
  public double getSpeedMph(double timeSec){
    return getSpeedMph(timeSec, this.getWeightPounds());
  }
}
```

And the `TrafficFactory` class can access these classes and their constructors to create objects as needed:

```
public class TrafficFactory {
  public static List<Vehicle> get(int vehiclesCount) {
    List<Vehicle> list = new ArrayList();
    for (int i = 0; i < vehiclesCount; i++){
      Vehicle vehicle;
      if (Math.random() <= 0.5) {
        vehicle = new CarImpl(2, 2000, 150);
      } else {
        vehicle = new TruckImpl(500, 3000, 300);
      }
      list.add(vehicle);
    }
    return list;
  }
}
```

The `random()` static method of the `Math` class generates a random decimal number between 0 and 1. We use it to make the resulting mix of traffic look somewhat real. And we have hardcoded, for now, the values we pass into each of the vehicles' constructors.

Now, we can run the following code (we discussed it already a few pages ago):

```java
public class TrafficApp {
  public static void main(String... args){
    double timeSec = 5;
    int vehiclesCount = 4;
    List<Vehicle> traffic = Vehicle.getTraffic(vehiclesCount);
    for(Vehicle vehicle: traffic){
      System.out.println("Loaded: " + vehicle.getSpeedMph(timeSec));
      if(vehicle instanceof Car){
        ((Car) vehicle).setPassengersCount(0);
        System.out.println("Car(no load): " +
                          vehicle.getSpeedMph(timeSec));
      } else {
        ((Truck) vehicle).setPayloadPounds(0);
        System.out.println("Truck(no load): " +
                          vehicle.getSpeedMph(timeSec));
      }
    }
  }
}
```

The result is:

```
Loaded: 98.0
Truck(no load): 105.0
Loaded: 98.0
Truck(no load): 105.0
Loaded: 83.0
Car(no load): 91.0
Loaded: 98.0
Truck(no load): 105.0
```

The calculated speed is the same because the input data is hardcoded in `TrafficFactory`. But before we move on and make the input data different, let's create a speed calculation test:

```java
package com.packt.javapath.ch08demo.traffic.impl;

class SpeedCalculationTest {
  @Test
  void speedCalculation() {
    double timeSec = 5;
    Vehicle vehicle = new CarImpl(2, 2000, 150);
    assertEquals(83.0, vehicle.getSpeedMph(timeSec));
    ((Car) vehicle).setPassengersCount(0);
    assertEquals(91.0, vehicle.getSpeedMph(timeSec));
```

```
        vehicle = new TruckImpl(500, 3000, 300);
        assertEquals(98.0, vehicle.getSpeedMph(timeSec));
        ((Truck) vehicle).setPayloadPounds(0);
        assertEquals(105.0, vehicle.getSpeedMph(timeSec));
    }
}
```

We could access the `CarImpl` and `TruckImpl` classes because the test belongs to the same package, although it's located in a different directory of our project (under the `test` directory, instead of `main`). On the classpath, they are placed according to their package, even if the source comes from another source tree.

We have tested our code and now we can concentrate on processing real data and creating the corresponding objects for the client in `TrafficFactory`. The implementation is decoupled from the interface and, until it is ready, we can keep it hardcoded, so the client can start writing and testing their code without waiting until our system is fully functional. That is another advantage of encapsulation and interface.

# Preferring aggregation over inheritance

Those who worked on real-life projects know that the requirements can change at any moment. In the case of our project, even before the second iteration was completed, new methods had to be added to the `Car` and `Truck` interfaces, while speed calculation grew in its own project. The programmers who worked on the implementation of the interfaces and those working on the speed calculation started to change the `CarImpl`, `TruckImpl`, and `VehicleImpl` files.

Not only that, but another project decided to use our speed calculation functionality, but they wanted to apply it to other objects, not cars and trucks. That is when we realized that we need to change our implementation in favor of aggregating the functionality instead of inheriting it, which is one of the recommended design strategies in general anyway, because it increases decoupling and facilitates more flexible design. Here is what it means.

We copy the `getSpeedMph()` method of the `VehicleImpl` class and put it in the `SpeedModelImpl` class in a new `com.packt.javapath.ch08demo.speedmodel.impl` package:

```
class SpeedModelImpl implements SpeedModel {
  public double getSpeedMph(double timeSec, int weightPounds,
                            int horsePower){
    double v = 2.0 * horsePower * 746 * timeSec * 32.174 / weightPounds;
    return Math.round(Math.sqrt(v) * 0.68);
```

```
    }
  }
```

We add `SpeedModelFactory` to the same package:

```
public class SpeedModelFactory {
  public static SpeedModel speedModel(){
    return new SpeedModelImpl();
  }
}
```

And we create a `SpeedModel` interface in the
`com.packt.javapath.ch08demo.speedmodel` package:

```
public interface SpeedModel {
  double getSpeedMph(double timeSec, int weightPounds, int horsePower);
  static SpeedModel getInstance(Month month, int dayOfMonth, int hour){
    return SpeedModelFactory.speedModel(month, dayOfMonth, hour);
  }
}
```

Now, we change the `VehicleImpl` class by adding a setter for the `SpeedModel` object and
by using this object in the speed calculations:

```
abstract class VehicleImpl implements Vehicle {
  private int weightPounds, horsePower;
  private SpeedModel speedModel;
  public VehicleImpl(int weightPounds, int horsePower) {
    this.weightPounds = weightPounds;
    this.horsePower = horsePower;
  }
  protected int getWeightPounds(){ return this.weightPounds; }
  protected double getSpeedMph(double timeSec, int weightPounds){
    if(this.speedModel == null){
      throw new RuntimeException("Speed model is required");
    } else {
      return speedModel.getSpeedMph(timeSec, weightPounds, horsePower);
    }
  }
  public void setSpeedModel(SpeedModel speedModel) {
    this.speedModel = speedModel;
  }
}
```

As you can see, the get SpeedMph () method now throws an exception (and stops working) if it is called before the SpeedModel object is set.

We also change TrafficFactory and let it set SpeedModel on the traffic objects:

```
public class TrafficFactory {
  public static List<Vehicle> get(int vehiclesCount) {
    SpeedModel speedModel = SpeedModelFactory.speedModel();
    List<Vehicle> list = new ArrayList();
    for (int i = 0; i < vehiclesCount; i++) {
      Vehicle vehicle;
      if (Math.random() <= 0.5) {
        vehicle = new CarImpl(2, 2000, 150);
      } else {
        vehicle = new TruckImpl(500, 3000, 300);
      }
      ((VehicleImpl)vehicle).setSpeedModel(speedModel);
      list.add(vehicle);
    }
    return list;
  }
}
```

Now, the speed model continues to be developed independently of the traffic model, and we accomplished all that without changing the client's code (such an internal code change that does not affect an interface is called **refactoring**). That is the benefit of decoupling based on encapsulation and interface. The behavior of the Vehicle object is now aggregated, which allow us to change its behavior without modifying its code.

Although the title of this section is *Preferring aggregation over inheritance*, it does not mean that inheritance should always be avoided. Inheritance has its own uses and is especially beneficial for polymorphic behavior. But when we talk about design flexibility and code reusability, it has two weaknesses:

- Java classes do not allow us to extend more than one parent, so, if the class is already a child, it cannot extend another class in order to reuse its method
- Inheritance requires a parent-child relationship between classes, while the same functionality is often shared by the unrelated classes

Sometimes, inheritance is the only way to solve the problem at hand and sometimes using it causes problems later. The reality is that we can never reliably predict what the future holds, so do not feel bad if the decision to use inheritance or not turns out to be wrong later.

# So many OOD principles and so little time

If you search for OOD principles on the internet, you can easily find many lists that include dozens of recommended design principles. And all of them make sense.

For example, here are the five most popular OOD principles often bundled together under the abbreviation SOLID (composed from the first letters of the principles' titles):

- **Single Responsibility Principle**: A class should have only one responsibility
- **Open Closed Principle**: A class should encapsulate its functionality (be closed) but be able to be extended
- **Liskov Substitution Principle**: An object should be replaceable (substituted) by its child and still not break the program
- **Interface Segregation Principle**: Many client-oriented interfaces are better than one general-purpose interface
- **Dependency Inversion Principle**: Code should depend on the interface, not implementations

And, as we have said before, there are many other good ideas about how to achieve better design. Should you study all of them? The answer very much depends on the way you prefer to learn new skills. Some people do it by experimenting, others by learning from other people's experience, and the majority learns from a combination of these approaches.

The good news is that the design criteria, OOP concepts, and the roadmap for a good design that we have discussed in this chapter are able to lead you to a solid OOP solution in most of the cases.

But if you decide to read more about OOD and see how other people have solved software design problems, do not hesitate to check them out. After all, that was how humanity got out of the caves and boarded a spacecraft – by passing their experience on to the next generation.

# Exercise – Design patterns

There are many OOD patterns that have shared software-design solutions of specific coding problems. OOD patterns are also often used by programmers as the way to talk about different implementations.

They are traditionally grouped into four categories: creational, behavioral, structural, and concurrency patterns. Read about them and:

- Name one pattern in each category
- Name three patterns we have used already

# Answer

The four patterns—one from each of the four categories—could be the following:

- **Creational patterns**: Factory method
- **Structural patterns**: Composite
- **Behavioral patterns**: Visitor
- **Concurrency patterns**: Messaging pattern

In this book, we have already used the following patterns:

- **Lazy initialization**: In Chapter 6, *Interfaces, Classes, and Object Construction*, we initialized the SingletonClassExample OBJECT static field, not automatically, but only when the getInstance() method was called
- **Singleton**: In Chapter 6, *Interfaces, Classes, and Object Construction*, see the SingletonClassExample class
- **Facade**: In Chapter 6, *Interfaces, Classes, and Object Construction*, when we created a Calculator interface that captures all possible interactions with the implemented functionality

# Summary

In this chapter, we revisited a high-level view of programming and Java programming in particular. We discussed design evolution in the process of software system development, starting with the earliest feasibility phase, going through high-level design, detailed design, and ending with coding and testing. We discussed the criteria for a good design, OOP concepts, the main OOD principles, and provided a roadmap to a good OOP design. The discussion was illustrated by code examples that demonstrated the application of all the OOD principles discussed.

In the next chapter, we will dive deeper into three core elements of Java programming: operators, expressions, and statements. We will define and discuss all Java operators, explore the most popular ones in more detail, and demonstrate them in specific examples, along with expressions and statements as well.

# Operators, Expressions, and Statements $9$

In this chapter, the three core elements of Java programming—operators, expressions, and statements—will be defined and explained in detail. The discussion will be supported by specific examples that illustrate the key aspects of these elements.

The following topics will be covered:

- What are the core elements of Java programming?
- Java operators, expressions, and statements
- Operator precedence and evaluation order of operands
- Widening and narrowing the conversion of primitive types
- Boxing and unboxing between primitive and reference types
- The `equals()` method of reference types
- Exercise – Naming the statements

## What are the core elements of Java programming?

In `Chapter 2`, *Java Language Basics*, we had an overview of many aspects of Java as a language, and even defined what statements are. Now, we will look closer into the core elements of Java more systematically.

The word "elements" is quite overloaded (playing on the analogy with method overload). In Chapter 5, *Java Language Elements and Types*, we introduced input elements, those that are identified by the Java specification: whitespace, comment, and token. That is how the Java compiler parses the source code and makes sense of it. The list of tokens includes identifiers, keywords, separators, literals, and operators. That is how the Java compiler adds more meaning to the tokens it encounters.

While discussing the input elements, we explained that they are used to build more complex elements of language. In this chapter, we will start with the operator token and show how an expression—a more complex Java element—is constructed with it.

But, not all Java operators are tokens. The instanceof and new operators are keywords, while the . operator (field access or method invocation), the :: method reference operator, and the ( type ) cast operator are separators.

As we said in Chapter 2, *Java Language Basics*, a statement in Java plays a role similar to a sentence in the English language, which expresses a complete thought. In a programming language, a statement is a complete line of code that performs some action.

An expression, on the other hand, is a part of a statement that evaluates to a value. Every expression can be a statement (if the resulting value is ignored), while most statements do not include expressions.

That is how the three core elements of Java—operator, expression, and statement—are related.

# Operators

Here is the list of all 44 operators in Java:

| Operators | Description |
| --- | --- |
| +, -, *, /, % | Arithmetic unary and binary operators |
| ++, -- | Increment and decrement unary operators |
| ==, != | Equality operators |
| <, >, <=, >= | Relational operators |
| !, &, \| | Logical operators |
| &&, \|\|, ?, : | Conditional operators |
| =, +=, -=, *=, /=, %= | Assignment operators |
| &=, \|=, ^=, <<=, >>=, >>>= | Assignment operators |
| &, \|, ~, ^, <<, >>, >>> | Bitwise operators |

| ->, :: | Arrow and method reference operators |
|---|---|
| new | Instance creation operator |
| . | Field access/method invocation operator |
| instanceof | Type comparison operator |
| ( target type ) | Cast operator |

Unary means used with a single operand, while binary means it requires two operands.

In the following subsections, we will define and demonstrate most of the operators, except the rarely used assignment operators &=, |=, ^=, <<=, >>=, and >>>=, and the bitwise operators.

Also, please notice that the & and | operators behave differently if applied to integer (bitwise) and Boolean (logical) values. In this book, we will discuss these operators only as logical operators.

The arrow operator -> and the method reference operator :: will be defined and discussed in Chapter 17, *Lambda Expressions and Functional Programming*.

# Arithmetic unary (+ -) and binary operators: + - * / %

The best way to understand operators is to see them in action. Here is our demo application code (with results captured in comments) that explains the unary operators + and -:

```
public class Ch09DemoApp {
  public static void main(String[] args) {
    int i = 2;   //unary "+" is assumed by default
    int x = -i;  //unary "-" makes positive become negative
    System.out.println(x);   //prints: -2
    int y = -x;  //unary "-" makes negative become positive
    System.out.println(y);   //prints: 2
  }
}
```

And the following code demonstrates the binary operators +, -, *, /, and %:

```
int z = x + y;             //binary "+" means "add"
System.out.println(z);     //prints: 0

z = x - y;                 //binary "-" means "subtract"
System.out.println(z);     //prints: -4
System.out.println(y - x); //prints: 4
```

```
z = x * y;
System.out.println(z);        //prints: -4

z = x / y;
System.out.println(z);        //prints: -1

z = x * y;
System.out.println(z % 3);    //prints: -1
System.out.println(z % 2);    //prints: 0
System.out.println(z % 4);    //prints: 0
```

As you have probably guessed, the % operator (called modulus) divides the left-hand operand by the right-hand operand and returns the remainder.

Everything looks logical and as expected. But, then we try to divide one integer by another integer with the remainder and do not get what was expected:

```
int i1 = 11;
int i2 = 3;
System.out.println(i1 / i2); //prints: 3 instead of 3.66...
System.out.println(i1 % i2); //prints remainder: 2
```

The result, i1/i2, should be bigger than 3. It has to be 3.66... or something similar. The problem is caused by the fact that all the numbers involved in the operation are integers. In such a case, Java assumes that the result should also be expressed as an integer and drops (without rounding) the fractional part.

Now, let's declare one of the operands as the double type, with the same value of 11, and try the division again:

```
double d1 = 11;
System.out.println(d1/i2);    //prints: 3.6666666666666665
```

This time, we got what was expected, and there are other ways to achieve the same result:

```
System.out.println((float)i1 / i2);   //prints: 3.6666667
System.out.println(i1 / (double)i2); //prints: 3.6666666666666665
System.out.println(i1 * 1.0 / i2);    //prints: 3.6666666666666665
System.out.println(i1 * 1f / i2);     //prints: 3.6666667
System.out.println(i1 * 1d / i2);     //prints: 3.6666666666666665
```

As you can see, you can cast any of the operands to the `float` or `double` types (depending on the precision you need), or you can include the `float` or `double` type number. You might remember from Chapter 5, *Java Language Elements and Types*, that a value with a fractional part is `double` by default. Or, you can explicitly select a type of the value added, as we did in the last two lines of the preceding code.

Whatever you do, just be careful while dividing two integers. If you do not want the fractional part to be dropped, cast at least one operand to `float` or `double` just in case (more about the cast operator in the *Cast operator: ( target type )* section later. Then, if you need, you can round up the result to any precision you prefer or cast it back to `int`:

```
int i1 = 11;
int i2 = 3;
float r = (float)i1 / i2;
System.out.println(r);          //prints: 3.6666667
float f = Math.round(r * 100f) / 100f;
System.out.println(f);          //prints: 3.67
int i3 = (int)f;
System.out.println(i3);         //prints: 3
```

Java integer division: if in doubt, make one of the operands `double` or `float`, or simply add a `1.0` multiplier to one of them.

In case of `String`, the binary operator `+` means concatenate and the operator is often called the concatenation operator:

```
String s1 = "Nick";
String s2 = "Samoylov";
System.out.println(s1 + " " + s2);  //prints: Nick Samoylov
String s3 = s1 + " " + s2;
System.out.println(s3);             //prints: Nick Samoylov
```

And just as a reminder, in Chapter 5, *Java Language Elements and Types*, we demonstrated that an arithmetic operation applied to the primitive type `char` uses the character's code point – a numeric value of the character:

```
char c1 = 'a';
char c2 = '$';
```

```
System.out.println(c1 + c2);       //prints: 133
System.out.println(c1/c2);         //prints: 2
System.out.println((float)c1/c2);  //prints: 2.6944444
```

These results make sense only if you remember that the code point of the symbol a is 97, while the code point of the symbol $ is 36.

Most of the time, the arithmetic operations in Java are quite intuitive and cause no confusion, except in two cases:

- When all operands of the division are integral
- When char variables are used as the operands of an arithmetic operator

# Incrementing and decrementing unary operators: ++ --

The following code shows how the ++ and -- operators work, depending on their position, before the variable (prefix) or after the variable (postfix):

```
int i = 2;
System.out.println(++i);          //prints: 3
System.out.println("i=" + i);     //prints: i=3
System.out.println(--i);          //prints: 2
System.out.println("i=" + i);     //prints: i=2

System.out.println(i++);          //prints: 2
System.out.println("i=" + i);     //prints: i=3
System.out.println(i--);          //prints: 3
System.out.println("i=" + i);     //prints: i=2
```

If placed as a prefix, it changes its value by 1 before the variable's value is returned. But when placed as a postfix, it changes its value by 1 after the variable's value is returned.

The ++x expression increments the x variable before returning the result, while the x++ expression returns the result first and increments the x variable afterward.

It takes time to get used to this. But once you do, it feels easy to write ++x; or x++, instead of x = x + 1;. Using prefix or postfix increments, in this case, does not make a difference because each of them increases x eventually:

```
int x = 0;
++x;
System.out.println(x);    //prints: 1
x = 0;
x++;
System.out.println(x);    //prints: 1
```

The difference between prefix and postfix appears only when the returned value is used, not the value of the variable that will have after the postfix returns, for example. Here is the demonstration code:

```
int x = 0;
int y = x++ + x++;
System.out.println(y);    //prints: 1
System.out.println(x);    //prints: 2
```

The value of y is formed by the first x++ returning 0 and then increasing x by 1. The second x++ gets 1 as the current x value and returns it, so the y value becomes 1. Meanwhile, the second x++ increases the value of x by 1 again, so the value of x becomes 2.

This functionality makes more sense if we include it in an expression:

```
int n = 0;
int m = 5*n++;
System.out.println(m);    //prints: 0
System.out.println(n);    //prints: 1
```

It allows us to use the current value of the variable first and then increase it by 1. So, the postfix increment (decrement) operator has the side effect of incrementing (decrementing) the variable value. As we have mentioned already, it is especially beneficial for array element access:

```
int k = 0;
int[] arr = {88, 5, 42};
System.out.println(arr[k++]);    //prints: 88
System.out.println(k);           //prints: 1
System.out.println(arr[k++]);    //prints: 5
System.out.println(k);           //prints: 2
System.out.println(arr[k++]);    //prints: 42
System.out.println(k);           //prints: 3
```

The same result can be achieved by setting k to −1 and moving ++ to the front:

```
int k = -1;
int[] arr = {88, 5, 42};
System.out.println(arr[k++]);  //prints: 88
System.out.println(k);         //prints: 1
System.out.println(arr[++k]);  //prints: 5
System.out.println(k);         //prints: 2
System.out.println(arr[++k]);  //prints: 42
System.out.println(k);         //prints: 3
```

But, using k=0 and k++ reads better and thus became a typical way to access the array components. However, it is only useful if you need to access the array elements by index. For example, if you need to access the array starting with index 2, then you need to use the index:

```
int[] arr = {1,2,3,4};
int j = 2;
System.out.println(arr[j++]);  //prints: 3
System.out.println(arr[j++]);  //prints: 4
```

But if you are going to access the array sequentially, starting from index 0, then there are more economical ways to do it. See Chapter 10, *Control Flow Statements*.

# Equality operators:  ==  !=

The equality operators == (means equals) and != (means not equals) compare values of the same type and return the Boolean value true if the operand's values are equal, or false otherwise. The integral and Boolean primitive type's equality is straightforward:

```
char a = 'a';
char b = 'b';
char c = 'a';
System.out.println(a == b);  //prints: false
System.out.println(a != b);  //prints: true
System.out.println(a == c);  //prints: true
System.out.println(a != c);  //prints: false

int i1 = 1;
int i2 = 2;
int i3 = 1;
System.out.println(i1 == i2);  //prints: false
System.out.println(i1 != i2);  //prints: true
System.out.println(i1 == i3);  //prints: true
```

```
System.out.println(i1 != i3);   //prints: false

boolean b1 = true;
boolean b2 = false;
boolean b3 = true;
System.out.println(b1 == b2);   //prints: false
System.out.println(b1 != b2);   //prints: true
System.out.println(b1 == b3);   //prints: true
System.out.println(b1 != b3);   //prints: false
```

In this code, the `char` type, as in the case of arithmetic operations, is treated as a numeric value that is equal to its code point. Otherwise, it is not easy to understand the results of the following line:

```
System.out.println((a + 1) == b); //prints: true
```

But the explanation for this line is obvious from the following results:

```
System.out.println(b - a);        //prints: 1
System.out.println((int)a);       //prints: 97
System.out.println((int)b);       //prints: 98
```

The code point of `a` is 97 and the code point of `b` is 98.

For the primitive types `float` and `double`, the equality operator seems to work in the same way. Here is an example of `double` type equality:

```
double d1 = 0.42;
double d2 = 0.43;
double d3 = 0.42;
System.out.println(d1 == d2);   //prints: false
System.out.println(d1 != d2);   //prints: true
System.out.println(d1 == d3);   //prints: true
System.out.println(d1 != d3);   //prints: false
```

But, that is because we compare numbers created as literals, with fixed fractional parts. If we compare the results of the following calculations, there is a good chance that the resulting value would never be equal to the expected result, because some numbers (such as $1/3$, for example) cannot be represented exactly. And what is it exactly in the case of $1/3$? Expressed as a decimal, it has a never-ending fractional part:

```
System.out.println((double)1/3);    //prints: 0.3333333333333333
```

That is why when comparing values of types `float` and `double`, it is much more reliable to use the relational operators <, >, <=, or => (see the next subsection).

In the case of object references, an equality operator compares the references themselves, not the objects and their values:

```
SomeClass c1 = new SomeClass();
SomeClass c2 = new SomeClass();
SomeClass c3 = c1;
System.out.println(c1 == c2);       //prints: false
System.out.println(c1 != c2);       //prints: true
System.out.println(c1 == c3);       //prints: true
System.out.println(c1 != c3);       //prints: false
System.out.println(new SomeClass() == new SomeClass());  //prints: false
```

Object equality based on the values they contain has to be performed using the equals() method. We talked about it in Chapter 2, *Java Language Basics*, and will discuss it more in the *Method equals() of reference types* section later.

# Relational operators: < > <= >=

Relational operators can only be used with primitive types:

```
int i1 = 1;
int i2 = 2;
int i3 = 1;
System.out.println(i1 > i2);      //prints: false
System.out.println(i1 >= i2);     //prints: false
System.out.println(i1 >= i3);     //prints: true
System.out.println(i1 < i2);      //prints: true
System.out.println(i1 <= i2);     //prints: true
System.out.println(i1 <= i3);     //prints: true

System.out.println('a' >= 'b');   //prints: false
System.out.println('a' <= 'b');   //prints: true

double d1 = 1/3;
double d2 = 0.34;
double d3 = 0.33;
System.out.println(d1 < d2);  //prints: true
System.out.println(d1 >= d3); //prints: false
```

In the preceding code, we see that int type values compare to each other as expected, and char type values compare to each other based on their numeric code point values.

Variables of the primitive type `char`, when used as operands with arithmetic, equality, or relational operators, assign numeric values equal to the code points of the characters they represent.

So far, nothing unexpected, except the last line. We have established that 1/3 expressed as a decimal should be 0.3333333333333333, which is bigger than 0.33. Why then does d1 >= d3 return `false`? If you said that it is because of integer division, you are correct. Even when assigned to a variable of type `double`, the result is 0.0 because the integer division 1/3 happens first, before the result is assigned to d1. Here is the code that demonstrates it:

```
double d1 = 1/3;
double d2 = 0.34;
double d3 = 0.33;
System.out.println(d1 < d2);    //prints: true
System.out.println(d1 >= d3);   //prints: false
System.out.println(d1);         //prints: 0.0
double d4 = 1/3d;
System.out.println(d4);         //prints: 0.3333333333333333
System.out.println(d4 >= d3);   //prints: true
```

But other than that, using `float` and `double` types with relational operators yields more predictable results than using them with equality operators.

 While comparing values of types `float` and `double`, use the relational operators <, >, <=, or => instead of the equality operators == and !=.

Like in experimental physics, think about precision while comparing values of `float` and `double` types.

# Logical operators:  !  &  |

Let's define each of the logical operators first:

- The unary operator ! returns `true` if the operand is `false` and returns `false` otherwise
- The binary operator & returns `true` if both of the operands are `true`
- The binary operator | returns true if at least one of the operands is true

Here is the demo code:

```
boolean x = false;
System.out.println(!x);  //prints: true
System.out.println(!!x); //prints: false
boolean y = !x;
System.out.println(y & x); //prints: false
System.out.println(y | x); //prints: true
boolean z = true;
System.out.println(y & z); //prints: true
System.out.println(y | z); //prints: true
```

Notice that the ! operator can be applied to the same value several times.

# Conditional operators: && || ? : (ternary)

We can reuse the previous code example, but with the && and || operators instead of the & and | operators:

```
boolean x = false;
boolean y = !x;
System.out.println(y && x); //prints: false
System.out.println(y || x); //prints: true
boolean z = true;
System.out.println(y && z); //prints: true
System.out.println(y || z); //prints: true
```

The results are not different, but there is a difference in the execution. The operators & and | always check values of both operands. Meanwhile, in the case of &&, if the operand on the left returns false, the && operator returns false without evaluating the operand on the right. And, in the case of ||, if the operand on the left returns true, the || operator returns true without evaluating the operand on the right. Here is the code that demonstrates this difference:

```
int i = 1, j = 3, k = 10;
System.out.println(i > j & i++ < k);   //prints: false
System.out.println("i=" + i);          //prints: i=2
System.out.println(i > j && i++ < k); //prints: false
System.out.println("i=" + i);          //prints: i=2
```

Both operators—& and &&—return false. But in the case of &&, the second operand, i++ < k, is not checked and the value of the variable i does not change. Such optimization saves time if the second operand takes time to evaluate.

The && and || operators do not evaluate the right-hand condition if the left-hand condition already failed the test (returned `false`) in the case of &&, or succeeded (returned `true`) in the case of ||.

Yet, the & operator is useful when it is necessary to always check the second operand. For example, the second operand might be a method that may throw an exception and change the flow of the logic under some rare condition.

The third conditional operator is called a ternary operator. Here's how it works:

```
int n = 1, m = 2;
System.out.println(n > m ? "n > m" : "n <= m");  //prints: n <= m
System.out.println(n > m ? true : false);         //prints: false
int max = n > m ? n : m;
System.out.println(max);                           //prints: 2
```

It evaluates the condition and, if it is true, returns the first entry (after the question mark, ?); otherwise, it returns the second entry (after the colon sign, :). It is a very convenient and compact way to select between two options instead of using the full `if-else` statement construct:

```
String result;
if(n > m){
   result = "n > m";
} else {
   result = "n <= m";
}
```

We will discuss such statements (called conditional statements) in Chapter 10, *Control Flow Statements*.

# Assignment operators (most popular): = += -= *= /= %=

Although we discuss them not the first, these are the most often used operators, especially the = simple assignment operator, which just assigns a value to a variable (also phrased as *assigns a variable a value*). We have seen examples of simple assignment usage many times already.

The only possible caveat in using simple assignment is when the type of the variable on the left is not the same as the value or variable type on the right. The difference in types can lead to the *narrowing* or *widening* of the value in the case of primitive types, or to *boxing* or *unboxing* when one type is a primitive type and another type is a reference type. We will discuss such assignments in the *Widening and narrowing conversion of primitive types* and *Boxing and unboxing between a primitive and reference types* sections later.

The rest of the assignment operators (`+= -= *= /= %=`) are called compound assignment operators:

- `x += 2;` assigns the result of this addition: `x = x + 2;`
- `x -= 2;` assigns the result of this subtraction: `x = x - 2;`
- `x *= 2;` assigns the result of this multiplication: `x = x * 2;`
- `x /= 2;` assigns the result of this division: `x = x / 2;`
- `x %= 2;` assigns the remainder of this division: `x = x + x % 2;`

The operation `x = x + x % 2;` is based on the operator precedence rules, which we are going to discuss in the *Operator precedence and evaluation order of operands* section later. According to these rules, the `%` operator (modulus) is executed first, then the `+` operator (addition), and then the result is assigned to the left-hand operand variable `x`. Here is the demonstration code:

```
int x = 1;
x += 2;
System.out.println(x);    //prints: 3
x -= 1;
System.out.println(x);    //prints: 2
x *= 2;
System.out.println(x);    //prints: 4
x /= 2;
System.out.println(x);    //prints: 2
x %= 2;
System.out.println(x);    //prints: 0
```

Again, every time we encounter integer division, we had better convert it to a `float` or `double` division, then round it if necessary or just cast it to an integer. In our example, we do not have any loss of the fractional part. But if we do not know the value of `x`, the code may look as follows:

```
x = 11;
double y = x;
y /= 3;                //That's the operation we wanted to do on x
```

```
System.out.println(y);        //prints: 3.6666666666666665
x = (int)y;
System.out.println(x);        //prints: 3

//or, if we need to round up the result:
double d = Math.round(y);     //prints: 4.0
System.out.println(d);
x = (int) d;
System.out.println(x);        //prints: 4
```

In this code, we have assumed that we do not know the value of x, so we switched to the double type to avoid the loss of the fractional part. After the result is calculated, we either cast it to int (and the fractional part is lost) or round it to the nearest integer.

In this simple division, we could lose the fractional part and get 3, even without converting to the double type. But in real-life calculations, the formula is usually not that simple, so one might never know exactly where the integer division might happen. That's why it is a good practice just to convert the values to float and double before starting the calculations.

# Instance creation operator: new

By now, we have seen examples of the new operator being used many times. It instantiates (creates an object of) a class by allocating memory for the new object and returning a reference to that memory. This reference is then typically assigned to a variable of the same type as the class used to create the object or the type of its parent, although we have also seen a case when the reference was never assigned. In Chapter 6, *Interfaces, Classes, and Object Construction*, for example, we used this code to demonstrate how the constructors are called:

```
new Child();
new Child("The Blows");
```

But such cases are very rare and most of the time we need a reference to the newly created object in order to invoke its methods:

```
SomeClass obj = new SomeClass();
obj.someMethod();
```

After the new operator is called and the memory is allocated, the corresponding (explicit or default) constructor initializes the state of the new object. We talked extensively about this Chapter 6, *Interfaces, Classes, and Object Construction*.

Since arrays are objects too, they can also be created using the `new` operator and any Java type:

```
int[] arrInt = new int[42];
```

The `[]` notation allows us to set the array length (max number of components, also called elements) – 42 in the preceding code. One potential source of confusion may come from the fact that at compile time, Java allows assigning values to components with indexes bigger than the array length:

```
int[] arrInt = new int[42];
arrInt[43] = 22;
```

But when the program is run, the line `arrInt[43] = 22` will throw an exception:

```
Exception in thread "main" java.lang.ArrayIndexOutOfBoundsException: 43
    at com.packt.javapath.ch09demo.OperatorsDemo.newOperator(OperatorsDemo.java:28)
    at com.packt.javapath.ch09demo.OperatorsDemo.main(OperatorsDemo.java:13)
```

It is also possible to create an array without using the `new` operator and using the array initializer instead:

```
int[] arrInt = {1,2,3,4};
```

 A class instance can only be created using the `new` operator. An array can be created using the `new` operator or the `{}` initializer.

We discussed this extensively in Chapter 5, *Java Language Elements and Types*. If not initialized explicitly, the values of an array are set to default values that depend on the type (we described them in Chapter 5, *Java Language Elements and Types*, too). Here is a code example:

```
int[] arrInt = new int[42];
//arrInt[43] = 22;
System.out.println(arrInt[2]);        //prints: 0
System.out.println(arrInt.length);    //prints: 42
int[] arrInit = {1,2,3,4};
System.out.println(arrInit[2]);       //prints: 3
System.out.println(arrInit.length);   //prints: 4
```

And, just to remind you, the index of the first element of an array is 0.

# Type comparison operator: instanceof

The instanceof operator requires two operands of a reference type. That is because it checks the parent-child relation of an object, including implementation of interfaces. It evaluates to true if the left-hand operand (an object reference) extends or implements the type on the right, and false otherwise. Obviously, every reference instanceof Object returns true because in Java, every class implicitly inherits the Object class. When instanceof is applied to an array of any type, it returns true for the right-hand operand Object only. And, since null is not an instance of any type, null instanceof returns false for any type. Here is the demo code:

```
interface IntrfA{}
class ClassA implements IntrfA {}
class ClassB extends ClassA {}
class ClassX implements IntrfA {}

private void instanceofOperator() {
    ClassA classA = new ClassA();
    ClassB classB = new ClassB();
    ClassX classX = new ClassX();
    int[] arrI = {1,2,3};
    ClassA[] arrA = {new ClassA(), new ClassA()};

    System.out.println(classA instanceof Object); //prints: true
    System.out.println(arrI instanceof Object);   //prints: true
    System.out.println(arrA instanceof Object);   //prints: true
//System.out.println(arrA instanceof ClassA);   //error

    System.out.println(classA instanceof IntrfA); //prints: true
    System.out.println(classB instanceof IntrfA); //prints: true
    System.out.println(classX instanceof IntrfA); //prints: true

    System.out.println(classA instanceof ClassA); //prints: true
    System.out.println(classB instanceof ClassA); //prints: true
    System.out.println(classA instanceof ClassB); //prints: false
//System.out.println(classX instanceof ClassA); //error

    System.out.println(null instanceof ClassA);   //prints: false
//System.out.println(classA instanceof null);    //error
    System.out.println(classA == null);           //prints: false
    System.out.println(classA != null);           //prints: true
}
```

Most of the results are straightforward and were probably expected. The only one that might have been expected is `classX instanceof ClassA`. Both `ClassX` and `ClassA` implement the same interface, `IntrfA`, so there is some affinity between them – each can be cast to the `IntrfA` interface:

```
IntrfA intA = (IntrfA)classA;
intA = (IntrfA)classX;
```

But that relation is not of parent-child type, so the `instanceof` operator cannot even be applied to them.

 The `instanceof` operator allows us to check whether the class instance (object) has a certain class as a parent or a certain interface implemented.

We see a similar problem with `classA instanceof null` because `null` does not refer to any object at all, although `null` is a literal of the reference type.

In the last two statements in the preceding code, we showed how the object reference can be compared to `null`. Such a comparison is often used before calling a method on the reference to make sure that the reference is not `null`. It helps to avoid the dreaded `NullPointerException`, which breaks the execution flow. We will talk more about exceptions in `Chapter 10`, *Control Flow Statements*.

# Preferring polymorphism over the instanceof operator

The `instance of` operator is very helpful. We have used it several times in this book. But, there are situations that may require us to revisit the decision to use it.

 Every time you think about using the `instanceof` operator, try to see if you can avoid it by using polymorphism.

To illustrate this tip, here is some code that can benefit from polymorphism instead of using the `intanceof` operator:

```
class ClassBase {
}
class ClassY extends ClassBase {
  void method(){
```

```
      System.out.println("ClassY.method() is called");
    }
  }
  class ClassZ extends ClassBase {
    void method(){
      System.out.println("ClassZ.method() is called");
    }
  }
  class SomeClass{
    public void doSomething(ClassBase object) {
      if(object instanceof ClassY){
        ((ClassY)object).method();
      } else if(object instanceof ClassZ){
        ((ClassZ)object).method();
      }
      //other code
    }
  }
```

If we run the following code snippet:

```
  SomeClass cl = new SomeClass();
  cl.doSomething(new ClassY());
```

We will see this:

```
ClassY.method() is called
```

Then, we notice that the methods in ClassY and ClassZ have the same signature, so we may add the same method to the base class, ClassBase:

```
  class ClassBase {
    void method(){
      System.out.println("ClassBase.method() is called");
    }
  }
```

And simplify the SomeClass implementation:

```
  class SomeClass{
    public void doSomething(ClassBase object) {
      object.method();
      //other code
    }
```

After calling `new SomeClass().doSomething(new ClassY())`, we still get the same result:

```
ClassY.method() is called
```

That is because `method()` is overridden in the child. The method implemented in `ClassBase` can do something or nothing. It does not matter because it is never going to be executed (unless you specifically call it by casting it from the child class using the `super` keyword).

And, while overriding, do not forget to use the `@Override` annotation:

```
class ClassZ extends ClassBase {
  @Override
  void method(){
    System.out.println("ClassY.method() is called");
  }
}
```

The annotation will help you to verify that you are not mistaken and the method in each of the child classes has the same signature as the one in the parent class.

# Field access or method invocation operator: .

Inside the class or interface, a field or a method of this class or interface can be accessed just by the name. But from outside the class or interface, the non-private field or method can be accessed using the dot (.) operator and:

- If the field or method is non-static (instance member), the object name
- If the field or method is static, the interface or class name

 A dot operator (.) can be used to access a non-private field or method. If the field or method is static, the dot operator is applied to the interface or class name. If the field or method is non-static, the dot operator is applied to the object reference.

We have seen many such examples already. So, we just summarize all the cases in one interface and the class that implements it. Let's assume that we have the following interface called `InterfaceM`:

```
interface InterfaceM {
```

```
String INTERFACE_FIELD = "interface field";
static void staticMethod1(){
  System.out.println("interface static method 1");
}
static void staticMethod2(){
  System.out.println("interface static method 2");
}
default void method1(){
  System.out.println("interface default method 1");
}
default void method2(){
  System.out.println("interface default method 2");
}
void method3();
}
```

We can use a dot operator (.) with it as follows:

```
System.out.println(InterfaceM.INTERFACE_FIELD);      //1: interface field
InterfaceM.staticMethod1();                  //2: interface static method
InterfaceM.staticMethod2();                  //3: interface static method
//InterfaceM.method1();                      //4: compilation error
//InterfaceM.method2();                      //5: compilation error
//InterfaceM.method3();                      //6: compilation error

System.out.println(ClassM.INTERFACE_FIELD);      //7: interface field
```

Cases 1, 2, and 3 are straightforward. Cases 4, 5, and 6 generate a compilation error because non-static methods can be accessed only via an instance (object) of a class that implements the interface. Case 7 is possible, but is not a recommended way to access interface fields (also called constants). Accessing them using the interface name (as in case 1) makes the code easier to understand.

Now let's create a ClassM class that implements the InterfaceM interface:

```
class ClassM implements InterfaceM {
  public static String CLASS_STATIC_FIELD = "class static field";
  public static void staticMethod2(){
    System.out.println("class static method 2");
  }
  public static void staticMethod3(){
    System.out.println("class static method 3");
  }
  public String instanceField = "instance field";
  public void method2(){
    System.out.println("class instance method 2");
  }
```

```
    public void method3(){
        System.out.println("class instance method 3");
    }
}
```

And here are all possible cases of using the dot operator ( . ) for the class field and method access:

```
//ClassM.staticMethod1();                            //8: compilation error
ClassM.staticMethod2();                              //9: class static method 2
ClassM.staticMethod3();                              //10: class static method 3

ClassM classM = new ClassM();
System.out.println(ClassM.CLASS_STATIC_FIELD);//11: class static field
System.out.println(classM.CLASS_STATIC_FIELD);//12: class static field
//System.out.println(ClassM.instanceField);      //13: compilation error
System.out.println(classM.instanceField);           //14: instance field
//classM.staticMethod1();                            //15: compilation error
classM.staticMethod2();                     //16: class static method  2
classM.staticMethod3();                     //17: class static method 3
classM.method1();                  //18: interface default method 1
classM.method2();                       //19: class instance method 2
classM.method3();                       //20: class instance method 3
}
```

Case 8 generates a compilation error because a static method belongs to the class or interface (in this case) where it is implemented.

Case 9 is an example of a static method hiding. A method with the same signature is implemented in the interface but hidden by the class implementation.

Cases 10 and 11 are straightforward.

Case 12 is possible but not recommended. Accessing a static class field using the class name makes the code easier to understand.

Class 13 is an obvious error because an instance field can be accessed only via an instance (object).

Class 14 is a correct version of case 13.

Class 15 is an error because a static method belongs to the class or interface (in this case) where it is implemented, not to the class instance.

Cases 16 and 17 are possible but are not recommended ways to access a static method. Using the class name (instead of the instance identifier) to access static method makes code easier to understand.

Case 18 demonstrates how an interface can provide a default implementation to a class. That is possible because `ClassM implements InterfaceM` effectively inherits all the methods and fields of the interface. We say effectively because the legally correct terminology is class *implements* interface. But in fact, a class that implements an interface acquires all the fields and methods of the interface in the same manner a child class inherits them.

Case 19 is an example of the class overriding the default implementation of the interface.

Case 20 is an example of the classic interface implementation. That was the original idea of an interface: to provide an abstraction of the API.

# Cast operator: (target type)

The cast operator is used for type casting, assigning a value of one type to a variable of another type. Usually, it is used to enable conversions that would otherwise not be allowed by the compiler. We used type casting, for example, when we discussed integer division, the `char` type as a numeric type, and assigning a class reference to a variable that has a type of one of the implemented interfaces:

```
int i1 = 11;
int i2 = 3;
System.out.println((float)i1 / i2);   //prints: 3.6666667

System.out.println((int)a);           //prints: 97

IntrfA intA = (IntrfA)classA;
```

There are two potential issues to watch while casting:

- In the case of primitive types, the value should be smaller than the maximum value the target type can hold (we will talk about this in detail in the *Widening and narrowing conversion of primitive types* section later)

- In the case of reference types, the left-hand operand should be a parent (even if indirect) of the right-hand operand, or the left-hand operand should be an interface implemented (even if indirectly) by the class represented by the right-hand operand:

```
interface I1{}
interface I2{}
interface I3{}
class A implements I1, I2 {}
class B extends A implements I3{}
class C extends B {}
class D {}
public static void main(String[] args) {
    C c = new C();      //1
    A a = (A)c;         //2
    I1 i1 = (I1)c;      //3
    I2 i2 = (I2)c;      //4
    I3 i3 = (I3)c;      //5
    c = (C)a;           //6
    D d = new D();      //7
    //a = (A)d;         //8 compilation error
    i1 = (I1)d;         //9 run-time error
}
```

In this code, case 6 is possible because we know that object a was originally cast based on object c, so we can cast it back to type C and expect it to be fully functional as an object of class C.

Case 8 does not compile because its parent-child relations can be verified by the compiler.

Case 9 is not so easy for the compiler for reasons that are outside the scope of this book. So, while writing code, the IDE will not give you a hint and you may think everything will work as you expect. But then at run-time, you can get ClassCastException:

```
Exception in thread "main" java.lang.ClassCastException: com.packt.javapath.ch09demo
    at com.packt.javapath.ch09demo.OperatorsDemo.castOperator(OperatorsDemo.java:40)
    at com.packt.javapath.ch09demo.OperatorsDemo.main(OperatorsDemo.java:17)
```

Programmers are as happy to see it as much as they like to see the NullPointerException or ArrayOutOfBoundException we demonstrated before. That's why casting to an interface has to be done with more care than to a class.

Typecasting is assigning a value of one type to a variable of another type. While doing it, make sure that the target type can hold the value and check it against the maximum target type value if necessary.

It is also possible to cast a primitive type to a matching reference type:

```
Integer integer1 = 3;                    //line 1
System.out.println(integer1);            //prints: 3
Integer integer2 = Integer.valueOf(4);
int i = integer2;                        //line 4
System.out.println(i);                   //prints: 4
```

In line 1 and line 4, casting is done implicitly. We will discuss such a casting (also called conversion, or boxing and unboxing) in more detail in the *Boxing and unboxing between a primitive and reference types* section later.

# Expressions

As we said at the beginning of this section, an expression exists only as a part of a statement, the latter being the complete action (we will discuss it in the next subsection). This means that an expression can be a building block of an action. Some expressions can even become a full action (an expression statement) after adding a semicolon to them.

The distinguishing feature of an expression is that it can be evaluated, which means it can produce something as the result of its execution. This something can be one of three things:

- A variable, such as `i = 2`
- A value, such as `2*2`
- Nothing, when the expression is an invocation of a method that returns nothing (void). Such an expression can only be the full action—an expression statement—with a semicolon at the end.

An expression typically includes one or more operators and is evaluated. It can produce a variable, a value (that is included in further evaluation), or can invoke a method that returns nothing (void).

An evaluation of an expression can also produce a side effect. That is, in addition to the variable assignment or returning a value, it can do something else, for example:

```
int x = 0, y;
y = x++;                    //line 2
System.out.println(y);      //prints: 0
System.out.println(x);      //prints: 1
```

The expression in line 2 assigns a value to variable y, but also has the side effect of adding 1 to the value of variable x.

By its form, the expression can be:

- A primary expression:
    - A literal (some value)
    - Object creation (with the new operator or with the { } array initializer)
    - Field access (with the dot operator for an external class or without it for this instance)
    - A method invocation (with the dot operator for an external class or without it for this instance)
    - A method reference (with the : : operator, in lambda expressions)
    - Array access (with the [ ] notation, which carries an index of the element to be accessed)
- A unary operator expression (x++ or -y, for example)
- A binary operator expression (x+y or x*y, for example)
- A ternary operator expression (x > y ? "x>y" : "x<=y", for example)
- A lambda expression i -> i + 1 (see Chapter 17, *Lambda Expressions and Functional Programming*)

The expressions are named according to the action they produce: an object creation expression, a cast expression, a method invocation expression, an array access expression, an assignment expression, and so on.

An expression that consists of other expressions is called a complex expression. Parentheses are often used to clearly identify each of the sub-expressions, instead of relying on the operator precedence (see the *Operators precedence and evaluation order of operands* section later).

# Statements

We actually defined a statement once in Chapter 2, *Java Language Basics*. It is a complete action that can be executed. It can include one or more expressions and ends with a semicolon ; .

A Java statement describes an action. It is a minimal construct that can be executed. It may or may not include one or more expressions.

The possible kinds of Java statements are:

- A class or interface declaration statement, such as class A {...}
- An empty statement that consists of only one symbol, ;
- A local variable declaration statement, int x;
- A synchronized statement – outside the scope of this book
- An expression statement, which can be one of the following:
  - A method invocation statement, such as method();
  - An assignment statement, such as x = 3;
  - An object creation statement, such as new SomeClass();
  - A unary increment or decrement statement, such as ++x ; --x; x++; x--;
- A control flow statement (see Chapter 10, *Control Flow Statements*):
  - A selection statement: if-else or switch-case
  - An iteration statement: for, while, or do-while
  - An exception handling statement, such as try-catch-finally or throw
  - A branching statement, such as break, continue, label:, return, assert

A statement can be *labeled* by placing an identifier and colon : in front of it. This label can be used by the branching statements break and continue to redirect the control flow. In Chapter 10, *Control Flow Statements*, we will show you how to do it.

Most often, statements compose a method body, and that is how programs are written.

# Operator precedence and evaluation order of operands

When several operators are used in the same expression, it might not be obvious how to execute them without established rules. For example, what is the value that is going to be assigned to variable x after the following right-hand expression is evaluated:

```
int x = 2 + 4 * 5 / 6 + 3 + 7 / 3 * 11 - 4;
```

We know how to do it because we have learned operator precedence in school—just apply the multiplication and division operators first from left to right, then addition and subtraction from left to right too. But, it turned out that the author actually wanted this sequence of operator execution:

```
int x = 2 + 4 * 5 / 6 + ( 3 + 7 / 3 * (11 - 4));
```

It yields a different result.

 Operator precedence and parentheses determines the sequence in which parts of an expression are evaluated. The evaluation order of operands defines for each operation the sequence in which its operands are evaluated.

The parentheses help to identify the structure of a complex expression and establish the sequence of evaluation, which overrides the operator precedence.

# Operator precedence

The Java specification does not provide operator precedence in one place. One has to pull it together from various sections. That's why different sources on the internet sometimes have a bit of a different sequence of operator execution, so do not be surprised, and if in doubt, experiment or just set the parentheses to guide the calculations in the sequence you need to.

The following list shows the operator precedence from the highest (the first executed) as the first in the list, to the lowest precedence at the end. Operators of the same level of precedence are executed by their position in the expression while moving from left to right (provided no parentheses are used):

- An expression that calculates the index of an array element inside the `[]` notation, such as `x = 4* arr[i+1]`; the field access and method invocation dot operator `.`, such as in `x = 3*someClass.COUNT` or `x = 2*someClass.method(2, "b")`
- Unary postfix increment `++` and decrement `--` operators, such as `x++` or `x--`, as in `int m = 5*n++`; notice that such an operator returns the old value of the variable before it increments/decrements its value, thus having the side effect of incrementing the value

- A unary prefix with the `++` and `--` operators, such as `++x` or `--x`; unary `+` and `-` operators, such as in `+x` or `-x`; the logical operator NOT, such as in `!b`, where b is a Boolean variable; unary bitwise NOT `~` (outside the scope of this book)
- A cast operator `()`, such as `double x = (double)11/3`, where 11 is cast to `double` first, thus avoiding the integer division problem of losing the fractional part; the instance creation operator `new`, such as in `new SomeClass()`
- Multiplicative operators `*`, `/`, `%`
- Additive operators `+`, `-`, string concatention `+`
- Bitwise shift operators `<<`, `>>`, `>>>`;
- Relational operators `<`, `>`, `>=`, `<=`, `instanceof`
- Equality operators `==`, `!=`
- The logical and bitwise operator `&`
- The bitwise operator `^`
- The logical and bitwise operator `|`
- The conditional operator `&&`
- The conditional operator `||`
- The conditional operator `?:` (ternary)
- The arrow operator `->`
- Assignment operators `=`, `+=`, `-=`, `*=`, `/=`, `%=`, `>>=`, `<<=`, `>>>=`, `&=`, `^=`, `|=`

If parentheses are present, then the expression inside the innermost parentheses is calculated first. For example, look at this code snippet:

```
int p1 = 10, p2 = 1;
int q = (p1 += 3)  +  (p2 += 3);
System.out.println(q);          //prints: 17
System.out.println(p1);         //prints: 13
System.out.println(p2);         //prints: 4
```

The assignment operators have the lowest precedence, but they are executed first if inside the parentheses, as in the preceding code. To prove this point, we can remove the first set of parentheses and run the same code again:

```
p1 = 10;
p2 = 1;
q = p1 += 3  +  (p2 += 3);
System.out.println(q);          //prints: 17
System.out.println(p1);         //prints: 17
System.out.println(p2);         //prints: 4
```

As you can see, now the first operator assignment += was executed last in the right-hand expression.

Using parentheses increases the readability of a complex expression.

You can take advantage of operator precedence and write an expression with very few parentheses, if any at all. But the quality of code is defined not only by its correctness. Being easy to understand, so that other programmers—maybe not so well versed in operator precedence—can maintain it is also one of the criteria for well-written code. Besides, even the code's author, after some time, may have difficulty trying to understand not-clearly-structured expressions.

# Evaluation order of operands

While evaluating an expression, parentheses and operator precedence are taken into account first. Then, those parts of the expression that have the same level of execution priority are evaluated as they appear when moving from left to right.

Using parentheses improves the understanding of a complex expression, but too many nested parentheses can obscure it. If in doubt, consider breaking the complex expression into several statements.

Eventually, the evaluation comes down to each operator and its operands. Operands of a binary operator are evaluated from left to right so that left-hand operand is fully evaluated before the evaluation of the right-hand operator starts. As we have seen, the left-hand operand can have a side effect that affects the right-hand operator's behavior. Here is a simplistic example:

```
int a = 0, b = 0;
int c = a++ + (a * ++b);        //evaluates to: 0 + (1 * 1);
System.out.println(c);          //prints: 1
```

In real-life examples, the expression can include methods with complex functionality behind and wide-reaching side effects. The left-hand operand can even throw an exception, so the right-hand operand will never be evaluated. But if the left-hand evaluation completes without exceptions, Java guarantees that both operands are fully evaluated before the operator is executed.

This rule does not apply though to conditional operators &&, ||, and ?: (see the *Conditional operators: && || ? : (ternary)* section).

# Widening and narrowing reference types

In the case of reference types, assigning a child object reference to the variable of the parent class type is called widening reference conversion or upcasting. The assigning of a parent class type reference to the variable of a child class type is called narrowing reference conversion or downcasting.

# Widening

For example, if a class, SomeClass, extends SomeBaseClass, the following declaration and initialization are possible:

```
SomeBaseClass someBaseClass = new SomeBaseClass();
someBaseClass = new SomeClass();
```

And, since every class extends the `java.lang.Object` class by default, the following declarations and initializations are possible too:

```
Object someBaseClass = new SomeBaseClass();
someBaseClass = new SomeClass();              //line 2
```

In line 2, we assigned a subclass instance reference to a variable of a superclass type. Methods present in a subclass but not in the superclass are not accessible via the reference of the superclass type. The assignment in line 2 is called a widening of the reference because it becomes less specialized.

# Narrowing

Assigning a parent object reference to the variable of the child class type is called narrowing reference conversion or downcasting. It is possible only after widening reference conversion has been applied first.

Here is a code example that demonstrates the case:

```
class SomeBaseClass{
    void someMethod(){
        ...
    }
}
class SomeClass extends SomeBaseClass{
    void someOtherMethod(){
        ...
    }
}
SomeBaseClass someBaseClass = new SomeBaseClass();
someBaseClass = new SomeClass();
someBaseClass.someMethod();                    //works just fine
//someBaseClass.someOtherMethod();             //compilation error
((SomeClass)someBaseClass).someOtherMethod(); //works just fine
//The following methods are available as they come from Object:
int h = someBaseClass.hashCode();
Object o = someBaseClass.clone();
//All other public Object's methods are accessible too
```

The narrowing conversion requires casting, and we discussed this in great detail when we talked about the cast operator (see the *Cast operator* section), including casting to an interface, which is another form of upcasting.

# Widening and narrowing conversion of primitive types

When a value (or variable) of one numeric type is assigned to a variable of another numeric type, the new type may hold a bigger number or smaller maximum number. If the target type can hold a bigger number, the conversion is widening. If otherwise, it is a narrowing conversion, which usually requires a typecasting using a cast operator.

## Widening

The maximum number a numeric type can hold is determined by the number of bits allocated to this type. To remind you, here is the number of bits for each numeric type representation:

- `byte`: 8 bit
- `char`: 16 bit
- `short`: 16 bit
- `int`: 32 bit
- `long`: 64 bit
- `float`: 32 bit
- `double`: 64 bit

The Java Specification defines 19 widening primitive conversions:

- `byte` to `short, int, long, float,` or `double`
- `short` to `int, long, float,` or `double`
- `char` to `int, long, float,` or `double`
- `int` to `long, float,` or `double`
- `long` to `float` or `double`
- `float` to `double`

In widening conversions between integral types and some conversions from integral types to floating-point values, the resulting value remains the same as the original one. But conversion from `int` to `float`, or from `long` to `float`, or from `long` to `double`, may result, according to the specification:

> *"in loss of precision - that is, the result may lose some of the least significant bits of the value. In this case, the resulting floating-point value will be a correctly rounded version of the integer value, using IEEE 754 round-to-nearest mode."*

Let's look at this effect through code examples and start with `int` type conversion to `float` and `double`:

```
int n = 1234567899;
float f = (float)n;
int r = n - (int)f;
System.out.println(r);     //prints: -46

double d = (double)n;
r = n - (int)d;
System.out.println(r);     //prints: 0
```

As the specification stated, only the conversion from `int` to `float` has lost precision. Conversion from `int` to `double` was just fine. Now, let's convert `long` type:

```
long l = 1234567899123456L;
float f = (float)l;
long rl = l - (long)f;
System.out.println(rl);     //prints: -49017088

double d = (double)l;
rl = l - (long)d;
System.out.println(rl);     //prints: 0

l = 12345678991234567L;
d = (double)l;
rl = l - (long)d;
System.out.println(rl);     //prints: -1
```

Conversion from `long` to `float` lost precision big time. Well, the specification warned us about it. But conversion from `long` to `double` looked fine at first. Then, we increased the `long` value approximately ten times and got a precision loss of -1. So, it depends on how big the value is too.

Despite that, the Java specification does not allow any runtime exceptions caused by widening conversion. In our examples, we did not encounter an exception either.

# Narrowing

The narrowing conversion of numeric primitive types occurs in the opposite direction—from the wider type to the narrower one—and typically requires casting. The Java specification identifies 22 narrowing primitive conversions:

- short to byte or char
- char to byte or short
- int to byte, short, or char
- long to byte, short, char, or int
- float to byte, short, char, int, or long
- double to byte, short, char, int, long, or float

It can result in a loss of magnitude of the value and possibly in loss of precision too. The narrowing procedure is more complicated than the widening one and discussion of it is beyond the scope of an introductory course. The least one can do is to make sure that the original value is smaller than the maximum value of the target type:

```
double dd = 1234567890.0;
System.out.println(Integer.MAX_VALUE); //prints: 2147483647
if(dd < Integer.MAX_VALUE){
  int nn = (int)dd;
  System.out.println(nn);              //prints: 1234567890
} else {
  System.out.println(dd - Integer.MAX_VALUE);
}

dd = 2234567890.0;
System.out.println(Integer.MAX_VALUE); //prints: 2147483647
if(dd < Integer.MAX_VALUE){
  int nn = (int)dd;
  System.out.println(nn);
} else {
  System.out.println(dd - Integer.MAX_VALUE); //prints: 8.7084243E7
}
```

As you can see from these examples, the narrowing conversion happens just fine when the number fits the target type, but we even do not try to convert if the original value is bigger than the maximum value of the target type.

Before casting, think about the maximum value the target type can hold, especially while narrowing the value type.

But there is more to it than just avoiding complete loss of value. Things get especially complicated with the conversion between type `char` and types `byte` or `short`. The reason for this is that type `char` is an unsigned numeric type, while types byte and short are signed numeric types, so some loss of information is possible.

# Methods of primitive type conversion

Casting is not the only way to convert one primitive type to another. Each of the primitive types has a corresponding reference type – a class called a wrapper class of a primitive type.

All wrapper classes are located in the `java.lang` package:

- `java.lang.Boolean`
- `java.lang.Byte`
- `java.lang.Character`
- `java.lang.Short`
- `java.lang.Integer`
- `java.lang.Long`
- `java.lang.Float`
- `java.lang.Double`

Most of them—except the `Boolean` and `Character` classes—extend the `java.lang.Number` class, which has the following abstract method declarations:

- `byteValue()`
- `shortValue()`
- `intValue()`
- `longValue()`
- `floatValue()`
- `doubleValue()`

This means that every `Number` class child has to implement all of them. Such methods are implemented in the `Character` class too, while the `Boolean` class has the `booleanValue()` method. These methods can be used to widen and narrow primitive types too.

In addition, each of the wrapper classes has methods that allow the conversion of `String` representation of a numeric value to the corresponding primitive numeric type or reference type, for example:

```
byte b = Byte.parseByte("3");
Byte bt = Byte.decode("3");
boolean boo = Boolean.getBoolean("true");
Boolean bool = Boolean.valueOf("false");
int n = Integer.parseInt("42");
Integer integer = Integer.getInteger("42");
double d1 = Double.parseDouble("3.14");
Double d2 = Double.valueOf("3.14");
```

After that, the previously listed methods (`byteValue()`, `shortValue()`, and so on) can be used to convert the value to another primitive type.

And each of the wrapper classes has the static method `toString(primitive value)` to convert the primitive type value to its `String` representation:

```
String s1 = Integer.toString(42);
String s2 = Double.toString(3.14);
```

The wrapper classes have many other useful methods of conversion from one primitive type to another, and to different formats and representations. So, if you need to something like that, look in the `java.lang` package at its numeric type class wrappers first.

One of the type conversions allows for creating a wrapper class object from the corresponding primitive type and vice versa. We will discuss such conversions in the next section.

# Boxing and unboxing between primitive and reference types

Boxing converts the value of a primitive type to an object of a corresponding wrapper class. Unboxing converts the object of a wrapper class to a value of the corresponding primitive type.

# Boxing

Boxing a primitive type can be done either automatically (called autoboxing) or explicitly using the `valueOf()` method available in each wrapper type:

```
int n = 12;
Integer integer = n; //an example of autoboxing
System.out.println(integer);       //prints: 12
integer = Integer.valueOf(n);
System.out.println(integer);       //prints: 12

Byte b = Byte.valueOf((byte)n);
Short s = Short.valueOf((short)n);
Long l = Long.valueOf(n);
Float f = Float.valueOf(n);
Double d = Double.valueOf(n);
```

Notice that the input value of the `valueOf()` method of the `Byte` and `Short` wrappers required casting because it was a narrowing of a primitive type, which we discussed in the previous section.

# Unboxing

Unboxing can be accomplished using the methods of the `Number` class implemented in each wrapper class:

```
Integer integer = Integer.valueOf(12);
System.out.println(integer.intValue());      //prints: 12
System.out.println(integer.byteValue());     //prints: 12
System.out.println(integer.shortValue());    //prints: 12
System.out.println(integer.longValue());     //prints: 12
System.out.println(integer.floatValue());    //prints: 12.0
System.out.println(integer.doubleValue());   //prints: 12.0
```

Similar to autoboxing, automatic unboxing is possible too:

```
Long longWrapper = Long.valueOf(12L);
long lng = longWrapper;       //implicit unboxing
System.out.println(lng);      //prints: 12
```

But, it is not called autounboxing. The term implicit unboxing is used instead.

# Method equals() of reference types

The equality operator, when applied to reference types, compares the reference values, not the content of the objects. It returns `true` only when both references (variable values) point to the same object. We have demonstrated it several times already:

```
SomeClass o1 = new SomeClass();
SomeClass o2 = new SomeClass();
System.out.println(o1 == o2);  //prints: false
System.out.println(o1 == o1);  //prints: true
o2 = o1;
System.out.println(o1 == o2);  //prints: true
```

This means that the equality operator returns `false` even when two objects of the same class with the same field values are compared. That is often not what programmers need. Instead, we usually need to consider two objects to be equal when they have the same type and the same field values. Sometimes, we even do not want to consider all the fields, but only those that identify the object as unique in our program logic. For example, if a person changes their hairstyle or dress, we still identify him or her as the same person, even if an object that describes the person has the field `hairstyle` or `dress`.

# Using the implementation of the base class Object

For such a comparison of objects—by the value of their fields—the `equals()` method is to be used. In Chapter 2, *Java Language Basics*, we already established that all reference types extend (implicitly) the `java.lang.Object` class, which has the `equals()` method implemented:

```
public boolean equals(Object obj) {
   return (this == obj);
}
```

As you can see, it compares only references using the equality operator, which means that if a class or one of its parents does not implement the `equals()` method (which overrides the implementation of the `Object` class), the result of using the `equals()` method will be the same as using the equality operator ==. Let's demonstrate this. The following class does not implement the `equals()` method:

```
class PersonNoEquals {
   private int age;
   private String name;

   public PersonNoEquals(int age, String name) {
      this.age = age;
      this.name = name;
   }
}
```

If we use it and compare the results of the `equals()` method and the == operator, we will see the following:

```
PersonNoEquals p1 = new PersonNoEquals(42, "Nick");
PersonNoEquals p2 = new PersonNoEquals(42, "Nick");
PersonNoEquals p3 = new PersonNoEquals(25, "Nick");
System.out.println(p1.equals(p2));      //false
System.out.println(p1.equals(p3));      //false
System.out.println(p1 == p2);           //false
p1 = p2;
System.out.println(p1.equals(p2));      //true
System.out.println(p1 == p2);           //true
```

As we expected, the results are the same, whether we use the `equals()` method or the == operator.

# Overriding the equals() method

Now, let's implement the `equals()` method:

```
class PersonWithEquals{
   private int age;
   private String name;
   private String hairstyle;

   public PersonWithEquals(int age, String name, String hairstyle) {
      this.age = age;
      this.name = name;
```

```
      this.hairstyle = hairstyle;
   }

   @Override
   public boolean equals(Object o) {
      if (this == o) return true;
      if (o == null || getClass() != o.getClass()) return false;
      PersonWithEquals person = (PersonWithEquals) o;
      return age == person.age && Objects.equals(name, person.name);
   }
}
```

Notice that, while establishing the objects' equality, we ignore the `hairstyle` field. Another aspect that requires comments is the use of the `equals()` method of the `java.utils.Objects` class. Here is its implementation:

```
public static boolean equals(Object a, Object b) {
   return (a == b) || (a != null && a.equals(b));
}
```

As you can see, it compares references first, then makes sure that one is not `null` (to avoid `NullPointerException`), then uses the `equals()` method of the `java.lang.Object` base class or the overriding implementation that might be present in a child passed in as a parameter value. In our case, we pass in parameter objects of type `String` that do have the `equals()` method implemented, which compares `String` type values, not just references (we will talk about it shortly). So, any difference in any field of objects, `PersonWithEquals`, will cause the method to return `false`.

If we run the test again, we will see this:

```
PersonWithEquals p11 = new PersonWithEquals(42, "Kelly", "Ponytail");
PersonWithEquals p12 = new PersonWithEquals(42, "Kelly", "Pompadour");
PersonWithEquals p13 = new PersonWithEquals(25, "Kelly", "Ponytail");
System.out.println(p11.equals(p12));     //true
System.out.println(p11.equals(p13));     //false
System.out.println(p11 == p12);          //false
p11 = p12;
System.out.println(p11.equals(p12));     //true
System.out.println(p11 == p12);          //true
```

Now, the `equals()` method returns `true` not only when references are equal (so they point to the same object), but also when the references are different but the objects they refer to have the same type and the same values of certain fields that are included in the object identification.

# Using the identification implemented in the parent class

We could create a base class, `Person`, that has only the two fields `age` and `name` and the `equals()` method, as implemented previously. Then, we could extend it with the `PersonWithHair` class (which has the additional field `hairstyle`):

```
class Person{
  private int age;
  private String name;
  public Person(int age, String name) {
    this.age = age;
    this.name = name;
  }
  @Override
  public boolean equals(Object o) {
    if (this == o) return true;
    if (o == null || getClass() != o.getClass()) return false;
    Person person = (Person) o;
    return age == person.age && Objects.equals(name, person.name);
  }
}
class PersonWithHair extends Person{
  private String hairstyle;
  public PersonWithHair(int age, String name, String hairstyle) {
    super(age, name);
    this.hairstyle = hairstyle;
  }
}
```

The objects of the `PersonWithHair` class would compare the same way as in the previous test of `PersonWithEquals`:

```
PersonWithHair p21 = new PersonWithHair(42, "Kelly", "Ponytail");
PersonWithHair p22 = new PersonWithHair(42, "Kelly", "Pompadour");
PersonWithHair p23 = new PersonWithHair(25, "Kelly", "Ponytail");
System.out.println(p21.equals(p22));    //true
System.out.println(p21.equals(p23));    //false
System.out.println(p21 == p22);         //false
p21 = p22;
System.out.println(p21.equals(p22));    //true
System.out.println(p21 == p22);         //true
```

That is possible because an object of `PersonWithHair` is of a type `Person` too, so take this line:

```
Person person = (Person) o;
```

The preceding line in the `equals()` method does not throw `ClassCastException`.

We can then create the `PersonWithHairDresssed` class:

```
PersonWithHairDressed extends PersonWithHair{
    private String dress;
    public PersonWithHairDressed(int age, String name,
                             String hairstyle, String dress) {
      super(age, name, hairstyle);
      this.dress = dress;
    }
}
```

If we run the same test again, it will yield the same results. But we think that dress and hairstyle are not part of the identification, so we can run the test to compare the children of `Person`:

```
Person p31 = new PersonWithHair(42, "Kelly", "Ponytail");
Person p32 = new PersonWithHairDressed(42, "Kelly", "Pompadour", "Suit");
Person p33 = new PersonWithHair(25, "Kelly", "Ponytail");
System.out.println(p31.equals(p32));    //false
System.out.println(p31.equals(p33));    //false
System.out.println(p31 == p32);         //false
```

That was not what we expected! The children were considered not equal because of this line in the `equals()` method of the `Person` base class:

```
if (o == null || getClass() != o.getClass()) return false;
```

The preceding line failed because the `getClass()` and `o.getClass()` methods return the child class name – the one that was instantiated with the `new` operator. To get out of this jam, we use the following logic:

- Our implementation of the `equals()` method is located in the `Person` class, so we know that the current object is of type `Person`
- To compare classes, all we need to do is to make sure that the other object is of type `Person` too

If we replace this line:

```
if (o == null || getClass() != o.getClass()) return false;
```

With the following code:

```
if (o == null) return false;
if(!(o instanceof Person)) return false;
```

The result will be this:

```
Person p31 = new PersonWithHair(42, "Kelly", "Ponytail");
Person p32 = new PersonWithHairDressed(42, "Kelly", "Pompadour", "Suit");
Person p33 = new PersonWithHair(25, "Kelly", "Ponytail");
System.out.println(p31.equals(p32));    //true
System.out.println(p31.equals(p33));    //false
System.out.println(p31 == p32);         //false
```

That is what we wanted, didn't we? This way, we have achieved the original idea of not including hairstyle and dress in the person's identification.

 In the case of object references, the equality operators == and != compare the references themselves - not the values of the objects' fields (states). If you need to compare object states, use the `equals()` method that has overridden the one in the `Object` class.

The `String` class and the wrapper classes of primitive types override the `equals()` method too.

# The equals() method of the String class

In Chapter 5, *Java Language Elements and Types*, we have already discussed this and even reviewed the source code. Here it is:

```
public boolean equals(Object anObject) {
  if (this == anObject) {
    return true;
  }
  if (anObject instanceof String) {
```

```
String aString = (String)anObject;
if (coder() == aString.coder()) {
  return isLatin1() ?
          StringLatin1.equals(value, aString.value)
        : StringUTF16.equals(value, aString.value);
}
}
return false;
}
```

As you can see, it overrides the Object class implementation in order to compare values, not just references. This code proves it:

```
String sl1 = "test1";
String sl2 = "test2";
String sl3 = "test1";

System.out.println(sl1 == sl2);                 //1: false
System.out.println(sl1.equals(sl2));            //2: false

System.out.println(sl1 == sl3);                 //3: true
System.out.println(sl1.equals(sl3));            //4: true

String s1 = new String("test1");
String s2 = new String("test2");
String s3 = new String("test1");

System.out.println(s1 == s2);                   //5: false
System.out.println(s1.equals(s2));              //6: false

System.out.println(s1 == s3);                   //7: false
System.out.println(s1.equals(s3));              //8: true

System.out.println(sl1 == s1);                  //9: false
System.out.println(sl1.equals(s1));             //10: true
```

You can see that the equality operator == sometimes compares the String object values correctly and sometimes doesn't. The equal() method, though, always compares the values correctly, even if they are wrapped in different objects, not just refer literals.

We included the equality operator in the test in order to clarify the cases of incorrect explanation of String values one can read on the internet more often than one might expect. The incorrect explanation is based on the JVM implementation that supports String instance immutability (read about String immutability and the motivation for it in Chapter 5, *Java Language Elements and Types*). The JVM does not store the same String value twice and reuses the value already stored in the area called the **string pool** in the process called **strings interning**. After learning about that, some people assume that using the equals() method with String values is unnecessary because the same value will have the same reference value anyway. Our test proves that, in the case of a String value wrapped in the class String, its value cannot be compared correctly by the equality operator and one must use the equals() method instead. There are also other cases when a String value is not stored in the string pool.

> To compare two String objects by value, always use
> the equals() method, not the equality operator ==.

In general, the equals() method is not as fast as the == operator. But, as we already pointed out in Chapter 5, *Java Language Elements and Types*, the equals() method of class String compares references first, which means there is no need to try to save performance time and compare references in the code before calling the equals() method. Just call the equals() method.

The ambiguity of String type behavior—sometimes like a primitive type, other times like a reference type—reminds me of the double nature of elementary particles in physics. Particles sometimes behave like small concentrated objects, but other times like waves. What is really going on behind the scenes, deep in the guts of the matter? Is something is immutable there too?

# The equals() method in wrapper classes of primitive types

If we run the test for a wrapper class, the results will be:

```
long ln = 42;
Integer n = 42;
System.out.println(n.equals(42));        //true
```

```
System.out.println(n.equals(ln));      //false
System.out.println(n.equals(43));      //false

System.out.println(n.equals(Integer.valueOf(42)));  //true
System.out.println(n.equals(Long.valueOf(42)));     //false
```

Based on our experience with the children of `Person`, we can quite confidently assume that the `equals()` methods of the wrapper classes include the comparison of class names. Let's look at the source code. Here is the `equals()` method of the `Integer` class:

```
public boolean equals(Object obj) {
  if (obj instanceof Integer) {
    return value == ((Integer)obj).intValue();
  }
  return false;
}
```

That is exactly what we expected. If an object is not an instance of the `Integer` class, it can never be considered equal to an object of another class, even if it carries exactly the same numeric value. It looks like the system of social classes in the olden days, doesn't it?

# Exercise – Naming the statements

What are the following statements called?

- `i++;`
- `String s;`
- `s = "I am a string";`
- `doSomething(1, "23");`

# Answer

The following statements are called:

- Increment statement: `i++;`
- Variable declaration statement: `String s;`
- Assignment statement: `s = "I am a string";`
- Method invocation statement: `doSomething(1, "23");`

# Summary

In this chapter, we learned what the three core elements of Java programming are—operators, expressions, and statements—and how they are related to each other. We walked you through all the Java operators, discussed the most popular ones with examples, and explained the potential issues with using them. A substantial part of this chapter was dedicated to data type conversion: widening and narrowing, boxing, and unboxing. The `equals()` method of reference types was also demonstrated and tested on specific examples for a variety of classes and implementations. The `String` class was used prominently and the popular incorrect explanation of its behavior was resolved.

In the next chapter, we will start writing the program logic—the backbone of any execution flow—using control flow statements, which are going to be defined, explained, and demonstrated in many examples: conditional statements, iterative statements, branching statements, and exceptions.

# 10
# Control Flow Statements

This chapter describes one particular kind of Java statement, called control statements, which allow the building of a program flow according to the logic of the implemented algorithm, which includes selection statements, iteration statements, branching statements, and exception handling statements.

In this chapter, we will cover the following topics:

- What is a control flow?
- Selection statements: `if, if....else, switch...case`
- Iteration statements: `for, while, do...while`
- Branching statements: `break, continue, return`
- Exception handling statements: `try...catch...finally, throw, assert`
- Exercise – Infinite loop

## What is a control flow?

A Java program is a sequence of statements that can be executed and produce some data or/and initiate some actions. To make the program more generic, some statements are executed conditionally, based on the result of an expression evaluation. Such statements are called control flow statements because, in computer science, control flow (or flow of control) is the order in which individual statements are executed or evaluated.

By convention, they are divided into four groups: selection statements, iteration statements, branching statements, and exception handling statements.

In the following sections, we will use the term block, which means a sequence of statements enclosed in braces. Here is an example:

```
{
   x = 42;
   y = method(7, x);
   System.out.println("Example");
}
```

A block can also include control statements – a doll inside a doll, inside a doll, and so on.

# Selection statements

The control flow statements of the selection statements group are based on an expression evaluation. For example, here is one possible format: `if(expression) do something`. Or, another possible format: `if(expression) {do something} else {do something else}`.

The expression may return a `boolean` value (as in the previous examples) or a specific value that can be compared with a constant. In the latter case, the selection statement has the format of a `switch` statement, which executes the statement or block that is associated with a particular constant value.

# Iteration statements

Iteration statements execute a certain statement or block until a certain condition is reached. For example, it can be a `for` statement that executes a statement or a block for each value of a collection of values, or until a certain counter reaches the predefined threshold, or some other condition is reached. Each cycle of the execution is called an iteration.

# Branching statements

Branching statements allow for breaking the current flow of the execution and continue executing from the first line after the current block, or from a certain (labeled) point in the control flow.

A `return` statement in a method is also an example of a branching statement.

# Exception handling statements

Exceptions are classes that represent events that happen during program execution and disrupt the normal execution flow. We have already seen examples of `NullPointerException`, `ClassCastException`, and `ArrayIndexOutOfBoundsException` generated under the corresponding conditions.

All the exception classes in Java have a common parent, the `java.lang.Exception` class, which in turn extends the `java.lang.Throwable` class. That's why all exception objects have common behaviors. They contain information about the cause of the exceptional condition and the location of its origination (line number of the class source code).

Each exception can be thrown either automatically (by JVM) or by the application code using the `throw` keyword. The method caller can catch the exception using the exception statements and perform some action based on the exception type and the message it (optionally) carries, or it can let the exception propagate further up the method call stack.

If none of the application methods in the stack catches the exception, it will eventually be caught by the JVM which will abort the application execution with an error.

So, the purpose of the exception handling statements is to generate (`throw`) and `catch` the exceptions.

# Selection statements

The selection statements have four variations:

- `if` statement
- `if...else` statement
- `if...else if-...-else` statement
- `switch...case` statement

# if

The simple `if` statement allows executing a certain statement or block conditionally, only when the result of the expression evaluation is `true`:

```
if(booelan expression){
   //do something
}
```

Here are a few examples:

```
if(true) System.out.println("true");    //1: true
if(false) System.out.println("false");  //2:

int x = 1, y = 5;
if(x > y) System.out.println("x > y");  //3:
if(x < y) System.out.println("x < y");  //4: x < y

if((x + 5) > y) {                        //5: x + 5 > y
   System.out.println("x + 5 > y");
   x = y;
}

if(x == y){                              //6: x == y
   System.out.println("x == y");
}
```

Statement 1 prints `true`. Statements 2 and 3 print nothing. Statement 4 prints x < y. Statement 5 prints x + 5 > y. We used braces to create a block because we wanted the x = y statement to be executed only when the expression of this `if` statement evaluates to `true`. Statement 6 prints x == y. We could avoid using braces here because there is only one statement to execute. We did it for two reasons:

- To demonstrate that braces can be used with a single statement too, thus forming a block of one statement.
- It is a good practice, in general, to have braces after `if`; it reads better and helps to avoid this frustrating error: you add another statement after if, assuming it is going to be executed only when the expression returns `true`:

```
if(x > y) System.out.println("x > y");
x = y;
```

But, the statement x = y in this code is executed unconditionally. If you think such an error doesn't happen very often, you will be surprised.

It is a good practice to always use braces { } with an `if` statement.

As we have mentioned already, it is possible to include a selection statement inside the selection statement to create a more refined logic for the control flow:

```
if(x > y){
   System.out.println("x > y");
   if(x == 3){
      System.out.println("x == 3");
   }
   if(y == 3){
      System.out.println("y == 3");
      System.out.println("x == " + x);
   }
}
```

It can go as deep (nested) as the logic requires.

# if...else

The `if...else` construct allows executing a certain statement or block if the expression evaluates to `true`; otherwise, another statement or block is executed:

```
if(Boolean expression){
   //do something
} else {
   //do something else
}
```

Here are two examples:

```
int x = 1, y = 1;
if(x == y){
   System.out.println("x == y");   //prints: x == y
   x = y - 1;
} else {
   System.out.println("x != y");
}

if(x == y){
   System.out.println("x == y");
} else {
   System.out.println("x != y");   //prints: x != y
}
```

You can see how easy it is to read this code when the braces { } are used consistently. And, as in the previous case of a simple if statement, each block can have another nested block with another if statement, and so on – as many blocks and as deeply nested as necessary.

# if...else if-...-else

You can use this form to avoid creating nested blocks and make the code easier to read and understand. For example, look at the following code snippet:

```
if(n > 5){
   System.out.println("n > 5");
} else {
   if (n == 5) {
      System.out.println("n == 5");
   } else {
      if (n == 4) {
         System.out.println("n == 4");
      } else {
         System.out.println("n < 4");
      }
   }
}
```

These nested `if...else` statements can be replaced by `if...else...if` statements as follows:

```
if(n > 5){
    System.out.println("n > 5");
} else if (n == 5) {
    System.out.println("n == 5");
} else if (n == 4) {
    System.out.println("n == 4");
} else {
    System.out.println("n < 4");
}
```

Such code is easier to read and understand.

If you don't need to do anything when `n < 4`, you can leave out the last catch-all-the-rest-options `else` clause:

```
if(n > 5){
    System.out.println("n > 5");
} else if (n == 5) {
    System.out.println("n == 5");
} else if (n == 4) {
    System.out.println("n == 4");
}
```

If you need to do something for each particular value, you can write, for example:

```
if(x == 5){
    //do something
} else if (x == 7) {
    //do something else
} else if (x == 12) {
    //do something different
} else if (x = 50) {
    //do something yet more different
} else {
    //do something completely different
}
```

But there is a dedicated selection statement for such cases, called `switch...case`, which is easier to read and understand.

# switch...case

The previous code example of the last section can be expressed as a `switch` statement, as follows:

```
switch(x){
  case 5:
    //do something
    break;
  case 7:
    //do something else
    break;
  case 12:
    //do something different
    break;
  case 50:
    //do something yet more different
    break;
  default:
    //do something completely different
}
```

The type of the expression that returns the value of the x variable can be either `char`, `byte`, `short`, `int`, `Character`, `Byte`, `Short`, `Integer`, `String`, or an `enum` type. Notice the `break` keyword. It forces the exit from the `switch...case` statement. Without it, the following statement, do something, would be executed. We will talk about the `break` statement in the *Branching statements* section later.

 The types that can be used in a `switch` statement are `char`, `byte`, `short`, `int`, `Character`, `Byte`, `Short`, `Integer`, `String`, and an `enum` type. The value set in a case clause has to be a constant.

Let's look at a method that takes advantage of the `switch` statement:

```
void switchDemo(int n){
  switch(n + 1){
    case 1:
      System.out.println("case 1: " + n);
      break;
    case 2:
      System.out.println("case 2: " + n);
      break;
    default:
      System.out.println("default: " + n);
      break;
  }
}
```

The following code demonstrates how the `switch` statement works:

```
switchDemo(0);       //prints: case1: 0
switchDemo(1);       //prints: case2: 1
switchDemo(2);       //prints: default: 2
```

And, similar to the `else` clause in an `if` statement, the default clause is not required in a `switch` statement if it is not needed for the program logic:

```
switch(n + 1){
  case 1:
    System.out.println("case 1: " + n);
    break;
  case 2:
    System.out.println("case 2: " + n);
}
```

# Iteration statements

Iteration statements are as fundamental for Java programming as selection statements. There is a good chance you will see and use them very often, too. Each iteration statement can be one of three forms: `while`, `do...while`, or `for`.

## while

The `while` statement executes a Boolean expression and a statement or a block repeatedly until the value of the expression evaluates as `false`:

```
while (Boolean expression){
  //do something
}
```

There are two things to note:

- Braces `{}` are not necessary when only one statement has to be repeatedly executed, but are recommended for consistency and better code understanding
- The statement may not be executed at all (when the very first expression evaluation returns `false`)

Let's look at some examples. The following loop executes the printing statement five times:

```
int i = 0;
while(i++ < 5){
  System.out.print(i + " ");    //prints: 1 2 3 4 5
}
```

Notice a different method used for printing: `print()` instead of `println()`. The latter adds an escape sequence `\n` after the printed line (we have explained what an escape sequence is in `Chapter 5`, *Java Language Elements and Types*), which moves the cursor to the next line.

And here is an example of calling a method that returns some value which is accumulated until the required threshold is reached:

```
double result = 0d;
while (result < 1d){
  result += tryAndGetValue();
  System.out.println(result);
}
```

The `tryAndGetValue()` method is very simple and unrealistic, written only for demo purposes:

```
double tryAndGetValue(){
   return Math.random();
}
```

If we run the last `while` statement, we will see something similar to the following:

```
0.04008814723807952
0.14761419247760388
0.9976253562971626
1.3936840361540992
```

The exact values will vary from run to run because the `Math.random()` method generates pseudo-random `double` values greater than or equal to 0.0 and less than 1.0. As soon as an accumulated value becomes equal to 1.0 or exceeds it, the loop exits.

It is tempting to make this loop simpler:

```
double result = 0d;
while ((result += tryAndGetValue()) < 1d){
   System.out.println(result);
}
```

Or even simpler yet:

```
double result = 0d;
while ((result += Math.random()) < 1d){
   System.out.println(result);
}
```

But if we run any of the last two `while` statement variations, we will get something like this:

```
0.824013192634479
0.9251526763091734
```

The printed value will never be equal or exceed 1.0 because the expression with the newly accumulated value is evaluated before entering the execution block. That is something to keep an eye on when the calculations are included in the expression, not in the execution block.

# do...while

Similarly to the `while` statement, the `do...while` statement executes the Boolean expression repeatedly and the statement or block until the value of the Boolean expression evaluates as `false`:

```
do {
    //statement or block
} while (Boolean expression)
```

But it executes the statement or the block first before the expression is evaluated, which means that the statement or block is executed at least once.

Let's look at some examples. The following code executes the printing statement six times (one more than the similar `while` statement):

```
int i = 0;
do {
    System.out.print(i + " ");    //prints: 0 1 2 3 4 5
} while(i++ < 5);
```

While the following code behaves the same way as a `while` statement:

```
double result = 0d;
do {
    result += tryAndGetValue();
    System.out.println(result);
} while (result < 1d);
```

If we run this code, we will see something similar to the following:

```
0.5907849135754448
0.8049481723535172
1.3318594841395899
```

That is because the value is printed after it is accumulated, and then the expression is evaluated before entering the execution block again.

The simplified do...while statement behaves differently. Here is an example:

```
double result = 0d;
do {
   System.out.println(result);
} while ((result += tryAndGetValue()) < 1d);
```

And here is the same code, but without using the tryAndGetValue() method:

```
double result = 0d;
do {
   System.out.println(result);
} while ((result += Math.random()) < 1d);
```

If we run any of the preceding two examples, we will get something like what's in the following screenshot:

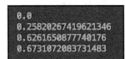

The initial value of the result variable is always printed first because the statement is executed at least once before the expression is evaluated the first time.

# for

The format of the basic for statement looks as follows:

```
for(ListInit; Boolean Expression; ListUpdate) block or statement
```

But, we will start with the most popular, much simpler, version and get back to the full version in the *For with multiple initializers and expressions* section later. The simpler basic for statement format looks like this:

```
for(DeclInitExpr; Boolean Expression; IncrDecrExpr) block or statement
```

This definition consists of the following components:

- `DeclInitExpr` is a declaration and initialization expression, like x = 1, that is evaluated only once at the very beginning of the `for` statement's execution
- Boolean Expression is a Boolean expression, like x < 10, that is evaluated at the beginning of each iteration – every time before executing the block or statement; if the result is `false`, the `for` statement terminates
- `IncrDecrExpr` is an increment or a decrement unary expression, like ++x, -- x, x++, x–, that is evaluated at the end of each iteration – after the block or statement is executed

Notice that we talk about expressions, not statements, although with added semicolons, they look like statements. The reason for that is that a semicolon serves as the separator between the expressions in the `for` statement. Let's look at an example:

```
for (int i=0; i < 3; i++){
   System.out.print(i + " ");   //prints: 0 1 2
}
```

In this code:

- `int i=0` is the declaration and initialization expression, evaluated only once at the very beginning
- `i < 3` is the Boolean expression, evaluated at the beginning of each iteration – before executing the block or statement; if the result is `false` ( i >= 3, in this case), the `for` statement execution terminates
- `i++` is the increment expression, evaluated after the block or statement is executed

And, as in the case of a `while` statement, the braces {} are not needed when only one statement has to be executed, but it is a good style to have them, so the code is consistent and easier to read.

None of the expressions in a `for` statement are required:

```
int k = 0;
for (;;){
   System.out.print(k++ + " ");       //prints: 0 1 2
   if(k > 2) break;
}
```

But using expressions in the statement declaration is more convenient and conventional, thus easier to understand. And here are other examples:

```
for (int i=0; i < 3;){
    System.out.print(i++ + " "); //prints: 0 1 2
}

for (int i=2; i > 0; i--){
    System.out.print(i + " "); //prints: 2 1
}
```

Notice how in the last example, the decrement operator is used to walk down the initial i value.

While using a `for` statement, or any iteration statement for that matter, make sure the exit condition will be reached (unless you deliberately create an infinite loop). That is the main concern around which the iteration statement is built.

# for enhanced

As we have mentioned already, a `for` statement is a very convenient way to access array components (elements):

```
int[] arr = {21, 34, 5};
for (int i=0; i < arr.length; i++){
    System.out.print(arr[i] + " ");   //prints: 21 34 5
}
```

Notice how we use the public property `length` of an array object to make sure we have reached all the array elements. But in such a case, when all the array has to be traversed, it is better (easier to write and to read) to use an enhanced `for` statement that has the following format:

```
<Type> arr = ...;              //an array or any Iterable
for (<Type> a: arr){
    System.out.print(a + " ");
}
```

As you can see from the comment, it is applicable to an array or a class that implements the interface `Iterable`. This interface has an `iterator()` method that returns an object of class `Iterator` which, in turn, has a method called `next()` that allows accessing the class members sequentially. We will talk about such classes, called collections, in Chapter 13, *Java Collections*. So, we can rewrite the last `for` statement example and use the enhanced `for` statement:

```
int[] arr = {21, 34, 5};
for (int a: arr){
  System.out.print(a + " ");   //prints: 21 34 5
}
```

In the case of a collection class that implements an interface `List` (and `List` extends `Iterable`), the sequential access to its members looks very similar:

```
List<String> list = List.of("Bob", "Joe", "Jill");
for (String s: list){
  System.out.print(s + " ");   //prints: Bob Joe Jill
}
```

But when not all elements of an array or collection have to be accessed, some other form of an iteration statement is probably better suited.

Also, please notice that since Java 8, many data structures can produce streams that allow writing much more compact code and avoid the use of for statements whatsoever. We will show you how to do it in Chapter 18, *Streams and Pipelines*.

# for with multiple initializers and expressions

Now, let's return to the basic `for` statement format once more. It allows much more variety in using it than many programmers even know about. And it is not because of a lack of interest or professional curiosity, but probably because this additional functionality usually is not needed. Yet, once in a while, when you read somebody's code or during a job interview, you may encounter the need to know the full picture. So, we decided to at least mention it.

The full format of `for` statements is built around lists of expressions:

```
for(ListInit; Boolean Expression; ListUpdate) block or statement
```

This definition consists of the following components:

- `ListInit`: May include a declaration list and/or an expression list
- `Expression`: Boolean expression
- `ListUpdate`: Expression list

The expression list members, separated by a comma, can be:

- **Assignment**: `x = 3`
- **Pre/postfix increment/decrement expression**: `++x --x x++ x--`
- **Method invocation**: `method(42)`
- **Object creation expression**: `new SomeClass(2, "Bob")`

The following two `for` statements produce identical results:

```
for (int i=0, j=0; i < 3 && j < 3; ++i, ++j){
  System.out.println(i + " " + j);
}
for (int x=new A().getInitialValue(), i=x == -2 ? x + 2 : 0, j=0;
  i < 3 || j < 3 ; ++i, j = i) {
  System.out.println(i + " " + j);
}
```

Where the `getInitialValue()` method has the following code:

```
class A{
  int getInitialValue(){ return -2; }
}
```

As you can see, even such a simple functionality can look very complex and even be confusing when multiple initializers, assignments, and expressions are excessively used. If in doubt, keep your code simple and easy to understand. Sometimes it is not easy, but in our experience, it can always be done, and being easy to understand is one of the most important criteria of good code quality.

# Branching statements

You have already seen the branching statements `break` and `return` in our examples. We will define and discuss them and the third member of the group—the branching statement `continue` —in this section.

# Break and labeled break

As you have probably noticed, the `break` statement is essential for the `switch...case` selection statements to be able to work (see the *switch...case* section for more information). If included in the execution block of an iteration statement, it causes the `for` or `while` statement to terminate immediately.

It is widely used in iteration statements while searching for a particular element in an array or collection. To demonstrate how it works, let's assume, for example, that we need to find a certain person by age and name among the students and teachers of a community college. Let's first create the classes `Person`, `Student`, and `Teacher`:

```
class Person{
  private int age;
  private  String name;
  public Person(int age,  String name) {
    this.age = age;
    this.name = name;
  }
  @Override
  public Boolean equals(Object o) {
    if (this == o) return true;
    Person person = (Person) o;
    return age == person.age &&
            Objects.equals(name, person.name);
  }
  @Override
  public String toString() {
    return "Person{age=" + age +
            ", name='" + name + "'}";
  }
}
class Student extends Person {
  private int year;

  public Student(int age, String name, int year) {
    super(age, name);
    this.year = year;
  }

  @Override
  public String toString() {
    return "Student{year=" + year +
        ", " + super.toString() + "}";
  }
}
```

```
class Teacher extends Person {
  private String subject;
  public Teacher(int age, String name, String subject) {
    super(age, name);
    this.subject = subject;
  }
  @Override
  public String toString() {
    return "Student{subject=" + subject +
           ", " + super.toString() + "}";
  }
}
```

Notice that the method equals() is implemented only in the base class Person. We identify a person by name and age only. Also, notice the use of the keyword super that allows us to access the constructor and toString() method of the parent class.

Let's assume that we are assigned to find a person (by name and age) in a community college database. So, we have created a collection of type List and we will iterate over it until we find a match:

```
List<Person> list =
  List.of(new Teacher(32, "Joe", "History"),
          new Student(29,"Joe", 4),
          new Student(28,"Jill", 3),
          new Teacher(33, "ALice", "Maths"));
Person personOfInterest = new Person(29,"Joe");
Person person = null;
for (Person p: list){
  System.out.println(p);
  if(p.equals(personOfInterest)){
    person = p;
    break;
  }
}
if(person == null){
  System.out.println("Not found: " + personOfInterest);
} else {
  System.out.println("Found: " + person);
}
```

If we run this program, the result will be:

```
Teacher{subject=History, Person{age=32, name='Joe'}}
Student{year=4, Person{age=29, name='Joe'}}
Found: Student{year=4, Person{age=29, name='Joe'}}
```

We have found the person we were looking for. But if we change our search and look for another person (just one year at age difference):

```
Person personOfInterest = new Person(30,"Joe");
```

The result will be:

```
Teacher{subject=History, Person{age=32, name='Joe'}}
Student{year=4, Person{age=29, name='Joe'}}
Student{year=3, Person{age=28, name='Jill'}}
Teacher{subject=Maths, Person{age=33, name='ALice'}}
Not found: Person{age=30, name='Joe'}
```

As you can see, the `break` statement allows exiting the loop as soon as the object of interest is found, thus not wasting time on iterating over all the collection, which may be quite large.

In `Chapter 18`, *Streams and Pipelines*, we will show you another (often more efficient) way to search a collection or an array. But iterating over the elements is still a viable way to do it in many cases.

The `break` statement can be used for searching a particular element in a multidimensional data structure, too. Let's assume we need to search a three-dimensional array and find the array of the lowest dimension that has the sum of its elements equal to or bigger than 4. Here is an example of such an array:

```
int[][][] data = {
        {{1,0,2},{1,2,0},{2,1,0},{0,3,0}},
        {{1,1,1},{1,3,0},{2,0,1},{1,0,1}}};
```

The lowest dimension array we are looking for is {1,3,0}. If the first dimension is x and the second dimension is y, then the location of this array is x=1, y=1, or [1][1]. Let's write a program that finds this array:

```
int[][][] data = {
        {{1,0,2},{1,2,0},{2,1,0},{0,3,0}},
        {{1,1,1},{1,3,0},{2,0,1},{1,0,1}}};
int threshold = 4;
int x = 0, y = 0;
Boolean isFound = false;
for(int[][] dd: data){
   y = 0;
   for(int[] d: dd){
      int sum = 0;
      for(int i: d){
         sum += i;
         if(sum >= threshold){
            isFound = true;
            break;
         }
      }
      if(isFound){
         break;
      }
      y++;
   }
   if(isFound){
      break;
   }
   x++;
}
System.out.println("isFound=" + isFound + ", x=" + x + ", y=" + y);
//prints: isFound=true, x=1, y=1
```

As you can see, we use a Boolean variable called `isFound` to facilitate exit from outer loops as soon as the desired result is found in the innermost loop. The boring need to check the value of the `isFound` variable made Java authors introduce a label – an identifier followed by a colon sign (`:`) that can be placed in front of a statement. The `break` statement can take advantage of it. Here is how the previous code can be changed using a label:

```
int[][][] data = {
        {{1,0,2},{1,2,0},{2,1,0},{0,3,0}},
        {{1,1,1},{1,3,0},{2,0,1},{1,0,1}}};
int threshold = 4;
int x = 0, y = 0;
Boolean isFound = false;
exit:
for(int[][] dd: data){
   y = 0;
   for(int[] d: dd){
      int sum = 0;
      for(int i: d){
         sum += i;
         if(sum >= threshold){
            isFound = true;
            break exit;
         }
      }
      y++;
   }
   x++;
}
System.out.println("isFound=" + isFound + ", x=" + x + ", y=" + y);
//prints: isFound=true, x=1, y=1
```

We still use the variable `isFound` but only for reporting purposes. The `exit:` label allows the `break` statement to specify which statement has to stop executing. This way, we do not need to write boilerplate code checking the `isFound` variable's value.

# Continue and labeled continue

The continue statement supports functionality similar to the one supported by the break statement. But instead of exiting the loop, it forces exiting the current iteration only, so the loop continues executing. To demonstrate how it works, let's assume that, as in the case with the break statement in the previous section, we need to search a three-dimensional array and find the array of the lowest dimension that has the sum of its elements equal to or bigger than 4. But this time, the sum should not include an element equal to 1. Here is the array:

```
int[][][] data = {
        {{1,1,2},{0,3,0},{2,4,1},{2,3,2}},
        {{0,2,0},{1,3,4},{2,0,1},{2,2,2}}};
```

Our program should find the following arrays:

- data[0][2] = {2,4,1}, sum = 6 (because 1 has to be skipped)
- data[0][3] = {2,3,2}, sum = 7
- data[1][1] = {1,3,4}, sum = 7 (because 1 has to be skipped)
- data[1][3]={2,2,2}, sum = 6

The sum of other array elements does not reach 4 if 1 is skipped.

Here is the program:

```
int[][][] data = {
        {{1,1,2},{0,3,0},{2,4,1},{2,3,2}},
        {{0,2,0},{1,3,4},{2,0,1},{2,2,2}}};
int threshold = 4;
int x = 0, y;
for(int[][] dd: data){
  y = 0;
  for(int[] d: dd){
    int sum = 0;
    for(int i: d){
      if(i == 1){
        continue;
      }
      sum += i;
    }
    if(sum >= threshold){
      System.out.println("sum=" + sum + ", x=" + x + ", y=" + y);
    }
    y++;
  }
  x++;
}
```

If we run it, the result will be:

```
sum=6, x=0, y=2
sum=7, x=0, y=3
sum=7, x=1, y=1
sum=6, x=1, y=3
```

As you can see, the results are exactly as we expected: all elements of 1 were skipped.

To demonstrate how the labeled continue statement can be used, let's change the requirements: not only the element 1 has to be skipped, but all the arrays that contain such an element have to be ignored too. In other words, we need to find arrays that do not contain 1 and have a sum of the elements equal to or bigger than 4.

Our program should find only two arrays:

- data[0][3] = {2,3,2}, sum = 7
- data[1][3] = {2,2,2}, sum = 6

Here is the code that does it:

```
int[][][] data = {
        {{1,1,2},{0,3,0},{2,4,1},{2,3,2}},
        {{0,2,0},{1,3,4},{2,0,1},{2,2,2}}};
int threshold = 4;
int x = 0, y;
for(int[][] dd: data){
  y = 0;
  cont: for(int[] d: dd){
    int sum = 0;
    for(int i: d){
      if(i == 1){
        y++;
        continue cont;
      }
      sum += i;
    }
    if(sum >= threshold){
      System.out.println("sum=" + sum + ", x=" + x + ", y=" + y);
    }
    y++;
  }
  x++;
}
```

As you can see, we have added a label called `cont:` and refer it in the `continue` statement, so the current iteration of the innermost loop and the iteration of the next outer loop stops executing. The outer loop then continues executing the next iteration. If we run the code, the results will be:

```
sum=7, x=0, y=3
sum=6, x=1, y=3
```

All the other arrays were skipped either because they contained 1 or the sum of their elements was less than 4.

# return

The `return` statement can be placed only in a method or a constructor. Its function is to return control to the invoker with or without a value.

In the case of a constructor, the `return` statement is not required. If placed in the constructor, it has to be the last statement that returns no value:

```
class ConstructorDemo{
  private int field;
  public ConstructorDemo(int i) {
    this.field = i;
    return;
  }
}
```

An attempt to place the `return` statement as not the last statement of a constructor or to make it return any value will result in a compilation error.

In the case of a method, if the method was declared as returning some type:

- The `return` statement is required
- The `return` statement has to be effectively (see the following example) the last statement of the method
- There may be several return statements, but one of them has to be effectively (see the following example) the last statement of the method, while the others have to be inside a selection statement; otherwise, a compilation error will be generated
- If the `return` statement does not return anything, it causes a compilation error
- If the `return` statement returns a type that is not the one declared in the method definition and not its subtype, it causes a compilation error
- Boxing, unboxing, and type widening are performed automatically, while type narrowing requires typecasting

The following example demonstrates the `return` statement being effectively the last statement of a method:

```
public String method(int n){
  if(n == 1){
    return "One";
  } else {
    return "Not one";
  }
}
```

The last statement of the method is a selection statement, but the `return` statement is the last one executed inside the selection statement.

Here's an example of a method with many return statements:

```
public static String methodWithManyReturns(){
   if(true){
      return "The only one returned";
   }
   if(true){
      return "Is never reached";
   }
   return "Is never reached";
}
```

Although in the method, only the first return statement always returned, the compiler does not complain and the method is executed without a runtime error. It just always returns a The only one returned literal.

The following examples of methods with several return statements are more realistic:

```
public Boolean method01(int n){
   if(n < 0) {
      return true;
   } else {
      return false;
   }
}

public Boolean sameAsMethod01(int n){
   if(n < 0) {
      return true;
   }
   return false;
}

public Boolean sameAsAbove(int n){
   return n < 0 ? true : false;
}

public int method02(int n){
   if(n < 0) {
      return 1;
   } else if(n == 0) {
      return 2;
   } else if (n == 1){
      return 3;
   } else {
      return 4;
   }
}
```

```
    }
    public int methodSameAsMethod02(int n){
      if(n < 0) {
        return 1;
      }
      switch(n) {
        case 0:
          return 2;
        case 1:
          return 3;
        default:
          return 4;
      }
    }
```

Here are examples of boxing, unboxing, and type widening and narrowing:

```
    public Integer methodBoxing(){
      return 42;
    }

    public int methodUnboxing(){
      return Integer.valueOf(42);
    }

    public int methodWidening(){
      byte b = 42;
      return b;
    }

    public byte methodNarrowing(){
      int n = 42;
      return (byte)n;
    }
```

We also can revisit the program that looks for a particular person in the list of teachers and students:

```
List<Person> list =
  List.of(new Teacher(32, "Joe", "History"),
          new Student(29,"Joe", 4),
          new Student(28,"Jill", 3),
          new Teacher(33, "ALice", "Maths"));
Person personOfInterest = new Person(29,"Joe");
Person person = null;
for (Person p: list){
  System.out.println(p);
  if(p.equals(personOfInterest)){
    person = p;
    break;
  }
}
if(person == null){
  System.out.println("Not found: " + personOfInterest);
} else {
  System.out.println("Found: " + person);
}
```

Using the return statements, we can now create the method `findPerson()`:

```
Person findPerson(List<Person> list, Person personOfInterest){
  Person person = null;
  for (Person p: list){
    System.out.println(p);
    if(p.equals(personOfInterest)){
      person = p;
      break;
    }
  }
  return person;
}
```

This method can be used as follows:

```
List<Person> list = List.of(new Teacher(32, "Joe", "History"),
        new Student(29,"Joe", 4),
        new Student(28,"Jill", 3),
        new Teacher(33, "ALice", "Maths"));
Person personOfInterest = new Person(29,"Joe");
Person person = findPerson(list, personOfInterest);
if(person == null){
  System.out.println("Not found: " + personOfInterest);
} else {
  System.out.println("Found: " + person);
}
```

Taking advantage of the new code structure, we can change the `findPerson()` method further and demonstrate greater variety in `return` statement usage:

```
Person findPerson(List<Person> list, Person personOfInterest){
  for (Person p: list){
    System.out.println(p);
    if(p.equals(personOfInterest)){
      return p;
    }
  }
  return null;
}
```

As you can see, we have replaced the `break` statement with the return statement. Is the code more readable now? Some programmers would say no, as they prefer to have one `return` statement to be the only source of the returned result. Otherwise, they argue, one has to study the code and see if there is another—the third—`return` statement that might return yet another value. If the code is not as simple, one is never sure that all possible returns have been identified. The programmers of the opposite camp would counter-argue that a method should be small, so finding all return statements is easy. But making a method small often forces the creation of deeply nested methods that are not so easy to understand. The argument may go on for a long time. That's why we leave it up to you to try and decide which style you prefer.

If the return type of a method is defined as `void`:

- The `return` statement is not required
- If the `return` statement is present, it does not return any value

- If the `return` statement returns some value, it causes a compilation error
- There may be several return statements, but one of them has to be effectively the last statement of the method, while the others have to be inside a selection statement; otherwise, a compilation error will be generated

To demonstrate the `return` statement without a value, we will use the `findPerson()` method again. If all we need to do is to print out the results, then the method can be changed as follows:

```
void findPerson2(List<Person> list, Person personOfInterest){
  for (Person p: list){
    System.out.println(p);
    if(p.equals(personOfInterest)){
      System.out.println("Found: " + p);
      return;
    }
  }
  System.out.println("Not found: " + personOfInterest);
  return;   //this statement is optional
}
```

And the client code will look much simpler:

```
List<Person> list = List.of(new Teacher(32, "Joe", "History"),
        new Student(29,"Joe", 4),
        new Student(28,"Jill", 3),
        new Teacher(33, "ALice", "Maths"));
Person personOfInterest = new Person(29,"Joe");
findPerson(list, personOfInterest);
```

Or it can be even more compact:

```
List<Person> list = List.of(new Teacher(32, "Joe", "History"),
        new Student(29,"Joe", 4),
        new Student(28,"Jill", 3),
        new Teacher(33, "ALice", "Maths"));
findPerson(list, new Person(29, "Joe");
```

As in the previous discussion, there are different styles for passing the parameters into a method. Some people prefer the more compact style as in the code here. Others argue that each parameter has to have a variable because the name of the variable carries additional information that helps to communicate the intent (like the name `personOfInterest`).

Such discussions are inevitable because the same code has to be understood and maintained by different people, and each development team has to find the style that suits the needs and preferences of all the team members.

# Exception handling statements

As we have explained in the introduction, an unexpected condition can cause JVM to create and throw an exception object, or the application code can do it. As soon as it happens, the control flow is transferred to the exception handling `try` statement (also called a `try-catch` or `try-catch-finally` statement) if the exception was thrown inside a `try` block. Here is an example of a caught exception:

```
void exceptionCaught(){
  try {
    method2();
  } catch (Exception ex){
    ex.printStackTrace();
  }
}

void method2(){
  method1(null);
}

void method1(String s){
  s.equals("whatever");
}
```

The method `exceptionCaught()` calls `method2()` which calls `method1()` and passes to it `null`. The line `s.equals("whatever")` throws `NullPointerException` which propagates through the method call stack until caught by the `try-catch` block of the method `exceptionCaught()` and its stack trace (which method called which method and in which line of the class) is printed:

```
java.lang.NullPointerException
    at com.packt.javapath.ch10demo.ExceptionHandlingDemo.method1(ExceptionHandlingDemo.java:21)
    at com.packt.javapath.ch10demo.ExceptionHandlingDemo.method2(ExceptionHandlingDemo.java:17)
    at com.packt.javapath.ch10demo.ExceptionHandlingDemo.exceptionCaught(ExceptionHandlingDemo.java:10)
    at com.packt.javapath.ch10demo.ExceptionHandlingDemo.main(ExceptionHandlingDemo.java:5)
```

From the stack trace, you can see that all the involved methods belong to the same class, ExceptionHandlingDemo. Reading from the bottom up, you can see that:

- The method main() called the method exceptionCaught() in line 5 of ExceptionHandlingDemo
- The method exceptionCaught() called method2() in line 10 of the same class
- The method2() called method1() in line 17
- The method1() has thrown java.lang.NullpointerException from line 21

If we don't see the code, we don't know if this exception was thrown deliberately. For example, method1() might look as follows:

```
void method1(String s){
  if(s == null){
    throw new NullPointerException();
  }
}
```

But usually, programmers add a message to indicate what the problem is:

```
void method1(String s){
  if(s == null){
    throw new NullPointerException("Parameter String is null");
  }
}
```

If that were the case, the stack trace would show a message:

```
java.lang.NullPointerException: Parameter String is null
    at com.packt.javapath.ch10demo.ExceptionHandlingDemo.method1(ExceptionHandlingDemo.java:22)
    at com.packt.javapath.ch10demo.ExceptionHandlingDemo.method2(ExceptionHandlingDemo.java:17)
    at com.packt.javapath.ch10demo.ExceptionHandlingDemo.exceptionCaught(ExceptionHandlingDemo.java:10)
    at com.packt.javapath.ch10demo.ExceptionHandlingDemo.main(ExceptionHandlingDemo.java:5)
```

But the message is not a reliable indicator of the custom exception. Some standard exceptions carry their own message, too. The exception package is better evidence of a custom exception or if the exception is one of the base classes (java.lang.Exception or java.langRuntimeException) and has a message in it. The following code, for example, customizes RuntimeException:

```
void method1(String s){
   if(s == null){
      throw new RuntimeException("Parameter String is null");
   }
}
```

And here is what the stack trace looks like with such a customized exception:

```
java.lang.RuntimeException: Parameter String is null
    at com.packt.javapath.ch10demo.ExceptionHandlingDemo.method1(ExceptionHandlingDemo.java:23)
    at com.packt.javapath.ch10demo.ExceptionHandlingDemo.method2(ExceptionHandlingDemo.java:17)
    at com.packt.javapath.ch10demo.ExceptionHandlingDemo.exceptionCaught(ExceptionHandlingDemo.java:10)
    at com.packt.javapath.ch10demo.ExceptionHandlingDemo.main(ExceptionHandlingDemo.java:5)
```

We will talk more about exception customization in the *Custom exceptions* section later.

If the exception is thrown outside a try...catch block, the program execution is terminated by JVM. Here is an example of an exception not caught by the application:

```
void exceptionNotCaught(){
   method2();
}

void method2(){
   method1(null);
}

void method1(String s){
   s.equals("whatever");
}
```

If we run this code, the result is:

```
Exception in thread "main" java.lang.NullPointerException
    at com.packt.javapath.ch10demo.ExceptionHandlingDemo.method1(ExceptionHandlingDemo.java:26)
    at com.packt.javapath.ch10demo.ExceptionHandlingDemo.method2(ExceptionHandlingDemo.java:22)
    at com.packt.javapath.ch10demo.ExceptionHandlingDemo.exceptionNotCaught(ExceptionHandlingDemo.java:10)
    at com.packt.javapath.ch10demo.ExceptionHandlingDemo.main(ExceptionHandlingDemo.java:6)
```

Now, let's talk about the exception handling statements and then come back to the discussion about the best way to handle the exceptions.

# throw

The `throw` statement consists of the keyword `throw` and either a variable or value of a reference type `java.lang.Throwable`, or the `null` reference. Since all the exceptions are children of `java.lang.Throwable`, any of the following throw statements is correct:

```
throw new Exception("Something happened");

Exception ex = new Exception("Something happened");
throw ex;

Throwable thr = new Exception("Something happened");
throw thr;

throw null;
```

If `null` is thrown, as it is in the last statement, then JVM converts it to a `NullPointerException`, so these two statements are equivalent:

```
throw null;

throw new NullPointerException;
```

And, just to remind you, the package `java.lang` does not need to be imported. You can refer to any of the package `java.lang` members—interface or class—by its name without using the fully qualified name (that includes package name too). That is why we are able to write `NullPointerException` without importing the class instead of using its fully qualified name, `java.lang.NullPointerException`. We will look into the content of the package `java.lang` in Chapter 12, *Java Standard and External Libraries*.

You can also create your own exception by extending `Throwable` or any of its children and throw them instead of standard exceptions of the package `java.lang`:

```java
class MyNpe extends NullPointerException{
    public MyNpe(String message) {
        super(message);
    }
    //whatever code you need to have here
}

class MyRuntimeException extends RuntimeException{
    public MyRuntimeException(String message) {
        super(message);
    }
    //whatever code you need to have here
}

class MyThrowable extends Throwable{
    public MyThrowable(String message) {
        super(message);
    }
    //whatever code you need to have here
}

class MyException extends Exception{
    public MyException(String message) {
        super(message);
    }
    //whatever code you need to have here
}
```

Why you would want to do that will become clear after reading the *Custom exceptions* section later.

# try...catch

When an exception is thrown inside a `try` block, it redirects control flow to its first `catch` clause (the one that catches `NullPointerException` in the following example):

```
void exceptionCaught(){
  try {
    method2();
  } catch (NullPointerException ex){
    System.out.println("NPE caught");
    ex.printStackTrace();
  } catch (RuntimeException ex){
    System.out.println("RuntimeException caught");
    ex.printStackTrace();
  } catch (Exception ex){
    System.out.println("Exception caught");
    ex.printStackTrace();
  }
}
```

If there are more than one `catch` clauses, the compiler forces you to arrange them so that the child exception is listed before the parent exception. In our previous example, `NullPointerException` extends `RuntimeException` extends `Exception`. If the thrown exception type matches the topmost `catch` clause, this `catch` block handles the exception (we will talk about what it means shortly). If the topmost clause does not match the exception type, the next `catch` clause gets the control flow and handles the exception if it matches the clause type. If not, the control flow is passed to the next clause until either the exception is handled or all the clauses are tried. If none of the clauses match, the exception is thrown further up until is it either handled by some try-catch block or it propagates all the way out of the program code. In such a case, JVM terminates the program execution (to be precise, it terminates the thread execution, but we will talk about threads in Chapter 11, *JVM Processes and Garbage Collection*).

Let's demonstrate this by running the examples. If we use the three `catch` clauses in the method `exceptionCaught()` as shown previously, and throw `NullPointerException` in `method1()` as follows:

```
void method1(String s){
  throw new NullPointerException("Parameter String is null");
}
```

The result will be like that shown in the following screenshot:

```
NPE caught
java.lang.NullPointerException: Parameter String is null
    at com.packt.javapath.ch10demo.ExceptionHandlingDemo.method1(ExceptionHandlingDemo.java:98)
    at com.packt.javapath.ch10demo.ExceptionHandlingDemo.method2(ExceptionHandlingDemo.java:88)
    at com.packt.javapath.ch10demo.ExceptionHandlingDemo.exceptionCaught(ExceptionHandlingDemo.java:46)
    at com.packt.javapath.ch10demo.ExceptionHandlingDemo.main(ExceptionHandlingDemo.java:5)
```

You can see that the topmost `catch` clause caught the exception as expected.

If we change `method1()` to throw a `RuntimeException`:

```
void method1(String s){
  throw new RuntimeException("Parameter String is null");
}
```

You probably will be not surprised to see that the second `catch` clause catches it. So, we are not going to demonstrate it. We better change `method1()` again and let it throw `ArrayIndexOutOfBoundsException`, which extends `RuntimeException`, but is not listed in any of the catch clauses:

```
void method1(String s){
  throw new ArrayIndexOutOfBoundsException("Index ... is bigger " +
                                           "than the array length ...");
}
```

If we run the code again, the result will be:

```
RuntimeException caught
java.lang.ArrayIndexOutOfBoundsException: Index ... is bigger than the array length ...
    at com.packt.javapath.ch10demo.ExceptionHandlingDemo.method1(ExceptionHandlingDemo.java:100)
    at com.packt.javapath.ch10demo.ExceptionHandlingDemo.method2(ExceptionHandlingDemo.java:88)
    at com.packt.javapath.ch10demo.ExceptionHandlingDemo.exceptionCaught(ExceptionHandlingDemo.java:46)
    at com.packt.javapath.ch10demo.ExceptionHandlingDemo.main(ExceptionHandlingDemo.java:5)
```

As you can see, the exception was caught by the first `catch` clause that matched its type. That is the reason the compiler forces you to list them so that a child is often listed before its parent, so the most specific type is listed first. This way, the first matched clause is always the best match.

Now, you probably fully expect to see any non-`RuntimeException` to be caught by the last `catch` clause. That is a correct expectation. But before we can throw it, we have to address the difference between *checked* and *unchecked* (also called *runtime*) exceptions.

# Checked and unchecked (runtime) exceptions

To understand why this topic is important, let's try to throw an exception of type `Exception` in `method1()`. For this test, we will use `InstantiationException`, which extends `Exception`. Let's assume there was a validation of input data (from some external source) and it turned out that they were not good enough for some object instantiation:

```
void method1(String s) {
   //some input data validation
   throw new InstantiationException("No value for the field" +
                                " someField of SomeClass.");
}
```

We wrote this code and suddenly the compiler generated an error, `Unhandled exception java.lang.InstantiationException`, although we do have a `catch` clause up in the client code that will match this type of exception (the last `catch` clause in the method `exceptionCaught()`).

The reason for the error is that all exception types that extend the `Exception` class but not its child `RuntimeException` are checked at compile time, hence the name. The compiler checks if such exceptions are handled in the method of their origination:

- If, in the method of the exception origination, there is a `try-catch` block that catches this exception and does not let it propagate outside the method, the compiler does not complain
- Otherwise, it checks if there is a `throws` clause in the method declaration that lists this exception; here is an example:

```
void method1(String s) throws Exception{
   //some input data validation
   throw new InstantiationException("No value for the field" +
                                " someField of SomeClass.");
}
```

The `throws` clause must list all the checked exceptions that can propagate outside the method. By adding `throws Exception`, we made the compiler happy even if we decide to throw any other checked exception because they are all of the type `Exception` and thus are covered by the new `throws` clause.

In the next section, `Throws`, you will read some pros and cons of using a base exception class in a `throws` clause, and in the section *Some best practices of exception handling*, later, we discuss some other possible solutions.

Meanwhile, let's continue discussing checked exception usage. In our demo code, we have decided to add the clause `throws Exception` to the `method1()` declaration. This change has immediately triggered the same error `Unhandled exception java.lang.InstantiationException` in `method2()`, which calls `method1()` but does not handle `Exception`. So, we had to add a `throws` clause to `method2()`, too:

```
void method2() throws Exception{
  method1(null);
}
```

Only the caller of `method2()`—the method `exceptionCaught()`—does not need to be changed because it handles the `Exception` type. The final version of the code is:

```
void exceptionCaught(){
  try {
    method2();
  } catch (NullPointerException ex){
    System.out.println("NPE caught");
    ex.printStackTrace();
  } catch (RuntimeException ex){
    System.out.println("RuntimeException caught");
    ex.printStackTrace();
  } catch (Exception ex){
    System.out.println("Exception caught");
    ex.printStackTrace();
  }
}

void method2() throws Exception{
  method1(null);
}

void method1(String s) throws Exception{
  throw new InstantiationException("No value for the field" +
                                    " someField of SomeClass.");
}
```

If we call the method `exceptionCaught()` now, the result will be:

```
Exception caught
java.lang.InstantiationException: No value for the field someField of SomeClass.
    at com.packt.javapath.ch10demo.ExceptionHandlingDemo.method1(ExceptionHandlingDemo.java:101)
    at com.packt.javapath.ch10demo.ExceptionHandlingDemo.method2(ExceptionHandlingDemo.java:88)
    at com.packt.javapath.ch10demo.ExceptionHandlingDemo.exceptionCaught(ExceptionHandlingDemo.java:46)
    at com.packt.javapath.ch10demo.ExceptionHandlingDemo.main(ExceptionHandlingDemo.java:5)
```

That is exactly what we expected. The last `catch` clause for the `Exception` type matched the `InstantiationException` type.

The unchecked exceptions—the descendants of the class `RuntimeExceptions` —are not checked at compile time, thus the name, and are not required to be listed in the `throws` clause.

Generally speaking, checked exceptions are (should be) used for recoverable conditions, while unchecked exceptions for unrecoverable conditions. We will talk more about it in the *What is exception handling?* and *Some best practices of exception handling* sections later.

# throws

A `throws` clause must list all checked exception classes (descendants of the class `Exception` but not descendants of the class `RuntimeException`) that the method or constructor can throw. It is allowed but not required to list the unchecked exception classes (descendants of the class `RuntimeException`) in a `throws` clause, too. Here is an example:

```
void method1(String s)
          throws InstantiationException, InterruptedException {
  //some input data validation
  if(some data missing){
    throw new InstantiationException("No value for the field" +
                                   " someField of SomeClass.");
  }
  //some other code
  if(some other reason){
    throw new InterruptedException("Reason..."); //checked exception
  }
}
```

Or, instead of declaring throwing two different exceptions, one can list only the base class in the `throws` clause:

```
void method1(String s) throws Exception {
  //some input data validation
  if(some data missing){
    throw new InstantiationException("No value for the field" +
                               " someField of SomeClass.");
  }
  //some other code
  if(some other reason){
    throw new InterruptedException("Reason..."); //checked exception
  }
}
```

However, it would mean that the variety and possible reasons for potential failures will be hidden from the client this way, so one must either:

- Handle the exceptions inside the method
- Assume that the client code will base its behavior on the content of the message (which is often not reliable and subject to change)
- Assume that the client will behave the same way no matter what the actual type exception can be
- Assume that the method will never throw any other checked exception and, if it does, the behavior of the client should not change

There are too many assumptions to feel comfortable declaring only a base class exception in the `throws` clause. But there are some best practices that avoid such a dilemma. We will talk about them in the *Some best practices for exception handling* section later.

# Custom exceptions

In this section, we promised to discuss the motivation for custom exception creation. Here are two examples:

```
//Unchecked custom exception
class MyRuntimeException extends RuntimeException{
  public MyRuntimeException(String message){
    super(message);
  }
  //whatever code you need to have here
}

//Checked custom exception
class MyException extends Exception{
  public MyException(String message){
    super(message);
  }
  //whatever code you need to have here
}
```

These examples don't look particularly useful until you realize that the comment `whatever code you need to have here` allows you put any data or functionality in your custom class and utilize the exception handling mechanism to propagate such an object from any code depth all the way up to any level you need it.

Since this is only an introduction to Java programming, such cases are beyond the scope of this book. We just wanted to make sure you know that such a capability exists, so you may search the internet when you need it or build your own innovative solution.

However, there is an ongoing discussion in the Java community on the topic of utilizing the exception handling mechanism for business purposes, which we will touch on in the *Some best practices of exception handling* section later.

# What is exception handling?

As we have mentioned already, checked exceptions were originally thought to be used for the recoverable conditions when a caller code may do something automatically and take another branch of execution, based on the type of the caught exception and maybe the data it carried. And that is the primary purpose and function of exception handling.

Unfortunately, such utilization of exceptions proved to be not very productive because as soon as an exceptional condition is discovered, the code is enhanced and makes such a condition one of the possible processing options, albeit not very often executed.

The secondary function is to document the error condition and all the related information for later analysis and code enhancement.

The third and no less important function of exception handling is to protect the application from complete failure. The unexpected condition happened, but hopefully such conditions are rare and the mainstream processing is still available for the application to continue working as it was designed.

The fourth function of exception handling is to provide a mechanism for information delivery in some special cases when other means are not as effective. This last function of exception handling remains controversial and not used very often. We will talk about it in the next section.

# Some best practices of exception handling

The Java exception handling mechanism was designed to address possible edge cases and unexpected program termination. The two categories of errors were expected to be:

- **Recoverable**: Those that can be remedied automatically based on the application logic
- **Unrecoverable**: Those that cannot be corrected automatically and which lead to program termination

The first category of errors was addressed by introducing checked exceptions (descendants of the Exception class), while the second became a realm of unchecked exceptions (descendants of the RuntimeException class).

Unfortunately, such categorization turned out to be not in line with the programming practicalities, especially for the areas of programming unrelated to the development of libraries and frameworks designed to be used by different users and organizations in a variety of environments and execution contexts. Typical application development was always able to fix the problem in the code directly without writing a complicated mechanism for recovery. The distinction is important because as an author of a library, you never know where and how your methods are going to be used, while as an application developer, one knows exactly the environment and the execution context.

Even the Java authors indirectly confirmed this experience by adding, as it stands at the time of writing, 15 unchecked exceptions and only nine checked exceptions to the `java.lang` package. If the original expectations were confirmed by the practice, one would expect only a few unrecoverable (unchecked) exceptions and many more types of recoverable (checked) exceptions. Meanwhile, even some of the checked exceptions of the `java.lang` package do not look as recoverable either:

- `ClassNotFoundException`: Thrown when JVM is not able to find the referred class
- `CloneNotSupportedException`: Thrown to indicate that the clone method in the object's class does not implement the `Cloneable` interface
- `IllegalAccessException`: Thrown when the currently executing method does not have access to the definition of the specified class, field, method, or constructor

In fact, one would be hard-pressed to find a situation when automatic recovery code is worth writing instead of just adding another branch of logic to the mainstream processing.

With that in mind, let's enumerate a few best practices that proved to be useful and effective:

- Always catch all exceptions
- Handle each exception as close to the source as possible
- Do not use checked exceptions unless you have to
- Convert third-party checked exceptions into unchecked by re-throwing them as `RuntimeException` with the corresponding message

- Do not create custom exceptions unless you have to
- Do not drive business logic by using the exception handling mechanism, unless you have to
- Customize the generic `RuntimeException` by using the system of messages and, optionally, enum type instead of using exception type to communicate the cause of the error

# finally

A `finally` block can be added to a `try` block with or without a `catch` clause. The format looks like the following:

```
try {
  //code of the try block
} catch (...){
  //optional catch block code
} finally {
  //code of the finally block
}
```

If present, the code in the `finally` block is always executed just before the method is exited. Whether the code in the `try` block has thrown an exception, and whether this exception was processed in one of the `catch` blocks or if the code in the `try` block did not throw an exception, the `finally` block is still executed every time just before the method returns the control flow to the caller.

Originally, the `finally` block was used to close some resources used in the `try` block that needed to be closed. For example, if the code has opened a connection to the database or has established a reading or writing connection with a file on a disk, such a connection has to be closed after the operation is completed or when an exception has been thrown. Otherwise, a connection that is not closed on time keeps the resources (necessary to maintain the connection) locked without being used. We will talk about JVM processes in Chapter 11, *JVM Processes and Garbage Collection*.

So, typical code looked like this:

```
Connection conn = null;
try {
  conn = createConnection();
  //code of the try block
} catch (...){
  //optional catch block code
} finally {
  if(conn != null){
    conn.close();
  }
}
```

It worked fine. But a new Java capability, called `try...with...resources`, allows closing the connection automatically if the connection class implements `AutoCloseable` (which most of the popular connection classes do). We will talk about the `try...with...resources` construct in Chapter 16, *Database Programming*. This development decreased the `finally` block's usefulness, and now it is used primarily for handling some code that cannot be executed using the `AutoCloseable` interface, yet has to be performed just before the method returns unconditionally. For example, we could refactor our `exceptionCaught()` method by taking advantage of the `finally` block as follows:

```
void exceptionCaught(){
  Exception exf = null;
  try {
    method2();
  } catch (NullPointerException ex){
    exf = ex;
    System.out.println("NPE caught");
  } catch (RuntimeException ex){
    exf = ex;
    System.out.println("RuntimeException caught");
  } catch (Exception ex){
    exf = ex;
    System.out.println("Exception caught");
  } finally {
    if(exf != null){
      exf.printStackTrace();
    }
  }
}
```

There are other cases of `finally` block use too, based on its guaranteed execution just before the control flow is returned to the method caller.

# Assert requires JVM option -ea

The branching `assert` statement can be used for validation of the data in application testing, especially for accessing rarely used execution paths or combinations of data. The unique aspect of this capability is that the code is not executed unless the JVM is run with the option –ea.

A full discussion of the `assert` statement's functionality and possible application is outside the scope of this book. We will just demonstrate its basic usage and how to turn it on using IntelliJ IDEA.

Look at the following code:

```
public class AssertDemo {
  public static void main(String... args) {
    int x = 2;
    assert x > 1 : "x <= 1";
    assert x == 1 : "x != 1";
  }
}
```

The first `assert` statement evaluates the expression x > 1 and stops program execution (and reports x <= 1) if the expression x > 1 evaluates to `false`.

The second `assert` statement evaluates the expression x == 1 and stops program execution (and reports x != 1) if the expression x == 1 evaluates to `false`.

If we run this program now, none of the `assert` statements will be executed. To turn them on, click **Run** in the IntelliJ IDEA menu and select **Edit Configurations**, as shown in the following screenshot:

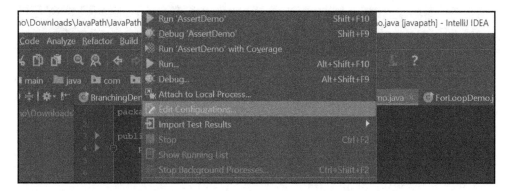

The **Run/Debug Configurations** screen will open. Type `-ea` in the field **VM options**, as shown in the following screenshot:

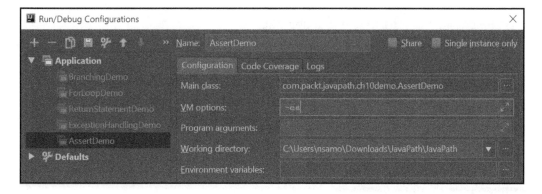

Then, click the **OK** button at the bottom of the screen.

If you run the `AssertDemo` program now, the result will be:

```
Exception in thread "main" java.lang.AssertionError: x != 1
        at com.packt.javapath.ch10demo.AssertDemo.main(AssertDemo.java:8)
```

The `-ea` option should not be used in production, except maybe temporarily for testing purposes, because it creates overhead and affects the application's performance.

# Exercise – Infinite loop

Write one or two examples of an infinite loop.

# Answer

Here is one possible infinite loop implementation:

```
while(true){
    System.out.println("try and stop me"); //prints indefinitely
}
```

The following is another one:

```
for (;;){
    System.out.println("try and stop me"); //prints indefinitely
}
```

And this one is an infinite loop, too:

```
for (int x=2; x > 0; x--){
    System.out.println(x++ + " "); //prints 2 indefinitely
}
```

In this code, the Boolean expression `x > 0` is always evaluated to `true` because x is initialized to 2 and then incremented and decremented by 1 in each iteration.

# Summary

This chapter described Java statements that let you build a program flow according to the logic of the implemented algorithm, using conditional statements, iteration statements, branching statements, and exception handling. An extensive discussion of Java exception helped you to navigate this complex and very often correctly used area. Best practices were provided for the most effective and least confusing exception handling.

In the next chapter, we will look under the hood of the JVM and discuss its processes and other aspects of its inner workings important that are for effective Java programming, including mechanism threads and garbage collection, which help an application to regain memory that is no longer in use.

# 11

# JVM Processes and Garbage Collection

This chapter allows readers to look under the hood of JVM and learn about its processes. The structure and behavior of JVM is more complex than just an executor of a sequence of instructions according to the coded logic. JVM finds and loads into the memory the `.class` files requested by the application, verifies them, interprets the bytecodes (translates them into platform-specific binary code), and passes the resulting machine code to the central processor (or processors) for execution, using several service threads in addition to the application threads. One of the service threads, called garbage collection, performs the important mission of releasing the memory from unused objects.

In this chapter, we will cover the following topics:

- What are JVM processes?
- JVM architecture
- Garbage collection
- Threads
- Exercise – Monitoring JVM while running an application

## What are JVM processes?

As we have established already in `Chapter 1`, *Java Virtual Machine (JVM) on Your Computer*, JVM does not know anything about the Java language and source code. It only knows how to read Byte Code. It reads the bytecodes and other information from `.class` files, interprets it (transforms it into the sequence of binary code instructions specific to a particular microprocessor, where JVM is running), and passes the result to the computer that executes it.

While talking about it, programmers often refer to JVM as *JVM instance* or *process*. This is because every time a `java` command is executed, a new *instance* of JVM is launched, dedicated to running the particular application in a separate process with the allocated memory size (default or passed in as the command option). Inside this JVM process, multiple threads are running, each with their own allocated memory; some are service threads created by the JVM, while others are application threads created and controlled by the application.

> Threads are lightweight processes that require less resource allocation than the JVM execution process.

That is the big picture of JVM executing the compiled code. But if you look closer and read the JVM Specification, you will discover that the word process in relation to JVM is overloaded many times. The JVM Specification identifies several other processes running inside the JVM that are usually not mentioned by programmers, except maybe the class loading process.

That is so because, most of the time, one can successfully write and execute Java programs without knowing more than that about JVM. But once in a while, some general understanding of JVM's internal workings helps to identify the root cause of certain related issues. That is why, in this section, we will provide a short overview of all the processes that happen inside JVM. Then, in the following sections, we will discuss JVM's memory structure and some other aspects of JVM functionality that may be useful to a programmer in more detail.

There are two subsystems that run all the JVM internal processes:

- Classloader, which reads `.class` files and populates method areas in JVM memory with the class-related data:
    - Static fields
    - Method bytecodes
    - Class metadata that describes the class
- Execution engine, which executes the bytecodes using:
    - Heap area for object instantiation
    - Java and native method stacks for keeping track of the methods called
    - A garbage collection process to reclaim the memory

The list of the processes that run inside the main JVM process includes:

- Processes performed by the classloader:
  - Class loading
  - Class linking
  - Class initialization
- Processes performed by the execution engine:
  - Class instantiation
  - Method execution
  - Garbage collection
  - Application termination

> The JVM architecture can be described as having two subsystems—the classloader and the execution engine—that run the service processes and application threads using runtime data memory areas: method area, heap, and application thread stacks.

The preceding list may give you the impression that these processes are executed sequentially. To some degree, this is true, if we talk about one class only. It is not possible to do anything with a class before loading. An execution of a method can begin only after all the previous processes are completed. However, the garbage collection, for example, doesn't happen immediately after the object stops being used (see the following section, *Garbage collection*). Also, an application can exit any time when an unhandled exception or some other error happens.

> Only the classloader processes are regulated by the JVM specification. The execution engine's implementation is largely at the discretion of each vendor. It is based on the language semantics and the performance goals set by the implementation authors.

The processes of the execution engine are not regulated by the JVM Specification. There is common sense, tradition, known and proven solutions, and the Java language specification that can guide a JVM vendor's implementation decisions, but there is no single regulatory document. The good news is that the most popular JVMs use similar solutions or, at least, that's how it looks from a high level of an introductory course. For vendor-specific details, see *Comparison of Java virtual machines* on Wikipedia (https://en.wikipedia.org/wiki/Comparison_of_Java_virtual_machines) and other sources available on the internet.

With this in mind, let's describe each of the seven processes listed previously in more detail.

# Loading

According to JVM Specification, the loading phase encompasses finding the `.class` file by its name and creating its representation in the memory.

The first class to be loaded is the one passed in the command line, with the method `main(String[])` in it. We previously described it in `Chapter 4`, *Your First Java Project*. The classloader reads the `.class` file, parses it according to the internal data structure, and populates the method area with static fields and method bytecodes. It also creates an instance of `java.lang.Class` that describes the class. Then, the classloader links (see section *Linking*) and initializes (see section *Initialization*) the class and passes it to the execution engine for running its bytecodes.

In the first project in `Chapter 4`, *Your First Java Project*, the `main(String[])` method did not use any other methods or classes. But in a real-life application, the `main(String[])` method is an entrance door into the application. If it calls a method of another class, that class has to be found on the classpath and read, parsed, and initialized; only then can its method be executed too. And so on. That is how a Java application starts and gets going.

In the following section, *How to execute the main(String[]) method*, we will show several ways a Java application can be started, including using an executable `.jar` file with a manifest.

Every class is allowed to have a `main(String[])` method and often does. Such a method is used to run the class independently as a standalone application for testing or demo purposes. The presence of such a method does not make the class main. The class becomes main only if it's identified as such in the `java` command line or in a `.jar` file manifest.

That said, let's continue with the discussion of the loading process.

If you look in the API of `java.lang.Class`, you will not see a public constructor there. The classloader creates its instance automatically and, by the way, is the same instance that is returned by the `getClass()` method that you can invoke on any object. It does not carry the class static data (that is maintained in the method area) or the state (they are in an object, created during the execution). It does not contain method bytecodes either (that is stored in the method area, too). Instead, the `Class` instance provides metadata that describes the class—its name, package, fields, constructors, method signatures, and so on. That is why it can be useful not only for JVM but also for application code, as we have seen in some examples already.

All the data created by the classloader in the memory and maintained by the execution engine is called a binary representation of the type.

If the `.class` file has errors or does not adhere to a certain format, the process is terminated. This means that some validation of the loaded class format and its bytecodes is performed by the loading process. But more verification follows at the beginning of the next process, called **linking**.

Here is the high-level description of the loading process. It performs three tasks:

- Finds and reads the `.class` file
- Parses it according to the internal data structure into the method area
- Creates an instance of `java.lang.Class` that carries the class metadata

# Linking

According to the JVM Specification, the linking is resolving the references of the loaded class, so the methods of the class can be executed.

Although JVM can reasonably expect that the `.class` file was produced by the Java compiler and all the instructions satisfy the constraints and requirements of the language, there is no guarantee that the loaded file was produced by the known compiler implementation or a compiler at all. That is why the first step of the linking process is *verification*, which makes sure that the binary representation of the class is structurally correct: that the arguments of each method invocation are compatible with the method descriptor, that the return instruction matches its method's return type, and so on.

After verification is successfully completed, the next step—*preparation*—follows. The interface or class (static) variables are created in the method area and initialized to the default values of their types. The other kinds of initializations – the explicit assignments specified by a programmer and static initialization blocks – are deferred to the process called **initialization** (see the next section, *Initialization*).

If the loaded bytecodes refer other methods, interfaces, or classes, the symbolic references are resolved into concrete references that point to the method area, which is done by the *resolution* process. If the referred interfaces and classes are not loaded yet, the classloader finds them and loads them as needed.

Here is the high-level description of the linking process. It performs three tasks:

- Verification of the binary representation of a class or an interface
- Preparation of static fields in the method area
- Resolution of symbolic references into concrete references that point to the method area

# Initialization

According to JVM Specification, the initialization is accomplished by executing the class initialization methods.

That is when the programmer-defined initialization (in static blocks and static assignments) is performed, unless the class was already initialized at the request of another class.

The last part of this statement is an important one because the class may be requested several times by different (already loaded) methods, and also because JVM processes are executed by different threads (see the definition of threads in the section *Threads*) and may access the same class concurrently. So, coordination (also called synchronization) between different threads is required, which substantially complicates JVM implementation.

# Instantiation

Technically, an instantiation process, triggered by the operator `new`, is the first step of the execution, and this section might not exist. But if the `main(String[])` method (which is static) uses only static methods of other classes, the instantiation never happens. That's why it is reasonable to identify this process as separate from the execution. Besides, this activity has very specific tasks:

- Allocating memory for the object (its state) in the heap area
- Initialization of the instance fields to the default values
- Creating thread stacks for Java and native methods

Execution starts when the first method—not a constructor—is ready to be executed. For every application thread, a dedicated runtime stack is created, where every method call is captured in a stack frame. If an exception happens, we get data from the current stack frames when we call the method `printStackTrace()`.

# Execution

The first application thread (called the *main* thread) is created when the `main(String[])` method starts executing. It can create other application threads. The execution engine reads the bytecodes, interprets them, and sends the binary code to the microprocessor for execution. It also maintains a count of how many times and how often each method was called. If the count exceeds a certain threshold, the execution engine uses a compiler, called JIT compiler, which compiles the method bytecodes into a native code. The next time the method is called, it will be ready without an interpretation. It substantially improves code performance.

The instruction currently being executed and the address of the next instruction are maintained in the **Program Counter** (**PC**) registers. Each thread has its own dedicated PC registers. It also improves performance and keeps track of the execution.

# Garbage collection

The **garbage collector** (**GC**) runs the process that identifies the objects that are not referenced anymore and so can be removed from the memory. There is a Java static method, `System.gc()`, that can be used programmatically to trigger the garbage collection, but the immediate execution is not guaranteed. Every GC cycle affects the application performance, so the JVM has to maintain a balance between the memory availability and the ability to execute the bytecodes quickly enough.

# Application termination

There are several ways an application can be terminated (and the JVM stopped) programmatically:

- Normal termination without an error status code
- Abnormal termination because of an unhandled exception or a forced programmatic exit with or without an error status code

If there are no exceptions and infinite loops, the `main(String[])` method completes with a `return` statement or after its last statement is executed. As soon as it happens, the main application thread returns the control flow to the JVM and the JVM stops executing, too.

That is the happy ending, and many applications enjoy it in real-life. Most of our examples, except those when we have demonstrated exceptions or infinite loops, have ended successfully, too.

However, there are other ways a Java application can exit, some of them quite graceful too. Others – not as much.

If the main application thread created child threads or, in other words, a programmer has written code that generates other threads, even the graceful exit may not be as easy. It all depends on the kind of the child threads created. If any of them is a user thread (the default), then the JVM instance continues to run even after the main thread exits.

Only after all user threads are completed does the JVM instance stop. It is possible for the main thread to request that the child user thread complete (we will talk about this in the following section, *Threads*). But until it exits, the JVM continues running, and this means that the application is still running too.

But if all child threads are daemon threads (see the following section, *Threads*) or there are no child threads running, the JVM instance stops running as soon as the main application thread exits.

 Without forced termination, the JVM instance continues running until the main application thread and all child user threads are completed. In the absence of child user threads or in the case where all the child threads are daemon, the JVM stops running as soon as the main application thread exits.

How the application exits in the case of an exception depends on the code design. We touched on it in the previous chapter while discussing the best practices of exception handling. If the thread captures all the exceptions in a try...catch block in main(String[]) or a similarly high-level method, then the control flow is returned back to the application code and it is up to the application (and the programmer who wrote the code) how to proceed – to try to recover, to log the error and continue, or to exit.

If, on the other hand, the exception remains unhandled and propagates into the JVM code, the thread (where the exception happened) stops executing and exits. Then, one of the following will occur:

- If there are no other threads, the JVM stops executing and returns an error code and the stack trace
- If the thread with an unhandled exception was not the main one, other threads (if present) continue running
- If the main thread has thrown an unhandled exception and the child threads (if present) are daemon, they exit too
- If there is at least one user child thread, the JVM continues running until all user threads exit

There are also ways to programmatically force the application to stop:

- `System.exit(0);`
- `Runtime.getRuntime().exit(0);`
- `Runtime.getRuntime().halt(0);`

All of the preceding methods force the JVM to stop executing any thread and exit with a status code passed in as the parameter (0, in our examples):

- Zero indicates normal termination
- The nonzero value indicates abnormal termination

If the Java command was launched by some script or another system, the value of the status code can be used for the automation of the decision making about the next step. But that is already outside the application and Java code.

The first two methods have identical functionality, because here is how `System.exit()` is implemented:

```
public static void exit(int status) {
    Runtime.getRuntime().exit(status);
}
```

To see the source code in IDE, just click on the method.

The Java Virtual Machine exits when some thread invokes the `exit()` method of the `Runtime` or `System` class, or the `halt()` method of the `Runtime` class, and the exit or halt operation is permitted by the security manager.

The difference between `exit()` and `halt()` is that `halt()` forces JVM to exit immediately, while `exit()` performs additional actions that can be set using the `Runtime.addShutdownHook()` method.

But all these options are rarely used in mainstream programming, so we are already stepping way beyond the scope of this book.

# JVM architecture

JVM architecture can be described in terms of the runtime data structure in the memory and in terms of the two subsystems that use the runtime data – the classloader and execution engine.

# Runtime data areas

Each of the runtime data areas of JVM memory belong to one of two categories:

- Shared areas, which include the following:
    - **Method area**: Class metadata, static fields, methods bytecodes
    - **Heap area**: Objects (state)
- Not shared areas, dedicated to each application thread, which include the following:
    - **Java stack**: Current and caller frames, each frame keeping the state of Java (not native) method invocation:
        - Values of local variables
        - Method parameters values
        - Values of operands for intermediate calculations (operand stack)
        - Method return value (if any)
    - **Program Counter (PC) register**: Next instruction to execute
    - **Native method stack**: The state of native method invocations

We have already discussed that a programmer has to be careful while using reference types to not modify the object itself unless it needs to be done. In a multithreaded application, if a reference to an object can be passed between threads, one has to be extra careful because of the possibility of the concurrent modification of the same data.

On the bright side, such a shared area can be and often is used as the means of communication between threads. We will talk about this in the upcoming *Threads* section.

# Classloader

The classloader performs the following three functions:

- Reads the `.class` file
- Populates the method area
- Initializes static fields not initialized by a programmer

# Execution engine

The execution engine does the following:

- Instantiates objects in the heap area
- Initializes static and instance fields, using initializers written by programmers
- Adds/removes frames to/from Java stack
- Updates the PC register with the next instruction to execute
- Maintains the native method stack
- Keeps counts of method calls and compiles popular ones
- Finalizes objects
- Runs garbage collection
- Terminates the application

# Threads

As we have mentioned already, the main application thread can create other - child - threads and let them run in parallel, either sharing the same core via time slicing or having a dedicated CPU for each thread. It can be done using the class `java.lang.Thread`, which implements the functional interface `Runnable`. The interface is called functional if it has only one abstract method (we will discuss functional interfaces in `Chapter 17`, *Lambda Expressions and Functional Programming*). The `Runnable` interface contains one method, `run()`.

There are two ways to create a new thread:

- Extend the `Thread` class
- Implement the `Runnable` interface and pass the object of the implementation into the constructor of the class `Thread`

# Extending the Thread class

Whatever method is used, we end up with a `Thread` class object that has the method `start()`. This method call starts the thread execution. Let's look at an example. Let's create a class called `AThread` that extends `Thread` and overrides its `run()` method:

```
public class AThread extends Thread {
   int i1, i2;
   public AThread(int i1, int i2) {
      this.i1 = i1;
      this.i2 = i2;
   }
   public void run() {
      for (int i = i1; i <= i2; i++) {
         System.out.println("child thread " + (isDaemon() ? "daemon" : "user")
+ " " + i);
         try {
            TimeUnit.SECONDS.sleep(1);
         } catch (InterruptedException e) {
            e.printStackTrace();
         }
      }
   }
}
```

Overriding the `run()` method is important because otherwise, the thread will do nothing. The `Thread` class implements the `Runnable` interface and has the `run()` method's implementation, but it looks as follows:

```
public void run() {
   if (target != null) {
      target.run();
   }
}
```

The variable `target` holds the value passed in the constructor:

```
public Thread(Runnable target) {
   init(null, target, "Thread-" + nextThreadNum(), 0);
}
```

But our `AThread` class does not pass any value to the parent class `Target`; the variable `target` is `null`, so the `run()` method in the `Thread` class does not do anything.

Now let's use our newly created thread. We expect it to increment variable i from i1 to i2 (these are parameters passed via the constructor) and print its value along with the Boolean value returned by the isDaemon() method, then wait (sleep) for 1 second and increment variable i again.

# What is daemon?

The word daemon has an ancient Greek origin, meaning a divinity or supernatural being of a nature between gods and humans and an inner or attendant spirit or inspiring force. But in computer science, this term has more mundane usage and is applied to a computer program that runs as a background process, rather than being under the direct control of an interactive user. That is why there are two types of threads in Java:

- User thread (default), initiated by an application (the main thread is one such example)
- Daemon threads that work in the background in support of user thread activity (garbage collection is an example of a daemon thread)

That is why all daemon threads exit immediately after the last user thread exits or is terminated by JVM after an unhandled exception.

# Running threads extending Thread

Let's use our new class, AThread, to demonstrate the behavior we have described. Here is the code we are going to run first:

```
Thread thr1 = new AThread(1, 4);
thr1.start();

Thread thr2 = new AThread(11, 14);
thr2.setDaemon(true);
thr2.start();

try {
  TimeUnit.SECONDS.sleep(1);
} catch (InterruptedException e) {
  e.printStackTrace();
}
System.out.println("Main thread exists");
```

In the preceding code, we create and immediately start two threads – a user thread, `thr1`, and a daemon thread, `thr2`. Actually, there is a user thread called `main` too, so we run two user threads and one daemon thread. Each of the child threads is going to print the incremented number four times, pausing for 1 second after each print. This means that each thread will be running for 4 seconds. The main thread will pause for 1 second too, but one time only, so it will run for approximately 1 second. Then, it prints `Main thread exists` and exists. If we run this code, we will see the following output:

```
child thread daemon 11
child thread user 1
Main thread exists
child thread daemon 12
child thread user 2
child thread user 3
child thread daemon 13
child thread daemon 14
child thread user 4
```

We execute this code on one shared CPU, so, although all three threads are running concurrently, they can only use CPU sequentially. Therefore, they cannot be run in parallel. On a multicore computer, each thread may be executed on a different CPU and the output may be slightly different, but not by much. In any case, you would see that the main thread exits first (after approximately 1 second) and the child threads run until completion, each for approximately 4 seconds in total.

Let's make user thread run for only 2 seconds:

```
Thread thr1 = new AThread(1, 2);
thr1.start();
```

The result is:

```
child thread daemon 11
child thread user 1
Main thread exists
child thread daemon 12
child thread user 2
child thread daemon 13
```

As you can see, the daemon thread did not run the full course. It managed to print 13, probably only because it had sent the message to the output device before the JVM responded to the last user thread exit.

# Implementing Runnable

The second way to create a thread is to use a class that implements `Runnable`. Here is an example of such a class that has almost exactly the same functionality as class `AThread`:

```
public class ARunnable implements Runnable {
    int i1, i2;

    public ARunnable(int i1, int i2) {
        this.i1 = i1;
        this.i2 = i2;
    }

    public void run() {
        for (int i = i1; i <= i2; i++) {
            System.out.println("child thread " + i);
            try {
                TimeUnit.SECONDS.sleep(1);
            } catch (InterruptedException e) {
                e.printStackTrace();
            }
        }
    }
}
```

The only difference is that there is no `isDaemon()` method in the `Runnable` interface, so we cannot print whether the thread is daemon or not.

# Runing threads implementing Runnable

And here is how this class can be used to create two child threads—one user thread and another a daemon thread—exactly as we have done before:

```
Thread thr1 = new Thread(new ARunnable(1, 4));
thr1.start();

Thread thr2 = new Thread(new ARunnable(11, 14));
thr2.setDaemon(true);
thr2.start();

try {
    TimeUnit.SECONDS.sleep(1);
} catch (InterruptedException e) {
    e.printStackTrace();
}
```

```
System.out.println("Main thread exists");
```

If we run the preceding code, the result will be the same as running threads based on a class that extends Thread.

# Extending Thread vs implementing Runnable

Implementing Runnable has the advantage (and in some cases, the only possible option) of allowing the implementation to extend another class. It is particularly helpful when you would like to add thread-like behavior to an existing class:

```
public class BRunnable extends SomeClass implements Runnable {
    int i;
    BRunnable(int i, String s) {
        super(s);
        this.i = i;
    }
    public int calculateSomething(double x) {
        //calculate result
        return result;
    }
    public void run() {
        //any code you need goes here
    }
}
```

You can even invoke the method run() directly, without passing the object into the Thread constructor:

```
BRunnable obj = new BRunnable(2, "whatever");
int i = obj.calculateSomething(42d);
obj.run();
Thread thr = new Thread (obj);
thr.start();
```

In the preceding code snippet, we have shown many different ways to execute the methods of the class that implements Runnable. So, implementing Runnable allows more flexibility in usage. But otherwise, there is no difference in functionality comparing to the extending of Thread.

The `Thread` class has several constructors that allow setting the thread name and the group it belongs to. Grouping of threads helps to manage them in the case of many threads running in parallel. The `Thread` class also has several methods that provide information about the thread's status and properties and allow us to control its behavior.

Threads—and any objects for that matter—can also talk to each other using the methods `wait()`, `notify()`, and `notifyAll()` of the base class `java.lang.Object`.

But all that is already outside the scope of the introductory course.

# How to execute the main(String[]) method

Before diving into the garbage collection process, we would like to review and summarize how to run an application from a command line. In Java, the following statements are used as synonyms:

- Run/execute main class
- Run/execute/start application
- Run/execute/start main method
- Run/execute/start/launch JVM or Java process

The reason for that is that each of the listed actions happens every time you execute one of them. There are also several ways to do it. We have already shown you how to run the `main(String[])` method using IntelliJ IDEA and the `java` command line. Now, we will just repeat some of what has been said already and add other variations that might be helpful for you.

# Using IDE

Any IDE allows running the main method. In IntelliJ IDEA, it can be done in three ways:

- By clicking on the green arrow next to the method name

- By selecting the class name from the drop-down menu (at the top line, to the left of the green arrow) and clicking the green arrow to the right of the menu:

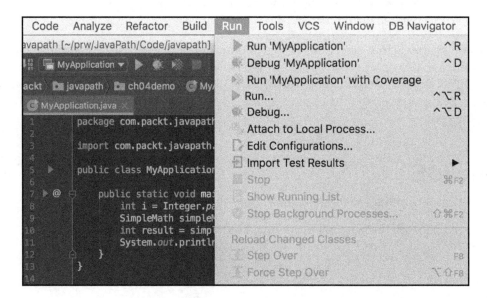

- By using the **Run** menu and selecting the name of the class:

In the preceding screenshot, you can also see the option **Edit configurations**. We have used it already to set the parameters that can be passed to the main method at the start. But there are more settings possible there:

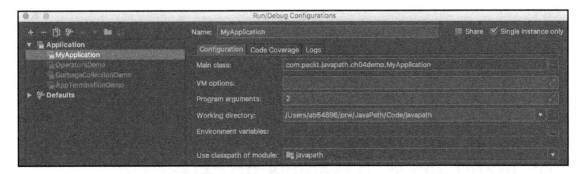

As you can see, it is possible to also set:

- **VM options**: The Java command options (we will do this in the next section)
- **Environment variables**: The way to set some parameters that can be read not only in the main method but anywhere in the application, using the System.getenv() method

For example, look at the following screenshot:

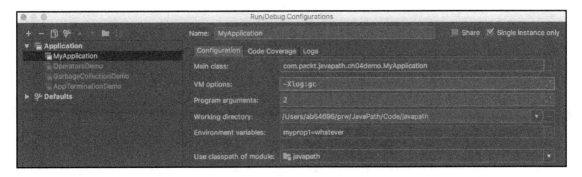

We have set the java command option -Xlog:gc and the environment variable myprop1=whatever. The IDE will use these settings to form the following java command:

```
java -Xlog:gc -Dmyprop1=whatever com.packt.javapath.ch04demo.MyApplication
2
```

The option -Xlog:gc tells JVM to display log messages from the garbage collection process. We will use this option in the next section to demonstrate how garbage collection works. The value of the variable myprop1 can be retrieved anywhere in the application using the following statement:

```
String myprop = System.getenv("myprop1");      //returns: "whatever"
```

And we have already seen how parameter 2 can be read in the main method as follows:

```
public static void main(String[] args) {
    String p1 = args[0];              //returns: "2"
}
```

# Command line with classes on classpath

Let's use the first program we created in Chapter 4, *Your First Java Project,* to demonstrate how to use the command line. Here is the program we wrote then:

```
package com.packt.javapath.ch04demo;
import com.packt.javapath.ch04demo.math.SimpleMath;
public class MyApplication {
    public static void main(String[] args) {
        int i = Integer.parseInt(args[0]);
        SimpleMath simpleMath = new SimpleMath();
        int result = simpleMath.multiplyByTwo(i);
        System.out.println(i + " * 2 = " + result);
    }
}
```

To run it from a command line, it has to be compiled first using the javac command. An IDE that uses Maven places the .class file in the directory target/classes. If you go into the root directory of your project or just click **Terminal** (bottom left corner in IntelliJ IDEA), you can run the following command:

**java -cp target/classes com.packt.javapath.ch04demo.MyApplication 2**

The result should be displayed as 2 * 2 = 4.

# Command line with a .jar file on classpath

To create a `.jar` file with the compiled application code, go to the project root directory and run the following commands:

```
cd target/classes
jar -cf myapp.jar com/packt/javapath/ch04demo/**
```

A `.jar` file with the classes `MyApplication` and `SimpleMath` is created. Now we can put it on the classpath and run the application again:

```
java -cp myapp.jar com.packt.javapath.ch04demo.MyApplication 2
```

The result will be displayed the same; `2 * 2 = 4`.

# Command line with an executable .jar file

It is possible to avoid specifying the main class in the command line. Instead, one can create an "executable" `.jar` file. It can be accomplished by placing the name of the main class—the one you need to run and that contains the main method—into the manifest file. Here are the steps:

- Create a text file, `manifest.txt` (the name actually does not matter, but it makes the intent clear) that contains the following one line: `Main-Class: com.packt.javapath.ch04demo.MyApplication`. There has to be a space after the colon (`:`) and there has to be an invisible new line symbol at the end, so make sure you have pressed the *Enter* key and the cursor has jumped to the beginning of the next line.
- Execute the command `cd target/classes` and go into the directory `classes`.
- Execute the following command: `jar -cfm myapp.jar manifest.txt com/packt/javapath/ch04demo/**`.

Notice the sequence of `jar` command options `fm` and the sequence of the following files; `myapp.jar manifest.txt`. They have to be the same, because `f` stands for the file the `jar` command is going to create and `m` stands for the manifest source. If you put the options as `mf`, then the files have to be listed as `manifest.txt myapp.jar`.

Now, run the following command:

```
java -jar myapp.jar 2
```

The result will be `2 * 2 = 4` again.

Equipped with the knowledge of how to run an application, we can now continue to the next section, where it is going to be needed.

# Garbage collection

Automatic memory management is an important aspect of JVM that relieves the programmer from the need to do it programmatically. In Java, the process that cleans up memory and allows you to reuse it is called **Garbage Collection** (**GC**).

# Responsiveness, throughput, and stop-the-world

The effectiveness of GC affects two major application characteristics – responsiveness and throughput. Responsiveness is measured by how quickly an application responds (brings necessary data) to the request. For example, how quickly a website returns a page, or how quickly a desktop application responds to an event. The smaller the response time, the better the user experience. Throughput, on the other hand, indicates the amount of work an application can do in a unit of time. For example, how many requests a web application can serve, or how many transactions a database can support. The bigger the number, the more value the application can potentially generate and the more user requests it can support.

Meanwhile, GC needs to move data around, which is impossible to accomplish while allowing data processing because the references are going to change. That's why GC needs to stop application threads from executing once in a while for a period of time called stop-the-world. The longer these periods are, the quicker GC does its job, and the longer an application freeze lasts, which can eventually grow big enough to affect both the application's responsiveness and throughput. Fortunately, it is possible to tune the GC behavior using `java` command options, but that is outside the scope of this book, which is more about introduction than solving complex problems. So, we will concentrate on a high-level view of the main activity of a GC; inspecting objects in the heap and removing those that don't have references in any thread stack.

# Object age and generations

The basic GC algorithm determines how old each object is. The term age refers to the number of collection cycles the object has survived. When JVM starts, the heap is empty and is divided into three sections: young generation, old or tenured generation, and humongous regions for holding the objects that are 50% the size of a standard region or larger.

The young generation has three areas, an Eden space and two survivor spaces, such as Survivor 0 (*S0*) and Survivor 1 (*S1*). The newly created objects are placed in Eden. When it is filling up, a minor GC process starts. It removes the un-referred and circular referred objects and moves others to the *S1* area. At the next minor collection, *S0* and *S1* switch roles. The referenced objects are moved from Eden and *S1* to *S0*.

At each of the minor collections, the objects that have reached a certain age are moved to the old generation. As the result of this algorithm, the old generation contains objects that are older than a certain age. This area is bigger than the young generation, and, because of that, the garbage collection here is more expensive and doesn't happen as often as in the young generation. But it is checked eventually (after several minor collections); the un-referenced objects are removed from there and the memory is defragmented. This cleaning of the old generation is considered a major collection.

# When stop-the-world is unavoidable

Some collections of objects in the old generation are done concurrently and some are done using stop-the-world pauses. The steps include:

- Initial marking of survivor regions (root regions) that may have references to objects in the old generation, done using stop-the-world pause
- Scanning of survivor regions for references into the old generation, done concurrently, while the application continues to run
- Concurrent marking of live objects over the entire heap, done concurrently, while the application continues to run
- Remark – completes the marking of live objects, done using stop-the-world pause
- Cleanup – calculates the age of live objects and frees regions (using stop-the-world) and returns them to the free list (concurrently)

The preceding sequence might be interspersed with the young generation evacuations because most of the objects are short-lived and it is easier to free a lot of memory by scanning the young generation more often. There is also a mixed phase (when G1 collects the regions already marked as mostly garbage in both the young and the old generations) and humongous allocation (where large objects are moved to or evacuated from humongous regions).

To demonstrate how GC works, let's create a program that produces more garbage than our usual examples:

```
public class GarbageCollectionDemo {
    public static void main(String... args) {
        int max = 99888999;
        List<Integer> list = new ArrayList<>();
        for(int i = 1; i < max; i++){
            list.add(Integer.valueOf(i));
        }
    }
}
```

This program generates close to 100,000,000 objects that take a chunk of heap and force GC to move them around from Eden, to S0, S1, and so on. As we have mentioned already, to see the log messages from GC, the option -Xlog:gc has to be included in the java command. We chose to use IDE for that, as we described in the previous section:

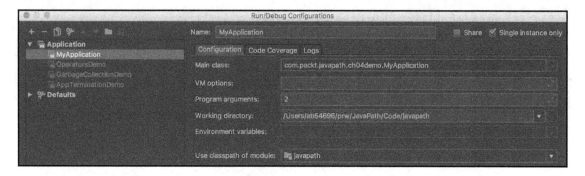

Then, we had run the program `GarbageCollectionDemo` and got the following output (we show only its beginning):

```
[0.024s][info][gc] Using G1
[0.392s][info][gc] GC(0) Pause Young (G1 Evacuation Pause) 47M->43M(256M) 74.748ms
[0.452s][info][gc] GC(1) Pause Young (G1 Evacuation Pause) 63M->65M(256M) 40.631ms
[0.499s][info][gc] GC(2) Pause Young (G1 Evacuation Pause) 75M->77M(256M) 36.899ms
[0.550s][info][gc] GC(3) Pause Young (G1 Evacuation Pause) 103M->104M(256M) 23.946ms
[0.604s][info][gc] GC(4) Pause Initial Mark (G1 Humongous Allocation) 118M->118M(768M) 41.259ms
[0.604s][info][gc] GC(5) Concurrent Cycle
[0.737s][info][gc] GC(5) Pause Remark 173M->173M(768M) 1.856ms
[0.772s][info][gc] GC(5) Pause Cleanup 210M->176M(768M) 0.773ms
[0.794s][info][gc] GC(5) Concurrent Cycle 190.287ms
[0.873s][info][gc] GC(6) Pause Young (G1 Evacuation Pause) 179M->180M(768M) 75.056ms
[0.975s][info][gc] GC(7) Pause Young (G1 Evacuation Pause) 213M->216M(768M) 67.878ms
[1.199s][info][gc] GC(8) Pause Young (G1 Evacuation Pause) 309M->310M(768M) 133.679ms
[1.351s][info][gc] GC(9) Pause Initial Mark (G1 Humongous Allocation) 351M->353M(2100M) 105.331ms
[1.351s][info][gc] GC(10) Concurrent Cycle
[1.922s][info][gc] GC(11) Pause Young (G1 Evacuation Pause) 531M->532M(2100M) 235.754ms
[2.045s][info][gc] GC(10) Pause Remark 659M->659M(2100M) 1.456ms
[2.194s][info][gc] GC(10) Pause Cleanup 741M->665M(2100M) 1.861ms
```

As you can see, the GC process goes through cycles and moves the objects as needed, pausing for a short time. We hope you got an idea of how GC works. The only thing we would like to mention is that there are a few occasions when full GC is performed, using stop-the-world pause:

- **Concurrent failure**: If during the marking phase the old generation gets full.
- **Promotion failure**: If during the mixed phase the old generation runs out of space.
- **Evacuation failure**: When the collector cannot promote objects to the survivor space and the old generation.
- **Humongous allocation**: When an application tries to allocate a very big object. If tuned properly, your applications should avoid full GC.

To help with GC tuning, the JVM provides platform-dependent default selections for the garbage collector, heap size, and runtime compiler. But fortunately, the JVM vendors improve and tune GC process all the time, so most of the applications work just fine with the default GC behavior.

# Exercise – Monitoring JVM while running an application

Read the Java official documentation and name a few tools that come with JDK installation that can be used to monitor JVM and the Java application.

## Answer

Jcmd, Java VisualVM, and JConsole, for example. Jcmd is particularly helpful as it is easy to remember and gives you the list of all Java processes that are currently running. Just type `jcmd` in the terminal window. That is an indispensable tool in case you are experimenting with several Java applications and some of them may not exit, whether because of a defect or because of such an intended design. Jcmd displays a **Process ID** (**PID**) for each running Java process, which you can use to stop it if need be by typing the command `kill -9 <PID>`.

## Summary

In this chapter, you have learned about the main Java processes that support any application's execution, the steps of a program's execution, and the main components of JVM architecture that compose the execution environment; runtime data areas, classloader, and execution engine. You have also learned about the lightweight processes called threads and how they can be used for concurrent processing. The summary of ways to run a Java application and the main features of the garbage collection process concluded the discussion about JVM.

In the next chapter, we will walk through several often used libraries – both standard (that come with JDK) and external open-source libraries. Pretty soon, you will know most of them very well, but to get there you need to start, and we will help you with our comments and examples.

# 12
# Java Standard and External Libraries

Even the first program we wrote in this book used a library included in the JDK, called a standard library. It is not possible to write a non-trivial program without using the standard libraries. That is why a solid familiarity with such libraries is as vital for successful programming as the knowledge of the language itself.

There are also non-standard libraries, which are called external libraries or third-party libraries because they are not included in JDK distribution, but they are used almost as often. They have long become permanent members of any programmer's toolkit. Meanwhile, keeping track of all the functionality available in these libraries is not as easy as staying abreast with Java itself. That is because IDE gives you a hint about the language possibilities, but it cannot advise about the functionality of a package that's not been imported yet. The only package that is imported automatically and does not require importing is `java.lang`, and that will be the first we are going to overview in this chapter.

The topics discussed in this chapter are:

- What are standard and external libraries?
- Java standard libraries overview
- Package `java.lang`
- Package `java.util`
- Packages `java.io` and `java.nio`
- Packages `java.sql` and `javax.sql`
- Package `java.net`
- Package `java.math`

- Packages `java.awt`, `javax.swing`, and `javafx`
- Java external libraries overview
- Library `org.junit`
- Library `org.mockito`
- Libraries `org.log4j` and `org.slf4j`
- Libraries `org.apache.commons`
- Exercise – Using `java.time.LocalDateTime`

# What are standard and external libraries?

A standard library (also called a class standard library) is a collection of classes and interfaces available for all implementations of the language. In simpler terms, this means that, it is a collection of `.class` files included in the JDK and ready to be used. Once you have installed Java, you get them as part of the installation and can start building your application code up using the classes of the standard library as building blocks that take care of a lot of low-level plumbing. The standard library's richness and ease of usage substantially contributed to Java's popularity.

These collections are organized by packages. That's why instead of saying Java standard library, which would be the correct way to refer to all these collections together, programmers call them Java standard libraries – because, in order to use them, you have to import the library packages as needed, so they are perceived as many libraries.

They are also standard because Maven adds them to the classpath automatically, so we do not need to list them in the `pom.xml` file as dependencies. And that is what separates standard libraries and external libraries; if you need to add a library (typically, a `.jar` file) as a dependency in the Maven configuration file `pom.xml`, this library is an external one, also called a third-party library. Otherwise, it is a standard library.

In the following sections, we will provide an overview for each category and look closer at a few of the most popular standard and external libraries.

# Java standard libraries

If you search "Java API" on the internet, you will find an online description of all the packages included in JDK. Some package names start with `java`. They are traditionally called core Java packages, while those that start with `javax` used to be called extensions. This was done so probably because the extensions were thought to be optional and maybe even released independently of JDK. There was also an attempt to promote former extension libraries to become a core package, but that would require the package's name to change from Java to Javax, which would have broken the already existing applications. So, the idea was abandoned, the extensions became as standard part of JDK as the core, and the distinction between core and extensions gradually disappeared.

That is why if you look at the official Java API on the Oracle website you will see listed as standard not only `java` and `javax` packages, but also `jdk`, `com.sun`, `org.xml`, and some other packages, too. These extra packages are primarily used by the tools or other specialized applications. In our book, we will concentrate mostly on the mainstream Java programming and talk only about `java` and `javax` packages.

# java.lang

This package is so fundamental for all the Java class libraries that it is not only not required to be listed in the Maven configuration `pom.xml` file as a dependency (all other packages of the Java standard library are not required to be listed as a dependency too), but its members are even not required to be imported in order to use them. Any member of any package, whether standard are not, has to be imported or used with its fully qualified name, except classes and interfaces of the `java.lang` package. The reason for that is that it contains the two most important and the most used classes of Java:

- `Object`: The base class of any other Java class (see `Chapter 2`, *Java Language Basics*)
- `Class`: Its instances carry metadata of every loaded class at runtime (see `Chapter 11`, *JVM Processes and Garbage Collection*)

In addition, the `java.lang` package includes:

- The classes `String`, `StringBuffer`, and `StringBuilders`, which support operations with type `String` (see Chapter 15, *Manage Objects, Strings, Time, and Random Numbers* for more details and examples of usage)
- The wrapper classes of all primitive types: `Byte`, `Boolean`, `Short`, `Character`, `Integer`, `Long`, `Float`, and `Double` (see Chapter 9, *Operators, Expressions, and Statements* for more details about wrapper classes and their usage)
- The `Number` class, the base class for the numeral wrapper classes listed previously
- The `System` class, which provides access to important system operations and the standard input and output (we have used the `System.out` object in every code example in this book)
- The `Runtime` class, which provides access to the execution environment
- The `Thread` class and the `Runnable` interface, fundamental for creating Java threads
- The `Iterable` interface used by the iteration statements (see Chapter 9, *Operators, Expressions, and Statements*)
- The `Math` class, which provides methods for basic numeric operations
- The `Throwable` class – the base class for all exceptions
- The exception class `Error` and all its children, used to communicate system errors that should not be caught by an application
- The `Exception` class and its many children, which represent checked exceptions (see Chapter 10, *Control Flow Statements*)
- The `RuntimeException` class and its many children, which represent unchecked exceptions, also called runtime exceptions (see Chapter 10, *Control Flow Statements*)
- The `ClassLoader` class, which allows loading classes and can be used to build customized classloaders
- The `Process` and `ProcessBuilder` classes, which allow creating external processes
- Many other useful classes and interfaces

# java.util

This is another very commonly used package. Most of its content is dedicated to support collections:

- The `Collection` interface – the base interface of many collection interfaces. It contains all the basic methods necessary to manage collection elements: `size()`, `add()`, `remove()`, `contains()`, `iterator()`, `stream()`, and others. Notice that the `Collection` interface extends the `Iterable` interface and inherits the `iterator()` method from it. This means that any implementation of the `Collection` interface can be used in iteration statements.
- Interfaces that extend the `Collection` interface: `List`, `Set`, `Queue`, `Deque`, and many others.
- Many classes that implement the forementioned interfaces: `ArrayList`, `LinkedList`, `HashSet`, `AbstractQueue`, `ArrayDeque`, and others.
- The `Map` interface and the classes that implement it: `HashMap`, `TreeMap`, and others.
- The `Collections` class, which provides many static methods for manipulating and converting collections.
- Many other collection interfaces, classes, and the related utilities.

We will talk more about collections and see examples of their usage in `Chapter 13`, *Java Collections*.

The `java.util` package also includes several other useful classes:

- The `Objects` class provides various objects-related utility methods, including null-safe `equals()` of two objects
- The `Arrays` class contains more than 200 static methods to manipulate arrays
- The `Formatter` class allows formatting of any primitive type, such as `String`, `Date`, and other types
- The classes `Optional`, `OptionalInt`, `OptionalLong`, and `OptionalDouble`, which help avoid `NullPointerException` by wrapping the actual value, nullable or not
- The `Properties` class helps to read and create key-value pairs used for configuration and similar purposes
- The `Random` class complements the `Math.random()` method by generating streams of pseudorandom numbers

- The `Stack` class allows creating a **last-in-first-out** (**LIFO**) stack of objects
- The `StringTokeneizer` class breaks `String` objects into the tokens separated by the specified delimiter
- The `StringJoiner` class constructs a sequence of characters separated by the specified delimiter and optionally surrounded by the specified prefix and suffix
- Many other useful utility classes, including internationalization support classes and base64 encoding and decoding

# java.time

That is the main Java API for managing dates, times, instants, and durations. The package includes:

- enum `Month`
- enum `DayOfWeek`
- The `Clock` class, which instantly returns the current date and time using a time zone
- The `Duration` and `Period` classes represent and compare amounts of time in different time units
- The `LocalDate`, `LocalTime`, `LocalDateTime` classes represent dates and times without time zones
- The `ZonedDateTime` class represents date-time with a time zone
- The `ZoneId` class identifies a time zone such as America/Chicago
- Some other classes that support date and time manipulation

The `java.time.format.DateTimeFormatter` class allows you to present date and time in accordance with **International Standards Organization** (**ISO**) formats and is based on patterns such as YYYY-MM-DD and others.

We will talk more about date and time processing and see code examples in Chapter 15, *Manage Objects, Strings, Time, and Random Numbers.*

# java.io and java.nio

The `java.io` and `java.nio` packages contain classes that support reading and writing data using streams, serialization, and the file system. The differences between these two packages are as follows:

- `java.io` allows us to read/write data as they go without caching
- `java.nio` creates a buffer and allows the program to move back and forth in the buffer
- The class methods of `java.io` block the stream until all the data is read or written
- `java.nio` stands for a non-blocking style of the data reading and writing

# java.sql and javax.sql

These two packages compose the **Java Database Connectivity** (**JDBC**) API, which allows accessing and processing data stored in a data source, typically a relational database. The package `javax.sql` complements the `java.sql` package by providing support for:

- `DataSource` interface as an alternative to the `DriverManager`
- Connection pooling and statement pooling
- Distributed transactions
- Rowsets

We will talk more about using these packages and see code examples in `Chapter 16`, *Database Programming*.

# java.net

The `java.net` package contains classes that support applications networking on two levels:

- Low-level networking, based on:
  - IP addresses
  - Sockets, which are basic bidirectional data communication mechanisms
  - Various network interfaces

- High-level networking, based on:
  - **Universal Resource Identifier (URI)**
  - **Universal Resource Locator (URL)**
  - Connections to the resource pointed to by URLs

# java.math

This package complements Java primitive types and the wrapper classes of the `java.lang` package by allowing working with much bigger numbers using the classes `BigDecimal` and `BigInteger`.

# java.awt, javax.swing, and javafx

The first Java library that supported building a **Graphical User Interface (GUI)** for desktop applications was **Abstract Window Toolkit (AWT)** in the `java.awt` package. It provided an interface to the native system of the executing platform that allowed the creation and management of windows, layouts, and events. It also had the basic GUI widgets (like text fields, buttons, and menus), provided an access to the system tray, and allowed users to launch a web browser and email client from the Java code. Its heavy dependence on the native code made AWT-based GUI look different on different platforms.

In 1997, Sun Microsystems and Netscape Communication Corporation introduced Java Foundation Classes, later called Swing and were put in the package `javax.swing`. The GUI components built with Swing could emulate the look and feel of some native platforms but also allowed users to plug in a look and feel that did not depend on the platform it was running on. It expanded the list of widgets the GUI could have by adding tabbed panels, scroll panes, tables, and lists. Swing components are called lightweight because they do not depend on the native code and are fully implemented in Java.

In 2007, Sun Microsystems announced JavaFX, which has eventually become a software platform for creating and delivering desktop applications across many different devices that is intended to replace Swing as the standard GUI library for Java SE. It is located in the packages that start with `javafx` and supports all major desktop OS and multiple mobile OS systems, including Symbian OS, Windows Mobile, and some proprietary real-time OS.

JavaFX adds to the arsenal of a GUI developer the support of smooth animation, web views, audio and video playback, and styles based on **Cascading Style Sheets** (**CSS**). However, Swing has more components and third-party libraries, so using JavaFX may require creating custom components and plumbing that was implemented in Swing long time ago already. That's why, although JavaFX is recommended as the first choice for desktop GUI implementation, Swing will remain part of Java for the foreseeable future, according to the official response on the Oracle website (`http://www.oracle.com/technetwork/java/javafx/overview/faq-1446554.html#6`). So, it is possible to continue using Swing, but, if possible, it's better to switch to JavaFX.

# Java external libraries

Various statistics include different names in the list of the 20 or 100 most used third-party libraries. In this section, we are going to discuss those of them that are included in most of these lists. All of them are open source projects.

# org.junit

JUnit is an open source testing framework that has the root package name `org.junit`. It was used throughout this book in several of our code examples. As you could see, it is very easy to set up and use (we have described the steps in `Chapter 4`, *Your First Java Project*):

- Add a dependency to the Maven configuration file `pom.xml`
- Create a test manually or right-click on the class name you would like to test, select **Go To**, then **Test**, then **Create New Test**, and then check the methods of the class you would like to test
- Write code for the generated test methods with the annotation `@Test`
- Add methods with the annotations `@Before` and `@After` if necessary

A "unit" is a minimal piece of code that can be tested, thus the name. The best testing practices consider a method as a minimal testable unit. That's why the unit tests are usually test methods.

# org.mockito

One of the problems a unit test often faces is the need to test a method that uses a third-party library, a data source, or a method of another class. While testing, you want to control all the inputs so that you can predict the expected results of the tested code exactly. That is where the technique of simulating or mocking the behavior of the objects the tested code interacts with comes in handy.

The open source framework Mockito (root package name `org.mockito`) allows you to accomplish exactly that – the creation of mock objects. It is quite easy and straightforward to use. Here is one simple case:

- Add a dependency to the Maven configuration file `pom.xml`
- Call the `mock()` method for the class you need to simulate: `SomelClass mo = Mockito.mock(SomeClass.class)`
- Set the value you need to be returned from a method: `Mockito.when(mo.doSomething(10)).thenReturn(20)`
- Now, pass the mocked object as a parameter into the method you are testing that calls the mocked method
- The mocked method returns the result you have predefined

Mockito has certain limitations. For example, you cannot mock static methods and private methods. Otherwise, it is a great way to isolate the code you are testing by reliably predicting the results of the used methods. The framework's name and logo are based on the word *mojitos* – a type of drink.

# org.apache.log4j and org.slf4j

Throughout this book, we have used the `System.out` object to display an output of the intermediate and final results. In the real-life application, one can do it too and redirect the output to a file, for example, for later analysis. After doing it for some time, you will notice that you need more details about each output – the date and time of each statement, or the class name where this statement was generated, for example. As the code base grows, you will find that it would be nice to send output from different subsystems or packages to different files, or turn off some messages when everything works as expected and turn them back on when an issue has been detected and more detailed information about code behavior is needed.

It is possible to write your own program that accomplishes all that, but there are several frameworks that do it based on the settings in a configuration file, which you can change every time you need to change the messages behavior. Such messages are called application logging messages, or application log, or log messages, and the two most popular frameworks used for that are called `log4j` (pronounced as *LOG-FOUR-JAY*) and `slf4j` (pronounced as *S-L-F-FOUR-JAY*).

In fact, these two frameworks are not rivals. The `slf4j` is a facade that provides a unified access to an underlying actually logging framework – one of them can be `log4j` too. Such a facade is especially helpful during a library development when programmers do not know in advance what kind of logging framework will be used by the application that uses the library. By writing code using `slf4j`, programmers allow users to later configure it to use any logging system.

So, if your code is going to be used only by the application that your team develops and is going to support in production, using just `log4j` is quite enough. Otherwise, consider using `slf4j`.

And, as in the case of any third-party library, before you can use any of the logging frameworks, you have to add a corresponding dependency to the Maven configuration file `pom.xml`.

# org.apache.commons

In the previous section, we talked about one package with the `org.apache` root name - the package `org.apache.log4j`.

The package `org.apache.commons` is another popular library, representing a project called Apache Commons that is maintained by open source community of programmers called Apache Software Foundation. This organization was formed from the Apache Group in 1999. The Apache Group has grown around the development of Apache HTTP Server since 1993. The Apache HTTP Server is an open source cross-platform web server that has remained the most popular since April 1996. From a Wikipedia article:

> *"As of July 2016, it was estimated to serve 46% of all active websites and 43% of the top million websites. The name "Apache" was chosen from respect for the Native American Apache Nation, well known for their superior skills in warfare strategy and their inexhaustible endurance. It also makes a pun on "a patchy web server"—a server made from a series of patches—but this was not its origin"*

The Apache Commons project has three parts:

- **Commons Sandbox**: A workspace for Java component development; you can contribute to the open source working there
- **Commons Dormant**: A repository of components that are currently inactive; you can use the code there, but have to build the components yourselves since these components probably will not be released in the near future
- **Commons Proper**: The reusable Java components, which compose the actual library `org.apache.commons`

In the following subsections, we will discuss only four of Commons Proper's most popular packages:

- `org.apache.commons.io`
- `org.apache.commons.lang`
- `org.apache.commons.lang3`
- `org.apache.commons.codec.binary`

There are, however, many more packages under `org.apache.commons` that contain thousands of useful classes that can easily be used and can help make your code elegant and efficient.

# org.apache.commons.io

All classes of the `org.apache.commons.io` package are contained in the root package and five subpackages:

- The root package, `org.apache.commons.io`, contains utility classes with static methods to perform common tasks, like a popular `FileUtils` class, for example, that allows doing all possible operations with files one can ever need:
    - Writing to a file
    - Reading from a file
    - Make a directory, including parent directories
    - Copying files and directories
    - Deleting files and directories
    - Converting to and from a URL
    - Listing files and directories by filter and extension
    - Comparing file content

- File last changed date
- Calculating a checksum

- The `org.apache.commons.io.input` package contains classes that support data input based on `InputStream` and `Reader` implementations, such as `XmlStreamReader` or `ReversedLinesFileReader`
- The `org.apache.commons.io.output` package contains classes that support data output based on `OutputStream` and `Writer` implementations, such as `XmlStreamWriter` or `StringBuilderWriter`
- The `org.apache.commons.io.filefilter` package contains classes that serve as file filters, such as `DirectoryFileFilter` or `RegexFileFilter`
- The `org.apache.commons.io.comparato` package contains various implementations of `java.util.Comparator` for files, such as `NameFileComparator`
- The `org.apache.commons.io.monitor` package provides a component for monitoring file system events (directory and file create, update, and delete events), such as `FileAlterationMonitor`, which implements `Runnable` and spawns a monitoring thread triggering any registered `FileAlterationObserver` at a specified interval

# org.apache.commons.lang and lang3

The package `org.apache.commons.lang3` is actually version 3 of the package `org.apache.commons.lang`. The decision to create a new package was forced by the fact that changes introduced in version 3 were backwardly incompatible. This means that existing applications that used the previous version of the `org.apache.commons.lang` package may stop working after the upgrade to version 3. But, in the majority of mainstream programming, adding 3 to an import statement (as the way to migrate to the new version) will probably not break anything.

According to the documentation *"the package org.apache.commons.lang3 provides highly reusable static utility methods, chiefly concerned with adding value to the java.lang classes."* Here are a few notable examples:

- The `ArrayUtils` class allows searching and manipulating arrays.
- The `ClassUtils` class provides some metadata about a class.
- The `ObjectUtils` class checks for `null` in an array of objects, compares objects, and calculates median and min/max of an array of objects in a null-safe manner.

- The `SystemUtils` class provides information about the execution environment.
- The `ThreadUtils` class finds information about currently running threads.
- The `Validate` class validates individual values and collections: compares them, checks for `null`, matches, and performs many other validations.
- The `RandomStringUtils` class generates `String` objects from the characters of various character sets.
- The `StringUtils` class is the favorite of many programmers. Here is the list of null-safe operations it provides:
  - `isEmpty`/`isBlank`: This checks if a `String` value contains text
  - `trim`/`strip`: This removes leading and trailing whitespace
  - `equals`/`compare`: This compares two strings null-safe
  - `startsWith`: This checks if a `String` value starts with a certain prefix null-safe
  - `endsWith`: This checks if a `String` value ends with a certain suffix null-safe
  - `indexOf`/`lastIndexOf`/`contains`: This provides null-safe index-of checks
  - `indexOfAny`/`lastIndexOfAny`/`indexOfAnyBut`/`lastIndexOfAnyBut`: This provides index-of any of a set of `String` values
  - `containsOnly`/`containsNone`/`containsAny`: This checks if a `String` value contains only/none/any of certain characters
  - `substring`/`left`/`right`/`mid`: This supports null-safe substring extractions
  - `substringBefore`/`substringAfter`/`substringBetween`: This performs substring extraction relative to other strings
  - `split`/`join`: This splits a `String` value into an array of substrings by certain delimiter and vice versa
  - `remove`/`delete`: This removes part of a `String` value
  - `replace`/`overlay`: This searches a `String` value and replaces one `String` value with another
  - `chomp`/`chop`: This removes the last part of a `String` value
  - `appendIfMissing`: This appends a suffix to the end of the `String` value if not present
  - `prependIfMissing`: This prepends a prefix to the start of the `String` value if not present

- `leftPad/rightPad/center/repeat`: This pads a `String` value
- `upperCase/lowerCase/swapCase/capitalize/uncapitalize`: This changes the case of a `String` value
- `countMatches`: This counts the number of occurrences of one `String` value in another
- `isAlpha/isNumeric/isWhitespace/isAsciiPrintable`: This checks the characters in a `String` value
- `defaultString`: This protects against a `null` input of `String` value
- `rotate`: This rotates (circular shift) characters in a `String` value
- `reverse/reverseDelimited`: This reverses characters or delimited groups of characters in a `String` value
- `abbreviate`: This abbreviates a `String` value using an ellipsis or another given `String` value
- `difference`: This compares `String` values and reports their differences
- `levenshteinDistance`: The number of changes needed to change one `String` value to another

## org.apache.commons.codec.binary

The content of this library is outside the scope of this introductory course. So, we will just mention that this library provides support for Base64, Base32, Binary, and Hexadecimal String encoding and decoding.

The encoding is necessary to make sure that the data you sent across different systems will not be changed on the way, due to the restrictions on the range of characters in different protocols. Besides, some systems interpret the sent data as control characters (a modem, for example).

# Exercise – Comparing String.indexOf() and StringUtils.indexOf()

What is the difference between the `indexOf()` method of the `String` class and the `indexOf()` method of the `StringUtils` class?

# Answer

The `indexOf()` method of the `String` class does not handle `null`. Here is some demo code:

```
String s = null;
int i = StringUtils.indexOf(s, "abc");      //return -1
s.indexOf("abc");                           //throws NullPointerException
```

# Summary

In this chapter, the reader has learned about the content of Java standard libraries included in the JDK and some of the most popular external libraries or third-party libraries. In particular, we have looked closely into the standard packages `java.lang` and `java.util`; compared the packages `java.io` and `java.nio`, `java.sql` and `javax.sql`, `java.awt`, `javax.swing` and `javafx`; and reviewed the packages `java.net` and `java.math`.

We have also made an overview of such popular external libraries as `org.junit`, `org.mockito`, `org.apache.log4j`, `org.slf4j`, and several packages of the Apache Commons project: `org.apache.commons.io`, `org.apache.commons.lang` and `org.apache.commons.lang3`, and `org.apache.commons.codec.binary`.

The next chapter will help the reader to become familiar with the most widely used Java classes in more detail. The code examples will illustrate the discussion of the functionality of the classes called collections: `List` and `ArrayList`, `Set` and `HashSet`, and `Map` and `HashMap`. We will also discuss the classes `Arrays` and `ArrayUtils`, `Objects` and `ObjectUtils`, `StringBuilder` and `StringBuffer`, `LocalDate`, `LocalTime`, and `LocalDateTime`.

# 13
# Java Collections

This chapter will help the reader to become more familiar with the most commonly used Java collections. The code examples illustrate their functionality and allow an experimentation that emphasizes the difference between different collection types and their implementations.

In this chapter, we will cover the following topics:

- What are collections?
- List and ArrayList
- Set and HashSet
- Map and HashMap
- Exercise – EnumSet methods

## What are collections?

When you read about the Java Collection Framework, you may assume there is something special about such an assemblage. Meanwhile, the word framework is quite overloaded and misused, as the word technology is one we have refused to use already. In the English language, the word framework means *a basic structure underlying a system, concept, or text.* In computer programming, a framework is a software system constructed so that its functionality can be customized by additional user-written code or configuration settings in order to fit the application-specific requirements.

But then we look closer into the content of the Java Collection Framework and realize that all its members belong to the `java.util` package, which is part of the Java Class Library, or Java standard library, as we have described it in the previous chapter. And, at the other extreme, the graphic user interfaces in the packages `java.awt`, `javax.swing`, or `javafx` have all the signs of a framework; they just provide gadgets and other graphic elements, which have to be filled by the application-specific content. And yet they belong to the Java Class Library too.

That's why we avoid using the word framework and mention it here only to explain what is hiding behind the title Java Collection Framework.

# The java.util package

The following interfaces and classes of the package `java.util` compose the Java Collections Framework:

- The interfaces that extend `java.util.Collection` (which in turn extends the `java.lang.Iterable` interface): List, Set, and Queue, to name the most popular ones
- The classes that implement the fore mentioned interfaces: ArrayList, HashSet, Stack, and LinkedList, as an example
- The classes that implement interface `java.util.Map` and its children: HashMap, HashTable, and TreeMap, to name just three of the most commonly used

As you can see, the Java Collection Framework, or just Java Collections, are composed of the interfaces that extend the `java.util.Collection` interface or the `java.util.Map` interface and the classes that implement these interfaces – all are contained in the `java.util` package.

Notice that those classes that implement—directly or indirectly—the Collection interface also implement the Iterable interface and thus can be used in iteration statements as described in Chapter 10, *Control Flow Statements*.

# Apache Commons collections

Project Apache Commons contains (in the package `org.apache.commons.collections`) multiple implementations of Java collection interfaces that complement the implementations in the `java.util` package. But, unless you work on an application that requires a particular collection algorithm, you probably won't need to use them. Nevertheless, we recommend that you look through the `org.apache.commons.collections` package API, so that you know its content in case you encounter a need to use it in the future.

# Collections vs arrays

All collections are data structures similar to arrays in the sense that they also contain elements, and each is represented by an object of a class. There are two significant differences between arrays and collections, though:

- An array requires assigning a size when instantiated, while a collection increases and decreases in size automatically when elements are added or removed.
- An element of a collection cannot be a value of a primitive type, but only a reference type, including wrapper classes such as `Integer` or `Double`. The good news is that you can add a primitive value:

  ```
  List list = new ArrayList();
  list.add(42);
  ```

  The boxing conversion (see `Chapter 9`, *Operators, Expressions, and Statements*) in the preceding statement will be applied to the primitive value automatically.

Although arrays are expected to provide better performance while accessing its elements, in practice, modern algorithms make the differences in performance of arrays and collections negligible, except in some very specialized cases. That is why the only reason you would have to use arrays is when some algorithms or methods require it.

# Here is what we are going to discuss

In the following subsections, we will discuss the most popular interfaces and classes of Java collections from standard libraries:

- The List interface and the ArrayList class – they preserve the order of the elements
- The Set interface and the HashSe class – they do not allow duplicate elements
- The Map and HashMap interfaces – they store objects by with a key and thus allow key-to-value mapping

Please notice that most of the methods described in the following sections come from the java.util.Collection interface – the parent interface of almost all the collections, except those that implement the java.util.Map interface.

# List - ArrayList preserves order

List is an interface, while the ArrayList class is its most often used implementation. Both are residing in the java.util package. The ArrayList class has a few more methods - in addition to those declared in the List interface. The removeRange() method, for example, is not present in the List interface but available in the ArrayList API.

# Prefer variable type List

It is a good practice, while creating an object of an ArrayList, to assign its reference to a variable of type List:

```
List listOfNames = new ArrayList();
```

More likely than not, using a variable of type ArrayList will not change anything in your program, not today, nor in the future:

```
ArrayList listOfNames = new ArrayList();
```

The preceding reference can still be passed to any method that accepts a parameter of type List. However, coding to an interface (that is what we do when we make the variable of an interface type) is a good habit in general because you never know when the requirements to your code might change and you would need to use another implementation of List, like the LinkedList class, for example. If the variable type was List, switching an implementation is easy. But if the variable type was ArrayList, changing it to List or to LinkedList requires tracking down all the places the variable was used and run various tests to make sure that ArrayList methods were not called anywhere. And if the code is complex, one can never be sure that all possible execution paths were checked and the code will not break in production. That's why we prefer to use an interface type for the variable that holds the reference to an object, unless you really need it to be the class type. We talked about this extensively in Chapter 8, *Object-Oriented Design (OOD) Principles*.

# Why is it called ArrayList?

The ArrayList class is named so because its implementation is based on an array. It actually uses an array behind the scenes. If you right-click on ArrayList in IDE and view the source code, here is what you are going to see:

```java
private static final Object[] DEFAULTCAPACITY_EMPTY_ELEMENTDATA = {};
public ArrayList() {
    this.elementData = DEFAULTCAPACITY_EMPTY_ELEMENTDATA;
}
```

It is just a wrapper around the array Object[]. And here is how method add(E) is implemented, for example:

```java
public boolean add(E e) {
    modCount++;
    add(e, elementData, size);
    return true;
}
private void add(E e, Object[] elementData, int s) {
    if (s == elementData.length)
        elementData = grow();
    elementData[s] = e;
    size = s + 1;
}
```

And if you study the source code more and look inside the method `grow()`, you will see how it increases the size of the array when new elements are added to the list:

```
private Object[] grow() {  return grow(size + 1); }

private Object[] grow(int minCapacity) {
   return elementData = Arrays.copyOf(elementData,
                               newCapacity(minCapacity));
}
private static final int DEFAULT_CAPACITY = 10;
private static final int MAX_ARRAY_SIZE = Integer.MAX_VALUE - 8;
private int newCapacity(int minCapacity) {
   // overflow-conscious code
   int oldCapacity = elementData.length;
   int newCapacity = oldCapacity + (oldCapacity >> 1);
   if (newCapacity - minCapacity <= 0) {
     if (elementData == DEFAULTCAPACITY_EMPTY_ELEMENTDATA)
       return Math.max(DEFAULT_CAPACITY, minCapacity);
     if (minCapacity < 0) // overflow
       throw new OutOfMemoryError();
     return minCapacity;
   }
   return (newCapacity - MAX_ARRAY_SIZE <= 0)
             ? newCapacity
             : hugeCapacity(minCapacity);
}
```

As you can see, when the allocated array size is not enough for storing another element, the new array is created with a minimum capacity of 10. All the already existing elements are copied to the new array using the `Arrays.copyOf()` method (we will talk about the `Arrays` class later in this chapter).

And that is why `ArrayList` was so named.

For using `List` and `ArrayList`, you do not need to know all that, unless you have to process really big lists of elements and the frequent copying of the underlying array affects the performance of your code. In such a case, consider using different data structures that have been designed specifically for the type of processing you need. But that is already outside the scope of this book. Besides, the vast majority of mainstream programmers have probably never used any collections that are not in the `java.util` package.

# Adding elements

The `List` interface provides two methods for adding an element:

- `add(E)`: This adds the element to the end of the list
- `add(index, E)`: This inserts the element into the specified (by index, starting with zero) position in the list by shifting the element the specified position (if any) and any subsequent elements to the right by adding 1 to their indices

Both methods can throw a `RuntimeException` if something goes wrong. So, putting a try-catch block around the method makes the code more robust (if the catch block does not simply rethrow the exception but does something meaningful). Read the documentation of the `List` interface API online and see what the names of the exceptions these methods can throw are and under which conditions they can happen.

The `add(E)` method also returns a Boolean value (`true/false`) that indicates the success of the operation. This method overrides the method in the `Collection` interface, so all Java collections that extend or implement the `Collection` interface have it. In the case of `List` implementations, this method most likely always returns `true` because list allows duplicate entries. By contrast, the implementations of the `Set` interface return `false` if such an element is present already because `Set` does not allow duplicates. We will discuss this in subsequent sections, as well as how the code determines if two elements are the same.

Now, let's look at the examples of the `add()` method of the `List` interface's usage:

```
List list = new ArrayList();
list.add(null);
list.add(1);
list.add("ss");
list.add(new A());
list.add(new B());
System.out.println(list);   //prints: [null, 1, ss, A, B]
list.add(2, 42);
System.out.println(list);   //prints: [null, 1, 42, ss, A, B]
```

In the preceding list, we have mixed up in the same list values of different types. The classes A and B, used in the preceding code, have parent-child relations:

```
class A {
  @Override
  public String toString() { return "A"; }
}
class B extends A {
  @Override
  public String toString() { return "B"; }
}
```

As you can see, we have added the toString() method to each of them, so we can see their objects printed in an expected format.

# size(), isEmpty(), clear()

These three methods are straightforward:

- size(): This returns count of elements in the list
- isEmpty(): This returns true if there is no elements in the list (size() returns 0)
- clear(): This removes all elements from the list so that isEmpty() returns true and size() returns 0

# Iterate and stream

Every collection that implements the Collection interface (which extends the Iterable interface) can be iterated over using the enhanced for statement discussed in Chapter 10, *Control Flow Statements*. Here is an example:

```
List list = new ArrayList();
list.add(null);
list.add(1);
list.add("ss");
list.add(new A());
list.add(new B());
for(Object o: list){
  //code that does something with each element
}
```

The `Iterable` interface also adds the following three methods to the `List` interface:

- `forEach(Consumer function)`: It applies the provided function to each collection element
- `iterator()`: It returns an object of class `Iterator` that allows walking through (iterating) each element of the collection and manipulating each of them as needed
- `splititerator()`: It returns an object of class `Splititerator` that allows splitting the collection for parallel processing (discussion of this functionality is outside the scope of this book)

In `Chapter 17`, *Lambda Expressions and Functional Programming*, we will explain how the function can be passed as a parameter, so for now, we just show an example of the `forEach()` method's usage (if we re-use the list created in the previous example):

```
list.forEach(System.out::println);
```

As you can see, the passed-in function take each element generated by the `forEach()` method and just prints it. It is called `Consumer` because it gets (consumes) the input and returns no value back it, just prints. If we run the preceding code, the result will be as follows:

The `forEach()` method provides the same functionality as the `for` statement (see the previous example) but requires writing less code. That is why programmers love functional programming (when a function can be treated as an object), because after writing the same boilerplate code hundreds of times, one can enjoy the shorthand style.

The `Iterator` interface returned by the `iterator()` method has the following methods:

- `next()`: It returns the next element in the iteration
- `hasNext ()`: It returns `true` if the iteration has more elements
- `forEachRemaining (Consumer<? super E> function)`: It applies the provided function to each of remaining elements
- `remove()`: It removes from the underlying collection the last element returned by this iterator

The methods `next()` and `hasNext()` are used by `for` statements behind the scenes. You can also use them and in fact reproduce the `for` statement functionality. But why? The `for` statements are doing it already. The only reason to use the `Iterator` interface we could think about is to remove some objects from the list (using the `remove()` method) while iterating over the list. This brings us to the point of discussing a mistake a beginner often makes.

Let's assume we would like to remove all the objects of type `String` from the following list:

```
List list = new ArrayList();
list.add(null);
list.add(1);
list.add("ss");
list.add(new A());
list.add(new B());
```

Here is the code that attempts to do it, but has a defect:

```
for(Object o: list){
  System.out.println(o);
  if(o instanceof String){
    list.remove(o);
  }
}
```

If we run the preceding code, the result will be as follows:

```
null
1
ss
Exception in thread "main" java.util.ConcurrentModificationException
    at java.base/java.util.ArrayList$Itr.checkForComodification(ArrayList.java:937)
    at java.base/java.util.ArrayList$Itr.next(ArrayList.java:891)
    at com.packt.javapath.ch13demo.ListDemo.iterate(ListDemo.java:29)
    at com.packt.javapath.ch13demo.ListDemo.main(ListDemo.java:10)
```

The `ConcurrentModificationException` was thrown because we tried to modify the collection while iterating over it. The `Iterator` class helps to avoid this problem. The following code works just fine:

```
System.out.println(list);   //prints: [null, 1, ss, A, B]
Iterator iter = list.iterator();
while(iter.hasNext()){
  Object o = iter.next();
  if(o instanceof String){
    iter.remove();
```

```
    }
  }
  System.out.println(list);   //prints: [null, 1, A, B]
```

We are not going to discuss why `Iterator` allows removing an element during the iteration and why the collection throws an exception in a similar situation for two reasons:

- It requires going much deeper into the JVM implementation than an introductory course allows.
- In `Chapter 18`, *Streams and Pipelines*, we will demonstrate a more compact way to do it using Java functional programming. Such a code looks so clean and elegant that many programmers working with Java 8 and higher almost never use `for` statements while working with collections and other data structures that generate streams.

There are also four other ways to iterate over a list of elements:

- `listIterator()` and `listIterator(index)`: Both return `ListIterator`, which is very similar to `Iterator` but allows going back and forth along the list (`Iterator` allows only going forth, as you have seen). These methods are rarely used, so we are going to skip their demonstration. But if you need to use them, look at the preceding `Iterator` example. The usage of `ListIterator` is very similar.
- `stream()` and `parallelStream()`: Both return the `Stream` object, which we are going to discuss in more detail in `Chapter 18`, *Streams and Pipelines*.

# Add using generics

Sometimes having different types in the same list is exactly what we want. But, most of the time, we would like the list to contain values of the same type. Meanwhile, code may have logical errors that allow a different type to be added to the list, which can have unexpected consequences. If it leads to throwing an exception, it is not as bad as some default conversion and incorrect results at the end, which may not be noticed for a long time, if ever.

To avoid such a problem, one can use generics that allow defining the expected type of the collection elements, so that the compiler can check and fail the case when a different type is added. Here is an example:

```
List<Integer> list1 = new ArrayList<>();
list1.add(null);
```

```
list1.add(1);
//list1.add("ss");              //compilation error
//list1.add(new A());           //compilation error
//list1.add(new B());           //compilation error
System.out.println(list1);  //prints: [null, 1]
list1.add(2, 42);
System.out.println(list1);  //prints: [null, 1, 42]
```

As you can see, a `null` value can be added anyway, because it is a default value of any reference type, while, as we have pointed out at the beginning of this section already, the elements of any Java collection can only be of a reference type.

Since a subclass has a type of any of its superclasses, the generic `<Object>` does not help to avoid the previously described problem, because every Java object has the `Object` class as its parent:

```
List<Object> list2= new ArrayList<>();
list2.add(null);
list2.add(1);
list2.add("ss");
list2.add(new A());
list2.add(new B());
System.out.println(list2);     //prints: [null, 1, ss, A, B]
list2.add(2, 42);
System.out.println(list2);     //prints: [null, 1, 42, ss, A, B]
```

But, the following generics are more restrictive:

```
List<A> list3= new ArrayList<>();
list3.add(null);
//list3.add(1);                 //compilation error
//list3.add("ss");             //compilation error
list3.add(new A());
list3.add(new B());
System.out.println(list3); //prints: [null, A, B]
list3.add(2, new A());
System.out.println(list3); //prints: [null, A, A, B]

List<B> list4= new ArrayList<>();
list4.add(null);
//list4.add(1);                 //compilation error
//list4.add("ss");             //compilation error
//list4.add(new A());          //compilation error
list4.add(new B());
System.out.println(list4); //prints: [null, B]
list4.add(2, new B());
System.out.println(list4); //prints: [null, B, B]
```

The only case when you might use a generic `<Object>` is when you would like to allow values of different types to be added to the list, but you do not want to allow the reference to the list itself to refer to a list with other generics:

```
List list = new ArrayList();
List<Integer> list1 = new ArrayList<>();
List<Object> list2= new ArrayList<>();
list = list1;
//list2 = list1;    //compilation error
```

As you can see, the list without generics (called raw type) allows its reference to refer to any other list with any generics, while the list with a generic `<Object>` does not allow its variable to refer to a list with any other generics.

The Java collection also allows a wildcard generic, `<?>`, which allows only `null` to be assigned to the collection:

```
List<?> list5= new ArrayList<>();
list5.add(null);
//list5.add(1);            //compilation error
//list5.add("ss");         //compilation error
//list5.add(new A());      //compilation error
//list5.add(new B());      //compilation error
System.out.println(list5); //prints: [null]
//list5.add(1, 42);        //compilation error
```

An example of the usage of the wildcard generics can be demonstrated as follows. Let's assume that we write a method that has `List` (or any collection, for that matter) as a parameter but we would like to ensure that this list will be not modified inside the method, which changes the original list. Here is an example:

```
void doSomething(List<B> list){
  //some othe code goes here
  list.add(null);
  list.add(new B());
  list.add(0, new B());
  //some other code goes here
}
```

If we use the preceding method, we get an undesirable side effect:

```
List<B> list= new ArrayList<>();
System.out.println(list); //prints: [B]
list.add(0, null);
System.out.println(list); //prints: [null, B]
doSomething(list);
System.out.println(list); //[B, null, B, null, B]
```

To avoid the side effect, one can write:

```
void doSomething(List<?> list){
  list.add(null);
  //list.add(1);              //compilation error
  //list.add("ss");           //compilation error
  //list.add(new A());        //compilation error
  //list.add(new B());        //compilation error
  //list.add(0, 42);          //compilation error
}
```

As you can see, this way the list cannot be modified, except by adding `null`. Well, it comes at a price of removing the generic, `<B>`. Now, it is possible that the passed-in list contains objects of different types, and the typecasting `(B)` will throw `ClassCastException`. Nothing comes free, but the possibilities are available.

> As in the case of an encapsulation, the best practice recommends using as many narrow (or specialized) a types for generics as possible. This ensures much lower chances of unexpected behavior.

To prevent the collection from being modified inside the method, it is possible to make the collection immutable. It can be done inside or outside the method (before passing it as the parameter). We will show you how to do it in the Chapter 14, *Managing Collections and Arrays*.

# Add collection

Two methods of the `List` interface allow adding the whole collection of objects to the existing list:

- `addAll(Collection<? extends E> collection)`: It adds the provided collection of objects to the end of the list.
- `addAll(int index, Collection<? extends E> collection)`: It inserts the provided elements into the list at the specified position. The operation shifts the element currently at that position (if any) and any subsequent elements to the right (increases their indices by the size of the provided collection).

Both methods throw several `RuntimeExceptions` if something goes wrong. Also, both methods return a Boolean value:

- `false`: If the list has not changed after this method invocation
- `true`: If the list has changed

As in the case of adding a single element, all `List` implementations of these methods most likely always return true because `List` allows duplicates, which is not the case for `Set` (we will discuss this shortly).

If you have read the description of generics a few pages back, you can guess what the notation `Collection<? extends E>` means. The generic `<? extends E>` means a type that is either `E` or a child of `E`, where `E` is the type used as the generics of the collection. To relate to our previous examples, observe the following, classes, `A` and `B`:

```
class A {
  @Override
  public String toString() { return "A"; }
}
class B extends A {
  @Override
  public String toString() { return "B"; }
}
```

We can add to `List<A>` objects of classes `A` and of `B`.

 The notation `addAll(Collection<? extends E> collection)` means this method allows the addition to `List<E>` objects of type `E` or any subtype of `E`.

As an example, we can do the following:

```
List<A> list = new ArrayList<>();
list.add(new A());
List<B> list1 = new ArrayList<>();
list1.add(new B());
list.addAll(list1);
System.out.println(list);    //prints: [A, B]
```

The `addAll(int index, Collection<? extends E> collection)` method acts very similar, but only starting from the specified index. And, of course, the value of the provided index should be equal to 0 or less than the length of the list.

> For the `addAll(int index, Collection<? extends E> collection)` method, the value of the provided index should be equal to 0 or less than the length of the list.

# Implementing equals() and hashCode()

This is a very important subsection because, more often than not, while creating a class, programmers are focused on the main functionality and forget to implement the `equals()` and `hashCode()` methods. It does not cause any problems until objects are compared using the `equals()` method or added to a collection and then searched or assumed to be unique (in the case of `Set`).

As we demonstrated in Chapter 9, *Operators, Expressions, and Statements,* the `equals()` method can be used for object identification. If a class does not override the default implementation of the `equals()` method in the base class `Object`, then every object is unique. Even if two objects of the same class have the same state, the default `equals()` method reports them as different. So, if you need two objects of the same class with the same state being treated as equal, you have to implement the `equals()` method in that class, so that it overrides the default implementation in `Object`.

Since every Java collection is using the `equals()` method while searching for the object among its elements, you have to implement it, because a typical business logic requires including the object state or at least some of the state values into consideration during the object identification process. You also have to decide on which level of the class inheritance chain two children should be considered equal, as we discussed in Chapter 9, *Operators, Expressions, and Statements,* while comparing objects of the classes `PersonWithHair` and `PersonWithHairDressed`; both extend the `Person` class. We decided then that the objects of these classes represent the same person if they are equal according to the `equals()` method implemented in the `Person` class. We also decided to consider for the purpose of the identification (equality) only the fields `age` and `name`, although the `Person` class may have had several other fields (such as `currentAddress`, for example) which are not relevant for the person's identification.

So, if you expect that the class you create will be used for generating objects that will be used as members of some Java collection, you'd better implement the `equals()` method. To do it, you have to make two decisions:

- On which level of the class inheritance hierarchy to implement the method
- Which fields of the object (which aspects of the object state, in other words) to include into the consideration

The `equals()` method is used by Java collections for the element identification. While implementing the `equals()` method, consider doing it in one of the parent classes and decide which fields to use while comparing two objects.

The method `hashCode()` is not used by the `List` implementation, so we will discuss it in more detail in relation to the implementations of the interfaces `Set` and `Map` in the following code. But since we are on the topic here, we would like to mention that the best Java programming practices recommend implementing the `hashCode()` method every time the `equals()` method is implemented. While doing it, use the same fields that the `equals()` method uses. For example, the `Person` class we implemented in Chapter 9, *Operators, Expressions, and Statements,* should look like this:

```
class Person{
    private int age;
    private String name, currentAddress;
    public Person(int age, String name, String currAddr) {
        this.age = age;
        this.name = name;
```

```
      this.currentAddress = currAddr;
   }
   @Override
   public boolean equals(Object o) {
      if (this == o) return true;
      if (o == null) return false;
      if(!(o instanceof Person)) return false;
         Person person = (Person)o;
         return age == person.getAge() &&
                  Objects.equals(name, person.getName());
   }
   @Override
   public int hashCode(){
      return Objects.hash(age, name);
   }
}
```

As you can see, we have added an implementation of the hashCode() method based on the hash() method of the Objects class, which we will discuss later in this chapter. We have also added a new field, but will not use it in either the equals() method nor in the hashCode() method, because we think it is not relevant for a person's identification.

 Every time you implement the equals() method, implement the hashCode() method as well, because the object of the class you create may be used not only in a List but in Set or Map too, which requires hashCode() to be implemented.

We will talk about the motivation of the hashCode() method's implementation for Set and Map in the corresponding sections of this chapter. We will also explain why we cannot use hashCode() for the purpose of the object identification, similar to like when we use the equals() method.

## Locating element

There are three methods in the List interface that allow checking the presence and location of an element in the list:

- contains(E): It returns true if the provided element is present in the list.
- indexOf(E): It returns an index (position) of the provided element in the list. If there are several such elements in the list, the smallest index is returned – the index of the first element from the left that equals the provided element.

- `lastIndexOf(E)`: It returns an index (position) of the provided element in the list. If there are several such elements in the list, the biggest index is returned – the index of the last element from the left that equals the provided element.

Here is the code that shows how to use these methods:

```
List<String> list = new ArrayList<>();
list.add("s1");
list.add("s2");
list.add("s1");

System.out.println(list.contains("s1"));    //prints: true
System.out.println(list.indexOf("s1"));      //prints: 0
System.out.println(list.lastIndexOf("s1")); //prints: 2
```

There are two things worth noticing:

- The first element in the list has an index of 0 (like an array, too)
- The preceding methods rely on the implementation of the `equals()` method to identify the provided object in the list

# Retrieving elements

There are two methods in the `List` interface that allow element retrieval:

- `get(index)`: It returns the element that has the provided index
- `sublist(index1, index2)`: It returns the list of elements starting with `index1` until (but not including) the element that has `index2`

The following code demonstrates how these methods can be used:

```
List<String> list = new ArrayList<>();
list.add("s1");
list.add("s2");
list.add("s3");

System.out.println(list.get(1));         //prints: s2
System.out.println(list.subList(0,2)); //prints: [s1, s2]
```

# Removing elements

There are four methods in the List interface that remove (delete) elements from the list:

- remove (index): It removes an element that has the provided index and returns the removed element
- remove (E): It removes the provided element and returns true if the list contained it
- removeAll (Collection): It removes the provided elements and returns true if the list has changed
- retainAll (Collection): It removes all the elements that are not in the provided collection and returns true if the list has changed

Two points we would like to make about these methods:

- The last three methods use the equals() method to identify the elements to be removed or retained
- If one or more elements were removed from the list, the indices of the remaining elements are recalculated

Let's look at the code examples now:

```
List<String> list = new ArrayList<>();
list.add("s1");
list.add("s2");
list.add("s3");
list.add("s1");

System.out.println(list.remove(1));       //prints: s2
System.out.println(list);                  //prints: [s1, s3, s1]
//System.out.println(list.remove(5));      //throws IndexOutOfBoundsException
System.out.println(list.remove("s1"));     //prints: true
System.out.println(list);                  //prints: [s3, s1]
System.out.println(list.remove("s5"));     //prints: false
System.out.println(list);                  //prints: [s3, s1]
```

In the preceding code, it is worth noticing that the list has two elements, s1 but only the first from the left is removed by the statement list.remove("s1"):

```
List<String> list = new ArrayList<>();
list.add("s1");
list.add("s2");
list.add("s3");
list.add("s1");
```

```
System.out.println(list.removeAll(List.of("s1", "s2", "s5")));   //true
System.out.println(list);                                         //[s3]
System.out.println(list.removeAll(List.of("s5")));                //false
System.out.println(list);                                         //[s3]
```

To save space, we have used the `of()` method to create a list, which we will discuss in Chapter 14, *Managing Collections and Arrays*. By contrast with the previous example, the statement `list.removeAll("s1","s2","s5")` in the preceding code removed both elements `s1` from the list:

```
List<String> list = new ArrayList<>();
list.add("s1");
list.add("s2");
list.add("s3");
list.add("s1");

System.out.println(list.retainAll(List.of("s1","s2","s5")));  //true
System.out.println(list);                                      //[s1, s2, s1]
System.out.println(list.retainAll(List.of("s1","s2","s5")));  //false
System.out.println(list);                                      //[s1, s2, s1]
System.out.println(list.retainAll(List.of("s5")));            //true
System.out.println(list);                                      //[]
```

Please note in the preceding code how the `retainAll()` method returns `false` the second time because the list was not changed. Also, notice how the statement `list.retainAll(List.of("s5")` clears the list because none of its elements were equal to any of the provided elements.

# Replacing elements

There are two methods in the `List` interface that allow replacing elements in the list:

- `set(index, E)`: It replaces the element that has the provided index with the provided element
- `replaceAll(UnaryOperator<E>)`: It replaces each element of the list with the result returned by the provided operation

Here is an example of the usage of the method `set()`:

```
List<String> list = new ArrayList<>();
list.add("s1");
list.add("s2");

list.set(1, null);
System.out.println(list);     //prints: [s1, null]
```

It is pretty straightforward and doesn't seem to require any comments.

The second method, `replaceAll()`, is based on the function `UnaryOperator<E>` – one of the Java functional interfaces introduced in Java 8. We will discuss it in `Chapter 17`, *Lambda Expressions and Functional Programming*. For now, we would just like to show the code examples. They seem quite simple, so you should be able to understand how it works. Let's assume we start with the following list:

```
List<String> list = new ArrayList<>();
list.add("s1");
list.add("s2");
list.add("s3");
list.add("s1");
```

And here are a few possible element modifications (just remember that the `replaceAll()` method replaces each element with the result returned by the provided function):

```
list.replaceAll(s -> s.toUpperCase()); //cannot process null
System.out.println(list);     //prints: [S1, S2, S3, S1]

list.replaceAll(s -> ("S1".equals(s) ? "S5" : null));
System.out.println(list);     //prints: [S5, null, null, S5]

list.replaceAll(s -> "a");
System.out.println(list);     //prints: [a, a, a, a]

list.replaceAll(s -> {
  String result;
  //write here any code you need to get the value
  // for the variable result based in the value of s
  System.out.println(s);    //prints "a" four times
  result = "42";
  return result;
});
System.out.println(list);     //prints: [42, 42, 42, 42]
```

In the last example, we have put the body of the operation in braces { } and added an explicit `return` statement, so you can see what we mean when we say the operation returns the result.

> While comparing the elements of a collection with a `String` literal or any other object using the `equals()` method, it is a good habit to invoke `equals()` on the literal, such as `"s1".equals(element)`, or on the object you use to compare with, such as `someObject.equals(element)`. It helps to avoid `NullPointerException` in case the collection has a `null` value.

The preceding examples of functions can be re-written as follows:

```
UnaryOperator<String> function = s -> s.toUpperCase();
list.replaceAll(function);

function = s -> ("S1".equals(s) ? "S5" : null);
list.replaceAll(function);

function = s -> "a";
list.replaceAll(function);

function = s -> {
  String result;
  //write here any code you need to get the value
  // for the variable result based in the value of s
  System.out.println(s);    //prints "a" four times
  result = "42";
  return result;
};
list.replaceAll(function);
```

This way, they can be passed around as any other parameters, and that is the power of functional programming. But again, we will talk more about it and explain all the syntax in `Chapter 17`, *Lambda Expressions and Functional Programming*.

# Sorting String and numeral types

As we have mentioned already, a collection of type `List` preserves an order of the elements, so, naturally, it has also an ability to sort the elements, and the `sort(Comparator<E>)` method serves this purpose. This method became possible after functional programming was introduced with Java 8. We will talk about it in Chapter 17, *Lambda Expressions and Functional Programming*.

Now, we will just show you a few examples and point where to look for the standard comparators. We start with the following list:

```
List<String> list = new ArrayList<>();
list.add("s3");
list.add("s2");
list.add("ab");
//list.add(null); //throws NullPointerException for sorting
                //      String.CASE_INSENSITIVE_ORDER
                //      Comparator.naturalOrder()
                //      Comparator.reverseOrder()
list.add("a");
list.add("Ab");
System.out.println(list);                       //[s3, s2, ab, a, Ab]
```

And here are a few examples of sorting:

```
list.sort(String.CASE_INSENSITIVE_ORDER);
System.out.println(list);                       //[a, ab, Ab, s2, s3]

list.sort(Comparator.naturalOrder());
System.out.println(list);                       //[Ab, a, ab, s2, s3]

list.sort(Comparator.reverseOrder());
System.out.println(list);                       //[Ab, a, ab, s2, s3]
```

The preceding sortings are not null-safe, as the preceding comments point out. You can know this by reading API documentation about the preceding comparators or just by experimenting with them. One often tries various edge cases even after reading the documentation, to understand the described functionality better and to see if you understand the description correctly.

There are also comparators that handle `null` values:

```
list.add(null);

list.sort(Comparator.nullsFirst(Comparator.naturalOrder()));
System.out.println(list);            //[null, Ab, a, ab, s2, s3]

list.sort(Comparator.nullsLast(Comparator.naturalOrder()));
System.out.println(list);            //[Ab, a, ab, s2, s3, null]
```

As you can see, many popular comparators can be found as static methods of class `java.util.Comparator`. But if you do not see a ready-to-use comparator you need, you can also write your own. For example, let's assume we need to sort null value so as if it is `String` value "null". For such a case, we can write a custom comparator:

```
Comparator<String> comparator = (s1, s2) ->{
   String s = (s1 == null ? "null" : s1);
   return s.compareTo(s2);
};
list.sort(comparator);
System.out.println(list);            //[Ab, a, ab, null, s2, s3]
```

There are also comparators for various number types in `Comparator` class:

- `comparingInt(ToIntFunction<? super T> keyExtractor)`
- `comparingLong(ToLongFunction<? super T> keyExtractor)`
- `comparingDouble(ToDoubleFunction<? super T> keyExtractor)`

We leave them for the readers to study on their own if they need to use these methods for numbers comparison. However, it seems that most mainstream programmers never use them; the ready-to-use comparators we have demonstrated are usually more than enough.

# Sorting custom objects

One of the more frequently encountered cases is the need to sort custom objects, such as `Car`, or `Person` type, for example. To do it, there are two options:

- Implement the `Comparable` interface. It has only one method, `compareTo(T)`, which accepts an object of the same type and returns a negative integer, zero, or a positive integer if this object is less than, equal to, or greater than the specified object. Such an implementation is called a natural ordering because objects that implement the `Comparable` interface can be ordered by the method `sort()` of a collection. Many of the examples of the previous subsection demonstrated how it works for the objects of type `String`. Comparators are returned by the methods `naturalOrder()`, `reverseOrder()`, `nullFirst()`, and `nullLast()` – they all are based on using the `compareTo()` implementation.

- Implement an external comparator that compares two objects of the type of collection elements using the static `comparing()` method of the `Comparator` class.

Let's see the code examples for each of the preceding options and discuss the pros and cons of each approach. First, let enhance the classes `Person`, `PersonWithHair`, and `PersonWithHairDressed` and implement the `Comparable` interface:

```
class Person implements Comparable<Person> {
  private int age;
  private String name, address;
  public Person(int age, String name, String address) {
    this.age = age;
    this.name = name == null ? "" : name;
    this.address = address;
  }
  @Override
  public int compareTo(Person p){
    return name.compareTo(p.getName());
  }
  @Override
  public boolean equals(Object o) {
    if (this == o) return true;
    if (o == null) return false;
    if(!(o instanceof Person)) return false;
      Person person = (Person)o;
      return age == person.getAge() &&
              Objects.equals(name, person.getName());
  }
  @Override
```

```
    public int hashCode(){ return Objects.hash(age, name); }
    @Override
    public String toString() { return "Person{age=" + age +
                                      ", name=" + name + "}";
    }
}
```

As you can see, we have added another instance field, address, but do not use it in either the equals(), hashCode(), or compareTo() methods. We did it just to show that it is completely up to you how to define the identity of the object of class Person and its children. We also implemented the toString() method (which prints only the fields included in the identity), so we can identify each object when they are displayed. And we have implemented the method of the Comparable interface, compareTo(), which is going to be used for sorting. Right now it takes into account only the name, so when sorted, the objects will be ordered by name.

The children of class Person did not change:

```
class PersonWithHair extends Person {
  private String hairstyle;
  public PersonWithHair(int age, String name,
                        String address, String hairstyle) {
    super(age, name, address);
    this.hairstyle = hairstyle;
  }
}

class PersonWithHairDressed extends PersonWithHair{
  private String dress;
  public PersonWithHairDressed(int age, String name,
          String address, String hairstyle, String dress) {
    super(age, name, address, hairstyle);
    this.dress = dress;
  }
}
```

Now we can create the list that we are going to sort:

```
List<Person> list = new ArrayList<>();
list.add(new PersonWithHair(45, "Bill", "27 Main Street",
                                               "Pompadour"));
list.add(new PersonWithHair(42, "Kelly","15 Middle Street",
                                               "Ponytail"));
list.add(new PersonWithHairDressed(34, "Kelly", "10 Central Square",
                                       "Pompadour", "Suit"));
list.add(new PersonWithHairDressed(25, "Courtney", "27 Main Street",
                                       "Ponytail", "Tuxedo"));

list.forEach(System.out::println);
```

Execution of the preceding code produces the following output:

```
Person{age=45, name=Bill}
Person{age=42, name=Kelly}
Person{age=34, name=Kelly}
Person{age=25, name=Courtney}
```

The persons are printed in the order they were added to the list. Now, let's sort them:

```
list.sort(Comparator.naturalOrder());
list.forEach(System.out::println);
```

The new order looks as follows:

```
Person{age=45, name=Bill}
Person{age=25, name=Courtney}
Person{age=42, name=Kelly}
Person{age=34, name=Kelly}
```

The objects are ordered alphabetically by name – that is how we have implemented the `compareTo()` method.

If we use the `reverseOrder()` comparator, the order shown be reversed:

```
list.sort(Comparator.reverseOrder());
list.forEach(System.out::println);
```

This is what we see if we run the preceding code:

```
Person{age=42, name=Kelly}
Person{age=34, name=Kelly}
Person{age=25, name=Courtney}
Person{age=45, name=Bill}
```

The order was reversed.

We can change our implementation of the `compareTo()` method and order the objects by age:

```
@Override
public int compareTo(Person p){
   return age - p.getAge();
}
```

Or we can implement it so that the `Person` objects will be sorted by both fields – first by name, then by age:

```
@Override
public int compareTo(Person p){
   int result = this.name.compareTo(p.getName());
   if (result != 0) {
     return result;
   }
   return this.age - p.getAge();
}
```

If we sort the list in natural order now, the result will be:

```
Person{age=45, name=Bill}
Person{age=25, name=Courtney}
Person{age=34, name=Kelly}
Person{age=42, name=Kelly}
```

You can see that the objects are ordered by name, but two persons with the same name Kelly are ordered by age too.

That is the advantage of implementing the `Comparable` interface – the sorting is always performed the same way. But this is also a disadvantage because to change the order, one has to re-implement the class. Besides, it might be not possible if the `Person` class comes to us from a library, so we cannot modify its code.

In such cases, the second option—using the `Comparator.comparing()` method—comes to the rescue. And, by the way, we can do it even when the `Person` class does not implement the `Comparable` interface.

The `Comparator.comparing()` method accepts a function as parameter. We will talk about functional programming in more detail in Chapter 17, *Lambda Expressions and Functional Programming*. For now, we will just say that the `Comparator.comparing()` method generates a comparator based on the field (of the class to be sorted) passed in as a parameter. Let's see an example:

```
list.sort(Comparator.comparing(Person::getName));
list.forEach(System.out::println);
```

The preceding code sorts `Person` objects by name. The only modification we had to do was adding the `getName()` method to the `Person` class. Similarly, if we add the `getAge()` method, we can sort the `Person` objects by age:

```
list.sort(Comparator.comparing(Person::getAge));
list.forEach(System.out::println);
```

Or we can sort them by both fields – exactly the same way we did it when implemented the `Comparable` interface:

```
list.sort(Comparator.comparing(Person::getName).thenComparing(Person::getAg
e));
list.forEach(System.out::println);
```

You can see in the preceding code how the sorting methods can be chained using `thenComparing()`.

Most of the classes usually have getters to access the fields value, so adding getters typically is not needed and any library class can be sorted this way.

# Comparing with another collection

Every Java collection implements the `equals()` method, which compares it with another collection. In the case of `List`, two lists are considered equal (the method `list1.equals(list2)` returns `true`) when:

- Each collection is of type `List`
- Each element of one list is equal to the element of another list in the same position

Here is the code that illustrates it:

```
List<String> list1 = new ArrayList<>();
list1.add("s1");
list1.add("s2");

List<String> list2 = new ArrayList<>();
list2.add("s1");
list2.add("s2");

System.out.println(list1.equals(list2)); //prints: true
list2.sort(Comparator.reverseOrder());
System.out.println(list2);               //prints: [s2, s1]
System.out.println(list1.equals(list2)); //prints: false
```

If two lists are equal, their `hashCode()` methods return the same integer value. But the equality of `hashCode()` results does not guarantee that the lists are equal. We will talk about the reason for that while discussing the `hashCode()` method implementation for the elements of the `Set` collection in the next section.

The `containsAll(Collection)` method of the `List` interface (or any collection that implements the `Collection` interface) returns `true` only if all elements of the provided collection are present in the list. If the size of the list and the size of the provided collection are equal, we can be sure that the same (well, equal) elements compose each of the compared collections. It does not guarantee though that the elements are of the same type, because they might be children of different generations with the `equals()` method implemented only in the common parent.

If not, we can find the difference using the methods `retainAll(Collection)` and `removeAll(Collection)`, described earlier in this section. Let's assume we have two lists as follows:

```
List<String> list1 = new ArrayList<>();
list1.add("s1");
list1.add("s1");
list1.add("s2");
list1.add("s3");
list1.add("s4");

List<String> list2 = new ArrayList<>();
list2.add("s1");
list2.add("s2");
list2.add("s2");
list2.add("s5");
```

We can find which elements in one list are not present in the other:

```
List<String> list = new ArrayList<>(list1);
list.removeAll(list2);
System.out.println(list);     //prints: [s3, s4]

list = new ArrayList<>(list2);
list.removeAll(list1);
System.out.println(list);     //prints: [s5]
```

Notice how we have created a temporary list to avoid corruption of the original one.

But this difference does not tell us about possibly duplicate elements present in each of the list. To find it, we can use the `retainAll(Collection)` method:

```
List<String> list = new ArrayList<>(list1);
list.retainAll(list2);
System.out.println(list);     //prints: [s1, s1, s2]

list = new ArrayList<>(list2);
list.retainAll(list1);
System.out.println(list);     //prints: [s1, s2, s2]
```

Now we have the full picture of the differences between the two lists.

Also, please, notice that the `retainAll(Collection)` method can be used to identify the elements that belong to each of the lists.

But neither `retainAll(Collection)` nor `removeAll(Collection)` guarantee that the compared list and the collection passed in contain elements of the same type. They might be a mix of children with a common parent that have the `equals()` method implemented in the parent only, and the parent type is the type of the list and the collection passed in.

# Converting to array

There are two methods that allow converting a list to an array:

- `toArray()`: It converts the list to array `Object[]`
- `toArray(T[])`: It converts the list to array `T[]`, where `T` is the type of the elements in the list

Both methods preserve the order of the elements. Here is the demo code that shows how to do it:

```
List<String> list = new ArrayList<>();
list.add("s1");
list.add("s2");

Object[] arr1 = list.toArray();
for(Object o: arr1){
  System.out.print(o);        //prints: s1s2
}

String[] arr2 = list.toArray(new String[list.size()]);
for(String s: arr2){
  System.out.print(s);        //prints: s1s2
}
```

Yet, there is another way to convert a list or any collection for that matter to an array – using a stream and functional programming:

```
Object[] arr3 = list.stream().toArray();
for (Object o : arr3) {
  System.out.print(o);        //prints: s1s2
}

String[] arr4 = list.stream().toArray(String[]::new);
for (String s : arr4) {
  System.out.print(s);        //prints: s1s2
}
```

Streams and functional programming have made many traditional coding solutions obsolete. We will discuss this in Chapter 17, *Lambda Expressions and Functional Programming* and in Chapter 18, *Streams and Pipeline*.

# List implementations

There are many classes that implement the `List` interface for various purposes:

- `ArrayList`: As we have discussed in this section, it is by far the most popular `List` implementation
- `LinkedList`: Provides fast adding and removing of the elements at the end of the list
- `Stack`: Provides a **last-in-first-out** (**LIFO**) storage for objects
- Many other classes referred to in the online documentation of the `List` interface.

# Set - HashSet does not allow duplicates

There was a reason for the creation of the `Set` interface; it was designed not to allow duplicate elements. A duplicate is identified using the `equals()` method, implemented in the class whose objects are elements of the set.

# Preferring variable type Set

As in the case of `List`, using type `Set` for the variable that holds a reference to the object of the class that implements the `Set` interface is a good programming practice called coding to an interface. It assures independence of the client code from any particular implementation. So, it is a good habit to write `Set<Person> persons = new HashSet<>()`, for example.

# Why is it called HashSet?

In programming, a hash value is a 32-bit signed integer that represents some data. It is used in such data structures as a `HashTable`. After a record is created in a `HashTable`, its hash value can be used later to quickly find and retrieve the stored data. A hash value is also called a hash code, digest, or simply hash.

In Java, the `hashCode()` method in the base `Object` class returns a hash value as the object representation, but it it does not take into account the values of any children's fields. This means that if you need the hash value to include the child object state, you need to implement the `hashCode()` method in that child class.

A hash value is an integer that represents some data. In Java, it represents an object.

The `HashSet` class uses hash value as a unique key to store and retrieve an object. Although the number of possible integers is big, the variety of objects is still bigger. So, it is quite possible that two not-equal objects have the same hash value. That is why each hash value in `HashSet` refers not to an individual object, but potentially a group of objects (called a bucket or bin). `HashSet` resolves this clash using the `equals()` method.

For example, there are several objects of class `A` stored in a `HashSet` object and you want to know if a particular object of class `A` is there. You call the `contains(object of A)` method on the `HashSet` object. The method calculates the hash value of the provided object and looks for a bucket with such a key. If none was found, the `contains()` method returns `false`. But if a bucket with such hash value exists, it may contain several objects of class `A`. That is when the `equals()` method comes into play. The code compares each of the objects in the bucket with the provided one using the `equals()` method. If one of the calls to `equals()` returns `true`, the `contains()` method returns `true`, thus confirming that such an object is stored in the already. Otherwise, it returns `false`.

That is why, as we have already stated while discussing the `List` interface, it is very important that, if the objects of the class you are creating are going to be elements of a collection, both methods—`equals()` and `hashCode()`—have to be implemented and use the same instance fields. Since `List` does not use a hash value, it is possible to get away using the `List` interface for the objects that do not have the `hashCode()` method implemented in a child of `Object`. But any collection that has "Hash" in its name will work incorrectly without it. Thus, the name.

# Adding elements

The `Set` interface provides only one method for adding a single element:

- `add(E)`: It adds the provided element `E1` to the set if there is not already such an element `E2` there such that the statement `Objects.equals(E1, E2)` returns `true`

The Objects class is a utility class located in the package java.util. Its equals() method compares two objects in a null-safe manner by returning true when both objects are null and using the equals() method otherwise. We will talk more about utility class Objects in this chapter in an upcoming section.

The add() method can throw a RuntimeException if something goes wrong. So, putting a try-catch block around the method makes the code more robust (if the catch block does not simply rethrow the exception but does something meaningful). Read the description of the Set interface API online and see what the names of the exceptions this method throws are and under which conditions they can occur.

The add(E) method also returns a Boolean value (true/false) that indicates the success of the operation. This method overrides the method in the Collection interface, so all Java collections that extend or implement the Collection interface have it. Let's look at an example:

```
Set<String> set = new HashSet<>();
System.out.println(set.add("s1"));   //prints: true
System.out.println(set.add("s1"));   //prints: false
System.out.println(set.add("s2"));   //prints: true
System.out.println(set.add("s3"));   //prints: true
System.out.println(set);             //prints: [s3, s1, s2]
```

Notice, first, how the add() method returns false when we try to add element s1 the second time. Then look at the last line of the code above and observe the following:

- Only one element s1 was added to the set
- The order of the elements is not preserved

The last observation is important. The Java Specification explicitly states that, by contrast with List, Set does not guarantee the order of the elements. It can be different when the same code is run on different JVM instances or even at different runs on the same instance. The factory methods Set.of() shuffle the unordered collections a bit while creating them (we will talk about collections factory methods in Chapter 14, *Managing Collections and Arrays*). This way, an inappropriate reliance on a certain order of the elements of Set and other unordered collections can be discovered earlier, before the code is deployed to the production environment.

# size(), isEmpty(), and clear()

These three methods are straightforward:

- `size()`: It returns count of elements in the set
- `isEmpty()`: It returns `true` if there is no elements in the list (`size()` returns 0)
- `clear()`: It removes all elements from the list, so that `isEmpty()` returns `true` and `size()` returns 0

# Iterate and stream

This `Set` functionality is not different from `List` as described previously, because every collection that implements the `Collection` interface also implements the `Iterable` interface (because `Collection` extends `Iterable`) Set can be iterated using a traditional enhanced `for` statement or its own method `forEach()`:

```
Set set = new HashSet();
set.add(null);
set.add(1);
set.add("ss");
set.add(new A());
set.add(new B());
for(Object o: set){
   System.out.println(o);
}
set.forEach(System.out::println);
```

In `Chapter 17`, *Lambda Expressions and Functional Programming,* we will explain how the function can be passed as a parameter of the method `forEach()`. The result of both iteration styles is the same:

```
null
ss
1
A
B
null
ss
1
A
B
```

The other related methods that come from the interface `Iterable` are the same as in the `List` interface too:

- `iterator()`: It returns an object of class `Iterator` that allows walking through (iterate) each element of the collection and manipulating each of them as needed
- `splititerator()`: It returns an object of class `Splititerator` that allows splitting the collection for parallel processing (discussion of this functionality is outside the scope of this book)

The `Iterator` interface returned by the `iterator()` method has the following methods:

- `next()`: It returns the next element in the iteration
- `hasNext ()`: It returns `true` if the iteration has more elements
- `forEachRemaining (Consumer<? super E> function)`: It applies the provided function to each of remaining elements
- `remove()`: It removes from the underlying collection the last element returned by this iterator

The `next()` and `hasNext()` methods are used by `for` statements behind the scenes.

It is also possible to iterate over collection elements using objects of the `Stream` class that can be obtained by the methods `stream()` and `parallelStream()`. We will show you how to do this in `Chapter 18`, *Streams and Pipelines*.

# Adding using generics

As in the case of `List`, generics can be used with `Set`, too (or any collection for that matter). The rules and `Set` behavior with generics are exactly the same as described for `List` in the section *List – ArrayList preserves order* (subsection *Add using generics*).

# Adding collection

The `addAll(Collection<? extends E> collection)` method adds the provided collection of objects to a set, but only those that are not present already in the set. The method returns the Boolean value `true` if the set was changed, and `false` otherwise.

The generic `<? extends E>` means type `E` or any subtype of `E`.

As an example, we can do the following:

```
Set<String> set1 = new HashSet<>();
set1.add("s1");
set1.add("s2");
set1.add("s3");

List<String> list = new ArrayList<>();
list.add("s1");

System.out.println(set1.addAll(list)); //prints: false
System.out.println(set1);              //prints: [s3, s1, s2]

list.add("s4");
System.out.println(set1.addAll(list)); //prints: true
System.out.println(set1);              //prints: [s3, s4, s1, s2]
```

# Implementing equals() and hashCode()

We have talked about implementing the methods `equals()` and `hashCode()` several times already and here will only repeat that, if your class is going to be used as a `Set` element, both methods have to be implemented. See the explanation in the preceding *Why is it called HashSet?* section.

# Locating element

The only `Set` functionality related to the location of a particular element directly is provided by the `contains(E)` method, which returns `true` if the provided element is present in the set. You can also iterate and locate the element this way, using the `equals()` method, but it is not a direct location.

# Retrieving elements

By contrast with `List`, it is not possible to retrieve an element from `Set` directly, because you cannot use index or another way to point to the object. But it is possible to iterate through the set as was described previously, in the subsection *Iterate and stream*.

# Removing elements

There are four methods in the `Set` interface that remove (delete) elements:

- `remove(E)`: It removes the provided element and returns `true` if the list contained it
- `removeAll(Collection)`: It removes the provided elements and returns `true` if the list has changed
- `retainAll(Collection)`: It removes all the elements that are not in the provided collection and returns `true` if the list has changed
- `removeIf(Predicate<? super E> filter)`: It removes all the elements that for which the provided predicate returns `true`

The first three methods behave the same way as with the `List` collection, so we will not repeat the explanations(see the subsection *Remove elements* of the section *List – ArrayList preserves order*).

As for the last of the listed methods, a predicate is a function that returns a Boolean value. It is another example of a functional interface (an interface that has only one abstract method) and functional programming.

 The notation `Predicate<? super E>` means a function that accepts a parameter of type `E` or any of its base (parent) class and returns a Boolean value.

We will talk more about functions in `Chapter 17`, *Lambda Expressions and Functional Programming*. Meanwhile, the following example shows how the `removeIf()` method can be used:

```
Set<String> set = new HashSet();
set.add(null);
set.add("s1");
set.add("s1");
set.add("s2");
```

```
set.add("s3");
set.add("s4");
System.out.println(set);    //[null, s3, s4, s1, s2]

set.removeIf(e -> "s1".equals(e));
System.out.println(set);    //[null, s3, s4, s2]

set.removeIf(e -> e == null);
System.out.println(set);    //[s3, s4, s2]
```

Please, notice how we put s1 first when trying to find the element e that equals s1. It does not match the way we express it in English, but it helps to avoid NullPointerException in case one of the elements is null (as it was in our case).

# Replacing elements

By contrast with List, it is not possible to replace an element in Set directly, because you cannot use index or another way to point to the object. But it is possible to iterate through the set as was described previously, or by using a Stream object (we will discuss this in Chapter 18, *Streams and Pipelines)* and check each element and see if this is the one you are looking to replace. Those elements that did not match the criteria, you can add to a new set. And those you would like to replace, skip and add another object (that will replace the one you skip) to the new set:

```
Set<String> set = new HashSet();
set.add(null);
set.add("s2");
set.add("s3");
System.out.println(set);    //[null, s3, s2]

//We want to replace s2 with s5
Set<String> newSet = new HashSet<>();
set.forEach(s -> {
  if("s2".equals(s)){
    newSet.add("s5");
  } else {
    newSet.add(s);
  }
});
set = newSet;
System.out.println(set);    //[null, s3, s5]
```

After we switch reference from original set to a new set (set = newSet), the original set will be eventually removed from memory by the garbage collector and the result will be the same as if we have just replaced that one element in the original set.

# Sorting

The Set interface does not allow sorting and does not guarantee order preservation. If you need these features added to the set, you can use the interfaces java.util.SortedSet or java.util.NavigableSet and their implementations java.util.TreeSet or java.util.ConcurrentSkipListSet.

# Comparing with another collection

Every Java collection implements the equals() method, which compares it with another collection. In the case of Set, two sets are considered equal (set1.equals(set2) returns true) when:

- Each collection is of type Set
- They have the same size
- Each element of one set is contained in another set

The following code illustrates the definition:

```
Set<String> set1 = new HashSet<>();
set1.add("s1");
set1.add("s2");

List<String> list = new ArrayList<>();
list.add("s2");
list.add("s1");

System.out.println(set1.equals(list)); //prints: false
```

The preceding collections are not equal because they are of different types. Now, let's compare two sets:

```
Set<String> set2 = new HashSet<>();
set2.add("s3");
set2.add("s1");

System.out.println(set1.equals(set2)); //prints: false

set2.remove("s3");
set2.add("s2");
System.out.println(set1.equals(set2)); //prints: true
```

The preceding sets are equal or not depending on the composition of their elements, even if the size of the sets is the same.

If two sets are equal, their `hashCode()` methods return the same integer value. But the equality of the `hashCode()` result does not guarantee that the sets are equal. We have talked about the reason for that while discussing the `hashCode()` method's implementation in the preceding subsection *Implement equals() and hashCode()*.

The `containsAll(Collection)` method of the `Set` interface (or any collection that implements the `Collection` interface for that matter) returns `true` only if all elements of the provided collection are present in the set. If the size of the set and the size of the provided collection are equal, we can be sure that the same (well, equal) elements compose each of the compared collections. It does not guarantee though that the elements are of the same type, because they might be children of different generations with the `equals()` method implemented only in the common parent.

If not, we can find the difference using the methods `retainAll(Collection)` and `removeAll(Collection)`, described earlier in this section. Let's assume we have two lists as follows:

```
Set<String> set1 = new HashSet<>();
set1.add("s1");
set1.add("s1");
set1.add("s2");
set1.add("s3");
set1.add("s4");

Set<String> set2 = new HashSet<>();
set2.add("s1");
set2.add("s2");
set2.add("s2");
set2.add("s5");
```

We can find which elements in one set are not present in the other:

```
Set<String> set = new HashSet<>(set1);
set.removeAll(set2);
System.out.println(set);      //prints: [s3, s4]

set = new HashSet<>(set2);
set.removeAll(set1);
System.out.println(set);      //prints: [s5]
```

Notice how we have created a temporary set to avoid corruption of the original one.

Since `Set` does not allow duplicate elements, there is no need to use the `retainAll(Collection)` method for the purpose of finding more differences between the sets, like we did for `List`. Instead, the `retainAll(Collection)` method can be used to find common elements in two sets:

```
Set<String> set = new HashSet<>(set1);
set.retainAll(set2);
System.out.println(set);      //prints: [s1, s2]

set = new HashSet<>(set2);
set.retainAll(set1);
System.out.println(set);      //prints: [s1, s2]
```

As you can from the preceding code, to find the common elements between two sets, it is enough to use the `retainAll()` method only once, no matter which set is the main and which one is used as a parameter.

Also, please notice that neither the `retainAll(Collection)` nor the `removeAll(Collection)` method guarantee that the compared set and the collection passed in contain elements of the same type. They might be a mix of children with a common parent that have the `equals()` method implemented in the parent only, and the parent type is the type of the set and the collection passed in.

# Converting to array

There are two methods that allow converting a set to an array:

- `toArray()`: It converts the set to array `Object[]`
- `toArray(T[])`: It converts the set to array `T[]`, where `T` is the type of the elements in the set

Both methods preserve the order of the elements only in the case the set preserves order too, such as `SortedSet` or `NavigableSet`, for example. Here is the demo code that shows how to do it:

```
Set<String> set = new HashSet<>();
set.add("s1");
set.add("s2");

Object[] arr1 = set.toArray();
for(Object o: arr1){
  System.out.print(o);         //prints: s1s2
}

String[] arr2 = set.toArray(new String[set.size()]);

for(String s: arr2){
  System.out.print(s);        //prints: s1s2
}
```

Yet, there is another way to convert a set, or any collection for that matter, to an array – using a stream and functional programming:

```
Object[] arr3 = set.stream().toArray();
for (Object o : arr3) {
  System.out.print(o);         //prints: s1s2
}

String[] arr4 = set.stream().toArray(String[]::new);
for (String s : arr4) {
  System.out.print(s);        //prints: s1s2
}
```

Streams and functional programming have made many traditional coding solutions obsolete. We will discuss them in `Chapter 17`, *Lambda Expressions and Functional Programming* and in `Chapter 18`, *Streams and Pipeline.*

# Set implementations

There are many classes that implement the Set interface for various purposes:

- We have discussed the HashMap class in this section; it is by far the most popular Set implementation
- The LinkedHashSet class stores unique elements in order
- The TreeSet class orders its elements based on their values natural order or using the Comparator provided at creation time
- Many other classes referred in the online documentation of the Set interface

# Map – HashMap stores/retrieves objects by key

The Map interface itself is not related to the Collection interface directly, but it uses the Set interface for its keys and Collection for its values. For example, for Map<Integer, String> map:

- Set<Integer> keys = map.keySet();
- Collection<String> values = map.values();

Each value is stored in a map with a unique key that is passed in along with the value when added to the map. In the case of Map<Integer, String> map:

```
map.put(42, "whatever");          //42 is the key for the value "whatever"
```

Then later, the value can be retrieved by its key:

```
String v = map.get(42);
System.out.println(v);      //prints: whatever
```

These are the basic map operations that convey the Map interface's purpose – to provide a storage for key-value pairs, where both—key and value—are objects and the class used as the key implements the equals() and hashCode() methods, which override the default implementations in the Object class.

Now, let's take a closer look at the Map interface, its implementation, and usage.

# Preferring variable type Map

As in the case of `List` and `Set`, using type `Map` for the variable that holds a reference to the object of the class that implements the `Map` interface is a good programming practice called coding to an interface. It assures independence of the client code from any particular implementation. So, it is a good habit to write `Map<String, Person> persons = new HashMap<>()` to store all persons as values by their key – a social security number, for example.

# Why is it called HashMap?

By now, it should be already obvious to you that the reason the `HashMap` class has "Hash" in its name that it stores the keys using their hash values, calculated by the `hashCode()` method. Since we have already discussed it at great length in the previous sections, we are not going to talk here about hash value and its usage; you can refer back to the subsection *Why is it called HashSet?* in the previous section of this chapter.

# Adding and maybe replace

The `Map` interface stores key-value pairs, also called entries, because in a `Map`, each key-value pair is also represented by the `Entry` interface, which is a nested interface of `Map` and thus referred as `Map.Entry`.

A key-value pair or an entry can be added to a `Map` using the following methods:

- `V put(K, V)`: It adds a key-value pair (or creates a key-value association). If the provided key exists already, the method overrides the old value and returns it (if the old value was `null`, then `null` is returned). If the provided key is not in the map already, the method returns `null`.
- `V putIfAbsent(K, V)`: It adds a key-value pair (or creates a key-value association). If the provided key exists already and the associated value is not `null`, the method does not override the old value but just returns it. If the provided key is not in the map already or if the associated value is `null`, the method overrides the old value and returns `null`.

The following code demonstrates the described functionality:

```
Map<Integer, String> map = new HashMap<>();
System.out.println(map.put(1, null));   //prints: null
System.out.println(map.put(1, "s1"));   //prints: null
System.out.println(map.put(2, "s1"));   //prints: null
System.out.println(map.put(2, "s2"));   //prints: s1
System.out.println(map.put(3, "s3"));   //prints: null
System.out.println(map);                //prints: {1=s1, 2=s2, 3=s3}

System.out.println(map.putIfAbsent(1, "s4"));  //prints: s1
System.out.println(map);                //prints: {1=s1, 2=s2, 3=s3}

System.out.println(map.put(1, null));   //prints: s1
System.out.println(map);                //prints: {1=null, 2=s2, 3=s3}

System.out.println(map.putIfAbsent(1, "s4"));  //prints: null
System.out.println(map);                //prints: {1=s4, 2=s2, 3=s3}

System.out.println(map.putIfAbsent(4, "s4"));  //prints: null
System.out.println(map);                //prints: {1=s4, 2=s2, 3=s3, 4=s4}
```

Notice that in a case where the returned value is `null`, there is some ambiguity about the result - whether the new entry was added (and replaced the entry with value `null`) or not. So, one has to pay attention while using the described methods on the maps that may contain a `null` value.

There are also the `compute()` and `merge()` methods, which allow you to add and modify data in the map, but their usage is much too complex for the introductory course, so we will leave them out of this discussion. Besides, they are not very often used in mainstream programming.

# size(), isEmpty(), and clear()

These three methods are straightforward:

- `size()`: It returns count of key-value pairs (entries) in the map
- `isEmpty()`: It returns `true` if there is nokey-value pairs (entries) in the map (`size()` returns 0)
- `clear()`: It removes allkey-value pairs (entries) from the map, so that `isEmpty()` returns `true` and `size()` returns 0

# Iterate and stream

There are several ways to iterate over the map content using the following `Map` methods, for example:

- `Set<K> keySet()`: It returns the keys associated with the values stored in the map. One can iterate over this set and retrieve from the map the value for each key (see the preceding section for who to iterate over a set).
- `Collection<V> values()`: It returns the values stored in the map. One can iterate over this collection.
- `Set<Map.Entry<K,V>> entrySet()`: It returns the entries (key-value pairs) stored in the map. One can iterate over this set and get the key and the value from each entry.
- `forEach (BiConsumer<? super K,? super V> action)`: It iterates over key-value pairs stored in the map and provides them as an input into the function `BiConsumer`, which accepts two parameters of the map key and value types and returns `void`.

 Here is how to read the notation `BiConsumer<? super K,? super V>`: It describes a function. The `Bi` in the function's name indicates that it accepts two parameters: one of type `K` or any of its superclasses and another of type `V` or any of its superclasses. The `Consumer` in the functions name indicates that it returns nothing (`void`).

We will talk more about functional programming in `Chapter 17`, *Lambda Expressions and Functional Programming*.

To demonstrate the preceding methods, we are going to use the following map:

```
Map<Integer, String> map = new HashMap<>();
map.put(1, null);
map.put(2, "s2");
map.put(3, "s3");
```

And here is how this map can be iterated:

```
for(Integer key: map.keySet()){
  System.out.println("key=" + key + ", value=" + map.get(key));
}
map.keySet().stream()
    .forEach(k->System.out.println("key=" + k + ", value=" + map.get(k)));
for(String value: map.values()){
  System.out.println("value=" + value);
```

```
    }
    map.values().stream().forEach(System.out::println);
    map.forEach((k,v) -> System.out.println("key=" + k + ", value=" + v));
    map.entrySet().forEach(e -> System.out.println("key=" + e.getKey() +
                                             ", value=" + e.getValue()));
```

All the preceding methods produce the same results, except the `values()` method, which returns only values. Which one to use is a matter of style, but it seems that `map.forEach()` requires fewer keystrokes to implement the iteration.

# Adding using generics

From our examples, you have seen already how generics can be used with `Map`. It provides a valuable help to a programmer by allowing the compiler to check the match between the map and the objects one tries to store in it.

# Adding another Map

The `putAll(Map<? extends K, ? extends V> map)` method adds each key-value pair from the provided map the same way the `put(K, V)` method does for one pair:

```
    Map<Integer, String> map1 = new HashMap<>();
    map1.put(1, null);
    map1.put(2, "s2");
    map1.put(3, "s3");

    Map<Integer, String> map2 = new HashMap<>();
    map2.put(1, "s1");
    map2.put(2, null);
    map2.put(4, "s4");

    map1.putAll(map2);
    System.out.println(map1); //prints: {1=s1, 2=null, 3=s3, 4=s4}
```

As you can see, the `putAll()` method adds a new pair or overrides a value in the existing pair (based on the key) and does not return anything.

# Implementing equals() and hashCode()

If you are going to use the class you are writing as a key in a `Map`, implementing both the `equals()` and `hashCode()` methods is very important. See the explanation in the preceding section, *Why is it called HashSet?* In our examples, we have used objects of the `Integer` class as keys. This class has an implementation of both these methods based on the integer value of the class.

The class that is going to be stored as a value in a `Map` has to implement the `equals()` method, at least (see the next subsection, *Locate element*).

# Locating element

The following two methods answer the question if the particular key of value is present in the map:

- `containsKey(K)`: It returns `true`, if the provided key is present already
- `containsValue(V)`: It returns `true`, if the provided value is present already

Both methods rely on the `equals()` method to identify the match.

# Retrieving elements

To retrieve elements from a `Map`, you can use any of the following four methods:

- `V get(Object K)`: It returns the value by the provided key, or `null` if the provided key is not in the map
- `V getOrDefault(K, V)`: It returns the value by the provided key, or the provided (default) value if the provided key is not in the map
- `Map.Entry<K,V> entry(K,V)`: A static method that converts the provided key-value pair into an immutable object of `Map.Entry` (immutable means it can be read, but cannot be changed)
- `Map<K,V> ofEntries(Map.Entry<? extends K,? extends V>... entries)`: It creates an immutable map based on the provided entries

The following code demonstrates these methods:

```
Map<Integer, String> map = new HashMap<>();
map.put(1, null);
map.put(2, "s2");
map.put(3, "s3");

System.out.println(map.get(2));                      //prints: s2
System.out.println(map.getOrDefault(2, "s4"));  //prints: s2
System.out.println(map.getOrDefault(4, "s4"));  //prints: s4

Map.Entry<Integer, String> entry = Map.entry(42, "s42");
System.out.println(entry);         //prints: 42=s42

Map<Integer, String> entries =
                Map.ofEntries(entry, Map.entry(43, "s43"));
System.out.println(entries);    //prints: {42=s42, 43=s43}
```

And it is always possible to retrieve elements of a map by iterating, as we have described in the subsection *Iterate and stream*.

# Removing elements

Two methods allow the direct removal of Map elements:

- `V remove(Object key)`: It removes an object associated with the key and returns its value, or, if such a key is not present in the map, returns `null`
- `boolean remove(Object key, Object value)`: It removes an object associated with the key only if the current value associated with the key equals the provided one; returns `true`, if the element was removed

Here is the code that illustrates the described behavior:

```
Map<Integer, String> map = new HashMap<>();
map.put(1, null);
map.put(2, "s2");
map.put(3, "s3");
System.out.println(map.remove(2));         //prints: s2
System.out.println(map);                   //prints: {1=null, 3=s3}
System.out.println(map.remove(4));         //prints: null
System.out.println(map);                   //prints: {1=null, 3=s3}
System.out.println(map.remove(3, "s4"));   //prints: false
System.out.println(map);                   //prints: {1=null, 3=s3}
System.out.println(map.remove(3, "s3"));   //prints: true
System.out.println(map);                   //prints: {1=null}
```

There is also another way to remove a `Map` element by key. If the key from the map is removed, the corresponding value is removed too. Here is the code that demonstrates it:

```
Map<Integer, String> map = new HashMap<>();
map.put(1, null);
map.put(2, "s2");
map.put(3, "s3");

Set<Integer> keys = map.keySet();

System.out.println(keys.remove(2));     //prints: true
System.out.println(map);                //prints: {1=null, 3=s3}

System.out.println(keys.remove(4));     //prints: false
System.out.println(map);                //prints: {1=null, 3=s3}
```

Similarly, the methods `removeAll(Collection)`, `retainAll(Collection)`, and `removeIf(Predicate<? super E> filter)` from the `Set` interface, described in the subsection *Remove elements* of the section *Set - HashSet does not allow duplicates,* can be used too.

# Replacing elements

To replace elements of the `Map`, one can use the following methods:

- `V replace(K, V)`: It replaces the value with the provided one only if the provided key is present in the map; returns the previous (replaced) value if such a key is present or `null` if such a key is not in the map
- `boolean replace(K, oldV, newV)` : It replaces the current value (`oldV`) with a new one (`newV`) only if the provided key is present in the map and is currently associated with the provided value `oldV`; returns `true` if the value was replaced
- `void replaceAll(BiFunction<? super K, ? super V, ? extends V> function)`: It allows you to replace the values using a provided function that takes two parameters—key and value—and returns a new value that will replace the current one in this key-value pair

Here is how to read the notation `BiFunction<? super K, ? super V, ? extends V>`: It describes a function. The `Bi` in the function's name indicates that it accepts two parameters: one of type `K` or any of its superclasses and another of type `V` or any of its superclasses. The `Function` part in the functions name indicates that it returns something. The returned value is listed the last. In this case, it is `<? extends V>`, which means value of type `V` or any of its subclasses.

Let's assume that the map we are going to change is as follows:

```
Map<Integer, String> map = new HashMap<>();
map.put(1, null);
map.put(2, "s2");
map.put(3, "s3");
```

Then, the code that illustrates the first two methods looks like this:

```
System.out.println(map.replace(1, "s1"));      //prints: null
System.out.println(map);                        //prints: {1=s1, 2=s2, 3=s3}

System.out.println(map.replace(4, "s1"));      //prints: null
System.out.println(map);                        //prints: {1=s1, 2=s2, 3=s3}

System.out.println(map.replace(1, "s2", "s1"));   //prints: false
System.out.println(map);                        //prints: {1=s1, 2=s2, 3=s3}

System.out.println(map.replace(1, "s1", "s2"));   //prints: true
System.out.println(map);                        //prints: {1=s2, 2=s2, 3=s3}
```

And here is the code that helps to understand how the last of the listed replacing methods works:

```
Map<Integer, String> map = new HashMap<>();
map.put(1, null);
map.put(2, null);
map.put(3, "s3");

map.replaceAll((k,v) -> v == null? "s" + k : v);
System.out.println(map);                    //prints: {1=s1, 2=s2, 3=s3}

map.replaceAll((k,v) -> k == 2? "n2" : v);
System.out.println(map);                    //prints: {1=s1, 2=n2, 3=s3}

map.replaceAll((k,v) -> v.startsWith("s") ? "s" + (k + 10) : v);
System.out.println(map);                    //prints: {1=s11, 2=n2, 3=s13}
```

Notice that we were able to use the `v.startsWith()` method only after we had replaced all the `null` values with something else. Otherwise, this line could throw a `NullPointerException` and we would need to change it for the following one:

```
map.replaceAll((k,v) -> (v != null && v.startsWith("s")) ?
                                    "s" + (k + 10) : v);
```

# Sorting

The `Map` interface does not allow sorting and does not guarantee order preservation. If you need these features added to the map, you can use the interfaces `java.util.SortedMap` or `java.util.NavigableMap`, and their implementations `java.util.TreeMap` or `java.util.ConcurrentSkipListMap`.

# Comparing with another collection

Every Java collection implements the `equals()` method, which compares it with another collection. In the case of `Map`, two maps are considered equal (`map1.equals(map2)` returns `true`) when:

- Both are `Map` objects
- One map has the same set of key-value pairs as another map

Here is the code that illustrates the definition:

```
Map<Integer, String> map1 = new HashMap<>();
map1.put(1, null);
map1.put(2, "s2");
map1.put(3, "s3");

Map<Integer, String> map2 = new HashMap<>();
map2.put(1, null);
map2.put(2, "s2");
map2.put(3, "s3");

System.out.println(map2.equals(map1)); //prints: true

map2.put(1, "s1");
System.out.println(map2.equals(map1)); //prints: false
```

If you think about it, the `map1.equals(map2)` method returns exactly the same result as the `map1.entrySet().equals(map2.entrySet())` method, because the `entrySet()` method returns `Set<Map.Entry<K,V>` and we know (see the subsection *Compare with another collection* for `Set`) that two sets are equal when each element of one set is contained in another set.

If two maps are equal, their `hashCode()` methods return the same integer value. But the equality of `hashCode()` results does not guarantee that the maps are equal. We have talked about the reason for that while discussing the `hashCode()` method's implementation for the elements of the `Set` collection in the previous section.

If two maps are not equal and there is a need to find out exactly what the difference is, there are a variety of ways to do it:

```
map1.entrySet().containsAll(map2.entrySet());
map1.entrySet().retainAll(map2.entrySet());
map1.entrySet().removeAll(map2.entrySet());

map1.keySet().containsAll(map2.keySet());
map1.keySet().retainAll(map2.keySet());
map1.keySet().removeAll(map2.keySet());

map1.values().containsAll(map2.values());
map1.values().retainAll(map2.values());
map1.values().removeAll(map2.values());
```

Using any combination of these methods, one can get the full picture of the difference between the two maps.

# Map implementations

There are many classes that implement the `Map` interface for various purposes:

- `HashMap`, which we have discussed in this section; it is by far the most popular `Map` implementation
- The `LinkedHashMap` class stores its key-value pairs in their insertion order
- The `TreeMap` class orders its key-value pairs based on the keys natural order or using the `Comparator` provided at creation time
- Many other classes referred to in the online documentation of the `Map` interface.

# Exercise – EnumSet methods

We did not talk about the collection `java.util.EnumSet`. It is lesser known but very useful class in cases where you need to work with some `enum` values. Look up its API online and write code that demonstrates the usage of its four methods:

- `of()`
- `complementOf()`
- `allOf()`
- `range()`

# Answer

Assuming the `enum` class looks like the following:

```
enum Transport { AIRPLANE, BUS, CAR, TRAIN, TRUCK }
```

Then the code that demonstrates the four methods of `EnumSet` may look like this:

```
EnumSet<Transport> set1 = EnumSet.allOf(Transport.class);
System.out.println(set1);    //prints: [AIRPLANE, BUS, CAR, TRAIN, TRUCK]

EnumSet<Transport> set2 = EnumSet.range(Transport.BUS, Transport.TRAIN);
System.out.println(set2);    //prints: [BUS, CAR, TRAIN]

EnumSet<Transport> set3 = EnumSet.of(Transport.BUS, Transport.TRUCK);
System.out.println(set3);    //prints: [BUS, TRUCK]

EnumSet<Transport> set4 = EnumSet.complementOf(set3);
System.out.println(set4);    //prints: [AIRPLANE, CAR, TRAIN]
```

# Summary

This chapter has made the reader familiar with the Java collections and the most popular ones - the `List`, `Set`, and `Map` interfaces. The code examples made their functionality more clear. The comments of the code attracted the reader's attention to the possible pitfalls and other useful details.

In the next chapter, we will continue to overview the most popular classes of the Java Standard Library and Apache Commons. Most of them are utilities, such as `Objects`, `Collections`, `StringUtils`, and `ArrayUtils`. Others are just classes, such as `StringBuilder`, `StringBuffer`, and `LocalDateTime`. Some help to manage collections; others, objects. What is common among them is that they belong to the small set of tools that every Java programmer has to master before they can become effective coders.

# 14
# Managing Collections and Arrays

The classes that we will be discussing in this chapter allow us to create, initialize, and modify objects of Java collections and arrays. They also allow the creation of unmodifiable and immutable collections. Some of these classes belong to Java standard libraries, others to popular Apache Commons libraries. Knowledge of these classes and familiarity with their methods are essential for any Java programmer.

We will cover the following areas of functionality:

- Managing collections
- Managing arrays

The list of the overviewed classes includes:

- `java.util.Collections`
- `org.apache.commons.collections4.CollectionUtils`
- `java.util.Arrays`
- `org.apache.commons.lang3.ArrayUtils`

## Managing collections

In this section, we will review how collection objects can be created and initialized, what immutable collections are, and how to perform basic operations over collections—copy, sort, and shuffle, for example.

# Initializing collections

We have already seen a few examples of collection constructors without parameters. Now, we are going to see other ways to create and initialize collection objects.

## Collection constructor

Each of the collection classes has a constructor that accepts a collection of elements of the same type. For example, here is how an object of class `ArrayList` can be created using the `ArrayList(Collection collection)` constructor and how an object of class `HashSet` can be created using the `HashSet<Collection collection)` constructor:

```
List<String> list1 = new ArrayList<>();
list1.add("s1");
list1.add("s1");

List<String> list2 = new ArrayList<>(list1);
System.out.println(list2);        //prints: [s1, s1]

Set<String> set = new HashSet<>(list1);
System.out.println(set);          //prints: [s1]

List<String> list3 = new ArrayList<>(set);
System.out.println(list3);        //prints: [s1]
```

We will show more examples of using such constructors in the *Using other objects and streams* subsection later.

## Instance initializer (double brace)

It is possible to use a double brace initializer for the collection initialization. It fits especially well when the collection is the value of an instance field, so it is initialized automatically during object creation. Here is an example:

```
public class ManageCollections {
  private List<String> list = new ArrayList<>() {
      {
           add(null);
           add("s2");
           add("s3");
      }
  };
  public List<String> getThatList(){
```

```
      return this.list;
   }
   public static void main(String... args){
      ManageCollections mc = new ManageCollections();
      System.out.println(mc.getThatList());    //prints: [null, s2, s3]
   }
}
```

We have added a getter and use it when the `main()` method runs. Unfortunately, the double brace initializer does not save any time typing compared with the traditional collection initialization in a constructor:

```
public class ManageCollections {
   private List<String> list = new ArrayList<>();
   public ManageCollections(){
        list.add(null);
        list.add("s2");
        list.add("s3");
   }
   public List<String> getThatList(){
        return this.list;
   }
   public static void main(String... args){
      ManageCollections mc = new ManageCollections();
      System.out.println(mc.getThatList());    //prints: [null, s2, s3]
   }
}
```

The only difference is that you need to type the `list` variable for each call of `add()` method. Besides, the double brace initializer has an overhead of creating an anonymous class with just an instance initializer and references to the enclosing class. It also has potentially more problems, so should be avoided.

The good news is that there is a much shorter and more convenient way to initialize a collection as the field value or as a local variable value:

```
private List<String> list = Arrays.asList(null, "s2", "s3");
```

The static method `asList()` of the `java.util.Arrays` class is very popular (we will talk about the `Arrays` class in more detail shortly). The only potential drawback is that such a list does not allow the addition of elements:

```
List<String> list = Arrays.asList(null, "s2", "s3");
list.add("s4");     // throws UnsupportedOperationException
```

But, we can always create a new collection by passing the initialized list into a constructor:

```
List<String> list = new ArrayList(Arrays.asList(null, "s2", "s3"));
list.add("s4");    //works just fine

Set<String> set = new HashSet<>(Arrays.asList(null, "s2", "s3"));
set.add("s4");    //works just fine as well
```

Notice that the constructors of collection classes accept any object that implements the `Collection` interface. It allows lists to be created from sets, and vice versa. But, the `Map` interface does not extend `Collection`, so `Map` implementations only allow a map to be created from another map:

```
Map<Integer, String> map = new HashMap<>();
map.put(1, null);
map.put(2, "s2");
map.put(3, "s3");

Map<Integer, String> anotherMap = new HashMap<>(map);
```

The types of keys and values of the new map have to be either the same as in the provided map or have to be parents of the types of the provided map:

```
class A{}
class B extends A{}
Map<Integer, B> mb = new HashMap<>();
Map<Integer, A> ma = new HashMap<>(mb);
```

For example, this is an acceptable assignment:

```
Map<Integer, String> map1 = new HashMap<>();
Map<Integer, Object> map2 = new HashMap<>(map1);
```

That is because the `HashMap` constructor limits the types just to the children of the map elements:

```
HashMap(Map<? extends K,? extends V> map)
```

There's a similar problem with the following code too:

```
class A {}
class B extends A {}
List<A> l1 = Arrays.asList(new B());
List<B> l2 = Arrays.asList(new B());
//List<B> l3 = Arrays.asList(new A()); //compiler error
```

The preceding code makes sense, doesn't it? `class B` has (inherits) all the non-private methods and fields of `class A`, but can have other non-private methods and fields that are not available in `class A`. Even if both classes are empty today, as in our example, tomorrow we may decide to add some methods to `class B`. So, the compiler protects us from such a case and does not allow a collection with elements of a parent type to be assigned to the collection of children. And that is the meaning of the generics in the following constructor definitions, as you see them in the Java Standard Library API's `java.util` package:

```
ArrayList(Collection<? extends E> collection)
HashSet(Collection<? extends E> collection)
HashMap(Map<? extends K,? extends V> map)
```

We hope that by now, you have become more comfortable with such generics. If in doubt, read the sections about generics in the previous chapter.

# Static initialization block

There is a similar solution for static field initialization. The static block can include the code necessary to generate values that have to be used for static field initialization:

```
class SomeClass{
    public String getThatString(){
        return "that string";
    }
}
public class ManageCollections {
  private static Set<String> set = new HashSet<>();
    static {
        SomeClass someClass = new SomeClass();
        set.add(someClass.getThatString());
```

```
            set.add("another string");
    }
    public static void main(String... args){
        System.out.println(set); //prints: [that string, another string]
    }
}
```

Since `set` is a static field, it cannot be initialized in a constructor because a constructor is called only when an instance is created, while a static field can be accessed without creating an instance. We also could rewrite the preceding code as follows:

```
private static Set<String> set =
    new HashSet<>(Arrays.asList(new SomeClass().getThatString(),
                                             "another string"));
```

But, you can argue that it looks somewhat awkward and difficult to read. So, the static initialization block might be a better choice if it allows more readable code to be written.

# Factory methods of()

Since Java 9, yet another option for creating and initializing a collection is available in each of the interfaces, including `Map`—the `of()` factory methods. They are called *factory* because they produce objects. There are eleven such methods, which accept from 0 to 10 parameters, each parameter being an element that has to be added to the collection, for example:

```
List<String> iList0 = List.of();
List<String> iList1 = List.of("s1");
List<String> iList2 = List.of("s1", "s2");
List<String> iList3 = List.of("s1", "s2", "s3");

Set<String> iSet1 = Set.of("s1", "s2", "s3", "s4");
Set<String> iSet2 = Set.of("s1", "s2", "s3", "s4", "s5");
Set<String> iSet3 = Set.of("s1", "s2", "s3", "s4", "s5", "s6",
                                    "s7", "s8", "s9", "s10");

Map<Integer, String> iMap = Map.of(1, "s1", 2, "s2", 3, "s3", 4, "s4");
```

Please note how the map is constructed: from a pair of values up to 10 such pairs.

We have decided to start the identificators for the above variables with "i" to indicate that these collections are immutable. We will talk about this in the next section.

Another feature of these factory methods is that they do not allow `null` as an element value. If added, `null` element will cause an error (`NullPointerException`) at runtime. The reason `null` is not allowed is because it had to be banned from most collections a long time ago. This issue is especially important for `Set` because a set provides keys to `Map` while the `null` key does not make much sense, does it? Look at the following code, for example:

```
Map<Integer, String> map = new HashMap<>();
map.put(null, "s1");
map.put(2, "s2");
System.out.println(map.get(null));      //prints: s1
```

You may also recall that the `put()` method of the `Map` interface returns `null` if there was no value associated with the key provided, or if the old value was `null`. This ambiguity is annoying, isn't it?

That's why the authors of Java 9 decided to start squeezing out `null` from the collections. There will probably always be special implementations of collections that allow `null`, but the most often used collections will eventually not allow `null`, and the factory methods we are describing now are the first step in that direction.

Another long-awaited feature added along with these factory methods is randomization of the order of the set elements. It means that the order is different every time the same set creation is executed. For example, if we run these lines:

```
Set<String> iSet3 = Set.of("s1", "s2", "s3", "s4", "s5", "s6",
                           "s7", "s8", "s9", "s10");
System.out.println(iSet3);
```

The output may be as follows:

```
[s10, s2, s1, s8, s7, s9, s4, s3, s6, s5]
```

But, if we run the same two lines again, the output will be different:

```
[s1, s2, s5, s6, s3, s4, s9, s10, s7, s8]
```

And every execution of set creation results in a different order of its elements. This is the randomization in action. It helps to uncover early the incorrect programmer's reliance on a certain element's order in places where order is not guaranteed.

# Using other objects and streams

In the *Constructor* subsection, we demonstrated how the `List<T>`
`Arrays.asList(T...a)` method can be used to generate a list of values, which
can then be passed in a constructor of any class that implements the
`Collection` interface (or any interface that extends the `Collection`, such as `List` and
`Set`, for example). As a reminder, we would like to mention that the `(T...a)` notation is
called varargs and means that the parameter can be passed in any of the following two
ways:

- As an unlimited comma-separated sequence of values of type T
- As an array of type T of any size

So, both the following statements create equal lists:

```
List<String> x1 = Arrays.asList(null, "s2", "s3");
String[] array = {null, "s2", "s3"};
List<String> x2 = Arrays.asList(array);
System.out.println(x1.equals(x2));        //prints: true
```

Another way to create a collection was added with Java 8, which introduced streams. Here
is one possible example of a list and set objects generation (we will talk about streams more
in `Chapter 18`, *Streams and Pipelines*):

```
List<String> list2 = Stream.of(null, "s2", "s3")
                     .collect(Collectors.toList());
System.out.println(list2);              //prints: [null, s2, s3]

Set<String> set2 = Stream.of(null, "s2", "s3")
                     .collect(Collectors.toSet());
System.out.println(set2);               //prints: [null, s2, s3]
```

If you read the documentation about the `Collectors.toList()` or
`Collectors.toSet()` methods, you will find it says that "*there are no guarantees on the type,
mutability, serializability, or thread-safety of the List returned; if more control over the returned List
is required, use toCollection(Supplier).*" They refer to the `toCollection(Supplier<C>`
`collectionFactory)` method of the `Collectors` class.

The `Supplier<C>` notation describes a function that takes no parameters
and produces a value of type `C`, hence the name.

In many cases (if not most), we do not care which class (implementation of List or Set) is returned. That is exactly the beauty of coding to an interface. But if we do, here is an example of how to use the toCollection() method which, according to the previous recommendation, is a better option than toList() or toSet():

```
List<String> list3 = Stream.of(null, "s2", "s3")
                .collect(Collectors.toCollection(ArrayList::new));
System.out.println(list3);                //prints: [null, s2, s3]

Set<String> set3 = Stream.of(null, "s2", "s3")
                .collect(Collectors.toCollection(HashSet::new));
System.out.println(set3);                //prints: [null, s2, s3]
```

If it looks strange to you that we create a collection, then stream it and reproduce the same collection again, but bear in mind that in real-life programming, you might be getting the Stream object only, while we create a stream in order for the example to work and also to show you which values to expect.

In the case of Map, the following code is also mentioned in the documentation as having "*no guarantees on the type*":

```
Map<Integer, String> m = new HashMap<>();
m.put(1, null);
m.put(2, "s2");
Map<Integer, String> map2 = m.entrySet().stream()
    .map(e -> e.getValue() == null ? Map.entry(e.getKey(), "") : e)
    .collect(Collectors.toMap(Map.Entry::getKey, Map.Entry::getValue));
System.out.println(map2);      //prints: {1=, 2=s2}
```

Please note how we are handling null by replacing it with an empty String literal, "", so as to avoid the dreaded NullPointerException. And here is the code that, similar to the toCollection() method previously, produces a map with the implementation of our choice, the HashMap class in this case:

```
Map<Integer, String> map3 = m.entrySet().stream()
    .map(e -> e.getValue() == null ? Map.entry(e.getKey(), "") : e)
    .collect(Collectors.toMap(e -> e.getKey(), e -> e.getValue(),
                                    (k,v) -> v, HashMap::new));
System.out.println(map3);      //prints: {1=, 2=s2}
```

If the examples provided look too complex to you, you are correct; they are complex even for experienced programmers. And there are two reasons for that:

- Functional programming is a different way of writing code than the one used in Java for the first twenty years of its existence
- It was introduced in Java only recently and there are not many utility methods built around it to make the code look simpler

The good news is that after some time, you will get used to it, and streams and functional programming will start looking simple to you. There is even a good chance you will prefer it over the traditional object-oriented code because using functions and streams makes the code more compact and yet more powerful and cleaner, especially when a lot of data (big data) has to be processed efficiently, which seems to be the current trend, stretching far into the future.

We will talk more about this in Chapter 17, *Lambda Expressions and Functional Programming*; in Chapter 18, *Streams and Pipelines*; and in Chapter 19, *Reactive Systems*.

# Immutable collections

In everyday language, the adjectives *immutable* and *unmodifiable* are used interchangeably. But in the case of Java collections, an unmodifiable collection can be changed. Well, it also depends on what kind of meaning you give to the word *change*. Here is what we mean by this.

## Immutable versus unmodifiable

There are eight static methods in the Collections class that make a collection *unmodifiable*:

- Set<T>  unmodifiableSet(Set<? extends T> set)
- List<T>  unmodifiableList(List<? extends T> list)
- Map<K,V>  unmodifiableMap(Map<? extends K, ? extends V> map)
- Collection<T> unmodifiableCollection (Collection<? extends T> collection)
- SortedSet<T>  unmodifiableSortedSet(SortedSet<T> sortdedSet)
- SortedMap<K,V>  unmodifiableSortedMap(SortedMap<K,? extends V> sortedMap),

- NavigableSet<T> unmodifiableNavigableSet(NavigableSet<T> navigableSet)

- NavigableMap<K,V> unmodifiableNavigableMap(NavigableMap<K,? extends V> navigableMap)

Here is an example of code that creates an unmodifiable list:

```
List<String> list = Arrays.asList("s1", "s1");
System.out.println(list);          //prints: [s1, s1]

List<String> unmodfifiableList = Collections.unmodifiableList(list);
//unmodfifiableList.set(0, "s1"); //UnsupportedOperationException
//unmodfifiableList.add("s2");    //UnsupportedOperationException
```

As you have probably expected, we can neither change the value of an element nor add a new element to an unmodifiable list. Nevertheless, we can change the underlying list because we still hold the reference to it. And this change will be picked up by the unmodifiable list created earlier:

```
System.out.println(unmodfifiableList);      //prints: [s1, s1]
list.set(0, "s0");
//list.add("s2");           //UnsupportedOperationException
System.out.println(unmodfifiableList);      //prints: [s0, s1]
```

As you can see, by changing the original list, we have managed to change the value of the element in the unmodifiable list created earlier. And that is the weakness of this way of creating unmodifiable collections, because they are basically just wrappers around regular ones.

The of() collection of factory methods do not have this weakness because they do not have two-step collection creation as in the case of unmodifiable collections. That is why there is no way to change the collection created by the of factory method. It is not possible to change either the collection composition nor any of its elements. The collections created this way are called "immutable." That is the difference between *unmodifiable* and *immutable* in the world of Java collections.

# Immutable without methods of()

To be fair, there are ways to create an immutable collection even without using the `of()` factory methods. Here is one way to do it:

```
List<String> iList =
        Collections.unmodifiableList(new ArrayList<>() {{
            add("s1");
            add("s1");
        }});
//iList.set(0, "s0");         //UnsupportedOperationException
//iList.add("s2");            //UnsupportedOperationException
System.out.println(iList);    //prints: [s1, s1]
```

The trick is not to have a reference to the original collection (the source of values) used to create the unmodifiable collection, so it cannot be used to change the underlying source.

And here is another way to create an immutable collection without using the `of()` factory methods:

```
String[] source = {"s1", "s2"};
List<String> iList2 =
        Arrays.stream(source).collect(Collectors.toList());
System.out.println(iList2);         //prints: [s1, s2]

source[0]="s0";
System.out.println(iList2);         //prints: [s1, s2]
```

It looks as if we have here the `source` reference to the original values. But, the stream does not maintain the reference between the value and its source. It copies each value before processing them, thus breaking the value's connection with its source. That is why our attempt to change the element of `iList2` by changing an element of the `source` array did not succeed. We will talk more about streams in Chapter 18, *Streams and Pipelines*.

The need for immutable collections arises from an effort to protect the collection object from modification when it is passed as a parameter into a method. As we have mentioned already, such modification would be a side effect that may introduce unexpected and difficult-to-trace defects.

Please note that the `of()` factory methods without parameters create empty immutable collections. They also might be needed when you need to call a method that requires a collection as a parameter, but you do not have data for it and also do not want to give the method a chance to modify the passed-in collection.

There are also three constants in the `Collections` class that provide immutable empty collections:

```
List<String> list1 = Collections.EMPTY_LIST;
//list1.add("s1");          //UnsupportedOperationException
Set<String> set1 = Collections.EMPTY_SET;
Map<Integer, String> map1 = Collections.EMPTY_MAP;
```

In addition, there are seven methods in the `Collections` class that create immutable empty collections too:

```
List<String> list2 = Collections.emptyList();
//list2.add("s1");          //UnsupportedOperationException
Set<String> set2 = Collections.emptySet();
Map<Integer, String> map2 = Collections.emptyMap();

SortedSet<String> set3 = Collections.emptySortedSet();
Map<Integer, String> map3 = Collections.emptySortedMap();
NavigableSet<String> set4 = Collections.emptyNavigableSet();
NavigableMap<Integer, String> map4 = Collections.emptyNavigableMap();
```

And the following methods of the `Collections` class create immutable collections with one element only:

- `Set<T> singleton(T object)`
- `List<T> singletonList(T object)`
- `Map<K,V> singletonMap(K key, V value)`

You can see how it works in the following code snippet:

```
List<String> singletonS1 = Collections.singletonList("s1");
System.out.println(singletonS1);
//singletonS1.add("s1");          //UnsupportedOperationException
```

All of these can be done using the `of()` factory methods. We have described it just for you to have a complete picture of the options available for immutable collection creation.

But the `List<T> nCopies(int n, T object)` method of the `Collections` class creates an immutable list of n copies of the same object in a more compact manner than the `of()` method:

```
List<String> nList = Collections.nCopies(3, "s1");
System.out.println(nList);
//nList.add("s1");          //UnsupportedOperationException
```

Similar code that uses the `of()` method is more verbose:

```
List<String> nList = List.of("s1", "s1", "s1");
```

If that does not look too bad for you, imagine that you need to create a list of 100 of the same objects.

## Methods add() and put() confusion

There is one aspect of immutable collection use that is a source of occasional confusion. You have seen from our examples that the immutable collections, like any Java collection, have the `add()` or `put()` methods. The compiler does not generate an error, only JVM at runtime does so. So, code that uses immutable collections should be well tested to avoid this kind of error in production.

# java.util.Collections class

All methods of the `java.util.Collections` class are static and stateless. The latter means that they do not maintain any state anywhere, and that their results do not depend on the history of calls but only on the values passed in as parameters.

There are many methods in the `Collections` class and you have seen some of them already in the previous section. We encourage you to look up the online documentation of this class. Here, we have grouped some of them for your convenience, so you can have a better overview of the methods of the `Collections` class.

## Copy

The `void copy(List<T> dest, List<T> src)` method copies elements of the `src` list to the `dest` list and preserves the element order. This method is very useful in case you need to make one list a sublist of another list:

```
List<String> list1 = Arrays.asList("s1","s2");
List<String> list2 = Arrays.asList("s3", "s4", "s5");
Collections.copy(list2, list1);
System.out.println(list2);    //prints: [s1, s2, "s5"]
```

While doing this, the `copy()` method does not consume additional memory - it just copies the values over the already allocated memory. It makes this method helpful for cases where the traditional way of copying lists of equal sizes is not acceptable:

```
List<String> list1 = Arrays.asList("s1","s2");
List<String> list2 = Arrays.asList("s3", "s4");
list2 = new ArrayList(list1);
System.out.println(list2);    //prints: [s1, s2]
```

This code abandons the values originally assigned to `list2` and allocates new memory for `list2` to hold a copy of `list1` values. The abandoned values sit in the memory until the garbage collector removes them and allows the reuse of the memory. Imagine these lists are of a substantial size, and you can appreciate that using `Collections.copy()`, which in this case removes a lot of overhead. It also helps to avoid the `OutOfMemory` exception.

## Sort and equals()

The two static sorting methods of the `Collections` class are:

- `void sort(List<T> list)`
- `void sort(List<T> list, Comparator<T> comparator)`

The first `sort(List<T>)` method accepts only lists with elements that implement the `Comparable` interface, which requires implementation of the `compareTo(T)` method. The order established by the `compareTo(T)` method implemented by each element is called *natural ordering*.

The second `sort()` method does not require the list elements to implement any particular interface. It uses the passed-in object of the class `Comparator` to establish the required order using the `Comparator.compare(T o1, T o2)` method. If the elements of the list implement `Comparable`, then their method `compareTo(T)` is ignored and the order is established by the method `Comparator.compare(T o1, T o2)` only.

 The order defined by the `Comparator` object (the `compare(T o1, T o2)` method) overrides the natural order defined by the `Comparable` interface (the method `compareTo(T)`).

For example, here is how the class `String` implements the interface `Comparable`:

```
List<String> no = Arrays.asList("a","b", "Z", "10", "20", "1", "2");
Collections.sort(no);
System.out.println(no);      //prints: [1, 10, 2, 20, Z, a, b]
```

For many people, the fact that `10` is placed in front of `2` and a capital `Z` is placed in front of the lowercase `a` probably does not look *natural*, but this term is not based on human perception. It is based on how the objects are going to be sorted when no comparator is provided. In such cases, they are ordered based on the implemented method, `compareTo(T)`. This implemented method can be considered to be *built into* the elements. That is why such an ordering is called *natural*.

 A natural ordering is one defined by the implementation of the interface `Comparable` (the method `compareTo(T)`).

Although it looks somewhat unexpected for humans, the `String` implementation of the `compareTo(T)` method is very helpful in many ordering cases. For example, we can use it for the implementation of the `Comparable` interface in our class `Person`:

```
class Person implements Comparable<Person>{
    private String firstName = "", lastName = "";
    public Person(String firstName, String lastName) {
        this.firstName = firstName;
        this.lastName = lastName;
    }
    public String getFirstName() { return firstName; }
    public String getLastName() { return lastName; }
    @Override
    public int compareTo(Person person){
        int result = this.firstName.compareTo(person.firstName);
        if(result == 0) {
            return this.lastName.compareTo(person.lastName);
        }
        return result;
    }
}
```

We compare first names first, and if they are equal, compare last names. This means that we would like `Person` objects to be ordered by first name, then by last name.

The `String` implementation of the `compareTo(T)` method returns the difference between the ordering positions of the first (or this) and the second objects. For example, the difference between the ordering positions of a and c is 2, and here is the result of their comparison:

```
System.out.println("a".compareTo("c"));    //prints: -2
System.out.println("c".compareTo("a"));    //prints: 2
```

This makes sense: a is placed before c, so its position is smaller when we count it from left to right.

Notice, though, that the `Integer` implementation of `compareTo(T)` does not return the difference in the ordering position. Instead, it returns 0 when objects are equal, -1 when this object is smaller than the method parameter, and 1 otherwise:

```
System.out.println(Integer.valueOf(3)
                      .compareTo(Integer.valueOf(3))); //prints: 0
System.out.println(Integer.valueOf(3)
                      .compareTo(Integer.valueOf(4))); //prints: -1
System.out.println(Integer.valueOf(3)
                      .compareTo(Integer.valueOf(5))); //prints: -1
System.out.println(Integer.valueOf(5)
                      .compareTo(Integer.valueOf(4))); //prints: 1
System.out.println(Integer.valueOf(5)
                      .compareTo(Integer.valueOf(3))); //prints: 1
```

We get the same results using `Comparator` and its method `compare(T o1, T o2)`:

```
Comparator<String> compStr = Comparator.naturalOrder();
System.out.println(compStr.compare("a", "c"));   //prints: -2

Comparator<Integer> compInt = Comparator.naturalOrder();
System.out.println(compInt.compare(3, 5));       //prints: -1
```

But, beware that the documentation of the methods `Comparable.compareTo(T)` and `Compartor.compare(T o1, T o2)` defines only the following return:

- 0 when the objects are equal
- -1 when the first object is smaller than the second one
- 1 when the first object is bigger than the second one

In the case of String, smaller, and bigger are defined according to their ordering position—smaller is placed in front of bigger in the ordered list. As you can see, the API documentation does not guarantee that the difference in the ordering position is returned for all types of objects.

 It is important to make sure that the method equals() is aligned with the method Comparable.compareTo(T) so that for equal objects, the method Comparable.compareTo(T) returns 0. Otherwise, one may get unpredictable sorting results.

That is why we add the following method equals() to our class Person:

```
@Override
public boolean equals(Object other) {
    if (other == null) return false;
    if (this == other) return true;
    if (!(other instanceof Person)) return false;
    final Person that = (Person) other;
    return this.firstName.equals(that.getFirstName()) &&
            this.lastName.equals(that.getLastName());
}
```

Now the method equals() is aligned with the method compareTo(T), so that compareTo(T) returns 0 when used for equal Person objects:

```
Person joe1 = new Person("Joe", "Smith");
Person joe2 = new Person("Joe", "Smith");
Person bob = new Person("Bob", "Smith");

System.out.println(joe1.equals(joe2));     //prints: true
System.out.println(joe1.compareTo(joe2)); //prints: 0

System.out.println(joe1.equals(bob));      //prints: false
System.out.println(joe1.compareTo(bob));   //prints: 8
System.out.println(joe2.compareTo(bob));   //prints: 8
```

The value 8 is returned because that is the difference between the positions of B and J in alphabetical order.

We have also added the following toString() method to our class Person too:

```
@Override
public String toString(){
    return this.firstName + " " + this.lastName;
}
```

It will allow us to demonstrate ordering results better, and that is what we are going to do now. Here is the demo code:

```
Person p1 = new Person("Zoe", "Arnold");
Person p2 = new Person("Alex", "Green");
Person p3 = new Person("Maria", "Brown");
List<Person> list7 = Arrays.asList(p1, p2, p3);
System.out.println(list7);  //[Zoe Arnold, Alex Green, Maria Brown]
Collections.sort(list7);
System.out.println(list7);  //[Alex Green, Maria Brown, Zoe Arnold]
```

As you can see, the order of the elements after sorting (the last line of the previous example) matches the one defined in the `compareTo(T)` method.

Now, let's create a comparator that sorts objects of class `Person` differently:

```
class OrderByLastThenFirstName implements Comparator<Person> {
    @Override
    public int compare(Person p1, Person p2){
        return (p1.getLastName() + p1.getFirstName())
                .compareTo(p2.getLastName() + p2.getFirstName());
    }
}
```

As you can see, the preceding comparator establishes an order based on the natural order of the last names first, and then the natural order of the first names. If we use this comparator with the same list and objects, we will get the following results:

```
Collections.sort(list7, new OrderByLastThenFirstName());
System.out.println(list7);  //[Zoe Arnold, Maria Brown, Alex Green]
```

As was expected, the `compareTo(T)` method was ignored and the passed-in `Comparator` object's order was enforced.

# Reverse and rotate

There are three static reverse-related, and one rotate-related, methods in the class `Collections`:

- `void reverse(List<?> list)`: Reverses the current order of elements
- `void rotate(List<?> list, int distance)` : Rotates the order of the elements by moving each of them to the right for the specified number of positions (distance)

- `Comparator<T> reverseOrder()`: Returns a comparator that creates an order that is the reverse of the natural ordering; applies only to elements that implement the `Comparable` interface
- `Comparator<T> reverseOrder(Comparator<T> comparator)`: Returns a comparator that reverses the order defined by the passed-in comparator

And here is the code that demonstrates the listed methods:

```
Person p1 = new Person("Zoe", "Arnold");
Person p2 = new Person("Alex", "Green");
Person p3 = new Person("Maria", "Brown");
List<Person> list7 = Arrays.asList(p1,p2,p3);
System.out.println(list7);  //[Zoe Arnold, Alex Green, Maria Brown]

Collections.reverse(list7);
System.out.println(list7);  //[Maria Brown, Alex Green, Zoe Arnold]

Collections.rotate(list7, 1);
System.out.println(list7);  //[Zoe Arnold, Maria Brown, Alex Green]

Collections.sort(list7, Collections.reverseOrder());
System.out.println(list7);  //[Zoe Arnold, Maria Brown, Alex Green]

Collections.sort(list7, new OrderByLastThenFirstName());
System.out.println(list7);  //[Zoe Arnold, Maria Brown, Alex Green]

Collections.sort(list7,
        Collections.reverseOrder(new OrderByLastThenFirstName()));
System.out.println(list7);  //[Alex Green, Maria Brown, Zoe Arnold]
```

# Search and equals()

There are five static search-related methods in the class `Collections`:

- `int binarySearch(List<Comparable<T>> list, T key)`
- `int binarySearch(List<T> list, T key, Comparator<T> comparator)`
- `int indexOfSubList(List<?> source, List<?> target)`
- `int lastIndexOfSubList(List<?> source, List<?> target)`
- `int frequency(Collection<?> collection, Object object)`

The `binarySearch()` methods search for the `key` value in the provided list. The important thing to notice is that the provided list must be *sorted* in *ascending* order because of the nature of the binary search. The algorithm compares the key to the middle element of the list; if they are unequal, the half in which the key cannot belong is ignored and the algorithm compares the key to the middle element of the other half of the list. The search continues until the element equal to the key is found or only one element is left to search and it is not equal to the key.

The `indexOfSubList()` and `lastIndexOfSubList()` methods return the position of the provided sublist in the provided list:

```
List<String> list1 = List.of("s3","s5","s4","s1");
List<String> list2 = List.of("s4","s5");
int index = Collections.indexOfSubList(list1, list2);
System.out.println(index);   //prints: -1

List<String> list3 = List.of("s5","s4");
index = Collections.indexOfSubList(list1, list3);
System.out.println(index);    //prints: 1
```

Please notice that the sublist should be exactly in the same order. Otherwise, it will not be found.

And the last method, `frequency(Collection, Object)`, returns the number of times the provided object appears in the provided collection:

```
List<String> list4 = List.of("s3","s4","s4","s1");
int count = Collections.frequency(list4, "s4");
System.out.println(count);          //prints: 2
```

If you are going to use these methods (or any other methods that search collections for that matter) and if the collections include objects of custom classes, you have to have the method `equals()` implemented. A typical search algorithm uses the method `equals()` for the identification of the object. If you do not implement the method `equals()` in your custom class, the method `equals()` from the base class `Object` is going to be used, which compares only the object references, not their states (values of their fields). Here is a demonstration of this behavior:

```
class A{}
class B extends A{}

List<A> list5 = List.of(new A(), new B());
int c = Collections.frequency(list5, new A());
System.out.println(c);              //prints: 0
```

```
A a = new A();
List<A> list6 = List.of(a, new B());
c = Collections.frequency(list6, a);
System.out.println(c);          //prints: 1
```

As you can see, the object of class A is found only if it is literally the same object. But if we implement the method equals(), then the object of class A is found according to the criteria we have put in the method equals() implementation:

```
class A{
    @Override
    public boolean equals(Object o){
        if (o == null) return false;
        return (o instanceof A);
    }
}
class B extends A{}

List<A> list5 = List.of(new A(), new B());
int c = Collections.frequency(list5, new A());
System.out.println(c);          //prints: 2

A a = new A();
List<A> list6 = List.of(a, new B());
c = Collections.frequency(list6, a);
System.out.println(c);          //prints: 2
```

Now, the count of objects A in each case is 2 because B extends A and thus has two types, B and A.

If we prefer to identify the object by exactly the current class name and not include its parent class in the consideration, we should implement the method equals() differently:

```
class A{
    @Override
    public boolean equals(Object o){
        if (o == null) return false;
        return o.getClass().equals(this.getClass());
    }
}
class B extends A{}

List<A> list5 = List.of(new A(), new B());
int c = Collections.frequency(list5, new A());
System.out.println(c);          //prints: 1

A a = new A();
```

```
List<A> list6 = List.of(a, new B());
c = Collections.frequency(list6, a);
System.out.println(c);          //prints: 1
```

The method `getClass()` returns the class name used when the object was created by the operator `new`. That is why the count in both cases is now `1`.

For the rest of this chapter, we are going to assume that the method `equals()` is implemented in the elements of the collections and arrays. Most of the time, we are going to use objects of the class `String` in our example. As we have mentioned earlier in `Chapter 9`, *Operators, Expressions, and Statements*, the class `String` has an `equals()` method implementation based on the string literal value, not on object reference only. And, as we have explained in the previous subsection, the class `String` also implements the interface `Comparable` so that it provides natural ordering.

# Comparing two collections

There is one straightforward static method for comparing two collections in the class `Collections`:

`boolean disjoint(Collection<?> c1, Collection<?> c2)`: Returns `true` if none of the elements of one collection equal any element of another collection

As you probably guessed, this method uses the method `equals()` to identify equal elements.

# Min and max elements

The following `Collections` class methods can be used to select the *biggest* and the *smallest* element of the provided collection:

- `T min(Collection<? extends T> collection)`
- `T max(Collection<? extends T>collection)`
- `T min(Collection<? extends T>collection, Comparator<T> comparator)`
- `T max(Collection<? extends T>collection, Comparator<T> comparator)`

The first two methods require the collection elements to implement `Comparable` (the method `compareTo(T)`), while the other two methods use an object of the class `Comparator` to compare the elements.

The smallest element is the one that is first in the sorted list; the biggest is on the opposite end of the sorted list. Here is the demonstration code:

```
Person p1 = new Person("Zoe", "Arnold");
Person p2 = new Person("Alex", "Green");
Person p3 = new Person("Maria", "Brown");
List<Person> list7 = Arrays.asList(p1,p2,p3);
System.out.println(list7);  //[Zoe Arnold, Alex Green, Maria Brown]

System.out.println(Collections.min(list7)); //prints: Alex Green
System.out.println(Collections.max(list7)); //prints: Zoe Arnold

Person min = Collections.min(list7, new OrderByLastThenFirstName());
System.out.println(min);                        //[Zoe Arnold]

Person max = Collections.max(list7, new OrderByLastThenFirstName());
System.out.println(max);                        //[Alex Green]
```

The first two methods use natural ordering to establish the order, while the second two use the comparator passed in as a parameter.

# Add and replace elements

The following are three static methods of the class `Collections` that add or replace elements in a collection:

- `boolean addAll(Collection<T> c, T... elements)`: Adds all the provided elements to the provided collection; if the provided element is `Set`, only unique elements are added. It performs significantly faster than the `addAll()` method of the corresponding collection type.
- `boolean replaceAll(List<T> list, T oldVal, T newVal)`: Replaces every element in the provided list that is equal to `oldValue` with the `newValue`; when `oldValue` is `null`, the method replaces every `null` value in the provided list with the `newValue`. It returns `true` if at least one element was replaced.
- `void fill(List<T> list, T object)`: Replaces every element in the provided list with the provided object.

# Shuffle and swap elements

The following three static methods of the class `Collections` shuffle and swap elements of the provided list:

- `void shuffle(List<?> list)`: Uses the default source of randomness to shuffle the positions of the elements in the provided list
- `void shuffle(List<?> list, Random random)`: Uses the provided source of randomness (we will talk about such sources in a corresponding section later) to shuffle the positions of the elements in the provided list
- `void swap(List<?> list, int i, int j)` : Swaps the element at position i in the provided list with the element at position j

# Converting to a checked collection

The following nine static methods of the class `Collections` convert the provided collection from a raw type (one without generics) to a certain type of element. The name *checked* implies that after the transformation, the type of each newly added element will be checked:

- `Set<E> checkedSet(Set<E> s, Class<E> type)`
- `List<E> checkedList(List<E> list, Class<E> type)`
- `Queue<E> checkedQueue(Queue<E> queue, Class<E> type)`
- `Collection<E> checkedCollection(Collection<E> collection, Class<E> type)`
- `Map<K,V> checkedMap(Map<K,V> map, Class<K> keyType, Class<V> valueType)`
- `SortedSet<E> checkedSortedSet(SortedSet<E> set, Class<E> type)`
- `NavigableSet<E> checkedNavigableSet(NavigableSet<E> set, Class<E> type)`
- `SortedMap<K,V> checkedSortedMap(SortedMap<K,V> map, Class<K> keyType, Class<V> valueType)`
- `NavigableMap<K,V> checkedNavigableMap(NavigableMap<K,V> map, Class<K> keyType, Class<V> valueType)`

Here is the demonstration code:

```
List list = new ArrayList();
list.add("s1");
list.add("s2");
list.add(42);
System.out.println(list);    //prints: [s1, s2, 42]

List cList = Collections.checkedList(list, String.class);
System.out.println(list);    //prints: [s1, s2, 42]

list.add(42);
System.out.println(list);    //prints: [s1, s2, 42, 42]

//cList.add(42);             //throws ClassCastException
```

You can observe that conversion does not affect the current elements of the collection. We have added objects of the String class and an object of the Integer class to the same list and were able to convert it to a checked list cList without any problem. We can continue adding to the original list objects of different types, but the attempt to add a non-String object to the checked list generates ClassCastException at runtime.

# Convert to a thread-safe collection

There are eight static methods in the class Collections that convert a regular collection to a thread-safe one:

- Set<T> synchronizedSet(Set<T> set)
- List<T> synchronizedList(List<T> list)
- Map<K,V> synchronizedMap(Map<K,V> map)
- Collection<T> synchronizedCollection(Collection<T> collection)
- SortedSet<T> synchronizedSortedSet(SortedSet<T> set)
- SortedMap<K,V> synchronizedSortedMap(SortedMap<K,V> map)
- NavigableSet<T> synchronizedNavigableSet(NavigableSet<T> set)
- NavigableMap<K,V> synchronizedNavigableMap(NavigableMap<K,V> map)

A thread-safe collection is constructed so that two application threads can only modify it sequentially without stepping on each other's temporary results. But, multithreaded processing is outside the scope of this book, so we'll leave it at that.

# Convert to another collection type

The four static methods that convert one type of collection into another include:

- `ArrayList<T> list(Enumeration<T> e)`
- `Enumeration<T> enumeration(Collection<T> c)`
- `Queue<T> asLifoQueue(Deque<T> deque)`
- `Set<E> newSetFromMap(Map<E,Boolean> map)`

The interface `java.util.Enumeration` is a legacy interface that came with Java 1, along with the legacy classes `java.util.Hashtable` and `java.util.Vector` that use it. It is very similar to the `Iterator` interface. In fact, an `Enumeration` type object can be converted into an `Iterator` type by using the `Enumeration.asIterator()` method.

All these methods are rarely used in mainstream programming, so we are listing them here only for completeness.

# Create enumeration and iterator

The following are also not-often-used static methods that allow the creation of an empty `Enumeration`, `Iterator`, and `ListIterator` - all are interfaces of the `java.util` package:

- `Iterator<T> empty iterator()`
- `ListIterator<T> emptyListIterator()`
- `Enumeration<T> emptyEnumeration()`

# Class collections4.CollectionUtils

The class `org.apache.commons.collections4.CollectionUtils` in the Apache Commons project contains static stateless methods that compliment the methods of the class `java.util.Collections`. They help to search, process, and compare Java collections. To use this class, you would need to add the following dependency to the Maven configuration file `pom.xml`:

```
<dependency>
  <groupId>org.apache.commons</groupId>
  <artifactId>commons-collections4</artifactId>
  <version>4.1</version>
</dependency>
```

There are many methods in this class, and more methods will probably be added over time. The just-reviewed `Collections` class will probably cover most of your needs, especially when you are just entering the field of Java programming. So, we are not going to spend time on explaining the purpose of each method, as we have done for the `Collections` class. Besides, the methods of `CollectionUtils` are created in addition to the methods of `Collections`, so they are more complex and nuanced and do not fit the scope of this book.

To give you an idea of the methods available in the class `CollectionUtils`, we have grouped them by related functionality:

- Methods that retrieve an element:
    - `Object get(Object object, int index)`
    - `Map.Entry<K,V> get(Map<K,V> map, int index)`
    - `Map<O,Integer> getCardinalityMap(Iterable<O> collection)`
- Methods that add an element or a group of elements to a collection:
    - `boolean addAll(Collection<C> collection, C[] elements)`
    - `boolean addIgnoreNull(Collection<T> collection, T object)`
    - `boolean addAll(Collection<C> collection, Iterable<C> iterable)`
    - `boolean addAll(Collection<C> collection, Iterator<C> iterator)`
    - `boolean addAll(Collection<C> collection, Enumeration<C> enumeration)`
- Methods that merge `Iterable` elements:
    - `List<O> collate(Iterable<O> a, Iterable<O> b)`
    - `List<O> collate(Iterable<O> a, Iterable<O> b, Comparator<O> c)`
    - `List<O> collate(Iterable<O> a, Iterable<O> b, boolean includeDuplicates)`
    - `List<O> collate(Iterable<O> a, Iterable<O> b, Comparator<O> c, boolean includeDuplicates)`
- Methods that remove or retain elements with or without criteria:
    - `Collection<O> subtract(Iterable<O> a, Iterable<O> b)`
    - `Collection<O> subtract(Iterable<O> a, Iterable<O> b, Predicate<O> p)`

- Collection<E> removeAll(Collection<E> collection, Collection<?> remove)
- Collection<E> removeAll(Iterable<E> collection, Iterable<E> remove, Equator<E> equator)
- Collection<C> retainAll(Collection<C> collection, Collection<?> retain)
- Collection<E> retainAll(Iterable<E> collection, Iterable<E> retain, Equator<E> equator)

- Methods that compare two collections:
  - boolean containsAll(Collection<?> coll1, Collection<?> coll2)
  - boolean containsAny(Collection<?> coll1, Collection<?> coll2)
  - boolean isEqualCollection(Collection<?> a, Collection<?> b)
  - boolean isEqualCollection(Collection<E> a, Collection<E> b, Equator<E> equator)
  - boolean isProperSubCollection(Collection<?> a, Collection<?> b)

- Methods that transform a collection:
  - Collection<List<E>> permutations(Collection<E> collection)
  - void transform(Collection<C> collection, Transformer<C,C> transformer)
  - Collection<E> transformingCollection(Collection<E> collection, Transformer<E,E> transformer)
  - Collection<O> collect(Iterator<I> inputIterator, Transformer<I,O> transformer)
  - Collection<O> collect(Iterable<I> inputCollection, Transformer<I,O> transformer)
  - Collection<O> R collect(Iterator<I> inputIterator, Transformer<I,O> transformer, R outputCollection)
  - Collection<O> R collect(Iterable<I> inputCollection, Transformer<I,O> transformer, R outputCollection)

- Methods that select and filter a collection:
  - Collection<O> select(Iterable<O> inputCollection, Predicate<O> predicate)

- Collection<O> R select(Iterable<O> inputCollection, Predicate<O> predicate, R outputCollection)
- Collection<O> R select(Iterable<O> inputCollection, Predicate<O> predicate, R outputCollection, R rejectedCollection)
- Collection<O> selectRejected(Iterable<O> inputCollection, Predicate<O> predicate),
- Collection<O> R selectRejected(Iterable<O> inputCollection, Predicate<O> predicate, R outputCollection)
- E extractSingleton(Collection<E> collection)
- boolean filter(Iterable<T> collection, Predicate<T> predicate)
- boolean filterInverse(Iterable<T> collection, Predicate<T> predicate)
- Collection<C> predicatedCollection(Collection<C> collection, Predicate<C> predicate)

- Methods that generate a union, an intersection, or a difference of two collections:
  - Collection<O> union(Iterable<O> a, Iterable<O> b)
  - Collection<O> disjunction(Iterable<O> a, Iterable<O> b)
  - Collection<O> intersection(Iterable<O> a, Iterable<O> b)

- Methods that create an immutable empty collection:
  - <T> Collection<T> emptyCollection()
  - Collection<T> emptyIfNull(Collection<T> collection)

- Methods that check collection size and emptiness:
  - int size(Object object)
  - boolean sizeIsEmpty(Object object)
  - int maxSize(Collection<Object> coll)
  - boolean isEmpty(Collection<?> coll)
  - boolean isNotEmpty(Collection<?> coll)
  - boolean isFull(Collection<Object> coll)

- Method that reverses an array:
  - void reverseArray(Object[] array)

This last method should probably belong to the utility class that handles arrays, and that is what we are going to discuss now.

# Manage arrays

In this section, we will review how array objects can be created and initialized, and where you can find methods that allow us to perform some operations over arrays—copy, sort, and compare, for example.

Although arrays have their place in some algorithms and legacy code, in practice an `ArrayList()` can do everything an array can do and does not require setting the size upfront. In fact, an `ArrayList` is using an array to store its elements at the back. So, the performance of an array and `ArrayList` is comparable too.

So, we are not going to discuss array management too much beyond the basics of creation and initialization. We will provide a short overview and references on where to find the array utility methods in case you need them.

# Initialize arrays

We have seen already a few examples of array construction. Now, we are going to review them and present other ways to create and initialize array objects.

## Creation expression

An array creation expression includes:

- The array element type
- The number of levels of nested arrays
- The length of the array for at least the first of the levels

Here are one-level array creation examples:

```
int[] ints = new int[10];
System.out.println(ints[0]);      //prints: 0

Integer[] intW = new Integer[10];
System.out.println(intW[0]);      //prints: null

boolean[] bs = new boolean[10];
```

```
System.out.println(bs[0]);          //prints: false

Boolean[] bW = new Boolean[10];
System.out.println(bW[0]);          //prints: 0

String[] strings = new String[10];
System.out.println(strings[0]);     //prints: null

A[] as = new A[10];
System.out.println(as[0]);          //prints: null
System.out.println(as.length);      //prints: 10
```

As we have shown in Chapter 5, *Java Language Elements and Types*, every Java type has a default initialization value, used during object creation when no value is assigned explicitly. Because an array is a class, its elements are initialized—like the instance fields of any class - even if a programmer does not assign values to them explicitly. The numeral primitive types have a default value of 0, and the boolean primitive type false, while all reference types have the default value null. The class A used in the previous example is defined as class A {}. And the length of the array is captured in the final public property, length.

The multi-level nested initialization looks as follows:

```
//A[][] as2 = new A[][10];                //compilation error
A[][] as2 = new A[10][];
System.out.println(as2.length);           //prints: 10
System.out.println(as2[0]);               //prints: null
//System.out.println(as2[0].length);      //NullPointerException
//System.out.println(as2[0][0]);          //NullPointerException

as2 = new A[2][3];
System.out.println(as2[0]);        //prints: ManageArrays$A;@282ba1e
System.out.println(as2[0].length); //prints: 3
System.out.println(as2[0][0]);     //prints: null
```

The first thing to notice is that an attempt to create an array without defining the length of the first-level array generates a compilation error. The second observation is that the length property of the multi-level array captures the length of the array of the first (top) level. The third is that every element of the top-level array is an array. The elements of the next-level array are also arrays if that is not the last level.

In our previous example, we did not set the second-level array length, so each element of the top-level array was initialized to null because that is the default value of any reference type (and an array is a reference type too). That is why an attempt to get the length or any value of the second-level array generated NullPointerException.

As soon as we set the length of the second-level array to three, we were able to get its length and the value of its first element (null because that is the default value). The strange printout ManageArrays$A;@282ba1e is the array binary reference because the object array does not have a toString() method implemented. The closest you can get is a static method, toString(), of the utility class java.util.Arrays (see the next section). It returns a String representation of all array elements:

```
System.out.println(Arrays.toString(as2));
        //prints: [[ManageArrays$A;@282ba1e, [ManageArrays$A;@13b6d03]
System.out.println(Arrays.toString(as2[0])); //[null, null, null]
```

It works just fine for the last (the deepest) nested array, but still prints a binary reference for the higher-level arrays. If you want to print out all the elements of all the nested arrays, use the Arrays.deepToString(Object[]) method:

```
System.out.println(Arrays.deepToString(as2));
        //the above prints: [[null, null, null], [null, null, null]]
```

 Please note that if array elements do not implement the toString() method, then the binary reference will be printed for those elements that are not null.

# Array initializer

An array initializer consists of a comma-separated list of expressions, enclosed in braces { }. The comma after the last expression is allowed and ignored:

```
String[] arr = {"s0", "s1", };
System.out.println(Arrays.toString(arr)); //prints: [s0, s1]
```

We often use this way of initializing an array in our examples because it is the most compact way to do it.

# Static initialization block

As in the case of collections too, a static block can be used to initialize an array static property when some code has to be executed:

```
class ManageArrays {
private static A[] AS_STATIC;
  static {
    AS_STATIC = new A[2];
    for(int i = 0; i< AS_STATIC.length; i++){
        AS_STATIC[i] = new A();
```

```
    }
    AS_STATIC[0] = new A();
    AS_STATIC[1] = new A();
  }
  //... the rest of class code goes here
}
```

The code in the static block is executed every time a class is loaded, even before the constructor is called. But if the field is not static, the same initialization code can be placed in the constructor:

```
class ManageArrays {
  private A[] as;
  public ManageArrays(){
    as = new A[2];
    for(int i = 0; i< as.length; i++){
        as[i] = new A();
    }
    as[0] = new A();
    as[1] = new A();
  }
  //the reat of class code goes here
}
```

# From collection

If there is a collection that can be used as the source for the array values, it has the method `toArray()`, which can be called as follows:

```
List<Integer> list = List.of(0, 1, 2, 3);
Integer[] arr1 = list.toArray(new Integer[list.size()]);
System.out.println(Arrays.toString(arr1)); //prints: [0, 1, 2, 3]
```

# Other possible methods

In a different context, there may be some other methods used to create and initialize an array. It is also a matter of the style you prefer. Here are examples of the variety of array creation and initialization methods you can choose from:

```
String[] arr2 = new String[3];
Arrays.fill(arr2, "s");
System.out.println(Arrays.toString(arr2));        //prints: [s, s, s]

String[] arr3 = new String[5];
```

```
Arrays.fill(arr3, 2, 3, "s");
System.out.println(Arrays.toString(arr3));
                              //prints: [null, null, s, null, null]
String[] arr4 = {"s0", "s1", };
String[] arr4Copy = Arrays.copyOf(arr4, 5);
System.out.println(Arrays.toString(arr4Copy));
                              //prints: [s0, s1, null, null, null]
String[] arr5 = {"s0", "s1", "s2", "s3", "s4" };
String[] arr5Copy = Arrays.copyOfRange(arr5, 1, 3);
System.out.println(Arrays.toString(arr5Copy));    //prints: [s1, s2]

Integer[] arr6 = {0, 1, 2, 3, 4 };
Object[] arr6Copy = Arrays.copyOfRange(arr6,1, 3, Object[].class);
System.out.println(Arrays.toString(arr6Copy));       //prints: [1, 2]

String[] arr7 = Stream.of("s0", "s1", "s2").toArray(String[]::new);
System.out.println(Arrays.toString(arr7));    //prints: [s0, s1, s2]
```

Out of six examples above, five used the class `java.util.Arrays` (see the next section) to fill or copy an array. And all of them used the method `Arrays.toString()` to print elements of the resulting array.

The first example assigns to all the elements of an array `arr2` values `s`.

The second example assigns the value `s` only to the elements from index 2 to index 3. Notice that the second index is not inclusive. That's why only one element of an array `arr3` is assigned the value.

The third example copies the `arr4` array and makes the new array longer in size. That is why the rest of the new array elements are initialized to the default value of `String`, which is `null`. Notice that we have put a trailing comma in the `arr4` array initializer to demonstrate that it is allowed and ignored. It does not look like a very important feature. We have pointed it out just in case you see it in other people's code and wonder how it works.

The fourth example creates a copy of an array using its elements from index 1 to 3. Again, the second index is not included, so only two elements are copied.

The fifth example not only creates a copy of the range of the elements but also converts them to the `Object` type, which is possible because the source array is of reference type.

And the last example is using the `Stream` class, which we are going to discuss in `Chapter 18`, *Streams and Pipelines*.

# Class java.util.Arrays

We have used the class `java.util.Arrays` already several times. It is the primary tool for array management. But, it used to be very popular with those who use collections too because the method `asList(T...a)` was the most compact way of creating and initializing a collection:

```
List<String> list = Arrays.asList("s0", "s1");
Set<String> set = new HashSet<>(Arrays.asList("s0", "s1");
```

But after a factory method, `of()`, was introduced in each of the collections, the popularity of the `Arrays` class dropped substantially. The following is a more natural way to create a collection:

```
List<String> list = List.of("s0", "s1");
Set<String> set = Set.of("s0", "s1");
```

This collection's objects are immutable. But if a mutable one is needed, it can be created as follows:

```
List<String> list = new ArrayList<>(List.of("s0", "s1"));
Set<String> set1 = new HashSet<>(list);
Set<String> set2 = new HashSet<>(Set.of("s0", "s1"));
```

We talked about this in great detail in the *Manage collections* section previously.

But if your code manages arrays, then you definitely need to use the class `Arrays`. It contains more than 160 methods. Most of them are overloaded with different parameters and array types. If we group them by method name, there will be 21 groups. And if we group them further by functionality, only the following 10 groups will cover all the `Arrays` class's functionalities:

- `asList()`: Creates an `ArrayList` object based on the provided array (see examples in the previous section)
- `binarySearch()`: Allows the searching of an array or just a part of it specified (by the range of indices)
- `compare()`, `mismatch()`, `equals()`, and `deepEquals()`: Compare two arrays or their parts (by the range of indices)
- `copyOf()` and `copyOfRange()`: Copy all arrays or just a part of them (by the range of indices)

- `hashcode()` and `deepHashCode()`: Generate a hash code value based on the provided array content
- `toString()` and `deepToString()`: Create a `String` representation of an array (see examples in the previous section)
- `fill()`, `setAll()`, `parallelPrefix()`, and `parallelSetAll()`: Set the value (fixed or generated by the provided function) of every element of an array or those specified by the range of indices
- `sort()` and `parallelSort()`: Sort elements of an array or only part of it (specified by the range of indices)
- `splititerator()`: Returns a `Splititerator` object for parallel processing of an array or part of it (specified by the range of indices)
- `stream()`: Generates a stream of array elements or some of them (specified by the range of indices); see `Chapter 18`, *Streams and pipelines*

All of these methods are helpful, but we would like to attract your attention to the `equals(a1, a2)` and `deepEquals(a1, a2)` methods. They are particularly helpful for array comparison because an array object does not allow to implement a custom method `equals(a)` and thus always uses the implementation of the class `Object` that compares only references.

By contrast, both `equals(a1, a2)` and `deepEquals(a1, a2)` methods compare not just references `a1` and `a2`, but, in the case of arrays, use the method `equals(a)` to compare elements. This means that non-nested arrays are compared by values of their elements and considered equal when either both arrays are `null` or they have equal length and the method `a1[i].equals(a2[i])` returns `true` for each index:

```
Integer[] as1 = {1,2,3};
Integer[] as2 = {1,2,3};
System.out.println(as1.equals(as2));              //prints: false
System.out.println(Arrays.equals(as1, as2));      //prints: true
System.out.println(Arrays.deepEquals(as1, as2));  //prints: true
```

As for nested arrays, the `equals(a1, a2)` method uses the method `equals(a)` to compare elements of the next level. But the elements of the nested array are arrays, so they are compared by reference only, not by the value of their elements. If you need to compare values of the elements on all nested levels, use the method `deepEquals(a1, a2)`:

```
Integer[][] aas1 = {{1,2,3}, {4,5,6}};
Integer[][] aas2 = {{1,2,3}, {4,5,6}};
System.out.println(Arrays.equals(aas1, aas2));      //prints: false
System.out.println(Arrays.deepEquals(aas1, aas2));  //prints: true
```

```
Integer[][][] aaas1 = {{{1,2,3}, {4,5,6}}, {{7,8,9}, {10,11,12}}};
Integer[][][] aaas2 = {{{1,2,3}, {4,5,6}}, {{7,8,9}, {10,11,12}}};
System.out.println(Arrays.deepEquals(aaas1, aaas2)); //prints: true
```

# Class lang3.ArrayUtils

The class `org.apache.commons.lang3.ArrayUtils` is a compliment to the class `java.util.Arrays`. It adds new methods to the array managing toolkit and the ability to handle `null` in cases when otherwise `NullPointerException` could be thrown.

Similarly to the`Arrays` class, the `ArrayUtils` class has many (around 300) overloaded methods that can be collected into 12 groups:

- `add()`, `addAll()`, and `insert()`: Add elements to an array
- `clone()`: Clones an array, similar to the method `copyOf()` in `java.util.Arrays` and the method `arraycopy()` of `java.lang.System`
- `getLength()`: Returns an array length and handles `null` (while the attempt to read the property `length` when an array is `null` throws `NullPointerException`)
- `hashCode()`: Calculates the hash value of an array, including nested arrays
- `contains()`, `indexOf()`, and `lastIndexOf()`: Search an array
- `isSorted()`, `isEmpty`, and `isNotEmpty()`: Check an array and handle `null`
- `isSameLength()` and `isSameType()`: Compare arrays
- `nullToEmpty()`: Converts a `null` array to an empty one
- `remove()`, `removeAll()`, `removeElement()`, `removeElements()`, and `removeAllOccurances()`: Remove elements
- `reverse()`, `shift()`, `shuffle()`, and `swap()`: Change the order of array elements
- `subarray()`: Extracts part of an array by the range of indices
- `toMap()`, `toObject()`, `toPrimitive()`, `toString()`, and `toStringArray()`: Convert an array to another type and handle `null` values

# Exercise – Sort list of objects

Name two methods that allow sorting a list of objects, and the prerequisites for their use.

## Answer

Two static methods of the class `java.util.Collections`:

- `void sort(List<T> list)`: Sorts a list of objects that implement the interface `Comparable` (the `compareTo(T)` method),
- `void sort(List<T> list, Comparator<T> comparator)`: Sorts objects according to the `Comparator` provided (the `compare(T o1, T o2)` method)

## Summary

In this chapter, we introduced the reader to the classes from the Java Standard Library and Apache Commons that allow the manipulating of collections and arrays. Every Java programmer has to know the capabilities of the classes `java.util.Collections`, `java.util.Arrays`, `org.acpache.commons.collections4.CollectionUtils`, and `org.acpache.commons.lang3.ArrayUtils`.

In the next chapter, we are going to discuss classes that, together with classes discussed in this chapter, belong to a group of the most popular utilities that every programmer has to master in order to become an effective coder.

# 15
# Managing Objects, Strings, Time, and Random Numbers

The classes that we will be discussing in this chapter, belong—together with Java collections and arrays discussed in the previous chapters—to the group of classes (mostly utilities from the Java Standard Library and Apache Commons) that every programmer has to master in order to become an effective coder. They also illustrate various software designs and solutions that are instructive and can be used as patterns for best coding practices.

We will cover the following areas of functionality:

- Managing objects
- Managing strings
- Managing time
- Manage random numbers

The list of the overviewed classes includes:

- `java.util.Objects`
- `org.apache.commons.lang3.ObjectUtils`
- `java.lang.String`
- `org.apache.commons.lang3.StringUtils`
- `java.time.LocalDate`
- `java.time.LocalTime`
- `java.time.LocalDateTime`
- `java.lang.Math`
- `java.util.Random`

# Managing objects

You may not need to manage arrays and may even not need to manage collections (for some time, at least), but you cannot avoid managing objects, which means that the classes described in this section you are probably going to use every day.

Although the `java.util.Objects` class was added to the Java Standard Libraries in 2011 (with the Java 7 release), while the `ObjectUtils` class has existed in the Apache Commons libraries since 2002, their use grew slowly. This may be partially explained by the small number of methods they had originally—only six in `ObjectUtils` in 2003 and only nine in `Objects` in 2011. However, they were very helpful methods that could make the code more readable and robust—less prone to errors. So, why these classes were not used more often from the very beginning remains a mystery. We hope that you start using them immediately with your very first project.

# Class java.util.Objects

The class `Objects` has only 17 methods—all static. We have already used some of them in the previous chapter when we implemented the class `Person`:

```
class Person implements Comparable<Person> {
    private int age;
    private String name;
    public Person(int age, String name) {
        this.age = age;
        this.name = name == null ? "" : name;
    }
    public int getAge(){ return this.age; }
    public String getName(){ return this.name; }
    @Override
    public int compareTo(Person p){
        int result = this.name.compareTo(p.getName());
        if (result != 0) {
            return result;
        }
        return this.age - p.getAge();
    }
    @Override
    public boolean equals(Object o) {
        if (this == o) return true;
        if (o == null) return false;
        if(!(o instanceof Person)) return false;
        Person person = (Person)o;
```

```
            return age == person.getAge() &&
                Objects.equals(name, person.getName()); //line 25
    }
    @Override
    public int hashCode(){
        return Objects.hash(age, name);
    }
    @Override
    public String toString() {
        return "Person{age=" + age + ", name=" + name + "}";
    }
}
```

We used the class `Objects` in the methods `equals()` and `hashCode()` previously. Everything worked fine. But, notice how we check the parameter `name` in the preceding constructor. If the parameter is `null`, we assign to the field `name` an empty `String` value. We did it to avoid `NullPointerException` in line 25. Another way to do it is to use the class `ObjectUtils` from the Apache Commons library. We will demonstrate it in the next section. Methods of the class `ObjectUtils` handle `null` values and make the conversion of a `null` parameter to an empty `String` unnecessary.

But first, let's review the methods of the class `Objects`.

# equals() and deepEquals()

We talked about the `equals()` method implementation extensively, but always assumed that it was invoked on a non-`null` object, `obj`, so the call `obj.equals(anotherObject)` could not generate `NullPointerException`.

Yet, sometimes we need to compare two objects, a and b, when one or both of them can be `null`. Here is typical code for such a case:

```
boolean equals(Object a, Object b) {
    return (a == b) || (a != null && a.equals(b));
}
```

This is the actual source code of the `boolean Objects.equals(Object a, Object b)` method. It allows comparing two objects using the method `equals(Object)` and handles cases where one or both of them are `null`.

Another related method of the class `Objects` is `boolean deepEquals(Object a, Object b)`. Here is its source code:

```
boolean deepEquals(Object a, Object b) {
    if (a == b)
        return true;
    else if (a == null || b == null)
        return false;
    else
        return Arrays.deepEquals0(a, b);
}
```

As you can see, it is based on `Arrays.deepEquals()`, which we discussed in the previous section. The demonstration code for these methods helps to understand the difference:

```
Integer[] as1 = {1,2,3};
Integer[] as2 = {1,2,3};
System.out.println(Arrays.equals(as1, as2));        //prints: true
System.out.println(Arrays.deepEquals(as1, as2));    //prints: true

System.out.println(Objects.equals(as1, as2));       //prints: false
System.out.println(Objects.deepEquals(as1, as2));   //prints: true

Integer[][] aas1 = {{1,2,3},{1,2,3}};
Integer[][] aas2 = {{1,2,3},{1,2,3}};
System.out.println(Arrays.equals(aas1, aas2));       //prints: false
System.out.println(Arrays.deepEquals(aas1, aas2));   //prints: true

System.out.println(Objects.equals(aas1, aas2));      //prints: false
System.out.println(Objects.deepEquals(aas1, aas2));  //prints: true
```

In the preceding code, `Objects.equals(as1, as2)` and `Objects.equals(aas1, aas2)` return `false` because arrays cannot override the method `equals()` of the class `Object` and are compared by references, not by value.

The method `Arrays.equals(aas1, aas2)` returns `false` for the same reason: because the elements of the nested array are arrays and are compared by references.

To summarize, if you would like to compare two objects, a and b, by the values of their fields, then:

- If they are not arrays and a is not `null`, use `a.equals(b)`
- If they are not arrays and both objects can be `null`, use `Objects.equals(a, b)`
- If both can be arrays and both can be `null`, use `Objects.deepEquals(a, b)`

That said, we can see that the method `Objects.deepEquals()` is the safest one, but it does not mean you must always use it. Most of the time, you will know whether the compared objects can be `null` or can be arrays, so you can safely use other `equals()` methods too.

# hash() and hashCode()

The hash values returned by the methods `hash()` or `hashCode()` are typically used as a key for storing the object in a hash-using collection, such as `HashSet()`. The default implementation in the `Object` superclass is based on the object reference in memory. It returns different hash values for two objects of the same class with the same values of the instance fields. That is why, if you need two class instances to have the same hash value for the same state, it is important to override the default `hashCode()` implementation using one of these methods:

- `int hashCode(Object value)`: calculates a hash value for a single object
- `int hash(Object... values)`: calculates a hash value for an array of objects (see how we used it in the class `Person` in our previous example)

Please notice that these two methods return different hash values for the same object when it is used as a single-element input array of the method `Objects.hash()`:

```
System.out.println(Objects.hash("s1"));        //prints: 3645
System.out.println(Objects.hashCode("s1"));    //prints: 3614
```

The only value that yields the same hash from both methods is `null`:

```
System.out.println(Objects.hash(null));        //prints: 0
System.out.println(Objects.hashCode(null));  //prints: 0
```

When used as a single not-null parameter, the same value has different hash values returned from the methods `Objects.hashCode(Object value)` and `Objects.hash(Object... values)`. The value `null` yields the same hash value, 0, returned from each of these methods.

Another advantage of using the class `Objects` for hash value calculation is that it tolerates `null` values, while the attempt to call the instance method `hashCode()` on the `null` reference generates `NullPointerException`.

# isNull() and nonNull()

These two methods are just thin wrappers around Boolean expressions, `obj == null` and `obj != null`:

- `boolean isNull(Object obj)`: returns the same value as `obj == null`
- `boolean nonNull(Object obj)`: returns the same value as `obj != null`

And here is the demo code:

```
String object = null;

System.out.println(object == null);            //prints: true
System.out.println(Objects.isNull(object));    //prints: true

System.out.println(object != null);            //prints: false
System.out.println(Objects.nonNull(object));   //prints: false
```

# requireNonNull()

The following methods of the class `Objects` check the value of the first parameter and, if the value is `null`, either throw `NullPointerException` or return the provided default value:

- `T requireNonNull(T obj)`: Throws `NullPointerException` without a message if the parameter is `null`:

```
String object = null;
try {
    Objects.requireNonNull(object);
} catch (NullPointerException ex){
    System.out.println(ex.getMessage());   //prints: null
}
```

- `T requireNonNull(T obj, String message)`: Throws `NullPointerException` with the message provided if the first parameter is `null`:

```
String object = null;
try {
    Objects.requireNonNull(object, "Parameter 'object' is null");
} catch (NullPointerException ex){
    System.out.println(ex.getMessage());
    //Parameter 'object' is null
```

```
    }
```

- T requireNonNull(T obj,
  Supplier<String> messageSupplier): returns the message generated by the
  provided function if the first parameter is null or, if the generated message or
  the function itself is null, throws NullPointerException:

```
String object = null;
Supplier<String> msg1 = () -> {
    String msg = "Msg from db";
    //get the corresponding message from database
    return msg;
};
try {
    Objects.requireNonNull(object, msg1);
} catch (NullPointerException ex){
    System.out.println(ex.getMessage());  //prints: Msg from db
}
Supplier<String> msg2 = () -> null;
try {
    Objects.requireNonNull(object, msg2);
} catch (NullPointerException ex){
    System.out.println(ex.getMessage());  //prints: null
}
Supplier<String> msg3 = null;
try {
    Objects.requireNonNull(object, msg3);
} catch (NullPointerException ex){
    System.out.println(ex.getMessage());  //prints: null
}
```

- T requireNonNullElse(T obj, T defaultObj): returns the first parameter
  value if it is non-null, or the second parameter value if it is non-null, or
  throws NullPointerException with the message defaultObj:

```
String object = null;
System.out.println(Objects.requireNonNullElse(object,
                        "Default value"));
                        //prints: Default value
try {
    Objects.requireNonNullElse(object, null);
} catch (NullPointerException ex){
    System.out.println(ex.getMessage());     //prints: defaultObj
}
```

- `T requireNonNullElseGet(T obj, Supplier<? extends T>` `supplier)`: returns the first parameter value if it is non-null, or the object produced by the provided function if it is non-null, or throws `NullPointerException` with the message `defaultObj`:

```
String object = null;
Supplier<String> msg1 = () -> {
    String msg = "Msg from db";
    //get the corresponding message from database
    return msg;
};
String s = Objects.requireNonNullElseGet(object, msg1);
System.out.println(s);                    //prints: Msg from db

Supplier<String> msg2 = () -> null;
try {
 System.out.println(Objects.requireNonNullElseGet(object, msg2));
} catch (NullPointerException ex){
 System.out.println(ex.getMessage()); //prints: supplier.get()
}
try {
 System.out.println(Objects.requireNonNullElseGet(object, null));
} catch (NullPointerException ex){
 System.out.println(ex.getMessage()); //prints: supplier
}
```

# checkIndex()

The following group of methods checks whether the index and the length of a collection or an array are compatible:

- `int checkIndex(int index, int` `length)`: throws `IndexOutOfBoundsException` if the provided `index` is bigger than `length - 1`
- `int checkFromIndexSize(int fromIndex, int size, int length)`: throws `IndexOutOfBoundsException` if the provided `index + size` is bigger than `length - 1`
- `int checkFromToIndex(int fromIndex, int toIndex, int length)`: throws `IndexOutOfBoundsException` if the provided `fromIndex` is bigger than `toIndex`, or `toIndex` is bigger than `length - 1`

Here is the demo code:

```
List<String> list = List.of("s0", "s1");
try {
    Objects.checkIndex(3, list.size());
} catch (IndexOutOfBoundsException ex){
    System.out.println(ex.getMessage());
                        //prints: Index 3 out-of-bounds for length 2
}
try {
    Objects.checkFromIndexSize(1, 3, list.size());
} catch (IndexOutOfBoundsException ex){
    System.out.println(ex.getMessage());
                //prints: Range [1, 1 + 3) out-of-bounds for length 2
}

try {
    Objects.checkFromToIndex(1, 3, list.size());
} catch (IndexOutOfBoundsException ex){
    System.out.println(ex.getMessage());
                    //prints: Range [1, 3) out-of-bounds for length 2
}
```

# compare()

The method `int compare(T a, T b, Comparator<T> c)` of the class `Objects` uses the provided comparator's method `compare(T o1, T o2)` for comparing the two objects. We have described already the behavior of the `compare(T o1, T o2)` method while talking about sorting collections, so the following results should be expected:

```
int diff = Objects.compare("a", "c", Comparator.naturalOrder());
System.out.println(diff);   //prints: -2
diff = Objects.compare("a", "c", Comparator.reverseOrder());
System.out.println(diff);   //prints: 2
diff = Objects.compare(3, 5, Comparator.naturalOrder());
System.out.println(diff);   //prints: -1
diff = Objects.compare(3, 5, Comparator.reverseOrder());
System.out.println(diff);   //prints: 1
```

As we have mentioned already, the method `compare(T o1, T o2)` returns the difference of positions of objects `o1` and `o2` in a sorted list for `String` objects and just −1, 0, or 1 for `Integer` objects. The API describes it as returning 0 when objects are equal and a negative number when the first object is smaller than the second; otherwise, it returns a positive number.

To demonstrate how the method `compare(T a, T b, Comparator<T> c)` works, let's assume that we want to sort objects of the class `Person` so that the name and age are arranged in a natural order of `String` and `Integer` classes, respectively:

```
@Override
public int compareTo(Person p){
    int result = Objects.compare(this.name, p.getName(),
                                    Comparator.naturalOrder());
    if (result != 0) {
        return result;
    }
    return Objects.compare(this.age, p.getAge(),
                                    Comparator.naturalOrder());
}
```

And here is the result of this new implementation of the `compareTo(Object)` method of the class `Person`:

```
Person p1 = new Person(15, "Zoe");
Person p2 = new Person(45, "Adam");
Person p3 = new Person(37, "Bob");
Person p4 = new Person(30, "Bob");
List<Person> list = new ArrayList<>(List.of(p1, p2, p3, p4));
System.out.println(list);//[{15, Zoe}, {45, Adam}, {37, Bob}, {30, Bob}]
Collections.sort(list);
System.out.println(list);//[{45, Adam}, {30, Bob}, {37, Bob}, {15, Zoe}]
```

As you can see, the `Person` objects are ordered by name in their natural order first, then by age in their natural order too. If we need to reverse the order of names, for example, we change the `compareTo(Object)` method to the following:

```
@Override
public int compareTo(Person p){
    int result = Objects.compare(this.name, p.getName(),
                                    Comparator.reverseOrder());
    if (result != 0) {
        return result;
    }
    return Objects.compare(this.age, p.getAge(),
                                    Comparator.naturalOrder());
}
```

The results looks as like we expected:

```
Person p1 = new Person(15, "Zoe");
Person p2 = new Person(45, "Adam");
Person p3 = new Person(37, "Bob");
```

```
Person p4 = new Person(30, "Bob");
List<Person> list = new ArrayList<>(List.of(p1, p2, p3, p4));
System.out.println(list);//[{15, Zoe}, {45, Adam}, {37, Bob}, {30, Bob}]
Collections.sort(list);
System.out.println(list);//[{15, Zoe}, {30, Bob}, {37, Bob}, {45, Adam}]
```

The weakness of the method `compare(T a, T b, Comparator<T> c)` is that it does not handle `null` values. Adding the `new Person(25, null)` object to the list triggers `NullPointerException` during sorting. In such cases, it is better to use the `org.apache.commons.lang3.ObjectUtils.compare(T o1, T o2)` method, which we are going to demonstrate in the next section.

# toString()

There are cases when you need to convert an `object` (which is a reference to some class type) to its `String` representation. When the reference `obj` is assigned a `null` value (the object is not created yet), writing `obj.toString()` generates `NullPointerException`. For such cases, using the following methods of the class `Objects` is a better choice:

- `String toString(Object o)`: returns the result of calling `toString()` on the first parameter when it is not `null` and `null` when the first parameter value is `null`
- `String toString(Object o, String nullDefault)`: returns the result of calling `toString()` on the first parameter when it is not `null` and the second parameter value `nullDefault` when the first parameter value is `null`

Here is the code that demonstrates how to use these methods:

```
List<String> list = new ArrayList<>(List.of("s0 "));
list.add(null);
for(String e: list){
    System.out.print(e);                        //prints: s0 null
}
System.out.println();
for(String e: list){
    System.out.print(Objects.toString(e)); //prints: s0 null
}
System.out.println();
for(String e: list){
    System.out.print(Objects.toString(e, "element was null"));
                                        //prints: s0 element was null
}
```

By the way, unrelated to the current discussion, please notice how we used the method `print()` instead of `println()` to show all the results in one line, because the method `print()` does not add an end-of-line symbol.

# Class lang3.ObjectUtils

The class `org.apache.commons.lang3.ObjectUtils` of the Apache Commons library complements the methods of the class `java.util.Objects` described previously. The scope of this book and the allocated size does not allow for a detailed review of all the methods of the class `ObjectUtils`, so we will describe them briefly, grouped by related functionality, and will demonstrate only those that are aligned with the examples we have provided already.

All the methods of the class `ObjectUtils` can be organized into seven groups:

- Object cloning methods:
    - `T clone(T obj)`: returns a copy of the provided object if it implements the interface `Cloneable`; otherwise, returns `null`.
    - `T cloneIfPossible(T obj)`: returns a copy of the provided object if it implements the interface `Cloneable`; otherwise, returns the original provided object.
- Methods that support object comparison:
    - `int compare(T c1, T c2)`: compares newly ordered positions of the two objects that implement the interface `Comparable`; allows any or both parameters to be `null`; places a `null` value in front of a non-null value.
    - `int compare(T c1, T c2, boolean nullGreater)`: behaves exactly as the previous method if the value of parameter `nullGreater` is `false`; otherwise, places a `null` value behind a non-null value. We can demonstrate the last two methods by using them in our class `Person`:

```
@Override
public int compareTo(Person p){
    int result = ObjectUtils.compare(this.name,
p.getName());
    if (result != 0) {
        return result;
    }
    return ObjectUtils.compare(this.age, p.getAge());
```

```
        }
```

The result of this change allows us to use a `null` value for the `name` field:

```
Person p1 = new Person(15, "Zoe");
Person p2 = new Person(45, "Adam");
Person p3 = new Person(37, "Bob");
Person p4 = new Person(30, "Bob");
Person p5 = new Person(25, null);
List<Person> list = new ArrayList<>(List.of(p1, p2,
p3, p4, p5));
System.out.println(list);  //[{15, Zoe}, {45, Adam},
{37, Bob}, {30, Bob}, {25, }]
Collections.sort(list);
System.out.println(list);  //[{25, }, {45, Adam}, {30,
Bob}, {37, Bob}, {15, Zoe}]
```

Since we have used the method `Objects.compare(T c1, T c2)`, the `null` value was placed in front of non-null values. By the way, have you noticed that we do not display `null` anymore? That is because we have changed the method `toString()` of the class `Person` as follows:

```
@Override
public String toString() {
    //return "{" + age + ", " + name + "}";
    return "{" + age + ", " + Objects.toString(name,
"") + "}";
}
```

Instead of just displaying the value of the field `name`, we used the method `Objects.toString(Object o, String nullDefault)`, which substitutes the object with the provided `nullDefault` value when the object is `null`. As to whether to use this method, in this case, is a matter of style. Many programmers would probably argue that we must display the actual value without substituting it for something else. But, we have done it just to show how the method `Objects.toString(Object o, String nullDefault)` could be used.

If we now use the second `compare(T c1, T c2, boolean nullGreater)` method, the `compareTo()` method of the class `Person` will look as follows:

```
@Override
public int compareTo(Person p){
    int result = ObjectUtils.compare(this.name,
p.getName(), true);
    if (result != 0) {
        return result;
    }
    return ObjectUtils.compare(this.age, p.getAge());
}
```

Then, `Person` objects with their `name` set to `null` will be shown at the end of the sorted list:

```
Person p1 = new Person(15, "Zoe");
Person p2 = new Person(45, "Adam");
Person p3 = new Person(37, "Bob");
Person p4 = new Person(30, "Bob");
Person p5 = new Person(25, null);
List<Person> list = new ArrayList<>(List.of(p1, p2,
p3, p4, p5));
System.out.println(list);
                //[{15, Zoe}, {45, Adam}, {37, Bob},
{30, Bob}, {25, }]
Collections.sort(list);
System.out.println(list);
                //[{45, Adam}, {30, Bob}, {37, Bob},
{15, Zoe}, {25, }]
```

And, to complete the discussion of `null` values, the preceding code will break with `NullPointerException` when a `null` object is added to the list: `list.add(null)`. To avoid the exception, you can use a special `Comparator` object that handles the `null` elements of a list:

```
Person p1 = new Person(15, "Zoe");
Person p2 = new Person(45, "Adam");
Person p3 = new Person(37, "Bob");
Person p4 = new Person(30, "Bob");
Person p5 = new Person(25, null);
List<Person> list = new ArrayList<>(List.of(p1, p2,
p3, p4, p5));
list.add(null);
```

```
System.out.println(list);
        //[{15, Zoe}, {45, Adam}, {37, Bob}, {30,
Bob}, {25, }, null]
Collections.sort(list,
Comparator.nullsLast(Comparator.naturalOrder()));
System.out.println(list);
        //[{45, Adam}, {30, Bob}, {37, Bob}, {15,
Zoe}, {25, }, null]
```

In this code, you can see how we have indicated the desire to see the `null` objects at the end of the list. Instead, we could use another `Comparator` that places null objects at the beginning of the sorted list:

```
Collections.sort(list,
Comparator.nullsFirst(Comparator.naturalOrder()));
System.out.println(list);
        //[null, {45, Adam}, {30, Bob}, {37, Bob},
{15, Zoe}, {25, }]
```

- `notEqual`:
  - `boolean notEqual(Object object1, Object object2)`: compares two objects for inequality, where either one or both objects may be `null`

- `identityToString`:
  - `String identityToString(Object object)`: returns the `String` representation of the provided object as if produced by the default method `toString()` of the base class `Object`
  - `void identityToString(StringBuffer buffer, Object object)`: appends the `String` representation of the provided object as if produced by the default method `toString()` of the base class `Object`
  - `void identityToString(StringBuilder builder, Object object)`: appends the `String` representation of the provided object as if produced by the default method `toString()` of the base class `Object`
  - `void identityToString(Appendable appendable, Object object)`: appends the `String` representation of the provided object as if produced by the default method `toString()` of the base class `Object`

The following code demonstrates two of these methods:

```
String s = "s0 " + ObjectUtils.identityToString("s1");
System.out.println(s);   //prints: s0
java.lang.String@5474c6c

StringBuffer sb = new StringBuffer();
sb.append("s0");
ObjectUtils.identityToString(sb, "s1");
System.out.println(s);   //prints: s0
java.lang.String@5474c6c
```

- `allNotNull` and `anyNotNull`:
    - `boolean allNotNull(Object... values)`: returns `true` when all values in the provided array are not `null`
    - `boolean anyNotNull(Object... values)`: returns `true` when at least one value in the provided array is not `null`
- `firstNonNull` and `defaultIfNull`:
    - `T firstNonNull(T... values)`: returns the first value from the provided array that is not `null`
    - `T defaultIfNull(T object, T defaultValue)`: returns the provided default value if the first parameter is `null`
- max, min, median, and mode:
    - `T max(T... values)`: returns the last in the ordered list of provided values that implement the `Comparable` interface; returns `null` only when all values are `null`
    - `T min(T... values)`: returns the first in the ordered list of provided values that implement the `Comparable` interface; returns `null` only when all values are `null`
    - `T median(T... items)`: returns the value that is in the middle of the ordered list of provided values that implement the `Comparable` interface; if the count of the values is even, returns the smallest of the two in the middle

- T median(Comparator<T> comparator, T... items): returns the value that is in the middle of the list of provided values ordered according to the provided Comparator object; if the count of the values is even, returns the smallest of the two in the middle
- T mode(T... items): returns the most frequently occurring item from the items provided; returns null when such an item occurs most often or when there is no one item that occurs most often; here is the code that demonstrates this last method:

```
String s = ObjectUtils.mode("s0", "s1", "s1");
System.out.println(s);      //prints: s1

s = ObjectUtils.mode("s0", "s1", "s2");
System.out.println(s);      //prints: null

s = ObjectUtils.mode("s0", "s1", "s2", "s1", "s2");
System.out.println(s);      //prints: null

s = ObjectUtils.mode(null);
System.out.println(s);      //prints: null

s = ObjectUtils.mode("s0", null, null);
System.out.println(s);      //prints: null
```

# Managing strings

The class String is used a lot. So, you have to have a good handle on its functionality. We talked already talked about String value immutability in Chapter 5, *Java Language Elements and Types*. We have shown that every time a String value is "modified", a new copy of the value is created, which means that in the case of multiple "modifications", many String objects are created, consuming memory and putting a burden on the JVM.

In such cases, it is advisable to use the class java.lang.StringBuilder or java.lang.StringBuffer because they are modifiable objects and do not have an overhead of creating String value copies. We will show how to use them and explain the difference between these two classes in the first part of this section.

After that, we will review the methods of the class String and then provide an overview of the class org.apache.commons.lang3.StringUtils, which complements the class String functionality.

# StringBuilder and StringBuffer

The classes `StringBuilder` and `StringBuffer` have exactly the same list of methods. The difference is that the methods of the class `StringBuilder` perform faster than the same methods of the class `StringBuffer`. That is because the class `StringBuffer` has an overhead of not allowing concurrent access to its values from different application threads. So, if you are not coding for multithreaded processing, use `StringBuilder`.

There are many methods in the classes `StringBuilder` and `StringBuffer`. But, we are going to show how to use only the method `append()`, which is by far the most popular, used for cases when multiple `String` value modifications are required. Its main function is to append a value to the end of the value already stored inside the `StringBuilder` (or `StringBuffer`) object.

The method `append()` is overloaded for all primitive types and for the classes `String`, `Object`, `CharSequence`, and `StringBuffer`, which means that a `String` representation of the passed-in object of any of these classes can be appended to the existing value. For our demonstration, we are going use only the `append(String s)` version because that is what you are probably going to use most of the time. Here is an example:

```
List<String> list =
    List.of("That", "is", "the", "way", "to", "build", "a", "sentence");
StringBuilder sb = new StringBuilder();
for(String s: list){
    sb.append(s).append(" ");
}
String s = sb.toString();
System.out.println(s);   //prints: That is the way to build a sentence
```

There are also methods `replace()`, `substring()`, and `insert()` in the class `StringBuilder` (and `StringBuffer`) that allow modifying the value further. They are used much less often than the method `append()` though, and we are not going to discuss them as they are outside the scope of this book.

# Class java.lang.String

The class String has 15 constructors and almost 80 methods. To talk details and demonstrate each of them is just too much for this book, so we will comment only on the most popular methods and just mention the rest. After you master the basics, you can read the online documentation and see what else you can do with other methods of the class String.

# Constructors

The constructors of the class String are useful if you are concerned that the strings your application creates consume too much memory. The problem is that String literals (abc, for example) are stored in a special area of the memory called the "string constant pool" and never garbage collected. The idea behind such a design is that String literals consume substantially more memory than numbers. Also, the handling of such large entities has an overhead that may tax the JVM. That is why the designers figured it is cheaper to store them and share them between all application threads than allocate new memory and then clean it up several times for the same value.

But if the rate of reuse of the String values is low, while the stored String values consume too much memory, creating a String object with a constructor may be the solution to the problem. Here is an example:

```
String veryLongText = new String("asdakjfakjn akdb aakjn... akdjcnak");
```

A String object created this way resides in the heap area (where all objects are stored) and is garbage collected when not used anymore. That is when the String constructor shines.

If necessary, you can use the method intern() of the class String to create a copy of the heap String object in the string constant pool. It allows us not only to share the value with other application threads (in multithreaded processing), but also to compare it with another literal value by reference (using the operator ==). If the references are equal, it means they point to the same String value in the pool.

But, mainstream programmers rarely manage the memory this way, so we will not discuss this topic further.

# format()

The method `String format(String format, Object... args)` allows insertion of the provided objects into specified locations of a string and formatting them as needed. There are many format specifiers in the class `java.util.Formatter`. We will demonstrate here only `%s`, which converts the passed-in object to its `String` representation by invoking it on the object method `toString()`:

```
String format = "There is a %s in the %s";
String s = String.format(format, "bear", "woods");
System.out.println(s); //prints: There is a bear in the woods

format = "Class %s is very useful";
s = String.format(format, new A());
System.out.println(s);  //prints: Class A is very useful
```

# replace()

The method `String replace(CharSequence target, CharSequence replacement)` in the `String` value replaces the value of the first parameter with the value of the second one:

```
String s1 = "There is a bear in the woods";
String s2 = s1.replace("bear", "horse").replace("woods", "field");
System.out.println(s2);     //prints: There is a horse in the field
```

There are also the methods `String replaceAll(String regex, String replacement)` and `String replaceFirst(String regex, String replacement)`, which have similar capabilities.

# compareTo()

We have already used the `int compareTo(String anotherString)` method in our examples. It returns the difference between the positions of this `String` value and the value of `anotherString` in an ordered list. It is used for the natural ordering of strings since it is an implementation of the `Comparable` interface.

The method `int compareToIgnoreCase(String str)` performs the same function but ignores the case of the compared strings and is not used for natural ordering because it is not an implementation of the `Comparable` interface.

# valueOf(Objectj)

The static method `String valueOf(Object obj)` returns `null` if the provided object is `null`, or calls the method `toString()` on the object provided.

# valueOf(primitive or char[])

Any primitive type value can be passed as the parameter into the static method `String valueOf(primitive value)`, which returns the String representation of the value provided. For example, `String.valueOf(42)` returns `42`. This group of methods includes the following static methods:

- `String valueOf(boolean b)`
- `String valueOf(char c)`
- `String valueOf(double d)`
- `String valueOf(float f)`
- `String valueOf(int i)`
- `String valueOf(long l)`
- `String valueOf(char[] data)`
- `String valueOf(char[] data, int offset, int count)`

# copyValueOf(char[])

The method `String copyValueOf(char[] data)` is equivalent to `valueOf(char[])`, while the method `String copyValueOf(char[] data, int offset, int count)` is equivalent to `valueOf(char[], int, int)`. They return a `String` representation of a char array or its subarray.

And the method `void getChars(int srcBegin, int srcEnd, char[] dest, int dstBegin)` copies characters from this `String` value into the destination character array.

# indexOf() and substring()

Various `int indexOf(String str)` and `int lastIndexOf(String str)` methods return the position of a substring in a string:

```
String s = "Introduction";
System.out.println(s.indexOf("I"));         //prints: 0
System.out.println(s.lastIndexOf("I"));     //prints: 0
System.out.println(s.lastIndexOf("i"));     //prints: 9
System.out.println(s.indexOf("o"));         //prints: 4
System.out.println(s.lastIndexOf("o"));     //prints: 10
System.out.println(s.indexOf("tro"));       //prints: 2
```

Notice that the position count starts from zero.

The method `String substring(int beginIndex)` returns the rest of the string value, starting from the position (index) passed in as the parameter:

```
String s = "Introduction";
System.out.println(s.substring(1));         //prints: ntroduction
System.out.println(s.substring(2));         //prints: troduction
```

The character with the `beginIndex` position is the first that is present in the preceding substring.

The method `String substring(int beginIndex, int endIndex)` returns the substring, starting from the position passed in as the first parameter, to the position passed in as the second parameter:

```
String s = "Introduction";
System.out.println(s.substring(1, 2));      //prints: n
System.out.println(s.substring(1, 3));      //prints: nt
```

As with the method `substring(beginIndex)`, the character with the `beginIndex` position is the first that is present in the preceding substring, while the character with the `endIndex` position is not included. The difference `endIndex - beginIndex` equals the length of the substring.

This means that the following two substrings are equal:

```
System.out.println(s.substring(1));                //prints: ntroduction
System.out.println(s.substring(1, s.length()));    //prints: ntroduction
```

# contains() and matches()

The method `boolean contains(CharSequence s)` returns `true` when the provided sequence of characters (substring) is present:

```
String s = "Introduction";
System.out.println(s.contains("x"));        //prints: false
System.out.println(s.contains("o"));        //prints: true
System.out.println(s.contains("tro"));      //prints: true
System.out.println(s.contains("trx"));      //prints: false
```

Other similar methods are:

- `boolean matches(String regex)`: uses a regular expression (not a subject of this book)
- `boolean regionMatches(int tOffset, String other, int oOffset, int length)`: compares regions of two strings
- `boolean regionMatches(boolean ignoreCase, int tOffset, String other, int oOffset, int length)`: same as above, but with the flag `ignoreCase` indicating whether to ignore the case

# split(), concat(), and join()

The methods `String[] split(String regex)` and `String[] split(String regex, int limit)` use the passed-in regular expression to split the strings into substrings. We do not explain regular expressions in this book. However, there is a very simple one that is easy to use even if you know nothing about regular expressions: if you just pass into this method any symbol or substring present in a string, the string will be broken (split) into parts separated by the passed-in value, for example:

```
String[] substrings = "Introduction".split("o");
System.out.println(Arrays.toString(substrings));
                                    //prints: [Intr, ducti, n]
substrings = "Introduction".split("duct");
System.out.println(Arrays.toString(substrings));
                                    //prints: [Intro, ion]
```

This code just illustrates the functionality. But the following code snippet is more practical:

```
String s = "There is a bear in the woods";
String[] arr = s.split(" ");
System.out.println(Arrays.toString(arr));
                    //prints: [There, is, a, bear, in, the, woods]
```

```
arr = s.split(" ", 3);
System.out.println(Arrays.toString(arr));
                              //prints: [There, is, a bear in the woods]
```

As you can see, the second parameter in the split() method limits the number of resulting substrings.

The method String concat(String str) adds the passed-in value to the end of the string:

```
String s1 =  "There is a bear";
String s2 =  " in the woods";
String s = s1.concat(s2);
System.out.println(s);  //prints: There is a bear in the woods
```

The concat() method creates a new String value with the result of concatenation, so it is quite economical. But if you need to add (concatenate) many values, using StringBuilder (or StringBuffer, if you need protection from concurrent access) would be a better choice. We discussed it in the previous section. Another option would be to use the operator +:

```
String s =  s1 + s2;
System.out.println(s);  //prints: There is a bear in the woods
```

The operator +, when used with String values, is implemented based on StringBuilder, so allows the addition of String values by modifying the existing one. There is no performance difference between using StringBuilder and just the operator + for adding String values.

The methods String join(CharSequence delimiter, CharSequence... elements) and String join(CharSequence delimiter, Iterable<? extends CharSequence> elements) are based on StringBuilder too. They assemble the provided values in one String value using the passed-in delimiter to separate the assembled values inside the created String result. Here is an example:

```
s = String.join(" ", "There", "is", "a", "bear", "in", "the", "woods");
System.out.println(s);  //prints: There is a bear in the woods

List<String> list =
            List.of("There", "is", "a", "bear", "in", "the", "woods");
s = String.join(" ", list);
System.out.println(s);  //prints: There is a bear in the woods
```

# startsWith() and endsWith()

The following methods return `true` when the String value starts (or ends) with the provided substring `prefix`:

- `boolean startsWith(String prefix)`
- `boolean startsWith(String prefix, int toffset)`
- `boolean endsWith(String suffix)`

Here is the demo code:

```
boolean b = "Introduction".startsWith("Intro");
System.out.println(b);              //prints: true

b = "Introduction".startsWith("tro", 2);
System.out.println(b);              //prints: true

b = "Introduction".endsWith("ion");
System.out.println(b);              //prints: true
```

# equals() and equalsIgnoreCase()

We have used the method `boolean equals(Object anObject)` of the class `String` several times already and have pointed out that it compares this `String` value with other objects. This method returns `true` only when the passed-in object is `String` with the same value.

The method `boolean equalsIgnoreCase(String anotherString)` does the same but also ignores case, so the strings `AbC` and `ABC` are considered equal.

# contentEquals() and copyValueOf()

The method `boolean contentEquals(CharSequence cs)` compares this `String` value with the `String` representation of an object that implements the interface `CharSequence`. The popular `CharSequence` implementations are `CharBuffer`, `Segment`, `String`, `StringBuffer`, and `StringBuilder`.

The method `boolean contentEquals(StringBuffer sb)` does the same but for `StringBuffer` only. It has slightly different implementation than `contentEquals(CharSequence cs)` and may have some performance advantages in certain situations, but we are not going to discuss such details. Besides, you probably will not even notice which of the two methods is used when you call `contentEquals()` on a `String` value unless you make an effort to exploit the difference.

# length(), isEmpty(), and hashCode()

The method `int length()` returns the number of characters in a `String` value. The method `boolean isEmpty()` returns `true` when there are no characters in the `String` value and the method `length()` returns zero.

The method `int hashCode()` returns a hash value of the `String` object.

# trim(), toLowerCase(), and toUpperCase()

The method `String trim()` removes leading and trailing whitespaces from a `String` value.

The following methods change the case of the characters in a `String` value:

- `String toLowerCase()`
- `String toUpperCase()`
- `String toLowerCase(Locale locale)`
- `String toUpperCase(Locale locale)`

# getBytes(), getChars(), and toCharArray()

The following methods convert the `String` value to a byte array, optionally encoding it using the given charset:

- `byte[] getBytes()`
- `byte[] getBytes(Charset charset)`
- `byte[] getBytes(String charsetName)`

And these methods convert all the `String` value to other types, or only part of it:

- `IntStream chars()`
- `char[] toCharArray()`
- `char charAt(int index)`
- `CharSequence subSequence(int beginIndex, int endIndex)`

# Get code point by index or stream

The following group of methods convert all the `String` value, or only part of it, into Unicode code points of its characters:

- `IntStream codePoints()`
- `int codePointAt(int index)`
- `int codePointBefore(int index)`
- `int codePointCount(int beginIndex, int endIndex)`
- `int offsetByCodePoints(int index, int codePointOffset)`

We explained Unicode code points in `Chapter` 5, *Java Language Elements and Types*. These methods are especially useful when you need to represent characters that *do not fit* into the two bytes of the `char` type. Such characters have code points bigger than `Character.MAX_VALUE`, which is `65535`.

# Class lang3.StringUtils

The class `org.apache.commons.lang3.StringUtils` of the Apache Commons library has more than 120 static utility methods that complement those of the class `String` we described in the previous section.

Among the most popular are the following static methods:

- `boolean isBlank(CharSequence cs)`: returns `true` when the passed-in parameter is an empty `String` "", `null`, or whitespace
- `boolean isNotBlank(CharSequence cs)`: returns `true` when the passed-in parameter is not an empty `String` "", `null`, or whitespace
- `boolean isAlpha(CharSequence cs)`: returns `true` when the passed-in parameter contains only Unicode letters

- `boolean isAlphaSpace(CharSequence cs)`: returns `true` when the passed-in parameter contains only Unicode letters and spaces (' ')
- `boolean isNumeric(CharSequence cs)`: returns `true` when the passed-in parameter contains only digits
- `boolean isNumericSpace(CharSequence cs)`: returns `true` when the passed-in parameter contains only digits and spaces (' ')
- `boolean isAlphaNumeric(CharSequence cs)`: returns `true` when the passed-in parameter contains only Unicode letters and digits
- `boolean isAlphaNumericSpace(CharSequence cs)`: returns `true` when the passed-in parameter contains only Unicode letters, digits, and spaces (' ')

We highly recommend you look through the API of this class and get a feel for what you can find there.

# Managing time

There are many classes in the `java.time` package and its sub-packages. They were introduced as a replacement for other—older—packages that handle date and time. The new classes are thread-safe (so better suited for multithreaded processing) and, no less important, are more consistently designed and easier to understand. Also, the new implementation follows the **International Standard Organization** (**ISO**) for date and time formats, but allows the use of any other custom format too.

We will describe the main five classes and demonstrate how to use them:

- `java.util.LocalDate`
- `java.util.LocalTime`
- `java.util.LocalDateTime`
- `java.util.Period`
- `java.util.Duration`

All these, and other classes of the `java.time` package and its sub-packages, are rich in various functionalities that cover all practical and any imaginable cases. But we are not going to cover all of them, just introduce the basics and most popular use cases.

# java.time.LocalDate

The class `LocalDate` does not carry time. It represents a date in ISO 8601 format, yyyy-MM-DD:

```
System.out.println(LocalDate.now());    //prints: 2018-04-14
```

As you can see, the method `now()` returns the current date as it is set on your computer: `April 14, 2018` was the date when this section was written.

Similarly, you can get the current date in any other timezone using the static method `now(ZoneId zone)`. The `ZoneId` object can be constructed using the static method `ZoneId.of(String zoneId)`, where `String zoneId` is any of the `String` values returned by the method `ZonId.getAvailableZoneIds()`:

```
Set<String> zoneIds = ZoneId.getAvailableZoneIds();
for(String zoneId: zoneIds){
    System.out.println(zoneId);
}
```

This code prints many timezone IDs, one of them being `Asia/Tokyo`. Now, we can find what the date is now, in that time zone:

```
ZoneId zoneId = ZoneId.of("Asia/Tokyo");
System.out.println(LocalDate.now(zoneId));    //prints: 2018-04-15
```

An object of `LocalDate` can represent any date in the past or in the future too, using the following methods:

- `LocalDate parse(CharSequence text)`: constructs an object from a string in ISO 8601 format, yyyy-MM-DD
- `LocalDate parse(CharSequence text, DateTimeFormatter formatter)` : constructs an object from a string in a format specified by the object `DateTimeFormatter`, which has many predefined formats
- `LocalDate of(int year, int month, int dayOfMonth)`: constructs an object form a year, month, and day
- `LocalDate of(int year, Month month, int dayOfMonth)`: constructs an object from a year, month (as enum constant), and day
- `LocalDate ofYearDay(int year, int dayOfYear)`: constructs an object from a year and day-of-year

The following code demonstrates these methods:

```
LocalDate lc1 =  LocalDate.parse("2020-02-23");
System.out.println(lc1);                         //prints: 2020-02-23

DateTimeFormatter formatter = DateTimeFormatter.ofPattern("dd/MM/yyyy");
LocalDate lc2 =  LocalDate.parse("23/02/2020", formatter);
System.out.println(lc2);                         //prints: 2020-02-23

LocalDate lc3 =  LocalDate.of(2020, 2, 23);
System.out.println(lc3);                         //prints: 2020-02-23

LocalDate lc4 =  LocalDate.of(2020, Month.FEBRUARY, 23);
System.out.println(lc4);                         //prints: 2020-02-23

LocalDate lc5 = LocalDate.ofYearDay(2020, 54);
System.out.println(lc5);                         //prints: 2020-02-23
```

Using the `LocalDate` object, you can get various values:

```
System.out.println(lc5.getYear());        //prints: 2020
System.out.println(lc5.getMonth());       //prints: FEBRUARY
System.out.println(lc5.getMonthValue());  //prints: 2
System.out.println(lc5.getDayOfMonth());  //prints: 23

System.out.println(lc5.getDayOfWeek());   //prints: SUNDAY
System.out.println(lc5.isLeapYear());     //prints: true
System.out.println(lc5.lengthOfMonth());  //prints: 29
System.out.println(lc5.lengthOfYear());   //prints: 366
```

The `LocalDate` object can be modified:

```
System.out.println(lc5.withYear(2021));       //prints: 2021-02-23
System.out.println(lc5.withMonth(5));         //prints: 2020-05-23
System.out.println(lc5.withDayOfMonth(5));    //prints: 2020-02-05
System.out.println(lc5.withDayOfYear(53));    //prints: 2020-02-22

System.out.println(lc5.plusDays(10));         //prints: 2020-03-04
System.out.println(lc5.plusMonths(2));        //prints: 2020-04-23
System.out.println(lc5.plusYears(2));         //prints: 2022-02-23

System.out.println(lc5.minusDays(10));        //prints: 2020-02-13
System.out.println(lc5.minusMonths(2));       //prints: 2019-12-23
System.out.println(lc5.minusYears(2));        //prints: 2018-02-23
```

The `LocalDate` objects can be compared:

```
LocalDate lc6 =  LocalDate.parse("2020-02-22");
LocalDate lc7 =  LocalDate.parse("2020-02-23");
System.out.println(lc6.isAfter(lc7));      //prints: false
System.out.println(lc6.isBefore(lc7));     //prints: true
```

There are many other helpful methods in the `LocalDate` class. If you have to work with dates, we recommend that you read the API of this class and other classes of the `java.time` package and its sub-packages.

# java.time.LocalTime

The class `LocalTime` contains the time without a date. It has methods similar to those of the class `LocalDate`.

Here is how an object of the `LocalTime` class can be created:

```
System.out.println(LocalTime.now());          //prints: 21:15:46.360904

ZoneId zoneId = ZoneId.of("Asia/Tokyo");
System.out.println(LocalTime.now(zoneId));   //prints: 12:15:46.364378

LocalTime lt1 =  LocalTime.parse("20:23:12");
System.out.println(lt1);                      //prints: 20:23:12

LocalTime lt2 =  LocalTime.of(20, 23, 12);
System.out.println(lt2);                      //prints: 20:23:12
```

Each component of the time value can be extracted from a `LocalTime` object as follows:

```
System.out.println(lt2.getHour());       //prints: 20
System.out.println(lt2.getMinute());     //prints: 23
System.out.println(lt2.getSecond());     //prints: 12
System.out.println(lt2.getNano());       //prints: 0
```

The object can be modified:

```
System.out.println(lt2.withHour(3));      //prints: 03:23:12
System.out.println(lt2.withMinute(10));   //prints: 20:10:12
System.out.println(lt2.withSecond(15));   //prints: 20:23:15
System.out.println(lt2.withNano(300));    //prints: 20:23:12:000000300

System.out.println(lt2.plusHours(10));    //prints: 06:23:12
System.out.println(lt2.plusMinutes(2));   //prints: 20:25:12
```

```
System.out.println(lt2.plusSeconds(2));      //prints: 20:23:14
System.out.println(lt2.plusNanos(200));      //prints: 20:23:14:000000200

System.out.println(lt2.minusHours(10));      //prints: 10:23:12
System.out.println(lt2.minusMinutes(2));     //prints: 20:21:12
System.out.println(lt2.minusSeconds(2));     //prints: 20:23:10
System.out.println(lt2.minusNanos(200));     //prints: 20:23:11.999999800
```

And two objects of the LocalTime class can be compared as well:

```
LocalTime lt3 =  LocalTime.parse("20:23:12");
LocalTime lt4 =  LocalTime.parse("20:25:12");
System.out.println(lt3.isAfter(lt4));       //prints: false
System.out.println(lt3.isBefore(lt4));      //prints: true
```

There are many other helpful methods in the LocalTime class. If you have to work with time, we recommend you read the API of this class and other classes of the java.time package and its sub-packages.

# java.time.LocalDateTime

The class LocalDateTime contains both date and time, and has all the methods the classes LocalDate and LocalTime have, so we are not going to repeat them here. We will only show how an object of LocalDateTime can be created:

```
System.out.println(LocalDateTime.now());   //2018-04-14T21:59:00.142804
ZoneId zoneId = ZoneId.of("Asia/Tokyo");
System.out.println(LocalDateTime.now(zoneId));
                                //prints: 2018-04-15T12:59:00.146038
LocalDateTime ldt1 =  LocalDateTime.parse("2020-02-23T20:23:12");
System.out.println(ldt1);                   //prints: 2020-02-23T20:23:12
DateTimeFormatter formatter =
         DateTimeFormatter.ofPattern("dd/MM/yyyy HH:mm:ss");
LocalDateTime ldt2 =
      LocalDateTime.parse("23/02/2020 20:23:12", formatter);
System.out.println(ldt2);                   //prints: 2020-02-23T20:23:12
LocalDateTime ldt3 = LocalDateTime.of(2020, 2, 23, 20, 23, 12);
System.out.println(ldt3);                   //prints: 2020-02-23T20:23:12
LocalDateTime ldt4 =
        LocalDateTime.of(2020, Month.FEBRUARY, 23, 20, 23, 12);
System.out.println(ldt4);                   //prints: 2020-02-23T20:23:12
LocalDate ld = LocalDate.of(2020, 2, 23);
LocalTime lt =  LocalTime.of(20, 23, 12);
LocalDateTime ldt5 = LocalDateTime.of(ld, lt);
System.out.println(ldt5);                   //prints: 2020-02-23T20:23:12
```

There are many other helpful methods in the `LocalDateTime` class. If you have to work with date and time, we recommend you read the API of this class and other classes of the `java.time` package and its sub-packages.

# Period and Duration

The classes `java.time.Period` and `java.time.Duration` are designed to contain an amount of time:

- The `Period` object contains an amount of time in units of years, months, and days
- The `Duration` object contains an amount of time in hours, minutes, seconds, and nanoseconds

The following code demonstrates their creation and use with the class `LocalDateTime`, but the same methods exist in the classes `LocalDate` (for `Period`) and `LocalTime` (for `Duration`):

```
LocalDateTime ldt1 = LocalDateTime.parse("2020-02-23T20:23:12");
LocalDateTime ldt2 = ldt1.plus(Period.ofYears(2));
System.out.println(ldt2); //prints: 2022-02-23T20:23:12

//The following methods work the same way:
ldt.minus(Period.ofYears(2));
ldt.plus(Period.ofMonths(2));
ldt.minus(Period.ofMonths(2));
ldt.plus(Period.ofWeeks(2));
ldt.minus(Period.ofWeeks(2));
ldt.plus(Period.ofDays(2));
ldt.minus(Period.ofDays(2));

ldt.plus(Duration.ofHours(2));
ldt.minus(Duration.ofHours(2));
ldt.plus(Duration.ofMinutes(2));
ldt.minus(Duration.ofMinutes(2));
ldt.plus(Duration.ofMillis(2));
ldt.minus(Duration.ofMillis(2));
```

Some other ways to create and use `Period` objects are demonstrated in the following code:

```
LocalDate ld1 =  LocalDate.parse("2020-02-23");
LocalDate ld2 =  LocalDate.parse("2020-03-25");

Period period = Period.between(ld1, ld2);
```

```
System.out.println(period.getDays());        //prints: 2
System.out.println(period.getMonths());       //prints: 1
System.out.println(period.getYears());        //prints: 0
System.out.println(period.toTotalMonths());   //prints: 1

period = Period.between(ld2, ld1);
System.out.println(period.getDays());         //prints: -2
```

Objects of `Duration` can be similarly created and used:

```
LocalTime lt1 =  LocalTime.parse("10:23:12");
LocalTime lt2 =  LocalTime.parse("20:23:14");
Duration duration = Duration.between(lt1, lt2);
System.out.println(duration.toDays());        //prints: 0
System.out.println(duration.toHours());       //prints: 10
System.out.println(duration.toMinutes());     //prints: 600
System.out.println(duration.toSeconds());     //prints: 36002
System.out.println(duration.getSeconds());    //prints: 36002
System.out.println(duration.toNanos());       //prints: 36002000000000
System.out.println(duration.getNano());       //prints: 0
```

There are many other helpful methods in the classes `Period` and `Duration`. If you have to work with the amount of time, we recommend you read the API of these classes and other classes of the `java.time` package and its sub-packages.

# Managing random numbers

Generating a truly random number is a big topic that does not belong to this book. But for the vast majority of practical purposes, the pseudo-random number generators provided by Java are good enough, and that is what we are going to discuss in this section.

There are two primary ways to generate a random number in Java Standard Library:

- The `java.lang.Math.random()` method
- The `java.util.Random` class

There is also the `java.security.SecureRandom` class, which provides a cryptographically strong random number generator, but it is outside the scope of an introductory course.

# Method java.lang.Math.random()

The static method `double random()` of the class `Math` returns a `double` type value greater than or equal to `0.0` and less than `1.0`:

```
for(int i =0; i < 3; i++){
    System.out.println(Math.random());
    //0.9350483840148613
    //0.0477353019234189
    //0.25784245516898985
}
```

We captured the result in the previous comments. But in practice, more often than not, a random integer from a certain range is required. To accommodate such a need, we can write a method that, for example, produces a random integer number from 0 (inclusive) to 10 (exclusive):

```
int getInteger(int max){
    return (int)(Math.random() * max);
}
```

Here is the result of one run of the previous code:

```
for(int i =0; i < 3; i++){
    System.out.print(getInteger(10) + " "); //prints: 2 5 6
}
```

As you can see, it generates a random integer value that can be one of the following 10 numbers: 0, 1, ..., 9. And here is the code that uses the same method and produces random integer numbers from 0 (inclusive) to 100 (exclusive):

```
for(int i =0; i < 3; i++){
    System.out.print(getInteger(100) + " "); //prints: 48 11 97
}
```

And when you need a random number between 100 (inclusive) and 200 (exclusive), you can just add 100 to the preceding result:

```
for(int i =0; i < 3; i++){
    System.out.print(100 + getInteger(100) + " "); //prints: 114 101 127
}
```

Including both ends of the range in the result can be done by rounding the generated `double` value:

```
int getIntegerRound(int max){
    return (int)Math.round(Math.random() * max);
}
```

When we used the preceding method, the results were:

```
for(int i =0; i < 3; i++){
    System.out.print(100 + getIntegerRound(100) + " "); //179 147 200
}
```

As you can see, the upper end of the range (the number 200) is included in the possible results set. The same effect can be achieved by just adding 1 to the requested upper range:

```
int getInteger2(int max){
    return (int)(Math.random() * (max + 1));
}
```

If we use the previous method, we can get the following result:

```
for(int i =0; i < 3; i++){
    System.out.print(100 + getInteger2(100) + " "); //167 200 132
}
```

But if you look at the source code of the `Math.random()` method, you will see that it uses the `java.util.Random` class and its `nextDouble()` method to generate a random double value. So, let's look at how to use the `java.util.Random` class directly.

# Class java.util.Random

The method `doubles()` of the class `Random` generates a `double` type value greater than or equal to `0.0` and less than `1.0`:

```
Random random = new Random();
for(int i =0; i < 3; i++){
    System.out.print(random.nextDouble() + " ");
    //prints: 0.8774928230544553 0.7822070124559267 0.09401796000707807
}
```

We can use the method `nextDouble()` the same way we used `Math.random()` in the previous section. But class have other methods that can be used without creating a custom `getInteger()` method when a random integer value of a certain range is required. For example, the `nextInt()` method returns an integer value between `Integer.MIN_VALUE` (inclusive) and `Integer.MAX_VALUE` (inclusive):

```
for(int i =0; i < 3; i++){
    System.out.print(random.nextInt() + " ");
                        //prints: -2001537190 -1148252160 1999653777
}
```

And the same method with a parameter allows us to limit the range of the returned values by the upper limit (exclusive):

```
for(int i =0; i < 3; i++){
    System.out.print(random.nextInt(11) + " "); //prints: 4 6 2
}
```

This code generates a random integer value between 0 (inclusive) and 10 (inclusive). And the following code returns a random integer value between 11 (inclusive) and 20 (inclusive):

```
for(int i =0; i < 3; i++){
    System.out.print(11 + random.nextInt(10) + " "); //prints: 13 20 15
}
```

Another way to generate a random integer from the range is by using the `IntStream` object returned by the method `ints(int count, int min, int max)`, where `count` is the number of requested values, `min` is the minimum value (inclusive), and `max` is the maximum value (exclusive):

```
String result = random.ints(3, 0, 101)
        .mapToObj(String::valueOf)
        .collect(Collectors.joining(" ")); //prints: 30 48 52
```

This code returns three integer values from 0 (inclusive) to 100 (inclusive). We will talk more about streams in `Chapter 18`, *Streams and Pipelines*.

# Exercise – Objects.equals() result

There are three classes:

```
public class A{}
public class B{}
public class Exercise {
    private A a;
    private B b;
    public Exercise(){
        System.out.println(java.util.Objects.equals(a, b));
    }
    public static void main(String... args){
        new Exercise();
    }
}
```

What is going to be displayed when we run the `main()` method of the `Exercise` class? `Error?` `False?` `True?`

# Answer

The display will show only one value: `True`. The reason is that both private fields—a and b—are initialized to `null`.

# Summary

In this chapter, we introduced the reader to the most popular utilities and some other classes from the Java Standard Library and Apache Commons libraries. Every Java programmer has to have a solid understanding of their capabilities in order to become an effective coder. Studying them also helps to get exposure to various software designs pattern and solutions that are instructive and can be used as patterns for best coding practices in any application.

In the next chapter, we are going to demonstrate to the reader how to write Java code that can manipulate—insert, read, update, and delete—data in a database. It will also provide a short introduction to SQL and basic database operations.

# 16
# Database Programming

This chapter explains how to write Java code that can manipulate—insert, read, update, delete—data in a database. It also provides a short introduction to the SQL language and basic database operations.

In this chapter, we will cover the following topics:

- What is **Java Database Connectivity (JDBC)**?
- How to create/delete a database
- Short overview of **Structured Query Language (SQL)**
- How to create/delete/modify a database table
- **Create, read, update, and delete (CRUD)** database data
- Exercise – Selecting unique first names

## What is Java Database Connectivity (JDBC)?

**Java Database Connectivity (JDBC)** is Java functionality that allows us to access and modify data in a database. It is supported by the JDBC API (the `java.sql`, `javax.sql`, and `java.transaction.xa` packages) and the database-specific implementation of an interface for the database access (called a database driver) provided by each database vendor.

When people say they are using JDBC, it means they write code that manages data in a database using the interfaces and classes of the JDBC API and a database-specific driver that knows how to connect the application with the particular database. Using this connection, an application can then issue requests written in **Structured Query Language** (**SQL**). Naturally, we are talking here only about the databases that understand SQL. They are called relational (or tabular) and compose the vast majority of the currently used databases, although some alternatives—a navigational database and NoSql, for example—are used too.

The `java.sql` and `javax.sql` packages are included in the Java Platform Standard Edition (Java SE). Historically, the `java.sql` package belonged to Java core, while the `javax.sql` package was considered a core extension. But later, the `javax.sql` package was included in the core too and the name was not changed to avoid breaking the existing application that used it. The `javax.sql` package contains the `DataSource` interface that supports the statement's pooling, distributed transactions, and rowsets. We will discuss each of these features in greater details in the following sections of this chapter.

Working with a database includes eight steps:

1. Install the database by following the vendor instructions.
2. Create a database user, a database, and the database schema – tables, views, stored procedures, and so on.
3. Add the dependency to the application on a `.jar` with the database-specific driver.
4. Connect to the database from the application.
5. Construct a SQL statement.
6. Execute a SQL statement.
7. Use the result of the execution.
8. Release (close) the database connection and other resources opened in the process.

Steps 1-3 are done only once, at the database setup before the application is run. Steps 4-8 are performed by the application repeatedly as needed. Steps 5-7 can be repeated multiple times with the same database connection.

# Connecting to the database

Here is the code fragment to connect to the database:

```
String URL = "jdbc:postgresql://localhost/javaintro";
Properties prop = new Properties( );
//prop.put( "user", "java" );
//prop.put( "password", "secretPass123" );
try {
  Connection conn = DriverManager.getConnection(URL, prop);
} catch(SQLException ex){
  ex.printStackTrace();
}
```

The commented lines show how you can set a user and password for your connection using the `java.util.Properties` class. The preceding is just an example of how to get a connection using the `DriverManger` class directly. Many keys for the passed-in properties are the same for all major databases, but some of them are database-specific. So, read your database vendor documentation for such details.

Alternatively, for passing user and password only, we could use an overloaded version, `DriverManager.getConnection(String url, String user, String password)`.

It is a good practice to keep the password encrypted. We are not going to show you how to do it, but there are plenty of guides available on the internet.

Another way of connecting to a database is to use the `DataSource` interface. Its implementation is included in the same `.jar` with the database driver. In the case of PostgreSQL, there are two classes that implemented the `DataSource` interface: `org.postgresql.ds.PGSimpleDataSource` and `org.postgresql.ds.PGConnectionPoolDataSource`. We can use them instead of `DriverManager`. The following is an example of creating a database connection using the `org.postgresql.ds.PGSimpleDataSource` class:

```
PGSimpleDataSource source = new PGSimpleDataSource();
source.setServerName("localhost");
source.setDatabaseName("javaintro");
source.setLoginTimeout(10);
Connection conn = source.getConnection();
```

To connect to the database using
the `org.postgresql.ds.PGConnectionPoolDataSource` class, we only need to replace
the first line in the preceding code with the following:

```
PGConnectionPoolDataSource source = new PGConnectionPoolDataSource();
```

Using the `PGConnectionPoolDataSource` class allows us to create a pool of `Connection`
objects in-memory. It is a preferred way because creating a `Connection` object takes time.
The pooling allows us to do it up-front and then reuse the already created objects as
needed. The pool size and other parameters can be set in the `postgresql.conf` file.

But whatever method of creating a database connection is used, we are going to hide it
inside the `getConnection()` method and use it in all our code examples in the same way.

With the object of the `Connection` class acquired, we can now access the database to add,
read, delete, or modify the stored data.

# Closing the database connection

Keeping a database connection alive requires a significant amount of resources memory
and CPU—so it is a good idea to close the connection and release the allocated resources as
soon as you do not need them anymore. In the case of the pooling, the `Connection` object,
when closed, is returned to the pool and consumes fewer resources.

Before Java 7, the way to close a connection was by invoking the `close()` method in a
`finally`-block with or without a catch-block:

```
Connection conn = getConnection();
try {
  //use object conn here
} finally {
  if(conn != null){
    conn.close();
  }
}
```

The code inside the `finally`-block is always executed, whether the exception inside the try-block was thrown or not. But since Java 7, the `try...with...resources` construct does the job just fine on any object that implements the `java.lang.AutoCloseable` or `java.io.Closeable` interfaces. Since the `java.sql.Connection` object implements `AutoCloseable`, we can rewrite the previous code snippet as follows:

```
try (Connection conn = getConnection()) {
  //use object conn here
}
catch(SQLException ex) {
  ex.printStackTrace();
}
```

The catch-clause is necessary because the auto-closeable resource throws `java.sql.SQLException`. One can argue that it does not save much in the way of typing. But the `close()` method of the `Connection` class can throw `SQLException` too, so the code with `finally`-block should be written more defensively:

```
Connection conn = getConnection();
try {
  //use object conn here
} finally {
  if(conn != null){
    try {
      conn.close();
    } catch(SQLException ex){
      //do here what has to be done
    }
  }
}
```

The preceding block already looks definitely like a more boilerplate code. Yet, even more, if we take into account that usually inside the `try`-block, some other code can throw `SQLException` too, then the preceding code should look as follows:

```
Connection conn = getConnection();
try {
  //use object conn here
} catch(SQLException ex) {
  ex.printStackTrace();
} finally {
  if(conn != null){
    try {
      conn.close();
    } catch(SQLException ex){
```

```
      //do here what has to be done
    }
  }
}
```

The boilerplate code grows, doesn't it? And that is not the end of the story. In the next
sections, you will learn that to send a database request, you also need to create
a java.sql.Statement, which throws SQLException and has to be closed too. Then the
preceding code grows even more:

```
Connection conn = getConnection();
try {
  Statement statement = conn.createStatement();
  try{
    //use statement here
  } catch(SQLException ex){
    //some code here
  } finally {
    if(statement != null){
      try {
      } catch (SQLException ex){
        //some code here
      }
    }
  }
} catch(SQLException ex) {
  ex.printStackTrace();
} finally {
  if(conn != null){
    try {
      conn.close();
    } catch(SQLException ex){
      //do here what has to be done
    }
  }
}
```

Now we can appreciate the try...with...resources construct in its full glory,
especially if we take into account that it allows us to include multiple auto-closeable
resources in the same clause:

```
try (Connection conn = getConnection();
  Statement statement = conn.createStatement()) {
  //use statement here
} catch(SQLException ex) {
  ex.printStackTrace();
}
```

And since Java 9, we can make it even simpler:

```
Connection conn = getConnection();
try (conn; Statement statement = conn.createStatement()) {
  //use statement here
} catch(SQLException ex) {
  ex.printStackTrace();
}
```

Now it is clear that the `try...with...resources` construct is a hands-down winner.

# Structured Query Language (SQL)

SQL is a rich language, and we do not have enough space to cover all its features. We just would like to enumerate a few of the most popular ones, so you become aware of their existence and can look them up as needed.

Similar to a Java statement, there is a SQL statement that expresses a database request like a complete sentence in the English language. Every statement can be executed either in a database console or by Java code using the JDBC connection. Programmers often test a SQL statement in a console before using it in the Java code because the turnaround in a console is much faster. One does not need to compile and execute a program while using a console.

There are SQL statements that create and delete a user and database. We will see the examples of such statements in the next section. There are also other statements related to a database as a whole, that are outside the scope of this book.

After a database is created, the following three SQL statements allow us to build and change the database structure – a table, function, constraint, or another database entity:

- `CREATE`: This statement creates a database entity
- `ALTER`: This statement changes a database entity
- `DROP`: This statement deletes a database entity

There are also various SQL statements that allow us to enquire about each database entity, which are outside the scope of this book too.

And there are four kinds of SQL statements that manipulate the data in the database:

- INSERT: This statement adds data to the database
- SELECT: This statement reads data from the database
- UPDATE: This statement changes data in the database
- DELETE: This statement deletes data from the database

One or several various clauses can be added to the preceding statements that identify the data requested (WHERE-clause), the order in which the results have to be returned (ORDER-clause), and similar.

The JDBC connection allows to wrap one or a combination of the preceding SQL statements in one of the three classes that provide a different functionality on the database side:

- java.sql.Statement: Just sends the statement to the database server for an execution
- java.sql.PreparedStatement: Caches the statement within a certain execution path on the database server, allowing it to be executed multiple times with different parameters in an efficient manner
- java.sql.CallableStatement: Executes a stored procedure in the database

We will start our demonstration with the statements that create and delete a database and its user.

# Creating a database and its structure

Look up how to download and install your preferred database server. A database server is a software system that maintains and manages the database. For our demonstrations, we are going to use PostgreSQL, a free, open source database server.

After the database server is installed, we'll use its console for creating a database and its user with the corresponding permissions. There are many ways to structure the data store and the system of users with different levels of access. In this book, we will introduce only the basic approach, which allows us to demonstrate the main JDBC capabilities.

# CREATE and DROP the database and its user

Read the database instructions and create, first, a `java` user and a `javaintro` database (or select any other name you prefer and use them instead in the provided code examples). Here is how we did it for PostgreSQL:

```
CREATE USER java SUPERUSER;
CREATE DATABASE javaintro OWNER java;
```

If you made a mistake and decide to start anew, you can delete the created user and database using the following statements:

```
DROP USER java;
DROP DATABASE javaintro;
```

We selected the `SUPERUSER` role for our user, but a good security practice recommends assigning such a powerful role to an administrator only. For an application, it is recommended to create a user who cannot create or change the database itself—its tables and constraints—but can only manage data. Also, it is a good practice to create another logical layer, called **schema**, that can have its own set of users and permissions. This way, several schemas in the same database could be isolated and each user (one of them is your application) can access only certain schemas. On an enterprise level, the common practice is to create synonyms for the database schema so that no application can access the original structure directly.

But, as we have mentioned already, for the purpose of this book, it is not needed, so we leave it to the database administrators who establish rules and guidelines suitable for the particular working conditions of each enterprise.

Now we can connect our application to the database.

# CREATE, ALTER, and DROP table

The standard SQL statement for the table creation looks like this:

```
CREATE TABLE tablename (
  column1 type1,
  column2 type2,
  column3 type3,
  ....
);
```

The limitations for a table name, column names, and types of values that can be used depend on the particular database. Here is an example of a command that creates table person in PostgreSQL:

```
CREATE TABLE person (
    id SERIAL PRIMARY KEY,
    first_name VARCHAR NOT NULL,
    last_name VARCHAR NOT NULL,
    dob DATE NOT NULL
);
```

As you can see, we have made the dob (date of birth) column not nullable. That imposes a constraint on our Person Java class that is going to represent the records of this table: its dob field cannot be null. And that was what we have done, you may recall, in Chapter 6, *Interfaces, Classes, and Objects Construction*, when we created our Person class, as follows:

```
class Person {
    private String firstName, lastName;
    private LocalDate dob;
    public Person(String firstName, String lastName, LocalDate dob) {
        this.firstName = firstName == null ? "" : firstName;
        this.lastName = lastName == null ? "" : lastName;
        if(dob == null){
            throw new RuntimeException("Date of birth is null");
        }
        this.dob = dob;
    }
    public String getFirstName() { return firstName; }
    public String getLastName() { return lastName; }
    public LocalDate getDob() { return dob; }
}
```

We did not set the size of the columns of the VARCHAR type, thus allowing those columns to store values of any length, while the integer type allows them to store numbers from 4,713 BC to 5,874,897 AD. NOT NULL was added because by default the column would be nullable, while we would like to make sure that all the columns are populated for each record. And our Person class supports it by setting first and last names to empty String values if they are null, as the parameters of the Person constructor.

We also identified the id column as PRIMARY KEY, which indicates that this column uniquely identifies the record. The SERIAL keyword means that we ask the database to generate the next integer value every time a new record is added, so each record will have a unique integer number. Alternatively, we could make PRIMARY KEY from the combination of first_name, last_name, and dob:

```
CREATE TABLE person (
   first_name VARCHAR NOT NULL,
   last_name VARCHAR NOT NULL,
   dob DATE NOT NULL,
   PRIMARY KEY (first_name, last_name, dob)
);
```

But there is a chance that there are two people who have the same name and who were born on the same day, so we decided not to do it and added another field and constructor to the Person class:

```
public class Person {
   private String firstName, lastName;
   private LocalDate dob;
   private int id;
   public Person(int id, String firstName,
                                 String lastName, LocalDate dob) {
      this(firstName, lastName, dob);
      this.id = id;
   }
   public Person(String firstName, String lastName, LocalDate dob) {
      this.firstName = firstName == null ? "" : firstName;
      this.lastName = lastName == null ? "" : lastName;
      if(dob == null){
         throw new RuntimeException("Date of birth is null");
      }
      this.dob = dob;
   }
   public String getFirstName() { return firstName; }
   public String getLastName() { return lastName; }
   public LocalDate getDob() { return dob; }
}
```

We will use the constructor that accepts id for constructing an object based on the record in a database, while the other constructor will be used to create an object before inserting a new record.

We run the preceding SQL statement in a database console and create this table:

```
demo> CREATE TABLE person (
javaintro(#        id SERIAL PRIMARY KEY,
javaintro(#        first_name VARCHAR NOT NULL,
javaintro(#        last_name VARCHAR NOT NULL,
javaintro(#        dob DATE NOT NULL
javaintro(#     );
CREATE TABLE
Time: 22.446 ms
demo>
```

If necessary, the table can be deleted by the DROP command:

```
DROP table person;
```

The existing table can be changed using the ALTER command. For example, we can add an address column:

```
ALTER table person add column address VARCHAR;
```

If you are not sure whether such a column exists already, you can add IF EXISTS or IF NOT EXISTS:

```
ALTER table person add column IF NOT EXISTS address VARCHAR;
```

But this possibility exists only since PostgreSQL 9.6.

Another important consideration of the database table creation is whether an index has to be added. An index is a data structure that helps to accelerate the data search in the table without having to check every table record. An index can include one or more columns of a table. For example, an index for a primary key is created automatically. If you bring up the description of the table we have created already, you will see:

```
demo> \d person
                        Table "public.person"

   Column    |       Type        |                   Modifiers
-------------+-------------------+----------------------------------------------------
 id          | integer           | not null default nextval('person_id_seq'::regclass)
 first_name  | character varying | not null
 last_name   | character varying | not null
 dob         | date              | not null

Indexes:
    "person_pkey" PRIMARY KEY, btree (id)

demo>
```

We can also add any index ourselves if we think (and have proven it through the experimentation) it will help the application's performance. For example, we can allow case-insensitive search by first and last name by adding the following index:

```
CREATE INDEX idx_names ON person ((lower(first_name), lower(last_name));
```

If the search speed improves, we leave the index in place. If not, it can be removed:

```
drop index idx_names;
```

We remove it because an index has an overhead of additional writes and storage space.

And we can remove a column from a table too:

```
ALTER table person DROP column address;
```

In our examples, we followed the naming convention of PostgreSQL. If you use a different database, we suggest you look up its naming convention and follow it, so the names you create align with those created automatically.

# Create, read, update, and delete (CRUD) data

So far, we have used a console to send SQL statements to the database. The same statements could be executed from Java code using the JDBC API, but tables are created only once, so there is not much sense in writing a program for a one-time execution.

But managing data is another matter. That is the primary purpose of a program we are going to write now. In order to do that, first, we add the following dependency to the pom.xml file because we have installed PostgreSQL 9.6:

```
<dependency>
  <groupId>org.postgresql</groupId>
  <artifactId>postgresql</artifactId>
  <version>42.2.2</version>
</dependency>
```

# INSERT statement

The SQL statement that creates (populates) data in the database has the following format:

```
INSERT INTO table_name (column1,column2,column3,...)
    VALUES (value1,value2,value3,...);
```

When several tables records have to be added, it looks like this:

```
INSERT INTO table_name (column1,column2,column3,...)
    VALUES (value1,value2,value3,...), (value11,value21,value31,...), ...;
```

Before writing a program, let's test our `INSERT` statement:

```
demo>
demo> insert into person (first_name, last_name, dob) values ('Jim', 'Adams', '1999-08-23');
INSERT 0 1
Time: 6.936 ms
demo>
```

It worked without an error and returned the number of inserted rows as 1, so we are going to create the following method:

```
void executeStatement(String sql){
  Connection conn = getConnection();
  try (conn; Statement st = conn.createStatement()) {
    st.execute(sql);
  } catch (SQLException ex) {
    ex.printStackTrace();
  }
}
```

We can execute the preceding method and insert another row:

```
executeStatement("insert into person (first_name, last_name, dob)" +
                        " values ('Bill', 'Grey', '1980-01-27')");
```

We will see the result of this and previous `INSERT`-statement execution in the next section, when we demonstrate `SELECT`-statement.

Meanwhile, we would like to discuss the most popular methods of the
`java.sql.Statement` interface:

- `boolean execute(String sql)`: It returns `true` if the executed statement
  returns data (as a `java.sql.ResultSet` object) that can be retrieved using
  the `ResultSet getResultSet()` method of
  the `java.sql.Statement` interface. It returns `false` if the executed statement
  does not return data (the SQL statement was probably updating or inserting
  some rows) and the subsequent call to the `int getUpdateCount()` method of
  the `java.sql.Statement` interface returns the number of the affected rows. For
  example, if we have added the print statements to our `executeStatement()`
  method, we would see the following results after inserting a row:

```java
void executeStatement(String sql){
  Connection conn = getConnection();
  try (conn; Statement st = conn.createStatement()) {
    System.out.println(st.execute(sql));        //prints: false
    System.out.println(st.getResultSet());      //prints: null
    System.out.println(st.getUpdateCount());    //prints: 1
  } catch (SQLException ex) {
    ex.printStackTrace();
  }
}
```

- `ResultSet executeQuery(String sql)`: It returns data as
  a `java.sql.ResultSet` object (the executed SQL statement is expected to be
  `SELECT`-statement). The same data can be also retrieved by the subsequent call to
  the `ResultSet getResultSet()` method of
  the `java.sql.Statement` interface. The `int getUpdateCount()` method of
  the `java.sql.Statement` interface returns −1. For example, if we change
  our `executeStatement()` method and use `executeQuery()`, the results of
  `executeStatement("select first_name from person")` would be:

```java
void executeStatement(String sql){
  Connection conn = getConnection();
  try (conn; Statement st = conn.createStatement()) {
    System.out.println(st.executeQuery(sql)); //prints: ResultSet
    System.out.println(st.getResultSet());      //prints: ResultSet
    System.out.println(st.getUpdateCount());    //prints: -1
  } catch (SQLException ex) {
    ex.printStackTrace();
  }
}
```

- `int executeUpdate(String sql)`: It returns the number of the affected rows (the executed SQL statement is expected to be UPDATE-statement). The same number returns the subsequent call to the `int getUpdateCount()` method of the `java.sql.Statement` interface. The subsequent call to the `ResultSet getResultSet()` method of the `java.sql.Statement` interface returns `null`. For example, if we change our `executeStatement()` method and use `executeUpdate()`, the results of `executeStatement("update person set first_name = 'Jim' where last_name = 'Adams'")` would be:

```java
void executeStatement4(String sql){
  Connection conn = getConnection();
  try (conn; Statement st = conn.createStatement()) {
    System.out.println(st.executeUpdate(sql));//prints: 1
    System.out.println(st.getResultSet());     //prints: null
    System.out.println(st.getUpdateCount());  //prints: 1
  } catch (SQLException ex) {
    ex.printStackTrace();
  }
}
```

# SELECT-statement

The SELECT-statement has the following format:

```
SELECT column_name, column_name
FROM table_name WHERE some_column = some_value;
```

When all the columns have to be selected, it looks like this:

```
SELECT * FROM table_name WHERE some_column=some_value;
```

Here is a more general definition of WHERE-clause:

```
WHERE column_name operator value
Operator:
   =    Equal
   <>   Not equal. In some versions of SQL, !=
   >    Greater than
   <    Less than
   >=   Greater than or equal
   <=   Less than or equal
   IN  Specifies multiple possible values for a column
   LIKE  Specifies the search pattern
   BETWEEN  Specifies the inclusive range of vlaues in a column
```

The `column_name` operator value constructs can be combined using the AND and OR logical operator and grouped by brackets, ( ).

In the previous statement, we have executed a `select first_name from person` SELECT-statement that returns all the first names recorded in the `person` table. Let's now execute it again and print out the results:

```
Connection conn = getConnection();
try (conn; Statement st = conn.createStatement()) {
  ResultSet rs = st.executeQuery("select first_name from person");
  while (rs.next()){
    System.out.print(rs.getString(1) + " "); //prints: Jim Bill
  }
} catch (SQLException ex) {
  ex.printStackTrace();
}
```

The `getString(int position)` method of the `ResultSet` interface extracts the `String` value from position 1 (the first in the list of columns in the SELECT-statement). There are similar getters for all primitive types, such as `getInt()` and `getByte()`.

It is also possible to extract the value from the `ResultSet` object by column name. In our case, it would be `getString("first_name")`. It is especially useful when the SELECT-statement looks like the following:

```
select * from person;
```

But bear in mind that extracting values from the `ResultSet` object by the column name is less efficient. The difference in performance is very small and becomes important only when the operation happens many times. Only the actual measuring and testing can tell if the difference is significant for your application or not. Extracting values by column name is especially attractive because it provides better code readability, which pays well in a long time during the application maintenance.

There are many other useful methods in the `ResultSet` interface. If your application reads data from a database, we highly recommend you read the documentation of the SELECT-statement and the `ResultSet` interface.

# UPDATE-statement

The data can be changed by the UPDATE-statement:

```
UPDATE table_name SET column1=value1,column2=value2,... WHERE-clause;
```

We have used such a statement to change the first name in one of the records from the original value John to a new value, Jim:

```
update person set first_name = 'Jim' where last_name = 'Adams'
```

Later, using the SELECT-statement, we will prove that the change was successful. Without the WHERE-clause, all the records of the table would be affected.

# DELETE-statement

The data can be deleted by the DELETE-statement:

```
DELETE FROM table_name WHERE-clause;
```

Without the WHERE-clause, all the records of the table are deleted. In the case of the person table, we can delete all the records using the delete from person SQL statement. The following statement deletes all the records with first name Jim from the person table:

```
delete from person where first_name = 'Jim';
```

# Using the PreparedStatement class

An object of PreparedStatement —a sub-interface of the Statement interface—is designed to be cached in the database and then used to efficiently execute the SQL statement multiple times for different input values. Similar to an object of Statement (created by the createStatement() method), it can be created by the prepareStatement() method of the same Connection object.

The same SQL statement that was used to generate the `Statement` object can be used to generate the `PreparedStatement` object, too. In fact, it is a good idea to consider using `PreparedStatement` for any SQL statement that is called multiple times because it performs better than `Statement`. To do it, all we need to change are these two lines in our preceding sample code:

```
try (conn; Statement st = conn.createStatement()) {
   ResultSet rs = st.executeQuery(sql);
```

Alternatively, we can use the `PreparedStatement` class the same way:

```
try (conn; PreparedStatement st = conn.prepareStatement(sql)) {
   ResultSet rs = st.executeQuery();
```

But the true usefulness of `PreparedStatement` shines because of its ability to accept parameters – the input values that substitute (in the order of their appearance) the `?` symbol. For example, we can create the following method:

```
List<Person> selectPersonsByFirstName(String sql, String searchValue){
   List<Person> list = new ArrayList<>();
   Connection conn = getConnection();
   try (conn; PreparedStatement st = conn.prepareStatement(sql)) {
      st.setString(1, searchValue);
      ResultSet rs = st.executeQuery();
      while (rs.next()){
         list.add(new Person(rs.getInt("id"),
                  rs.getString("first_name"),
                  rs.getString("last_name"),
                  rs.getDate("dob").toLocalDate())));
      }
   } catch (SQLException ex) {
      ex.printStackTrace();
   }
   return list;
}
```

We can use the preceding method to read those records form the `person` table that match the `WHERE`-clause. For example, we can find all the records that have the first name `Jim`:

```
String sql = "select * from person where first_name = ?";
List<Person> list = selectPersonsByFirstName(sql, "Jim");
for(Person person: list){
   System.out.println(person);
}
```

The result will be:

```
Person{firstName='Jim', lastName='Adams', dob=1999-08-23, id=1}
```

The `Person` object is printed this way because we have added the
following `toString()` method:

```
@Override
public String toString() {
  return "Person{" +
          "firstName='" + firstName + '\'' +
          ", lastName='" + lastName + '\'' +
          ", dob=" + dob +
          ", id=" + id +
          '}';
}
```

The same result we would get from running the following code:

```
String sql = "select * from person where last_name = ?";
List<Person> list = selectPersonsByFirstName(sql, "Adams");
for(Person person: list){
    System.out.println(person);
}
```

It is not a bad idea to always use prepared statements for CRUD operations. They might be
a little slower if executed only once, but you can test to see whether this is the price you're
willing to pay. What you get with prepared statements is consistent (better readable) code,
more security (prepared statements are not vulnerable to SQL injection attack), and one
fewer decision to make – just reuse the same code everywhere.

# Exercise – Selecting unique first names

Write an SQL statement that selects all the names from the person table without duplicates.
For example, assume that there are three records in the `person` table that have these first
names: `Jim`, `Jim`, and `Bill`. The SQL statement you write must return `Jim` and `Bill`,
without repeating the name `Jim` twice.

We did not explain how to do it; you have to read the SQL documentation
to find out how to select unique values.

# Answer

Use the `distinct` keyword. The following SQL statement returns unique first names:

```
select distinct first_name from person;
```

# Summary

This chapter explained how to write Java code that can manipulate—insert, read, update, delete—data in a database. It also provided a short introduction to the SQL language and basic database operations. The reader has learned what JDBC is, how to create and delete a database and a table, and how to write a program that manages data in a table.

In the next chapter, the reader will learn the concept of functional programming. We will provide an overview of functional interfaces that come with JDK, explain how to use them in lambda expressions, and look at how to use lambda expressions in datastream processing.

# 17
# Lambda Expressions and Functional Programming

This chapter explains the concept of functional programming. It provides an overview of the functional interfaces that come with JDK, explains how to use them in lambda expressions, and how to write lambda expressions in the most concise style.

In this chapter, we will cover the following topics:

- Functional programming
- Functional interfaces
- Lambda expressions
- Method references
- Exercise – Using method references for creating a new object

## Functional programming

Functional programming allows us to treat a block of code (a function) like an object, passing it as a parameter or as a return value of a method. This feature is present in many programming languages. It does not require us to manage the object state. The function is stateless. Its result depends only on the input data, no matter how many times it was called. This style makes the outcome more predictable, which is the most attractive aspect of functional programming.

Without functional programming, the only way to pass a functionality as a parameter in Java would be through writing a class that implements an interface, creating its object, and then passing it as a parameter. But even the least involved style—using the anonymous class—requires writing too much of the boilerplate code. Using functional interfaces and lambda expressions makes the code shorter, clearer, and more expressive.

Adding it to Java increases parallel programming capabilities by shifting the responsibility for parallelism from the client code to the library. Before that, in order to process elements of Java collections, the client code had to iterate over the collection and organize processing. In Java 8, new (default) methods were added that accept a function (the implementation of a functional interface) as a parameter and then apply it to each element of the collection in parallel or not, depending on the internal processing algorithm. So, it is the library's responsibility to organize parallel processing.

Throughout this chapter, we will define and explain these Java features—functional interfaces and lambda expressions—and demonstrate their applicability in code examples. They make functions the first-class citizens of the language on the same level of importance as objects.

# What is a functional interface?

In fact, you have already seen elements of functional programming in our demonstration code. One example is the `forEach(Consumer consumer)` method, available for every `Iterable`, where `Consumer` is a functional interface. Another example is the `removeIf(Predicate predicate)` method, available for every `Collection` object. The passed-in `Predicate` object is a function – an implementation of a functional interface. Similarly, the `sort(Comparator comparator)` and `replaceAll(UnaryOperator uo)` methods in the `List` interface and several `compute()` methods in `Map` are examples of functional programming.

A functional interface is an interface that has only one abstract method, including those that were inherited from the parent interface.

To help avoid runtime errors, an `@FunctionalInterface` annotation was introduced in Java 8 that tells the compiler about the intent, so the compiler can check to see whether there is truly only one abstract method in the annotated interface. Let's review the following interfaces of the same line of inheritance:

```
@FunctionalInterface
interface A {
  void method1();
  default void method2(){}
  static void method3(){}
}
```

```
@FunctionalInterface
interface B extends A {
   default void method4(){}
}

@FunctionalInterface
interface C extends B {
   void method1();
}

//@FunctionalInterface   //compilation error
interface D extends C {
   void method5();
}
```

Interface A is a functional interface because it has only one abstract method: method1(). Interface B is also a functional interface because it has only one abstract method too – the same method1() inherited from interface A. Interface C is a functional interface because it has only one abstract method, method1(), which overrides the abstract method1() method of the parent interface A. Interface D cannot be a functional interface because it has two abstract methods – method1(), from the parent interface A, and method5().

When the @FunctionalInterface annotation is used, it tells the compiler to check on the presence of only one abstract method, and it warns the programmer, who reads the code, that this interface has only one abstract method intentionally. Otherwise, the programmer may waste time enhancing the interface only to discover later that it cannot be done.

For the same reason, the Runnable and Callable interfaces that existed in Java since its early versions were annotated in Java 8 as @FunctionalInterface. It makes this distinction explicit and serves as a reminder to its users and to those who might attempt to add another abstract method:

```
@FunctionalInterface
interface Runnable {
   void run();
}
@FunctionalInterface
interface Callable<V> {
   V call() throws Exception;
}
```

As you can see, creating a functional interface is easy. But before doing that, consider using one of the 43 functional interfaces provided in the java.util.function package.

# Ready-to-use standard functional interfaces

Most of the interfaces provided in the `java.util.function` package are specializations of the following four interfaces: `Function`, `Consumer`, `Supplier`, and `Predicate`. Let's review them and then have a short overview of the rest of the 39 standard functional interfaces.

## Function<T, R>

The notation of this and other functional `<indexentry content="standard functional interfaces:function">` interfaces includes listing of the types of the input data (`T`) and the returned data (`R`). So, `Function<T, R>` means that the only abstract method of this interface accepts an argument of type `T` and produces a result of type `R`. You can find the name of that abstract method by reading the online documentation. In the case of the `Function<T, R>` interface, its method is `R apply(T)`.

After learning all that, we can create an implementation of this interface using an anonymous class:

```
Function<Integer, Double> multiplyByTen = new Function<Integer, Double>(){
  public Double apply(Integer i){
    return i * 10.0;
  }
};
```

It is up to the programmer to decide which actual type will be `T` (the input parameter) and which type will be `R` (the returned value). In our example, we have decided that the input parameters will be of the `Integer` type and the result will be of the `Double` type. As you have probably realized by now, the types can be reference types only, and the boxing and unboxing of primitive types is performed automatically.

We can now use our new `Function<Integer, Double> multiplyByTen` function any way we need. We can just use it directly, as follows:

```
System.out.println(multiplyByTen.apply(1)); //prints: 10.0
```

Or we can create a method that accepts this function as a parameter:

```
void useFunc(Function<Integer, Double> processingFunc, int input){
  System.out.println(processingFunc.apply(input));
}
```

We can then pass our function into this method and let the method use it:

```
useFunc(multiplyByTen, 10);     //prints: 100.00
```

We can also create a method that will generate a function whenever we need one:

```
Function<Integer, Double> createMultiplyBy(double num){
  Function<Integer, Double> func = new Function<Integer, Double>(){
    public Double apply(Integer i){
      return i * num;
    }
  };
  return func;
}
```

Using the preceding method, we can write the following code:

```
Function<Integer, Double> multiplyByFive = createMultiplyBy(5);
System.out.println(multiplyByFive.apply(1)); //prints: 5.0
useFunc(multiplyByFive, 10);                 //prints: 50.0
```

In the next section, we will introduce lambda expressions and will show how they can be used to express the functional interface implementation with much less code.

# Consumer<T>

By looking at the `Consumer<T>` interface definition, you can already guess that this interface has an abstract method that accepts a parameter of the `T` type <indexentry content="standard functional interfaces:Consumer">and does not return anything. From the documentation of the `Consumer<T>` interface, we learn that its abstract method is `void accept(T)`, which means that, for example, we can implement it as follows:

```
Consumer<Double> printResult = new Consumer<Double>() {
  public void accept(Double d) {
    System.out.println("Result=" + d);
  }
};
printResult.accept(10.0);            //prints: Result=10.0
```

Or we can create a method that will generate the function:

```
Consumer<Double> createPrintingFunc(String prefix, String postfix){
  Consumer<Double> func = new Consumer<Double>() {
    public void accept(Double d) {
      System.out.println(prefix + d + postfix);
    }
  };
  return func;
}
```

Now we can use it as follows:

```
Consumer<Double> printResult = createPrintingFunc("Result=", " Great!");
printResult.accept(10.0);    //prints: Result=10.0 Great!
```

We can also create a new method that not only accepts a processing function as a parameter but also a printing function too:

```
void processAndConsume(int input,
                  Function<Integer, Double> processingFunc,
                              Consumer<Double> consumer){
  consumer.accept(processingFunc.apply(input));
}
```

We can then write the following code:

```
Function<Integer, Double> multiplyByFive = createMultiplyBy(5);
Consumer<Double> printResult = createPrintingFunc("Result=", " Great!");
processAndConsume(10, multiplyByFive, printResult); //Result=50.0 Great!
```

As we have mentioned before, in the next section, we will introduce lambda expressions and will show how they can be used to express the functional interface implementation with much less code.

# Supplier<T>

Here is a trick question: guess the input and the output types of the abstract method of the Supplier<T> interface. The answer is: it accepts no parameters and returns the T type. As you understand now, the difference is in the name of the interface itself. It should give you a hint: the consumer just consumes and returns nothing, while the supplier just supplies without any input. The abstract method of the Supplier<T> interface is T get().

Similar to the previous functions, we can write the supplier generating method:

```
Supplier<Integer> createSuppplier(int num){
    Supplier<Integer> func = new Supplier<Integer>() {
        public Integer get() { return num; }
    };
    return func;
}
```

We can now write a method that accepts only functions:

```
void supplyProcessAndConsume(Supplier<Integer> input,
                             Function<Integer, Double> process,
                             Consumer<Double> consume){
    consume.accept(processFunc.apply(input.get()));
}
```

Notice how the output type of the `input` function is the same as the input of the `process` function, which returns the same type as consumed by the `consume` function. It makes the following code possible:

```
Supplier<Integer> supply7 = createSuppplier(7);
Function<Integer, Double> multiplyByFive = createMultiplyBy(5);
Consumer<Double> printResult = createPrintingFunc("Result=", " Great!");
supplyProcessAndConsume(supply7, multiplyByFive, printResult);
                                        //prints: Result=35.0 Great!
```

At this point, we hope, you start to appreciate the value functional programming brings to the table. It allows us to pass around chunks of functionality that can be plugged into the middle of an algorithm without needing to create an object. Static methods do not require creating an object either, but they are shared by all application threads because they are unique in the JVM. Meanwhile, each function is an object and can be either unique in the JVM (if assigned to a static variable) or created for each processing thread (which typically is the case). It has very little coding overhead and can have even less plumbing when used in a lambda expression – the topic of our next section.

So far, we have demonstrated how a function can be plugged into the existing control-flow expression. And now we will describe the last missing piece – a function that represents the decision-making construct that can be passed around as an object too.

# Predicate<T>

This is an interface that represents a Boolean-valued function that has a single method: `boolean test(T)`. Here is an example of a method that creates a `Predicate<Integer>` function:

```
Predicate<Integer> createTestSmallerThan(int num){
    Predicate<Integer> func = new Predicate<Integer>() {
      public boolean test(Integer d) {
        return d < num;
      }
    };
    return func;
}
```

We can use it to add some logic to the processing method:

```
void supplyDecideProcessAndConsume(Supplier<Integer> input,
                                   Predicate<Integer> test,
                                   Function<Integer, Double> process,
                                   Consumer<Double> consume){
    int in = input.get();
    if(test.test(in)){
      consume.accept(process.apply(in));
    } else {
      System.out.println("Input " + in +
                    " does not pass the test and not processed.");
    }
}
```

And the following code demonstrates its usage:

```
Supplier<Integer> input = createSuppplier(7);
Predicate<Integer> test = createTestSmallerThan(5);
Function<Integer, Double> multiplyByFive = createMultiplyBy(5);
Consumer<Double> printResult = createPrintingFunc("Result=", " Great!");
supplyDecideProcessAndConsume(input, test, multiplyByFive, printResult);
        //prints: Input 7 does not pass the test and not processed.
```

Let's set the input to 3, for example:

```
Supplier<Integer> input = createSuppplier(3)
```

The preceding code would result in the following output:

```
Result=15.0 Great!
```

# Other standard functional interfaces

The other 39 functional interfaces in the `java.util.function` package are variations of the four interfaces we have just reviewed. These variations are created in order to achieve one or any combination of the following:

- Better performance by avoiding autoboxing and unboxing via the explicit usage of the integer, double, or long primitives
- Allowing two input parameters
- A shorter notation

Here are just a few of examples:

- `IntFunction<R>` with the `R apply(int)` method provides shorter notation (without generics for the input parameter type) and avoids autoboxing by requiring the `int` primitive as the parameter
- `BiFunction<T,U,R>` with the `R apply(T,U)` method allows two input parameters
- `BinaryOperator<T>` with the `T apply(T,T)` method allows two input parameters of the `T` type and returns a value of the same `T` type
- `IntBinaryOperator` with the `int applAsInt(int,int)` method accepts two parameters of the `int` type and returns the value of the `int` type

If you are going to use functional interfaces, we encourage you to study the API of the interfaces of the `java.util.functional` package.

# Chaining standard functions

Most of the functional interfaces in the `java.util.function` package have default methods that allow us to build a chain (also called a pipe or pipeline) of functions that pass the result of one as the input parameter to another, thus composing a new complex function. For example:

```
Function<Double, Long> f1 = d -> Double.valueOf(d / 2.).longValue();
Function<Long, String> f2 = l -> "Result: " + (l + 1);
Function<Double, String> f3 = f1.andThen(f2);
System.out.println(f3.apply(4.));              //prints: 3
```

As you can see from the preceding code, we have created a new f3 function by combining the f1 and f2 functions using the andThen() method. That's the idea behind the methods we are going to explore in this section. First, we express the functions as anonymous classes and, in the following section, we introduce the lambda expressions that we used in the preceding example.

# Chain two Function<T,R>

We can use the andThen(Function after) default method of the Function interface. We have already created the Function<Integer, Double> createMultiplyBy() method:

```
Function<Integer, Double> createMultiplyBy(double num){
  Function<Integer, Double> func = new Function<Integer, Double>(){
    public Double apply(Integer i){
      return i * num;
    }
  };
  return func;
```

We can also write another method that creates a subtracting function with the Double input type, so we can chain it to the multiplying function:

```
private static Function<Double, Long> createSubtractInt(int num){
  Function<Double, Long> func = new Function<Double, Long>(){
    public Long apply(Double dbl){
      return Math.round(dbl - num);
    }
  };
  return func;
}
```

Now we can write the following code:

```
Function<Integer, Double> multiplyByFive = createMultiplyBy(5);
System.out.println(multiplyByFive.apply(2));   //prints: 10.0

Function<Double, Long> subtract7 = createSubtractInt(7);
System.out.println(subtract7.apply(11.0));   //prints: 4

long r = multiplyByFive.andThen(subtract7).apply(2);
System.out.println(r);                          //prints: 3
```

As you can see, the `multiplyByFive.andThen(subtract7)` chain acts effectively as `Function<Integer, Long> multiplyByFiveAndSubtractSeven`.

The `Function` interface has another default method, `Function<V,R> compose(Function<V,T> before)`, that also allows us to chain two functions. The function that has to be executed first can be passed as the `before` parameter into the `compose()` method of the second function:

```
boolean r = subtract7.compose(multiplyByFive).apply(2);
System.out.println(r);                          //prints: 3
```

# Chain two Consumer<T>

The `Consumer` interface has the `andThen(Consumer after)` method too. We have already written the method that creates the printing function:

```
Consumer<Double> createPrintingFunc(String prefix, String postfix){
  Consumer<Double> func = new Consumer<Double>() {
    public void accept(Double d) {
      System.out.println(prefix + d + postfix);
    }
  };
  return func;
}
```

And now we can create and chain two printing functions, as follows:

```
Consumer<Double> print21By = createPrintingFunc("21 by ", "");
Consumer<Double> equalsBy21 = createPrintingFunc("equals ", " by 21");
print21By.andThen(equalsBy21).accept(2d);
//prints: 21 by 2.0
//        equals 2.0 by 21
```

As you can see in the `Consumer` chain, both functions consume the same value in the sequence defined by the chain.

# Chain two Predicate<T>

The `Supplier` interface does not have default methods, while the `Predicate` interface has one static method, `isEqual(Object targetRef)`, and three default methods: `and(Predicate other)`, `negate()`, and `or(Predicate other)`. To demonstrate usage of the `and(Predicate other)` and `or(Predicate other)` methods, for example, let's write the methods that create two `Predicate<Double>` functions. One function checks whether the value is smaller than the input:

```
Predicate<Double> testSmallerThan(double limit){
  Predicate<Double> func = new Predicate<Double>() {
    public boolean test(Double num) {
      System.out.println("Test if " + num + " is smaller than " + limit);
      return num < limit;
    }
  };
  return func;
}
```

Another function checks whether the value is bigger than the input:

```
Predicate<Double> testBiggerThan(double limit){
  Predicate<Double> func = new Predicate<Double>() {
    public boolean test(Double num) {
      System.out.println("Test if " + num + " is bigger than " + limit);
      return num > limit;
    }
  };
  return func;
}
```

Now we can create two `Predicate<Double>` functions and chain them:

```
Predicate<Double> isSmallerThan20 = testSmallerThan(20d);
System.out.println(isSmallerThan20.test(10d));
    //prints: Test if 10.0 is smaller than 20.0
    //        true

Predicate<Double> isBiggerThan18 = testBiggerThan(18d);
System.out.println(isBiggerThan18.test(10d));
    //prints: Test if 10.0 is bigger than 18.0
    //        false

boolean b = isSmallerThan20.and(isBiggerThan18).test(10.);
System.out.println(b);
    //prints: Test if 10.0 is smaller than 20.0
    //        Test if 10.0 is bigger than 18.0
```

```
//          false

b = isSmallerThan20.or(isBiggerThan18).test(10.);
System.out.println(b);
    //prints: Test if 10.0 is smaller than 20.0
    //          true
```

As you can see, the `and()` method required execution of each of the functions, while the `or()` method did not execute the second function as soon as the first one in the chain returned `true`.

# identity() and other default methods

Functional interfaces of the `java.util.function` package have other helpful default methods. The one that stands out is the `identity()` method, which returns a function that always returns its input argument:

```
Function<Integer, Integer> id = Function.identity();
System.out.println(id.apply(4));             //prints: 4
```

The `identity()` method is very helpful when some procedure requires providing a certain function, but you do not want the provided function to change anything. In such cases, you create an identity function with the necessary output type. For example, in one of our previous code snippets, we may decide that the `multiplyByFive` function should not change anything in the `multiplyByFive.andThen(subtract7)` chain:

```
Function<Double, Double> multiplyByFive = Function.identity();
System.out.println(multiplyByFive.apply(2.));   //prints: 2.0

Function<Double, Long> subtract7 = createSubtractInt(7);
System.out.println(subtract7.apply(11.0));      //prints: 4

long r = multiplyByFive.andThen(subtract7).apply(2.);
System.out.println(r);                          //prints: -5
```

As you can see, the `multiplyByFive` function did not do anything with the input parameter 2, so the result (after 7 was subtracted) is -5.

Other default methods are mostly related to conversion and boxing and unboxing, but also extracting minimum and maximum values of two parameters. If you are interested, you can look through the API of interfaces of the `java.util.function` package and get a feeling for the possibilities.

# Lambda expressions

The examples in the previous section (that used anonymous classes for the implementation of functional interfaces) looked bulky and felt excessively verbose. For one, there was no need to repeat the interface name, because we had declared it already as the type for the object reference. And, second, in the case of a functional interface that had only one abstract method, there is no need to specify the method name that has to be implemented. The compiler and Java runtime can figure it out. All we need is to provide the new functionality. Lambda expressions were introduced for exactly this purpose.

# What is a lambda expression?

The term lambda comes from lambda calculus—a universal model of computation that can be used to simulate any Turing machine. It was introduced by mathematician, Alonzo Church, in the 1930s. A lambda expression is a function, implemented in Java as an anonymous method, that also allows us to omit modifiers, return types, and parameter types. That makes for a very compact notation.

The syntax of a lambda expression includes the list of parameters, an arrow token ->, and a body. The list of parameters can be empty (), without brackets (if there is only one parameter), or a comma-separated list of parameters surrounded by brackets. The body can be a single expression or a statement block.

Let us look at a few examples:

- `()  -> 42;` always returns 42
- `x -> x + 1;` increments the x variable by 1
- `(x, y)  -> x * y;` multiplies x by y and returns the result
- `(char x)  -> x == '$';` compares the value of the x variable and the $ symbol, and returns a Boolean value
- `x -> {  System.out.println("x=" + x);  };` prints the x value with the x= prefix

# Re-implementing functions

We can rewrite our functions, created in the previous section, using lambda expressions, as follows:

```
Function<Integer, Double> createMultiplyBy(double num){
  Function<Integer, Double> func = i -> i * num;
  return func;
}
Consumer<Double> createPrintingFunc(String prefix, String postfix){
  Consumer<Double> func = d -> System.out.println(prefix + d + postfix);
  return func;
}
Supplier<Integer> createSuppplier(int num){
  Supplier<Integer> func = () -> num;
  return func;
}
Predicate<Integer> createTestSmallerThan(int num){
  Predicate<Integer> func = d -> d < num;
  return func;
}
```

We don't repeat the name of the implemented interface because it is specified as the return type in the method signature. And we do not specify the name of the abstract method either because it is the only method of the interface that has to be implemented. Writing such a compact and efficient code became possible because of the combination of the lambda expression and functional interface.

Looking at the preceding examples, you probably realize that there is no need to have methods that create a function anymore. Let's change the code that calls the `supplyDecideProcessAndConsume()` method:

```
void supplyDecideProcessAndConsume(Supplier<Integer> input,
                                   Predicate<Integer> test,
                                   Function<Integer, Double> process,
                                         Consumer<Double> consume){
  int in = input.get();
  if(test.test(in)){
    consume.accept(process.apply(in));
  } else {
    System.out.println("Input " + in +
              " does not pass the test and not processed.");
  }
}
```

Let's revisit the following lines:

```
Supplier<Integer> input = createSuppplier(7);
Predicate<Integer> test = createTestSmallerThan(5);
Function<Integer, Double> multiplyByFive = createMultiplyBy(5);
Consumer<Double> printResult = createPrintingFunc("Result=", " Great!");
supplyDecideProcessAndConsume(input, test, multiplyByFive, printResult);
```

We can change the preceding code to the following without changing the functionality:

```
Supplier<Integer> input = () -> 7;
Predicate<Integer> test = d -> d < 5.;
Function<Integer, Double> multiplyByFive = i -> i * 5.;;
Consumer<Double> printResult =
                d -> System.out.println("Result=" + d + " Great!");
supplyDecideProcessAndConsume(input, test, multiplyByFive, printResult);
```

We can even inline the preceding functions and write the preceding code in one line like this:

```
supplyDecideProcessAndConsume(() -> 7, d -> d < 5, i -> i * 5.,
                d -> System.out.println("Result=" + d + " Great!"));
```

Notice how much more transparent the definition of the printing function has become. That is the power and the beauty of lambda expressions in combination with functional interfaces. In `Chapter 18`, *Streams and Pipelines*, you will see that lambda expressions are, in fact, the only way to process streamed data.

# Lambda limitations

There are two aspects of a lambda expression that we would like to point out and clarify, which are:

- If a lambda expression uses a local variable created outside it, this local variable has to be final or effectively final (not re-assigned in the same context)
- The `this` keyword in a lambda expression refers to the enclosing context, and not the lambda expression itself

# Effectively final local variable

As in the anonymous class, the variable, created outside and used inside the lambda expression, becomes effectively final and cannot be modified. You can write the following:

```
int x = 7;
//x = 3;          //compilation error
int y = 5;
double z = 5.;
supplyDecideProcessAndConsume(() -> x, d -> d < y, i -> i * z,
           d -> { //x = 3;          //compilation error
                  System.out.println("Result=" + d + " Great!"); } );
```

But, as you can see, we cannot change the value of the local variable used in the lambda expression. The reason for this restriction is that a function can be passed around and executed in different contexts (different threads, for example), and the attempt to synchronize these contexts would defeat the original idea of the stateless function and independent distributed evaluation of the expression. That is why all the local variables used in the lambda expression are effectively final, meaning that they can either be declared final explicitly or become final by virtue of their usage in a lambda expression.

There is one possible workaround for this limitation. If the local variable is of a reference type (but not String or a primitive wrapping type), it is possible to change its state even if this local variable is used in the lambda expression:

```
class A {
  private int x;
  public int getX(){ return this.x; }
  public void setX(int x){ this.x = x; }
}
void localVariable2(){
  A a = new A();
  a.setX(7);
  a.setX(3);
  int y = 5;
  double z = 5.;
  supplyDecideProcessAndConsume(() -> a.getX(), d -> d < y, i -> i * z,
           d -> { a.setX(5);
    System.out.println("Result=" + d + " Great!"); } );
}
```

But this workaround should be used only when really needed and has to be done with care because of the danger of unexpected side effects.

# The this keyword interpretation

One principal difference between the anonymous class and lambda expressions is the interpretation of the `this` keyword. Inside an anonymous class, it refers to the instance of the anonymous class. Inside a lambda expression, `this` refers to the instance of the class that surrounds the expression, also called an *enclosing instance, enclosing context,* or *enclosing scope.*

Let's write a `ThisDemo` class that illustrates the difference:

```
class ThisDemo {
  private String field = "ThisDemo.field";
  public void useAnonymousClass() {
    Consumer<String> consumer = new Consumer<>() {
      private String field = "AnonymousClassConsumer.field";
      public void accept(String s) {
        System.out.println(this.field);
      }
    };
    consumer.accept(this.field);
  }
  public void useLambdaExpression() {
    Consumer<String> consumer = consumer = s -> {
      System.out.println(this.field);
    };
    consumer.accept(this.field);
  }

}
```

As you can see, `this` inside the anonymous class refers to the anonymous class instance, while `this` in the lambda expression refers to the enclosing class instance. Lambda expressions just do not have and cannot have a field. If we execute the preceding methods, the output confirms our assumptions:

```
ThisDemo d = new ThisDemo();
d.useAnonymousClass();    //prints: AnonymousClassConsumer.field
d.useLambdaExpression(); //prints: ThisDemo.field
```

The lambda expression is not a class instance and cannot be referred to by `this`. According to Java Specification, such an approach *allows more flexibility for implementations* by *treating [this] the same as in the surrounding context.*

# Method references

Let's look at our last implementation of the call to
the `supplyDecidePprocessAndConsume()` method:

```
supplyDecideProcessAndConsume(() -> 7, d -> d < 5, i -> i * 5.,
                        d -> System.out.println("Result=" + d + " Great!"));
```

The functions we have used are pretty trivial. In real-life code, each of them may require a
multiple-line implementation. In such a case, to put a code block inline would make the
code almost unreadable. In such cases, referring to the methods with the necessary
implementation helps. Let's assume we have the following `Helper` class:

```
public class Helper {
  public double calculateResult(int i){
    // Maybe many lines of code here
    return i* 5;
  }
  public static void printResult(double d){
    // Maybe many lines of code here
    System.out.println("Result=" + d + " Great!");
  }
}
```

The lambda expressions in the `Lambdas` class may refer to the methods of the `Helper` and
`Lambdas` classes, as follows:

```
public class Lambdas {
  public void methodReference() {
    Supplier<Integer> input = () -> generateInput();
    Predicate<Integer> test = d -> checkValue(d);
    Function<Integer, Double> multiplyByFive =
                              i -> new Helper().calculateResult(i);
    Consumer<Double> printResult = d -> Helper.printResult(d);
    supplyDecideProcessAndConsume(input, test,
                                  multiplyByFive, printResult);
  }
  private int generateInput(){
    // Maybe many lines of code here
    return 7;
  }
  private static boolean checkValue(double d){
    // Maybe many lines of code here
    return d < 5;
  }
}
```

The preceding code reads better already, and the functions may be inlined again:

```
supplyDecideProcessAndConsume(() -> generateInput(), d -> checkValue(d),
            i -> new Helper().calculateResult(i), Helper.printResult(d));
```

But in such cases, the notation can be made even more compact. When a one-line lambda expression consists of a reference to an existing method, it is possible to further simplify the notation by using a method reference without listing the parameters.

The syntax of the method reference is `Location::methodName`, where `Location` indicates where (in which object or class) the `methodName` method can be found, and the two colons (`::`) serve as a separator between the location and the method name. If there are several methods with the same name at the specified location (because of the method overload), the reference method is identified by the signature of the abstract method of the functional interface implemented by the lambda expression.

Using the method reference, the preceding code under `methodReference()` method in the `Lambdas` class can be rewritten as follows:

```
Supplier<Integer> input = this::generateInput;
Predicate<Integer> test = Lambdas::checkValue;
Function<Integer, Double> multiplyByFive = new Helper()::calculateResult;;
Consumer<Double> printResult = Helper::printResult;
supplyDecideProcessAndConsume(input, test, multiplyByFive, printResult);
```

To inline such functions makes even more sense:

```
supplyDecideProcessAndConsume(this::generateInput, Lambdas::checkValue,
            new Helper()::calculateResult, Helper::printResult);
```

You have probably noticed that we have intentionally used different locations and two instance methods and two static methods in order to demonstrate the variety of possibilities.

If it feels like too much to remember, the good news is that a modern IDE (IntelliJ IDEA is one example) can do it for you and convert the code you are writing into the most compact form.

# Exercise – Using the method reference to create a new object

Use the method reference to express creating a new object. Let's assume that we have `class A{}`. Replace the following `Supplier` function declaration with another one that uses the method reference:

```
Supplier<A> supplier = () -> new A();
```

## Answer

The answer is:

```
Supplier<A> supplier = A::new;
```

# Summary

This chapter introduced the concept of functional programming. It provided an overview of the functional interfaces that come with JDK and demonstrated how to use them. It also discussed and demonstrated lambda expressions and how effectively they can improve code readability.

The next chapter will make the reader familiar with the powerful concept of datastreams processing. It explains what streams are, how to create them and process their elements, and how to build processing pipelines. It also shows how easily you can organize stream processing in parallel.

# 18
# Streams and Pipelines

The lambda expressions described and demonstrated in the previous chapter, together with functional interfaces, added a powerful functional programming capability to Java. It allows for passing behaviors (functions) as parameters to the libraries optimized for the performance of the data processing. This way, an application programmer can concentrate on the business aspects of the developed system, leaving the performance aspects to the specialists: the authors of the library. One example of such a library is the `java.util.stream` package, which is going to be the focus of this chapter.

We will introduce the concept of data streams processing, and will explain what streams are, how to process them, and how to build processing pipelines. We will also show how easily one can organize stream processing in parallel.

In this chapter, the following topics will be covered:

- What is a stream?
- Creating a stream
- Intermediate operations
- Terminal operations
- Stream pipelines
- Parallel processing
- Exercise – Multiplying all of the stream elements

## What is a stream?

The best way to understand a stream is to compare it to a collection. The latter is a data structure stored in memory. Every collection element is computed *before* being added to the collection. In contrast, an element emitted by a stream exists somewhere else (in the source) and is computed *on demand*. So, a collection can be a source for a stream.

In Java, a stream is an object of a `Stream`, `IntStream`, `LongStream`, or `DoubleStream` interface of the `java.util.stream` package. All methods present in the `Stream` interface are also available (with corresponding type changes) in the `IntStream`, `LongStream`, or `DoubleStream` specialized *numeric* stream interfaces. Some of the numeric stream interfaces have a few extra methods, such as `average()` and `sum()`, specific to the numeric values.

In this chapter, we will mostly speak about the `Stream` interface and its methods. But everything introduced can be equally applied to the numeric stream interfaces, too. At the end of the chapter, we will also review a few methods that are available in the numeric stream interfaces, but not in the `Stream` interface.

A stream represents some source of data—a collection, an array, or a file, for example—and generates (produces, emits) some values (stream elements of the same type as the stream) sequentially, as soon as the previously emitted element has been processed.

The `java.util.stream` package allows for the declarative presentation of the procedures (functions) that can be applied to the emitted elements, also in parallel. Today, with the machine learning requirements of massive data processing and the fine-tuning of operations having become ubiquitous, this feature reinforces the position of Java among the few modern programming languages of choice.

# Stream operations

Many of the methods of the `Stream` interface (those that have a functional interface type as a parameter) are called operations, because they are not implemented as traditional methods. Their functionalities are passed into the methods as a functions. The methods themselves are just shells that call a method of the functional interface, assigned as the type of the method parameter.

For example, let us look at the `Stream<T> filter (Predicate<T> predicate)` method. Its implementation is based on the call to the `boolean test(T)` method of the `Predicate<T>` function. So, instead of saying, "We use the `filter()` method of the `Stream` object to select some of the stream elements and skip others," the programmers prefer to say, "We apply the `filter` operation that allows some of the stream elements to get through, and skips others." It sounds similar to the statement, "We apply an operation of addition." It describes the nature of the action (operation), not the particular algorithm, which is unknown until the method receives the particular function.

So, there are three groups of methods in the `Stream` interface:

- Static factory methods that create `Stream` objects.
- Intermediate operations, which are instance methods that return `Stream` objects.
- Terminal operations, which are instance methods that return some type other than `Stream`.

Stream processing is organized typically as a pipe using a fluent (dot-connected) style (see the *Stream pipeline* section). A `Stream` factory method or another stream source starts such a pipe, and a Terminal operation produces the pipe result or a side effect, and ends the pipe (thus, the name). An intermediate operation can be placed between the originating `Stream` object and the Terminal operation. It processes the stream elements (or not, in some cases), and returns the modified (or not modified) `Stream` object, so the next intermediate or Terminal operation can be applied.

Examples of intermediate operations are as follows:

- `filter()`: This selects only elements matching a criterion.
- `map()`: This transforms elements according to a function.
- `distinct()`: This removes duplicates.
- `limit()`: This limits a stream to the specified number of elements.
- `sorted()`: This transforms unsorted stream into a sorted one.

There are some other methods that we will discuss in the *Intermediate operations* section.

The processing of the stream elements actually begins only when a Terminal operation starts executing. Then, all of the intermediate operations (if present) start processing. The stream closes (and cannot be reopened) as soon as the Terminal operation finishes execution. Examples of Terminal operations are `forEach()`, `findFirst()`, `reduce()`, `collect()`, `sum()`, `max()`, and other methods of the `Stream` interface that do not return `Stream`. We will discuss them in the *Terminal operations* section.

All of the Stream methods support parallel processing, which is especially helpful in the case of a large amount of data processed on a multi-core computer. One must make sure that the processing pipeline does not use a context state that can vary across different processing environments. We will discuss this in the *Parallel processing* section.

# Creating a stream

There are many ways to create a stream—an object of the Stream type or any of the numeric interfaces. We have grouped them by classes and interfaces that have methods creating Stream objects. We did so for the reader's convenience, to provide a better overview, so that it will be easier for the reader to find them if needed.

## Stream interface

This group of Stream factories is composed of static methods that belong to the Stream interface.

### empty(), of(T t), ofNullable(T t)

The following three methods create either empty or single-element Stream objects:

- Stream<T> empty(): Creates an empty sequential Stream object.
- Stream<T> of(T t): Creates a sequential single-element Stream object.
- Stream<T> ofNullable(T t): Creates a sequential Stream object containing a single element if the t parameter is non-null; otherwise, creates an empty Stream.

The following code demonstrates the usage of the preceding methods:

```
Stream.empty().forEach(System.out::println);     //prints nothing
Stream.of(1).forEach(System.out::println);       //prints: 1

List<String> list = List.of("1 ", "2");
//printList1(null);                               //NullPointerException
printList1(list);                                 //prints: 1 2

void printList1(List<String> list){
    list.stream().forEach(System.out::print);;
}
```

Notice how the first call to the `printList1()` method generates `NullPointerException` and prints 1 2 when the list is not `null`. To avoid the exception, we could implement the `printList1()` method as follows:

```
void printList1(List<String> list){
    (list == null ? Stream.empty() : list.stream())
                                    .forEach(System.out::print);
}
```

Instead, we have used the `ofNullable(T t)` method, as you can see in the following implementation of the `printList2()` method:

```
printList2(null);                                   //prints nothing
printList2(list);                                   //prints: [1 , 2]

void printList2(List<String> list){
    Stream.ofNullable(list).forEach(System.out::print);
}
```

That is the use case that has motivated the creation of the `ofNullable(T t)` method. But you may have noticed that a stream created by `ofNullable()` emitting the list as one object: it is printed as [1 , 2].

To process each element of the list in this case, we would need to add an intermediate `Stream` operation, `flatMap()`, that converts each element to a `Stream` object:

```
Stream.ofNullable(list).flatMap(e -> e.stream())
                        .forEach(System.out::print);        //prints: 1 2
```

We will discuss `flatMap()` method further in the *Intermediate operations* section.

The function passed into the `flatMap()` operation in the preceding code can be expressed as a method reference, too:

```
Stream.ofNullable(list).flatMap(Collection::stream)
                        .forEach(System.out::print);        //prints: 1 2
```

# iterate(Object, UnaryOperator)

Two static methods of the Stream interface allow us to generate a stream of values using an iterative process similar to the traditional for loop:

- Stream<T> iterate(T seed, UnaryOperator<T> func): Creates an **infinite** sequential Stream object, based on the iterative application of the second parameter (a func function) to the first seed parameter, producing a stream of seed, f(seed), and f(f(seed)) values.
- Stream<T> iterate(T seed, Predicate<T> hasNext, UnaryOperator<T> next): Creates a finite sequential Stream object based on the iterative application of the third parameter (the next function) to the first seed parameter, producing a stream of seed, f(seed), and f(f(seed)), values, as long as the third parameter (the hasNext function) returns true.

The following code demonstrates the usage of these methods:

```
Stream.iterate(1, i -> ++i).limit(9)
        .forEach(System.out::print);        //prints: 123456789

Stream.iterate(1, i -> i < 10, i -> ++i)
        .forEach(System.out::print);        //prints: 123456789
```

Notice that we were forced to add a limit() intermediate operator to the first pipeline to avoid generating an infinite number of values.

# concat(Stream a, Stream b)

The Stream<T> concatenate(Stream<> a, Stream<T> b) static method of the Stream interface creates a stream of values based on two Stream objects, a and b, passed in as the parameters. The newly created stream consists of all the elements of the first parameter, a, followed by all of the elements of the second parameter, b. The following code demonstrates this method of Stream object creation:

```
Stream<Integer> stream1 = List.of(1, 2).stream();
Stream<Integer> stream2 = List.of(2, 3).stream();

Stream.concat(stream1, stream2)
        .forEach(System.out::print);        //prints: 1223
```

Notice that the 2 element is present in both original streams, and consequently, it is present twice in the resulting stream.

# generate(Supplier)

The `Stream<T> generate(Supplier<T> supplier)` static method of
the `Stream` interface creates an infinite stream, where each element is generated by the
provided `Supplier<T>` function. Here are two examples:

```
Stream.generate(() -> 1).limit(5)
        .forEach(System.out::print);        //prints: 11111

Stream.generate(() -> new Random().nextDouble()).limit(5)
        .forEach(System.out::println);      //prints: 0.38575117472619247
                                            //        0.5055765386778835
                                            //        0.6528038976983277
                                            //        0.4422354489467244
                                            //        0.06770955839148762
```

Since the stream is infinite, we have added a `limit()` operation.

# of(T... values)

The `Stream<T> of(T... values)` method accepts varargs, or an array of values, and
creates a Stream object with the provided values as the stream elements:

```
Stream.of("1 ", 2).forEach(System.out::print);        //prints: 1 2
//Stream<String> stringStream = Stream.of("1 ", 2); //compile error

String[] strings = {"1 ", "2"};
Stream.of(strings).forEach(System.out::print);        //prints: 1 2
```

Notice that in the first line of the preceding code, a `Stream` object accepts elements of
different types if there is no type specified in the generics of the `Stream` reference
declaration. In the next line, the generics define the type of the `Stream` object as `String`,
and the same mix of element types generates a compile error. Generics definitely help
programmers to avoid many mistakes, and should be used wherever possible.

The `of(T... values)` method can also be used for the concatenation of multiple streams.
Let's assume, for example, that we have the following four streams, and we would like to
concatenate into one:

```
Stream<Integer> stream1 = Stream.of(1, 2);
Stream<Integer> stream2 = Stream.of(2, 3);
Stream<Integer> stream3 = Stream.of(3, 4);
Stream<Integer> stream4 = Stream.of(4, 5);
```

We expect the new stream to emit the values 1, 2, 2, 3, 3, 4, 4, and 5. First, we try the following code:

```
Stream.of(stream1, stream2, stream3, stream4)
    .forEach(System.out::print);
        //prints: java.util.stream.ReferencePipeline$Head@58ceff1j
```

The preceding code did not do what we hoped. It treated each stream as an object of the `java.util.stream.ReferencePipeline` internal class, which is used in the `Stream` interface implementation. So, we have added a `flatMap()` operation that converts each stream element into a stream (we will describe it in the *Intermediate operations* section):

```
Stream.of(stream1, stream2, stream3, stream4)
    .flatMap(e -> e).forEach(System.out::print);    //prints: 12233445
```

The function we passed into `flatMap()` as a parameter (`e -> e`) may look like it's doing nothing, but that is because each element of the stream is a stream already, so we did not need to transform it. By returning an element as the result of the `flatMap()` operation, we have told the pipeline to treat it as a `Stream` object. That was done, and the expected result was displayed.

# The Stream.Builder interface

The `Stream.Builder<T> builder()` static method returns an internal (located inside the interface `Stream` interface) `Builder` interface that can be used to construct a `Stream` object. The `Builder` interface extends the `Consumer` interface, and has the following methods:

- `void accept(T t)`: Adds an element to the stream (this method comes from the `Consumer` interface).
- `default Stream.Builder<T> add(T t)`: Calls the `accept(T)` method and returns `this`, thus allowing chaining `add(T)` methods in a fluent, dot-connected style.
- `Stream<T> build()`: Transitions this builder from the constructing state to the built state. After this method is called, no new elements can be added to the stream.

Using the `add()` method is straightforward:

```
Stream.<String>builder().add("cat").add(" dog").add(" bear")
        .build().forEach(System.out::print);   //prints: cat dog bear
```

Just notice the `<String>` generics that we have added in front of the `builder()` method. This way, we tell the builder that the stream we are creating will have `String` type elements. Otherwise, it will add them as `Object` types.

The `accept()` method is used when the builder is passed as a parameter of the `Consumer` type, or when you do not need to chain the methods that add the elements. For example, here is how the builder is passed in as a `Consumer` object:

```
Stream.Builder<String> builder = Stream.builder();
List.of("1", "2", "3").stream().forEach(builder);
builder.build().forEach(System.out::print);       //prints: 123
```

There are also cases where there is no need to chain the methods while adding the stream elements. The following method receives a list of `String` objects, and adds some of them (those that contain the character a) to a stream:

```
Stream<String> buildStream(List<String> values){
    Stream.Builder<String> builder = Stream.builder();
    for(String s: values){
        if(s.contains("a")){
            builder.accept(s);
        }
    }
    return builder.build();
}
```

Notice that we have added the `<String>` generics the `Stream.Builder` interface for the same reason—to tell the builder that the elements we are adding should be treated as `String` types.

When the preceding method is called, it produces the expected result:

```
List<String> list = List.of("cat", " dog", " bear");
buildStream(list).forEach(System.out::print);       //prints: cat bear
```

# Other classes and interfaces

In Java 8, two default methods were added to the `java.util.Collection` interface:

- `Stream<E> stream()`: Returns a stream of the elements of this collection.
- `Stream<E> parallelStream()`: Returns (possibly) a parallel stream of the elements of this collection. We say possibly because the JVM attempts to split the stream into several chunks and process them in parallel (if there are several CPUs) or virtually parallel (using the time-sharing of the CPU). This is not always possible; it depends, in part, on the nature of the requested processing.

It means that all of the collection interfaces that extend this interface, including `Set` and `List`, have these methods. Here is an example:

```
List<Integer> list = List.of(1, 2, 3, 4, 5);
list.stream().forEach(System.out::print);    //prints: 12345
```

We will discuss parallel streams further in the *Parallel processing* section.

Eight static overloaded `stream()` methods were added to the `java.util.Arrays` class, too. They create streams of different types from a corresponding array, or its subset:

- `Stream<T> stream(T[] array)`: Creates `Stream` from the provided array.
- `IntStream stream(int[] array)`: Creates `IntStream` from the provided array.
- `LongStream stream(long[] array)`: Creates `LongStream` from the provided array.
- `DoubleStream stream(double[] array)`: Creates `DoubleStream` from the provided array.
- `Stream<T> stream(T[] array, int startInclusive, int endExclusive)`: Creates `Stream` from the specified range of the provided array.
- `IntStream stream(int[] array, int startInclusive, int endExclusive)`: Creates `IntStream` from the specified range of the provided array.
- `LongStream stream(long[] array, int startInclusive, int endExclusive)`: Creates `LongStream` from the specified range of the provided array.
- `DoubleStream stream(double[] array, int startInclusive, int endExclusive)`: Creates `DoubleStream` from the specified range of the provided array.

Here is an example of creating a stream from the subset of an array:

```
int[] arr = {1, 2, 3, 4, 5};
Arrays.stream(arr, 2, 4).forEach(System.out::print);    //prints: 34
```

Notice that we have used the `Stream<T> stream(T[] array, int startInclusive, int endExclusive)` method, which means we have created `Stream` and not `IntStream`, although all of the elements in the created stream are integers, as in `IntStream`. The difference is that `IntStream` provides some numeric-specific operations not available in `Stream` (see the *Numeric stream interfaces* section).

The `java.util.Random` class allows us to create numeric streams of pseudorandom values:

- `IntStream ints()` and `LongStream longs()`: Create an unlimited stream of pseudorandom values of the corresponding type.
- `DoubleStream doubles()`: Creates an unlimited stream of pseudorandom double values, each between zero (inclusive) and one (exclusive).
- `IntStream ints(long streamSize)` and `LongStream longs(long streamSize)`: Create a stream of the specified number of pseudorandom values of the corresponding type.
- `DoubleStream doubles(long streamSize)`: Creates a stream of the specified number of pseudorandom double values, each between zero (inclusive) and one (exclusive).
- `IntStream ints(int randomNumberOrigin, int randomNumberBound)`, `LongStream longs(long randomNumberOrigin, long randomNumberBound)`, and `DoubleStream doubles(long streamSize, double randomNumberOrigin, double randomNumberBound)`: Create an infinite stream of pseudorandom values of the corresponding type, each value equal to or larger than the first parameter, and smaller than the second parameter.

Here is an example of one of the preceding methods:

```
new Random().ints(5, 8)
            .limit(5)
            .forEach(System.out::print);    //prints: 56757
```

The `java.nio.File` class has six static methods to create streams of lines and paths:

- `Stream<String> lines(Path path)`: Creates a stream of lines from the file specified by the provided path.
- `Stream<String> lines(Path path, Charset cs)`: Creates a stream of lines from the file specified by the provided path. Bytes from the file are decoded into characters using the provided charset.
- `Stream<Path> list(Path dir)`: Creates a stream of the entries in the specified directory.
- `Stream<Path> walk(Path start, FileVisitOption... options)`: Creates a stream of the entries of the file tree rooted at a given starting file.
- `Stream<Path> walk(Path start, int maxDepth, FileVisitOption... options)`: Creates a stream of the entries of the file tree rooted at a given starting file to the specified depth.
- `Stream<Path> find(Path start, int maxDepth, BiPredicate<Path, BasicFileAttributes> matcher, FileVisitOption... options)`: Creates a stream of the entries of the file tree rooted at a given starting file to the specified depth that match the provided predicate.

Other classes and methods that create streams include:

- `IntStream stream()` of the `java.util.BitSet` class: Creates a stream of indices for which `BitSet` contains a bit in the set state.
- `Stream<String> lines()` of the `java.io.BufferedReader` class: Creates a stream of lines read from the `BufferedReader` object, typically from a file.
- `Stream<JarEntry> stream()` of the `java.util.jar.JarFile` class: Creates a stream of the ZIP file entries.
- default `IntStream chars()` of the `java.lang.CharSequence` interface: Creates a stream of int zero-extending the char values from this sequence.
- default `IntStream codePoints()` of the `java.lang.CharSequence` interface: Creates a stream of code point values from this sequence.
- `Stream<String> splitAsStream(CharSequence input)` of the `java.util.regex.Pattern` class: Creates a stream from the provided sequence around matches of this pattern.

There is also the `java.util.stream.StreamSupport` class, which contains static, low-level utility methods for library developers. That is outside the scope of this book.

# Intermediate operations

We have already seen how a `Stream` object that represents a source and emits elements can be created. As we have mentioned already, the operations (methods) provided by the `Stream` interface can be divided into three groups:

- The methods that create a `Stream` object based on a source.
- Intermediate operations that accept a function and produce a `Stream` object that emits the same, or modified, values.
- Terminal operations that complete the stream processing, close it, and produce the result.

In this section, we will review the intermediate operations that, in turn, can be grouped by their functionalities.

# Filtering

This group includes operations that remove duplicates, skip some of the elements, and limit the number of processed elements, only selecting those that are needed:

- `Stream<T> distinct()`: Compares stream elements using the `Object.equals(Object)` method, and skips the duplicates.
- `Stream<T> skip(long n)`: Ignores the provided number of stream elements that are emitted first.
- `Stream<T> limit(long maxSize)`: Allows only the provided number of stream elements to be processed.
- `Stream<T> filter(Predicate<T> predicate)`: Allows only those elements that result in `true` (when processed by the provided `Predicate` function).
- Default `Stream<T> dropWhile(Predicate<T> predicate)`: Skips the first elements of the stream that result in `true` when processed by the provided `Predicate` function.
- Default `Stream<T> takeWhile(Predicate<T> predicate)`: Allows only the first elements of the stream that result in `true` (when processed by the provided `Predicate` function) to be processed.

The following code demonstrates how the preceding operations work:

```
Stream.of("3", "2", "3", "4", "2").distinct()
                            .forEach(System.out::print);   //prints: 324
List<String> list = List.of("1", "2", "3", "4", "5");
list.stream().skip(3).forEach(System.out::print);         //prints: 45
list.stream().limit(3).forEach(System.out::print);        //prints: 123
list.stream().filter(s -> Objects.equals(s, "2"))
                            .forEach(System.out::print);   //prints: 2
list.stream().dropWhile(s -> Integer.valueOf(s) < 3)
                            .forEach(System.out::print);   //prints: 345
list.stream().takeWhile(s -> Integer.valueOf(s) < 3)
                            .forEach(System.out::print);   //prints: 12
```

Notice that we were able to reuse the `List<String>` source object, but could not reuse the `Stream` object. Once it has been closed, it cannot be reopened.

# Mapping

This group includes arguably the most important intermediate operations. They are the only intermediate operations that modify the elements of the stream. They *map* (transform) the original stream element value to a new one:

- `Stream<R> map(Function<T, R> mapper)`: Applies the provided function to each element of the `T` type of this stream, and produces a new element value of the `R` type.

- `IntStream mapToInt(ToIntFunction<T> mapper)`: Converts this stream to an `IntStream` of the `Integer` values.

- `LongStream mapToLong(ToLongFunction<T> mapper)`: Converts this stream to a `LongStream` of the `Long` values.

- `DoubleStream mapToDouble(ToDoubleFunction<T> mapper)`: Converts this stream to a `DoubleStream` of the `Double` values.

- `Stream<R> flatMap(Function<T, Stream<R>> mapper)`: Applies the provided function to each element of the `T` type of this stream and produces a `Stream<R>` object that emits elements of the `R` type.

- `IntStream flatMapToInt(Function<T, IntStream> mapper)`: Converts each element of the `T` type to a stream of `Integer` values, using the provided function.

- `LongStream flatMapToLong(Function<T, LongStream> mapper)`:
  Converts each element of the `T` type to a stream of `Long` values, using the provided function.
- `DoubleStream flatMapToDouble(Function<T, DoubleStream> mapper)`:
  Converts each element of the `T` type to a stream of `Double` values, using the provided function.

The following are examples of the usage of these operations:

```
List<String> list = List.of("1", "2", "3", "4", "5");
list.stream().map(s -> s + s)
            .forEach(System.out::print);          //prints: 1122334455
list.stream().mapToInt(Integer::valueOf)
            .forEach(System.out::print);              //prints: 12345
list.stream().mapToLong(Long::valueOf)
            .forEach(System.out::print);              //prints: 12345
list.stream().mapToDouble(Double::valueOf)
            .mapToObj(Double::toString)
            .map(s -> s + " ")
            .forEach(System.out::print);//prints: 1.0 2.0 3.0 4.0 5.0
list.stream().mapToInt(Integer::valueOf)
            .flatMap(n -> IntStream.iterate(1, i -> i < n, i -> ++i))
            .forEach(System.out::print);          //prints: 1121231234
list.stream().map(Integer::valueOf)
            .flatMapToInt(n ->
                    IntStream.iterate(1, i -> i < n, i -> ++i))
            .forEach(System.out::print);          //prints: 1121231234
list.stream().map(Integer::valueOf)
            .flatMapToLong(n ->
                    LongStream.iterate(1, i -> i < n, i -> ++i))
            .forEach(System.out::print);          //prints: 1121231234;
list.stream().map(Integer::valueOf)
            .flatMapToDouble(n ->
                    DoubleStream.iterate(1, i -> i < n, i -> ++i))
            .mapToObj(Double::toString)
            .map(s -> s + " ")
            .forEach(System.out::print);
                //prints: 1.0 1.0 2.0 1.0 2.0 3.0 1.0 2.0 3.0 4.0
```

In the preceding examples, in the case of `Double` values, we converted a numeric value to a `String`, and added space, so the result will be printed with a space between the numbers. These examples are very simple—just conversion with minimal processing. But in real life, each `map` or `flatMap` operation can accept a (function of any level of complexity) that does something really useful.

# Sorting

The following two intermediate operations sort the stream elements. Naturally, such an operation cannot be finished until all of the elements are emitted, so it creates a lot of overhead, slows down performance, and has to be used either for the small size streams:

- `Stream<T> sorted()`: Sorts the stream elements in a natural order (according to their `Comparable` interface implementation).
- `Stream<T> sorted(Comparator<T> comparator)`: Sorts the stream elements in the order according to the provided `Comparator<T>` object.

Here is a demo code:

```
List<String> list = List.of("2", "1", "5", "4", "3");
list.stream().sorted().forEach(System.out::print);   //prints: 12345
list.stream().sorted(Comparator.reverseOrder())
             .forEach(System.out::print);             //prints: 54321
```

# Peeking

A `Stream<T> peek(Consumer<T> action)` intermediate operation applies the provided `Consumer` function to each stream element and does not change this `Stream` (returns the same element value it has received) because the `Consumer` function returns `void` and cannot affect the value. This operation is used for debugging.

The following code shows how it works:

```
List<String> list = List.of("1", "2", "3", "4", "5");
list.stream().peek(s-> {
    if("3".equals(s)){
        System.out.print(3);
    }
}).forEach(System.out::print);   //prints: 123345
```

# Terminal operations

The Terminal operations are the most important operations of a stream pipeline. It is easy to accomplish everything without a need for any other operations. We have used already the `forEach(Consumer<T>)` Terminal operation to print each element. It does not return a value; thus, it is used for its side effects. But the `Stream` interface has many more powerful Terminal operations that do return values. The central among them is a `collect()` operation, which has two forms, `R collect(Collector<T, A, R> collector)` and `R collect(Supplier<R> supplier, BiConsumer<R, T> accumulator, BiConsumer<R, R> combiner)`. These allow us to compose practically any process that can be applied to a stream. The classic example is as follows:

```
List<String> asList = stringStream.collect(ArrayList::new,
                                            ArrayList::add,
                                            ArrayList::addAll);
```

As you can see, it is implemented in a way suited for parallel processing. It uses the first function to produce a value based on the stream element, accumulates the result using the second function, and then combines the accumulated results from all of the threads that processed the stream.

However, having only one such generic Terminal operation would force the programmers to write the same functions repeatedly. That is why the API authors added the `Collectors` class, which generates many specialized `Collector` objects without the need to create three functions for every `collect()` operation. In addition to that, the API authors added even more specialized Terminal operations, which are much simpler and easier to use to the `Stream` interface.

In this section, we will review all of the Terminal operation of the `Stream` interface, and, in the `Collecting` subsection, look at the vast population of `Collector` objects produced by the `Collectors` class.

We will start with the most simple Terminal operation, which allows for processing each element of a stream one at a time.

# Processing each element

There are two Terminal operations in this group:

- `void forEach(Consumer<T> action)`: Applies the provided action (process) for each element of the stream.

- void forEachOrdered(Consumer<T> action): Applies the provided action (process) for each element of the stream in an order defined by the source, regardless of whether the stream is sequential or parallel.

If the order in which you need the elements to be processed is important for your application, and it has to be in the order the values were arranged in the source, use the second method—especially if can foresee that your code is going to be executed on a computer with several CPUs. Otherwise, use the first one, as we have done in all our examples.

It is not unusual to see this operation being used for *any kind* of stream processing, especially when the code is written by an inexperienced programmer. For the following example, we have created the Person class:

```java
class Person {
    private int age;
    private String name;
    public Person(int age, String name) {
        this.name = name;
        this.age = age;
    }
    public String getName() { return this.name; }
    public int getAge() {return this.age; }
    @Override
    public String toString() {
        return "Person{" + "name='" + this.name + "'" +
                        ", age=" + age + "}";
    }
}
```

We are going to use this class throughout our discussion of Terminal operations. For this example, we are going to read comma-separated values (age and name) from a file and create Person objects. We have placed the following persons.csv file (**Comma-Separated Values (CSV)**) in the resources folder:

```
23 , Ji m
 2 5 , Bob
15 , Jill
 17 , Bi ll
```

Notice the spaces that we have added outside and inside of the values. We have done it in order to take the opportunity to show you some simple, but very useful, tips for working with real-life data. Here is how an inexperienced programmer may write the code that reads this file and creates a list of `Person` objects:

```
List<Person> persons = new ArrayList<>();
Path path = Paths.get("src/main/resources/persons.csv");
try (Stream<String> lines = Files.newBufferedReader(path).lines()) {
    lines.forEach(s -> {
        String[] arr = s.split(",");
        int age = Integer.valueOf(StringUtils.remove(arr[0], ' '));
        persons.add(new Person(age, StringUtils.remove(arr[1], ' ')));
    });
} catch (IOException ex) {
    ex.printStackTrace();
}
persons.stream().forEach(System.out::println);
                                //prints: Person{name='Jim', age=23}
                                //        Person{name='Bob', age=25}
                                //        Person{name='Jill', age=15}
                                //        Person{name='Bill', age=17}
```

You can see that we used the `String` method, `split()`, to break each line by a comma that separates the values, and that we have used the `org.apache.commons.lang3.StringUtils` class to remove spaces from each value. The preceding code also provides a real-life example of the `try-with-resources` construct, which is used to close the `BufferedReader` object automatically.

Although this code works fine in small examples and on a single-core computer, it might create unexpected results with a long stream and parallel processing. That is, the reason that lambda expressions require all variables to be final, or effectively final, because the same function can be executed in a different context.

In contrast, here is the correct implementation of the preceding code:

```
List<Person> persons = new ArrayList<>();
Path path = Paths.get("src/main/resources/persons.csv");
try (Stream<String> lines = Files.newBufferedReader(path).lines()) {
    persons = lines.map(s -> s.split(","))
        .map(arr -> {
            int age = Integer.valueOf(StringUtils.remove(arr[0], ' '));
            return new Person(age, StringUtils.remove(arr[1], ' '));
        }).collect(Collectors.toList());
} catch (IOException ex) {
    ex.printStackTrace();
}
```

```
persons.stream().forEach(System.out::println);
```

To improve readability, one can create a method that does the job of mapping:

```
public List<Person> createPersons() {
    List<Person> persons = new ArrayList<>();
    Path path = Paths.get("src/main/resources/persons.csv");
    try (Stream<String> lines = Files.newBufferedReader(path).lines()) {
        persons = lines.map(s -> s.split(","))
                    .map(this::createPerson)
                    .collect(Collectors.toList());
    } catch (IOException ex) {
        ex.printStackTrace();
    }
    return persons;
}
private Person createPerson(String[] arr){
    int age = Integer.valueOf(StringUtils.remove(arr[0], ' '));
    return new Person(age, StringUtils.remove(arr[1], ' '));
}
```

As you can see, we used the `collect()` operation and the `Collector` function created by the `Collectors.toList()` method. We will see more of the `Collector` functions created by the `Collectors` class in the *Collect* subsection.


# Counting all elements

The `long count()` Terminal operation of the `Stream` interface looks straightforward and benign. It returns the number of elements in this stream. Those who are used to working with collections and arrays may use the `count()` operation without thinking twice. Here is an example that proves it works just fine:

```
long count = Stream.of("1", "2", "3", "4", "5")
        .peek(System.out::print)
        .count();
System.out.print(count);                        //prints: 5
```

As you can see, the code that implements the method count was able to determine the stream size without executing all the pipe. The values of elements were not printed by the `peek()` operation, which proves that the elements were not emitted. But it is not always possible to determine the stream size at the source. Besides, the stream may be infinite. So, one has to use `count()` with care.

Since we are on the topic of counting elements, we would like to show you another possible way to determine the stream size, using the `collect()` operation:

```
int count = Stream.of("1", "2", "3", "4", "5")
          .peek(System.out::print)          //prints: 12345
          .collect(Collectors.counting());
System.out.println(count);                  //prints: 5
```

You can see that the implementation of the `collect()` operation does not even attempt to calculate the stream size at the source (because, as you can see, the pipe was fully executed and each element was printed by the `peek()` operation). This is because the `collect()` operation is not as specialized as the `count()` operation. It just applies the passed-in collector to the stream, and the collector counts the elements provided to it by the `collect()` operation. You could consider this an example of bureaucratic myopia: every operator does its job as expected, but the overall performance is wanting.

# Matching all, any, or none

There are three (seemingly very similar) Terminal operations that allow us to asses whether all, any, or none of the stream elements have a certain value:

- `boolean allMatch(Predicate<T> predicate)`: Returns `true` when each of this stream elements returns `true`, when used as a parameter of the provided `Predicate<T>` function

- `boolean anyMatch(Predicate<T> predicate)`: Returns `true` when one of this stream elements returns `true`, when used as a parameter of the provided `Predicate<T>` function

- `boolean noneMatch(Predicate<T> predicate)`: Returns `true` when none of the stream elements return `true`, when used as a parameter of the provided `Predicate<T>` function.

The following are examples of their usage:

```
List<String> list = List.of("1", "2", "3", "4", "5");
boolean found = list.stream()
        .peek(System.out::print)          //prints: 123
        .anyMatch(e -> "3".equals(e));
System.out.print(found);                  //prints: true      <= line 5
found = list.stream()
        .peek(System.out::print)          //prints: 12345
        .anyMatch(e -> "0".equals(e));
System.out.print(found);                  //prints: false
```

```
boolean noneMatches = list.stream()
        .peek(System.out::print)            //prints: 123
        .noneMatch(e -> "3".equals(e));
System.out.print(noneMatches);              //prints: false
noneMatches = list.stream()
        .peek(System.out::print)            //prints: 12345
        .noneMatch(e -> "0".equals(e));
System.out.print(noneMatches);              //prints: true   <= line 17
boolean allMatch = list.stream()
        .peek(System.out::print)            //prints: 1
        .allMatch(e -> "3".equals(e));
System.out.print(allMatch);                 //prints: false
```

Let's look at the results of the preceding example more closely. Each of these operations triggers the stream pipe execution, and at least one element of the stream is processed every time. But look at the `anyMatch()` and `noneMatch()` operations. Line 5 states that there is at least one element equal to 3. The result was returned *after only three first elements* had been processed. Line 17 states that there was no element equal to 0 *after all of the elements* of the stream had been processed.

The question is, which of these two operations should you when you use would like to know whether the stream *does not contain* the v value? If `noneMatch()` is used, *all of the elements are going to be processed*. But if `anyMatch()` is used, all of the elements are going to be processed *only if there is no v value* in the stream. It seems that the `noneMatch()` operation is useless, because when `anyMatch()` returns `true`, it means the same as when `noneMatch()` returns `false`, while the `anyMatch()` operation achieves it with fewer elements processed. This difference grows in significance with the growth of the stream size and the chance that there is an element with the v value. It seems that the only reason for having the `noneMatch()` operation is for code readability, when processing time is not important, because the stream size is small.

The `allMatch()` operation does not have an alternative, and, similar to `anyMatch()`, either returns when the first non-matching element is encountered or requires processing all of the stream elements.

# Finding any or first

The following Terminal operations allow us to find any, or the first, element of the stream:

- Optional<T> findAny(): Returns Optional with the value of any element of the stream, or an empty Optional if the stream is empty.
- Optional<T> findFirst(): Returns Optional with the value of the first element of the stream, or an empty Optional if the stream is empty.

The following example illustrates these operations:

```
List<String> list = List.of("1", "2", "3", "4", "5");

Optional<String> result = list.stream().findAny();
System.out.println(result.isPresent());    //prints: true
System.out.println(result.get());          //prints: 1

result = list.stream().filter(e -> "42".equals(e)).findAny();
System.out.println(result.isPresent());    //prints: true
//System.out.println(result.get());        //NoSuchElementException

result = list.stream().findFirst();
System.out.println(result.isPresent());    //prints: true
System.out.println(result.get());          //prints: 1
```

As you can see, they return the same results. That is because we are executing the pipe in a single thread. The differences between these two operations are more prominent in parallel processing. When the stream is broken into several parts for parallel processing, the findFirst() operation always returns the first element of the stream if the stream is not empty, while the findAny() operation returns the first element only in one of the processing threads.

Let's discuss the java.util.Optional class in more detail.

# Class Optional

The object of java.util.Optional is used to avoid returning null, as it may cause a NullPointerException. Instead, an Optional object provides methods that can be used to check the value presence and to substitute it if there is no value. For example:

```
List<String> list = List.of("1", "2", "3", "4", "5");

String result = list.stream().filter(e -> "42".equals(e))
        .findAny().or(() -> Optional.of("Not found")).get();
```

```
System.out.println(result);                          //prints: Not found

result = list.stream().filter(e -> "42".equals(e))
                        .findAny().orElse("Not found");
System.out.println(result);                          //prints: Not found
Supplier<String> trySomethingElse = () -> {
    //Code that tries something else
    return "43";
};
result = list.stream().filter(e -> "42".equals(e))
                    .findAny().orElseGet(trySomethingElse);
System.out.println(result);                          //prints: 43

list.stream().filter(e -> "42".equals(e))
    .findAny().ifPresentOrElse(System.out::println,
            () -> System.out.println("Not found"));  //prints: Not found
```

As you can see, if the Optional object is empty, then:

- The or() method of the Optional class allows for returning an alternative Optional object (with a value).
- The orElse() method allows for returning an alternative value.
- The orElseGet() method allows for providing the Supplier function, which returns an alternative value.
- The ifPresentOrElse() method allows for providing two functions: one that consumes the value from the Optional object, and another that does something if the Optional object is empty.

# Min and max

The following Terminal operations return the minimum or maximum value of the stream elements, if present:

- Optional<T> min(Comparator<T> comparator): Returns the minimum element of this stream, using the provided Comparator object.
- Optional<T> max(Comparator<T> comparator): Returns the maximum element of this stream, using the provided Comparator object.

Here is the demonstration code:

```
List<String> list = List.of("a", "b", "c", "c", "a");
String min = list.stream().min(Comparator.naturalOrder()).orElse("0");
System.out.println(min);     //prints: a

String max = list.stream().max(Comparator.naturalOrder()).orElse("0");
System.out.println(max);     //prints: c
```

As you can see, in the case of non-numerical values, the minimum element is the one that is first (when ordered from the left to the right), according to the provided comparator; the maximum, accordingly, is the last element. In the case of numeric values, the minimum and maximum are just that—the biggest and the smallest number among the stream elements:

```
int mn = Stream.of(42, 33, 77).min(Comparator.naturalOrder()).orElse(0);
System.out.println(mn);     //prints: 33
int mx = Stream.of(42, 33, 77).max(Comparator.naturalOrder()).orElse(0);
System.out.println(mx);     //prints: 77
```

Let's look at another example, assuming that there is a `Person` class:

```
class Person {
    private int age;
    private String name;
    public Person(int age, String name) {
        this.age = age;
        this.name = name;
    }
    public int getAge() { return this.age; }
    public String getName() { return this.name; }
    @Override
    public String toString() {
        return "Person{name:" + this.name + ",age:" + this.age + "}";
    }
}
```

The task is to find the oldest person in the following list:

```
List<Person> persons = List.of(new Person(23, "Bob"),
                               new Person(33, "Jim"),
                               new Person(28, "Jill"),
                               new Person(27, "Bill"));
```

In order to do that, we can create the following `Compartor<Person>`:

```
Comparator<Person> perComp = (p1, p2) -> p1.getAge() - p2.getAge();
```

Then, using this comparator, we can find the oldest person:

```
Person theOldest = persons.stream().max(perComp).orElse(null);
System.out.println(theOldest);   //prints: Person{name:Jim,age:33}
```

# The toArray() operation

These two Terminal operations generate an array that contains the stream elements:

- `Object[] toArray()` : Creates an array of objects; each object is an element of this stream.
- `A[] toArray(IntFunction<A[]> generator)`: Creates an array of the stream elements using the provided function.

Let's look at an example:

```
List<String> list = List.of("a", "b", "c");
Object[] obj = list.stream().toArray();
Arrays.stream(obj).forEach(System.out::print);     //prints: abc

String[] str = list.stream().toArray(String[]::new);
Arrays.stream(str).forEach(System.out::print);     //prints: abc
```

The first example is straightforward. It converts elements to an array of the same type. As for the second example, the representation of `IntFunction` as `String[]::new` is probably not obvious, so let's walk through it.

`String[]::new` is a method reference that represents the following lambda expression:

```
String[] str = list.stream().toArray(i -> new String[i]);
Arrays.stream(str).forEach(System.out::print);     //prints: abc
```

And that is already `IntFunction<String[]>`, which, according to its documentation, accepts an `int` parameter and returns the result of the specified type. It can be defined by using an anonymous class, as follows:

```
IntFunction<String[]> intFunction = new IntFunction<String[]>() {
    @Override
    public String[] apply(int i) {
        return new String[i];
    }
};
```

You may recall (from `Chapter 13`, *Java Collections*) how we converted a collection to an array:

```
str = list.toArray(new String[list.size()]);
Arrays.stream(str).forEach(System.out::print);    //prints: abc
```

You can see that the `toArray()` operation of the `Stream` interface has a very similar signature, except that it accepts a function, instead of just an array.

# The reduce operation

This Terminal operation is called *reduce* because it processes all of the stream elements and produces one value. It *reduces* all of the stream elements to one value. But this is not the only operation that does it. The *collect* operation reduces all of the values of the stream element into one result, too. And, in a way, all Terminal operations reduce. They produce one value after processing of all the elements.

So, you may look at *reduce* and *collect* as synonyms that help to add structure and classification to many operations available in the `Stream` interface. Also, the operations in the *reduce* group can be viewed as specialized versions of the *collect* operation, because `collect()` can be tailored to provide the same functionality, too.

With that, let's look at the group of *reduce* operations:

- `Optional<T> reduce(BinaryOperator<T> accumulator)`: Reduces the elements of this stream by using the provided associative function that defines the logic of the element aggregation. Returns `Optional` with the reduced value, if available.
- `T reduce(T identity, BinaryOperator<T> accumulator)`: Provides the same functionality as the previous `reduce()` version, but with the `identity` parameter used as the initial value for an accumulator, or a default value, if a stream is empty.
- `U reduce(U identity, BiFunction<U,T,U> accumulator, BinaryOperator<U> combiner)`: Provides the same functionality as the previous `reduce()` version, but, in addition, uses the `combiner` function to aggregate the results when this operation is applied to a parallel stream. If the stream is not parallel, the combiner function is not used.

For a demonstration of the `reduce()` operation, we are going to use the same `Person` class that that we before:

```
class Person {
    private int age;
    private String name;
    public Person(int age, String name) {
        this.age = age;
        this.name = name;
    }
    public int getAge() { return this.age; }
    public String getName() { return this.name; }
    @Override
    public String toString() {
        return "Person{name:" + this.name + ",age:" + this.age + "}";
    }
}
```

We are also going to use the same list of `Person` objects as the source for our stream examples:

```
List<Person> list = List.of(new Person(23, "Bob"),
                            new Person(33, "Jim"),
                            new Person(28, "Jill"),
                            new Person(27, "Bill"));
```

Now, using the `reduce()` operation, let's find the oldest person in this list:

```
Person theOldest = list.stream()
    .reduce((p1, p2) -> p1.getAge() > p2.getAge() ? p1 : p2).orElse(null);
System.out.println(theOldest);        //prints: Person{name:Jim,age:33}
```

The implementation is somewhat surprising, isn't it? We were talking about the "accumulator," but we did not accumulate anything. We just compared all of the stream elements. Well, apparently, the accumulator saves the result of the comparison and provides it as the first parameter for the next comparison (with the next element). One could say that the accumulator, in this case, accumulates the results of all previous comparisons. In any case, it does the job we wanted it to do.

Let's now accumulate something explicitly. Let's assemble all of the names from the list of people in one comma-separated list:

```
String allNames = list.stream().map(p->p.getName())
                    .reduce((n1, n2) -> n1 + ", " + n2).orElse(null);
System.out.println(allNames);        //prints: Bob, Jim, Jill, Bill
```

The notion of accumulation, makes a bit more sense in this case, doesn't it?

Now, let's use the identity value to provide an initial value:

```
String allNames = list.stream().map(p->p.getName())
                  .reduce("All names: ", (n1, n2) -> n1 + ", " + n2);
System.out.println(allNames);        //All names: , Bob, Jim, Jill, Bill
```

Notice that this version of the `reduce()` operation returns the value, not the `Optional` object. That is because, by providing the initial value, we guarantee that this value will be present in the result, even if the stream turns out to be empty.

But the resulting string does not look as pretty as we had hoped. Apparently, the provided initial value is treated as any other stream element, and a comma is added after it by the accumulator we created. To make the result look pretty again, we could use the first version of the `reduce()` operation again, and add the initial value this way:

```
String allNames = "All names: " + list.stream().map(p->p.getName())
                  .reduce((n1, n2) -> n1 + ", " + n2).orElse(null);
System.out.println(allNames);        //All names: Bob, Jim, Jill, Bill
```

We have decided to use a space as a separator, instead of a comma, for demonstration purposes:

```
String allNames = list.stream().map(p->p.getName())
                  .reduce("All names:", (n1, n2) -> n1 + " " + n2);
System.out.println(allNames);        //All names: Bob, Jim, Jill, Bill
```

Now, the result looks better. While demonstrating the `collect()` operation in the next subsection, we will show you another way to create a comma-separated list of values with a prefix.

Now, let's look at how to use the third form of the `reduce()` operation—the one with three parameters, the last one is called a combiner. Adding the combiner to the preceding `reduce()` operation does not change the result:

```
String allNames = list.stream().map(p->p.getName())
                  .reduce("All names:", (n1, n2) -> n1 + " " + n2,
                                        (n1, n2) -> n1 + " " + n2 );
System.out.println(allNames);        //All names: Bob, Jim, Jill, Bill
```

That is because the stream is not parallel, and the combiner is used only with a parallel stream.

If we make the stream parallel, the result changes:

```
String allNames = list.parallelStream().map(p->p.getName())
                    .reduce("All names:", (n1, n2) -> n1 + " " + n2,
                                          (n1, n2) -> n1 + " " + n2 );
System.out.println(allNames);
        //All names: Bob All names: Jim All names: Jill All names: Bill
```

Apparently, for a parallel stream, the sequence of elements is broken into subsequences, each being processed independently; their results are aggregated by the combiner. When doing so, the combiner adds the initial value (identity) to each of the results. Even if we remove the combiner, the result of the parallel stream processing remains the same, because a default combiner behavior is provided:

```
String allNames = list.parallelStream().map(p->p.getName())
                    .reduce("All names:", (n1, n2) -> n1 + " " + n2);
System.out.println(allNames);
        //All names: Bob All names: Jim All names: Jill All names: Bill
```

In the previous two forms of `reduce()` operations, the identity value was used by the accumulator. In the third form, with the `U reduce(U identity, BiFunction<U,T,U> accumulator, BinaryOperator<U> combiner)` signature, the identity value is used by the combiner (notice that, the `U` type is the combiner type).

To get rid of the repetitive identity value in the result, we have decided to remove it from the second parameter in the combiner:

```
allNames = list.parallelStream().map(p->p.getName())
      .reduce("All names:", (n1, n2) -> n1 + " " + n2,
          (n1, n2) -> n1 + " " + StringUtils.remove(n2, "All names:"));
System.out.println(allNames);       //All names: Bob, Jim, Jill, Bill
```

As you can see, the result now looks much better.

In our examples so far, the identity played not only the role of an initial value, but also of the identifier (a label) in the result. When the elements of the stream are numeric, the identity looks more like the initial value only. Let's look at the following example:

```
List<Integer> ints = List.of(1, 2, 3);
int sum = ints.stream().reduce((i1, i2) -> i1 + i2).orElse(0);
System.out.println(sum);                          //prints: 6

sum = ints.stream().reduce(Integer::sum).orElse(0);
System.out.println(sum);                          //prints: 6

sum = ints.stream().reduce(10, Integer::sum);
```

```
System.out.println(sum);                            //prints: 16

sum = ints.stream().reduce(10, Integer::sum, Integer::sum);
System.out.println(sum);                            //prints: 16
```

The first two stream pipes are exactly the same, except that the second pipe uses a method reference instead of a lambda expression. The third and the fourth pipes have the same functionality too. They both use an initial value of 10. Now the first parameter makes more sense as the initial value than the identity, isn't it? In the fourth pipe, we added a combiner but it is not used because the stream is not parallel.

Let's make it parallel and see what happens:

```
List<Integer> ints = List.of(1, 2, 3);
int sum = ints.parallelStream().reduce(10, Integer::sum, Integer::sum);
System.out.println(sum);                            //prints: 36
```

The result is 36 because the initial value of 10 was added three times—with each partial result. Apparently, the stream was broken into three subsequences. But that is not always the case, it changes as the stream grows and the number of CPUs on the computer increases. So, one cannot rely on a certain fixed number of subsequences and it is better not to use it for such cases, and add to the result if needed:

```
List<Integer> ints = List.of(1, 2, 3);

int sum = ints.parallelStream().reduce(0, Integer::sum, Integer::sum);
System.out.println(sum);                            //prints: 6

sum = 10 + ints.parallelStream().reduce(0, Integer::sum, Integer::sum);
System.out.println(sum);                            //prints: 16
```

# The collect operation

Some of the usages of the `collect()` operation are very simple and recommended for any beginner, while other cases can be complex and inaccessible even for a seasoned programmer. Together with the operations discussed already, the most popular cases of `collect()` we present in this section are more than enough for all the needs a beginner may have. Add the operations of numeric streams we are going to present in the *Numeric stream interfaces* section, and the covered material may easily be all a mainstream programmer will need for the foreseeable future.

As we have mentioned already, the collect operation is very flexible, and allows us to customize the stream processing. It has two forms:

- R collect(Collector<T, A, R> collector): Processes the elements of this stream of the T type using the provided Collector and producing the result of the R type via an intermediate accumulation of the A type
- R collect(Supplier<R> supplier, BiConsumer<R, T> accumulator, BiConsumer<R, R> combiner): Processes the elements of this stream of the T type using the provided functions:
  - Supplier<R>: Creates a new result container
  - BiConsumer<R, T> accumulator: A stateless function that adds an element to the result container
  - BiConsumer<R, R> combiner: A stateless function that merges two partial result containers, adds the elements from the second result container into the first result container.

Let's look at the second form of the collect() operation. It is very similar to the reduce() operation, with the three parameters we have just demonstrated. The biggest difference is that the first parameter in the collect() operation is not identity or initial value, but the container—an object—that is going to be passed between functions and that maintains the state of the processing. For the following example, we are going to use the Person1 class as the container:

```
class Person1 {
    private String name;
    private int age;
    public Person1(){}
    public String getName() { return this.name; }
    public void setName(String name) { this.name = name; }
    public int getAge() {return this.age; }
    public void setAge(int age) { this.age = age;}
    @Override
    public String toString() {
        return "Person{name:" + this.name + ",age:" + age + "}";
    }
}
```

As you can see, the container has to have a constructor without parameters and setters, because it should be able to receive and keep the partial results—the name and age of the person that is the oldest, so far. The `collect()` operation will use this container while processing each element and, after the last element is processed, will contain the name and the age of the oldest person. Here is the list of people, which should be familiar to you:

```
List<Person> list = List.of(new Person(23, "Bob"),
                            new Person(33, "Jim"),
                            new Person(28, "Jill"),
                            new Person(27, "Bill"));
```

And here is the `collect()` operation that should find the oldest person in the list:

```
Person1 theOldest = list.stream().collect(Person1::new,
    (p1, p2) -> {
        if(p1.getAge() < p2.getAge()){
            p1.setAge(p2.getAge());
            p1.setName(p2.getName());
        }
    },
    (p1, p2) -> { System.out.println("Combiner is called!"); });
```

We tried to inline the functions in the operation call, but it looks a bit difficult to read, so here is the better version of the same code:

```
BiConsumer<Person1, Person> accumulator = (p1, p2) -> {
    if(p1.getAge() < p2.getAge()){
        p1.setAge(p2.getAge());
        p1.setName(p2.getName());
    }
};
BiConsumer<Person1, Person1> combiner = (p1, p2) -> {
    System.out.println("Combiner is called!");          //prints nothing
};
theOldest = list.stream().collect(Person1::new, accumulator, combiner);
System.out.println(theOldest);          //prints: Person{name:Jim, age:33}
```

The `Person1` container object is created only once—for the first element processing (in this sense, it is similar to the initial value of the `reduce()` operation). Then it is passed to the accumulator that compared it with the first element. The `age` field in the container was initialized to the default value of zero and thus, the age and name of the first element were set in the container as the parameters of the oldest person, so far.

When the second element (the `Person` object) of the stream was emitted, its `age` field was compared with the `age` value currently stored in the container (the `Person1` object), and so on, until all elements of the stream were processed. The result is shown in the preceding comments.

The combiner was never called because the stream is not parallel. But when we make it parallel, we need to implement the combiner as follows:

```
BiConsumer<Person1, Person1> combiner = (p1, p2) -> {
    System.out.println("Combiner is called!");   //prints 3 times
    if(p1.getAge() < p2.getAge()){
        p1.setAge(p2.getAge());
        p1.setName(p2.getName());
    }
};
theOldest = list.parallelStream()
                .collect(Person1::new, accumulator, combiner);
System.out.println(theOldest);   //prints: Person{name:Jim,age:33}
```

The combiner compares the partial results (of all the stream subsequences) and comes up with the final result. Now we see the `Combiner is called!` message printed three times. But, as in the case of the `reduce()` operation, the number of partial results (the stream subsequences) may vary.

Now let's look at the first form of the `collect()` operation. It requires an object of the class that implements the `java.util.stream.Collector<T,A,R>` interface where `T` is the stream type, `A` is the container type, and `R` is the result type. One can use the `of()` method of the `Collector` interface to create a necessary `Collector` object:

- `static Collector<T,R,R> of(Supplier<R> supplier, BiConsumer<R,T> accumulator, BinaryOperator<R> combiner, Collector.Characteristics... characteristics)`
- `static Collector<T,A,R> of(Supplier<A> supplier, BiConsumer<A,T> accumulator, BinaryOperator<A> combiner, Function<A,R> finisher, Collector.Characteristics... characteristics).`

The functions one has to pass to the preceding methods are similar to those we have demonstrated already. But we are not going to do it for two reasons. First, it is somewhat more involved and pushes beyond the scope of this introductory course, and, second, before doing that, one has to look in the `java.util.stream.Collectors` class that provides many ready-to-use collectors. As we have mentioned already, together with the operations discussed in this book and the numeric streams operations we are going to present in the *Numeric stream interfaces* section, they cover the vast majority of the processing needs in mainstream programming, and there is a good chance you would never need to create a custom collector at all.

# Class collectors

The `java.util.stream.Collectors` class provides more than 40 methods that create `Collector` objects. We are going to demonstrate only the simplest and most popular ones:

- `Collector<T,?,List<T>> toList()`: Creates a collector that collects the stream elements into a `List` object.
- `Collector<T,?,Set<T>> toSet()`: Creates a collector that collects the stream elements into a `Set` object.
- `Collector<T,?,Map<K,U>> toMap (Function<T,K> keyMapper, Function<T,U> valueMapper)`: Creates a collector that collects the stream elements into a `Map` object.
- `Collector<T,?,C> toCollection (Supplier<C> collectionFactory)`: Creates a collector that collects the stream elements into a `Collection` object of the type specified by the collection factory.
- `Collector<CharSequence,?,String> joining()`: Creates a collector that concatenates the elements into a `String` value.
- `Collector<CharSequence,?,String> joining (CharSequence delimiter)`: Creates a collector that concatenates the elements into a delimiter-separated `String` value.
- `Collector<CharSequence,?,String> joining (CharSequence delimiter, CharSequence prefix, CharSequence suffix)`: Creates a collector that concatenates the elements into a delimiter-separated `String` value with the provided prefix and suffix.
- `Collector<T,?,Integer> summingInt(ToIntFunction<T>)`: Creates a collector that calculates the sum of the results generated by the provided function applied to each element. The same method exists for the `long` and `double` types.

- `Collector<T,?,IntSummaryStatistics>`
  `summarizingInt(ToIntFunction<T>)`: Creates a collector that
  calculates the sum, min, max, count, and average of the results generated by the
  provided function applied to each element. The same method exists for
  the `long` and `double` types.
- `Collector<T,?,Map<Boolean,List<T>>> partitioningBy (Predicate<?`
  `super T> predicate)`: Creates a collector that partitions the elements
  according to the provided `Predicate` function.
- `Collector<T,?,Map<K,List<T>>> groupingBy(Function<T,U>)`: Creates a
  collector that groups elements into a `Map` with keys generated by the provided
  function.

The following demo code shows how to use the collectors created by these methods. First,
we demonstrate usage of the `toList()`, `toSet()`, `toMap()`,
and `toCollection()` methods:

```
List<String> ls = Stream.of("a", "b", "c").collect(Collectors.toList());
System.out.println(ls);                    //prints: [a, b, c]

Set<String> set = Stream.of("a", "a", "c").collect(Collectors.toSet());
System.out.println(set);                    //prints: [a, c]

List<Person> persons = List.of(new Person(23, "Bob"),
                               new Person(33, "Jim"),
                               new Person(28, "Jill"),
                               new Person(27, "Bill"));
Map<String, Person> map = persons.stream()
    .collect(Collectors.toMap(p->p.getName() + "-" + p.getAge(), p->p));
System.out.println(map); //prints: {Bob-23=Person{name:Bob,age:23},
                                    Bill-27=Person{name:Bill,age:27},
                                    Jill-28=Person{name:Jill,age:28},
                                    Jim-33=Person{name:Jim,age:33}}
Set<Person> personSet = persons.stream()
                        .collect(Collectors.toCollection(HashSet::new));
System.out.println(personSet);   //prints: [Person{name:Bill,age:27},
                                    Person{name:Jim,age:33},
                                    Person{name:Bob,age:23},
                                    Person{name:Jill,age:28}]
```

The `joining()` method allows concatenating the `Character` and `String` values in a delimited list with a prefix and suffix:

```
List<String> list = List.of("a", "b", "c", "d");
String result = list.stream().collect(Collectors.joining());
System.out.println(result);            //abcd

result = list.stream().collect(Collectors.joining(", "));
System.out.println(result);            //a, b, c, d

result = list.stream()
          .collect(Collectors.joining(", ", "The result: ", ""));
System.out.println(result);            //The result: a, b, c, d

result = list.stream()
       .collect(Collectors.joining(", ", "The result: ", ". The End."));
System.out.println(result);            //The result: a, b, c, d. The End.
```

The `summingInt()` and `summarizingInt()` methods create collectors that calculate the sum and other statistics of the `int` values produced by the provided function applied to each element:

```
List<Person> list = List.of(new Person(23, "Bob"),
                            new Person(33, "Jim"),
                            new Person(28, "Jill"),
                            new Person(27, "Bill"));
int sum = list.stream().collect(Collectors.summingInt(Person::getAge));
System.out.println(sum);   //prints: 111

IntSummaryStatistics stats =
     list.stream().collect(Collectors.summarizingInt(Person::getAge));
System.out.println(stats);       //IntSummaryStatistics{count=4, sum=111,
                                 //   min=23, average=27.750000, max=33}
System.out.println(stats.getCount());    //4
System.out.println(stats.getSum());      //111
System.out.println(stats.getMin());      //23
System.out.println(stats.getAverage());  //27.750000
System.out.println(stats.getMax());      //33
```

There are also `summingLong()`, `summarizingLong()`, `summingDouble()`, and `summarizingDouble()` methods.

The `partitioningBy()` method creates a collector that groups the elements by the provided criteria and put the groups (lists) in a `Map` object with a `boolean` value as the key:

```
List<Person> list = List.of(new Person(23, "Bob"),
                            new Person(33, "Jim"),
                            new Person(28, "Jill"),
                            new Person(27, "Bill"));
Map<Boolean, List<Person>> map =
    list.stream().collect(Collectors.partitioningBy(p->p.getAge() > 27));
System.out.println(map);
                //{false=[Person{name:Bob,age:23}, Person{name:Bill,age:27}],
                // true=[Person{name:Jim,age:33}, Person{name:Jill,age:28}]}
```

As you can see, using the `p.getAge() > 27` criteria, we were able to put all the people in two groups—one is below or equals 27 years of age (the key is `false`), and the other is above 27 (the key is `true`).

And, finally, the `groupingBy()` method allows us to group elements by a value and put the groups (lists) in a `Map` object with this value as a key:

```
List<Person> list = List.of(new Person(23, "Bob"),
                            new Person(33, "Jim"),
                            new Person(23, "Jill"),
                            new Person(33, "Bill"));
Map<Integer, List<Person>> map =
        list.stream().collect(Collectors.groupingBy(Person::getAge));
System.out.println(map);
                //{33=[Person{name:Jim,age:33}, Person{name:Bill,age:33}],
                // 23=[Person{name:Bob,age:23}, Person{name:Jill,age:23}]}
```

To be able to demonstrate the preceding method, we changed our list of `Person` objects by setting the age on each of them either to 23 or to 33. The result is two groups by their age.

There are also overloaded `toMap()`, `groupingBy()`, and `partitioningBy()` methods as well as the following, often overloaded too, methods that create corresponding `Collector` objects:

- `counting()`
- `reducing()`
- `filtering()`
- `toConcurrentMap()`
- `collectingAndThen()`

- maxBy() and minBy()
- mapping() and flatMapping()
- averagingInt(), averagingLong(), and averagingDouble()
- toUnmodifiableList(), toUnmodifiableMap(), and toUnmodifiableSet()

If you cannot find the operation you need among those discussed in this book, search the Collectors API first, before building your own Collector object.

# Numeric stream interfaces

As we have mentioned already, all the three numeric interfaces, IntStream, LongStream, and DoubleStream,have methods similar to the methods in the Stream interface, including methods of the Stream.Builder interface. This means that everything we have talked so far in this chapter equally applies to any of the numeric stream interfaces. That is why, in this section, we will only talk about those methods that are not present in the Stream interface:

- The range(lower,upper) and rangeClosed(lower,upper) methods in the IntStream and LongStream interfaces. They allow us to create a stream from the values in the specified range.
- The boxed() and mapToObj() intermediate operations, which convert a numeric stream to Stream.
- The mapToInt(), mapToLong(), and mapToDouble() intermediate operations, which convert a numeric stream of one type to a numeric stream of another type.
- The flatMapToInt(), flatMapToLong(), and flatMapToDouble() intermediate operations, which convert a stream to a numeric stream.
- The sum() and average() Terminal operations, which calculate sum and average of the numeric stream elements.

# Creating a stream

In addition to the methods of the Stream interface that create streams, the IntStream and LongStream interfaces allow us to create a stream from the values in the specified range.

# range(), rangeClosed()

The `range(lower, upper)` method generates all the values sequentially, starting from the `lower` value and ending with the value just before `upper`:

```
IntStream.range(1, 3).forEach(System.out::print);   //prints: 12
LongStream.range(1, 3).forEach(System.out::print);  //prints: 12
```

The `rangeClosed(lower, upper)` method generates all the values sequentially, starting from the `lower` value and ending with the `upper` value:

```
IntStream.rangeClosed(1, 3).forEach(System.out::print);   //prints: 123
LongStream.rangeClosed(1, 3).forEach(System.out::print);  //prints: 123
```

# Intermediate operations

In addition to the `Stream` intermediate operations, the `IntStream`, `LongStream`, and `DoubleStream` interfaces also have number-specific intermediate operations: `boxed()`, `mapToObj()`, `mapToInt()`, `mapToLong()`, `mapToDouble()`, `flatMapToInt()`, `flatMapToLong()`, and `flatMapToDouble()`.

# boxed() and mapToObj()

The `boxed()` intermediate operation converts (boxes) elements of the primitive numeric type to the corresponding wrapper type:

```
//IntStream.range(1, 3).map(Integer::shortValue)        //compile error
//                     .forEach(System.out::print);
IntStream.range(1, 3).boxed().map(Integer::shortValue)
                             .forEach(System.out::print);   //prints: 12
//LongStream.range(1, 3).map(Long::shortValue)          //compile error
//                     .forEach(System.out::print);
LongStream.range(1, 3).boxed().map(Long::shortValue)
                             .forEach(System.out::print);   //prints: 12
//DoubleStream.of(1).map(Double::shortValue)            //compile error
//                .forEach(System.out::print);
DoubleStream.of(1).boxed().map(Double::shortValue)
                             .forEach(System.out::print);   //prints: 1
```

In the preceding code, we have commented out the lines that generate compilation errors because the elements generated by the `range()` method are of primitive types. By adding the `boxed()` operation, we convert the primitive values to the corresponding wrapping type and can then process them as a reference type.

The `mapToObj()` intermediate operation does a similar transformation, but it is not as specialized as the `boxed()` operation and allows to use an element of the primitive type to produce an object of any type:

```
IntStream.range(1, 3).mapToObj(Integer::valueOf)
                     .map(Integer::shortValue)
                     .forEach(System.out::print);        //prints: 12
IntStream.range(42, 43).mapToObj(i -> new Person(i, "John"))
                     .forEach(System.out::print);
                              //prints: Person{name:John,age:42}
LongStream.range(1, 3).mapToObj(Long::valueOf)
                     .map(Long::shortValue)
                     .forEach(System.out::print);        //prints: 12
DoubleStream.of(1).mapToObj(Double::valueOf)
                     .map(Double::shortValue)
                     .forEach(System.out::print);        //prints: 1
```

In the preceding code, we have added the `map()` operation just to prove that the `mapToObj()` operation does the job and creates a wrapping type object as expected. Also, by adding the stream pipe that produces the `Person` objects, we have demonstrated how the `mapToObj()` operation can be used to create an object of any type.

# mapToInt(), mapToLong(), and mapToDouble()

The `mapToInt()`, `mapToLong()`, `mapToDouble()` intermediate operations allow us to convert a numeric stream of one type to a numeric stream of another type. For the demonstration code, we convert the list of `String` values to a numeric stream of different types by mapping each `String` value to its length:

```
list.stream().mapToInt(String::length)
                     .forEach(System.out::print); //prints: 335
list.stream().mapToLong(String::length)
                     .forEach(System.out::print); //prints: 335
list.stream().mapToDouble(String::length)
     .forEach(d -> System.out.print(d + " "));    //prints: 3.0 3.0 5.0
```

The elements of the created numeric streams are of a primitive type:

```
//list.stream().mapToInt(String::length)
//              .map(Integer::shortValue)    //compile error
//              .forEach(System.out::print);
```

And since we are on this topic, if you would like to convert elements to a numeric wrapping type, the `map()` intermediate operation is the way to do it (instead of `mapToInt()`):

```
list.stream().map(String::length)
            .map(Integer::shortValue)
            .forEach(System.out::print);   //prints: 335
```

## flatMapToInt(), flatMapToLong(), and flatMapToDouble()

The `flatMapToInt()`, `flatMapToLong()`, `flatMapToDouble()` intermediate operations produce a numeric stream of a corresponding type:

```
List<Integer> list = List.of(1, 2, 3);

list.stream().flatMapToInt(i -> IntStream.rangeClosed(1, i))
                        .forEach(System.out::print);     //prints: 112123
list.stream().flatMapToLong(i -> LongStream.rangeClosed(1, i))
                        .forEach(System.out::print);     //prints: 112123
list.stream().flatMapToDouble(DoubleStream::of)
            .forEach(d -> System.out.print(d + " "));   //prints: 1.0 2.0 3.0
```

As you can see, in the preceding code, we have used `int` values in the original stream. But it can be a stream of any type:

```
List<String> str = List.of("one", "two", "three");
str.stream().flatMapToInt(s -> IntStream.rangeClosed(1, s.length()))
                        .forEach(System.out::print);   //prints: 12312312345
```

## Terminal operations

The additional Terminal operations of numeric streams are pretty straightforward. There are two of them:

- `sum()`: Calculates the sum of the numeric stream elements
- `average()`: Calculates the average of the numeric stream elements

## sum() and average()

If you need to calculate a sum or an average of the values of numeric stream elements, the only requirement for the stream is that it should not be infinite. Otherwise, the calculation never finishes:

```
int sum = IntStream.empty().sum();
System.out.println(sum);          //prints: 0

sum = IntStream.range(1, 3).sum();
System.out.println(sum);          //prints: 3

double av = IntStream.empty().average().orElse(0);
System.out.println(av);           //prints: 0.0

av = IntStream.range(1, 3).average().orElse(0);
System.out.println(av);           //prints: 1.5

long suml = LongStream.range(1, 3).sum();
System.out.println(suml);         //prints: 3

double avl = LongStream.range(1, 3).average().orElse(0);
System.out.println(avl);          //prints: 1.5

double sumd = DoubleStream.of(1, 2).sum();
System.out.println(sumd);         //prints: 3.0

double avd = DoubleStream.of(1, 2).average().orElse(0);
System.out.println(avd);          //prints: 1.5
```

As you can see, using these operations on an empty stream is not a problem.

# Parallel processing

We have seen that changing from a sequential stream to a parallel stream can lead to incorrect results if the code was not written and tested for processing a parallel stream. The following are a few more considerations related to the parallel stream.

# Stateless and stateful operations

There are stateless operations, such as `filter()`, `map()`, and `flatMap()`, which do not keep data around (do not maintain state) while moving from processing from one stream element to the next. And there are stateful operations, such as `distinct()`, `limit()`, `sorted()`, `reduce()`, and `collect()`, which may pass the state from previously processed elements to the processing of the next element.

Stateless operations usually do not pose a problem when switching from a sequential stream to a parallel one. Each element is processed independently and the stream can be broken into any number of sub-streams for independent processing.

With stateful operations, the situation is different. To start with, using them for an infinite stream may never finish processing. Also, while discussing the `reduce()` and `collect()` stateful operations, we have demonstrated how switching to a parallel stream can produce a different result if the initial value (or identity) is set without parallel processing in mind.

And there are performance considerations too. Stateful operations often require processing all the stream elements in several passes using buffering. For large streams, it may tax JVM resources and slow down, if not completely shut down, the application.

That is why a programmer should not take switching from a sequential to a parallel stream lightly. If stateful operations are involved, the code has to be designed and tested to be able to perform the parallel stream processing without negative effects.

# Sequential or parallel processing?

As we indicated in the previous section, parallel processing may or may not produce better performance. One has to test every use case before deciding to use it. Parallelism can yield better performance, but the code has to be designed and possibly optimized to do it. And each assumption has to be tested in the environment as close to the production as possible.

However, there are a few considerations one can take into account while deciding between sequential and parallel processing:

- Small streams typically are processed faster sequentially (well, what is "small" for your environment should be determined through testing and measuring the performance)

- If stateful operations cannot be replaced with stateless ones, design the code carefully for the parallel processing or just avoid it completely
- Consider parallel processing for the procedures that require extensive calculations, but think about bringing the partial results together for the final result

# Exercise – Multiplying all the stream elements

Multiply all the values of the following list using a stream:

```
List<Integer> list = List.of(2, 3, 4);
```

## Answer

```
int r = list.stream().reduce(1, (x, y) -> x * y);
System.out.println(r);    //prints: 24
```

# Summary

This chapter introduced the powerful concept of data-streams processing and provided many examples of functional programming usage. It explained what streams are, how to process them, and how to build processing pipelines. It also demonstrated how one can organize stream processing in parallel and some of the possible pitfalls.

In the next chapter, we are going to discuss reactive systems, their advantages, and possible implementations. You will learn about asynchronous non-blocking processing, reactive programming, and microservices, all with code examples that demonstrate the main principles on which these reactive systems are based.

# 19
# Reactive Systems

In the final chapter of this book, we'll break the flow of the connected narrative and jump closer to real-life professional programming. As more data gets processed and services become more sophisticated, the need for more adaptive, highly scalable, and distributed applications grows exponentially. That is what we are going to address in this chapter—how such a software system may look in practice.

In this chapter, we will cover the following topics:

- How to process a lot of data quickly
- Microservices
- Reactive systems
- Exercise – Creating `io.reactivex.Observable`

## How to process a lot of data quickly

There are many measurable performance characteristics that can be applied to an application. Which ones to use depends on the purpose of the application. They are usually listed as non-functional requirements. The most typical set includes the following three:

- **Throughput**: The number of requests processed per a unit of time.
- **Latency**: The time elapsed between the moment a request was submitted and the moment the *first* byte of the response is received. It is measured in seconds, milliseconds, and so on.
- **Memory footprint**: The amount of memory—min, max, or average— that the application consumes.

In practice, latency is often calculated as the inverse of the throughput. These characteristics vary as a load grows, so the non-functional requirements typically include the maximum value for each of them under the average and maximum load.

Often, the improvements in throughput and latency are only at the expense of the memory, unless adding a faster CPU can improve all three characteristics. But that depends on the nature of the processing. For example, an input/output (or another interaction) with a low-performance device can impose a limit, and no change in the code can improve the application performance.

There are also subtle nuances in the measuring of each of the characteristics. For example, instead of measuring latency as the average of all requests, we can use the maximum latency among 99% of the fastest (least latency) requests. Otherwise, it looks like an average wealth number obtained by dividing the wealth of a billionaire and a person at the bottom of the income pyramid by two.

When evaluating application performance, one has to answer the following:

- Can the requested upper limit of the latency ever be exceeded? If yes, how often, and by how much?
- How long can the period of poor latency be, and how often it is allowed to happen?
- Who/what measures the latency in production?
- What is the expected peak load, and how long is it expected to last?

Only after all of these (and similar questions) have been answered, and the non-functional requirements have been established, can we start designing the system, testing it, tweaking, and testing again. There are many programming techniques that prove to be effective in achieving the required throughput with an acceptable memory consumption.

In this context, the terms *asynchronous, non-blocking, distributed, scalable, reactive, responsive, resilient, elastic,* and *message-driven* became ubiquitous, just synonyms of *high performance*. We are going to discuss each of these terms so that the reader can understand the motivation that brought *microservices* and *reactive systems* to life, which we are going to present in the next two sections of this chapter.

# Asynchronous

**Asynchronous** means that the requestor gets the response *immediately,* but the result is not there. Instead, the requestor receives an object with methods that allow us to check whether the result is ready. The requestor calls this method periodically, and, when the result is ready, retrieves it using another method on the same object.

The advantage of such a solution is that the requestor can do other things while waiting. For example, in Chapter 11, *JVM Processes and Garbage Collection*, we demonstrated how a child thread can be created. So, the main thread can create a child thread that sends a non-asynchronous (also called blocking) request, and waits for its return, doing nothing. The main thread, meanwhile, can continue executing something else, periodically calling the child thread object to see whether the result is ready.

That is the most basic of asynchronous call implementations. In fact, we we already used it when we processed a parallel stream. The parallel stream operations create child threads behind the scenes, break the stream into segments, and assign each segment to a dedicated thread, then aggregate the results from each segment in the final one. In the previous chapter, we wrote functions that did the aggregating job. As a reminder, these functions are called combiners.

Let's compare the performance of the same functionality when processing sequential and parallel streams.

## Sequential versus parallel streams

To demonstrate the difference between sequential and parallel processing, let's imagine a system that collects data from 10 physical devices (sensors) and calculates an average. The interface of such a system could look like the following:

```
interface MeasuringSystem {
    double get(String id);
}
```

It has only one method, get(), which receives an ID of a sensor and returns the result of the measurement. Using this interface, we can implement many different systems, which are able to call different devices. For demonstration purposes, we are not going to write a lot of code. All we need is to put a delay of 100 milliseconds (to imitate the time it takes to collect the measurement from the sensor) and return some number. We can implement the delay as follows:

```
void pauseMs(int ms) {
    try{
        TimeUnit.MILLISECONDS.sleep(ms);
    } catch(InterruptedException ex){
        ex.printStackTrace();
    }
}
```

As for the resulting number, we will use `Math.random()` to simulate the difference of the measurements received from different sensors (that is why we need to find an average—to offset the errors and other idiosyncrasies of an individual device). So, our demo implementation may look as follows:

```
class MeasuringSystemImpl implements MeasuringSystem {
    public double get(String id){
        demo.pauseMs(100);
        return 10. * Math.random();
    }
}
```

Now, we realize that our `MeasuringInterface` is a functional interface, because it has only one method. This means we can use one of the standard functional interfaces from the `java.util.function` package; namely, `Function<String, Double>`:

```
Function<String, Double> mSys = id -> {
    demo.pauseMs(100);
    return 10. + Math.random();
};
```

So, we can discard our `MeasuringSystem` interface and `MeasuringSystemImpl` class. But we can leave the `mSys` (*Measuring System*) identificator that reflects the idea behind this function: it represents a measuring system that provides access to its sensors and allows us to collect data from them.

Now, let's create a list of sensor IDs:

```
List<String> ids = IntStream.range(1, 11)
        .mapToObj(i -> "id" + i).collect(Collectors.toList());
```

Again, in real life, we would need to collect the IDs of real devices, but for demo purposes, we just generate them.

Finally, we will create the `collectData()` method, which calls all the sensors and calculates an average across all the received data:

```
Stream<Double> collectData(Stream<String> stream,
                           Function<String, Double> mSys){
    return  stream.map(id -> mSys.apply(id));
}
```

As you can see, the method receives a stream that provides IDs and a function that uses each ID to get a measurement from a sensor.

Here is how we are going to call this method from the `averageDemo()` method, using the `getAverage()` method:

```
void averageDemo() {
    Function<String, Double> mSys = id -> {
        pauseMs(100);
        return 10. + Math.random();
    };
    getAverage(() -> collectData(ids.stream(), mSys));
}

void getAverage(Supplier<Stream<Double>> collectData) {
    LocalTime start = LocalTime.now();
    double a = collectData.get()
                    .mapToDouble(Double::valueOf).average().orElse(0);
    System.out.println((Math.round(a * 100.) / 100.) + " in " +
        Duration.between(start, LocalTime.now()).toMillis() + " ms");
}
```

As you can see, we create the function that represents the measuring system and pass it into the `collectData()` method, along with the stream of IDs. Then, we create the `SupplierStream<Double>` function as the `() -> collectData(ids.stream(), mSys)` lambda expression, and pass it as the `collectData` parameter into the `getAverage()` method. Inside of the `getAverage()` method, we call the `get()` of the supplier, and thus invoke `collectData(ids.stream(), mSys)`, which returns `Stream<Double>`. We then convert it to `DoubleStream` with the `mapToDouble()` operation, so we can apply the `average()` operation. The `average()` operation returns an `Optional<Double>` object, and we call its `orElse(0)` method, which returns either the calculated value or zero (if, for example, the measuring system could not connect to any of its sensors and returned an empty stream). The last line of the `getAverage()` method prints the result and the time it took to calculate it. In real code, we would return the result and use it for other calculations. But for our demonstration, we just print it.

Now, we can compare the performance of sequential stream processing to parallel stream processing:

```
List<String> ids = IntStream.range(1, 11)
                .mapToObj(i -> "id" + i).collect(Collectors.toList());
Function<String, Double> mSys = id -> {
        pauseMs(100);
        return 10. + Math.random();
```

```
};
getAverage(() -> collectData(ids.stream(), mSys));
                                        //prints: 10.46 in 1031 ms
getAverage(() -> collectData(ids.parallelStream(), mSys));
                                        //prints: 10.49 in 212 ms
```

As you can see, processing a parallel stream is five times faster than processing a sequential stream.

Although behind the scenes, the parallel stream uses \ asynchronous processing, this is not what programmers have in mind when talking about processing requests asynchronously. From the application perspective, it is just parallel (also called concurrent) processing. It is faster than sequential processing, but the main thread has to wait until all of the calls are made and all of the data retrieved. If each call takes at least 100 ms (as it does in our case), then the processing of all the calls cannot be completed in less time.

Of course, we can create a child thread and let it place all the calls, and wait until they complete, while the main thread does something else. We can even create a service that does it, so the application can just tell such a service what to do (pass the sensor IDs, in our case) and continue doing something else. Later, the main thread can call the service again, and get the result or pick it up in some agreed-upon place. That would be the truly asynchronous processing that the programmers are talking about.

But before writing such a code, let's look at the `CompletableFuture` class located in the `java.util.concurrent` package. It does everything we described, and even more.

# Using the CompletableFuture class

Using the `CompletableFuture` object, we can separate sending the request for data to the measuring system (and creating the `CompletableFuture` object) from getting the result from the `CompletableFuture` object. This is exactly the scenario we described when explaining what asynchronous processing is. Let's demonstrate it in the code. Similar to the way we submitted the requests to a measuring system, we can do it using the `CompletableFuture.supplyAsync()` static method:

```
List<CompletableFuture<Double>> list = ids.stream()
        .map(id -> CompletableFuture.supplyAsync(() -> mSys.apply(id)))
        .collect(Collectors.toList());
```

The difference is that the `supplyAsync()` method does not wait for the call to the measuring system to return. Instead, it immediately creates a `CompletableFuture` object and returns it, so that a client can use this object to retrieve the value returned by the measuring system at any time. There are also methods that allow us to check whether the value was returned at all, but that is not the point of this demonstration, which is to show how the `CompletableFuture` class can be used to organize asynchronous processing.

The created list of `CompletableFuture` objects can be stored anywhere. We have chosen to store it in a `Map`. In fact, we have created a `sendRequests()` method that can send any number of requests to any number of measuring systems:

```
Map<Integer, List<CompletableFuture<Double>>>
                sendRequests(List<List<String>> idLists,
                            List<Function<String, Double>> mSystems){
    LocalTime start = LocalTime.now();
    Map<Integer, List<CompletableFuture<Double>>> requests
                                            = new HashMap<>();
    for(int i = 0; i < idLists.size(); i++){
        for(Function<String, Double> mSys: mSystems){
            List<String> ids = idLists.get(i);
            List<CompletableFuture<Double>> list = ids.stream()
              .map(id -> CompletableFuture.supplyAsync(() -> mSys.apply(id)))
              .collect(Collectors.toList());
            requests.put(i, list);
        }
    }
    long dur = Duration.between(start, LocalTime.now()).toMillis();
    System.out.println("Submitted in " + dur + " ms");
    return requests;
}
```

As you can see, the preceding method accepts two parameters:

- `List<List<String>> idLists`: A collection (list) of lists of sensor IDs, each list specific to a particular measuring system.
- `List<Function<String, Double>> mSystems`: List of measuring systems, each represented as `Function<String, Double>`, that has a single `apply()` method that accepts a sensor ID and returns a double value (measurement result). The systems in this list are in the same order as the sensor ID lists in the first parameter, so we can match IDs to the system by their positions.

Then, we create the `Map<Integer, List<CompletableFuture<Double>>>` object to store lists of the `CompletableFuture` objects. We generate them in a `for`-loop, and then store them in a `Map` with a key that is just some sequential number. The `Map` is returned to the client and can be stored anywhere, for any period of time (well, there are some limitations that can be modified, but we are not going to discuss them here). Later, when the client has decided to get the results of the requests, the `getAverage()` method can be used to retrieve them:

```
void getAverage(Map<Integer, List<CompletableFuture<Double>>> requests){
    for(List<CompletableFuture<Double>> list: requests.values()){
        getAverage(() -> list.stream().map(CompletableFuture::join));
    }
}
```

The preceding method accepts the `Map` object created by the `sendRequests()` method and iterates over all the values (lists of the `ComputableFuture` objects) stored in `Map`. For each list, it creates a stream that maps each element (object of `ComputableFuture`) to the result of the `join()` method called on the element. This method retrieves the value returned from the corresponding call to a measuring system. If the value is not available, the method waits for some time (a configurable value), and either quits (and returns `null`), or, eventually, receives the value from the call to the measuring system, if available. Again, we are not going to discuss all the guards placed around failures, to keep the focus on the main functionality.

The `() -> list.stream().map(CompletableFuture::join)` function is actually passed into the `getAverage()` method (which should be familiar to you), which we used while processing the streams in the previous example:

```
void getAverage(Supplier<Stream<Double>> collectData) {
    LocalTime start = LocalTime.now();
    double a = collectData.get()
                    .mapToDouble(Double::valueOf).average().orElse(0);
    System.out.println((Math.round(a * 100.) / 100.) + " in " +
        Duration.between(start, LocalTime.now()).toMillis() + " ms");
}
```

This method calculates the average of all the values emitted by the passed-in stream, prints it, and also captures the time it took to process the stream (and calculate the average).

Now, let's use the new methods and see how performance is improved:

```
Function<String, Double> mSys = id -> {
    pauseMs(100);
    return 10. + Math.random();
};
List<Function<String, Double>> mSystems = List.of(mSys, mSys, mSys);
List<List<String>> idLists = List.of(ids, ids, ids);

Map<Integer, List<CompletableFuture<Double>>> requestLists =
        sendRequests(idLists, mSystems);  //prints: Submitted in 13 ms

pauseMs(2000);   //The main thread can continue doing something else
                 //for any period of time
getAverage(requestLists);              //prints: 10.49 in 5 ms
                                       //        10.61 in 0 ms
                                       //        10.51 in 0 ms
```

For simplicity, we reused the same measuring system (and its IDs) to imitate working with three measuring systems. You can see that the requests for all three systems are submitted in 13 ms. The `sendRequests()` method exists, and the main thread is free to do something else for at least two seconds. That is how much time it takes to actually send all the requests and receive the response, because of `pauseMs(100)`, used for each call to a measuring system. Then, we calculate an average for each system, and it takes almost no time. That is what programmers mean when they talk about processing requests asynchronously.

The `CompletableFuture` class has many methods, and has support from several other classes and interfaces. For example, the pause period of two seconds to collect all of the data can be decreased by using a thread pool:

```
Map<Integer, List<CompletableFuture<Double>>>
                sendRequests(List<List<String>> idLists,
                        List<Function<String, Double>> mSystems){
    ExecutorService pool = Executors.newCachedThreadPool();
    LocalTime start = LocalTime.now();
    Map<Integer, List<CompletableFuture<Double>>> requests
                                        = new HashMap<>();
    for(int i = 0; i < idLists.size(); i++){
        for(Function<String, Double> mSys: mSystems){
            List<String> ids = idLists.get(i);
            List<CompletableFuture<Double>> list = ids.stream()
              .map(id -> CompletableFuture.supplyAsync(() -> mSys.apply(id),
                                                          pool))
              .collect(Collectors.toList());
            requests.put(i, list);
        }
```

```
    }
    pool.shutdown();
    long dur = Duration.between(start, LocalTime.now()).toMillis();
    System.out.println("Submitted in " + dur + " ms");
    return requests;
}
```

There is a variety of such pools, for different purposes and different performances. But all of that does not change the overall system design, so we will omit such details.

So, the power of asynchronous processing is great. But who benefits from it?

If you have created an application that collects data and calculates an average for each measuring system on demand, then from the client's point of view, it still takes a lot of time, because the pause (for two seconds, or less if we use a thread pool) is still included in the client's wait time. So, the advantage of asynchronous processing is lost for the client, unless you have designed your API so that the client can submit the request and walk away to do something else, then pick up the results later.

That is the difference between a *synchronous* (or *blocking*) API, when a client waits (blocked) until the result is returned, and an *asynchronous* API, when a client submits a request and walks away to do something else, then gets the results later.

The possibility of an asynchronous API enhances our understanding of latency. Usually, by latency, programmers mean the time between the moment the request was submitted and the time the first byte of the response has been received *during the same call to the API*. But if the API is asynchronous, the definition of latency changes to, "The moment the request was submitted and the time the result is available for the client to collect." The latency during each call, in such cases, is assumed to be much smaller than the time between the call to place the request and the call to collect the result.

There is also a notion of the *non-blocking* API, which we are going to discuss in the next section.

# Non-blocking

For the client of an application, the notion of a non-blocking API only tells us that the application is probably scalable, reactive, responsive, resilient, elastic, and message-driven. In the following sections, we are going to discuss all of these terms, but for now, we hope you can derive a sense of what each of them means from the names themselves.

Such a statement means two things:

- Being non-blocking does not affect the protocol of communication between the client and the application: it may be synchronous (blocking) or asynchronous. Non-blocking is an implementation detail; it is a view of the API from inside the application.
- Non-blocking is the implementation that helps the application to be all of the following: scalable, reactive, responsive, resilient, elastic, and message-driven. This means it is a very important design concept that resides at the foundation of many modern applications.

It's know that blocking APIs and non-blocking APIs are not opposites. They describe different aspects of the application. The blocking API describes how a client interacts with it: the client calls, and stays connected until the response is provided. The non-blocking API describes how the application is implemented: it does not dedicate an execution thread to each of the requests, but provides several lightweight worker threads that do the processing asynchronously and concurrently.

The term non-blocking came into use with the `java.nio` (NIO stands for non-blocking input/output) package that provides support for intensive input/output (I/O) operations.

# The java.io versus java.nio package

Writing and reading data to and from external memory (a hard drive, for example) is a much slower operation than other processes that happen in the memory. The already existing classes and interfaces of the `java.io` package worked fine, but once in a while, the performance would bottleneck. The new `java.nio` package was created to provide more effective I/O support.

The `java.io` implementation was based on stream processing, which, as we saw in the previous section, is basically a blocking operation, even if some kind of concurrency is happening behind the scenes. To increase the speed, the `java.nio` implementation was based on reading/writing to/from a buffer in the memory. Such a design allowed us to separate the slow process of filling/emptying the buffer and the fast reading/writing from/to it. In a way, it is similar to what we have done in our example of the `CompletableFuture` class usage. The additional advantage of having data in a buffer is that it is possible to inspect it, going there and back along the buffer, which is impossible when reading sequentially from the stream. It has allowed for more flexibility during data processing.

In addition, the `java.nio` implementation introduced another middleman process, called a channel, which provided bulk data transfers to and from buffers. The reading thread gets data from a channel, and only receives what is currently available, or nothing at all (if there is no data is in the channel). If data is not available, the thread, instead of remaining blocked, can do something else—reading/writing to/from other channels, for example. The same way the main thread in our `CompletableFuture` example was free to do whatever had to be done while the measuring system was reading data from its sensors. This way, instead of dedicating a thread to one I/O process, a few worker-threads can serve many I/O processes.

Such a solution was called a non-blocking I/O, and was later applied to other processes, the most prominent being the events processing in an *event loop*, also called a *run loop*.

# Event loop, or run loop

Many non-blocking systems of processing are based on the event (or run) loop—a thread that is continually executed, receives events (requests, messages), and then dispatches them to the corresponding *event handlers*. There is nothing special about the event handlers. They are just methods (functions) dedicated, by the programmer, for processing a particular event type.

This design is called a *reactor design pattern*, defined as *an event handling pattern for handling service requests delivered concurrently to a service handler*. It also provided the name for the *reactive programming* and *reactive systems* that *react* to some events, and process them accordingly. We will talk about reactive systems later, in a dedicated section.

Event loop-based design is widely used in operating systems and graphical user interfaces. It is available in Spring WebFlux in Spring 5, and implemented in JavaScript and its popular executing environment, Node.js. The last one uses an event loop as its processing backbone. The Vert.x toolkit is built around the event loop, too. We will show some examples of the latter in the *Microservices* section.

Before the adoption of the event loop, a dedicated thread was assigned to each incoming request—much like in our demonstration of stream processing. Each of the threads requires the allocation of a certain amount of resources that is not request-specific, so some of the resources—mostly memory allocation—are wasted. Then, as the number of requests grows, the CPU needs to switch its context from one thread to another more often, to allow more or less concurrent processing of all the requests. Under the load, the overhead of switching the context becomes substantial enough to affect the performance of an application.

Implementing an event loop has addressed these two issues:

- It eliminated the waste of resources by avoiding the creation of a thread dedicated to each request, and keeping it around until the request was processed. With an event loop in place, a much smaller memory allocation is needed for each request to capture its specifics. It made it possible to keep many more requests in memory, so that they can be processed concurrently.
- The overhead of the CPU context-switching became much smaller, too, because of the diminishing context size.

The non-blocking API is how the processing of the requests is implemented. With it, the systems are able to handle a much bigger load (to be more scalable and elastic), while remaining highly responsive and resilient.

# Distributed

The notion of what is distributed has changed over time. It used to mean an application running on several computers, connected via a network. It even had the synonym name of parallel computing, because each instance of the application did the same thing. Such an application improved system resilience. The failure of one computer did not affect the system as a whole.

Then, another meaning was added: an application spread across several computers, so each of its components contributed to the result produced by the application as a whole. Such a design was usually used for the calculation- or data-heavy tasks that required a lot of CPU power, or required lots of data from many different sources.

When a single CPU became powerful enough to handle the computation load of thousands of older computers and cloud computing, especially systems such as AWS Lambda serverless computing platforms, it removed the notion of an individual computer from consideration at all; *distributed* may mean any combination of one application, or its components, running on one, or many, computers.

The examples of a distributed system include big data processing systems, distributed file or data storage systems, and ledger systems, such as blockchain or Bitcoin, that can also be included in the group of data storage systems under the subcategory of *smart* data storage systems.

When programmers call a system *distributed* today, they typically mean the following:

- The system can tolerate a failure of one, or even several, of its constituting components.
- Each system component has only a limited, incomplete view of the system.
- The structure of the system is dynamic, and may change during the execution.
- The system is scalable.

# Scalable

Scalability is the ability to sustain a growing load without significant degradation of the latency/throughput. Traditionally, it was achieved by breaking the software system into tiers: a front tier, middle tier, and backend tier, for example. Each tier was composed of multiple deployments of the copies of the same group of components responsible for the particular type of processing.

The front tier components were responsible for the presentation, based on the request and the data they received from the middle tier. The middle tier components were responsible for computations and decision-making, based on the data coming from the front tier and the data they could read from the backend tier. They also sent data to the backend for storage. The backend tier stored the data, and provided it to the middle tier.

Adding copies of components, each tier allowed us to stay abreast with the increasing load. In the past, it was only possible by adding more computers to each tier. Otherwise, there would be no resources available for the newly deployed components' copies.

But, with the introduction of cloud computing, and especially the AWS Lambda services, scalability is achieved by adding only new copies of the software components. The fact that more computers are added to the tier (or not) is hidden from the deployer.

Another recent trend in distributed-system architecture allowed us to fine-tune the scalability by scaling up not only by a tier, but also by a particular small, functional part of a tier, and providing one, or several, particular kinds of services, called microservices. We will discuss this and show some examples of microservices in the *Microservices* section.

With such an architecture, the software system becomes a composition of many microservices; each may be duplicated as many times as needed, to support the required increase in the processing power. In this sense, we can talk about scalability on the level of one microservice only.

# Reactive

The term *reactive* is usually used in the context of reactive programming and reactive systems. Reactive programming (also called Rx programming) is based on programming with asynchronous data streams (also called reactive streams). It was introduced to Java in the `java.util.concurrent` package, with Java 9. It allows a `Publisher` to generate a stream of data, to which a `Subscriber` can asynchronously subscribe.

As you have seen, we were able to process data asynchronously even without this new API, by using `CompletableFuture`. But, after writing such a code a few times, one notices that most of it is just plumbing, so one gets the feeling there has to be an even simpler and more convenient solution. That's how the Reactive Streams initiative (`http://www.reactive-streams.org`) was born. The scope of the effort is defined as follows:

> *The scope of Reactive Streams is to find a minimal set of interfaces, methods and protocols that will describe the necessary operations and entities to achieve the goal—asynchronous streams of data with non-blocking back pressure.*

The term *non-blocking back pressure* refers to one of the problems of asynchronous processing—a coordination of the speed rate of the incoming data with the ability of the system to process it, without the need to stop (block) the data input. The solution is to inform the source that the consumer has a difficulty in keeping up with the input, but the processing should react to the change of the rate of incoming data in a more flexible manner than just blocking the flow (thus, the name reactive).

In addition to standard Java libraries, several other libraries already exist that implemented the Reactive Streams API: RxJava, Reactor, Akka Streams, and Vert.x are among the most known. We will use RxJava 2.1.13 in our examples. You can find the RxJava 2.x API at `http://reactivex.io`, under the name ReactiveX, which stands for Reactive Extension.

Let's first compare two implementations of the same functionality, using the `java.util.stream` package and the `io.reactivex` package of RxJava 2.1.13, which can be added to the project with the following dependency:

```
<dependency>
    <groupId>io.reactivex.rxjava2</groupId>
    <artifactId>rxjava</artifactId>
    <version>2.1.13</version>
</dependency>
```

The sample program is going to be very simple:

- Create a stream of integers: 1, 2, 3, 4, 5.
- Filter only even numbers (2 and 4).
- Calculate the square root of each of the filtered numbers.
- Calculate the sum of all the square roots.

Here is how it can be implemented using the `java.util.stream` package:

```
double a = IntStream.rangeClosed(1, 5)
        .filter(i -> i % 2 == 0)
        .mapToDouble(Double::valueOf)
        .map(Math::sqrt)
        .sum();
System.out.println(a); //prints: 3.414213562373095
```

And the same functionality implemented with RxJava looks as follows:

```
Observable.range(1, 5)
        .filter(i -> i % 2 == 0)
        .map(Math::sqrt)
        .reduce((r, d) -> r + d)
        .subscribe(System.out::println); //prints: 3.414213562373095
```
RxJava is based on the Observable object (which plays the role of
Publisher) and Observer that subscribes to the Observable and waits for
data to be emitted.

In addition to the `Stream` functionality, `Observable` has significantly different capabilities.
For example, a stream, once closed, cannot be reopened, while an `Observable` object can
be used again. Here is an example:

```
Observable<Double> observable = Observable.range(1, 5)
        .filter(i -> i % 2 == 0)
        .doOnNext(System.out::println)      //prints 2 and 4 twice
        .map(Math::sqrt);
observable
        .reduce((r, d) -> r + d)
        .subscribe(System.out::println);   //prints: 3.414213562373095
observable
        .reduce((r, d) -> r + d)a
        .map(r -> r / 2)
        .subscribe(System.out::println);   //prints: 1.7071067811865475
```

In the preceding example, as you can see from the comments, the `doOnNext()` operation was called twice, which means the `observable` object emitted values twice. But if we do not want `Observable` running twice, we can cache its data by adding the `cache()` operation:

```
Observable<Double> observable = Observable.range(1,5)
        .filter(i -> i % 2 == 0)
        .doOnNext(System.out::println)   //prints 2 and 4 only once
        .map(Math::sqrt)
        .cache();
observable
        .reduce((r, d) -> r + d)
        .subscribe(System.out::println); //prints: 3.414213562373095
observable
        .reduce((r, d) -> r + d)
        .map(r -> r / 2)
        .subscribe(System.out::println);  //prints: 1.7071067811865475
```

As you can see, the second usage of the same `Observable` took advantage of the cached data, allowing for better performance. There is more functionality available in the `Observable` interface and RxJava, which the format of this book does not allow us to describe. But we hope you get the idea.

Writing code using RxJava, or another asynchronous-streams library, constitutes reactive programming. It realizes the goal declared in the Reactive Manifesto (`https://www.reactivemanifesto.org`) as building reactive systems that are responsive, resilient, elastic, and message-driven.

# Responsive

It seems that this term is self-explanatory. The ability to respond in a timely manner is one of the primary qualities every client demands from any system. It is possible to achieve this using many different approaches. Even traditional blocking APIs can be supported by enough servers and other infrastructure, to provide the expected responsiveness under a very big load. Reactive programming just helps to do it using less hardware.

It comes with a price, as reactive code requires changing the way we used to do it, even five years ago. But after some time, this new way of thinking becomes as natural as any other already-familiar skill. We will see a few more examples of reactive programming in the following sections.

# Resilient

Failures are inevitable. The hardware crashes, the software has defects, unexpected data is received, or an unexpected and poorly-tested execution path was taken—any of these events, or a combination of them, can happen at any time. Resilience is the ability of the system to withstand such a situation and continue to deliver the expected results.

It can be achieved using redundancy of the deployable components and hardware, using isolation of parts of the system from each other (so the domino effect becomes less probable), designing the system so that the lost piece can be replaced automatically or an appropriate alarm raised so that qualified personnel can interfere, and through other measures.

We have talked about distributed systems already. Such an architecture makes the system more resilient by eliminating a single point of failure. Also, breaking the system into many specialized components that talk to each other using messages allows for a better tuning of the duplication of the most critical parts, and creates more opportunities for their isolation and potential failure containment.

# Elastic

The ability to sustain the biggest possible load is usually associated with scalability. But the ability to preserve the same performance characteristics under varying loads is called elasticity. A client of an elastic system should not notice any difference between the idle periods and the periods of the peak load.

The non-blocking reactive style of implementation facilitates this quality. Also, breaking the program into smaller parts and converting them into services that can be deployed and managed independently allows for fine-tuning the resource allocation. Such small services are called microservices, and many of them can together comprise a reactive system that can be both scalable and elastic. We will discuss these solutions in more detail in the following sections.

# Message-driven

We have already established that the components' isolation and system distribution are two aspects that help to keep the system responsive, resilient, and elastic. Loose and flexible connections is an important condition that supports these qualities, too. And the asynchronous nature of the reactive system simply does not leave the designer any other choice but to build communication between components on messages.

It creates a *breathing space* around each component, without which the system would be a tightly coupled monolith, susceptible to all kinds of problems, not to mention a maintenance nightmare.

With that, we are going to look at the architectural style that can be used to build an application as a collection of loosely coupled services that provide the required business functionality—microservices.

# Microservices

In order for a deployable unit of code to be qualified as a microservice, it has to possess the following characteristics:

- The size of the source code of one microservice should be smaller than the size of a traditional application. Another size criteria is that one programmer's team should be able to write and support several of them.
- It has to be deployed independently. Naturally, one microservice typically cooperates and expects cooperation from other systems, but that should not prevent our ability to deploy it.
- If a microservice uses a database to store data, it has to have its own schema, or a set of tables. This statement is still under debate, especially in cases when several services modify the same data set or interdependent datasets. If the same team owns all of the related services, it is easier to accomplish. Otherwise, there are several possible strategies to ensure independent microservice development and deployment.
- It has to be stateless, in the sense that its state should not be kept in memory, unless the memory is shared. If one instance of the service has failed, another should be able to accomplish what was expected from the service.
- It should provide a way to check its *health*—that the service is up and running and ready to do the job.

That said, let's look over the field of toolkits for microservice implementation. One can definitely write microservices from scratch, but before doing that, it is always worth looking at what is out there already, even if you find that nothing fits your particular needs.

The two most popular toolkits are Spring Boot (`https://projects.spring.io/spring-boot`) and raw J2EE. The J2EE community founded the MicroProfile (`https://microprofile.io`) initiative, with a declared goal of optimizing Enterprise Java for a microservices architecture. KumuluzEE (`https://ee.kumuluz.com`) is a lightweight open source microservice framework, compliant with MicroProfile.

A list of some other frameworks, libraries, and toolkits includes the following (in alphabetical order):

- **Akka**: A toolkit for building highly concurrent, distributed, and resilient message-driven applications for Java and Scala (`https://akka.io/`).
- **Bootique**: A minimally opinionated framework for runnable Java applications (`https://bootique.io/`).
- **Dropwizard**: A Java framework for developing ops-friendly, high-performance, RESTful web services (`https://www.dropwizard.io/`).
- **Jodd**: A set of Java microframeworks, tools, and utilities, under 1.7 MB (`https://jodd.org/`).
- **Lightbend Lagom**: An opinionated microservice framework built on Akka and Play (`https://www.lightbend.com/`).
- **Ninja**: A fullstack web framework for Java (`http://www.ninjaframework.org/`).
- **Spotify Apollo**: A set of Java libraries used by Spotify for writing microservices (`http://spotify.github.io/apollo/`).
- **Vert.x**: A toolkit for building reactive applications on the JVM (`https://vertx.io/`).

All of the frameworks, libraries, and toolkits listed support HTTP/JSON communication between microservices. Some of them also have an additional way of sending messages. If they do not, any lightweight messaging system can be used. We mention it here because, as you may recall, message-driven asynchronous processing is a foundation for the elasticity, responsiveness, and resilience of a reactive system composed of microservices.

To demonstrate the process of microservice building, we will use Vert.x, an event-driven non-blocking lightweight polyglot toolkit (components can be written in Java, JavaScript, Groovy, Ruby, Scala, Kotlin, or Ceylon). It supports an asynchronous programming model and a distributed event bus that reaches into in-browser JavaScript, allowing for the creation of real-time web applications.

# Vert.x basics

The building block in Vert.x world is a class that implements the `io.vertx.core.Verticle` interface:

```
package io.vertx.core;
public interface Verticle {
  Vertx getVertx();
  void init(Vertx vertx, Context context);
```

```
    void start(Future<Void> future) throws Exception;
    void stop(Future<Void> future) throws Exception;
}
```

The implementation of the preceding interface is called a verticle. Most of the method names of the preceding interface are self-explanatory. The getVertex() method provides access to the Vertx object—the entry point into the Vert.x Core API that has methods that allow us to build the following functionalities necessary for microservice building:

- Creating DNS clients
- Creating periodic services
- Creating Datagram sockets
- Deploying and undeploying verticles
- Providing access to the shared data API
- Creating TCP and HTTP clients and servers
- Providing access to the event bus and filesystem

All of the deployed verticles can talk to each other via either standard HTTP protocol or using io.vertx.core.eventbus.EventBus, forming a system of microservices. We will show how one can build a reactive system of microservices using verticles and RxJava implementations from the io.vertx.rxjava package.

A Verticle interface implementation can be created easily, by extending the io.vertx.rxjava.core.AbstractVerticle class:

```
package io.vertx.rxjava.core;
import io.vertx.core.Vertx;
import io.vertx.core.Context;
import io.vertx.core.AbstractVerticle
public class AbstractVerticle extends AbstractVerticle {
    protected io.vertx.rxjava.core.Vertx vertx;
    public void init(Vertx vertx, Context context) {
        super.init(vertx, context);
        this.vertx = new io.vertx.rxjava.core.Vertx(vertx);
    }
}
```

As you can see, the preceding class extends the io.vertx.core.AbstractVerticle class:

```
package io.vertx.core;
import java.util.List;
import io.vertx.core.Verticle;
import io.vertx.core.json.JsonObject;
```

```
public abstract class AbstractVerticle implements Verticle {
    protected Vertx vertx;
    protected Context context;
    public void init(Vertx vertx, Context context) {
        this.vertx = vertx;
        this.context = context;
    }
    public Vertx getVertx() { return vertx; }
    public JsonObject config() { return context.config(); }
    public String deploymentID() { return context.deploymentID(); }
    public List<String> processArgs() { return context.processArgs(); }
    public void start(Future<Void> startFuture) throws Exception {
        start();
        startFuture.complete();
    }
    public void stop(Future<Void> stopFuture) throws Exception {
        stop();
        stopFuture.complete();
    }
    public void start() throws Exception {}
    public void stop() throws Exception {}
}
```

As you can see, all you need to do is extend the
`io.vertx.rxjava.core.AbstractVerticle` class and implement the `start()` method.
The new verticle will be deployable, even without implementing the `start()` method, but
it will do nothing useful. The code in the `start()` method is the entry point into the
functionality of your application.

To use Vert.x and execute the examples, the following dependencies have to be added to
the project:

```
<dependency>
    <groupId>io.vertx</groupId>
    <artifactId>vertx-web</artifactId>
    <version>${vertx.version}</version>
</dependency>
<dependency>
    <groupId>io.vertx</groupId>
    <artifactId>vertx-rx-java</artifactId>
    <version>${vertx.version}</version>
</dependency>
```

The `vertx.version` property can be set in the `properties` section of the `pom.xml` file:

```
<properties>
    <vertx.version>3.5.1</vertx.version>
</properties>
```

What makes a verticle reactive is the underlying implementation of an event loop (a thread) that receives an event (request) and delivers it to a handler—a method in a verticle, or another dedicated class, that is processing this type of the event. Programmers typically describe them as functions associated with each event type. When a handler returns, the event loop invokes the callback, implementing the reactor pattern we talked about in the previous section.

For certain types of procedures that are blocking by nature (JDBC calls or long computations, for example), a worker verticle can be executed asynchronously, not through the event loop (so, not to block it), but by a separate thread, using the `vertx.executeBlocking()` method. The golden rule of an event loop-based application design is, *Don't Block the Event Loop!* Violating this rule stops the application in its tracks.

# The HTTP server as a microservice

As an example, here is a verticle that acts as an HTTP server:

```java
package com.packt.javapath.ch18demo.microservices;
import io.vertx.rxjava.core.AbstractVerticle;
import io.vertx.rxjava.core.http.HttpServer;
public class HttpServer1 extends AbstractVerticle{
    private int port;
    public HttpServer1(int port) {
        this.port = port;
    }
    public void start() throws Exception {
        HttpServer server = vertx.createHttpServer();
        server.requestStream().toObservable()
           .subscribe(request -> request.response()
               .end("Hello from " + Thread.currentThread().getName() +
                                    " on port " + port + "!\n\n"));
        server.rxListen(port).subscribe();
        System.out.println(Thread.currentThread().getName() +
                                " is waiting on port " + port + "...");
    }
}
```

In the preceding code, the server is created, and the stream of data from a possible request is wrapped into an `Observable`. The data emitted by the `Observable` is passed to the function (a request handler) that processes the request and generates a necessary response. We also told the server which port to listen to, and can now deploy several instances of this verticle, to listen on different ports:

```
vertx().getDelegate().deployVerticle(new HttpServer1(8082));
vertx().getDelegate().deployVerticle(new HttpServer1(8083));
```

There is also an `io.vertx.rxjava.core.RxHelper` helper class that can be used for deployment. It takes care of some of the details that are not important for the current discussion:

```
RxHelper.deployVerticle(vertx(), new HttpServer1(8082));
RxHelper.deployVerticle(vertx(), new HttpServer1(8083));
```

Whichever method is used, you will see the following messages:

```
vert.x-eventloop-thread-0 is waiting on port 8082...
vert.x-eventloop-thread-0 is waiting on port 8083...
```

These messages confirm what we had expected: the same event loop thread is listening on both ports. We can now place a request to any of the running servers, using the standard `curl` command, for example:

```
curl localhost:8082
```

The response is going to be the one we hardcoded:

```
Hello from vert.x-eventloop-thread-0 on port 8082!
```

# Periodic service as a microservice

Vert.x also allows us to create a periodic service, which does something at a regular interval. Here is an example:

```
package com.packt.javapath.ch18demo.microservices;
import io.vertx.rxjava.core.AbstractVerticle;
import java.time.LocalTime;
import java.time.temporal.ChronoUnit;
public class PeriodicService1 extends AbstractVerticle {
  public void start() throws Exception {
    LocalTime start = LocalTime.now();
    vertx.setPeriodic(1000, v-> {
      System.out.println("Beep!");
```

```
            if(ChronoUnit.SECONDS.between(start, LocalTime.now()) > 3 ){
                vertx.undeploy(deploymentID());
            }
        });
        System.out.println("Vertical PeriodicService1 is deployed");
    }
    public void stop() throws Exception {
        System.out.println("Vertical PeriodicService1 is un-deployed");
    }
}
```

As you can see, this vertical, once deployed, prints the `Beep!` message every second, and after three seconds, is automatically un-deployed. If we deploy this vertical, we will see:

```
Vertical PeriodicService1 is deployed
Beep!
Beep!
Beep!
Beep!
Vertical PeriodicService1 is un-deployed
```

The first `Beep!` comes out when the vertical starts, then there are three more messages every second, and the vertical is un-deployed, as was expected.

# The HTTP client as a microservice

We can use periodic service verticals to send messages to the server vertical using the HTTP protocol. In order to do it, we need a new dependency, so we can use the `WebClient` class:

```
<dependency>
    <groupId>io.vertx</groupId>
    <artifactId>vertx-web-client</artifactId>
    <version>${vertx.version}</version>
</dependency>
```

With that, the periodic service that sends messages to the HTTP server vertical looks like this:

```
package com.packt.javapath.ch18demo.microservices;
import io.vertx.rxjava.core.AbstractVerticle;
import io.vertx.rxjava.core.buffer.Buffer;
import io.vertx.rxjava.ext.web.client.HttpResponse;
import io.vertx.rxjava.ext.web.client.WebClient;
import rx.Single;
```

```
import java.time.LocalTime;
import java.time.temporal.ChronoUnit;
public class PeriodicService2 extends AbstractVerticle {
    private int port;
    public PeriodicService2(int port) {
        this.port = port;
    }
    public void start() throws Exception {
        WebClient client = WebClient.create(vertx);
        Single<HttpResponse<Buffer>> single = client
                .get(port, "localhost", "?name=Nick")
                .rxSend();
        LocalTime start = LocalTime.now();
        vertx.setPeriodic(1000, v-> {
            single.subscribe(r-> System.out.println(r.bodyAsString()),
                            Throwable::printStackTrace);
            if(ChronoUnit.SECONDS.between(start, LocalTime.now()) >= 3 ){
                client.close();
                vertx.undeploy(deploymentID());
                System.out.println("Vertical PeriodicService2 undeployed");
            }
        });
        System.out.println("Vertical PeriodicService2 deployed");
    }
}
```

As you can see, this periodic service accepts the port number as a parameter of its constructor, then sends a message to this port on the localhost every second, and undeploys itself after three seconds. The message is the value of the name parameter. By default, it is the GET request.

We will also modify our server vertical to read the value of the name parameter:

```
public void start() throws Exception {
    HttpServer server = vertx.createHttpServer();
    server.requestStream().toObservable()
            .subscribe(request -> request.response()
                .end("Hi, " + request.getParam("name") + "! Hello from " +
            Thread.currentThread().getName() + " on port " + port + "!"));
    server.rxListen(port).subscribe();
    System.out.println(Thread.currentThread().getName()
                                    + " is waiting on port " + port + "...");
}
```

We can deploy both verticals:

```
RxHelper.deployVerticle(vertx(), new HttpServer2(8082));
RxHelper.deployVerticle(vertx(), new PeriodicService2(8082));
```

The output will be as follows:

```
Vertical PeriodicService2 deployed
vert.x-eventloop-thread-0 is waiting on port 8082...
Hi, Nick! Hello from vert.x-eventloop-thread-0 on port 8082!
Hi, Nick! Hello from vert.x-eventloop-thread-0 on port 8082!
Vertical PeriodicService2 undeployed
Hi, Nick! Hello from vert.x-eventloop-thread-0 on port 8082!
```

# Other microservices

In principle, the whole system of microservices can be built based on the messages sent using the HTTP protocol, with each microservice implemented as an HTTP server or having an HTTP server as the front for the message exchange. Alternatively, any other messaging system can be used for the communication.

In the case of Vert.x, it has its own messaging system-based on the event bus. In the next section, we will demonstrate it and use it as an illustration of how a reactive system may look.

The size of our sample microservices may leave the impression that microservices have to be as fine-grained as object methods. In some cases, it is worth considering whether a particular method needs to be scaled, for example. The truth is, this architectural style is novel enough to allow for definite size recommendations, and the existing frameworks, libraries, and toolkits are flexible enough to support practically any size of independently deployable services. Well, if a deployable, independent service is as big as a traditional application, then it probably won't be called a microservice, but *an external system*, or something similar.

# Reactive systems

Those familiar with the concept of **event-driven architecture** (**EDA**) may have noticed that it closely resembles the idea of a reactive system. Their descriptions use very similar language and diagrams. The difference is that EDA deals with only one aspect of a software system—the architecture. The idea of a reactive system, on the other hand, is more about the code style and execution flow, including an emphasis on using asynchronous data streams, for example. So, a reactive system can have EDA, and EDA can be implemented as a reactive system.

Let's look at another set of examples that provides a glimpse into how a reactive system may look, if implemented using Vert.x. Notice that the Vert.x API has two source trees: one starts with `io.vertx.core`, and the other with `io.vertx.rxjava`. Since we are discussing reactive programming, we are going to use packages under `io.vertx.rxjava`, called the rx-fied Vert.x API.

# Message-driven system

Vert.x has a feature that directly supports both the message-driven architecture and EDA. It is called an event bus. Any verticle has access to the event bus, and can send any message to any address (which is just a string) using the `io.vertx.core.eventbus.EventBus` class, or its cousin, `io.vertx.rxjava.core.eventbus.EventBus`. We are only going to use the latter, but similar (not rx-fied) functionality is available in `io.vertx.core.eventbus.EventBus`, too. One, or several, verticles can register themselves as a message consumer for a certain address. If several verticles are consumers for the same address, then the `rxSend()` method of `EventBus` delivers the message only to one of these consumers, using a round-robin algorithm to pick the receiver of the next message. Alternatively, the `publish()` method, as you would expect, delivers the message to all consumers with the same address. Here is the code that sends the message to the specified address:

```
vertx.eventBus().rxSend(address, msg).subscribe(reply ->
    System.out.println("Got reply: " + reply.body()),
    Throwable::printStackTrace );
```

The rxSend() method returns the Single<Message> object that represents a message that can be received, and the subscribe() method to ... well... subscribe to it.
The Single<Message> class implements the reactive pattern for a single value response. The subscribe() method accepts two Consumer functions: the first processes the reply, the second processes the error. In the preceding code, the first function just prints the reply:

```
reply -> System.out.println("Got reply: " + reply.body())
```

The second action prints the stack trace of the exception, if it happens:

```
Throwable::printStackTrace
```

As you already know, the preceding construct is called a method reference. The same function, as a lambda expression, would look like the following:

```
e -> e.printStackTrace()
```

A call to the publish() method looks similar:

```
vertx.eventBus().publish(address, msg)
```

It publishes the message to many consumers potentially, so the method does not return a Single object, or any other object that can be used to get a reply. Instead, it just returns an EventBus object; if needed, more event bus methods can be called.

# Message consumer

The message consumer in Vert.x is a verticle that registers with the event bus as a potential receiver of the messages sent or published to the specified address:

```
package com.packt.javapath.ch18demo.reactivesystem;
import io.vertx.rxjava.core.AbstractVerticle;
public class MsgConsumer extends AbstractVerticle {
    private String address, name;
    public MsgConsumer(String id, String address) {
        this.address = address;
        this.name = this.getClass().getSimpleName() +
                            "(" + id + "," + address + ")";
    }
    public void start() throws Exception {
        System.out.println(name + " starts...");
        vertx.eventBus().consumer(address).toObservable()
         .subscribe(msg -> {
            String reply = name + " got message: " + msg.body();
            System.out.println(reply);
```

```
              if ("undeploy".equals(msg.body())) {
                  vertx.undeploy(deploymentID());
                  reply = name + " undeployed.";
                  System.out.println(reply);
              }
              msg.reply(reply);
          }, Throwable::printStackTrace );
          System.out.println(Thread.currentThread().getName()
                  + " is waiting on address " + address + "...");

      }
  }
```

The `consumer(address)` method returns an object of
`io.vertx.rxjava.core.eventbus.MessageConsumer<T>`, which represents a stream
of messages to the provided address. This means that one can convert the stream into an
`Observable` and subscribe to it to receive all of the messages sent to this address.
The `subscribe()` method of the `Observable` object accepts two `Consumer` functions: the
first processes the received message, and the second is executed when an error happens. In
the first function, we have included the `msg.reply(reply)` method, which sends the
message back to the source of the message. And you probably remember that the sender is
able to get this reply if the original message was sent by the `rxSend()` method. If
the `publish()` method was used instead, then the reply sent by the `msg.reply(reply)`
method goes nowhere.

Also, notice that when the `undeploy` message is received, the message consumer
undeploys itself. This method is usually only used during automatic deployment, when the
old version is replaced by the newer one without shutting down the system.

Because we are going to deploy several message consumers with the same address for the
demonstration, we have added the `id` parameter and included it in the `name` value. This
value serves as a prefix in all of the messages, so we can trace how the message propagates
across the system.

You have probably realized that the preceding implementation is just a shell that can be
used to invoke some useful functionalities. The received message can be a command to do
something, data to be processed, data to be stored in the database, or anything else. And
the reply can be an acknowledgment that the message was received, or some other
expected result. If the latter is the case, the processing should be very fast, to avoid blocking
the event loop (remember the golden rule). If the processing cannot be done quickly, the
replay can also be a callback token, used by the sender later to retrieve the result.

# Message sender

The message sender we will demonstrate is based on the HTTP server implementation we demonstrated in the *Microservices* section. It is not necessary to do it this way. In real-life code, a vertical typically sends messages automatically, either to get data it needs, to provide data some other vertical wants, to notify another vertical, to store data in the database, or for any other reason. But for demonstration purposes, we have decided that the sender will listen to some port for messages, and we will send it messages manually (using the `curl` command) or automatically, via some periodic service described in the *Microservices* section. That is why the message sender looks a bit more complex than the message consumer:

```
package com.packt.javapath.ch18demo.reactivesystem;
import io.vertx.rxjava.core.AbstractVerticle;
import io.vertx.rxjava.core.http.HttpServer;
public class EventBusSend extends AbstractVerticle {
    private int port;
    private String address, name;
    public EventBusSend(int port, String address) {
        this.port = port;
        this.address = address;
        this.name = this.getClass().getSimpleName() +
                    "(port " + port + ", send to " + address + ")";
    }
    public void start() throws Exception {
        System.out.println(name + " starts...");
        HttpServer server = vertx.createHttpServer();
        server.requestStream().toObservable().subscribe(request -> {
          String msg = request.getParam("msg");
          request.response().setStatusCode(200).end();
          vertx.eventBus().rxSend(address, msg).subscribe(reply -> {
            System.out.println(name + " got reply:\n  " + reply.body());
          },
          e -> {
            if(StringUtils.contains(e.toString(), "NO_HANDLERS")){
                vertx.undeploy(deploymentID());
                System.out.println(name + " undeployed.");
            } else {
                e.printStackTrace();
            }
          });
        });
        server.rxListen(port).subscribe();
        System.out.println(Thread.currentThread().getName()
                            + " is waiting on port " + port + "...");
    }
}
```

```
    }
```

Most of the preceding code is related to the HTTP server functionality. The few lines that send the message (received by the HTTP server) are these ones:

```
vertx.eventBus().rxSend(address, msg).subscribe(reply -> {
    System.out.println(name + " got reply:\n  " + reply.body());
}, e -> {
    if(StringUtils.contains(e.toString(), "NO_HANDLERS")){
        vertx.undeploy(deploymentID());
        System.out.println(name + " undeployed.");
    } else {
        e.printStackTrace();
    }
});
```

After the message is sent, the sender subscribes to the possible reply and prints it (if the reply was received). If an error happens (an exception is thrown during message sending), we can check whether the exception (converted to the `String` value) contains literal `NO_HANDLERS`, and un-deploy the sender if so. It took us a while to figure out how to identify the case when there are no consumers assigned to the address, for which this sender is dedicated to sending messages. If there are no consumers (all are un-deployed, most likely), then there is no need for the sender, so we un-deploy it.

It is a good practice to clean up and un-deploy all of the verticles that are not needed anymore. But if you run the verticles in IDE, chances are, all the verticles are stopped as soon as you stop the main process (that has created the verticles) in your IDE. If not, run the `jcmd` command and see whether there are still Vert.x verticles running. The first number for each of the listed processes is the process ID. Identify the verticles that you do not need anymore and use the `kill -9 <process ID>` command to stop them.

Now, let's deploy two message consumers, and send them messages via our message sender:

```
String address = "One";
Vertx vertx = vertx();
RxHelper.deployVerticle(vertx, new MsgConsumer("1",address));
RxHelper.deployVerticle(vertx, new MsgConsumer("2",address));
RxHelper.deployVerticle(vertx, new EventBusSend(8082, address));
```

After you run the preceding code, the Terminal shows the following messages:

```
MsgConsumer(1,One) starts...
MsgConsumer(2,One) starts...
EventBusSend(port 8082, send to One) starts...
vert.x-eventloop-thread-1 is waiting on address One...
vert.x-eventloop-thread-0 is waiting on address One...
vert.x-eventloop-thread-2 is waiting on port 8082...
```

Notice the different event loops running to support each verticle.

Now, let's send a few messages, using the following commands from a terminal window:

```
curl localhost:8082?msg=Hello!
curl localhost:8082?msg=Hi!
curl localhost:8082?msg=How+are+you?
curl localhost:8082?msg=Just+saying...
```

The plus sign (+) is necessary because a URL cannot contain spaces and has to be *encoded*, which means, among other things, replacing spaces with plus sign + or %20. In response to the preceding commands, we will see the following messages:

```
MsgConsumer(2,One) got message: Hello!
EventBusSend(port 8082, send to One) got reply:
  MsgConsumer(2,One) got message: Hello!
MsgConsumer(1,One) got message: Hi!
EventBusSend(port 8082, send to One) got reply:
  MsgConsumer(1,One) got message: Hi!
MsgConsumer(2,One) got message: How are you?
EventBusSend(port 8082, send to One) got reply:
  MsgConsumer(2,One) got message: How are you?
MsgConsumer(1,One) got message: Just saying...
EventBusSend(port 8082, send to One) got reply:
  MsgConsumer(1,One) got message: Just saying...
```

As expected, the consumers received messages by turns, according to the round-robin algorithm. Now, let's deploy all of the verticles:

```
curl localhost:8082?msg=undeploy
curl localhost:8082?msg=undeploy
curl localhost:8082?msg=undeploy
```

Here are the messages displayed in response to the preceding commands:

```
MsgConsumer(1,One) got message: undeploy
MsgConsumer(1,One) undeployed.
EventBusSend(port 8082, send to One) got reply:
  MsgConsumer(1,One) undeployed.
MsgConsumer(2,One) got message: undeploy
MsgConsumer(2,One) undeployed.
EventBusSend(port 8082, send to One) got reply:
  MsgConsumer(2,One) undeployed.
EventBusSend(port 8082, send to One) undeployed.
```

According to the preceding messages, all of our verticals are un-deployed. If we submit the `undeploy` message again, we will see:

```
curl localhost:8082?msg=undeploy
curl: (7) Failed to connect to localhost port 8082: Connection refused
```

That is because the sender is undeployed, and there is no HTTP server that listens to port `8082` of the localhost.

# Message publisher

We implemented the message publisher very similarly to the message sender:

```
package com.packt.javapath.ch18demo.reactivesystem;

import io.vertx.rxjava.core.AbstractVerticle;
import io.vertx.rxjava.core.http.HttpServer;

public class EventBusPublish extends AbstractVerticle {
    private int port;
    private String address, name;
    public EventBusPublish(int port, String address) {
        this.port = port;
        this.address = address;
        this.name = this.getClass().getSimpleName() +
                "(port " + port + ", publish to " + address + ")";
    }
    public void start() throws Exception {
        System.out.println(name + " starts...");
        HttpServer server = vertx.createHttpServer();
        server.requestStream().toObservable()
                .subscribe(request -> {
                    String msg = request.getParam("msg");
                    request.response().setStatusCode(200).end();
```

```
                    vertx.eventBus().publish(address, msg);
                    if ("undeploy".equals(msg)) {
                        vertx.undeploy(deploymentID());
                        System.out.println(name + " undeployed.");
                    }
                });
            server.rxListen(port).subscribe();
            System.out.println(Thread.currentThread().getName()
                    + " is waiting on port " + port + "...");
        }
    }
```

The publisher differs from the sender only by this section:

```
                vertx.eventBus().publish(address, msg);
                if ("undeploy".equals(msg)) {
                    vertx.undeploy(deploymentID());
                    System.out.println(name + " undeployed.");
                }
```

Since one cannot get a reply while publishing, the preceding code is much simpler than the message-sending code. Also, since all of the consumers recieve the undeploy message at the same time, we can assume that they are all going to be un-deployed, and the publisher can un-deploy itself. Let's test it by running the following program:

```
String address = "One";
Vertx vertx = vertx();
RxHelper.deployVerticle(vertx, new MsgConsumer("1",address));
RxHelper.deployVerticle(vertx, new MsgConsumer("2",address));
RxHelper.deployVerticle(vertx, new EventBusPublish(8082, address));
```

In response to the preceding code execution, we get the following messages:

```
MsgConsumer(1,One) starts...
MsgConsumer(2,One) starts...
EventBusPublish(port 8082, publish to One) starts...
vert.x-eventloop-thread-2 is waiting on port 8082...
```

Now, we issue the following command in another terminal window:

```
curl localhost:8082?msg=Hello!
```

The messages in the terminal window where the verticals are running are as follows:

```
MsgConsumer(1,One) got message: Hello!
MsgConsumer(2,One) got message: Hello!
```

As expected, both consumers with the same address receive the same message. Now, let's un-deploy them:

```
curl localhost:8082?msg=undeploy
```

The verticals respond with these messages:

```
MsgConsumer(1,One) got message: undeploy
MsgConsumer(2,One) got message: undeploy
EventBusPublish(port 8082, publish to One) undeployed.
MsgConsumer(1,One) undeployed.
MsgConsumer(2,One) undeployed.
```

If we submit the undeploy message again, we will see:

```
curl localhost:8082?msg=undeploy
curl: (7) Failed to connect to localhost port 8082: Connection refused
```

With that, we have completed our demonstration of a reactive system composed of microservices. Adding methods and classes that do something useful will make it closer to the real-life system. But we will leave that as an exercise for the reader.

# Reality check

We have run all of the previous examples in one JVM process. If necessary, Vert.x instances can be deployed in different JVM processes and clustered by adding the -cluster option to the run command, when the verticals are deployed not from IDE, but from a command line. Clustered verticals share the event bus, and the addresses are visible to all Vert.x instances. This way, more message consumers can be deployed if the consumers of certain addresses cannot process the requests (messages) in a timely manner.

Other frameworks that we mentioned earlier have similar capabilities. They make microservice creation easy, and may encourage breaking the application into tiny, single-method operations, with the expectation of assembling a very resilient and responsive system. However, these are not the only criteria of good software. System decomposition increases the complexity of its deployment. Also, if one development team is responsible for many microservices, the complexity of versioning so many pieces in different stages (development, test, integration test, certification, staging, and production) may lead to confusion. The deployment process may become so complex that slowing down the rate of changes is necessary to keep the system in sync with the market requirements.

In addition to the developing of microservices, many other aspects have to be addressed to support a reactive system:

- A monitoring system has to be set up to provide insight into the state of the application, but its development should not be so complex as to pull the development resources away from the main application.

- Alerts have to be installed to warn the team about possible and actual issues in a timely manner, so they can be addressed before affecting the business.

- If possible, self-correcting automated processes have to be implemented. For example, the retry logic has to be implemented, with a reasonable upper limit of attempts before declaring a failure.

- A layer of circuit breakers has to protect the system from the domino effect when the failure of one component deprives other components of necessary resources.

- An embedded testing system should be able to introduce disruptions and simulate load increases to ensure that the application's resilience and responsiveness do not degrade over time. For example, the Netflix team has introduced a *chaos monkey*—a system that is able to shut down various parts of the production system and test its ability to recover. They use it even in production, because a production environment has a specific configuration, and no test in another environment can guarantee that all possible issues are found.

As you have probably realized by now, before committing to a reactive system, the team has to weigh all the pros and cons to understand exactly why they need a reactive system, and the price of its development. It is an old adage that *no value can be added for free*. The awesome power of reactive systems comes with a corresponding growth of complexity, not only during development, but also during system tuning and maintenance.

Yet, if the traditional systems cannot solve the processing problem that you face, or if you're passionate about everything reactive and love the concept, by all means, go for it. The ride will be challenging, but the reward will be worth it. As another old adage states, *what is easily achievable is not worth the effort*.

# Exercise – Creating io.reactivex.Observable

Write code that demonstrates several ways to create `io.reactivex.Observable`. In each example, subscribe to the created `Observable` object and print the emitted values.

We did not discuss this so you will need to study the RxJava2 API and look up examples on the internet.

# Answer

Here are six of the methods that allow you to create `io.reactivex.Observable`:

```
//1
Observable.just("Hi!").subscribe(System.out::println); //prints: Hi!
//2
Observable.fromIterable(List.of("1","2","3"))
          .subscribe(System.out::print); //prints: 123
System.out.println();
//3
String[] arr = {"1","2","3"};
Observable.fromArray(arr).subscribe(System.out::print); //prints: 123
System.out.println();
//4
Observable.fromCallable(()->123)
          .subscribe(System.out::println); //prints: 123
//5
ExecutorService pool = Executors.newSingleThreadExecutor();
Future<String> future = pool
        .submit(() -> {
            Thread.sleep(100);
            return "Hi!";
        });
Observable.fromFuture(future)
          .subscribe(System.out::println); //prints: Hi!
pool.shutdown();
//6
Observable.interval(100, TimeUnit.MILLISECONDS)
          .subscribe(v->System.out.println("100 ms is over"));
                                   //prints twice "100 ms is over"
try { //this pause gives the above method a chance to print the message
    TimeUnit.MILLISECONDS.sleep(200);
} catch (InterruptedException e) {
    e.printStackTrace();
}
```

# Summary

In this last chapter of the book, we have provided the reader with a glimpse into real-life professional programming and a short overview of the challenges of the trade. We have revisited many of the modern terms used in relation to big data processing using highly-scalable responsive and resilient reactive systems that are able to solve the challenging processing, problems of the modern age. We have even provided code examples of such systems, which may serve as the first step for your real-life project.

We hope that you remain curious, that you will continue studying and experimenting, and that you will eventually build a system that will solve a real problem and bring more happiness to the world.

# Other Books You May Enjoy

If you enjoyed this book, you may be interested in these other books by Packt:

**C++ Data Structures and Algorithms**
Wisnu Anggoro

ISBN: 978-1-78883-521-3

- Know how to use arrays and lists to get better results in complex scenarios
- Build enhanced applications by using hashtables, dictionaries, and sets
- Implement searching algorithms such as linear search, binary search, jump search, exponential search, and more
- Have a positive impact on the efficiency of applications with tree traversal
- Explore the design used in sorting algorithms like Heap sort, Quick sort, Merge sort and Radix sort
- Implement various common algorithms in string data types
- Find out how to design an algorithm for a specific task using the common algorithm paradigms

## Learning Rust

Paul Johnson, Vesa Kaihlavirta

ISBN: 978-1-78588-430-6

- Set up Rust for Windows, Linux, and OS X
- Write effective code using Rust
- Expand your Rust applications using libraries
- Interface existing non-Rust libraries with your Rust applications
- Use the standard library within your applications
- Understand memory management within Rust and speed efficiency when passing variables
- Create more complex data types
- Study concurrency in Rust with multi-threaded applications and sync threading techniques to improve the performance of an application problem

# Leave a review - let other readers know what you think

Please share your thoughts on this book with others by leaving a review on the site that you bought it from. If you purchased the book from Amazon, please leave us an honest review on this book's Amazon page. This is vital so that other potential readers can see and use your unbiased opinion to make purchasing decisions, we can understand what our customers think about our products, and our authors can see your feedback on the title that they have worked with Packt to create. It will only take a few minutes of your time, but is valuable to other potential customers, our authors, and Packt. Thank you!

# Index

primitive types 127
reference types 127

# U

Unicode table
  reference 140
user threads 389

# V

varargs 35
variables
  about 128, 129
  array component 129
  class variable 129
  constructor parameter 129
  declaration 129

definition 129
exception parameter 129
final variable (constant) 131, 132
initialization 130
instance variable 129
lambda parameter 129
local variable 129
method parameter 129
Vert.x
  basics 664, 667
  reference 664

# W

wait() method 61
while statement 334
World Wide Web (WWW) 175

CPSIA information can be obtained
at www.ICGtesting.com
Printed in the USA
LVHW060112200919
631682LV00004B/76/P